6th edition

programming and planning
in early childhood settings

6th edition

programming and planning

in early childhood settings

leonie **arthur**   bronwyn **beecher**   elizabeth **death**   sue **dockett**   sue **farmer**

Programming and Planning in Early Childhood Settings
6th Edition
Leonie Arthur
Bronwyn Beecher
Elizabeth Death
Sue Dockett
Sue Farmer

Publishing manager: Dorothy Chiu
Publishing editor: Ann Crabb
Developmental editor: James Cole
Project editor: Michaela Skelly
Art direction: Olga Lavecchia
Cover designer: Sarah Rudledge
Text designer: Astred Hicks (Designcherry)
Editor: Julie Wicks
Proofreader: Jade Jakovcic
Indexer: Julie King
Permissions/Photo researcher: QBS Learning
Cover: iStockphoto/billnoll (blue paper background), iStockphoto/Chris Elwell (windmill), iStockphoto/ollo (feather), iStockphoto/SelectStock (boy pirate); Shutterstock/Aleksangel, Shutterstock/donatas 1205 (green line), Shutterstock/KsushaArt (yellow dot), Shutterstock/Luis Carlos Torres (blue cellophane), Shutterstock/My Good Images, Shutterstock/Photka (sand), ShutterstockTzidosun (fish).
Typesetter: Cenveo Publisher Services

Any URLs contained in this publication were checked for currency during the production process. Note, however, that the publisher cannot vouch for the ongoing currency of URLs.

Previously published in 2012

For product information and technology assistance,
in Australia call **1300 790 853**;
in New Zealand call **0800 449 725**

For permission to use material from this text or product, please email
aust.permissions@cengage.com

National Library of Australia Cataloguing-in-Publication Data
Author: Arthur, Leonie, author.
Title: Programming and Planning in Early Childhood Settings / Leonie Arthur, Bronwyn Beecher, Elizabeth Death, Sue Dockett, Sue Farmer.
Edition: 6th edition
ISBN: 9780170264105 (paperback)
Subjects: Educational planning.
             Early childhood education.
Other Authors/Contributors: Beecher, Bronwyn, 1951- , author., Death, Elizabeth, author., Dockett, Sue, author., Farmer, Sue, author.
Dewey Number: 372.11

Cengage Learning Australia
Level 7, 80 Dorcas Street
South Melbourne, Victoria Australia 3205

Cengage Learning New Zealand
Unit 4B Rosedale Office Park
331 Rosedale Road, Albany, North Shore 0632, NZ

For learning solutions, visit **cengage.com.au**

Printed in China by China Translation & Printing Services.
2 3 4 5 6 7 18 17 16 15

Brief contents

Contents

Contents

Preface

This is the sixth edition of *Programming and Planning in Early Childhood Settings*. It retains all of the chapters from the fifth edition, but in a rearranged order and with extensive new content in each chapter and in accompanying materials online. We have updated each chapter to incorporate current policies and practices in early childhood education in Australia.

Since the publication of the last edition there have continued to be many developments, both within Australia and internationally, in the area of early childhood education. At the time of going to print in 2012 the National Curriculum for Australian schools was still under development, and the *National Quality Standard* was yet to be mandated. At the time of writing this latest edition educators were working closely with these documents and we have used many examples from the field in this edition to illustrate this.

There are more explicit references in this edition to *Belonging, Being and Becoming: The Early Years Learning Framework for Australia*, *My Place, My Time* and the *National Quality Standard* throughout the book. The names of some chapters have changed to reflect consistency in language with these curriculum documents and to make it easier for readers to make connections between the book and the assessment standards and curriculum framework.

The book explores the principles and practices of *The Early Years Learning Framework for Australia* and the *Melbourne Declaration on Educational Goals for Young Australians* and how they are enacted in practice in a range of educational settings. Throughout the book there is a strong focus on respect for diversity and difference, partnerships, play-based pedagogies, learning environments, documentation and assessment for learning, intentional teaching, reflective practice and continuity of learning. There is more information in this edition on continuity of learning and transition to school, with specific strategies to support children, families and educators to experience a smooth transition and to strengthen relationships and communication across prior to school and school settings.

There are many new examples and new photographs that provide real life experiences of educators putting theory into practice. These include more examples of learning environments, both outdoors and indoors, more examples of educators working with and assessing learning for under threes and more examples from regional and remote communities. There is a stronger focus on working in Aboriginal and Torres Strait Islander communities and there are extensive examples from early childhood settings in central Australia, with a specific focus on working in Aboriginal communities. There is also a greater emphasis in planning learning environments that promote engagement with and appreciation of the natural environment and address issues of sustainability.

We recognise that the book's readership is diverse. The challenge is to cater for university-based teacher education students as well as students studying in the vocational education sector and early childhood practitioners. To cater for this diversity of readers, each chapter has margin definitions of key terms and the book includes a glossary. Where possible we have included student perspectives and the perspectives of early career practitioners as well as experienced professionals. There are also more questions for reflection in each chapter that are addressed specifically to students and the *Journeys of change* chapter includes a range of early career educators as well as more experienced educators.

The structure of the book is based on the key roles of educators – understanding the broad political and policy context of early childhood, understanding the early childhood/school setting and being able to clearly articulate their own philosophy, working in partnerships with families, understanding children's learning and development, documenting and assessing children's learning, making curriculum decisions based on sound understandings of curriculum approaches and pedagogies and the role of physical and social environments in learning, and engaging in

reflection, evaluation and planning for change. All of these aspects are addressed in one or more of the book's chapters.

In each edition since 1993 we have renamed and re-ordered the chapters. This edition is no exception. We have done this based on feedback from the users of previous editions. However, there is no definitive answer to the ordering of chapters. The reality is that the book is not designed to be read in a linear fashion from beginning to end. Teacher-educators, students and practitioners can use the chapters in any order. To facilitate the use of the book in multiple ways each chapter refers the reader to other chapters in the book where relevant issues are discussed in more detail.

While we have aimed to avoid the unnecessary duplication of content, it is inevitable that some issues are discussed in more than one chapter. This is often necessary to set the context or because there are key issues that are explored in different ways in different chapters.

As in previous editions, the book aims to provide a range of theoretical perspectives. We encourage students and practitioners to develop their own philosophy and their own contextually responsive curriculum approaches and frameworks, and to engage in reflection on their own practices and in processes of change. To facilitate this ongoing professional learning, each chapter includes a number of questions for reflection throughout as well as questions for individual reflection and group discussion at the end of the chapter.

We hope that the book encourages lively debate amongst educators and contributes to reflective discussion, informed decision-making and pedagogical leadership.

About the authors

Leonie Arthur (B. A./Dip. Ed. University of New England, B. Ed. (EC) with Distinction Mitchell College of Advanced Education, M. Ed. (Applied Linguistics) University of Sydney, Ed. D. University of Western Sydney) has worked in long day care, preschool and the early years of school. She currently works in early childhood curriculum and literacy at the University of Western Sydney and her recent research has focused on effective pedagogies, practitioner research and literacy learning. Leonie is a co-author of *Play and Literacy in Children's Worlds* and *Literacies, Communities and Under 5s* and co-author and co-editor of *Diverse Literacies in Early Childhood*; she was also one of the members of the CSU led consortium that developed the *Early Years Learning Framework*.

Bronwyn Beecher (Dip. Teach Wagga Wagga Teachers College, Grad. Dip. Ed. Studies Riverina College of Advanced Education, M. Ed. Studies University of Wollongong, M. Ed. (Hons) University of Wollongong, Ed.D, University of Western Sydney) has worked in the early years of school. For many years she worked in early childhood education in the School of Education, University of Western Sydney and currently manages the KU Early Language and Literacy Initiative (KU ELLI). Her research examines family and community partnerships, strengthening pedagogical practice and children's literacy learning. Bronwyn is a co-author of *Play and Literacy in Children's Worlds*, *Literacies, Communities and Under 5s* and a co-editor and co-author of *Diverse Literacies in early Childhood*.

Elizabeth Death (Dip. Teach (EC) Mitchell College of Advanced Education, B. Ed. (EC) with Distinction Mitchell College of Advanced Education) has worked within the early childhood profession for more than 30 years. Her experience spans directing and teaching in preschool and long day care settings, early intervention, lecturing at University of Western Sydney and Charles Sturt University, teaching at TAFE, early childhood policy adviser for the NSW Minister for Education, consultancy and service group management across New South Wales, the Australian Capital Territory and Queensland. Elizabeth held the position of Director, Community Services with MacDonnell Shire (now regional) Council Central Australia, overseeing children services, youth services, aged care and community safety across twelve remote and very remote indigenous communities. Elizabeth's current position is General Manager, Early Childhood Policy and Regulation for the Northern Territory Government Department of Education. This role includes the implementation of the Education and Care Services National Law and Regulations, the Australian Early Development Index, early childhood policy development and oversight of key initiatives for our most vulnerable children in remote and very remote Northern Territory, such as Families as First Teachers and the Australian Abecedarian Approach.

Sue Dockett (B.Ed (Pre-Primary) (Hons), M.Ed (Hons), PhD University of Sydney) is Professor, Early Childhood Education at Charles Sturt University. Sue has worked as an educator and academic in the field of early childhood for over 30 years. Over many years, she has researched experiences of educational transitions, particularly the transition to school. With Bob Perry, she has published widely in this area both nationally and internationally. Much of this research has focused on children's experiences and expectations, as well as those of families, educators and communities at times of transition. She is co-author of *Transition to School: Perceptions, Expectations and Experiences* (with Bob Perry), co-editor of *Transitions to School – International Research, Policy and Practice* (with Bob Perry and Anne Petriwskyj) and *Varied Perspectives on Play and Learning: Theory and Research on Early years Education* (with Bob Perry and Ole Fredrik Lillemyr).

Sue Farmer (Cert IV, Assessment & Workplace Training (TAFE), Dip. Teach. (EC) Sydney Kindergarten Teachers College, Grad. Dip. Ed. Studies Institute of Early Childhood, M.Ed. University of Sydney) has worked in a wide range of early childhood education and care settings and management positions since the mid-1970s. She worked at the University of Western Sydney for many years and more recently within the TAFE system. Sue has been involved in many early childhood professional organisations . Her recent projects with the Inclusion Support Agency (Gold Coast) focused on providing mentoring in early childhood settings and developing the publication *Journeys of Inclusion*. Sue is currently the coordinator of an Early Childhood Intervention service, as well as being involved in various inclusive practice projects in mainstream settings.

Acknowledgements

The authors would like to acknowledge the following people and settings for their significant contributions and examples of practice appearing within this book:

- Cape Byron Rudolph Steiner School, particularly Julie McVeigh and John O'Brien, for their unique contributions.

- Gold Coast Inclusion Support Agency, particularly Joanne Goodwin, for their commitment to excellence in the area of inclusion and working with Aboriginal and Torres Strait Islander communities. Thanks for their many innovative ideas, photographs and insightful reflections.

- Integricare Children's Centre Homebush – Kurralee. Thanks in particular to Jenny Green for sharing reflections on organisational climate and examples of pedagogical documentation proformas that encourage collaboration between educators and families and Carla Paszti for sharing examples of her documentation.

- Keiraville Community Preschool, particularly Margaret Gleeson, for ongoing support and contributions in sharing documentation of children's learning. Thanks to the families and children for the photographs.

- Kingscliff Mini School for their ongoing support, encouragement and contributions, especially the current staff of Lindy Andrews and Vicki Schaefer, as well as Sharon Martin for her long term inspiration. Thanks also to the families and children who shared their involvement at the service through photographs.

- KU Hebersham Preschool, especially Amanda Kupke, Kelly Keith, Michelle Munro and Debbie Weisenbach for their support and contributions of the program. Thanks to the families and children for the photographs.

- KU Killarney Heights Preschool, in particular Jane Pethers and Kylie Kennemore.

- KU Macquarie Fields Preschool, especially Glenys Gadoll, Jackie Staudinger and Alison O'Hea for their support and contributions of the program. Thanks to the families and children for the photographs.

- MacDonnell Regional Council Children's Services, in particular Margaret Harrison, Hannah Scully and the families and children of Watiyawanu (Mt Liebig community).

- Mary Bailey House, Santa Sabina College, especially Jackie Baxter, Cathy Merlino, Kathryn Graham, Kathy Dowdell, Mariam Raihani and Lyne Cooke and the families and children for sharing inspiring examples of their documentation and their processes of analysing children's learning.

- Our Lady of Lourdes Catholic School, Seven Hills, especially Lesley Studans and Carol Cividin. Thanks for sharing their reflections on supporting children's constructivist learning through investigation, interests and family experiences in the curriculum. Thanks to children and families for photographs.

- Parkes Early Childhood Centre, in particular Lindy Farrant and Bronnie Dean.

- Rebecca Leacock for her contribution to inclusive environments.

- Robert Townsend Public School, chiefly Jan Rogers and Linda Green. Thanks for sharing program development and the school's strategic planning.

- Tonia Godhard for her continued contribution both to this book and the early childhood education and care profession.

We would also like to thank the following centres for their ongoing support and inspiration over many years:

- Cherry Tree Kindergarten, particularly Ana Levar, Sarah Cunningham, Sharon Gillespie and Jodie Edwards.

- Earlwood Children's Centre, Canterbury Council, including previous staff Fran Bastion, Nicole Tytherleigh, Jacqui Bolt and Marisa Rodriguez.

- KU Phoenix Pre-School staff, children and families for their many ideas, examples and photographs, especially Ros Meager, Kim Tegel, Tracey Hogan and Bev Tolhurst.

- Paddington Children's Centre (UnitingCare) staff for their commitment to excellence and their many contributions, in particular, Natalie Cordukes.
- Rainbow Children's Centre staff including Ballina Early Intervention, for their support, enthusiasm, examples of innovative practice and individual contributions, especially Leo Prendergast. Thanks also to the families and children who shared their documentation and learning.
- Summer Hill Children's and Community Centre (UnitingCare), in particular Roberta DeSousa, Averil Dudman, Emma Hawkings and Phyll Latta.
- Tigger's Honeypot Children's Centre staff for their support, enthusiasm and individual contributions, especially Sylvia Turner and Jemma Carlisle for continuing the journey.

Thanks also to the staff, families, children and management of the following services for sharing their stories, ideas and for their input: Hinchinbrook Children's Centre; Werrington TAFE Children's Centre; KU Children's Services, Botany Downs Kindergarten; Liverpool City Council; and Ballina Public School.

In addition we would like to thank the following individuals for their contributions: Naomi Beech, Melinda Casey, Sheridan Dudley, Lynette Funnell, Bronwyn Glass, Miriam Giugni, Joanne Goodwin, Christine Legg, Monique Beange, Ana Levar, Helen Meredith, Christie Roe and Rebecca Watson. Special thanks to Michele Howell, who has sadly passed away since the last edition.

We are also indebted to our colleagues at the University of Western Sydney, Charles Sturt University and Rainbow Children's Centre, especially Ballina Early Intervention, with whom we have shared ideas and sought advice, as well as to all the students who have contributed to our thinking.

Our thanks also go to our families, in particular Leo Prendergast, Toby Arthur, Bob and Will Perry, and Allen Nash, Thom and Grace Richards for their ongoing support and inspiration. We thank them for their patience and goodwill, their willingness to share photographs and anecdotes, as well as their understanding.

The authors and Cengage Learning would like to thank the following reviewers for their, time, expertise and insight:

- Wendy Boyd – Southern Cross University
- Carla Jeffrey – LaTrobe University
- Michael McGirr – The Northern Sydney Institute
- Janet Moles – Deakin University
- Hilary Monk – Monash University
- Katie O'Brien – Australian Catholic University
- Alicia Olson – University of Sydney
- Prathyusha Sanagavarapu – University of Western Sydney
- Reesa Sorin – James Cook University
- Erin Taylor – Australian Catholic University
- Anne Tietzel – University of the Sunshine Coast
- Katarzyna Wieczorek-Ghisso – Australian Catholic University

Resource guide

For the student

As you read this text you will find a wealth of features to assist you with your learning.

The **chapter learning focus** gives you a broad overview of what the chapter will cover.

Numerous real-life **examples** demonstrate how the concepts and theory you are learning about have been applied in real-life settings by specific child-care centres and professionals.

Key terms are highlighted throughout the text, with **definitions** located in the margins for easy reference.

Reflection points encourage you to pause and reflect on the material you have just read, as well as on your own practices, to facilitate your ongoing learning.

At the end of each chapter you'll find several tools to help you to review key concepts and extend your learning.

The **conclusion and reflection** section includes further **Questions for reflection** that encourage you to develop your own philosophy and explore the issues further.

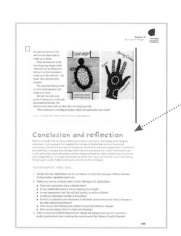

The **list of key terms** is a handy checklist to help you revise terminology.

The **key weblinks** section suggests useful websites to help you find more information.

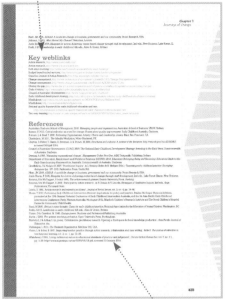

For quick reference, a full list of key terms is available in the **glossary** at the back of the book.

A **recommended resources** section highlights key resources for further reading.

A comprehensive list of **references** concludes each chapter.

Online resources

Visit **http://login.cengagebrain.com** and use the access code that comes with this book for 12 months' access to:

- the *Programming and Planning in Early Childhood Settings* **CourseMate Express** website. You'll find: online research activities; revision quizzes; matching pairs activities; flashcards and crosswords to help you revise key terms; online video activities; weblinks, and more. **CourseMateExpress**

- **Search me! education.** Fast and convenient, this resource provides you with 24-hour access to full-text articles from hundreds of scholarly and popular journals and newspapers, including *The Australian* and *The New York Times*. Use the **Search me! education keywords** at the end of each chapter to get you started; then try your own search terms to explore topics further and find current references. Search me!

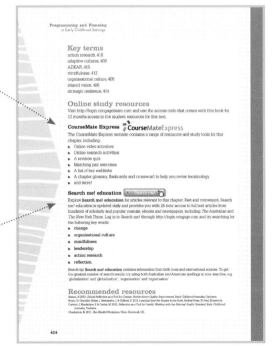

For the instructor

Cengage Learning is pleased to provide you with a selection of resources that will help you prepare for your lectures. These teaching tools are available on the instructor's companion website accessible via http://login.cengage.com.

Instructor's guide

The **instructor's guide** provides you with a wealth of content to help you set up and administer your subject. It includes chapter outlines, suggestions for student activities, and further investigations for students. Available via the instructor's companion website.

PowerPoint™ presentations

These **PowerPoint** presentations cover the main concepts addressed within the chapters of the text and can be edited to suit your subject. Use these slides to enhance your lecture presentations or as student handouts. Available via the instructor's companion website.

Artwork files

These digital files of tables and pictures from the text can be used in a variety of media. You can use them in your learning management system, add them to PowerPoint presentations or copy them onto student materials. Available via the instructor's companion website.

CHAPTER ONE

SETTING THE SCENE

Chapter learning focus

This chapter will investigate:

- government policies and priorities

- changing worlds and childhoods

- contemporary perspectives of children's learning

- what contemporary theories mean in practice.

Introduction

This is the sixth edition of *Programming and Planning in Early Childhood Settings*. It retains all of the chapters from the fifth edition, but in a rearranged order and with extensive new content in each chapter and accompanying online materials. Since the last edition, educators in Australian prior-to-school settings and outside school hours care have been working with the *National Quality Framework* (ACECQA, 2011), including *Belonging, Being and Becoming: The Early Years Framework for Australia*, *My Time Our Place: Framework for Outside School Hours Care in Australia* and the *National Quality Standard*.

In 2013 the Australian Council for Early Children's Quality Authority released a *Report on the National Quality Framework and Regulatory Burden*, reviewing the success of the *National Quality Framework* in reducing unnecessary compliance burdens on early childhood services. Key themes explored in the report were opportunities to simplify the *National Quality Standard*, reduce the number of administrative requirements, set clearer expectations and improve communication about administrative requirements, and remove operational impediments (ACECQA, 2013, pp. 10–23). Subsequently changes have been undertaken to amend legislation and the Australian Government announced a 2014 review of the *National Quality Framework* content of the Standard, implementation, workforce availability, governance and regulatory agencies.

At the time of writing, the Australian Government Productivity Commission *Inquiry into Child Care and Early Learning* is being undertaken into 'future options for childcare and early childhood learning, with a focus on developing a system that supports workforce participation and addresses children's learning and development needs' (Australian Government Productivity Commission, 2014). In particular, the inquiry will address issues of affordability, including levels of government assistance, accessibility, flexibility and transition to school.

Since the last edition, educators in the school sector have begun implementation of the Australian Curriculum in the areas of English, mathematics, science and history, and documents for Foundation to Year 10 or Year 12 are shortly to be released for other curriculum areas (*see* Australian Curriculum and Assessment Authority). As well as the review of early childhood education, in 2014 the Australian Government also launched a review of the national curriculum for schools.

This chapter provides an overview of the policy context in the early childhood and school sectors. It also considers the changing worlds and contemporary theories of childhood and children's learning and the implications of these theories for practice. These ideas are then elaborated on in the following chapters.

Government policies priorities

> - Early years are a critical time for children learning (Shonkoff + Phillips, 2000; Shonkoff et al, 2009)
> - need to remember that it is equally important to ~~focus~~ help other years.

Australian Government policies and priorities in the a

- the importance of the early years
- equity and social justice
- national learning and curriculum documents
- quality assurance.

The importance of the early years

The early years are recognised at both national and international levels as a critical time for children's learning (*see* Shonkoff & Phillips, 2000; Shonkoff et al., 2009). Consequently, there is a focus at government level on strengthening families and communities in order to provide children with a good start in life. The importance of early childhood policy has been emphasised within organisations such as UNESCO and the World Bank. Along with other OECD countries, Australia is committed to developing early childhood policy and to assessing quality within early childhood provisions. The *National Early Childhood Development Strategy, Investing in the Early Years* was developed by the Council of Australian Governments (COAG) 'to ensure that by 2020 all children have the best start in life to create a better future for themselves and for the nation' (COAG, 2009, p. 4).

One of the challenges facing such commitments is the balance between a focus on investment in early childhood as a means of securing the future and a focus on improving the present. Dahlberg and Moss (2005) are critical of the focus on investments and commitments motivated primarily by economic consideration. For example, investment in early childhood can be promoted as a means of ensuring the supply of a well-qualified workforce, both by providing early childhood services as a support for currently working families and as a means of training a future workforce. Such a focus can be seen in a number of Australian policy documents, where recognition of the aging nature of the current workforce is provided as one aspect of a rationale for ensuring that young children have access to early childhood education.

Investing in early childhood has become a catchcry of economists, community health professionals and early childhood educators. For example, Grunewald and Rolnick (2003) note the importance of policymakers identifying the educational investments that yield the highest return for each dollar invested. James Heckman (cited in Vimpani, 2005) notes similar outcomes:

> People who participate in enriched early childhood programs are more likely to complete school and much less likely to require welfare benefits, become teen parents or participate in criminal activities.

Few can argue with the importance of supporting children and families. However, we need to be cautious about assessing the value of early childhood programs only in terms of children's future contributions to society. It is equally important to focus on programs that improve the lives of children, families and communities in the present. It is also necessary to recognise that investing in early childhood is unlikely to solve all societal problems, and investments promoting the wellbeing of children after they reach the age of five, and often into later life, will continue to be needed. It is critical to balance the focus on future contributions of young children to society with recognition of the importance of what happens in their lives in the present. The early years need to be seen as important in their own right as well as being a foundation for life outcomes.

Much of the recognition of the significance of the early years has been drawn from research on early brain development (*see* Chapter 3). Brain research also points to the significance of secure and caring relationships in children's early years. One possible consequence of this research can be a shift from focusing on early childhood education and care as necessary for parents' workforce participation to a focus on children's development, socialisation and learning (Press & Hayes, 2000). The introduction in many countries, including Australia, of national standards for early childhood education and care and outside school hours care programs, with the aim of lifting quality, reflects governments' emphasis on the requirements of children. At the same time, the increasing recognition of the early years is reflected in government policies and programs aimed at supporting children's wellbeing by strengthening families and communities.

For example, the Australian Government funded the *Stronger Families and Communities Strategy* from 2000 to 2009. This strategy highlighted the role of families, communities, governments and the corporate sector in building social support networks and strengthening relationships (Press & Hayes, 2000). Many programs, such as the Early Childhood – Invest to Grow, Child Care Links and Supported Playgroups, target families living in poverty or isolation, Indigenous families, and culturally and linguistically diverse (CALD) families. An evaluation of the *Stronger Families and Communities Strategy* found that there were many benefits, including community mapping, the development of services and programs that met community needs, the development of services that engaged hard-to-reach families, community capacity building and improvements in parenting self-efficacy (Social Policy Research Centre and the Australian Institute of Family Studies, 2009).

Since 2009, a range of early intervention and prevention programs, including early learning and literacy, parenting and family support and early development programs, have been funded through the Family Support Program within the Australian Government Department of Families, Housing, Community Services and Indigenous Affairs. The *Stronger Futures in the Northern Territory* program was introduced in July 2012 in place of the Northern Territory National Emergency Response Act 2007 in order to work with Aboriginal people in the Northern Territory to provide safe and healthy environments for children and families (Australian Government, 2013).

In 2009, all Australian state and territory governments endorsed the *National Framework for Protecting Australia's Children 2009–2020*, which placed children's interests at the centre of everything educators do (Commonwealth of Australia, 2009). This strategy aims to build family and community capacity and includes investment in family support and child protection services and the promotion of the safety and wellbeing of all children. This strategy has identified six outcomes:

1. Children live in safe and supportive families and communities.
2. Children and families access adequate support to promote safety and intervene early.
3. Risk factors for child abuse and neglect are addressed.
4. Children who have been abused or neglected receive the support and care they need for their safety and wellbeing.
5. Indigenous children are supported and safe in their families and communities.
6. Child sexual abuse and exploitation is prevented and survivors receive adequate support.

Commonwealth of Australia, 2009, p. 11

Actions associated with this strategy include:
- the establishment of child and family centres and children's services hubs
- an expansion of the Communities for Children program
- an expansion of family support programs for vulnerable families and children
- expansion of mental health programs such as KidsMatters and MindMatters
- universal access to early childhood education and care in the year prior to formal schooling
- a *National Quality Framework for Early Childhood Education and Care*
- a National Early Years Workforce Strategy
- increased funding for disadvantaged schools
- the appointment of a National Children's Commissioner
- the implementation of a nationally-consistent approach to *Working with Children* checks
- new Child and Family Centres across Australia – it is expected that the National Partnership Agreement on Indigenous Early Childhood Development will complete 38 of these centres across Australia.

The action plan for 2012–15 focuses on the develop[ment] [of] [pa]rtnerships for [the]
solutions, in particular recognising that there is a need [...]
and linguistically diverse families and communities.

One of the aims of the *National Framework for Prote*[ction]
is universal access to a year of preschool education in [...]
intended to better prepare children for formal full-time [...]
more positive school outcomes. The idea that a presch[ool]
delivered by a degree-qualified early childhood teache[r]
However, few of those involved in early childhood serv[ice]
programs. In supporting calls for families and children [...]
of early childhood services that best meet their needs, [...]
affordable, accessible and of high quality. The move to [...]
services is essential to ensure that all children have access to a quality program. Accompanying
this is a need to consider what is meant by 'preparing' children for school and the implications
of this. In this book, we advance the notion that children make a positive start to school when
all those around them are working together to promote positive, meaningful and engaging
experiences, rather than a sense that prior-to-school settings need to ensure that young children
have a requisite set of skills or abilities (Dockett & Perry, 2007). Clearly, a critical element of this
involves educators at all levels working together to support children in the present and the future.

The focus on the importance of the early years is also reflected in the Commonwealth and
state governments' commitment to the Australian Early Development Index (AEDI). The AEDI is
implemented across Australia as a population measure of children's preparedness for school and
as a means to consider funding allocations for services within communities. The AEDI is
completed by teachers of children in the first year of formal schooling. For each child,
teachers are asked to rate children's overall development across five domains: physical
health and wellbeing; social competence; emotional maturity; language and cognitive
skills; and communication skills and general knowledge. While data are collected about
individual children, these data are reported at the community level, enabling
communities to identify what works well, as well as ways to improve the supports
provided for children and families. The community profiles generated from the data
reflect the proportions of children starting school across the community who are
perceived by teachers to be developmentally vulnerable, as well as those who
are perceived to be developing well. Community measures, such as the AEDI, allow
communities to monitor what happens to their children and families and to plan to
change local resources, provision or supports to improve children's life chances (Centre
for Community Child Health and the Telethon Institute for Child Health Research, 2009).

While the focus on population measures, rather than individual measures, of readiness is
acknowledged, there is still some concern that what [...]
limited picture of what is important as children cross [...]
services and school. For example, it is well establishe[d]
supports, as well as school provisions for all children [...]
(Dockett & Perry, 2009). Further, the value of informa[tion]
prior-to-school educators needs to be considered in [...]

What is the AEDI community profile for the children starting school in your early childhood or school local community? What resources and support services would be useful to further support children in your local area?

Equity and social justi[ce]

One of the key reasons the Australian Government de[...]
and a national school curriculum was to promote better educational outcomes for all Australians.
The intention is to provide a high-quality curriculum for children and young people regardless of
where they live, their ability or the type of early childhood service or school they attend.

All ministers of education across Australia have signed the *Melbourne Declaration on
Educational Goals for Young Australians*, which includes a commitment to ensuring that
socio-economic disadvantage is no longer a significant determinant of educational outcomes
(MCEETYA, 2008). The MCEETYA goals include promotion of equity and excellence in schooling

Handwritten notes:

- AEDI implemented across Australia as a measure of childrens preparedness for school.
- AEDI completed by teachers in the childrens first formal year of schooling.
- Each child is rated on their overall development across 5 stages:
  - Physical health + wellbeing
  - Social competence
  - Emotional maturity
  - Language + cognitive skills
  - Communication + general knowledge

Melb declaration goals:
- promotion of equity + excellence in schools
- All Aust become 'successful learners + active + informed citizens' (MCEETYA)

as well as the goal that all Australians become 'successful learners, confident and creative individuals and active and informed citizens' (MCEETYA, 2008). These goals underpin the *National Quality Framework* for early childhood education and school aged care as well as the Australian Curriculum for Foundation to Year 12.

One of the underpinning principles of *The Early Years Learning Framework* (EYLF) and *My Place, Our Time* is equity and social justice. Similarly, in the school system, terms such as 'inclusion' and 'equal opportunity' are used in the Australian Curriculum documents to reflect this commitment to equity and social justice.

Australian Government policies and funding initiatives support inclusive practices. Inclusion refers to the active participation and meaningful involvement of children with disabilities and additional needs in the same early childhood programs and community settings as other typically developing children. Current research indicates that the most effective form of early childhood intervention is to support children in the environments in which they spend most of their time; that is, in the home and mainstream early childhood services. The federally-funded Inclusion and Professional Support Program aims to remove the barriers to access for children with additional needs through the provision of inclusion support and is available to federally-funded child care services (approved for child care benefit) and Budget Based Funded programs, for example Multifunctional Aboriginal Children's Services. This funding supports the inclusion of children with ongoing high support needs. Each state government also provides inclusion support funding for early childhood services and schools. Many of these state-funded programs are under review at present.

In the past few years, policy and funding for children with additional needs has moved towards what is known as 'person-centred approaches', which provide funds to families/children who are approved to receive this funding. Helping Children with Autism, funded through the Department of Social Services, is one such scheme. Person-centred funding, which will become a national approach under the National Disability Insurance Scheme, allows individuals to choose services they wish to access with the funds available. While this can be seen as a positive step for individuals, especially adults, there are some concerns about what this may mean for education, especially early childhood intervention services which are often small community-based services dependent on current government funding for their existence rather than a 'user pays' system. While policy supports inclusive practice, it is unclear whether funding itself will support this approach appropriately in the future.

The introduction of a national quality standard for early childhood services – which mandates staff–child ratios, staffing qualifications and national curriculum frameworks for early childhood education and school aged care with underpinning principles, practices and learning outcomes – is designed to ensure quality early education and care for all children (ACECQA, 2011).

By signing up to the *National Quality Framework*, states and territories have committed to the provision of universal access to a year of early childhood education. As a consequence, most Australian children now have access to some form of early childhood education and care program in the year before they start school. Data on access and attendance has been difficult to collect. The Australian Institute of Health and Welfare (AIHW) and Australian Bureau of Statistics (ABS) developed data standards through the Early Childhood Education and Care National Minimum Data Set (ECEC NMDS) to provide a nationally consistent approach to data collection (the ECEC Collection). Estimates from the ABS National Early Childhood Education and Care (ECEC) Collection for 2012 indicate that 89 per cent of children were enrolled in a preschool program (including long day care programs) in the year before full-time schooling and 86 per cent of children were attending a preschool program for at least one hour in the reference week (according to data provided by DEEWR from the ABS 2012 National ECEC Collection). Despite new partnership agreements, this figure is similar to that from 2008 (AIHW, 2013). In addition, preschool program attendance rates were higher among children in two parent families where at least one family member was employed and in families with a higher parental income than single parent, unemployed and low income families, indicating that early childhood education and care is still not accessible or affordable for many families.

Although access to early childhood education and care has improved, Australia ranks near the bottom (30/34) of OECD countries for the percentage of three- to five-year-olds attending early learning or preschool services. While Australia meets the OECD benchmarks for subsidised and regulated child care services and staff with tertiary qualifications, it does not meet the benchmark for subsidised and accredited early education services for four-year-olds, overall staff training, staff–child ratios or the percentage of GDP spent on early childhood services (UNICEF Innocenti Research Centre, 2008).

Greishaber (2009) notes the importance of equitable access to quality early childhood programs that is not dependent on family income or employment status, and not restricted by special education requirements, language, ethnicity or race. The Federal Government's commitment to the provision of early childhood/preschool education for all children in the year before school aims to address issues of access, although the cost of services is still a barrier to access for many families. In addition, culturally responsive services and staff and the availability of qualified staff in rural and remote regions are all issues that impact on the accessibility of quality education and care for all children.

Ratings of children's development were collected through the AEDI for 96.5 per cent of children in the first year of formal full-time schooling (almost 290 000 children across almost 7500 government and non-government schools). Analysis of these data indicates that teachers rate many children as vulnerable on one or more of the rated domains. While most Australian children are reported to be doing well across each of the five domains measured by the AEDI (physical health and wellbeing, social competence, emotional maturity, language and cognitive skills, and communication skills and general knowledge) 22 per cent of children are rated as vulnerable in one or more domain and 10.8 per cent of children across two or more domains (Royal Children's Hospital Centre for Community Child Health and the Murdoch Children's Research Institute, 2013). While this is an improvement from 23.5 per cent and 11.8 per cent respectively in 2009, it still represents a substantial number of children who are considered by their teachers to be vulnerable in one or more domain. The Australian Research Alliance for Children and Youth aim to reduce the percentage of children identified as developmentally vulnerable in one or more area to 15 per cent by 2020 (ARACY, 2013). They argue that this requires the nation to address issues of income disparity and child poverty, and family health outcomes.

Currently, for the 46 indicators where comparable data are available, Australia is ranked in the top third of OECD countries for less than one-quarter (12/46) of the indicators of child and youth wellbeing, in the middle third for almost half (20/46) and in the bottom third for around one-quarter (14/46) of indicators, including the areas of health, education, child poverty and participation. Australia is in the bottom third for infant mortality, income inequality and unemployed families. In fact, the data indicate that income inequality and unemployment are increasing in Australia. In 2013, 2.2 million Australians lived below the poverty line, which means that 600 000 children under 15 live in households where no one has a job (Skattebol et al., 2012). Australia does not meet the OECD benchmark for a national plan with priority for disadvantaged children or for child poverty (UNICEF Innocenti Research Centre, 2008).

AEDI data indicate that Aboriginal and Torres Strait Islander children are almost twice as likely to be considered developmentally vulnerable as non-Indigenous children (Children's Hospital Centre for Community Child Health and the Murdoch Children's Research Institute, 2013). However, there are some improvements, with a change from almost 50 per cent of Aboriginal and Torres Strait Islander children being vulnerable in one or more development domain in 2009 to 43 per cent in 2012. These data also point to the importance of educators demonstrating cultural competence in their interactions with Aboriginal and Torres Strait Islander children, families and communities and, through this, developing responsive educational contexts that identify and build upon the strengths of those involved. The development of more appropriate training pathways for local Aboriginal and Torres Strait Islander educators and the availability of culturally-competent pedagogical leaders are essential to this strategy.

In 2008, the then Deputy Prime Minister of Australia, Julia Gillard, announced that the Australian Government aimed to halve the Indigenous gap in literacy and numeracy achievements and in Year 12 completion within a decade (DEEWR, 2008). The *Closing the Gap* strategy was agreed to by all Australian state and territory leaders in 2008 and includes targets in the areas of infant mortality, life expectancy, education and employment. Education targets included 'ensuring that all Indigenous four-year-olds living in remote communities have access to early childhood education' (COAG, 2012) by 2013 and 'halving the gap for Indigenous students in reading, writing and numeracy' (COAG, 2012) by 2018. While some data suggests that there has been progress towards these goals, at the time of writing (2014) it is not clear that the stated goals have been met.

The National Partnership Agreement on Early Childhood Education has seen increases in early childhood education programs in remote communities. It is important to note that the target is access rather than attendance and, as early childhood education is not compulsory, the agreed target is 95 per cent enrolment. The *Prime Minister's Report on Closing the Gap* (Australian Government, 2013) indicated that 91 per cent of Indigenous children in remote areas were enrolled in a preschool program in 2011 and it was anticipated that 95 per cent would be achieved in 2013. However, as the Prime Minister's Report (Australian Government, 2013, p. 23) notes, it is not enough merely to have access to children's services: 'Children need to attend regularly and families need to be engaged to achieve maximum benefits and the programs offered need to be of high quality and culturally relevant'.

Strategies directed towards improved school outcomes for Indigenous students include the National Plan for School Improvement, with additional funding to schools with Aboriginal or Torres Strait Islander students enrolled, and the Parental and Community Engagement Program, which encourages parental participation in educational decision-making and support for children's learning at home. Analysis of the National Assessment Program – Literacy and Numeracy (NAPLAN) results indicate there has been some lessening of the gap between Indigenous and non-Indigenous students for reading, writing and numeracy, with the percentage of Indigenous students at or above the NAPLAN National Minimum Standards in Year 3 Reading increasing by 5.9 percentage points between 2008 and 2012.

However, Indigenous students were meeting the target points for 2012 in only three out of eight areas assessed by NAPLAN (Australian Government, 2013). In some areas (Years 3, 5 and 7 reading and Year 9 numeracy) the gap between Indigenous and non-Indigenous students had narrowed between 2008 and 2012, in some cases quite substantially (for example, by 4.7 percentage points in Year 3 reading), and in other cases fairly modestly (0.6 percentage points in Year 5 reading). While 96.4 per cent of non-Indigenous children assessed in 2012 were meeting at least the minimum standard for persuasive writing in Year 3, this was only the case for 78.3 percent of Indigenous children (Australian Government, 2013). In four of the eight areas assessed the gap had increased, with the largest increase being 5 percentage points in Year 3 numeracy (Australian Government, 2013). There are also pronounced differences in achievement according to location, with Indigenous students in remote locations generally achieving poorer results than students in urban and regional areas. For example, only 20.3 per cent of Indigenous Year 5 students in very remote areas achieved at or above national minimum standards in reading in 2012 compared to 76.0 per cent in metropolitan areas (Australian Government, 2013).

Similar concerns are raised in the data from international assessments of literacy, numeracy and science of fifteen year olds in the Program of International Student Assessment (PISA). While Australia has improved from 'high quality, low equity' in 2000 to 'high quality, medium equity' in 2009 and 'high-quality, high equity' in 2012, meaning that education systems are ranked as high quality and student background have a less significant impact on performance than the OECD average, closer interrogation of the data shows that there are still different outcomes according to class, ethnicity and geographical location.

While many students are doing well, with Australia ranked 17th in mathematics, equal 8th in science and equal 10th in reading out of 65 countries, 42 per cent of Australian 15-year-olds did not meet minimum standards in maths, and 36 per cent for reading. Despite being ranked as 'high equity', PISA 2012 data shows that Australian students who have Indigenous, rural and/or low socio-economic backgrounds are more likely to achieve at lower levels than other Australian

students (Thomson, 2013). For example, Australian students in the lowest 25 per cent of socio-economic status performed much worse on PISA than the rest of Australian students and those in the top 25 per cent of socio-economic status performed significantly better (Thomson, de Borteli & Buckley, 2013). This difference is equivalent to around two-and-a-half years of schooling for reading, maths and science for the students in the highest socio-economic group compared to those in the lowest, and in NSW there is a three year differential. There are also significant gaps based on gender, Indigenous and immigrant status, and particular intersections such as Indigenous boys living in remote areas where students are underperforming. There are also differences across jurisdictions, with Tasmania and the Northern Territory rated as 'low quality, low equity' for mathematical literacy (Thomson, de Borteli & Buckley, 2013). These data suggest that while government policies to promote equity in education are important, there is still some way to go before it can be claimed that Australian education – at both school and prior-to-school levels – is equitable. For example, responsive schools in very remote areas providing culturally appropriate gender segregated schooling environments may improve attendance, and therefore learning outcomes, for older Indigenous boys.

National learning and curriculum documents

There has been a move internationally to the codification of curriculum at a national level. In Australia, this includes *Belonging, Being and Becoming: The Early Years Learning Framework for Australia* (EYLF), introduced in July 2009 for all early childhood settings; *My Place, Our Time: Framework for Outside School Hours Care in Australia*; and the Australian Curriculum, a national curriculum for school students, implemented from 2011.

The EYLF and *My Place, Our Time* are frameworks to support informed curriculum decisions, not curriculums in themselves. They include a vision for children, underpinning principles and practices and expectations for children's learning that are expressed as learning outcomes. The five core principles are 'secure, respectful and reciprocal relationships; partnerships with families; high expectations and equity; respect for diversity; and ongoing learning and reflective practice' (DEEWR, 2009, p. 10). They encourage educators to utilise pedagogical practices that reflect holistic approaches to learning and teaching, are responsive to children, use a play-based approach, include intentional teaching and the creation of learning environments that have a positive impact on children's learning, demonstrate value for the cultural and social contexts of children's families, support continuity of learning, and assess and monitor children's learning in order to support children's achievement of learning outcomes (DEEWR, 2009, p. 14). They include five broad learning outcomes – children have a strong sense of identity, children are connected with and contribute to their world, children have a strong sense of wellbeing, children are confident and involved learners and children are effective communicators.

The *Melbourne Declaration on Educational Goals for Young Australians*, supported by all ministers of education, takes a similar approach. This document includes the promotion of equity as one of the goals of Australian schooling (MCEETYA, 2008, p. 7). It also emphasises the importance of 'an appreciation of and respect for social, cultural and religious diversity, and a sense of global citizenship', and highlights the importance of partnerships between educators, families and communities. Education for the 21st century needs to equip children and young people with the 'knowledge, understanding, skills and values' necessary to engage confidently with the opportunities and challenges they will face (MCEETYA, 2008, p. 4). This document highlights the importance of aesthetic, moral, spiritual, social and emotional learning as well as the intellectual and physical aspects. This means that education in prior-to-school and school settings should include a focus on areas such as social interaction, problem solving and digital media, and should reinforce values of democracy, equity, justice and respect for others.

While the outcomes for the prior-to-school sector and outside school-hours care are broad and integrated across curriculum and developmental areas, the achievement standards in the national school curriculum are linked to specific curriculum areas and specific years of schooling. At the time of writing, the Australian Curriculum and Assessment Authority (ACARA) national curriculum for the areas of English, mathematics, science, the arts, geography and history were being implemented and languages, health and physical education, technologies and civics and citizenship were being developed (*see* the ACARA website for updates). These curriculum areas have been developed for year groups with the first year of school referred to as the Foundation year. Extracts from the achievement standards for the Foundation year are listed in Table 1.1.

Learning outcomes in documents for preschool children focus on rich expectations for learning, while outcomes in national school curriculum documents appear to be much narrower

TABLE 1.1 Extracts from the achievement standards for the Foundation year, Australian Curriculum.

CURRICULUM AREA	ACHIEVEMENT STANDARDS – FOUNDATION YEAR
Mathematics	By the end of the Foundation year, students make connections between number names, numerals and quantities up to 10. They compare objects using mass, length and capacity. Students connect events and the days of the week. They explain the order and duration of events. They use appropriate language to describe location. Students count to and from 20 and order small collections. They group objects based on common characteristics and sort shapes and objects. Students answer simple questions to collect information.
English	By the end of the Foundation year, students use predicting and questioning strategies to make meaning from texts. They recall one or two events from texts with familiar topics. They read short, predictable texts with familiar vocabulary and supportive images, drawing on their developing knowledge of concepts about print and sound and letters. They identify the letters of the English alphabet and use the sounds represented by most letters. They listen for rhyme, letter patterns and sounds in words. They identify and describe likes and dislikes about familiar texts, objects, characters and events. When writing, students use familiar words and phrases and images to convey ideas. Their writing shows evidence of sound and letter knowledge, beginning writing behaviours and experimentation with capital letters and full stops. They correctly form known upper- and lower-case letters.
Science	By the end of the Foundation year, students describe the properties and behaviour of familiar objects. They suggest how the environment affects them and other living things. Students share observations of familiar objects and events.
History	By the end of the Foundation year, students identify similarities and differences between families. They recognise how important family events are commemorated. Students sequence familiar events in order. They pose questions about their past. Students relate a story about their past using a range of texts.
Geography	By the end Foundation year, students describe the features of familiar places and recognise why some places are special to people. They recognise that places can be represented on maps and a globe and why places are important to people. Students observe the familiar features of places and represent these features and their location on pictorial maps and models. They share observations in a range of texts and use everyday language to describe direction and location. Students reflect on their learning to suggest ways they can care for a familiar place.

Source: © 2012 by Australian Curriculum Assessment and Reporting Authority (ACARA)

in focus. For many educators, there is concern that the national curriculum for schools potentially reduces opportunities for student learning in terms of diversity and complexity. It is up to educators working in the first years of school to incorporate the content requirements of the national curriculum with integrated approaches to pedagogy that acknowledge the complexity of learning and promote depth of understanding as well as the engagement of all students. Effective education for the 21st century requires inquiry, problem solving, collaboration and meaning making that goes across curriculum areas. As Reid (2009, in Marsh, 2010, p. 26) argues, 'the approach to issues, problems and challenges of the contemporary world requires us to cross established disciplinary boundaries, not remain trapped within them'.

There is potential for *The Early Years Learning Framework* to have a 'push-up' effect into schools. The framework provides many opportunities for stronger links across prior-to-school and school settings and greater continuity of learning. The learning outcomes of the EYLF are consistent with the *Melbourne Declaration on the Education Goals for Young Australians*. In addition, the use of terms such as 'outcomes' and 'assessment' in the early childhood sector provides a shared language across early childhood settings and schools and has the potential for educators in prior-to-school settings to clearly articulate children's learning in ways that are accessible to the school community.

This shared language aligns the discourses of early childhood more closely with those of the school sector and has the potential to provide benefits in terms of greater recognition of the significance of early childhood programs and improved status for early childhood educators. However, there are also concerns that the stronger emphasis on learning and assessment and mandated learning outcomes will mean that discourses of care will become marginalised, that educators will become de-professionalised and that there will be a 'push-down' of school curriculum (Ortlipp et al., 2011). There are dangers that with the focus on 'preschool' education and transition to school, some administrators, educators and families will perceive that young children need an academic, teacher-directed curriculum. Children's preparation for school is interpreted by some to mean children's ability to demonstrate a narrow range of skills (Pianta & Cox, 1999) with little recognition of the social and interpersonal areas of learning that are equally as important as academic skills (La Paro & Pianta, 2000; MCEETYA, 2008).

It is essential to continue to promote the value of play in young children's learning in order to counter the push towards a more formal academic curriculum. Play environments enriched with culturally relevant resources provide opportunities for children to explore processes and concepts, to develop positive dispositions towards learning and to use literacy and numeracy for a range of purposes (*see* Figure 1.1). Play encourages exploration, risk taking, social networks and engagement with learning (Hall, 2000; Wood & Attfield, 1996/2005) and provides a social context for learning where children are able to draw on their everyday worlds and feelings and use a range of resources and media to represent meanings (Marsh & Millard, 2000). In play, children are able to explore and reflect on interests and issues that are relevant to their lives.

Source: KU Phoenix Preschool

FIGURE 1.1 Play environments provide opportunities for children to explore processes and concepts, develop positive dispositions towards learning and use literacy and numeracy for a range of purposes.

Quality assurance

The *National Quality Framework* for early childhood and outside school-hours care and the Australian Curriculum are designed to provide quality education and care for all Australian children. While national standards such as these support equity and social justice, there are also concerns that accountability regimes can enforce standardised practices, predictability and control, and imply that there is one set of 'best practices' and one way of measuring outcomes.

In the school sector, student performance is increasingly measured against predetermined educational outcomes and national benchmarks are used to assess literacy and numeracy. This focus on national standards, measuring and reporting can help to make schools more accountable to their communities and to improve student learning (Press & Hayes, 2000). However, the increased focus on NAPLAN, the publication of data such as NAPLAN results on the MySchool website and the potential to link school funding and teacher promotion to these results mean that these tests present a major equity issue (Marsh, 2010). Marsh alerts us to the dangers of these 'high stake' tests, including concerns that school curricula will become narrower as teachers 'teach to the test', the potential for many students to be disengaged as the curriculum content is not meaningful and the de-professionalisation of teachers. There are also implications for the early childhood years when academic curriculum is 'pushed down' into the earlier years and children are faced with greater academic demands in order to meet the requirements of future tests.

The demands of bureaucratic reporting and attention to the technicalities of teaching often leave educators with little time to engage in more meaningful professional experiences. Many educators involved in an inquiry into public education in New South Wales, for example, complained that there is little time 'to reflect on their teaching practice, to discuss pedagogical issues with colleagues, or to engage in innovative teaching programs' (New South Wales Teachers Federation and Federation of P & C Associations of New South Wales, 2002, p. ix).

Accountability issues are often at the fore in discussions of starting school. As noted above, the AEDI has been implemented across Australia to provide a picture of children's developmental preparedness for school. This is a population measure and is reported in terms of the percentage of a particular population that is considered to be developmentally on track, or developmentally vulnerable, across several developmental domains. In addition to this, several states and territories have introduced a measure of individual children's abilities – particularly in terms of literacy and numeracy – at the time of children starting school. These assessments have various names in different jurisdictions, but have many similarities. While it seems sensible for educators in schools to have an accurate, up-to-date picture of children's skills and understandings, there remain some challenges with such assessments, their timing and their purposes. For example, it is reasonable to ask about the impact of information from prior-to-school educators and how this, along with information from families, could be used to provide the same picture. There are also questions of how the results of such assessments are used – for example, do they provide the basis for allocation to specific classes, access to special education resources or form the basis of major educational decisions? In any formal assessment of young children's learning, it is important to heed the cautions expressed by Meisels (2007) relating to the nature and purpose of such assessments and to consider the equity and social justice implications of assuming that all children start school with similar experiences, backgrounds and understandings.

A second challenge of accountability in the early years of school relates to what counts as evidence of children's learning and how this can be documented. Sometimes teachers in the early years of school report pressure from teachers of later years, and sometimes parents, to ensure that their children are prepared for major tests, such as NAPLAN, selective schools tests and the like. As noted in Chapter 8, there are many ways to document the breadth and depth of children's learning. One of these involves using some form of standardised testing, or sometimes teacher-developed or school-developed tests.

Cautions about the formal assessment of young children are noted by Bowman et al. (2001). Of particular importance is the recognition that young children's abilities are emerging, not fixed, and that assessment at any one point may provide a limited view of children's capabilities. Rather than have major educational decisions based on formal assessments that may present a

limited view of children's abilities and capabilities, educators need to advocate for a wide range of approaches to assessment, over time, using contexts and materials that are familiar to children, and with a clear purpose and clear links to plans for future learning.

We encourage early childhood educators to take notions of accountability seriously – it is important that children, families, communities and administrators are aware of the learning and teaching that occurs within early childhood settings. However, we are firmly committed to the view that the use of standardised testing has the potential to mask, rather than reveal, children's learning. We are keen to suggest that educators can learn a great deal about children from less formal methods, such as observations and conversations. While these strategies may be less formal, the documentation can be even more impressive than a test score, as many of the Learning Stories included in Chapter 8 demonstrate, and these methods of assessment provide clear directions for future learning.

In prior-to-school settings, there is also an increased focus on accountability, predominantly through regulations and accreditation systems. The *National Standard for Early Childhood Education and Care and Outside School Hours Care* (ACECQA, 2011) provides a national accountability framework for these service types for the first time in Australia. The National Standard emphasises:

1. educational program and practice
2. children's health and safety
3. physical environment
4. staffing arrangements (including the number of staff looking after children)
5. relationships with children
6. collaborative partnerships with families and communities
7. leadership and service management.

The National Standard includes a focus on staff qualifications in recognition of the fact that qualified staff are an essential component in the provision of 'good quality children's services' (Press, 2005). There is a range of research that supports the critical role of qualified staff in providing early childhood programs that result in positive outcomes for children. Since the 1970s, research has indicated that early childhood teacher education impacts significantly on the type of education and care that is provided for young children (Honig & Hirallal, 1998; Howes et al., 1998; Phillips et al., 2001). Early childhood programs that have qualified staff and high ratios of staff to children have immediate and long-term benefits for children (*see*, for example, Wylie et al., 2006).

Specialised qualifications in early childhood education are reflected in more child-centred beliefs about child rearing and more positive care giving in centre-based care (Burchinal et al., 2002; Phillips et al., 2001). Research in the USA by the National Institute for Child Health and Human Development (1996; 2002) indicated that specialist qualifications were associated with more planned experiences for children and more warm and sensitive care-giving behaviours. In the United Kingdom the *Effective Provision of Preschool Education* study found that the provision of highly qualified staff promoted the creation of quality learning environments and effective pedagogies and resulted in better outcomes for children (Sylva et al., 2003). This study found that early childhood settings where staff had teaching qualifications recorded the highest quality ratings and had positive staff–child interactions, and settings where staff had low-level qualifications recorded the lowest outcomes for children (Siraj-Blatchford et al., 2003). Research in the school sector also highlights the positive impact of teacher quality on student outcomes (Hattie, 2003; Rowe, 2004).

At the time of writing, there is a requirement that when there are 25 or more children in a long day care or preschool service there is an early childhood teacher in attendance for a minimum of six hours a day or for 60 per cent of the operating hours for a service that operates for less than 50 hours per week. Long day care and preschool services with less than 25 children (based on approved places) must have access to an early childhood teacher for at least 20 per cent of the time that the service provides education and care. In addition, at least half of all educators required to meet the relevant educator-to-child ratios in long day care and preschool services need to hold or be working towards a diploma-level early childhood education and care qualification or a higher qualification and the remainder of the staff need to hold or be working towards a Certificate III qualification. In family day care, all coordinators need to have a Diploma early childhood education and care qualification or above and all family day care educators are required to have (or be actively working towards) a Certificate III early childhood education and care qualification, or equivalent.

By 1 January 2020 there will be a requirement for a second early childhood teacher to be in attendance six hours a day or 60 per cent of the operating hours for services operating less than 50 hours a week when long day care and preschool services are being provided to more than 80 children, and for three hours a day or 30 per cent of the operating hours for services operating less than 50 hours per week for long day and preschool services for 60 to 80 children (ACECQA, 2013).

The national early childhood staffing qualification standard combined with the move to universal access requires greater numbers of qualified staff working in early childhood settings. Between 1997 and 2010, the early childhood workforce almost doubled in size (Productivity Commission, 2011). However, according to the Productivity Commission, approximately 72 per cent of the workforce is on a part-time, casual or seasonal basis and turnover of staff is high in some areas. This is particularly the case for early childhood teachers, many of whom leave early childhood settings to teach in primary schools, and for educators in Indigenous, rural and remote services.

Submissions to the Productivity Commission revealed both high levels of job satisfaction and high levels of stress, poor morale and the perception that there is a lack of public recognition for the work of early childhood educators. Similarly, in 2006 the Victorian Government's Community Services Minister's Advisory Council found that 71 per cent of all child care workers said that the job is stressful and only 51 per cent of all workers expressed an intention to remain working in the sector for five years or more. *Big Steps in Childcare* (2010), a document published by the United Voice union that covers many educators in early childhood services, has argued that there is a workforce crisis in Australian early childhood education, highlighting the high staff turnover in early childhood services and attributing this predominantly to low wages, with lack of pay parity for teachers across the prior-to-school and school sectors a major issue for early childhood teachers. Other issues focus on poor workforce conditions, which include lack of time for programming and staff professional development.

Early childhood educators report that they spend significant time complying with a large regulatory and administrative burden (Productivity Commission, 2011). The requirement to meet externally imposed standards increases educators' workloads while at the same time implying that they cannot be trusted to make professional judgements. The dominant control over curricula exercised by government authorities and the often narrow prescriptions of acceptable practice do not acknowledge the professionalism of educators or the diversity of the contexts in which they work. Early childhood educators who participated in a study conducted by Fenech et al. (2006) stated that the Australian accreditation system in practice at the time impeded their relationships with families and overemphasised risks to the detriment of children's learning. Requirements were often found to be time-consuming as well as 'excessive, unnecessary and repetitive' (Fenech et al., 2006, p. 54). Similarly, Bretherton (2010) found that regulatory burdens influenced educators to leave the early childhood field.

Educators in prior-to-school education have long expressed concerns that their profession has little recognition and is undervalued (CCCAC, 2001; Community Services Ministers Advisory Council, 2006; Elliott, 2006; Fenech, 2006). Traditionally, governments, parents and the broader community have viewed staff in early childhood settings as carers, rather than educators, resulting in poor wages and low status (Productivity Commission, 2011). This, along with the poor working conditions in prior-to-school settings, impacts on the number and quality of students attracted to early childhood teacher education and diploma-level courses and available for employment (ACTU, 2003). Low status and poor working conditions also make it difficult to retain educators in the field.

There was hope that the introduction of the EYLF would help improve the status of the early childhood profession by making the work of early childhood educators more visible to families, community members and other professionals (Ortlipp et al., 2011). While the introduction of a learning framework with learning outcomes along with national standards can raise the status of the early childhood profession, accountability requirements placed on educators can also serve to detract from the self-image and morale of educators, and lower the status and standing of teaching in the community. The mandating of national curriculum documents and learning frameworks heralds a move away from the autonomous professional towards a more regulated profession (Ortlipp et al., 2011). There are concerns about the extent to which mandatory learning frameworks or a focus on the achievement of government-initiated and mandated outcomes might de-professionalise early childhood practice (Alvestad & Duncan, 2006; Ortlipp et al., 2011).

It is essential that educators continue to be proactive in raising community awareness of the complexity of educators' roles in both the prior-to-school and school sectors and in advocating for recognition for the work that they do. Sumsion (2006) argues for a politically active early childhood profession that is proactive in promoting the importance of early childhood work and influential in policy decisions. She suggests that early childhood educators can work towards transforming the world through critical imagination, critical literacy and critical action.

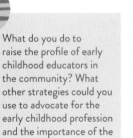

What do you do to raise the profile of early childhood educators in the community? What other strategies could you use to advocate for the early childhood profession and the importance of the early years?

In addition to staff qualifications, other components in the National Standard focus on the educational program, the physical environment and children's health and safety. National standards can provide early childhood educators with clear expectations and guidelines, give protection to children and families and offer educators 'power, confidence and direction' (Fenech et al., 2006, p. 53). A regulatory framework that is regularly monitored and enforced is an essential component in the provision of 'quality early childhood programs' (Press, 2005). There is compelling international evidence of the importance of structural variables being mandated through regulations. Documents such as the EYLF and the *National Standard* can provide a unifying framework that supports educators in their professional decision making (Alvested & Duncan, 2006).

However, there has been much critique of concepts such as 'quality care' and the notion that there is one set of practices that is appropriate for all communities and that can be measured objectively (*see*, for example, Grieshaber, 2002). Postmodern theorists such as Foucault (1970) have argued that some forms of specialised knowledge such as 'quality care' become 'regimes of truth … that sometimes work against social justice by excluding, rather than including, different ways of understanding and living in the world' (Campbell & Page, 2003, p. 290). According to Dahlberg et al. (2007), the term 'quality' is prescriptive, does not reflect the diversity or complexity of family contexts and early childhood settings and does not allow for a range of practices. The concept of quality assumes that there is such a thing as objective, scientific truth and that quality is a universal construct that can be measured by prescribed outcomes. Trying to define one set of best practice and applying it universally contradicts much of what we know about the importance of contexts and the ways in which contexts influence interactions and outcomes.

As Moss (2001a, p. 126) notes, the Reggio Emila region of Italy (see Malaguzzi, 1998) has managed to develop a world-renowned program 'without the benefit of prescriptive guidelines on content or methods, quality assurance or accreditation schemes, inspection systems, Baseline Assessments or other "outcome" indicators or research'. In Reggio Emilia, the emphasis is on contextualised practice rather than a set of abstract external standards. Quality 'must be considered within a socio-cultural, economic and political context as well as take account of relevant research concerning children's growth and development' (Goodfellow, 2002, p. 8). Rather than the notion of one set of 'quality' practices, Dahlberg and her colleagues (2007) argue that there should be an emphasis on ongoing self-reflection and evaluation and on quality improvement that is context-specific. Goodfellow recommends that educators move away from trying to identify the one best way to achieve a specific goal and instead focus on 'wise practice', which emphasises 'introspective examination and … opportunities to explore our own values and beliefs as well as the insights and understandings framed within our workplaces' (2002, p. 5).

Dahlberg et al. (2007) encourage a focus on ethical dimensions of choice that take account of complexity and diversity. Luke (2003) also argues that quality assurance must take account of context. He notes that Canadian school reform literature demonstrates that accountability to other professionals is a stronger indicator of improvements in pedagogy than standardisation of centralised forms of accountability. Rather than prescriptive codes, Moss (2001b) argues for an 'ethic of care' where respect for diversity and responsiveness to difference are foregrounded. Woodrow and Brennan (2001) also suggest a focus on connections, relationships and conflicting responsibilities rather than a focus on rights and rules. Moss (2001b, p. 6) argues that rather than being bound by rules, early childhood professionals need to be their 'own moral agents', prepared to accept responsibility for the decisions they make.

Changing worlds and childhoods

There have been major social, economic and technological changes in the late 20th and early 21st centuries in many parts of the world resulting in changing experiences of childhoods. Most children now experience a range of technologies as part of everyday life. In 2010–11, 79 per cent of Australian households had home Internet access, an increase of 12 per cent from 2006–07; 73 per cent of these were broadband connections (ABS, 2012). The 13.3 million people using the Internet at home emailed (91%), read research, news and general items (87%) and completed financial activities, as in banking or paying bills (64%). The 2012 *Children's Participation in Cultural and Leisure Activities* survey (ABS, 2012 [April]) indicated that 90 per cent of all children aged five to 14 years used the Internet, an 11 per cent increase since 2010. This included 79 per cent of five- to eight-year-old children using the Internet. Children most commonly accessed the Internet from home (2.3 million) as well as from school (2.2 million). In 2012, 29 per cent of children used their own mobile phones, including two per cent of children aged five to eight years. While most children used a computer at school, interestingly the home was reported as the more common site of Internet use. These statistics indicate that many children use computers and the Internet as part of their social worlds, meaning that they can access a range of texts, including those of popular culture.

Books, magazines, television programs, movies, websites, food, computer games and collectables are all increasingly interrelated and are frequently connected to children's popular culture (Buckingham, 2000). Even when children do not have access to the latest DVDs, computer

FIGURE 1.2 Popular culture and technology are significant parts of everyday life for most children growing up in Australia.

games and toys, popular culture characters and narratives are part of children's social worlds and 'funds of knowledge' (Moll et al., 1992). Popular culture provides many children with a shared frame of reference on which they draw in their play as they share and discuss narratives and reinvent characters and plots (Jones Diaz et al., 2007). Popular culture, media and technology also play a significant role in children's identity construction and in the production of culture and knowledge (Anderson & Cavallaro, 2002; Kenway & Bullen, 2001).

Children's access to a range of technologies and popular culture and their active role in their own learning suggests that the line between childhood and adulthood is indeed an arbitrary one. The power that children have through their ability to independently access information and entertainment and to access 'adult' knowledge challenges traditional images of children as dependent, morally pure and incompetent. An alternative view is that children are competent users of technology, active agents in their own learning and very aware of the world beyond their family.

However, it is important not to assume that children are 'digital natives' or that all children have access to technologies. The proliferation of technologies in some communities may serve to widen the gap for children living and learning in very remote locations. For many children in remote locations, effective Internet access may only be available at the educational setting. Educators have a responsibility to support the development of all children's computer literacy.

> What experiences do the children you work with have with technologies and popular culture? How is this reflected in their play?

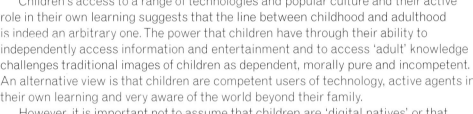

Contemporary perspectives of children's learning

This book draws on contemporary perspectives of children's learning that are influenced by sociocultural theory, postmodernism, the sociology of childhood, poststructuralist theory and the reconceptualising early childhood movement. Possibilities in all children's learning are signalled from these perspectives. Although these perspectives differ in some aspects, they recognise the 'meaning-making competencies of children as a basis for all learning' (Malaguzzi, 1998, p. 81). The image is of a strong child with agency on their own learning within intricate and rapidly changing sociocultural contexts (Clarke & Moss, 2001; Dahlberg et al., 2007; Gutierrez et al., 2007).

Sociocultural theory

Sociocultural–historical perspectives on learning recognise the family context as the site where children learn the 'cultural tools' (Vygotsky, 1978) of their family. The social interactions of family life (Heath, 1983; Rogoff, 2003) become highly significant. Children learn the culturally relevant tools, concepts and practices from co-constructing understandings, creating and sharing meanings and establishing shared understandings of their everyday family life; in other words, the world as they know it. For example, children learn about getting dressed, having meals, interacting with others, working, attending religious settings and shopping. They build expertise with family concepts and values on how to look, talk, act, think and feel from participating in everyday family practices and from paying attention to how their family responds to their attempts.

McInerney and McInerney state that 'children are wrapped around by their culture (represented by ... tools, social structures and language) and this directs the form and extent that cognitive development takes' (2006, p. 57). They suggest that cultural groups evolve through the 'collective activity' of their members and that 'individuals are therefore both part of, and the product of, this collective culture'. From this, learning differs for each child and needs to be understood within particular cultural and social contexts (Rogoff, 2003). Sociocultural theorists such as Rogoff highlight the key role of families and communities in children's learning. Through participation in family and community life, children establish their 'funds of knowledge' (Moll et al., 1992), social networks and 'virtual school bags' (Thomson, 2002). They become knowledgeable and skilled with the ideas and activities practised within their family and community. Sociocultural perspectives suggest that children learn best when the curriculum is connected to their everyday lives and interests.

Sociocultural theory challenges us to examine our ideas and assumptions about traditional early childhood practice to analyse how relevant and useful these are for children from diverse families and cultures. Critiquing understandings – for example, on transmission approaches to curriculum or learning through play with minimal educator mediation – leads us to investigate ways in which children participate in diverse family and community life and learn through observation and responsive interactions (Fleer, 2003; Gestwicki, 2010; Razfar & Guiérrez, 2003; Rogoff, 2003). Purposeful participation with others in family activities, rather than one-on-one activities devoid of their known sociocultural context, enable children to learn (Gee, 1990; Wertsch, 1991).

Postmodernism

Postmodern and poststructural perspectives often co-exist. Postmodern perspectives identify changes in society while poststructural perspectives recognise transformations for each person (Mac Naughton, 2003). Postmodernity regards the changing world as complex, confusing and unclear and disputes modern perspectives of objective universal truths (Foucault, 1972; 1974) of many phenomena, including children's learning. Some argue learning should be understood only within local contexts (Grieshaber & Cannella, 2001; Mac Naughton, 2003) – that there is no single pathway of development for every child or no one set of appropriate practices for every child. When educators work non-critically with modern truths of predetermined stages, simplistic outcomes or continuums in children's learning, they work from naive understandings (Mac Naughton, 2003). Modern truths – for example, bounded sets of knowledge established through scientific inquiry as in developmental psychology or educational psychology – do not seem to always recognise children's unique, dynamic and contradictory learning in a culturally diverse world (Fleer et al., 2006; Mac Naughton, 2003).

Postmodern perspectives analyse modern perspectives concerning the notion of dichotomies – for example, appropriate and inappropriate behaviour – and maintain that there are many truths, many views of the world and multiple pathways and patterns of learning and behaving. Postmodern theorists challenge taken-for-granted assumptions and the privileging of certain positions, such as developmental psychology, and work to 'expand the range of perspectives possible for early childhood education' (Grieshaber & Cannella, 2001, p. 4).

Postmodern and poststructural perspectives explain 'family' and 'community' as contexts for children's learning. They focus on social practice through **habitus**, **social capital** and **social field** based on the theorising of Bourdieu (1993) and/or **discourse** based on the work of Foucault (1972; 1978). Family life offers intricate experiences for learning when viewed with these concepts. As children determine particular ways of thinking, valuing and acting from engaging in the practices of their family, they 'become themselves' (Webb et al., 2002, p. xii) and establish habitus (Bourdieu, 1990; McNay, 2000; Robinson & Jones Diaz, 2006). Usually children maintain these practices across different contexts, only slightly changing their habitus over time. Habitus also refers to how individuals function within these practices (Webb et al., 2002). In early childhood or school settings, for example, children use their **cultural capital** from family habitus during moments of social practice (Bourdieu, 1993). Their cultural capital includes symbolic and representational knowledge that may reflect forms of advantage or disadvantage, depending on the values in the social field or context (Corson, 1998; Robinson & Jones Diaz, 2006). For example, children's habitus involving family practices with television, the Internet and computer games may have cultural capital, depending on the values of the educators and the curricula in the educational setting.

We all have values and patterns of behaviour, such as ways of interacting, and family and community experiences and knowledge that have cultural and **linguistic capital** in different social fields. Some children's linguistic and cultural capital may include experiences with books in English, visits to museums and children's birthday parties. Other children may have different

Habitus

As children engage in the practices of their family, they develop particular ways of thinking, valuing and acting which they use as they move across contexts such as home and school.

Social capital

Social capital includes relationships, friendships and social networks that provide support to individuals and group solidarity.

Social field

Individuals experience different social contexts or social fields depending on where they are, for example, at home, at church, in the classroom, at the park or out bush and so on. People usually interact and relate in response to functioning of the social field and what is considered important knowledge or capital in that field.

Discourse

Socially constructed ways of being, speaking, feeling and acting that represent particular values and world views.

Cultural capital

Culture includes ways of being and doing and particular forms of knowledge. Our culture is not always valued in all social fields. What has cultural capital in the playground or at home may not have cultural capital in the early childhood setting.

Linguistic capital

There are many different languages and different ways of using language. The power and status of Standard English means that diverse languages and ways with language are valued in some social fields but not in others.

experiences, such as playing with hand-held computer games, riding bikes, hunting, watching television, telling stories and communicating in a language other than English. Educational settings tend to operate as if all children have access to the cultural capital of the dominant group, meaning that many children are unable to 'cash in' their cultural capital in the classroom and extend their learning.

It follows that in educational settings, children, families and educators often use differing capital reflecting their differing habitus (Robinson & Jones Diaz, 2006). The classroom field determines which capital is valuable and often this materialises as inequality for children whose habitus does not resemble that valued in the setting. Some families and some children will be privileged while others will be disadvantaged in educational settings if educators maintain a deficit view of family habitus, linguistic and cultural capital and disregard how they may marginalise children's learning (Henderson, 2005; Kamler & Comber, 2005). For example, educational settings which only value the practices of reading English-language books and writing on paper disadvantage children whose habitus primarily involves television and DVD viewing and computer gaming (Bartlett, 2003; Jones Diaz et al., 2007; Arthur et al., 2014).

Children's cultural capital changes when they move from field to field. They draw on this capital to enter groups and try changing their cultural capital to social capital by interacting and networking to build relationships and friendships with educators and children. Social capital in this way relates to accessing social relations, networks and institutions from being a group member (Bourdieu & Wacquant, 1992). For example, children's understandings of Buzz Lightyear, when shared with peers in the field of the outdoors/playground, may constitute significant cultural capital to convert to social capital when others show interest in this cultural capital (Arthur et al., 2014), even though it may be discounted in classrooms.

The habitus and capital of many Australian families includes languages and dialects other than Standard Australian English. The AEDI data indicate that approximately 20 per cent of Australian children starting school speak a language or languages other than English at home (Royal Children's Hospital Centre for Community Child Health and the Murdoch Children's Research Institute, 2013). Issues of cultural and linguistic capital are significant for these children and families. Power relations operate in contexts where Standard English is the official language in educational and other institutional settings, and Aboriginal languages, dialects such as Aboriginal English and community languages other than English are perceived to be subordinate. Children notice these power relations and this shapes their perceptions of their own languages and dialects and their acceptability and status in the community. This influences children's willingness to identify with and to use their own language as well as their recognition of how their family is treated by the educational setting. Negative attitudes to languages and dialects other than Standard English result in language loss (Wong Fillmore, 1991). Equal status needs to be given to all languages and dialects in educational settings. At the same time, for reasons of equity and social justice, all children need to have access to, and develop proficiency in, the dominant language, Standard English, as an additional language or dialect, rather than at the expense of their home language, family literacy practices and family relationships (Wong Fillmore, 1991; Ordoñez-Jasis & Ortiz, 2007).

Poststructuralism

Structural perspectives theorise the world as systems of meaning or structures; for example, socialisation theory or developmental psychology. These structures or systems are understood as universal and applicable to all people. In contrast, poststructural perspectives 'address the complexities of the relationship between the child, the adult and their cultural context ... [and] focus attention on the constitutive roles of gender, race, class and disability in children's learning and development' (Mac Naughton, 1995, p. 36). The shifting transformations for each person are recognised from this poststructural perspective (Mac Naughton, 2003).

Agency

Agency refers to a person's ability to act on and shape their own life.

Poststructural theorists argue that people have **agency** in their own lives – they can act on and shape their own identities. This means that we are not only shaped by our environment, but we can determine our identities and actions. Agency is seen as 'the power of individuals to actively participate in the construction of self through the process of subjectification' (Robinson & Jones Diaz, 2006, p. 180). In this way, agency relates to what individuals knowingly and unconsciously think and feel about themselves and their relationships to the world. Foucault concluded that individuals can take active roles in shaping their identities (McNay, 2000) and can resist the 'technologies of domination' circulating in society (Robinson & Jones Diaz, 2006).

Poststructuralists draw on the work of Foucault (1970, 1974, 1978, 1989) to argue that humans act in the world using discourses, or frameworks, that include ways of looking, speaking, thinking, feeling and being (Mac Naughton, 2003). Discourses are socially constructed ideas, practices, values, belief systems, words and images that involve emotional, social and institutional frameworks and practices through which meaning is constituted in our lives. Foucault regarded discourses as 'the practices that systematically form the objects of which they speak' (1974, p. 49) and he defined knowledge as 'constituted in discourses operating in society, which are historically and culturally formed' (Robinson & Jones Diaz, 2006, p. 29). Another interpretation explains discourse as shaping who is likely to speak, what they are likely to say and with what authority (Ball, 1990), signalling the importance of meaning and social relations as discourse. And another interpretation explains discourse as the cumulative production of a 'particular version of events' from multiple sources; for example, groups of 'meanings, metaphors, representations, images, stories, statements' (Burr, 1995, p. 48).

Discourses materialising and moving around society represent different knowledge, ideas and practices through integrating values, actions, culture and language (Foucault, 1972). Humans act in the world influenced by many cultural discourses in various forms; for example, propositional, emotional, social and institutional patterns and practices. Educators may or may not take for granted current forms of discourse involving people's ways of looking, thinking, feeling, acting and being (Mac Naughton, 2003). Educators can decide which discourse they choose to take up as active agents constructing their own lives; however, this choice is not totally free. Particular discourses about what it means to be a boy, or a girl, a 'good' parent, a 'good' educator are dominant in many communities within society, which act to silence and marginalise alternative discourses. Powerful institutions – for example, the media and entertainment industries – influence the availability and desirability of different discourses (Mac Naughton, 2003). Children, families and educators are influenced by the available discourses and the power of discourses; for example, the dominance of Barbie and Buzz Lightyear images in discourses available to boys and girls. It is possible to resist these dominant discourses but people who do so are often frowned upon by others.

Poststructural theorists analyse the power relationships between discourses that result in some people's ways of being and doing to be regarded as 'normal' and others regarded as a 'problem'. Feminist poststructuralists focus on gender and the ways in which identities are shaped and limited by our understandings of being male and female. Theorists, such as Davies (1989; 1993), question 'regimes of truth that dictate life roles and expectations' and critique the 'relationships among gender, power and education' (Grieshaber & Cannella, 2001, p. 12). Though children's biological sex is usually permanent, children change how they compose their gender according to their sociocultural context (Blaise, 2005; Davies, 2003; Robinson & Jones Diaz, 2006). Gender lives in these contexts and not the individual (Thorne, 1993). So femininity and masculinity influence and emerge from discursive practice as children act intentionally with their habitus in social fields, according to Bourdieu (McNay, 2003). They perform gender roles in fluid and contradictory ways as they position themselves through the many ways to be a boy or a girl (Butler, 1990; Davies, 2003; Robinson & Jones Diaz, 2006). They try to get their gender 'right', especially with playmates (Butler, 1990) and in the current social order (Davies, 2003). Children are likely to retain gender understandings from outside sociocultural practices but also use their agency to anticipate and transcend gender understandings in the present. Even though children construct gender in broad and complex ways, inequities exist as narrow interpretations of gender still discriminate against anyone who differs from the hegemonic 'tough boys' and 'pretty girls' ideal (Blaise, 2005; Mac Naughton, 2003; Robinson & Jones Diaz, 2006).

Postmodern and poststructural theorists argue that everyone has multiple identities that are socioculturally constructed, shifting and multifaceted (Dahlberg et al., 2007). Individuals are all

members of multiple and overlapping communities at work, at home and at school, and in relation to their interests, ethnic origin, sexuality and so on (Kalantsiz, 1997). Everyone negotiates their identities across different contexts and engage in different discourses in various situations. In diverse sociocultural contexts, gender, class, ethnicity, religion, race and family education levels intersect to build cultural identities (Hill et al., 1998) and children concurrently shape their identities through participating in various communities (Carr, 2001; Gregory et al., 2004). Their languages, literacies and cultures enable them to fashion their identities across situations just as adults would. These understandings contest modern perspectives on identity as 'predetermined, rigid and universal forms through socialisation and reproduction'; instead, 'identity, both across groups and within individuals, is understood as complex and multiple, fragmented and ambitious, contradictory and contextualised' (Dahlberg et al., 2007, p. 57). Children are regarded by these theorists as 'inscribed in multiple and overlapping identities, in whose constructions they are active participants' (Dahlberg et al., 2007, p. 57).

In addition, postmodern perspectives are grounded in critical theory and encourage the examination of issues of power, control and social justice (Grieshaber & Cannella, 2001). Bourdieu's theory of social practice focuses on the significance of language in constructing power relations and highlights the way that educational institutions privilege some groups and marginalise others (Bourdieu, 1986).

The sociology of childhood

The sociology of childhood (James et al., 1998) critiques the term 'development' for its emphasis on the differences between children and adults that results in the view of children as 'needy' and 'becoming'. Instead, the sociology of childhood focuses on valuing each child's current experience and understandings, and their 'being'. Children are seen to take actions and establish their power, or not, and to shape their own experiences and structures which affect their lives (Alanen, 2001; Alanen et al., 2005; Lehtinen, 2004). Young children understand how to make decisions and take action. They understand how to organise resources such as space and time as well as social action resources, such as fellowship, friendship, popularity and trust (Lehtinen, 2004). As a result there is increased value placed on the learning occurring in the early childhood years as legitimate in its own right, rather than as preparation for formal school learning and adulthood. There is also a strong focus on children's competencies and an acknowledgement of children's strengths, agency and voice. In their introduction to *The Art of Awareness*, Curtis and Carter (2000, p. xiii) suggest that:

> if we begin to value who children are, not just what we want them to be, a shift
> happens in the way we think about learning and teaching. Our jobs become
> more engaging and fulfilling. We also begin to envision a larger purpose for
> our profession – making childhood visible and valued for the ways in which
> it can enrich our humanity and contribute to our collective identity.

The importance of researching with children, as opposed to research conducted 'on' children, and of listening to children has been highlighted in much recent research (for example, Clark, 2005; Cox & Robinson-Pant, 2010; Dockett & Perry, 2005; Kinney & Wharton, 2008; Schiller, 2005; Smith et al., 2005). Dencik (2006) has described childhood as the constantly changing 'lifespace of childhood'. Within this changing lifespace, children encounter a wide range of interactions and artefacts that are not necessarily familiar to their families. Perspectives of children and childhood need to reflect engagement in many different worlds. Adult views of children need to draw on children's own perspectives of their experiences and expectations (*see* Figure 1.3). Seeking children's perspectives about issues in which they are involved, or issues that impact upon them, is a relatively recent development in areas such as health, education and community involvement, yet it is a critical element of the UN *Convention on the Rights of the Child* (United Nations, 1989). Children's rights theory and the sociology of childhood offer theoretical support for approaches that regard children as competent commentators on their own experiences and that respect children's input as valid and reliable, with views that deserve to be taken seriously (Freeman, 1998;

Mayall, 2002). Such approaches do not seek to deny the importance of providing appropriate support for children; rather they emphasise the importance of such support, in the context of institutions that are 'responsive and flexible in their work for children' (Prout & Hallett, 2003, p. 2). The NSW Commission for Children and Young People and the ACT Department of Education, Youth and Family Services provide useful strategies for effective consultation with children and young people.

Reconceptualising early childhood

The reconceptualist movement grew out of critiques in the 1980s of the dominance of developmentally appropriate practice in the early childhood field and the marginalisation of diverse children and families. The first reconceptualising early childhood conference was held in the USA in 1991, followed by an edited volume of essays and research studies (Kessler & Swadener, 1992). There is now an international group of reconceptualists who apply postmodern, poststructuralist and critical theories to the analysis of questions of early childhood education, focusing particularly on issues of identity, power relations, social justice and social change (Jipson, 2001).

The reconceptualists challenge and resist 'dominant knowledges, ideologies and practices' (Jipson, 2001, p. 4). Traditional early childhood knowledges, including child development theory, early childhood curricula and the role of the educator, are challenged and taken-for-granted assumptions are critically examined from cultural and historical perspectives. Discussions within the reconceptualising early childhood movement have challenged the traditional focus on developmental discourses and highlighted the significance of sociocultural contexts.

FIGURE 1.3 Contemporary theories view young children as competent and social learners.

One area where ideas have been reconceptualised is the image of the child. Traditional assumptions of the 'universal child' constructed within developmental theory have been challenged by the reconceptualist movement as well as postmodern and poststructuralist theories. For many, the prevailing view of childhood is of innocence, immaturity and naïvety (Woodrow, 1999): childhood is seen as 'the Golden Age of life' (Dahlberg et al., 2007, p. 49). Cultural artefacts such as movies, books, posters and greeting cards contribute to and reflect our images of the child; frequently children are portrayed as 'cute', 'sweet' and 'innocent'. Hilton (1996) maintains that this mythological idealised view of childhood innocence was laid down by the sociocultural elite in the early 20th century and does not reflect the reality of most children's lives in contemporary society. However, as Woodrow and Brennan (2001) note, the image of the child as innocent in early childhood is pervasive and resilient and positions the educator as a protector of children. The view of children as innocent also denies them any agency in their own lives.

Another prevalent image portrays children as 'evil', 'out of control' monsters (Prout, 2003); this gives rise to an emphasis on rules and conformity, with educators exercising power and control over children (Woodrow & Brennan, 2001). Children can also be viewed as embryonic adults; this image draws on developmental and socialisation theories and the notion of children gradually becoming adults. The child can be viewed as a 'knowledge, identity and culture reproducer' and as a 'labour market supply factor' (Dahlberg et al., 2007, p. 49). These images position the educator as a facilitator of children's development.

Educators and policymakers have 'choices to make about who we think the child is' (Dahlberg et al., 2007, p. 43). The educator's image of the child impacts the services that they provide for children as well as the ways that they interact with children, whether children have a voice in the decisions that affect their lives and the pedagogies that the educator draws on in early childhood settings and schools.

Dominant images of the child as innocent, evil or an embryonic adult have 'shaped discussions, policy and practice' (Dahlberg et al., 2007, p. 49) and 'offer limited space for conceptualizing childhood or change' (Woodrow & Brennan, 2001, p. 25). These views of the child tend to blind us to the realities of children's lives and lead to universal conceptions of the child that reinforce stereotypes and existing power relations and ignore issues of social justice (Woodrow & Brennan, 2001).

Postmodern and poststructural theories as well as the sociology of childhood and the reconceptualist movement have challenged traditional notions of 'the child' and 'childhood' as universal categories. The fact that children's lives vary in different cultures and in different centuries supports the view that images of children are created by communities. The reality is that children's experiences vary greatly and there are many childhoods (Dahlberg et al., 2007). Contemporary theories emphasise the historical and social construction of childhood (*see*, for example, Dahlberg et al., 2007; Prout, 2003). These theories recognise the rapid changes taking place in children's worlds and challenge dominant images of children as innocent and incompetent. Instead, children are described as competent social beings actively engaged in the co-construction of 'knowledge, identity and culture' (Dahlberg et al., 2007, p. 49). The focus is on children as strong, capable and rich, rather than dependent, weak and poor (Chiwela, 2010; James et al., 1998; Malaguzzi, 1993; Rinaldi, 2005).

What contemporary theories mean in practice

Dynamic and complex early childhood settings, changing worlds and childhoods, and contemporary perspectives on children's learning challenge educators to find ways of working with children and families where they:

- engage in reflective practice, critical action and change
- understand the importance of cultural contexts in children's learning
- respect diversity and focus on equity and social justice
- build effective partnerships with families, children and communities
- enhance relationships and collaborative learning environments
- focus on dispositions and processes of learning
- provide meaningful curriculum that connects to children's social worlds and extends learning
- engage in intentional teaching, drawing on a repertoire of pedagogies
- document children's learning in ways that acknowledge children's strengths and make children's thinking visible to children, families and staff.

Each of these aspects is explored in brief below and in detail in the chapters that follow.

Reflective practice

Effective educators engage in ongoing reflection and 'active and critical engagement in learning' (Arthur, 2010, p. 1). These processes of inquiry and critical reflection on their practices enable them to make decisions about curriculum that are responsive to cultural context and support more equitable outcomes for children (Arthur, 2010; Mac Naughton & Williams, 2009). Rather than a focus on external standards that codify 'quality care', what is important are the processes of critical thinking, self-reflection and evaluation. Moss (2001a, p. 131) argues that working with 'complexity, values, diversity, subjectivity and multiple perspectives' requires educators to focus on making meaning of what is going on. The aim is to increase understandings of practices; educators may choose to then engage in assessment of practices and make judgements as to the value of these.

Moss (2001a, p. 131) argues that while quality is related to a pedagogy of 'conformity and normalization, control and management', meaning making, on the other hand, focuses on choice, interpretation and the co-construction of understandings, thus promoting multiple perspectives and dissensus rather than always striving for consensus. A focus on meaning making highlights the role of educators as professional decision makers engaged in reflective practice. As Goodfellow (2002, p. 8) notes, 'where the determinants of quality are placed within the local context of individual service provision and as part of ongoing practices then assessment is somewhat reliant on a sense of trust emanating from the professionalism and the integrity of staff'.

There are a number of tools that can assist educators to reflect on and critically evaluate practice. The Early Childhood Australia *Code of Ethics* is designed to 'provide a framework for reflection' (Early Childhood Australia, 2006). The preamble to the code states that it is not intended to be a set of rules, but rather provides a set of principles that encourage critical reflection and decision making. As Stonehouse (1991) has noted, a code of ethics helps to clarify core values and guide practice. Newman and Pollnitz's (2001) Ethical Response Cycle also assists early childhood professionals to analyse contextually specific relationships and complexities, to reflect and negotiate and to make informed decisions. The EYLF (DEEWR, 2009) and the *Educators Guide* (DEEWR, 2010) also encourage educators to engage in ongoing reflection on their practices. In a context of rapid sociocultural, historical, political, economic and technological change, it is increasingly important that educators are aware of the broad issues that impact on children's services. Educators need to be 'able to manage and respond effectively to change and its inherent demands, challenges and tensions' (Sumsion & Goodfellow, 2002, p. 1). The processes of reflection and the implementation of change are addressed further in Chapters 4, 5, 6 and 11.

Cultural contexts

For many educators, the defining characteristic of an early childhood program has been its focus on child development. This has involved the incorporation of developmentally appropriate practice (DAP) as outlined by Bredekamp in 1987, Bredekamp and Copple in 1997 and, more recently, Copple and Bredekamp in 2009. Child development theory has provided the basis for curriculum for children and guided the interactions of adults in many early childhood programs. In this way, it has influenced the expectations educators have of children and the nature of the experiences provided within early childhood settings.

Yet sociocultural, postmodern and poststructuralist theorists argue that child development and DAP do not take sufficient account of the social and cultural contexts in which children live (Dahlberg et al., 2007; Fleer, 2010). There has also been criticism that, as a discipline, the traditional base for child development – developmental psychology – has become limited and outdated. The idea of diverse contexts for learning challenges traditional notions of a universal, predictable pathway of learning and the concept of developmentally appropriate practice. Dahlberg et al. (2007) argue that the term 'developmentally appropriate practice' and the associated language is prescriptive and constraining. From a sociocultural perspective, learning occurs in diverse social and cultural contexts and different pedagogies are needed to cater for different children in different contexts, rather than there being a dichotomy of appropriate/inappropriate practices as DAP suggests.

Some specific criticisms of child development theory and DAP have been directed towards:
- the focus on the individual rather than children in social, cultural and political contexts
- the idea that developmental theory is described as 'normative', with the implication that any who do not fit the theory are in some way 'not normal'
- the notion that children are in the process of 'becoming' adults and the assumption that adult ways of thinking are more valued than those of children
- the recognition that theories are themselves cultural constructions, reflecting the dominant practices and beliefs of a specific cultural context
- the assumption that there is a universal pattern of development for all children, so that all children are described as going through the same stages at about the same ages.

If any of these criticisms are valid, what does it mean for early childhood educators and their understandings of what is appropriate for young children? Should we abandon child development as the basis for early childhood programs?

This would be a major shift in early childhood education, given the predominant role of developmental theory in the history of the field. It would require educators to say that what they have learned about children through the lens of child development is wrong. And yet, many have learned a great deal about children using developmental theory as a base. All educators know of children who illustrated very clearly the stages described by Piaget (1963), the moral understanding outlined by Kohlberg (1975) or the psychosexual stages of Erikson (1963). At the same time, we can all identify children who did not neatly fit within these frameworks, and for whom planning was difficult because they were described as different – they did not fit with expectations.

There is certainly a need to update educators understanding of child development. There is a sense that developmental theory is static – once it has been learned, it is learned for life! However, much knowledge about children and child development is changing. It is possible that perceptions of child development are limited by what has been previously learned and never updated or reflected upon.

Despite this, educators cannot continue to embrace developmental theory in its entirety without some critique. This does not suggest removing developmental theory from their repertoire. However, it does suggest some careful consideration of the assumptions and expectations underlying developmental theory, and it advises a need to continually read and reflect on what developmental theory is actually saying and how it is relevant to the social and cultural contexts in which all educators all exist. One example here is the work of Piaget (1963) and the development of his grand theory of cognitive development. Piaget's influence has been significant and it is still felt very strongly in early childhood education. Yet, the influence of Piaget in the broader field of developmental psychology has decreased over time as other perspectives of cognitive development, such as sociocultural perspectives, and other understandings of children's capabilities have entered the developmental literature.

When asked to discuss what should be done with developmental theory, Walsh (2002) concluded that there is a need to, 'Update it and extend it; it's not sufficient, but it's necessary'. How can this be achieved?

The authors suggest that an awareness of child development can provide a useful basis for helping early childhood educators understand children and families when they:

- consider multiple perspectives and multiple ways of explaining how children develop and learn
- recognise that the usefulness of theories is directly related to the contexts in which they are applied
- acknowledge that children exist in social contexts and that understanding children involves understanding their contexts
- realise that theories change, and so do their implications for practice
- challenge, question and reflect on assumptions underpinning theories.

Rogoff (2003) argues that development can be understood only in a cultural context: 'people develop as participants in cultural communities. Their development can be understood only in light of the cultural practices and circumstances of their communities – which also change' (pp. 3–4). This is a significant change to conceptualisations of development based on common expectations of development at similar ages. Recognising the importance of cultural context means expecting and valuing differences: 'different cultural communities may expect children to engage in activities at vastly different times in childhood and may regard "timetables" of development in other communities as surprising or even dangerous' (Rogoff, 2003, p. 4).

These principles underpin this book. Chapter 3 considers some of the major challenges and achievements for young children in the early childhood years. In this book children are not considered in specific age ranges or at specific stages; rather, they are considered in context and with an aim to suggest multiple ways of interpreting and understanding situations. There is a focus on young children as competent and capable, with consideration of their strengths, rather than starting from what they cannot do or do not understand. This is not to suggest that children are the same as adults; rather, they are active actors and inter-actors within their contexts; they are actively working to understand the world in which they exist and, at the same time, changing that world by their very participation and interactions.

Respect for diversity

Sociocultural, postmodern and poststructuralist theorists highlight the diversity of viewpoints, practices and feelings. These theorists encourage educators to respect and work with differences in children's experiences and family expectations. The promotion of partnerships between families, communities, educators and children helps educational settings to connect to the 'funds of knowledge' (Moll et al., 1992) children bring from home and to thus make their learning visible in the classroom.

Contemporary theories of learning encourage educators to explore multiple pathways of learning. As Reid (2003, p. 5) argues, 'recognising the complexity of development is central to reconceptualising educational practice to help all children, not just the "good" ones, learn'. At the same time educators are challenged to explore multiple pedagogies and to question the effects of different pedagogical practices on different groups of children. A repertoire of pedagogies is needed to effectively cater for children's diverse experiences and learning styles. Pedagogies are explored in further detail in Chapters 7, 8 and 10.

From a postmodern and poststructuralist perspective there is an essential role for the educator in working with children to challenge dominant discourses and to construct possibilities for alternative ways of being and doing. As Pelo (2006) notes, educators are agents of social change. Educators can work with children to 'transform the possibilities' for individuals and groups, and transform society to promote equity and social justice (Mac Naughton, 2003, p. 188). Mac Naughton (2003) outlines the tasks of an educator who holds a transforming philosophy as:

- attempting to change ideas, practices, stories and emotions that are oppressive and that produce inequality
- promoting equal opportunity
- opening up possibilities for all children
- helping children to recognise and deal with what is fair and unfair
- creating a democratic classroom
- building children's social action skills.

Taking a critical approach involves 'analysing relationships between language, social groups, social practices and power' (Knobel & Healy, 1998, p. 4) and challenging the power structures and social practices that privilege some groups over others. This means challenging existing hierarchical power relations and including the practices of diverse social and cultural communities in educational settings. Pelo (2006) and Giugni (2006) provide practical examples of ways in which educators can draw on children's interests and curiosity to explore issues of power and social justice.

Collaborative partnerships

Sociocultural theories highlight the ways in which children learn through interactions within their families and communities. The family is a key influence on children's learning; therefore, it is essential that children's family and community experiences, and the family's perceptions of their children's learning and interests, are taken into account and included in the program. Educators are responsible for finding out about children's worlds through developing and maintaining strong and meaningful partnerships with families and children. The importance of effective partnerships between homes and educational settings that enable parents and educators to engage in dialogue, examine issues and develop shared understandings cannot be understated. These partnerships create opportunities for educators to find ways to connect the early childhood and school curriculum to children's worlds and for children to draw on their expertise and investigate and extend their interests in the early childhood or school setting, resulting in authentic and dynamic learning opportunities (Gestwicki, 2010; Kinney & Wharton, 2008).

Collaborative partnerships between families, educators, children and communities mean that there is exchange of information between partners rather than the one-way transmission of knowledge and information from educators to other parties. Hughes and Mac Naughton (2002) suggest that effective partnerships between families and educators give family members

a voice and a role in decision making and encourage the negotiation of shared meanings. These processes foster the development of learning communities. Partnerships with families are discussed more fully in Chapter 2, and the inclusion of children's and families' voices in documentation and planning in Chapters 8 and 10.

Relationships and communities of practice

Contemporary views of curriculum in Australia and New Zealand focus on processes of learning, relationships, dispositions, values and social responsibility (DEEWR, 2009; New Zealand Ministry of Education, 1996). There is much emphasis in contemporary curriculum documents on the pedagogy of relationships and the role that interactions play in children's learning. The *Melbourne Declaration on Educational Goals for Young Australians* (MCEETYA, 2008) also highlights the importance of working collaboratively and effective communication.

Sociocultural theorists highlight the importance of relationships, social engagement and social interactions. Learning takes place through complex sets of relationships. Lave and Wenger (1991) use the terms 'situated learning' and '**communities of practice**' to reflect the collaborative nature of knowledge building. 'Communities of practice are groups of people who share a concern or a passion for something they do and learn how to do it better as they interact regularly' (Wenger, n.d.). Early childhood educators working in the same centre or school, or for the same organisation, may be a community of practice or educators may form communities of practice when they join professional associations such as Early Childhood Australia or form networking groups across organisations in a local government area. The community of practice 'acts as a living curriculum' (Wenger, n.d.) – particularly for student teachers, trainees and staff with little experience – although it is important to emphasise that everyone is learning from each other.

Wenger (1998) emphasises that a community of practice is more than a group of individuals working for the same organisation. A community of practice has similar experiences, a shared domain of interest and shared knowledge. In an early childhood context a community of practice may have a shared interest in documentation or in literacy, for example, and engage in joint activities and discussions around this interest. Membership of the group requires a commitment to a shared interest and to collaborative reflection and problem solving. Communities of practice build relationships and promote meaningful and productive interactions that facilitate collective learning and knowledge building. In this way new knowledge and learning are located within local communities and are contextually relevant. Communities of practice 'develop a shared repertoire of resources: experiences, stories, tools, ways of addressing recurring problems – in short a shared practice' (Wenger, n.d.).

Effective communities of practice ensure that there are opportunities for all members to participate to the full and develop a sense of trust where participants can negotiate meanings with others. Wenger (2000) argues that communities of practice require learning energy, strong relationships and feelings of belonging, and reflection to be effective. Relationships and communities of practice are discussed further in Chapter 9.

Citizenship and democracy

The *Melbourne Declaration on Educational Goals for Young Australians* includes the importance of children and young people acting 'with moral and ethical integrity', appreciating 'social, cultural, linguistic and religious diversity' and acknowledging 'the value of Indigenous cultures' and working towards reconciliation (MCEETYA, 2008, p. 9). Also of importance are values of 'democracy, equity and justice, and participation in Australia's civic life', cultural literacy, environmental sustainability and local and global citizenship (MCEETYA, 2008).

Contemporary theories and research have challenged early childhood educators to reconsider traditional notions of children and childhood. Children are now viewed as 'citizens with entitlements and rights' (Early Childhood Australia, 2006). Children are active agents who process and construct meanings and identities, rather than passive recipients of knowledge.

Communities of practice

Communities of practice are groups of people with shared experiences and interests who interact regularly with each other to engage in collaborative reflection and learning (Wenger, n.d.).

Democracy, Giroux argues, is grounded in the notion of the citizen as an active and critical agent upholding principles of 'sociality and community' (Giroux, 1989, p. 34). Democratic classrooms listen to the views of children and young people and design curriculum that centres on issues that are of concern to children. This means viewing children as citizens and enabling them to set the agenda, including children's voices in the curriculum, involving children in decision making and including a range of tools to enable children to express their ideas (Mac Naughton & Williams, 2009). Through projects that investigate big ideas, children often become interested in broader issues, such as environmental sustainability, and are supported to become ethical democratic citizens. Children's roles in documentation and planning are discussed further in Chapter 8.

Dispositions and processes of learning

There is also a focus in contemporary curriculum on the processes of learning, such as investigation, problem solving, inquiry and critical thinking, and **dispositions** of learning, such as curiosity and persistence. Dispositions are 'relatively enduring habits of mind and action' (Katz & Chard, 1989, p. 30). Dispositions and learning processes are essential to learning in a world that is rapidly changing. Effective learners draw on a repertoire of dispositions in their interactions with their world (Carr, 2001).

Learning processes such as inquiry, problem solving and hypothesising are also essential for effective learning. As well as having literacy, numeracy and ICT skills, successful learners are able to 'think deeply and logically, and obtain and evaluate evidence' (MCEETYA, 2008, p. 8). Successful learners are also 'creative, innovative and resourceful, and are able to solve problems in ways that draw upon a range of learning areas' (MCEETYA, 2008, p. 8). Dispositions and processes of learning are discussed further in Chapter 8.

Dispositions
These are acquired through experiences within families and communities, including educational settings. They are tendencies to respond in characteristic ways – for example, with creativity – across different situations.

Meaningful curriculum

Partnerships with families and the ongoing exchange of knowledge between home and the early childhood setting can help to bring family and community funds of knowledge into the setting. Sharing information gives children, families and communities a voice in the early childhood setting and school and enables the educator to act as a bridge between the children's worlds and the world of the early childhood setting or school (Moll et al., 1992). Without the support of parents and educators to help them to make these connections, children may struggle to understand complex concepts introduced in the early childhood setting and school (Blaise & Nuttall, 2011) and educators may struggle to understand the complexities of children's worlds.

On the other hand, a curriculum that connects to children's everyday lives and funds of knowledge provides many opportunities for children to display their existing understandings and to build confidence in themselves as learners (Arthur, 2010). For example, Marsh (2000) found that connecting what happens at the early childhood setting to funds of knowledge about popular media culture supports children to locate new understandings within a familiar discourse (Marsh, 2000). The *Te Whāriki* of New Zealand (New Zealand Ministry of Education, 1996) along with Margaret Carr's and Wendy Lee's work on Learning Stories (Carr, 2001; Carr & Lee, 2012), the EYLF (DEEWR, 2009) and Australian state curriculum documents, such as the *Victorian Essential Learning Standards* (VCAA, 2009), also encourage pedagogies that celebrate children's competencies and challenge their thinking.

The emphasis in current approaches to early childhood curriculum is on investigations and projects that build on children's strengths and interests and that respond to children's questions, rather than one-off experiences based on what adults perceive children are interested in or need to know. Planning needs to be flexible and based on possibilities rather than the rigid implementation of preplanned experiences. This means that there is often a greater focus on retrospective documentation that includes reflections on children's responses to experiences, and the interactions that occurred, rather than on preplanning.

This does not mean that there is no need for planned experiences, or that there is no place for adult input into children's experiences and interactions. As noted in *Belonging, Being and*

Becoming: The Early Years Learning Framework, educators use a range of pedagogies which include:

- Being responsive to children
- Planning and implementing learning through play
- Intentional teaching
- Providing continuity in experiences and enabling children to have successful transitions
- Assessing and monitoring children's learning to inform provisions and to support children achieving learning outcomes.

DEEWR, 2009, p14.

Plans provide possible directions that can later be reflected on and changed. In this way educators can compare their 'intentions for the children with the children's own intentions and interests' (Perry, 1997, p. 51). Effective programs are flexible and responsive to children's ideas, strengths and skills while also including carefully planned experiences, resources and strategies that encourage collaborative exploration, investigation, problem solving and discovery (Arthur et al., 2003).

Effective curriculum interconnects learning across discipline areas, investigates meaningful, significant content and focuses on deep knowledge. These approaches to curriculum and a range of pedagogies are detailed in Chapter 7, methods for assessing children's learning are explored in Chapter 8 and planned and spontaneous learning environments are examined in Chapter 10.

Intentional teaching

Sociocultural theories of learning highlight the role of interactions in children's learning. Thoughtful, sensitive interactions between educators and children can support, challenge and extend children's learning. This is termed 'intentional teaching' in the EYLF (DEEWR, 2009). In conversations with children, or in what is sometimes referred to as 'sustained shared thinking' (Siraj-Blatchford et al., 2003), educators listen carefully and ask questions and make comments that provoke children's thinking and extend learning. When educators use specific language in these conversations to talk about concepts such as size and patterns, processes such as writing and arts techniques such as modelling, they can scaffold children's learning (Arthur et al., 2010). Educators can also use specific language to support children to compare texts and engage in critical literacy. There is a very important role for educators in mediating children's interactions with texts and supporting children's critical thinking about a range of texts, including texts of popular culture.

Although contemporary theories view children as competent and capable, it is important to avoid the creation of a new binary of the competent/incompetent child (Malaguzzi, 1998; Buckingham, 2000). As Hughes and Mac Naughton (2001, p. 127) argue, children are neither sponges nor free agents, but rather they:

> actively and continually construct and reconstruct their identity(ies) or sense(s) of self, but they do so within discursive repertoires that are increasingly liable to be dominated by the major corporations within the cultural and communications industries.

The collaborative deconstruction of dominant narratives and oppressive practices and the reconstruction of alternatives assist us to work towards 'achieving a more egalitarian and inclusive society' (Morrell, 2002, p. 72).

Pedagogies are discussed further in Chapters 7 and 9.

Assessment

Views of children as competent learners, an emphasis on collaborative partnerships and moves towards curriculum that focuses on interactions and learning processes require ways of thinking about, documenting and assessing children's learning that are respectful of children's ideas and funds of knowledge. The Reggio Emilia experience in Italy (Edwards et al., 1993/1998), as well as emergent curriculum (Jones & Nimmo, 1994), interest-based projects (Helm & Katz, 2001; Helm, 2011; Katz & Chard, 1989) and the reconceptualist movement (Swadener & Kessler, 1991), have long encouraged documentation of children's learning in ways that value children's ideas and help make children's learning visible.

The work in Australia of Fleet, Patterson and Robertson (Fleet & Patterson, 1998; Fleet, Patterson & Robertson, 2006; 2012) has also challenged educators to think 'beyond the boxes' (Fleet & Patterson, 1998) of prescriptive planning and to explore innovative methods of documentation. Fleer and her colleagues (Fleer et al., 2004; Fleer et al., 2006; Fleer, 2010) advocate the use of sociocultural approaches to observation and assessment and highlight the critical role of documentation in representing children's learning and providing feedback that informs practice.

This book encourages educators to engage in and document decisions about children's learning that honour children's strengths and interests, promote collaboration between educators, children, families and communities and make children's learning visible. Documentation is explored further in Chapter 8.

Conclusion and reflection

This chapter examined the national agenda for early childhood and school education, which includes the opportunities for all Australian children with education to be successful learners and effective citizens in the 21st century, irrespective of their location, ability and socio-economic resources. The expanded concept of childhoods was investigated, recognising change for children and families in their worlds. Further contemporary perspectives on children's learning were identified, along with their implications for practice in early childhood settings and schools.

Questions for reflection

1. What theories do you bring to your work with children? What other theories could you draw on that may provide new insights?

2. What is your image of the child? How are these views reflected in your daily curriculum?

3. What are the experiences and funds of knowledge of the children with whom you work? How do you connect your curriculum to children's family and community experiences and funds of knowledge?

Key terms

agency, 18
communities of practice, 26
cultural capital, 17
discourse, 17
dispositions, 27
habitus, 17
linguistic capital, 17
social capital, 17
social field, 17

Online study resources

Visit http://login.cengagebrain.com and use the access code that comes with this book for 12 months access to the student resources for this text.

CourseMate Express

The CourseMate Express website contains a range of resources and study tools for this chapter, including:

- Online video activities
- Online research activities
- A revision quiz
- Matching pair exercises
- A list of key weblinks
- A chapter glossary, flashcards and crossword to help you revise terminology
- and more!

Search me! education ▶ Search me! 🖱️

Explore **Search me! education** for articles relevant to this chapter. Fast and convenient, Search me! education is updated daily and provides you with 24-hour access to full text articles from hundreds of scholarly and popular journals, ebooks and newspapers, including *The Australian* and *The New York Times*. Log in to Search me! through http://login.cengage.com and try searching for the following key words:

- sociology of childhood
- reconceptualising early childhood
- sociocultural theory
- reflective practice.

Search tip: **Search me! education** contains information from both local and international sources. To get the greatest number of search results, try using both Australian and American spellings in your searches, e.g. 'globalisation' and 'globalization'; 'organisation' and 'organization'

Recommended resources

Fleer, M 2010, *Early Learning and Development: Cultural-historical Concepts in Play*, Cambridge University Press, Cambridge.

Ministerial Council on Education, Employment, Training and Youth Affairs (MCEETYA) 2008, *Melbourne Declaration on Educational Goals for Young Australians*, MCEETYA, http://www.curriculum.edu.au/verve/_resources/National_Declaration_on_the_Educational_Goals_for_Young_Australians.pdf, accessed 15 June 2011.

Key weblinks

ACARA, http://www.acara.edu.au/default.asp
ACECQA, http://www.acecqa.gov.au/
ARACY, http://www.aracy.org.au/
Big Steps, http://www.bigsteps.org.au
Early Childhood Australia, http://www.earlychildhoodaustralia.org.au
Inclusion and Professional Support Program (IPSP): http://education.gov.au/inclusion-and-professional-support-program

References

ABS, *see* Australian Bureau of Statistics

ACARA, *see* Australian Curriculum, Assessment and Reporting Authority

Alanen, L 2001, 'Childhood as a generational condition: Children's daily lives in a central Finland town', in L Alanen & B Mayall (eds), *Conceptualising Child–adult Relationships*, Routledge-Falmer, London, pp. 129–44.

Alanen, L, Kiili, J, Kuukka, A & Lehtinen, AR 2005, 'Health, well being and children's agency', in *GEMS of the Health Promotion Research Programme*, Tampere, Finland, Cancer Society of Finland and Academy of Finland.

Alvestad, M & Duncan, J 2006, '"The value is enormous: it's priceless I think!": New Zealand preschool teachers' understandings of the early childhood curriculum in New Zealand: a comparative perspective', *International Journal of Early Childhood*, vol. 38, no. 1, pp. 31–45.

Anderson, K & Cavallaro, D 2002, 'Parents or pop culture? Children's heroes and role models', *Childhood Education*, Spring, pp. 161–8.

Arthur, L 2010, *The Early Years Learning Framework: Building Confident Learners*, Early Childhood Australia: Canberra.

Arthur, L, Beecher, B, Harrison, C & Morandini, C 2003, 'Sharing the lived experiences of children', *Australian Journal of Early Childhood*, vol. 28, no. 2, pp. 8–13.

Arthur, L, McArdle, F & Papic, M 2010, *Stars are Made of Glass: Children as Capable and Creative Communicators*, Early Childhood Australia, Canberra.

Australian Bureau of Statistics (ABS) 2012, *Year Book Australia, 2012*, Cat. 1301.0, http://www.abs.gov.au/ausstats/abs@.nsf/Lookup/by%20Subject/1301.0~2012~Main%20Features~Use%20of%20information%20technology~174, accessed 30 January 2014.

Australian Bureau of Statistics (ABS) 2012, *Children's Participation in Cultural and Leisure Activities*, Australia, April 2012, Cat. 4901.0, http://www.abs.gov.au/ausstats/abs@.nsf/cat/4901.0, accessed 30 January 2014.

Australian Children's Education and Care Quality Authority, 2013, *Report on the National Quality Framework & Regulatory Burden*, http://www.scseec.edu.au, accessed 31 January 2014.

Australian Council for Trade Unions (ACTU) 2003, *A Fair Australia: Child Care Policy*, Melbourne, ACTU.

Australian Curriculum, Assessment and Reporting Authority (ACARA), *Foundation Year*, http://www.australiancurriculum.edu.au/FoundationYear?, accessed 11 February 2014

Australian Government Department of Social Services, 2013, *Protecting Children is Everyone's Business*, http://www.dss.gov.au/our-responsibilities/families-and-children/publications-articles/protecting-children-is-everyones-business, accessed 24 January 2014.

Australian Government, 2013, *Closing the Gap: Prime Ministers Report*, http://www.dss.gov.au/our-responsibilities/indigenous-australians/programs-services/closing-the-gap/closing-the-gap-prime-ministers-report-2013, accessed 30 January 2014.

Australian Government Productivity Commission, *Inquiry into Child Care and Early Learning*, http://pc.gov.au/projects/inquiry/childcare, accessed 31 January 2014

Australian Institute of Health and Welfare, 2013, *Australia's Welfare 2013*, http://aihw.gov.au/publication-detail/?id=60129543825, accessed 30 January 2014.

Australian Research Alliance for Children and Youth 2013, *The Nest: A National Plan for Child and Youth Wellbeing*, http://www.aracy.org.au/documents/item/162.

Ball, SG (ed.) 1990, *Foucault and Education: Disciplines and Knowledge*, Routledge, London.

Bandura, A 2001, 'Social cognitive theory: An agentic perspective', *Annual Review of Psychology*, no. 52, pp. 1–26.

Bartlett, L 2003, 'Social studies of literacy and comparative education', *Current Issues in Comparative Education*, vol. 5, no. 2, pp. 67–75.

Berk, L 2001, *Awakening Children's Minds: How Parents and Teachers can make a Difference*, Oxford University Press, Oxford.

Blaise, M 2005, 'A feminist poststructural study of children "doing" gender in an urban kindergarten classroom', *Early Childhood Research Quarterly*, vol. 20, no. 1, pp. 85–108.

Blaise, M & Nuttall, J 2011, *Learning to Teach in the Early Years Classroom*, Oxford University Press, South Melbourne.

Bourdieu, P 1986, *Distinction: A Social Critique of the Judgement of Taste*, Routledge, London.

Bourdieu, P 1990, *The Logic of Practice*, Polity Press, Cambridge.

Bourdieu, P 1993, *Sociology in Question*, Sage, London.

Bourdieu, P & Wacquant, LJD 1992, *An Invitation to Reflexive Sociology*, University of Chicago Press, Chicago.

Bowman, BT, Donovan, MS & Burns, MS (eds) 2001, *Eager to Learn: Educating our Preschoolers*, National Academy Press, Washington, DC.

Bredekamp, S 1987, *Developmentally Appropriate Practice in Early Childhood Programs Serving Children from Birth through Age 8*, National Association for the Education of Young Children, Washington, DC.

Bredekamp, S & Copple, C 1997, *Developmentally Appropriate Practice in Early Childhood Programs Serving Children from Birth through Age 8*, National Association for the Education of Young Children, Washington, DC.

Buckingham, D 2000, *After the Death of Childhood*, Polity Press in assoc. with Blackwell Publishers, Cambridge, UK.

Burchinal, M, Howes, C & Kontos, S 2002, 'Structural predictors of child care quality in child care', *Early Childhood Research Quarterly*, vol. 17, no. 1, pp. 87–105.

Burr, V 1995, *An Introduction to Social Constructionism*, Routledge, London.

Butler, J 1990, *Gender Trouble: Feminism and the Subversion of Identity*, New York, Routledge.

Campbell, S & Page, J 2003, 'Curriculum contexts: Becoming an early childhood professional' in G Mac Naughton (ed.), *Shaping Early Childhood Practices: Learners, Curriculum and Contexts*, Open University Press, Maidenhead, pp. 282–301.

Carr, M 2001, *Assessment in Early Childhood Settings: Learning Stories*, Paul Chapman, London.

Carr, M & Lee, W 2012, *Learning Stories: Constructing Learner Identities in Early Education*, Sage, London.

CCCAC, *see* Commonwealth Child Care Advisory Council

Centre for Community Child Health and the Telethon Institute for Child Health Research 2009, *A Snapshot of Early Childhood Development in Australia*, Australian Government Department of Education, Employment and Workplace Relations, Canberra, http://www.aedi.org.au, accessed 13 March 2011.

Children's Services Branch, ACT Department of Education, Youth and Family Services & Mac Naughton, G, Smith K & Lawrence, H (n.d.), *Hearing Young Children's Voices*, ACT Department of Education, Youth and Family Services, Canberra.

Chiwela, GM 2010, 'Participatory school governance: Children in decision-making in the Zambian context', in S Cox, SC Dyer, A Robinson-Pant & AM Schweisfurth (eds), *Children as Decision Makers in Education: Sharing Experiences across Cultures*, Continuum, London, pp. 59–68.

Clark, A 2005, 'Listening to and involving young children', *Early Childhood Development and Care*, vol. 175, no. 6, pp. 489–505.

Clarke, A & Moss, P 2001, *Listening to Young Children: The Mosaic Approach*, National Children's Bureau, London.

Council of Australian Governments (2009). *National Early Childhood Development Strategy, Investing in the Early Years*, Commonwealth of Australia, Canberra.

Commonwealth of Australia 2009, *Protecting Children is Everyone's Business: A National Framework for Protecting Australia's Children 2009–2020*, http://www.coag.gov.au/node/224, accessed 31 January, 2014.

Commonwealth of Australia 2009, *Investing in the Early Years—A National Early Childhood Development Strategy*, Council of Australian Governments, https://www.coag.gov.au/sites/default/files/national_ECD_strategy.pdf, accessed 12 April 2014.

Commonwealth Child Care Advisory Council 2001, *Child Care: Beyond 2001: A Report to the Minister for Family and Community Services*, Commonwealth of Australia, Canberra.

Community Services Ministers Advisory Council 2006, *National Children's Services Workforce Study*, Victorian Government Department of Human Services, Melbourne.

Copple, C & Bredekamp, S 2009, *Developmentally Appropriate Practice in Early Childhood Programs Serving Children from Birth through Age 8*, National Association for the Education of Young Children, Washington, DC.

Cox, S & Robinson-Pant, M 2010, 'Children as researchers: A question of risk?', in S Cox, C Dyer, A Robinson-Pant & M Schweisfurth (eds), *Children as Decision Makers in Education: Sharing Experiences across Cultures*, Continuum, London, pp. 143–51.

Curtis, D & Carter, M 2000, *The Art of Awareness: How Observations can Transform your Teaching*, Redleaf Press, St Paul, MN.

Dahlberg, G & Moss, P 2005, *Ethics and Politics in Early Childhood Education*, RoutledgeFalmer, London.

Dahlberg, G, Moss, P & Pence, A 1999/2007, *Beyond Quality in Early Childhood Education and Care: Postmodern Perspectives*, Falmer Press, London.

Davies, B 1989/2003, *Frogs and Snails and Feminist Tales: Preschool Children and Gender*, Allen & Unwin, Sydney.

Davies, B 1993, *Shards of Glass*, Allen & Unwin, Sydney.

DEEWR 2008, *Second Reading Speech – Indigenous Education (Targeted Assistance) Amendment (2008 Measures No. 1)* Bill 2008, http://parlinfo.aph.gov.au/parlInfo/search/summary/summary.w3p;query=BillId_Phrase%3A%22s932%22%20Dataset%3Ahansardr,hansards%20Title%3A%22second%20reading%22;rec=0 accessed 6 June 2014.

DEEWR 2009, *Belonging, Being and Becoming: The Early Years Learning Framework for Australia*, Australian Government Department of Education, Employment and Workplace Relations, Canberra.

DEEWR 2010, *Educators Belonging, Being and Becoming: Educators Guide to the Early Years Learning Framework for Australia*, Australian Government Department of Education, Employment and Workplace Relations, Canberra.

Dencik, L 2006, 'Parent-child relationships in early childhood', *Keynote Address to the European Early Childhood Education Research Association Annual Conference*, September, Reykjavik, Iceland.

Dockett, S & Perry, B 2005, 'Researching with children: Insights from the Starting School Research Project', *Early Childhood Development and Care*, vol. 175, no. 6, pp. 507–21.

Dockett, S & Perry, B 2007, *Transitions to School*, University of New South Wales Press, Sydney.

Dockett S & Perry B 2009 'Readiness for school: A relational construct', *Australasian Journal of Early Childhood*, vol. 34, no. 1, pp. 20–6.

Early Childhood Australia 2006, *Early Childhood Australia's Code of Ethics*, http://www.earlychildhoodaustralia.org.au/code_of_ethics/early_childhood_australias_code_of_ethics.html, accessed 15 June 2011.

Edwards, C, Gandini, L & Forman, G 1993/1998, *The Hundred Languages of Children*, Ablex, Greenwich, CN.

Elliott, A 2006, *Early Childhood Education: Pathways to Quality and Equity for all Children*, ACER Press, Camberwell, Victoria.

Erikson, E 1963, *Childhood and Society*, 2nd edn., Norton, New York.

Fenech, M 2006, 'The impact of regulatory environments on early childhood professional practice: A review of conflicting discourses', *Australian Journal of Early Childhood*, vol. 31, no. 2, pp. 49–57.

Fenech, M, Sumsion, J & Goodfellow, J 2006, 'The regulatory environment in long day care: A "double-edged sword" for early childhood professional practice', *Australian Journal of Early Childhood*, vol. 31, no. 3, pp. 49–58.

Fleer, M 2003, 'Early childhood education as an evolving "community of practice" or as lived "social reproduction": Researching the taken-for-granted', *Contemporary Issues in Early Childhood*, vol. 4, no. 1, pp. 64–79.

Fleer, M 2010, *Early Learning and Development: Cultural-historical Concepts in Play*, Cambridge University Press, Cambridge.

Fleer, M, Edwards, S, Hammer, M, Kennedy, A, Ridgway, A, Robbins, J & Richardson, C 2004, 'Moving from a constructivist-developmental framework for planning to a sociocultural approach: Foregrounding the tension between individual and community', *Journal of Australian Research in Early Childhood Education*, vol. 11, no. 2, pp. 70–87.

Fleer, M, Edwards, S, Hammer, M, Kennedy, A, Ridgway, A, Robbins, J & Surman, L 2006, *Early Childhood Learning Communities: Sociocultural Research in Practice*, Pearson, Sydney.

Fleet, A & Patterson, C 1998, 'Beyond the boxes: Planning for real knowledge and live children', *Australian Journal of Early Childhood*, vol. 23, no. 4, pp. 31–5.

Fleet, A, Patterson, C & Robertson, J (eds) 2006, *Insights: Behind Early Childhood Pedagogical Documentation*, Pademelon Press, Castle Hill, NSW.

Fleet, A, Patterson, C & Robertson, J (eds) 2012, *Conversations: Behind Early Childhood Pedagogical Documentation*, Pademelon Press, Castle Hill, NSW.

Foucault, M 1970, *The Order of Things: An Archeology of Human Sciences*, Tavistock, London.

Foucault, M 1972/1974/1989, *The Archeology of Knowledge*, Tavistock, London.

Foucault, M 1977, *Discipline and Punish: The Birth of the Prison*, trans. A. Sheridan, Vintage Books, New York.

Foucault, M 1978, *History of Sexuality: An Introduction*, Penguin, London.

Freeman, M 1998, 'The sociology of childhood and children's rights', *The International Journal of Children's Rights*, vol. 6, pp. 433–44.

Gee, J 1990, *Social Linguistics and Literacies: Ideology in Discourse*, Taylor and Francis, London.

Gestwicki, C 2010, *Home, School and Community*, Wadsworth & Cengage, Belmont, CA.

Giroux, HA 1989, *Schooling for Democracy: Critical Pedagogy in the Modern Age*, Routledge, London.

Giugni, M 2006, 'The power and the passion: Popular culture and pedagogy', in A Fleet, C Patterson & J Robertson (eds), *Insights: Behind Early Childhood Pedagogical Documentation*, Pademelon Press, Castle Hill, NSW, pp. 205–24.

Goodfellow, J 2002, *Report of the National Childcare Accreditation Council Environmental Scan*, National Childcare Accreditation Council, Sydney.

Gregory, E, Long, S & Volk, D (eds) 2004, *Many Pathways to Literacy: Young Children Learning with Siblings, Grandparents, Peers and Communities*, Routledge Falmer, New York.

Grieshaber, S 2002, 'A national system of childcare accreditation: Quality assurance or a technique of normalisation?', in G Cannella & J Kincheloe (eds), *Kidworld: Childhood Studies, Global Perspectives and Education*, Peter Lang, New York, pp. 161–80.

Grieshaber, S 2009, 'Equity and quality in the early years of schooling', *Curriculum Perspectives*, vol. 29, no. 1, pp. 91–7.

Grieshaber, S & Cannella, G 2001, 'From identity to identities: Increasing possibilities in early childhood education', in S Grieshaber & G Cannella (eds) *Embracing Identities in Early Childhood Education: Diversity and Possibilities*, Teachers College Press, New York.

Grunewald, R & Rolnick, A 2003, 'Early childhood development: Economic development with a high public return', *Fedgazette, the Federal Reserve Bank of Minneapolis*, http://www.minneapolisfed.org/publications_papers/pub_display.cfm?id=3832, accessed 1 April 2011.

Gutierrez, KD, Larson, J, Enciso, P & Ryan, C 2007, 'Discussing expanded spaces for learning', *Language Arts*, vol. 85, no. 1, pp. 69–77.

Hall, N 2000, 'Literacy, play and authentic experience', in K Roskos & J Christie (eds), *Play and Literacy in Early Childhood: Research from Multiple Perspectives*, Lawrence Erlbaum Associates, Mahwah, NJ.

Hattie, J 2003, *Teachers Make a Difference: What is the Research Evidence?*, Australian Council of Educational Research, Canberra.

Heath, SB 1983, *Ways with Words: Language, Life and Work in Community and Classrooms*, Cambridge University Press, Cambridge, UK.

Helm, J & Katz, L 2001, *Young Investigators: The Project Approach in the Early Years*, Teachers College Press, New York.

Helm, J 2011, *Young Investigators: The Project Approach in the Early Years*, 2nd edn., Teachers College Press, New York.

Henderson, R 2005, *The Social and Discursive Construction of Itinerant Farm Workers Children as Literacy Learners*, Unpublished doctoral manuscript, James Cook University, Townville.

Hill, S, Comber, B, Louden, W, Rivalland, J & Reid, J 1998, *100 Children go to School: Connections and Disconnections in Literacy Development in the Year Prior to School and the First Year of School*, vol. 1, Department of Education, Employment, Training and Youth Affairs, Canberra.

Hilton, M 1996, 'Introduction: The children of this world', in M Hilton (ed.), *Potent Fictions: Children's Literacy and the Challenge of Popular Culture*, Routledge, London.

Honig, AD & Hirallal, A 1998, 'Which counts more for excellence in childcare staff – years in service, education level or ECE coursework?', *Early Child Development and Care*, vol. 145, no. 1, pp. 31–46.

Howes, C, Galinsky, E, Shinn, M, Clements, M, Sibley, A, Abbott-Shim, M & McCarthy, J 1998, *The Florida Child Care Quality Improvement Study: 1996 Report*, Families and Work Institute, New York.

Hughes, P & Mac Naughton, G 2001, 'Fractured or manufactured: Gendered identities and culture in the early years', in S Grieshaber & G Cannella (eds), *Embracing Identities in Early Childhood Education: Diversity and Possibilities*, Teachers College Press, New York.

Hughes, P & Mac Naughton, G 2002, 'Preparing early childhood professionals to work with parents: The challenges of diversity and dissensus', *Australian Journal of Early Childhood*, vol. 28, no. 2, pp. 14–20.

James, A, Jenks, C & Prout, A 1998, *Theorizing Childhood*, Polity Press, Canberra.

Jipson, J 2001, 'Resistance and representation: Rethinking childhood education', in J Jipson & R Johnson (eds), *Resistance and Representation: Rethinking Childhood Education*, Peter Lang, New York.

Jones, E & Nimmo, J 1994, *Emergent curriculum*, National Association for the Education of Young Children, Washington, DC.

Jones Diaz, C, Beecher, B & Arthur, L 2007, 'Children's worlds: Globalisation and critical literacy', in L Makin, C Jones Diaz & C McLachlan (eds), *Literacies in Childhood*, Elsevier, Sydney.

Kalantzis, M 1997, *Education for Cultural Diversity: A Professional Development Program*, Centre for Workplace Communication and Culture, Sydney.

Kamler, B & Comber, B (eds) 2005, *Turn-around Pedagogies: Literacy Interventions for At-risk Students*, Primary English Teaching Association, Newtown, NSW.

Katz, L & Chard, S 1989, *Engaging Children's Minds: The Project Approach*, Ablex, Norwood, NJ.

Kenway, J & Bullen, E 2001, *Consuming Children: Education–Entertainment–Advertising*, Open University Press, Buckingham, UK.

Kessler, S & Swadener, B (eds) 1992, *Reconceptualizing the Early Childhood Curriculum*, Teachers College Press, New York.

Kinney, L & Wharton, P 2008, *An Encounter with Reggio Emilia: Children's Early Learning made Visible*, Routledge, Oxon.

Knobel, M & Healy, A 1998, 'Critical literacies: An introduction', in M Knobel & A Healy (eds), *Critical Literacies in the Primary Classroom*, Primary English Teaching Association, Sydney.

Kohlberg, L 1975, 'The cognitive-developmental approach to moral education', *Phi Delta Kappa*, vol. 56, no. 10, pp. 670–7.

La Paro, K & Pianta, RC 2000, 'Predicting children's competence in the early school years: A meta-analytic review', *Review of Educational Research*, vol. 70, no. 4, pp. 443–84.

Lave, J & Wenger, E 1991, *Situated Learning: Legitimate Peripheral Participation*, University of Cambridge Press, Cambridge.

Lehtinen, A 2004, *Children as Agents – The Core Elements of Agency*, Unpublished manuscript, Jyvaskyla, Finland.

Luke, A 2003, 'Making literacy policy and practice with a difference : generational change, professionalisation and literate futures', *Australian Journal of Language and Literacy*, 26(3), pp. 58–82. http://eprints.qut.edu.au/31650/ accessed 6 June 2014.

Mac Naughton, G 1995, 'A post-structuralist analysis of learning in early childhood settings', in M Fleer (ed.), *DAPcentrism: Challenging Developmentally Appropriate Practice*, Australian Early Childhood Association, Canberra.

Mac Naughton, G 2003, *Shaping Early Childhood: Learners, Curriculum and Contexts*, Open University Press, Maidenhead, UK.

Mac Naughton, G & Williams, G 2009, *Techniques for Teaching Young Children*, 3rd edn., Pearson, Frenchs Forest, NSW.

Malaguzzi, L 1993/1998, 'History, ideas and basic philosophy', in C Edwards, L Gandini & G Foreman (eds), *The Hundred Languages of Children*, Ablex, Norwood, NJ.

Marsh, C 2010, *Becoming a Teacher: Knowledge, Skills and Issues*, Pearson, Frenchs Forest, NSW.

Marsh, J 2000, 'Teletubby tales: Popular culture in the early childhood language and literacy curriculum', *Contemporary Issues in Early Childhood*, vol. 1, no. 2, pp. 119–33, http://www.wwwords.co.uk, accessed 13 March 2011.

Marsh, J & Millard, E 2000, *Literacy and Popular Culture: Using Children's Culture in the Classroom*, Paul Chapman Publishing Limited, London.

Mayall, B 2002, *Towards a Sociology for Childhood: Thinking from Children's Lives*, Open University Press, Buckingham

McInerney, D & McInerney, V 2006, *Educational Psychology: Constructing Learning*, 4th edn., Pearson, Sydney.

McNay, L 2000, *Gender and Agency: Reconfiguring the Subject in Feminist and Social Theory*, Polity Press, Cambridge.

McNay, L 2003, 'Agency, participation and indeterminacy in feminist theory', *Feminist Theory*, vol. 4, no. 2, pp. 139–48.

Meisels, SJ 2007, 'Accountability in early childhood: No easy answer', in RC Pianta, MJ Cox & KL Snow (eds), *School Readiness and the Transition to Kindergarten in the Era of Accountability*, Paul H Brookes, Baltimore, pp. 31–47.

Ministerial Council on Education, Employment, Training and Youth Affairs (MCEETYA) 2008, *Melbourne Declaration on Educational Goals for Young Australians*, MCEETYA.

Moll, L, Amanti, C, Neff, D & Gonzalez, N 1992, 'Funds of knowledge for teaching: Using a qualitative approach to connect homes and classrooms', *Theory into Practice*, vol. 31, no. 2, pp. 132–41.

Morrell, E 2002, 'Toward a critical pedagogy of popular culture: Literacy development among urban youth', *Journal of Adolescent and Adult Literacy*, vol. 46, no. 1, pp. 72–8.

Moss, P 2001a, 'The otherness of Reggio', in L Abbott & C Nutbrown (eds), *Experiencing Reggio: Implications for Pre-school Provision*, Open University Press, Buckingham.

Moss, P 2001b, 'Making space for ethics', *Australian Journal of Early Childhood*, vol. 26, no. 4, pp. 1–6.

National Institute for Child Health and Human Development (NICHD): Early Child Care Research Network 1996, 'Characteristics of infant childcare: Factors contributing to positive care giving', *Early Childhood Research Quarterly*, vol. 11, no. 3, pp. 269–306.

National Institute for Child Health and Human Development (NICHD): Study of Early Child Care 2002, 'Early child care and children's development prior to school entry: Results from the NICHD Study of Early Child Care', *American Educational Research Journal*, vol. 39, no. 1, pp. 33–164.

New South Wales Department of Community Services (DoCS) 2002, *New South Wales Curriculum Framework for Children's Services: The Practice of Relationships, Essential Provisions for Children's Services*, New South Wales Department of Community Services, Sydney.

New South Wales Teachers Federation and Federation of P & C Associations of New South Wales 2002, *Inquiry into the Provision of Public Education in New South Wales: First Report*, May 2002, http://nswtf.org.au/files/first_report.pdf, accessed 15 June 2011.

New Zealand Ministry of Education 1996, *Te Whāriki: He Whāriki Matauranga monga Mokopuna o Aotearoa – Early Childhood Curriculum*, Learning Media Limited, Wellington.

Newman, L & Pollnitz, L 2001, *Is My Response Ethical? A Reflective Process to Guide the Practice of Early Childhood Students and Professionals*, University of Western Sydney & University of Newcastle, Kingswood, NSW.

NICHD, *see* National Institute for Child Health and Human Development

NSW DoCS, *see* New South Wales Department of Community Services

Ordoñez-Jasis, R & Ortiz, RW 2007, 'Reading their words: Working with diverse families to enhance children's early literacy development', in D Koralek (ed.), *Spotlight on Young Children and Families*, National Association for Education of Young Children, Washington, DC, pp. 44–9.

Ortlipp, M, Arthur, L & Woodrow, C 2011, 'Discourses of the early years learning framework: Constructing the early childhood professional', *Contemporary Issues in Early Childhood*, vol. 12, no. 1, pp. 56–70.

Patterson, C & Fleet, A 2003, *Meaningful Planning: Rethinking Teaching and Learning Relationships*, Research in Practice Series, vol. 10, no. 1, Australian Early Childhood Association, Canberra.

Pelo, A 2006, 'At the crossroads: Pedagogical documentation and social justice', in A Fleet, C Patterson & J Robertson (eds), *Insights: Behind Early Childhood Pedagogical Documentation*, Pademelon Press, Castle Hill, NSW, pp. 173–90.

Perry, R 1997, *Teaching Practice: A Guide for Early Childhood Students*, Routledge, London and New York.

Phillips, D, Mekos, D, Scarr, S, McCartney, K & Abbott-Shim, M 2001, 'Within and beyond the classroom door: Assessing quality in child care centers', *Early Childhood Research Quarterly*, vol. 15, no. 4, pp. 475–96.

Piaget, J 1963, *Origins of Intelligence in Children*, Norton, New York.

Pianta, RC & Cox, M (eds) 1999, *The Transition to Kindergarten*, Brookes, Baltimore, MD.

Press, F 2005, *What about the Kids? Policy Directions for Improving the Experiences of Infants and Young Children in a Changing World*, New South Wales Commission for Children and Young People, Commission for Children and Young People and Child Guardian, NIFTeY, http://kids.nsw.gov.au/uploads/documents/What_about_the_kids_full.pdf, accessed 15 June 2011.

Press, F & Hayes, A 2000, *OECD Thematic Review of Early Childhood Education and Care Policy*, Australian background report, Department of Education, Training and Youth Affairs, Canberra.

Productivity Commission 2011, *Early Childhood Development Workforce*, Research Report, http://www.pc.gov.au/__data/assets/pdf_file/0018/113850/07-early-childhood-chapter4.pdf, accessed 27 March 2014.

Prout, A 2003, 'Participation, policy and childhood', in C Hallett & A Prout (eds), *Hearing the Voices of Children: Social Policy for a New Century*, RoutledgeFalmer, London, pp. 11–25.

Prout, A & Hallett, C 2003, 'Introduction', in C Hallett & A Prout (eds), *Hearing the Voices of Children: Social Policy for a New Century*, RoutledgeFalmer, London, pp. 1–8.

Razfar, A & Guiérrez, K 2003, 'Reconceptualising early childhood literacy: The sociocultural influence', in N Hall, J Larson & J Marsh (eds), *Handbook of Early Childhood Literacy*, Sage, London, pp. 34–47.

Reid, J 2003, 'From bad to worse?: Troubling development in preschool settings', *Australian Journal of Early Childhood*, vol. 28, no. 1, pp. 1–5.

Rinaldi, C 2005, *In Dialogue with Reggio Emilia: Listening, Researching, and Learning*, Routledge, New York.

Robinson, KH & Jones Diaz, C 2006, *Diversity and Difference in Early Childhood Education: Issues for Theory and Practice*, Open University Press, Maidenhead.

Rogoff, B 2003, *The Cultural Nature of Human Development*, Oxford University Press, Oxford.

Rowe, K 2004, 'In good hands? The importance of teacher quality', *Educare News*, no. 149, pp. 4–14.

Royal Children's Hospital Centre for Community Child Health and the Murdoch Childrens Research Institute, 2013, *A Snapshot of Early Childhood Development in Australia 2012*, Melbourne, Australian Government.

Schiller, W 2005, 'Children's perspectives of live arts performances: A longitudinal study', *Early Childhood Development and Care*, vol. 175, no. 6, pp. 543–52.

Shonkoff, J & Phillips, D (eds) 2000, *From Neurons to Neighborhoods: The Science of Early Childhood Development*, National Academy Press, Washington, DC.

Shonkoff, JP, Boyce, WT & McEwen, BS 2009, 'Neuroscience, molecular biology, and the childhood roots of health disparities: Building a new framework for health promotion and disease prevention', *The Journal of the American Medical Association*, vol. 301, no. 21, pp. 2252–9.

Siraj-Blatchford, I, Sylva, K, Taggart, B, Sammons, P, Melhuish, E & Elliot, K 2003, *Technical Paper 10: The Effective Provision of Pre-School Education (EPPE) Project: Intensive Case Studies of Practice*, Institute of Education, University of London, https://www.education.gov.uk/publications/eOrderingDownload/ RBX16-03.pdf, accessed 15 June 2011.

Smith, A, Duncan, J & Marshall, K 2005, 'Children's perspectives on their learning: Exploring methods', *Early Childhood Development and Care*, vol. 175, no. 6, pp. 473–88.

Social Policy Research Centre and the Australian Institute of Family Studies 2009, *National Evaluation (2004–2008) of the Stronger Families and Communities Strategy 2004–2009*, Australian Government Department of Families, Housing, Community Services and Indigenous Affairs, Canberra.

Stonehouse, A 1991, *Our Code of Ethics at work*, Australian Early Childhood Resource Booklets, no. 2, May.

Sumsion, J 2006, 'From Whitlam to economic rationalism', *Australian Journal of Early Childhood*, vol. 31, no. 1, pp. 1–9.

Sumsion, J & Goodfellow, J 2002, 'Identifying generic skills through curriculum mapping: A critical evaluation', paper presented at the annual conference of the Australian Association for Research in Education, Brisbane, December 2002.

Swadener, B & Kessler, S (eds) 1991, 'Reconceptualising early childhood education', special issue, *Early Education and Development*, vol. 2, no. 2.

Sylva, K, Melhuish, E, Simmons, P, Siraj-Blatchford, I, Taggart, B & Elliott, K 2003, *The Effective Provision of Preschool Education (EPPE) Project, Summary of Findings*, Institute of Education, University of London.

Sylva, K, Melhuish, E, Simmons, P, Siraj-Blatchford, I & Taggart, B 2010, *Early Childhood Matters: Evidence from the Effective Preschool and Primary Education Project*, Routledge, London.

Thomson, P 2002, *Schooling the Rustbelt Kids; Making the Difference in Changing Times*, Allen & Unwin, Crows Nest, NSW.

Thomson, S, De Bortoli, L, & Buckley, S 2013, *PISA 2012: How Australia measures up*, http://www.acer.edu.au/documents/PISA-2012-Report.pdf, accessed 25 January 2014.

Thomson, S 2013, 'New PISA results show education decline – it's time to stop the slide', *The Conversation*, 3 December 2013, https://theconversation.com/new-pisa-results-show-education-decline-its-time-to-stop-the-slide-21054, accessed 25 January 2014.

Thorne, B 1993, *Gender Play: Girls and Boys in School*, Open University Press, Buckingham.

UNICEF Innocenti Research Centre, 2008. *The Child Care Transition: A League Table of Early Childhood Education and Care in Economically Advanced Countries*, Report Card 8.

United Nations 1989, *Convention on the Rights of the Child*, New York.

United Voice 2010, 'Big steps in childcare: The childcare workforce crisis', *Big Steps*, Redfern, NSW, http://www.bigsteps.org.au, accessed 15 June 2011.

Victorian Curriculum and Assessment Authority (VCAA) 2009, *Essential Learning Standards*, VCAA, Melbourne.

Vimpani, G 2005, 'The case for national investment in early childhood', *Centre for Policy Development*, http://cpd.org.au/2005/11/the-case-for-national-investment-in-early-childhood/, accessed 13 April 2014.

Vygotsky, L 1978, *Mind in Society: The Development of Higher Psychological Processes*, Harvard University Press, Cambridge, MA.

Walsh, D 2002, 'What to do with developmental theory? Update it and extend it: It's not sufficient, but it's necessary', paper presented at the annual meeting of the American Educational Research Association, New Orleans, April.

Webb, J, Schirato, T & Danaher, G 2002, *Understanding Bourdieu*, Allen & Unwin, Crows Nest, NSW.

Wenger, E 1998, *Communities of Practice: Learning, Meaning, and Identity*, Cambridge University Press, Cambridge.

Wenger, E 2000, 'Communities of practice and social learning systems', *Organization*, vol. 7, no. 2, pp. 225–46.

Wenger, E n.d., *Communities of Practice: A Brief Introduction*, http://www.ewenger.com/theory, accessed 12 June 2011.

Wertsch, JV 1991, *Voices of the Mind: A Sociocultural Approach to Mediated Action*, Harvard University Press, Cambridge, MA.

Wong Fillmore, L 1991, 'When learning a second language means losing the first', *Early Childhood Research Quarterly*, vol. 6, no. 3, pp. 323–46.

Wood, E & Attfield, J 1996/2005, *Play, Learning and the Early Childhood Curriculum*, Chapman Publishing, London.

Woodrow, C 1999, 'Revisiting images of the child in early childhood education: Reflections and considerations', *Australian Journal of Early Childhood*, vol. 24, no. 4, pp. 7–12.

Woodrow, C & Brennan, M 2001, 'Interrupting dominant images: Critical and ethical issues', in J Jipson & R Johnson (eds), *Resistance and Representation: Rethinking Childhood Education*, Peter Lang, New York.

Wylie, C, Hogden, E, Ferrell, H & Thompson, J 2006, *Contributions of Early Childhood Education to Age-14 Competence: Evidence of the Longitudinal Competent Children*, Competent Learners study, Ministry of Education, Wellington, New Zealand.

• CHAPTER TWO •

CHILDREN IN THE CONTEXT OF THEIR FAMILIES AND COMMUNITIES

Chapter learning focus

This chapter will investigate:

- the role of families and communities in children's learning

- relationships and a sense of belonging

- continuity of learning and transitions

- collaborative partnerships

- building connections

- respect for diversity

- high expectations and equity

- putting respect for diversity, high expectations and equity and cultural competence into practice

- ongoing learning and reflective practice.

Introduction

The *Melbourne Declaration on the Educational Goals for Young Australians* identifies two broad goals – 'Australian schooling promotes equity and excellence' and 'all young Australians become: successful learners; confident and creative individuals; and active and informed citizens' (MCEETYA, 2008, p. 7). These goals provide the policy framework for the Australian Curriculum (ACARA, n.d.) and curriculum frameworks for prior to school – *Belonging, Being and Becoming: The Early Years Learning Framework for Australia* (DEEWR, 2009) – and outside school hours care – *My Time, Our Place: Framework for School Aged Care in Australia* (DEEWR, 2011). In order to support equitable access to successful learning for all children, educators need to respect diversity and difference and work collaboratively with all families and communities (MCEETYA, 2008; DEEWR, 2009; 2011). *The Early Years Learning Framework for Australia* (DEEWR, 2009) and *My Time, Our Place* (DEEWR, 2011) reflect these understandings through the principles of:

- secure, respectful and reciprocal relationships

- partnerships

- high expectations and equity

- respect for diversity

- ongoing learning and reflective practice.

This chapter draws on these principles and the practice of cultural competency, and links these to practical strategies for working collaboratively with families and communities. It highlights the role of families and communities in children's learning and development and the importance of partnerships between and among educators, children and families. It describes strategies for communicating with families and promoting continuity of learning between homes and early childhood settings and between early childhood settings and schools. It also explores practical strategies that demonstrate respect for diversity, high expectations for all and a commitment to equity and cultural competence. The chapter concludes by emphasising the importance of reflective practice.

The role of families and communities in children's learning

Sociocultural theory maintains that children's learning is situated in the social and cultural contexts of their families and communities. As children observe family and community members, participate in daily events and engage in collaborative experiences, they learn about the processes, concepts and practices that are valued within their community.

Family and community experiences include everyday activities such as shopping, going to the movies, attending a church or mosque or going hunting out bush. When children engage in these everyday experiences within their families and communities they develop their own 'configurations of knowledge, narratives and interests' (Thomson, 2002, p. 8). A child in one family may be learning a great deal about relationships, literacy and numeracy, for example, as they participate in family experiences such as watching television and DVDs, reading the train timetable, filling out the footy tipping sheet or reheating food in the microwave. Other children learn as they participate in shared book experiences, play card games and interact with tablet computers.

There is a breadth and depth of experiences in children's homes and communities. Children come to early childhood settings and schools with their 'virtual school bag full of things they have already learned at home, with their friends and in and from the world in which they live' (Thomson, 2002, p. 1). It is important that educators value these '**funds of knowledge**' (Moll et al.1992; Gonzalez, 2005). All families and communities have the potential to provide 'ample and positive resources' for children (Moll et al. 1992, p. 134); however, these resources vary across social, cultural, linguistic and economic contexts. Moll and his colleagues point out that children from low socio-economic and culturally and linguistically diverse communities have a great deal of information and expertise about life and everyday literacy practices in their own communities, but these 'funds of knowledge' are often not recognised or built upon in educational settings.

> **What are the funds of knowledge of the families and children you work with?**

Funds of knowledge

The skills, knowledge, networks and everyday practices that children acquire as they participate in family and community life.

Building relationships and a sense of belonging

In order for children, families and community members to feel a sense of 'belonging' in an early childhood or outside school hours care setting, in keeping with the concepts of *Belonging, Being and Becoming: The Early Years Learning Framework for Australia* (EYLF) (DEEWR, 2009) and *My Time, Our Place: Framework for School Aged Care in Australia* (DEEWR, 2011), it is crucial that educators are sensitive and responsive to diversity and difference, and engage in critical reflection about their partnerships and pedagogies.

It is important for educators to reflect on the extent to which children and their families and community members feel that they belong in the early childhood setting or school and develop strategies that support **collaborative partnerships** and build connections between home and the early childhood setting or school. 'The three concepts, belonging, being and becoming, are an overarching framework for connecting people, places, things and everyday life' (Giugni, n.d., p. 11). To feel a sense of belonging, children, families and communities need to experience respectful attitudes and interactions that appreciate diversity and see the strengths in difference (Gonzalez-Mena, 2008). 'How teachers build and form relationships with children and their families matters, and contributes to children's sense of belonging and wellbeing' (Blaise & Nuttall, 2011, p. 167).

Collaborative partnerships

Involve two-way communication and negotiation where educators and family members share information, exchange ideas and work towards shared goals.

Respect for children's family practices, beliefs and values within the early childhood setting, outside school hours care and school, is foundational to children feeling a sense of security and belonging. Educators need to find out about, value and reflect the diversity of the local community within their settings. Because Standard Australian English, book-based literacies and Anglo-Celtic culture have power and status within most Australian educational settings, many families with diverse practices are often reluctant to share their families' experiences with educators as they do not see them valued within the educational setting. 'Typically, school expectations of families reflect behaviours, value orientations, and capabilities of middle class families' (Tutwiler, 2012, p. 40). Families who speak a language other than English, have non-mainstream values or practices or are not able to participate in school events may be judged as 'disinterested' or 'bad' parents. Some parents get the message that they do not belong in early childhood settings and schools because their language and social practices are not respected (Hill et al., 2002). All educators have the responsibility of recognising the capabilities of all families and building positive relationships with them.

Source: Summer Hill Children's and Community Centre and Earlwood Children's Centre

FIGURE 2.1 Resources that reflect children's everyday cultures can be included throughout the curriculum; for example, in the literacy area, dramatic play and construction. Photographs of the local community add authenticity to resources, such as props for block construction.

Source: Kingscliff Mini School (community preschool)

FIGURE 2.2 Creating a welcoming environment for when families first arrive at the centre encourages a sense of belonging. This centre involved local Aboriginal and Torres Strait Islander Elders in developing its entrance; the Elders worked with children to create artworks and a bush tucker garden, which are meaningful to the local area.

Continuity of learning and transitions

The importance of continuity of learning and successful transitions between early childhood settings and schools is recognised in the EYLF (DEEWR, 2009). Transitions between settings and homes are also recognised as important in *My Time, Our Place* (DEEWR, 2011). In addition, *The National Quality Standard for Early Childhood Education and Care and School Age Care* (ACECQA, n.d.), which operates across Australian early childhood services and school age care, includes an emphasis in Quality Area 6 (element 6.3.2) of 'continuity of learning and transitions for each child by sharing relevant information and clarifying responsibilities' (ACECQA, 2013, p. 11). Children and families make transitions between home, school and out of school hours care and these documents emphasise the importance of complementary relationships across these contexts to ensure children are confident and comfortable with the changes.

Epstein and associates (2008) report that children and young people are more likely to experience academic success when the three spheres of school, community and family are closely linked. When educators are aware of, and value, children's interests, experiential learning and knowledge networks within their families and communities, there is more likely to be congruence between children's family and educational contexts.

The importance of congruence between children's home and educational settings has been highlighted in research studies for some time (Breen et al., 1994; Hill et al., 1998; Hill et al., 2002). In some cases, the 'language, social and textual practices of the home and the school [are] ... similar, creating an easy connection between home and school values and attitudes' (Hill et al., 2002, p. 7). For example, Abby's 'virtual school bag' contains experiences with English language picture books and DVDs and visits to museums, so she has many experiences she is able to take out and use in the classroom. Lily is interested in computer-based texts and popular media culture, and she is a competent speaker of Mandarin. If Lily's experiences are not valued in her early childhood setting or school, she may not have many opportunities to use the resources in her 'virtual school bag'. If connections between her home and the early childhood setting/school are not present, it may be difficult for her to engage with school curricula and literacies (Hill et al., 2002).

If only one set of experiences is held up as the norm in educational settings, children such as Lily, whose experiences do not match those of the dominant group, are likely to become marginalised. As Campbell and Green (2000, p. 3) notes:

> A classroom is a kind of club with insiders – those who understand the rules of the game because they come from clubs/homes that have similar beliefs, values, rituals, rules and ways of using language – and outsiders.

When only mainstream, Standard Australian English language, book-based experiences are valued, children such as Lily quickly learn that their cultural and linguistic capital (Bourdieu, 1990), or funds of knowledge, are not valued within the school or early childhood setting – and so become outsiders in the classroom. Consequently, they may not talk to educators about their interests or ideas, they learn not to take anything out of their virtual school bag and so they do not have opportunities to demonstrate their understandings in the classroom. On the other hand, when educators hold broad views of learning and are respectfully aware of the diversity of funds of knowledge, they are able to move beyond limiting 'deficit' views to develop positive partnerships with children and families. In these situations there is likely to be a substantial degree of congruence between home and early childhood settings/schools (Cairney, 2000; Lingard et al., 2002; Makin et al., 1999).

Building on children's prior and current experiences helps them to feel secure, confident and connected to familiar people, places, events and understandings. This is particularly important when children are making the transition from home to an early childhood setting or from an early childhood setting to school. Transition to school is more likely to be a positive experience

Can you identify the predominant 'rules of the game' for the families and children you work with? What can you do to break down entry barriers for 'perceived' outsiders?

when there are collaborative partnerships between educators across prior-to-school and school settings, and with families and children (Dockett & Perry, 2006; Ashton et al., 2008). These partnerships 'encourage shared understanding of cultural and social values, which enables staff to plan experiences relevant for all children' (Ashton et al., 2008, p. 15).

Educators may need to step outside their own comfort zones in order to facilitate these important partnerships. At times, acknowledging personal bias and our own 'cultural norms' can challenge our ability to embrace another's diversity.

Much of the current research around educational transitions draws on Bronfenbrenner's (Bronfenbrenner & Morris, 1998) bioecological theory, which promotes a focus on the processes, person, contexts and time elements of transition (*see* Chapter 3). This means attending to a range of factors when considering transition, including the ways in which different contexts (such as the family, community and setting) work together to support relationships between and among children and adults, educators and families, as well as children and their peers.

Transition is recognised as a time of continuity and change; some things endure and other elements change over time. This can be seen in terms of relationships, where some relationships (such as those in the family) are ongoing, but others change, with some relationships being lost and others built. Change and continuity are often evident for children who enter a new setting, but it is important to recognise that educational transitions are also family transitions, not only involving family members but also resulting in some changes for the family (Dockett, Perry, & Kearney, 2012).

Families provide ongoing support during transitions. What happens at home and within communities influences how children feel about making transitions, the experiences they have to support transitions and how they manage transitions. The experiences of family members also contribute to the ways in which transitions are enacted.

A range of international evidence from research and practice points to the importance of transition as a process that occurs over time and involves multiple participants – including children, families, communities, educators and other professionals. This research has contributed to the development of the *Transition to School Position Statement* (Educational Transitions and Change, 2011), which characterises transition to school in terms of opportunities, aspirations, expectations and entitlements for all involved – children, families, educators, school organisations and communities. Examples from the *Position Statement* highlight:

Opportunities for:

- children to continue shaping their identities and to extend their existing knowledge, skills and understandings through interactions with adults, peers and family
- families and educators to collaborate with a range of others in ways that strengthen and support each child's ongoing learning and development
- educators to build relationships with children, families, other educators and communities that provide the basis for effective learning and teaching interactions and
- communities to recognise the transition to school as an important event in the lives of children and families.

Aspirations as:

- children look forward to making friends and engaging with learning at school
- families work towards positive educational outcomes for their children
- educators work towards professional partnerships that create strong and supportive educational environments for all children
- educational organisations and system aim to promote positive educational trajectories and outcomes for all children.

Expectations as:

- children start school expecting to learn and face challenges and to have support from peers and sensitive adults as they engage within these
- families expect that their knowledge of their children will be respected at school and that educators will draw on this, as well as their own expertise and that of other professionals, to create the best possible learning environments for their children
- educators expect to have support and appropriate professional recognition as they create positive learning and teaching environments, partnerships with families, other educators and professionals
- communities expect schools to attend to the wellbeing of all children.

Entitlements as:

- children access high quality education that demonstrates respect for existing competencies, cultural heritage and histories
- families are confident that their children will have access to education that promotes equity and excellence and that attends to the wellbeing of all children
- educators receive professional regard and ongoing professional support
- communities are regarded as essential contributors to children's education.

Educational Transitions and Change Research Group, © 2011 Research Institute
for Professional Practice, Learning and Education, Charles Sturt University.

Collaborative partnerships with families and communities

Collaborative partnerships between educators, families and communities are one of the seven Quality Areas in the *National Quality Standard for Early Childhood Education and Care and School Aged Care* (*see Guide to the National Quality Standard*, ACECQA, 2013), which is mandatory for the majority of Australian early childhood and school aged care settings. The value of partnerships between educators and families is also affirmed in the Australian Curriculum for Foundation to Year 12. The *Melbourne Declaration on Educational Goals for Young Australians*, endorsed by all ministers of education, also advocates partnerships between students, educators, families and the broader community (MCEETYA, 2008). Partnerships are essential for supporting and extending children's learning and for equitable outcomes. 'Open, honest, respectful, reliable, friendly and helpful communication' between educators and families provides a source of social support to all families (Rolfe & Armstrong, 2010, p. 65). For Aboriginal and Torres Strait Islander communities, family and community involvement is an essential component of culturally strong programming and of support for families (Guilfoyle et al., 2010). Involvement may take many different forms and will need to be negotiated sensitively and respectfully within each Aboriginal and Torres Strait Islander community, with one possible result being an Elder choosing to engage in a cultural mentor relationship. Educators will need to research and develop a greater understanding of their reciprocal cultural responsibilities in such circumstances.

Educators need to take the initiative in promoting partnerships with families. It is the educator's responsibility to develop strategies and confidence in effective communication with all families, not just the families with whom they feel comfortable or the families who initiate communication, and to provide support for all families.

Strong partnerships between educators, families and communities are highlighted as a strategy to 'maximise student engagement and achievement' in the *Melbourne Declaration on Educational Goals for Young Australians* (MCEETYA, 2008, p. 10). Partnerships between the significant people in children's lives enable 'a two-way flow of information that constructs curriculum that is equitable, engaging and relevant to the children, families and their communities' and supports continuity of learning (Beecher & Jones Diaz, 2014, p. 62). Collaborative partnerships between home and educational settings, families and educators facilitate the exchange of information and development of shared understandings. These partnerships strengthen educators' sociocultural awareness of children's home and community contexts and knowledge networks, which can then be included in the curriculum. When children's real-world knowledge and experiences are included in the classroom, children are likely to have the opportunity to demonstrate their competencies and to bridge to new knowledge so that they become insiders in the classroom. 'Learning outcomes are most likely to be achieved when early childhood educators work in partnership with families' (DEEWR, 2009, p. 12).

Effective partnerships involve:

- trust
- reciprocal respect and valuing of each other's knowledge
- sensitivity to diverse perspectives where each partner can share insights
- ongoing, open, respectful communication
- empathy
- recognition of the partner's strengths
- collaboration
- shared decision making.

(DEEWR, 2009; Stonehouse & Gonzalez-Mena, 2008)

Collaborative partnerships involve both educators and family members making a commitment and sharing relevant information and are 'built on mutual benefit' (Puckett & Diffily, 2004, p. 174) and the 'integration of different wisdoms' (Spaggiari, 1993, p. 97).

Partnerships require open communication. It is not necessary that both partners agree, but that they are able to appreciate each other's perspectives. Stonehouse and Gonzalez-Mena (2008) assert that effective partnerships require a genuine acceptance and acknowledgement of diversity where families and educators will sometimes have conflicting views. Rather than viewing disagreements as a problem, they can enable different perspectives to be shared, new questions asked and new means of investigation proposed (Lyotard, 1984). Open communication acknowledges the expertise that families as well as educators bring to discussions and challenges assumptions that effective partnerships are based on families adapting to or fitting in with setting or school expectations.

Partnerships are different from parent involvement. Parent involvement may include fundraising, parent help in the classroom, working bees or involvement in the parent group in a management or advisory capacity. Family or parent involvement generally does not promote family members as active decision makers; rather, educators are considered as experts and the ones with the power (Mac Naughton & Hughes, 2003; Stonehouse & Gonzalez-Mena, 2008). This involvement is generally at the invitation of staff and on the educator's terms, and is concerned with what the parent can do for the setting or how the setting can better educate the parent. These are what Mac Naughton and Hughes call conforming relationships because the aim is for families and children to conform to setting expectations.

Families who share the educator's culture, language and values are generally more likely to become involved than those from diverse communities. Steps need to be taken to encourage all families to be involved in whatever way they feel is appropriate. Families are more likely to become involved when educators are welcoming and encourage family contributions, when families are aware of the value of their input and when decision-making is seen as a shared responsibility (Briggs & Potter, 1999; DEST, 2006). Issues such as employment commitments and care for younger children also need to be considered (Briggs & Potter, 1999).

While family involvement is not a partnership, it can lead to a partnership (Stonehouse & Gonzalez-Mena, 2008). It is important that any parent involvement is viewed as an opportunity for forming connections that support the child (Stonehouse & Gonzalez-Mena, 2008), not as a way of getting tasks done. Asking family members to engage in meaningless tasks such as cutting fruit or covering books, often in isolation from the children, does not encourage families to return and does not build partnerships between educators, families and children. This type of parent involvement is 'shallow, ineffectual, unrewarding and even frustrating to those involved' (Briggs & Potter, 1999, p. 433).

Inviting family members to suggest meaningful ways in which they might be genuinely involved in their child's education can strengthen meaningful partnerships. These partnerships have the potential to transform relationships (Mac Naughton & Hughes, 2003) as they challenge the traditional knowledge–power links between educators and families by acknowledging that there is not a fixed body of knowledge about children that educators possess and parents lack. In **transformative relationships** the voice and expertise of family members is acknowledged and educators and families are able to build collaborative relationships where family members are invited to 'form policies, manage resources and evaluate services [and to make] decisions about what and how children should learn' (Mac Naughton & Hughes, 2003, p. 269). For families to be involved in decision making, as advocated in Standard 6.3 of the National Standard (ACECQA, 2013), the situation to be decided should be clear and families must possess all the relevant information (Briggs & Potter, 1999).

Educators can support family members in their role as the child's first teacher and enhance collaborative partnerships between educators and families by:

- involving families in the development and evaluation of the setting's philosophy, goals, policies and program
- talking with families about their values and their expectations for their child
- including families in the processes of documenting children's learning
- connecting the curriculum to children's home and community experiences and interests
- building a sense of community within the setting by providing multiple ways for families to choose how to be a part of the setting community
- bringing the broader community into the setting for events or as resources
- providing information to families about the early childhood setting and its program
- exchanging information with the family about the child's experiences, interests, relationships, dispositions and learning
- linking families with relevant community organisations and networks.

Transformative relationships

Involve educators reflecting on their interactions with families and repositioning families as experts so that there is a two-way exchange of knowledge between the educator and families.

What strategies do you use to acknowledge families as experts and develop collaborative partnerships?

Building connections

Educators must take responsibility for building connections with families and communities and facilitating the exchange of information with all families, despite many of the barriers to effective communication. Effective communication between families and educators takes time, effort and energy. It is essential to acknowledge any barriers to communication and find strategies that support open communication.

Barriers to effective communication

It is important to recognise and respect that not all families have positive attitudes towards or trust educational settings. Some family members will not have had positive experiences of education, or with institutions in general, and may not trust educators. Family members who have any additional needs may feel intimidated by educators, or feel they are being judged – based on their past experience and skills. Where family members have had previous negative experiences with educational settings, it may be necessary for educators to reach out in many ways and over considerable time, in order to build trusting relationships. Adults' own experiences of education impact on their attitudes and approaches to educational settings for their children (Turunen & Dockett, 2013). When adults recall feelings of alienation from school, or remember that resources and practices did not reflect or value their culture, educators face the challenge of providing evidence that things have changed.

Family and community arguments, deaths or other significant incidents will not always be shared with or be obvious to educators, particularly in Aboriginal and Torres Strait Islander communities. Trusting families, observing but not judging and allowing time for communication is critical. Remember, your time frame will not necessarily be in sync with families who may have significant front-of-mind cultural responsibilities.

Often staff are disappointed when families are not actively seeking information about how their children are engaging with the program and sometimes mistakenly believe that these families 'don't care'. These issues may arise because of cultural differences, limited English language proficiency, or lack of familiarity with school curriculum and the procedures and protocols of the setting. Educators must be careful not to judge families' responses from their own cultural perspective. As Siraj-Blatchford and Clarke (2000) note, many ethnic minority and working-class families respect and trust educators. They do not question educators' decisions, unlike many middle-class Anglo-Celtic families who ask questions and are proactive. Conversely, some families may feel that their perspectives are not valued in the setting and that even when they do provide information or ask questions, they feel that their voice will not be heard.

At times, families may be reluctant to disclose what they see as personal information to educators (Hughes & Mac Naughton, 2000). When families are trying to cope with difficult life circumstances they may also be reluctant to share information with staff for fear of being judged a 'bad' parent. Parents experiencing difficulties may also mistrust and reject educators' assessments of their child's learning difficulties (Hill et al., 2002). At these times it may be appropriate for educators to provide families with information about support services that are available and to facilitate access for families to appropriate assistance.

Some families may experience difficulties in finding time to participate in the setting's activities or to engage in conversations with staff. This may be due to work commitments and/or because of the need to pick up children from multiple care arrangements. Some parents are required to work longer hours than others or may have less flexibility in their work hours. There is often an expectation that families with children with additional needs have high levels of participation in their child's education, and they may be expected to take on the role of 'teacher' as well as parent. However, like any other parent they face the same issues of employment commitments, being a parent to all their children, including those without additional needs, and everyday life. Educators also may find it difficult to make time to engage in meaningful interactions with families, and the physical environment may not be conducive to productive, confidential exchanges (Mac Naughton, 2004).

Effective communication

It is essential that educators take the initiative in communicating with families, rather than wait for families to initiate interactions. This means developing attitudes, policies and communication strategies that are reflective of, and sensitive to, diverse family contexts and that open up possibilities for discussion. It is important for educators to be aware of their own expectations of families, to be alert to possible stereotypes and not to make judgments about families. Stereotypes and assumptions can disrupt communication, particularly when educators and families are from different cultural backgrounds.

Effective communication requires appropriate staff time and a physical space where staff and families can talk meaningfully and confidentially. Siraj-Blatchford and Clarke (2000) note that educators need to get to know families and take steps to build family members' confidence so that they are more likely to share information that enables educators to gain insights into children's experiences.

Effective communication involves:
- equal access to information for all families
- use of bilingual staff or interpreters and translators
- opportunities for all families to be involved in the service and to share information with educators

- daily verbal communication that includes meaningful conversations about issues of importance
- written communication that goes beyond administrative issues and that is tailored to individuals
- processes that identify at least one educator who is available for communication with each family
- encouragement for families to share ideas and practices with each other as well as educators so that there is an understanding and acceptance of difference
- professional boundaries that build trust and avoid unethical issues.

(De Gioia, 2009; Mac Naughton & Hughes, 2003; Rolfe & Armstrong, 2010)

When educators adopt these practices, relationships with families are likely to be respectful and collaborative, providing opportunities for an open and ongoing exchange of information with all families.

Exchanging information with families

If educators are to understand children's strengths and interests, it is important they find out about children's home and community experiences as well as family expectations and values. When gathering this information, educators must be clear as to why they are requesting families to divulge information and how this will help them to work with children in their centre or class. It is important to think about whether there is a 'right to know' about what happens in a child's home and what information it is necessary to collect. Educators must be respectful of families' wishes not to divulge information and must treat information professionally and ethically. This means respecting diverse perspectives, recording all information in a professional manner, maintaining confidentiality and not making judgements about families' child-rearing practices and lifestyles. All families have valuable knowledge about their children. However, it is essential to recognise the power relationships that exist between educators and many families and to take steps to develop relationships with all families, including those who are different from us (Blaise & Nuttall, 2011).

The following list offers suggestions as to the types of information that may enhance understandings of the child's family and community context. Not all of this information will be shared in one exchange. Some information will be obtained initially as part of the enrolment process and can then be added to over time through regular meetings and social events. Possible areas of discussion may include:

- family members
- languages
- beliefs and practices
- everyday experiences
- family expectations
- community groups and events
- expertise.

Family members significant in a child's life will vary from immediate to extended family and significant family friends. It is important to respect diverse family structures and living arrangements. It is not necessary to know about parents' marital status or issues such as family breakdown unless parents choose to share this information.

Where families have experienced migration or have been refugees, it is useful to know their country of origin, the length of time they have been in the new country and their experiences of migration, displacement or detention. Again, it is important to be sensitive to traumas that families may have faced and to respect a family's right not to divulge this information.

It is important to find out about the *language/s* that children experience within their families and communities. Children may speak different languages with different family members, such as English with one parent and Spanish with another parent, or English with parents and siblings and Greek with grandparents. For Aboriginal and Torres Strait Islander families it is important to find out about different dialects that may be spoken, and the contexts in which these dialects

are used. Information about languages and dialects used at home enables educators to provide relevant resources, or to work with families to develop relevant resources.

It is not necessary to know families' religious *beliefs*, although some families may wish to share this information. However, there may be particular beliefs or values that a family feels strongly about, such as peace or social justice, or particular cultural *practices*, which they may choose to share with staff. In some families, there may be specific foods that are not eaten because of religious affiliations or family beliefs. There may be special cultural or religious events that a family celebrates which they would like to share with staff and have included in the early childhood setting or school. Every family has different child-rearing practices. These include different practices at sleep or rest time, different beliefs and practices regarding food and different expectations regarding self-help skills. It is important that educators ask families about their everyday practices and routines, and the words that they use with children at these times. This information enables educators to provide continuity between home and the early childhood setting.

Children will have a range of *everyday experiences* within their families and communities that contribute to their funds of knowledge. These experiences may involve languages other than English, popular media culture, sport, play with siblings or peers, visits to family members, sorry camp, bush trips and family outings to parks or restaurants. Children will have a range of literacy and numeracy experiences, including television and DVD viewing, card and board games, shopping, commuting, computer and video games, shared book experiences, dreaming stories, songs and conversations. Many families listen to or participate in music, engage in visual arts experiences and share stories. It is useful to find out about any favourite songs, stories, books, DVDs and creative arts experiences that the child may have at home and in their community. Educators can use this information to connect setting experiences to children's family and community contexts and, if appropriate, invite family and community members to share stories, music or visual arts.

It is also useful for educators to know about families' beliefs and *expectations* regarding children's learning. Families will have different views on the role of play and academic experiences in children's learning, different expectations of the setting in regards to children's learning and different views on what school readiness entails. Families' perspectives will often be influenced by their own experiences as children and their own education as well as the media and other families' experiences. The emphasis on play in many early childhood programs is not shared by all families. Some families, particularly those who experienced schooling in contexts where there is a stronger focus on an academic curriculum, may value a more structured program with significant teacher direction and a strong emphasis on academic learning. Families that include children with additional needs may feel pressured to focus on academic learning and a deficit approach, which can be a focus in many intervention and therapy programs, rather than supporting their child's play. It is important for educators to find out about and respect family perspectives while also being proactive in promoting the play-based pedagogies advocated in contemporary curriculum documents. Engaging in ongoing dialogue with families can assist with the development of shared understandings and shared goals for children.

Educators also need to be aware of each family's expectations for their child's language learning. Some bilingual parents will want their children to retain their home language while others may believe that it is more important for the child to learn English. In some cases children may attend language schools on Saturday mornings to extend their home language. It is important to be sensitive to family perspectives while also challenging dominant monolingual discourses that privilege Standard English language at the expense of community languages and non-standard dialects.

Educators in some very remote Aboriginal and Torres Strait Islander communities will be challenged to develop their language skills in a local language to enable true engagement with families and children, such as the dialect Luritja, which is the predominant language spoken in Watiyawanu/Mt Liebig in Central Australia (*see* Chapter 10). It is critical to maintain a relevant program where families and children feel safe and able to share traditional culture and expectations for learning. The amount of time required to achieve this outcome will vary according to each individual and community. When educators demonstrate trust and respect by working alongside and trusting families and children, rather than taking over and 'doing it all', educators will be rewarded for their patience with increased participation in the program by both children and families.

Families may be involved in particular *community groups*, such as a cultural or religious group, or be members of clubs or associations and attend *community events*. Children may also be involved in these groups and events and participate in music, dance, language or sport activities. Knowledge of children's connections with community groups provides insights into their interests and funds of knowledge. Knowledge of family members' association with different groups means that families may be able to help to connect the setting to local groups and events.

Family members all have different areas of interest and *expertise*, whether it is storytelling, painting, gardening, music, a language, cooking or sports. Knowledge of the interests and hobbies of extended family members as well as parents can provide insights into children's interests and expertise and open up opportunities for family involvement. Educators can encourage all families to share their expertise with children in the ways in which they feel comfortable. However, educators also need to acknowledge that family members may not choose to share their expertise.

Based on these exchanges of information with families and using Bronfenbrenner's bioecological model (*see* Chapter 3) educators can identify the many relationships and influences in a child's life and the strengths that the child brings to the setting. This is illustrated in the example for the Osborne Family in Figure 2.3.

Initial information

The first point of contact between families and the early childhood setting is a crucial step in setting the tone of family–service communication. Careful orientation of a family to the service and the service to the family enables trust to grow and dialogue to begin. This is the first step in developing 'respectful and supportive relationships with families' (*National Quality Standard* 6.1, ACECQA, 2013, p. 11). When a family member or carer initially telephones or visits, they will have a range of expectations that will guide decisions about whether the service is the most appropriate environment for their child/children. Questions may include such aspects as: Is the service affordable? Do the opening hours suit? Is the environment welcoming and caring? Will my family's cultural values be respected? Will my child be safe? Allowing the parent/carer (grandparents are often involved in this decision) to guide the initial conversation will ensure their critical questions are answered in full.

If the conversation is driven by cost and availability, rather than children, culture, care and educational provisions, this may reinforce decisions based purely on pragmatics. If information about culture, care and education as well as cost and waiting lists is offered, families will sense that the key focus of the service is children and community. Recording family requirements and expectations at this point will begin the important process of understanding through shared information.

The follow-up written information the staff at the early childhood setting provides will further shape the family's impression of the service. A waiting-list package (translated if required) that includes service history, management structure, mission statement and/or philosophy, adult/child ratios, staff qualifications, a current newsletter, a brochure that guides informed choices and enrolment priority guidelines, combined with an invitation to view the centre (either before or after an offer of placement) reinforces a welcoming environment.

Accommodating family schedules is important when setting appointments to view the early childhood setting. 'Showcasing' times of the day or rigidly setting times may not suit the family. Educators should be comfortable with sharing every part of the day, recognising that families may be restricted by work, family or cultural commitments requiring early morning, lunchtime, late afternoon or evening appointments. These appointments provide an opportunity to share the practicalities of the early childhood setting's philosophy and allow families to evaluate the program through observing interactions, provisions, environment, tone and staff. In some

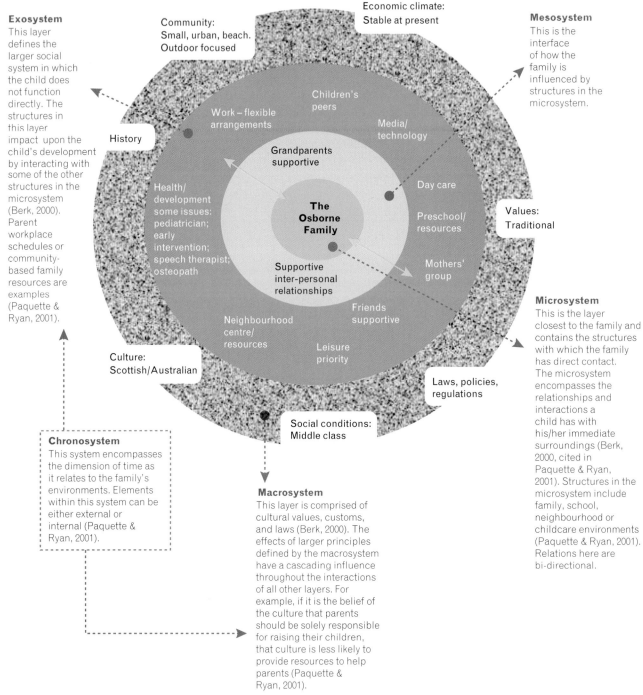

Source: Michele Howell, adapted from Paquette & Ryan, 2001

FIGURE 2.3 Bioecological systems diagram for the Osborne family.

environments families may need to build up their own confidence to enter the setting, so to be asked to return at a time more suitable to the educator may result in another child never accessing early childhood services.

Enrolment forms and enrolment surveys are excellent tools to establish family expectations and reinforce the value of family–service communication. Educators should question the traditional enrolment form structure and ensure that the language is inclusive, that the content is clearly written, comprehensive and useful, and that all legal requirements (such as the *Privacy Act*) are met. For many families, particularly when literacy in Standard Australian English may be a challenge, a face-to-face discussion can be the most effective way to gain family information. The provision of enrolment forms and information in other languages and/or the engagement of translators will determine the success of these initial exchanges for many families. Educators will need to be sensitive to individual family requirements and facilitate meaningful exchanges where families feel empowered rather than deficient due to differences in literacy competence.

A permission section for a parent signature allows families to question or approve critical policies and practices on enrolment. The addition of a comprehensive Family and Community Handbook, translated into relevant community languages, ensures that families are well informed and able to clearly express their desires and expectations.

Staff and families can continue to share further critical information during family orientation visits to the setting and/or, if appropriate, through home visits. These visits provide opportunities for information to be collected and staff–family relationships to be initiated. This enables educators and families to establish preferred communication pathways for ongoing communication, which may include communication books/pockets, emails, Facebook or other electronic media such as SMS, daily diaries, routine charts and conversation on arrival/ departure. Regular evaluation of these communication strategies ensures that they remain effective for families.

Ongoing exchange of information

It is important that educators explore a range of strategies for maintaining ongoing communication with families and, with family input, select those that are most appropriate for the different families using the setting.

For some families, written communication will be the most appropriate method to share information, whereas for other families oral communication may be more appropriate. Information may need to be translated into relevant community languages for families who are more proficient in their home language than English. It is also important to remember that not all family members are literate. Bilingual speakers will not necessarily be literate in their home language or in English. Those for whom English is their first language may not always be confident with literacy either.

One communication method is not going to suit all families, so it is necessary to utilise a variety of methods that incorporate both written and oral forms of communication that range from formal to informal. Broad-based comprehensive approaches that include a mixture of formal and informal communication are most effective.

Following is a range of communication strategies that educators may choose to use when developing effective communication with families. Strategies should be regularly evaluated as to their appropriateness for families.

ONGOING CONVERSATIONS

A welcoming physical space can encourage family members to spend time at the setting and to engage in conversations with educators and children. For some families this will be a space with adult-sized furniture such as a sofa in the foyer or family room. In other contexts a welcoming physical space may be an indoor space with floor mats or a space outdoors under the trees. Displays of photographs and samples of children's work on the walls or in booklets, or a computer or tablet loaded with images of children engaged in projects can provide opportunities for reflection and conversation.

INTERVIEWS

More formal conversations can occur during interviews between educators and family members. It is essential that interviews provide opportunities for families to share information about their children with staff and to ask questions; interviews should not be just for staff to tell parents about the child's experiences and progress. Interviews should be held several times during the year so that information can be updated periodically, and educators and families remain well informed. At these times, educators and family members can share artefacts from children's experiences, such as samples of the child's writing, drawing and paintings, photographs of the child engaged in experiences, and narratives about the child's play and social interactions. Children can also participate in these interviews and contribute their perspectives on their interests and learning.

CONFERENCES

Educators, families and professionals from support services may meet to develop an individualised program for a child. This may be particularly useful where a child has an additional need or requires additional support. Conferences enable all participants to share their insights and contribute to setting goals, developing plans and evaluating progress towards goals. Where appropriate it is useful for children to be involved in these conferences and to participate in goal setting and evaluations.

FAMILY MEETINGS

Meetings with multiple families as a group can be less intimidating for families than interviews as they involve a number of parents and the educators who work with a class or a group of children. When educators move beyond notions of family meetings as times for 'telling' families about the setting's program, or what they should do at home, there are many opportunities for shared decision making. These meetings enable both educators and families to share information, tell stories, discuss issues and make decisions together (Puckett & Diffily, 2004). Family meetings can be an appropriate time to discuss the setting's philosophy and program, evaluate policies and procedures and set group goals. Formal strategies for encouraging family involvement include family representation on the setting's management committee or school board.

In some settings, family meetings may include extended family and community Elders from the local Aboriginal or Torres Strait Islander community who have specific expectations of the role of the early childhood service within the broader community. These meetings may be planned by the educator but are often impromptu with a delegation of Elders attending the service unannounced. It is vital to recognise the importance of such meetings and respect the time and suggestions offered by the community to engage with the service.

FAMILY INVOLVEMENT IN THE PROGRAM

Immediate and extended family members can be involved in early childhood settings and schools in many different ways. This may include sharing expertise in a particular area, such as telling a story in a language other than English or playing a musical instrument. It may mean spending time at the setting playing with children, sharing books or listening to children read. It could be writing 'welcome' in a community language for the 'Welcome to the centre' sign (*see* Figure 2.4) or working in the school's bush tucker or community garden. It is important for educators to provide different opportunities for participation and to recognise that family members will participate in different ways and at different levels (Farmer, 2009). In some environments, families will want to remain with the children for an extended period of time, sharing in the care and education of their children throughout the day. This may include bathing and nappy change on arrival, sharing meals with their child, washing clothes, playing and learning alongside children and educators.

FIGURE 2.4 Welcome signs in relevant community languages give families the message that their language and culture are valued in the setting.

Gathering information about family strengths, skills and interests is one way of finding out how family members might wish to be involved in the setting. When families are invited to share their skills they feel that they have something valuable to offer and this can motivate them to develop these skills further and works to enhance confidence (Farmer, 2009). Involving family and community members within the early childhood setting and school is also a way of providing an inclusive environment for children when staff may only reflect one language, gender or set of skills (Farmer, 2009). Family attendance on excursions or at special events such as concerts, the screening of a child-created video or an open day or evening is another strategy for family involvement.

SOCIAL EVENTS

Social events can include a grandparents' or seniors' day, family barbecues or picnics, or coffee mornings. These events encourage family participation in the life of the setting and foster social relationships between staff, children and families, and among families. When family members are working it may be most appropriate for these social events to be held at night or on weekends. While some of these events may also be opportunities for fundraising, it is important that educators, children and families are able to get together simply for social purposes. It is important to consider families' financial situations when organising social events. Educators need to be sensitive to children's diverse family situations and extend open invitations that are inclusive of all family structures. During celebrations such as Mother's Day and Father's Day educators should not assume that children live in a traditional family.

COLLABORATIVE PROFESSIONAL DEVELOPMENT

Families can join with staff in discussions on a selected topic – such as anti-bias curriculum or literacy – where issues can be raised and diverse approaches explored. The inclusion of family members ensures that families' perspectives are heard and taken into consideration in future plans. The addition of a guest speaker can also encourage critique of existing practices and the examination of new ideas.

Families, educators and children can also participate in workshops offered by community organisations, parents or staff, where they are able to learn more about skills such as working with clay, establishing worm farms or cooking. These workshops can be significant social and learning events for families, children and staff.

SHARING RESOURCES

Communication and connections between the educational setting and the home and local community can be facilitated when families and children are encouraged to bring resources to the setting from home. These may be food packaging materials for collage or dramatic play, or other literacy resources

Source: KU Hebersham Preschool

FIGURE 2.5 Social events and workshops for educators, families and children support collaborative learning.

that reflect children's home and community experiences. Families can contribute bilingual resources such as old newspapers or restaurant menus; children's favourite music, books or DVDs for sharing; or photographs from a family event. The opportunity to share resources gives families the message that their experiences are valued in the setting and opens up further dialogue between educators, children and families.

The development of bilingual storybooks is one positive way of valuing the child's culture and demonstrating respect for the family's home language and skills. For example, families in the early childhood service in Walungurru/Kintore, a remote Central Australian community, liaised with the educator and a language specialist to develop a board book based on the adventures of a community pig. The children and families dictated the text, illustrated the book and each child received a copy to take home. The book continues to delight the children and demonstrates the value of and respect for community input as well as being an important literacy tool.

QUESTIONNAIRES

Educators can create their own short questionnaires focused on a particular topic, such as children's literacy and numeracy experiences and interests at home or issues families want included in parent seminars. 'Information update sheets' (Stonehouse & Gonzalez-Mena, 2008)

can be a fast and effective way of obtaining current information from families. Older children can complete questionnaires themselves about topics such as their weekend interests or the languages they speak at home and in the community. Questionnaires can also be a useful way of obtaining families' perspectives on the program as a whole or on particular policies. Pictorial questionnaires are a practical method of collecting data when English literacy may present a barrier.

LITERACY AND NUMERACY QUILTS

The idea of a literacy or numeracy quilt originated with *ECLIPSE: Early childhood literacy includes parents, staff and education – literacy in early childhood* (Department of Education and Children's Services South Australia, 1997). This idea was adapted in the professional development conducted for *Literacies, communities and under 5s* (Jones Diaz et al., 2001) and has also been used with educators and families in Chile (Woodrow, Arthur & Newman, 2014). Families can be encouraged to write, draw or collage examples of the sorts of literacy and/or numeracy experiences that their child engages in at home on colourful pieces of paper or post-it notes or provide photographs that illustrate family literacy and numeracy practices. The examples can then be attached to a piece of fabric to create a literacy or numeracy patchwork quilt. If the quilt is hung in the foyer and paper, pens and nappy pins left nearby, parents are able to quickly add more ideas to the quilt. The quilt provides staff with insights into children's home and community experiences with literacy and/or numeracy that assist them to plan appropriate experiences.

FIGURE 2.6 A literacy quilt can capture and display family literacy practices

NOTICEBOARDS

Noticeboards are a useful way to keep families informed about what is happening at the setting. This can include information about meetings, children's projects and community information. It is important that they are checked regularly and kept up-to-date. Family members can also add items to the noticeboard, including flyers about community events and information about local support agencies.

POSTBOXES

A postbox in the foyer area can provide a quick and easy method for families and children to share information and items from home. Families and children can contribute examples of children's drawings and writing from home, a photograph of a family experience, tickets from a movie the child has seen recently or a note letting staff know that a family member is visiting from overseas. When children participate in the creation of artefacts at home and the reading and viewing of these in the classroom, collaboration between educators, families and children is enhanced. Knowledge of children's family and community experiences can also assist staff to provide meaningful experiences for children.

Children may also have their own letterboxes (*see* Figure 2.7) where peers, family members and educators can leave notes, photographs and drawings. These letterboxes encourage relationships and communication as well as children's literacy development.

Source: Earlwood Children's Centre

FIGURE 2.7 The provision of children's letterboxes encourages the exchange of notes, photographs and drawings.

MASCOTS

The early childhood setting or school may have a soft toy that becomes a mascot and goes home with different children for a night or a week. Children and families may write about what the mascot did while at their house and/or use drawings and photography to record experiences. There may be a camera that accompanies the mascot to encourage this recording. The sharing of the journal with educators and classmates provides many insights into children's family experiences and provides a meaningful literacy experience for children.

NEWSLETTERS

Newsletters enable educators and children to share children's experiences at the setting with families and provide an opportunity for educators to explain why they do things the way they do. They can include information about projects, units of work being implemented and what children are learning. Transcripts of children's conversations or webs of their thinking can provide families with insights into their children's learning and encourage collaboration.

Newsletters can also include the titles of children's favourite books, the words of new poems or songs and information about excursions or visitors that invite connections between the home and the setting. Newsletters can encourage family input into the program by asking for suggestions, requesting resources that families can contribute from home and including brief surveys that families can complete. There can be a page for family contributions, or families can be responsible for putting together the newsletter in consultation with staff. Older children can also contribute to the newsletter or produce their own newsletter. Newsletters can be paper-based and/or electronic.

COMMUNICATION POCKETS

Communication pockets can contain photocopies of articles that may be of interest to families, information about local community events, recipes from group-cooking experiences and photographs of children. Educators may also include narratives of the children's day; these can be written once and then photocopied for each child in the group. The involvement of children in the construction of notes to families can also aid in the development of partnerships and connections between homes and early childhood settings. Communication pockets can also become a means for two-way communication if families and children are able to leave items such as photographs, notes or drawings for staff.

TELEPHONE, EMAILS, WEBSITES, BLOGS AND WIKIS

Many families who do not have time to spend at the setting appreciate the use of technology as a communication tool. Educators can telephone families as a quick way of sharing information. When the educator and family member speak different languages, a telephone interpreter service can be a useful aid to communication. Email is also an effective communication tool for many families as they are able to respond to messages in their own time. Settings can also establish their own website or information sharing Facebook page (being aware of protocols for confidentiality) and use this to provide information to families and to share children's experiences. Photographs and samples of children's artwork may also be added, provided that permission has been obtained from families. Educators may also establish a blog or wiki as a way of sharing information and engaging in a dialogue with families.

COMMUNICATION BOOKS

Communication books encourage two-way communication between educators and families and can also include children's input. Educators and family members can use the communication book to share examples of what the child has experienced and said during the day or over the weekend and any special events that are coming up, as well as to exchange information about health and nutrition as in Example 2.1.

 EXAMPLE 2.1
A page from a communication book, with entries from a family member
and staff member

FRI 16th.

SHE IS GREAT HAD A MORNING
SLEEP VERY KEEN TO PLAY

2 BOTTLES IN FRIDGE.

YOUR THE BEST. X

16.4.04
Lola played happily this morning.
She enjoyed all of the baby toys —
shaking them, tasting them, grasping
them and dropping them.
Lola became a little distressed at
around 11am — she wouldn't eat
her lunch. We then gave her a bottle
which she very happily drank and
then she ate some of her lunch.
Lola took some time to settle off
to sleep.
Have a great weekend -Ö-
Love Jenny

Source: Paddington Children's Centre , 2004

DOCUMENTATION OF CHILDREN'S LEARNING

Documentation of children's experiences and projects through the use of annotated photographs, samples of drawing and writing, examples of constructions, transcripts of conversations, along with commentary and analysis, provides families with information about their child's experiences and learning. Pedagogical documentation can help to make children's learning visible for families and encourages educators, families and children to discuss learning together. Thoughtful documentation of 'dynamic learning processes at work draws parents into deeper connections' (Fraser & Gestwicki, 2001, p. 71) and encourages families to contribute resources to projects and to continue investigations with children at home (Helm, 2011).

Photographs of children engaged in experiences are particularly useful in documenting children's learning. Where these are accompanied by the child's interpretation or meaning of the experience, much can be learned about what is important for the child and their understandings. While wary of the assumption that photographs themselves reflect learning, educators can use photographs to share children's days with families and to document children's projects and experiences. Walters (2006) notes that photographs can be easily accessed by family members who have little English language proficiency and by those who are not confident with literacy.

Documentation can be for an individual child and for groups of children, paper-based or digital and can be organised into a portfolio or journal that is added to over time. Family members and children can add to the portfolios by contributing samples or photographs from home, making comparisons between the child's experiences and responses at home and at the early childhood setting, and engaging in analysis of the meaning of the portfolio items.

Individual portfolios or journals can go home with children so that families and children have the chance to add entries in their own time. An effective strategy to enhance communication between home and the early childhood setting or school is to have a camera that is lent to each family for a few days or a week to enable them to capture everyday family experiences for sharing at the setting. Children can also contribute to the documentation of their learning by deciding on drawings or photographs they want included and telling an accompanying narrative. Children can also be the ones who take the photographs, providing their own perspectives on learning.

Source: KU Phoenix Preschool

FIGURE 2.8 Displays of children's narratives and drawings make children's ideas and thinking visible to children, families and staff.

The strategies listed above provide opportunities for educators and families to collaborate in exchanging information, sharing insights and making joint decisions. These processes promote collaborative partnerships that are respectful and inclusive of diverse perspectives, and that foster dialogue where issues can be discussed and changes to practices suggested in a climate of open communication.

The principles of the EYLF and *My Place, Our Time*, as well as the Australian Curriculum and the *Melbourne Declaration on the National Goals for Education* all emphasise the importance of respecting diversity and difference, enacting cultural competence and holding high expectations and developing strategies that focus on equity. These principles and practices are discussed in the following section.

Respect for diversity

Educators need to be aware of and respect the diverse family structures, experiences, values, languages, abilities and beliefs of the children and families they work with. Respect for diversity is one of the principles that underpins the EYLF and *My Time, Our Place*. Educators who respect diversity acknowledge the strengths of children and their families and communities, and understand and work with the complexities of families and communities (DEEWR, 2009).

All families have different life experiences, family composition, interests and abilities and each setting can draw on this diversity to support authentic inclusion of diversity and difference. It is crucial that educators view the diversity of children's family and community experiences positively, and not as problems or deficits. If diversity is viewed as a positive resource, then families and educators are more willing to share this richness with others. It is important to explore the diversity that exists within educational settings and the wider community, and the strengths within families, and not to make deficit assumptions and judgements about families and communities.

The families and communities that children belong to are diverse in many ways, including:

- ethnicity
- language
- beliefs and values
- geographic location
- family structure
- gender and sexuality
- abilities
- health
- economic circumstances.

All of these aspects contribute to an individual's culture. It is important to remember that everyone has a culture – culture is not something that only 'others' have.

Families and communities are *ethnically diverse*. Approximately 29 per cent of the Australian population aged 15 years and over was born overseas (ABS, 2010). The greatest numbers of overseas-born Australians come from Britain and New Zealand, followed by China, India and Vietnam, with many of the more recent arrivals coming from China and India. There are also significant numbers of Australians with Filipino, South African and Malaysian ancestry. Many families are recent arrivals, with 8 per cent of the population of people over 15 in 2010 having arrived within the last 10 years (ABS, 2012).

What are the languages of the children and families you work with? How do you incorporate these in the setting?

Families and children are also *linguistically diverse*. Over 400 languages are spoken in Australia, including the many different languages that are spoken by Aboriginal and Torres Strait Islander Australians. At least 19 per cent of the population speaks a language other than English at home (ABS, 2012). The five most commonly spoken languages other than English are Mandarin, Italian, Arabic, Cantonese and Greek. In addition, over 50 000 people speak an Australian Indigenous language (including Australian Creoles), which equates to 12 per cent of all Indigenous Australians (ABS, 2010b). Indigenous languages are more likely to be spoken in remote areas, with approximately 56 per cent of the Indigenous population in very remote areas speaking an Indigenous language at home compared to around 1 per cent in cities.

Families also have many different ways of using language, which are reflected in their social and regional dialects (that is, different varieties of a language). There are many varieties of English, based on geographical and social differences. There are differences based on the country we live in (for example, differences between Australian, Singaporean and South African dialects of English) and the region (such as differences between states in Australia and between urban and regional areas). There are also social differences that result in dialects such as Aboriginal English. Often the first language for many Aboriginal children, Aboriginal English is a dialect of English influenced by local Aboriginal languages, which means there are many different varieties of Aboriginal English throughout Australia. It is important to note that Aboriginal English is not 'bad language' or 'bad English'. Many Aboriginal people use Aboriginal English in their family and community contexts and use Standard Australian English (or Academic English) when interacting with non-Indigenous people (Eades, 1993/2000). Some Aboriginal families will use Standard Australian English in all contexts and other families may use Aboriginal English in all circumstances. It is important that educators are respectful of all languages and dialects and do not make judgements about the language used by children and their families.

Accessing early childhood services and schools can be difficult for many families when they feel that they, or their culture and language, are not valued by those operating the service or others utilising that service. For example, in many communities, Indigenous families tend to participate in prior-to-school services less often than non-Indigenous families. The latest available data suggests that just over 60 per cent of Aboriginal and Torres Strait Islander children are enrolled in preschool programs in the year before school, compared with an average of 70 per cent for all Australian children (ABS, 2009a; FaHCSIA, 2010). While caution is required in interpreting these data – in terms of questioning enrolment as opposed to attendance, the definition of preschool, which does not include long day care, and the availability of services, particularly in remote communities – the data do suggest that many Indigenous children do not access preschool. One of the key reasons for Indigenous families' low levels of participation in early childhood services is a lack of cultural sensitivity (Mann et al., 2011). The *cultural competence* of educators within these services strongly influences the attendance patterns of children and families. Many Indigenous families are not comfortable using services that are not inclusive of the language and cultural practices that are important within their specific communities (MCEETYA, 2001; New South Wales Aboriginal Education Consultative Group & NSW Department of Education and Training, 2004). Employment of Aboriginal staff, flexibility of services, cost and transport are also key factors in Aboriginal families accessing early childhood services (ARACY, 2007; FaHCSIA, 2009; Mann et al., 2011).

Families have different *beliefs* and *values*; these include beliefs about family roles, how children learn, what they believe is important for children and their visions for society. Some families will follow particular religions while others will have strongly held world views. Family beliefs and values are often reflected in everyday practices such as ways of interacting with others, children's eating and sleeping routines, expectations about independence and/or interdependence, strategies for guiding children's behaviour and expectations around social responsibility and civic participation. Some of these beliefs and practices will be very different from the educators own and can be quite confronting at times. It may be difficult to understand why a two-year-old is not toilet trained or a baby is carried around until she falls asleep. The educator may become frustrated when a child doesn't arrive at the centre until lunchtime or feel that children are not showing respect when they look away or don't answer when they are spoken to. This is because these behaviours are being viewed through our own cultural lens. When the educator feels 'upset, offended or disturbed by a family's behaviour or practice, that's a clue to look at the bigger picture to understand the meaning behind the behaviour' (Gonzalez-Mena, 2008, p. 41). It does not mean the educator will always accept the family's practices, but being able to understand different beliefs and values opens up possibilities for discussion and negotiation.

Australia is also very diverse *geographically*. While the majority of Australians live on the coastal fringe, there are many diverse communities in this coastal area, characterised by different beliefs, values and practices. Other communities are located in inland regional towns, rural areas and remote regions of Australia. Children develop a sense of place and belonging in these communities. These different geographical locations provide different types of experiences for children and, as they interact with people and place, they develop their own interests and 'funds of knowledge' (Moll et al., 1992; Gonzalez et al., 2005). For example, they might be interested in and knowledgeable about whales and fishing if they live in the coastal regions of Australia, be experts on tractors if they live in a farming community or adept at catching lizards or digging for honey ants if from a remote Central Australian community.

Communities all have different resources. In some cases children will have strong connections with extended family members who are able to provide many rich experiences for children. In other communities children may be isolated from extended family but have access to a range of services such as outside school hours care, libraries, art galleries and museums. Some families will have lived in the one area for generations and others will be transient, moving many times due to work or family commitments or to seek employment and housing.

Children experience a range of *family structures* including sole-parent families, multi-family households, same-sex couples as parents, extended families and grandparents or other relatives as guardians. Family breakdown is an issue for many families, with estimates that almost half of all marriages will end in divorce (Human Rights and Equal Opportunity Commission [HREOC], 2005). Many children experience a range of family structures, including blended and stepfamilies, as part of the shared care arrangements after separation and divorce. A growing number of Australian families are sole-parent families. In 2010, approximately 20 per cent of Australian families with children under 15 were sole-parent families, with 3 per cent of these being lone-father families (ABS, 2012).

The age profile of families has also shifted in the last decade as young people increasingly postpone marriage and childbirth. The median age of Australian mothers giving birth is 30.7 (ABS, 2011). While many mature-age parents are often highly involved in their children's lives and may have high expectations for their children, the actual circumstances of mature-age parents are diverse and often differ from the myth that older parents are all financially secure and career-focused (Powell, 2004).

Family members also have different *sexual preferences* and the number of children with same-sex couples as parents is increasing. There was a total of 33 714 same-sex couples in 2011, which was 32 per cent higher than the number recorded in the 2006 census (ABS, 2012). With the increasing availability of technologies and the options of adoption and surrogacy, as well as blended families that include children from previous relationships, many same-sex couples are parents. The last census indicated that approximately 22 per cent of female same-sex couples have children living with them in the family home.

It is essential that educators are open to and accepting of different family structures and sexual preferences. Skattebol and Ferfolja (2007) highlight the many issues faced by lesbian parents when they place their children in early childhood services and are required to decide whether to make their sexuality visible. Many of the lesbian mothers involved in this study feared that their children would be considered 'freaks' or would experience homophobia and discrimination. Despite their concerns about homophobic reactions, the mothers all emphasised the importance of disclosing their sexuality and challenging heteronormative discourses. They also stressed the value of the early childhood setting including resources that reflect diverse families and of being inclusive and respectful in their interactions.

This diversity of family types highlights the importance of educators being open to a range of ways that 'families function in terms of gendered roles, biological and social connections' (Skattebol & Ferfolja, 2007, p. 17). It is important that educators are aware of and sensitive to diverse family structures and include all the significant adults in the child's life in their communication with families.

Many children are cared for by grandparents, with 43 per cent of Australian children cared for by a grandparent some of the time (ABS, 2007). There is also evidence that Australian courts are giving custody of children to grandparents in an increasing number of cases, with the number of families with children cared for by grandparents increasing (Brennan et al., 2013) and almost half of these grandparents being sole-parent families (ABS, 2005). In 2012, almost 41 000 children and young people across Australia were the subject of care and protection orders issued by child protection authorities (AIHW, 2012a), with more than half cared for by relatives, often grandparents (AIHW, 2012a). Grandparents caring for their grandchildren provide a stable and caring environment but generally have lower financial resources and may experience social, financial and health problems that impact on the whole family (Brennan et al., 2013). The Social Policy Research Centre study found that 80 per cent of the children cared for by grandparents had emotional and behavioural problems related to previous abuse and abandonment (Brennan et al., 2013).

Parents, children or extended family members may have *additional needs* or *health* issues. Families with children with additional needs tend to face extra commitments, such as attending appointments with specialists, early intervention services and therapists, which place extra stress on finances and impact on all members of the family. Employment difficulties can occur, especially if parents do not work in organisations that support family-friendly practices. Many parents may have to change jobs or work part-time to attend to their children's needs. Furthermore, many families may need to pay for additional services that their children require due to long waiting lists in health services and poor funding for many services supporting children with additional needs.

A number of children are living with chronic illnesses such as diabetes, asthma, and eczema, with 10–20 per cent of children affected (Sydney Children's Hospital, 2013). These illnesses and the often time-consuming and costly medical procedures involved place financial strain and stresses on family relationships and often create feelings of anxiety, resentment and guilt (Ashton, 2004). Children with chronic illness often experience long periods of absence from education or care and disrupted relationships with peers, which all impact on their learning (Ashton, 2004; Dockett, 2004; Shiu, 2004). Early childhood settings have a key role in working with families and support services to help all children to live as full a life as possible.

Employment opportunities for families vary and this impacts on families' *economic circumstances*. Despite the economic prosperity of recent years, the impact of the global financial crisis continues to be felt and to have implications on employment. In 2009, even before the full effect of the crisis was felt, 12 per cent of families with dependent children and 44 per cent of sole-parent families had no one in the family in paid employment. Almost half of these families included a child under five years of age (ABS, 2009b). However, joblessness is concentrated in some areas more than others, with the most disadvantaged areas of Australia having at least one-third of families unemployed. Other families may have one or both parents in paid employment but on low incomes, often in casual employment.

Current data indicate that one in six Australian children grow up in poverty, with nearly 600 000 or 17.3 per cent of children living below the poverty line (Cass, 2013). Children's experiences of poverty may include poorly serviced neighbourhoods, limited access to early childhood and outside school hours' services and poor life choices (Cass, 2013; Redmond, 2013). More than half of the children living in poverty are Aboriginal and Torres Strait Islanders (ARECY, n.d.). Australian Institute of Health and Welfare data show that Aboriginal and Torres Strait Islander children experience higher death rates than the national average and are less likely to have achieved the reading and numeracy minimum standards (AIHW, 2012b).

Families living in poverty often experience more instances of flexible households, with more separations and instances of blended families, and more experiences of moving home in search of employment than people who are economically better off (Skattebol et al., 2012). Poverty, and constant moving, makes it difficult for children to develop and maintain relationships. The participants in one recent study of living in poverty reported that secure relationships were more important to them than money, educational attainment or employment (Skattebol et al., 2012).

Many families experience some form of discrimination based on their race, ethnic origin, language, socio-economic class, geographic location, gender, sexual preference or the responsibilities for caring for children with chronic illness or additional needs, making it difficult for them to find employment or adequate housing, or to access appropriate education or training. The intersections of racism, sexism, class prejudice and lack of understanding about children with additional needs and chronic illnesses compound the discrimination and inequalities experienced by many families. Members of minority groups may also experience verbal abuse and vilification. It is essential that educators are aware of the discrimination that some families experience and work to ensure this does not occur in the early childhood setting. This means addressing issues of bias with young children and with members of staff by dealing with oppressive behaviour and discussing similarities and differences with children.

Many families are isolated from, or have minimal contact with, mainstream society. Families can be isolated socially, economically and culturally as well as physically (Fegan & Bowes, 2009).

Isolation exacerbates social disadvantage and creates a range of difficulties for families who are raising children in circumstances where they have little access to social supports and community connections (Joinking, 2003). Poverty results not only in lack of material possessions but also in a feeling of social exclusion, and it is this exclusion that children and young people find most difficult (Saunders, 2011). In their study on the impact of poverty on Australian children and young people, Skattebol et al. (2012, p. 8) found that children and young people living in poverty were excluded from 'a range of institutions, activities or environments', often because they could not afford to participate and because they lacked private or public transport to travel to these amenities. For many families the cost of care prohibits their access to children's services. A recent survey of Aboriginal families in the inner west of Sydney found that one of the main barriers to children's participation in early childhood services was the cost (Mann et al., 2011).

High expectations and equity

Alongside respect for diversity, another underpinning principle of the EYLF and *My Time, Our Place* is high expectations and equity.

The 'authentic' pedagogies research in the United States (Newmann, 1996), *Productive Pedagogies* (Queensland Department of Education, 2001) and *Fair Go* research (Fair Go, 2006; Munns et al., 2013) have demonstrated that effective pedagogies are characterised by high expectations of learners. Effective educators provide intellectual challenge for all learners in ways that demonstrate respect for each child's cultural context and that build connections between home and the early childhood setting or school. This means promoting inclusion and putting in place strategies to support all children to succeed (DEEWR, 2009).

Cultural competency

Includes respect for diversity and a focus on equity and social justice.

Educators in early childhood settings and schools need to develop and enact **cultural competency** to work effectively with children, families and staff who may have diverse experiences, values and beliefs. The EYLF (DEEWR, 2009) and the supporting *Educators' Guide* (DEEWR, 2010) highlight the importance of cultural competency, or what is sometimes referred to as cultural literacy.

Cultural competency includes respect for diversity and a focus on equity and social justice (DEEWR, 2009). 'At the heart of cultural competence is the ability to interact respectfully, constructively and positively with children, families, staff and community' (DEEWR, 2010, p. 21).

Cultural competency involves:

- awareness of our own cultural influences and values, beliefs and practices
- continual assessment of our own and the setting's attitudes and values towards difference
- understanding different cultural values, beliefs and practices
- respectful partnerships
- being aware of the power relationships between dominant and minority cultures
- the ability to adapt interactions and services to meet the needs of families and communities.

(DEEWR, 2010; Victorian Aboriginal Child Care Agency, 2008)

Culturally competent educators question taken-for-granted assumptions and world views, and don't assume that their way of seeing and doing things is the only way, or the best way. To be culturally competent means the educator thinks critically about the ways in which they interact with children, staff, families and community members and examines whether their interactions open up possibilities for relationships and meaningful exchanges of information or whether they limit communication and reinforce stereotypes. Moving beyond cultural competence, culturally proficient educators highly value diversity, and engage in ongoing research to extend their knowledge base and improve relationships. In Indigenous communities in particular, cultural proficiency includes promotion of self-determination for Aboriginal and Torres Strait Islander communities (Victorian Aboriginal Child Care Agency, 2008). It is always important to view learning as two-way in Aboriginal and Torres Strait Islander communities and to ensure that services are targeted to meet the expectations of the community and not predetermined by the educator.

Putting respect for diversity, cultural competency and high expectations and equity into practice

Figure 2.9 suggests key elements that need to be considered when educators reflect on their practices and plan in ways that demonstrate *respect for diversity, high expectations and equity* and *cultural competence*. The starting point within this process will depend on what the setting or school is currently implementing that reflects these principles and practices. A starting point may be collaborating with stakeholders to explore *philosophical perspectives*, and then critically reflecting on each element and the extent to which it articulates shared beliefs about diversity and equity. Alternatively, educators and families could start with critical reflection on *attitudes and values*, and/or the ways in which children respond to diversity. It is also important to examine the extent to which the setting is *accessible* to families and communities with diverse languages, beliefs and practices. This means evaluating the extent to which the diversity of the local community is reflected in the enrolments at the setting and the extent to which the setting's philosophies, policies and pedagogies demonstrate respect for diversity. In other cases it may be appropriate to start with a critical evaluation of the existing *policies* or with policy development. Another starting point could be a critical evaluation of the existing *pedagogies* and the extent to which they encourage respect for diversity and equitable outcomes.

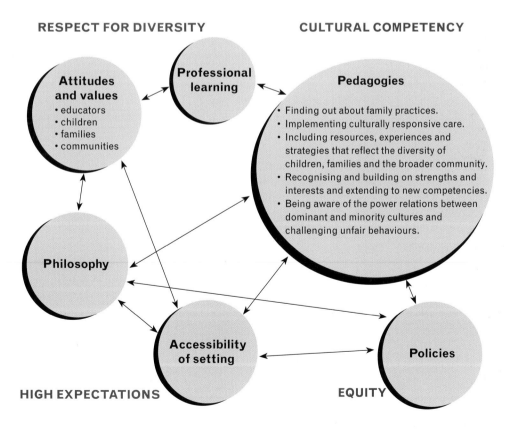

FIGURE 2.9 Putting principles of respect for diversity, cultural competency, high expectations and equity into practice.

In order to implement culturally responsive *pedagogies*, educators need to *find out about children's home and community experiences and their 'funds of knowledge'* (Gonzalez et al., 2005). This involves establishing and maintaining positive partnerships with families and engaging in 'collaborative dialogue, where participants learn with support from each other' (Ashton et. al., 2008, p. 10). Where staff and families are from different cultural and linguistic contexts, it is essential that educators find out about the languages spoken by family members and their cultural communication practices. Knowing about aspects such as body language, forms of address, eye contact and personal space can help promote effective cross-cultural communication.

When educators have effective partnerships with families they are able to find out about family care-giving practices, routines and interaction styles and consider ways of being responsive to these in the early childhood program and classroom. *Culturally responsive care and pedagogies* require educators to be knowledgeable about and sensitive to children's family and community experiences and to respect different beliefs and practices. Respect for cultural and religious beliefs may be as simple as supporting a family's wishes regarding dietary requirements or children's dress, such as the wearing of the hijab. In other cases it may involve negotiating ways to respect family wishes; for example, balancing the need to wear particular items of jewellery or religious artefacts while also ensuring that the environment is safe for all children. It is also helpful to ask families about the occasions they celebrate so that these can also be celebrated at the setting. The inclusion of a range of celebrations such as NAIDOC, Lunar New Year, Hanukkah and Diwali as well as Christmas and Easter demonstrates respect for diverse beliefs. Calendars from organisations such as UNICEF display diverse images while also providing useful information about celebrations relevant to different communities.

When educators are knowledgeable about the experiences, social practices and languages that children bring from home, they are able to *include resources, experiences and strategies that reflect the diversity of children, families and the broader community* and support all children to achieve learning outcomes. These familiar resources and experiences assist children to feel a sense of belonging – to feel that 'school is for me' (Fair Go Team, 2006; Munns et al., 2013) – and provide opportunities for children to display their funds of knowledge and build on their strengths.

Regardless of the diversity within the setting, it is essential that all children are exposed to diverse languages, beliefs, practices, family structures and interaction styles and are encouraged to develop positive attitudes towards difference. Resources should reflect the diversity of the children, families and staff as well as the broader community. Books, posters, puzzles and dramatic play materials that reflect diverse family structures, languages, cultural practices, locations, sexualities and abilities help children to find materials they can connect with while also broadening children's appreciation of difference. The inclusion of diverse resources may be as simple as providing red paint during Lunar New Year celebrations, including books with images of sole-parent and lesbian families or taking photos of the local community and displaying these in the centre or school.

The inclusion of a range of images, fabrics, textures and artefacts within the environment 'all work with the child's senses to develop knowledge about their world' and is a particularly useful way of introducing diversity to very young children (Barron, n.d.). Older children can explore different art mediums such as watercolour, batik and ink, and techniques such as weaving and bead making. The addition of a range of writing implements, such as pen and ink and fine brushes, along with posters of scripts in different languages, can encourage children to explore literacy in relevant community languages.

The integration of diverse languages and literacies in early childhood settings and schools demonstrates respect for linguistic diversity and assists bilingual children to maintain and extend their home language. For infants and toddlers, everyday interactions, music, songs, rhymes, finger plays and stories in their home language will support home language development while also assisting monolingual children to understand that meaning can be expressed in different languages. Older children will also appreciate a range of texts, including books, DVDs, newspapers, magazines, computer games and Internet sites that represent the languages of the children, families and staff as well as the broader community. Environmental print, such as posters and signs, that are inclusive of a range of languages will encourage children to experiment with different scripts.

Educators should be aware of the power relations between dominant and 'minority' languages and cultures, be alert to any incidents of negative *attitudes*, disrespect or discriminatory behaviour within the setting or school and respond in ways that indicate these attitudes and behaviours are unacceptable. It is vital that educators observe children's play and listen to what children have to say. Gathering information about children's understanding of difference as well as group dynamics and the power relations between children can assist educators to support children's understanding of diversity and social justice and to enact justice in their relationships with others. Where appropriate, educators should participate in experiences and use group discussions to challenge children's thinking and introduce alternative perspectives. The Australian Curriculum for Foundation to Year 12 emphasises interpersonal relationships and harmony. The EYLF (DEEWR, 2009) and *My Time, Our Place* (DEEWR, 2011) also encourage children to develop positive relationships with others, to respect diversity and to develop social and civic skills.

Ongoing learning and reflective practice

Reflective practice supports educators in their analysis of what is working well and areas that could be improved. It is important that educators recognise the different cultural and family influences that are present in children's lives, and reflect on the extent to which they value diverse experiences and practices and incorporate these in the setting or classroom. Reflective practice also involves analysing the ways that power relations can oppress people (Siraj-Blatchford & Clarke, 2000) and taking action to transform relationships. When educators recognise that all families have valuable knowledge, initiate interactions with all families instead of just the families they feel comfortable with and understand that educator–family relationships involve power relationships, then it is possible to develop transformative relationships (Blaise & Nuttall, 2011).

Ongoing learning and reflective practice are one of the five underpinning principles of The EYLF and *My Time, Our Place*. Effective educators continually reflect on their practices and seek ways to engage in ongoing learning that includes professional reading, connecting with and learning from families and communities, networking with other professionals and engaging in critical reflection on 'questions of philosophy, ethics and practice' (DEEWR, 2009, p. 13). This includes reflection on relationships and partnerships with families, the extent to which diversity is respected and the curriculum supports high expectations and equity, and staff members' levels of cultural competence.

Conclusion and reflection

Effective educators work in partnerships with families to understand children in their social and cultural context. They find out about and build on the strengths and interests that children bring from home in order to extend children's learning. The use of culturally responsive resources along with high expectations and critical reflection provide a program where all children are supported to succeed.

Programming and Planning
in Early Childhood Settings

Questions for reflection

1. What is your philosophy regarding working with diversity? How do you put this philosophy into practice? Critically examine areas such as policies, pedagogies, resources, intercultural communication and strategies for dealing with bias and promoting social justice. Identify strengths and challenges and plan for professional learning.

2. What strategies do you currently use (as an educator or as a student) to find out about children's family and community experiences? Implement some additional strategies outlined in this chapter. What new information about children's funds of knowledge have you gained?

3. How do you include children's funds of knowledge in your early childhood setting or classroom or in your programming as a student? What additional strategies could you use to assist children to be able to demonstrate their competencies in the setting or classroom?

Key terms

collaborative partnerships, 37

cultural competency, 60

funds of knowledge, 37

transformative relationships, 43

Online study resources

Visit http://login.cengagebrain.com and use the access code that comes with this book for 12 months access to the student resources for this text.

CourseMate Express

The CourseMate Express website contains a range of resources and study tools for this chapter, including:

- Online video activities
- Online research activities
- A revision quiz
- Matching pair exercises
- A list of key weblinks
- A chapter glossary, flashcards and crossword to help you revise terminology
- and more!

Search me! education

Explore **Search me! education** for articles relevant to this chapter. Fast and convenient, Search me! education is updated daily and provides you with 24-hour access to full text articles from hundreds of scholarly and popular journals, ebooks and newspapers, including *The Australian* and *The New York Times*. Log in to Search me! through http://login.cengage.com and try searching for the following key words:

- **collaborative partnerships**
- **cultural and linguistic capital**
- **funds of knowledge.**

Search tip: **Search me! education** contains information from both local and international sources. To get the greatest number of search results, try using both Australian and American spellings in your searches, e.g. 'globalisation' and 'globalization'; 'organisation' and 'organization'

Recommended resources

Moll, L, Amanti, C, Neff, D & Gonzalez, N 1992, 'Funds of knowledge for teaching: Using a qualitative approach to connect homes and classrooms', *Theory into Practice*, vol. 31, no. 2, pp. 132–41.

Munns, G., Cole, B. & Sawyer, W. (Eds.). *Teachers for a Fair Go*. London: Routledge.

Key weblinks

Charles Sturt University, http://www.csu.edu.au/special/teach-ec/RESOURCES/PDF/You're%20in%20new%20county-low%20res.pdf

Early Childhood Australia *Code of Ethics*,
   http://www.earlychildhoodaustralia.org.au/code_of_ethics/early_childhood_australias_code_of_ethics.html

Educational Transitions and Change (ETC) Research Group, 2011, *Transition to School: Position Statement*. Albury-Wodonga: Research Institute for Professional Practice, Learning and Education, Charles Sturt University. Available from
   http://www.csu.edu.au/research/ripple/research-groups/etc/Position-Statement.pdf

Families Australia, http://www.familiesaustralia.org.au/

Ministerial Council on Education, Employment, Training and Youth Affairs 2008, *Melbourne Declaration on Educational Goals for Young Australians*, Author, Canberra, http://www.curriculum.edu.au/verve/_resources/National_Declaration_on_the_Educational_Goals_for_Young_Australians.pdf

References

ABS, *see* Australian Bureau of Statistics

ACECQA, *see* Australian Children's Education & Care Quality Authority

AIHW, *see* Australian Institute of Health and Welfare

ARACY, *see* Australian Research Alliance for Children & Youth

Alloway, N, Freebody, P, Gilbert, P & Muspratt, S 2002, *Boys' Literacy and Schooling: Expanding the Repertoires of Practice*, Commonwealth Department of Education, Science and Training (DEST), Canberra.

Arthur, L, Beecher, B, Dockett, S, Farmer, S & Death, E 1996, *Programming and Planning in Early Childhood Settings*, 2nd edn., Harcourt Brace, Sydney.

Ashton, J 2004, 'Life after the shock!: The impact on families of caring for young children with chronic illness', *Australian Journal of Early Childhood*, vol. 29, no. 1, pp. 22–6.

Ashton, J, Woodrow, C, Johnston, C, Wangmann, J, Singh, L & James, T 2008, 'Partnerships in learning: Linking early childhood services, families and schools for optimal development', *Australasian Journal of Early Childhood*, vol. 33, no. 2, pp. 10–16.

Australian Bureau of Statistics 2013, 4102.0 *Australian Social Trends*, July 2013, http://www.abs.gov.au/AUSSTATS/abs@.nsf/Lookup/4102.0Main+Features10July+2013, accessed 31 January 2014.

Australian Bureau of Statistics, 2012, 2071.0 *Reflecting a Nation: Stories from the 2011 Census: 2012–2013*. http://www.abs.gov.au/ausstats/abs@.nsf/mf/2071.0, accessed 31 January 2014.

Australian Bureau of Statistics 2011, 3301.0 *Births Australia, 2010*, http://www.abs.gov.au/ausstats/abs@.nsf/Products/EB94F978573DD478CA25793300167581, accessed 31 January 2014.

Australian Bureau of Statistics, 2010, 47130.0 *Population Characteristics Aboriginal and Torres Strait Islanders*, latest issue released 2010, http://www.abs.gov.au/ausstats/abs@.nsf/mf/4713.0, accessed 31 January 2014.

Australian Bureau of Statistics 2005, *Australian Social Trends: Family Functioning: Grandparents Raising Their Grandchildren*, http://www.abs.gov.au/AUSSTATS/abs@.nsf/Previousproducts/5E98BEE015D25F60CA25703B0080CCB8?opendocument, accessed 31 March 2014.

Australian Bureau of Statistics 2009a, *Directory of Education and Training Statistics – National Preschool Census*, http://www.abs.gov.au/AUSSTATS/abs@.nsf/Lookup/1136.0Main+Features5042009, accessed 31 January 2014.

Australian Bureau of Statistics 2009b, *Australian Social Trends – Jobless Families*, http://www.abs.gov.au/AUSSTATS/abs@.nsf/Lookup/4102.0Main+Features10Dec+2009, accessed 31 January 2014.

Australian Children's Education & Care Quality Authority n.d., *National Quality Standards*, ACECQA, http://www.acecqa.gov.au/national-quality-framework/the-national-quality-standard, accessed 27 March 2014.

Australian Children's Education & Care Quality Authority 2013, 'Quality areas, standards and elements', in *Guide to the National Quality Standards* (p. 11), ACECQA, http://www.acecqa.gov.au/national-quality-framework/the-national-quality-standard, accessed 27 March 2014.

Australian Institute of Health and Welfare (AIHW) (2012a), *Child Protection Australia 2010–11*, Australian Institute of Health and Welfare, Canberra.

Australian Institute of Health and Welfare 2012b, *Australia's Health 2012*, http://www.aihw.gov.au/publication-detail/?id=10737422172, accessed 12 April 2014.

Australian Government Productivity Commission 2005, *Overcoming Indigenous Disadvantage: Key Indicators 2005*, Author, Canberra.

Australian Research Alliance for Children & Youth (ARACY) 2007, *Evidence into Action Topical Paper—Indigenous Early Learning and Care*, http://www.aracy.org.au/publications-resources/command/download_file/id/215/filename/Indigenous_Early_Learning_and_Care.pdf, accessed 31 March 2014.

Barron, J n.d., *Exploring Culture through the Arts with Under Threes*, FKA Resource No. 123.

Beecher, B & Arthur, L 2001, *Play and Literacy in Children's Worlds*, Primary English Teaching Association, Sydney.

Beecher, B & Jones Diaz, C 2014, 'Extending children's literacies through partnerships between children, families, educators and communities', in L Arthur, J Ashton & B Beecher, *Diverse Literacies in Early Childhood*, ACER, Melbourne.

Berryman, M & Atvars, K 1999, 'Networking: Helping Maori Whanau close the literacy gap', paper presented at the *Innovations for Effective Schooling* Conference, Auckland, New Zealand, August 1999.

Blaise, M & Nuttall, J 2011, *Learning to Teach in the Early Years Classroom*, Oxford University Press, South Melbourne.

Bourdieu, P 1984/1993, *Sociology in Question*, 1993 English trans. R Nice, Sage, London.

Breen, M, Louden, W, Barratt-Pugh, C, Rivalland, J, Rohl, M, Rhydwen, M, Lloyd, S & Carr, T 1994, *Literacy in its Place: An Investigation of Literacy Practices in Urban and Rural Communities*, Department of Employment, Education and Training, Canberra.

Brennan, D, Cass, B, Flaxman, S, Hill, T, Jenkins, B, McHugh, M, Purcal, C, & Valentine, K. 2013, *Grandparents Raising Grandchildren: Towards Recognition, Respect and Reward* (SPRC Report 14/13). SPRC, University of New South Wales.

Briggs, F & Potter, G 1999, *The Early Years of School: Teaching and Learning*, 3rd edn., Longman, Melbourne.

Bronfenbrenner, U, & Morris, P 1998, 'The ecology of human developmental processes', in W Damon & R M Lerner (eds.), *Handbook of Child Psychology: Theoretical Models of Human Development* (5th edn., vol. 1) (pp. 993–1029), Wiley, New York.

Cairney, T 2000, 'The home-school connection in literacy and language development', in R Campbell & D Green (eds), *Literacies and Learners: Current Perspectives*, Prentice Hall, Sydney.

Carr, M 2001, *Assessment in Early Childhood Settings: Learning Stories*, Paul Chapman, London.

Cass, B 2013, *Beneath the Surface: National Trends and the Lived Experience of Child Poverty in Australia*, Presentation at ACOSS Policy Forum 12 November 2013.

Centre for Community Child Health 2001, *The Heart of Partnership in Family Day Care: Carer–parent Communication*, Royal Children's Hospital, Melbourne.

Centre for Community Child Health and Royal Children's Hospital, 'Working with culturally and linguistically diverse families', *Childcare and Children's Health*, http://www.rch.org.au/emplibrary/ecconnections/CCH_Vol10_No1Mar2007.pdf, accessed 31 March 2014.

COAG, *see* Council of Australian Governments

Corson, D 1998, *Changing Education for Diversity*, Open University Press, Philadelphia, PA.

Council of Australian Governments (COAG) 2009, *National Quality Standard for Early Childhood Education and Care and School Age Care*, Early Childhood Development Steering Committee, COAG, Canberra.

De Gioia, K 2009, 'Parent and staff expectations for continuity of home practices in the child care centre for families with diverse cultural backgrounds', *Australasian Journal of Early Childhood*, vol. 34, no. 3, pp. 9–18.

DEEWR, *see* Department of Education, Employment and Workplace Relations

Department of Education and Children's Services South Australia 1997, *ECLIPSE: Childhood Literacy Includes Parents, Staff and Education – Literacy in Early Childhood*, Author, Adelaide.

Department of Education, Employment and Workplace Relations (DEEWR) 2009, *Belonging, Being and Becoming: The Early Years Learning Framework for Australia*, Author, Canberra.

Department of Education, Employment and Workplace Relations (DEEWR) 2010, *Belonging, Being and Becoming: Educators' Guide to the Early Years Learning Framework for Australia*, Author, Canberra.

Department of Education, Employment and Workplace Relations (DEEWR) 2011, *My Time, Our Place: Framework for School Aged Care in Australia*, Author, Canberra.

Department of Families, Housing, Community Services and Indigenous Affairs (FaHCSIA) 2009, *Footprints in Time: The Longitudinal Study of Indigenous Children – Key Summary Report from Wave 1*, Author, Canberra.

Department of Families, Housing, Community Services and Indigenous Affairs (FaHCSIA) 2010, *Closing the Gap: Prime Minister's Report*, Author, Canberra.

Dockett, S 2004, '"Everyone was really happy to see me!": The importance of friendships in the return to school of children with chronic illness', *Australian Journal of Early Childhood*, vol. 29, no. 1, pp. 27–32.

Dockett, S & Perry, B 2006, *Transitions to School: Perceptions, Expectations, Experiences*, University of New South Wales Press, Sydney.

Dockett, S, Perry, B, & Kearney, E 2012, 'Family transitions as children start school', *Family Matters*, vol. 90, 57–67.

Eades, D 1993/2000, *Aboriginal English*, PEN093, Primary English Teaching Association, Sydney.

Educational Transitions and Change (ETC) Research Group, 2011, *Transition to School: Position Statement Poster*. Albury-Wodonga: Research Institute for Professional Practice, Learning and Education, Charles Sturt University, http://www.csu.edu.au/faculty/educat/edu/transitions/publications/School-Transition-Poster.pdf, accessed 30 March 2014.

Educational Transitions and Change (ETC) Research Group, 2011, *Transition to School: Position Statement*. Albury-Wodonga: Research Institute for Professional Practice, Learning and Education, Charles Sturt University, http://www.csu.edu.au/research/ripple/research-groups/etc/Position-Statement.pdf, accessed 30 March 2014.

Epstein, J, Sanders, M, Simon, B, Salinas, K, Jansorn, N & Van Voorhis, F 2008, *School, Family, and Community Partnerships: Your Handbook for Action*, 3rd edn., Corwin Press, Thousand Oaks, CA.

FaHSCIA, *see* Department of Families, Housing, Community Services and Indigenous Affairs

Fair Go Team 2006, *School is for Me: Pathways to Student Engagement*, Priority Schools Funding Program, NSW Department of Education and Training, Sydney.

Families Australia n.d., *Our Children, Our Concern, Our Responsibility: A Case for Commonwealth Investment in the Prevention of Child Abuse and Neglect*, http://www.familiesAustralia.org.au, accessed 9 March 2004.

Farmer, S 2009, 'Building relationships – honouring family diversity', *SCAN Scene*, vol. 7, no. 2, SDN Children's Services, Newtown.

Fegan, M & Bowes, J 2009, 'Isolation in rural, remote and urban communities', in J Bowes (ed.), *Children, Families and Communities: Contexts and Consequences*, 3rd edn., Oxford University Press, Melbourne.

Fraser, S & Gestwicki, C 2001, *Authentic Childhood: Exploring Reggio Emilia in the Classroom*, Delmar/Thomson, Albany, NY.

Gonzalez, N, Moll, L & Amanti, C (eds) 2005, *Funds of Knowledge: Theorising Practices in Households and Classrooms*, Lawrence Erlbaum & Associates, New Jersey.

Gonzalez-Mena, J 2008, *Diversity in Early Childhood Education: Honoring Differences*, 5th edn., McGraw-Hill, New York, NY.

Green, D 2000, 'The nature of language: The culture of texts', in R Campbell & D Green (eds), *Literacies and Learners: Current Perspectives*, Prentice Hall, Sydney.

Guigni, M n.d., *Inclusion through Relatedness: Learning 'With': Inclusion Support Facilitators Encountering the Early Years Learning Framework*, Australian Government, Canberra.

Guilfoyle, A, Saggers, S, Sims, M & Hutchins, T 2010, 'Culturally strong child care programs for Indigenous children, families and communities', *Australasian Journal of Early Childhood*, vol. 35, no. 3, pp. 68–75.

Helm, J 2011, *Young investigators: The Project Approach in the Early Years*, Teachers College Press, New York.

Hill, S, Comber, B, Louden, W, Rivalland, J & Reid, J 1998, *100 Children go to School: Connections and Disconnections in Literacy Development in the Year Prior to School and the First Year of School*, vol. 1, Department of Education, Employment, Training and Youth Affairs, Canberra.

Hill, S, Comber, B, Louden, W, Rivalland, J & Reid, J 2002, *100 Children Turn 10*, vol. 1, Department of Education, Science and Training, Canberra.

HREOC, *see* Human Rights and Equal Opportunity Commission

Hughes, P & Mac Naughton, G 2000, 'Consensus, dissensus or community: The politics of parent involvement in early childhood education', *Contemporary Issues in Early Childhood*, vol. 1, no. 3, http://www.wwwords.co.uk/ciec/, accessed 10 June 2011.

Human Rights and Equal Opportunity Commission (HREOC) 2005, *Striking the Balance: Women, Men, Work and Family*, Sex Discrimination Unit, HREOC, Sydney, http://www.humanrights.gov.au/sex_discrimination/publication/strikingbalance/index.html, accessed 10 June 2011.

Joinking, A 2003, 'Families on the margins: Strategies for building resilience', paper presented at the *Australian Social Policy* Conference, Sydney, 9–11 July 2003.

Jones Diaz, C, Beecher, B, Arthur, L, Ashton, J, Hayden, J, Makin, L, McNaught, M & Clugston, L 2001, *Literacies, Communities and Under 5S*, New South Wales Department of Community Services and New South Wales Department of Education and Training, Sydney.

Jones Diaz, C & Harvey, N 2007, 'Other words, other worlds: Bilingual identities and literacy', in L Makin, C Jones Diaz & C McLachlan (eds), *Literacies in childhood: Changing Views, Challenging Practices*, Elsevier, Sydney.

Kenner, C & Kress, G 2003 'The multisemiotic resources of biliterate children', *Journal of Childhood Literacy*, vol. 3, no. 2, pp. 179–202.

Lingard, B, Martino, W, Mills, M & Bahr, M 2002, *Addressing the Educational Needs of Boys*, Commonwealth Department of Education, Science and Training, Canberra.

Lyotard, J 1984, *The Postmodern Condition: A Report on Knowledge*, University of Minneapolis Press, Minneapolis, MN.

Mac Naughton, G 2004, 'Children, staff and parents: Building respectful relationships in New Zealand and Australian early childhood contexts – the Australian context', *Australian Journal of Early Childhood*, vol. 29, no. 1, pp. 1–7.

Mac Naughton, G & Hughes, P 2003, 'Parents and communities', in G Mac Naughton, *Shaping Early Childhood: Learners, Curriculum and Contexts*, Open University Press, Maidenhead, UK.

Makin, L, Hayden, J, Holland, A, Arthur, L, Beecher, B, Jones Diaz, C & McNaught, M 1999, *Mapping Literacy Practices in Early Childhood Services*, New South Wales Department of Education and Training and New South Wales Department of Community Services, Sydney.

Mann, D, Knight, S & Thomson, J 2011, *Aboriginal Access to Preschool: What Attracts and Retains Aboriginal and Torres Strait Islander Families in Preschools – A Small Qualitative Study of Inner Sydney Mainstream Preschools*, SDN Child and Family Services, Sydney.

Marsh, J & Millard, E 2000, *Literacy and Popular Culture: Using Children's Culture in the Classroom*, Paul Chapman Publishing Limited, London.

MCEETYA, *see* Ministerial Council on Education, Employment, Training and Youth Affairs

Ministerial Council on Education, Employment, Training and Youth Affairs, 2001, *Effective Learning Issues for Indigenous Children Aged 0–8 Years – Discussion paper*, MCEETYA Taskforce on Indigenous Education, Carlton, Vic.

Ministerial Council on Education, Employment, Training and Youth Affairs, 2008, *Melbourne Declaration on Educational Goals for Young Australians*, MCEETYA, Canberra, http://www.curriculum.edu.au/verve/_resources/National_Declaration_on_the_Educational_Goals_for_Young_Australians.pdf, accessed 31 January 2014.

Moll, L, Amanti, C, Neff, D & Gonzalez, N 1992, 'Funds of knowledge for teaching: Using a qualitative approach to connect homes and classrooms', *Theory into Practice*, vol. 31, no. 2, pp. 132–41.

Mundine, K & Giugni, M 2006, *Diversity and Difference: Lighting the Spirit of Identity*, Early Childhood Australia, Canberra.

Munns, G, Arthur, L, Hertzberg, M, Sawyer, W & Zammit, K 2011, 'A fair go for students in poverty', in T Wrigley, P Thomson & R Lingard (eds), *Changing Schools: Alternative Ways to Make a World of Difference*, Routledge, London.

Munns, G, Cole, B & Sawyer, W (Eds.), *Exemplary Teachers of Students in Poverty*. Routledge, London.

New South Wales Aboriginal Education Consultative Group & NSW Department of Education and Training 2004, *The Report of the Review of Aboriginal Education*, NSW Department of Education and Training, Sydney.

Newmann, F & Associates 1996, *Authentic Achievement: Restructuring Schools for Intellectual Quality*, Josey Bass, San Francisco.

Paquette, D & Ryan, J 2001, *Bronfenbrenner's Ecological Systems Theory*, http://www.floridahealth.gov/AlternateSites/CMS-Kids/providers/early_steps/training/documents/bronfenbrenners_ecological.pdf, accessed 18 September 2010.

Powell, K 2004, 'Working with mature-age parents', *Every Child*, vol. 10, no. 1, pp. 4–6.

Press, F 2005, *What about the Kids? Policy Directions for Improving the Experiences of Infants and Young Children in a Changing World*, New South Wales Commission for Children and Young People, Commission for Children and Young People and Child Guardian, NIFTeY.

Puckett, M & Diffily, D 2004, *Teaching Young Children: An Introduction to the Early Childhood Profession*, 2nd edn., Harcourt Brace, Fort Worth, TX.

Redman, G 2013, 'Beneath the surface: National trends and the lived experience of child poverty in Australia', paper presented at the ACOSS Policy Forum, *Turning the Tide on Child Poverty in Australia*, 13 November 2013.

Rolfe, S & Armstrong, K 2010, 'Early childhood professionals as a source of social support: The role of parent-professional communication', *Australasian Journal of Early Childhood*, vol. 35, no. 3, pp. 60–7.

Rowan, L, Knobel, M, Bigum, C & Lankshear, C 2002, *Boys, Literacies and Schooling: The Dangerous Territories of Gender-based Literacy Reform*, Open University Press, Buckingham.

Saunders, PG, 2011, *Down and Out: Poverty and Exclusion in Australia*, The Policy Press, Bristol.

Shiu, S 2004, 'Maintaining the thread: Including young children with chronic illness in the primary classroom', *Australian Journal of Early Childhood*, vol. 29, no. 1, pp. 33–8.

Shockley, B, Michalove, B & Allen, J 1996, *Engaging Families: Connecting Home and School Communities*, Heinemann, Portsmouth, NH.

Siraj-Blatchford, I & Clarke, P 2000, *Supporting Identity, Diversity and Language in the Early Years*, Open University Press, Buckingham.

Skattebol, J & Ferfolja, T 2007, 'Voices from an enclave: Lesbian mothers' experiences of child care', *Australian Journal of Early Childhood*, vol. 32, no. 1.

Skattebol, J, Saunders, P, Redmond, G, Bedford, M & Cass, B, 2012, *Making a Difference: Building on Young People's Experiences of Economic Adversity, Final Report*, NSW Social Policy Research Centre, University of NSW.

Spaggiari, S 1993/1998, 'The community–teacher partnership in the governance of the schools', in C Edwards, L Gandini & G Forman (eds), *The Hundred Languages of Children*, Ablex, Norwood, NJ.

Stonehouse, A & Gonzalez-Mena, J 2008, *Making Links: A Collaborative Approach to Planning and Practice in Early Childhood Services*, 2nd edn., Pademelon Press, Sydney.

Sydney Children's Hospital 2013, *Fact Sheet: Chronic Illness*, http://www.sch.edu.au/health/factsheets/joint/?chronic_illness.htm, accessed 31 March 2014.

Thomson, P 2002, *Schooling the Rustbelt Kids: Making the Difference in Changing Times*, Allen & Unwin, Crows Nest, NSW.

Turunen, TA & Dockett, S 2013, 'Family members' memories about starting school. Intergenerational aspects', *Australasian Journal of Early Childhood*, vol. 32, no. 2, pp. 103–10.

Tutwiler, S 2012, 'Family diversity', in G. Olsen & M. Fuller (eds.), *Home and School Relations: Teachers and Parents Working Together*, 4th edn., Pearson, Boston.

Victorian Aboriginal Child Care Agency 2008, *Aboriginal Cultural Competence Framework*, Victorian Government Department of Human Services, Melbourne.

Walters, K 2006, *Capture the Moment: Using Digital Photography in Early Childhood Settings*, Early Childhood Australia, Canberra.

CHAPTER THREE

THINKING ABOUT CHILDREN: PLAY, LEARNING AND DEVELOPMENT

Chapter learning focus

This chapter will investigate:

- theoretical bases for learning, development and play
- children's development
- children's learning
- children's play and play-based pedagogy.

Introduction

Early childhood education has recently embraced *Belonging, Being and Becoming: The Early Years Learning Framework* (EYLF) for Australia. The introduction to this document emphasises 'early childhood as a vital period in children's learning and development' (DEEWR, 2009, p. 5). This framework emphasises the importance of children's learning and development, supported by quality teaching and learning, which is in turn underpinned by **play-based learning**. At the same time, the Australian Curriculum for the compulsory years of school is being developed and implemented (Australian Curriculum, Assessment and Reporting Authority (ACARA), 2010).

Both documents emphasise the importance of children's learning and note some specific outcomes for learning in the early childhood years. However, each document reflects a different focus on that learning. The EYLF, in keeping with the consideration of young children aged birth to five years, reflects a holistic approach to learning and development, embedded within play-based environments, and includes broad learning outcomes. The Australian Curriculum is focused much more on specific learning outcomes across a range of subject areas, associated with definite years of schooling. Both documents are relevant for early childhood educators, even when they may work in only one sector. One of the basic tenets of early childhood education is that it is important to recognise what children bring with them to any given situation, as well as the experiences they are likely to meet in the future. Indeed, when combined with consideration of the present for children and their families, the basis of the EYLF is noted in the title – *Belonging, Being and Becoming*.

This chapter provides an overview of learning, development and play in the early childhood years. It does not aim to be a complete guide to children's learning, development and play. Rather, the aim of the chapter is to consider how understandings of children's learning, development and play inform the ways in which educators plan educational programs that are relevant, interesting and meaningful for children.

Play-based learning

A context for learning through which children organise and make sense of their social worlds, as they engage actively with people, objects and representations. (DEEWR, 2009, p. 6)

Theoretical bases for learning, development and play

Over the last century, educators have drawn on a range of theories of development and learning, including maturational theory (Gessell), psychoanalytic theory (Freud), psychosocial theory (Erikson), behavioural theory (Skinner), social learning theory (Bandura) and theories of cognitive development (Piaget, Vygotsky). They have also drawn on theories of social play (Parten), cognitive connection and play (Piaget) and theories emphasising particular types of play, such as sociodramatic play (Smilanksy). Each of these theories has contributed to the knowledge base of early childhood education. As theories evolve, so too does our understanding of children, and their learning, development and play. More recent theories have increased our knowledge of the ways children solve problems and process information (information processing theory: Miller), the ways in which social and cultural contexts shape and are shaped by children (sociocultural theory: Rogoff) and the importance of contexts and bioecological systems in development (bioecological theory: Bronfenbrenner). A characteristic of later theories is the recognition of the complexity and diversity of children, their lives and experiences. The range of theories, and ways of considering children, has led to the awareness that adequate explanations of their lives and experiences often involve more than one theoretical approach. Rather than adopting one theoretical stance and using this alone as the lens through which educators observe and plan for children, this book encourages educators to:

- consider multiple perspectives and multiple ways of explaining how children learn, develop and play
- recognise that the usefulness of theories is directly related to the contexts in which they are applied
- acknowledge that children exist in social contexts and that understanding children involves understanding their contexts
- realise that theories change, and so do their implications for practice
- challenge, question and reflect on assumptions underpinning theories.

Educators make professional judgements about educational environments, experiences and interactions. Underpinning these professional judgements are their own experiences, beliefs and values; their knowledge of children, families and communities; and their professional knowledge and skills (DEEWR, 2009). Much of educators' professional knowledge is also drawn from an understanding of theoretical perspectives. This understanding is constantly changing, as theory and practice interact and as theories evolve.

Many of the theories educators use in interactions with children have a developmental basis – they describe the changes, usually in terms of progressions, that occur for children over time. In this way, educators develop expectations about the physical, social, emotional, cognitive and language development of young children. Other theories explore the role of the contexts in which children exist – their families, communities and educational settings – and the impact of these on development and learning. Still other theories challenge educators to think beyond the changes that occur for children and families to consider why some changes occur in particular ways for some children and families, and not others. Such theories challenge assumptions, question the role of power within early childhood education and require educators to engage with issues of social justice and equity. This chapter draws on several theories to provide an overview of development, learning and play. This chapter begins by considering two theoretical perspectives that have become prominent in recent years: bioecological and cultural-historical theories. These theories provide the basis for much current thinking about children and early childhood education.

Ecological theory

Bronfenbrenner's (1979) ecological theory, represented by a series of nested concentric circles locating the child in the centre, is well known to early childhood educators. With a key focus on the interactions between children and contexts, this theory has been used to highlight the many and varied contexts in which children exist and the importance of positive and reciprocal interactions within and across these contexts. In developing his later bioecological theory, Bronfenbrenner retained this focus on the interrelationships between people and context, while expanding the focus on the role of individuals in influencing their own development (Bronfenbrenner & Morris, 2006). Bronfenbrenner's later theory – **bioecological theory** – emphasises four elements: process, person, context and time.

Processes are the progressively more complex reciprocal interactions that occur between the individual and their environment. Regular, ongoing interactions are labelled as **proximal processes**. Bronfenbrenner considered these the drivers of development, as it is through consistent interactions with people, objects and symbols that individuals make sense of their world and their roles within it (Bronfenbrenner & Morris, 2006). For example, interactions between young children as they play, or interactions between adults and young children, provide opportunities to develop understandings of their environment and the people within it. Consistent, reciprocal interactions can promote feelings of security, trust and respect. The nature of proximal processes is influenced by the characteristics that each person brings to the interaction.

The characteristics of each individual – the **person** element – influence interactions. In bioecological theory, Bronfenbrenner emphasised the importance of demand characteristics (such as age and physical appearance), resource characteristics (including emotional, social and material resources) and force characteristics (such as temperament and motivation). Each of these characteristics was described as impacting on the ways individuals interacted with the environment as well as the ways in which others interacted with the individual.

The third element of bioecological theory – **context** – is often the most recognised. The notion of nested systems includes those in which individuals interact (microsystems), overlapping contexts (mesosystems) that influence the actions and interactions of individuals, even though they are not direct participants in these contexts (exosystem), and the broader societal and cultural context (macrosystem).

The concept of **time** assumed a critical role in bioecological theory. Interactions within a specific activity are the focus of micro-time, while meso-time refers to activities and interactions that occur consistently within an individual's environment. For example, a positive interaction may occur between an adult and child as they read a book. If this occurs regularly, it can serve as a prompt for development and learning, as both child and adult built reciprocal patterns of interaction – possibly around questions and answers, patterns of word play or of personal interaction. The concept of macro-time is also introduced in reference to the chronosystem, which recognises that developmental processes vary according to the specific historical time in which individuals are located (Bronfenbrenner & Morris, 2006). Life course theory (Elder 1998) pays particular attention to the chronosystem, arguing that people who inhabit different time periods can experience the same event in different ways. This element highlights the importance of time and timing in development, as well as the related processes of continuity and change.

Bioecological theory acknowledges multiple influences on development. These include the individual themselves as well as the people and environment with whom they interact. It reminds us that the relationships educators form with children are critical to their development, providing the basis for proximal processes. These patterns of reciprocal interaction influence experiences and expectations.

Bioecological theory

A theory of development that emphasises the elements of process, person, context and time.

Proximal processes

Ongoing interactions between the individual and the people, objects and/or symbols in their environment.

Person

Individual characteristics, including physical characteristics, resources and individual attributes.

Context

Refers to the immediate contexts in which individuals exist, as well as more general social and cultural contexts.

Time

Refers to the time involved in immediate interactions as well as the impact of historical time on development.

Elements of bioecological theory and starting school

Processes – as children start school, they engage in a range of reciprocal interactions with others at school – both adults and children. Repeated patterns of interaction can promote learning as, for example, children are encouraged to participate in literacy activities or engage with peers. Educators are keen to promote positive patterns of interaction as negative patterns that are established early can contribute to feelings of insecurity or incompetence.

Person – the characteristics of individuals influence their experiences. As they start school, children who are outgoing and very pleased to be at school will approach experiences with vigour; children who feel unhappy or unsupported, or who feel that they do not 'fit in', may face challenges as they start school. Children who are well supported with resources – emotional, social and material – can draw on these to manage challenging situations.

Context – starting school is a time when many contexts come together – typically, school, home and prior-to-school settings. The compatibility of these contexts, and the ways in which people within these interact, will influence how children experience the transition to school.

Time – starting school happens within a particular historical time. Recognising the impact of this broad sense of time on experiences of starting school allows us to explore differences across generations. Also, the focus on time directs our attention to things that happen in the moment – or within specific experiences.

Starting school is a time of interactions among the child's immediate settings: family, early childhood setting and school.

Cultural-historical theory

What do you remember about starting school? In what ways are your memories similar to, or different from, those of other members of your family?

There is increasing recognition of the role of social and cultural contexts for learning and development within early childhood education. Much of this recognition has come with greater understanding of the theoretical position originally described by Vygotsksy (1978) and enhanced by the perspectives of other researchers. The essence of this position is that children's social and cultural contexts influence their development and learning, just as children themselves influence these contexts. While this position is often referred to as sociocultural theory, in recent years the term **cultural-historical theory** has gained prominence.

For several years, understandings of children's development, as exemplified in concepts such as Developmentally Appropriate Practice (DAP) (Bredekamp & Copple, 1997), provided definitive examples of what was expected of children at specific stages. While many educators considered these examples with caution, in recent years there have been strong moves to reconceptualise this approach to early childhood education, particularly by acknowledging the diversity of children, their contexts and their development. An essential step in this process has been recognising the importance of sociocultural perspectives, which 'take into account the social, historical and cultural dimensions of everyday activities' (Fleer et al., 2004, p. 175).

In cultural-historical theory, the guidance and support of adults, or others more expert than the child, are significant influences in the child's development and learning. The importance of the social context is stressed, with the idea that the child exists within society and cannot be separated out and studied away from that society. Vygotsky described all higher mental functions as having social origins; that is, they first appear in interactions between people before they are then internalised by those individuals. In other words, learning was regarded as social in origin.

Building on Vygotskian theory, Rogoff (2003) has emphasised the importance of children's culture and the ways in which this influences development and learning. The learning of all children will reflect those things that are important in a particular culture. As children interact with others who have more experience and expertise, they are guided and supported in their learning. Think of a parent reading a story to a child, and the child grappling with the words and the storyline. The adult may well provide clues as to what the words mean, ask the child to look at the pictures to see what is happening or even remind the child that she/he had read that word on the page before. This is **guided participation** on the part of the adult that helps children achieve or perform at a level they could not attain on their own. The level of guidance can vary as the parent regulates the experience, offering implicit or explicit support. Children, though, don't just passively participate in interactions. They are active in using the strategies suggested, in making sense of what they are doing and in guiding the experience in their own ways.

Rogoff (2003) has highlighted the pivotal role of culture in development: 'people develop as participants in cultural communities. Their development can be understood only in light of the cultural practices and circumstances of their communities – which also change' (pp. 3–4). To consider the importance of culture in development and learning, Rogoff has proposed the following orienting concepts:

- Culture isn't just what *other* people do.
- Understanding one's own cultural heritage, as well as other cultural communities, requires taking the perspective of people of contrasting backgrounds.
- Cultural practices fit together and are connected.
- Cultural communities continue to change, as do individuals.
- There is not likely to be One Best Way.

B Rogoff, *The Cultural Nature of Human Development*, p. 368, © 2003 Oxford University Press.

What is culture? Schweder et al. (1998) focused on the symbolic and behavioural expectations that are passed from generation to generation. These include ideas, beliefs, values, rituals and practices. When considered in relation to early childhood, this approach to culture could include: family expectations for their children, how they approach discipline, gender roles and expectations, ideas about wellbeing, and expectations for children's behaviour at such times as sleeping, eating and playing (Shonkoff & Phillips, 2000). All of these could have an impact on how children learn and develop (*see* also Chapter 2, which discusses working with diversity).

Cultural-historical theory

Focuses on the role of culture – including values, beliefs and skills – in development. Social interaction with more knowledgeable others is a key driver of development.

Guided participation

Shared interactions between expert and less expert participants.

FIGURE 3.1 Children learn what is important in their culture.

Culture is not static, nor is it homogeneous. Everyone exists within several cultures. These can be influenced by race, ethnicity, common nationality or language. Culture is complex. Within this, there is a need to consider how particular types, or aspects, of development and learning are facilitated by cultural contexts. By situating development in cultural contexts, educators are able to consider development as adaptive; that is, to consider why some developments occur and why they are important in a particular context. The skills and abilities of young children need to be understood in relation to the 'learning opportunities and expectations that are embedded in the important social interactions in the child's typical environment' (Shonkoff & Phillips, 2000, p. 68).

Children's development

With these two theoretical perspectives in mind, we explore some of the identifiable patterns of development that have come to provide the basis for much early childhood education. In asking educators to question and reflect upon what they know, understand and believe about early childhood education, particularly child development, it is not suggested that information about development areas or expectations is redundant; rather, educators are invited to consider what they know and to reflect upon interpretations of that same information with consideration for social and cultural contexts.

For example, rather than rejecting notions of milestones of development, it is suggested educators consider the ways in which such milestones were constructed, the groups with whom they were developed, when and how the supporting research was conducted and the implications for practice that have derived from these. Then educators might consider the impact of social and cultural contexts on these milestones, and construct interpretations of children's development from different perspectives. The following brief overview of developmental areas is provided to provoke this reflection.

Physical and motor development

BRAIN DEVELOPMENT

Recent advances in understanding brain development among young children support the view that the genetic make-up of any individual is important, but also emphasise the role of the environment in contributing to developmental outcomes. Children's genetic make-up guides the basic structure (cells and wiring) of the brain, but it is the experiences children have that develop and strengthen specific connections. Specific experiences activate specific connections in the brain. Connections that are activated often will become strong; those that are rarely activated can be discarded. The result is that the neural circuits in children's brains that come to work most efficiently are those that are activated often.

The broad promulgation of the brain research has highlighted the importance of the early years and promoted greater attention to the experiences of children during this time. However, many interpretations of the research have resulted in 'oversimplifications and misunderstandings' (Twardosz, 2012, p. 106). In reviewing these, Twardosz reminds us that brain development is not confined to the early years; indeed, modification as a result of experience continues throughout life. The notion of sensitive periods also needs consideration as, even when there is agreement about these, there is no sense that the entire brain is subject to these same periods. Finally, Twardosz cautions that the attention to providing stimulation to foster specific areas of brain development – particularly through well-marketed commercial materials – may generate short-term changes, but not necessarily lead to longer-term impacts.

Much brain development does happen in the prenatal period, and it is during this time that some environmental factors – such as toxic chemicals – can have serious consequences on that development. Further brain development occurs after birth as brain cells develop, migrate and form connections, all the while building up pathways that guide each individual's understandings and thoughts. These pathways continue to develop throughout life. An interesting way to view the changes that occur in brain development over the first few years of life has been shared on the website for the US organisation, Zero to Three (http://www.zerotothree.org > Behavior & Development > Brain Development > Baby Brain Map).

With the greater prominence of research about the brain, there have been many questions about what parents and early childhood educators can do to provide the 'right' sort of experiences to support and enhance development. Mac Naughton (2004) cautions that much of the focus on developing 'the right environment' or 'the right tools to stimulate brain development' assumes a simple and direct causal connection between what happens in an early childhood context and later life experiences. One of the most important outcomes from the brain research has been 'increased appreciation for the importance of the environment, beginning with prenatal conditions and continuing with the wide range of settings individuals encounter throughout their lives' (Twardosz, 2012, p. 114).

CAPABLE INFANTS

Very young infants actively make sense of their environment through use of their senses and their reactions to particular actions and interactions (*see* Figures 3.2 and 3.3). Once again, this represents a clear interaction between the characteristics infants are born with and the experiences they have that refine and help develop skills in these areas.

FIGURE 3.2 Infants are capable in many ways.

Far from being totally 'helpless', infants have an amazing range of skills and abilities from birth. As well, growth, development and learning in the early years proceed at an amazing pace. Infants soon replace the reflexes they have at birth with motor skills that demonstrate greater control and coordination, providing some clear indications of the development of their nervous system, as well as their sense of agency in interactions. From this early age, children develop a sense that they can influence what happens around them.

As young children acquire motor skills, their environment and their perspectives change. The perspectives of adults around them also change, as parents celebrate their child sitting up, rolling over, crawling or taking first steps. There is wide variation in the timing of the acquisition of these skills. In general, children develop control of their head and upper body first; hence, infants hold up their head well before they can walk. Berk (2009, p. 146) reminds us that motor skills do not develop in isolation. Rather, she states that each new skill is a joint product of:

- central nervous system development
- movement possibilities of the body
- goals the child has in mind
- environmental supports for the skill.

Performing a new skill has as much to do with its context as it does with development. An eager, encouraging and positive caregiver can provide a supportive environment and materials that help children set goals and move towards achieving these. If an infant has spotted a new toy, can move sufficiently to reach it, thinks it is reachable and knows there is encouragement to reach it, then she/he is likely to try to reach it. If, on the other hand, the infant has learned that the environment is not supportive – for example, if the caregiver routinely takes the toy away – then the reaching out may not occur.

There are many charts listing milestones of physical and motor development in infancy. These can provide a useful guide for children's development, but they must be read with caution. Many charts use Western populations as their normative sample. When children from diverse cultural backgrounds or contexts are compared with these samples, they are often described as lacking skills or delayed. Cultural variations in child-rearing patterns and styles also mean that

FIGURE 3.3 Infants make sense of their environment in different ways.

some actions are encouraged more than others. This does not automatically mean that children who do not meet these normative milestones have developmental problems. In fact, they often have expertise in different areas.

Planning for children is often focused on achieving the next developmental milestone. While support may be needed to assist children where development and learning are delayed, it is also important to look beyond skill acquisition to other aspects of each child's unique strengths and emergent development. Assessing children on skills that may be important in one context may miss a wide range of skills that are different, but equally valuable.

Infants have often been described as relying on sensorimotor understandings of their world. The infant who reaches to grasp objects and then places them in the mouth is using the senses of touch and taste to explore those objects. From birth, infants respond to differences in tastes and smells. Newborns can discriminate the smell of their own mother from other mothers, and react much as adults do to smells such as rotten eggs (they turn away) and chocolate (they relax their facial muscles) (Berk, 2009).

Many infants and the adults who care for them engage in a lot of play. Some of the exciting times with infants are the playtimes where infants emit a great chortle as they react to a game of 'peekaboo', respond to tickling or laugh with a great grin. As well as providing great enjoyment, these interactions promote communication and social relationships. The sense of closeness and value children experience in these interactions contributes to relationships, and the pattern of responsiveness sets up some of the patterns of conversation relevant to that context. Many infants enjoy the company of others and play in ways that engage them: making eye contact, smiling, reaching and responding in play interactions. Much of the play of infants has been called sensorimotor play because it relies on senses and motor actions. Infants can be content to play on their own, sometimes using their own body in repeated movements, and other times using some of the resources to hand, such as toys or other people.

Recent research has highlighted the ways in which infant agency can be promoted through play. Degotardi (2013) explores ways in which infants develop intentionality and autonomy and describes studies in which adults have been attentive to interpreting infants' perspectives and intentions. Indeed, she argues that such attentiveness is at the core of high quality interactions between adults and infants. In these interactions, adults note not only the physical actions of infants, but also engage with their mental actions – their thoughts, preferences, perspectives and intentions. This can be seen in adult conversations that refer to infants' mental worlds – using terms such as *want*, *need* and *think*. Combined with sensitive observations, responsive interactions can facilitate relationships that build a shared sense of **agency**, where adults and infants contribute to shared understandings. These interactions reflect the competence of infants.

> What opportunities are afforded for infants to demonstrate agency in your setting?

Agency

When children exercise choice within a given social and cultural context.

DEVELOPMENT IN LATER YEARS

Some of the most obvious changes in physical and motor growth and development occur during infancy. However, throughout the early childhood years a great deal is happening for children as their physical and motor skills become more refined and used in different ways. It is also important to note that one of the most significant changes for children themselves relates to their own sense of 'getting bigger'.

Dramatic weight and height gains are observed in the early years of life, accompanied by significant changes in body proportions. Changes in the development of muscles, often described as children 'losing their baby fat', cause children to look different as they get older. For example, most toddlers look to be slimmer than they were as babies, and preschoolers look slimmer than they were as toddlers.

Underpinning these changes is growth in the skeletal system. As children's bones grow, they also begin to harden and some bones fuse. This process is far from complete in the early childhood years, but it does result in major increases in strength and endurance. It is also a process that can reflect a wide range of differences. For example, the quality of the nutrition children receive can have an impact on the rate and pace of development. A diet low in calcium can have implications for the development of strong, hard bones.

Physical changes in muscle and bone strengths, as well as children's changing size and proportions, are reflected in their motor skills. Children's balance and their centre of gravity change as their shape changes. Observing both a toddler and a preschooler running illustrates some of these changes as the toddler often appears top-heavy and relatively uncoordinated, and the preschooler seems more streamlined and coordinated in comparison. Changes in muscle strength and balance open the way for changes in motor skills. The initial hesitant run soon becomes a more confident sprint, sometimes accompanied by elements of jumping, hopping, galloping and/or skipping.

There are many charts listing the milestones of both gross (large) and fine (small) motor development. As with all generalised charts, these need to be read with caution and considered in a specific context. One of the fascinating things about motor skills is that they develop with practice. Practice itself can take many forms, from the organised practice associated with sports and sporting teams to the everyday play of children in a range of contexts. Children who have both the opportunities and the inclination to practise specific skills can often surprise adults with their abilities. Similarly, children who have never had the opportunity to practise some skills will most likely seem uncoordinated when they first attempt these. How other children and adults react to these initial attempts will have a big influence on whether or not these skills are attempted again. Children's images of themselves (self-concept) and the images they believe others hold of them (self-esteem) are influenced by experiences such as these.

Much of children's play involves a wide range of physical and motor activities, and most children are keen to be involved in physical activities (*see* Figure 3.4). It is not unusual to see a group of children attending early childhood services or school running around the perimeter of the playground, chasing each other or seemingly running around for no apparent reason. Play also provides a wonderful context in which children can experiment with and practise such skills. Adults can sometimes be tempted to channel those skills into organised team sporting activities, such as soccer, netball, cricket or hockey, particularly as children reach school age. Given the incredible individual differences among children, it is not surprising that some children thrive as they engage in these sports. It is also not surprising that others find the social as well as the physical expectations of such sports overwhelming. It is often the children who are not so good at the sport who find participation difficult. Not only can the required skill elude them, but the social pressure of 'letting the team down' can be very distressing. Children who are confident and competent in using the required skills are more likely to enjoy such sports than those who are not.

Many young children will be involved in organised sporting activities. Given current concerns about the rates of childhood obesity, coupled with parental concerns about

FIGURE 3.4 Children's play involves a wide range of physical and motor activities.

Should we exclude young children from team sports? Should we make sure that teams consist of players with varying abilities?

children spending too much time in front of the television or computer, there may well be pressure on educators to introduce more formal, organised sporting activities for young children. Responding to these calls will require a sound understanding of the importance of children's play, understanding of the specific context and an awareness of the children, families and communities involved.

Social development

Close relationships are the context for children's play, development and learning: 'what young children learn, how they react to events and people around them, and what they expect from themselves and others' (Shonkoff & Phillips, 2000, p. 226) depend greatly on their close relationships, particularly with parents and family.

ATTACHMENT

'Healthy development depends on the quality and reliability of a young child's relationships with the important people in his or her life, both within and outside the family' (National Scientific Council on the Developing Child, 2009, p. 1). The strong emotional ties between infants and their caregivers – **attachment** – provide an important context for development. Many children experience strong emotional connections with their parents and with caregivers outside the family (*see* Figure 3.5). Having strong emotional ties to a few people enables infants, as well as older children, to feel secure and confident in their environment. The feelings of security and comfort that are part of attachment enable young children to explore and interact, knowing that a secure base is always close by. Children who do not have secure attachments are reported to grow and develop in different ways from infants who do have such ties (Berk, 2009).

The development of early secure attachments is linked with a wide range of future competencies. These include emotional understanding and self-regulation, forming positive relationships in later years, a strong sense of self and positive social skills. In considering the nature of secure attachment relationships, it is important to acknowledge cultural variation. Just as not all cultural groups interact in the same ways, not all infant–parent dyads will demonstrate attachment in the same ways.

The nature of attachment is influenced by the opportunities that are available to form strong bonds between infants and caregivers and the quality of that care giving. Infant characteristics – such as **temperament** and physical wellbeing – also influence attachment relationships. For example, not all babies snuggle or like to be held; some become quite tense and agitated at physical contact.

Adults have many special relationships; young children can and do benefit from the same. Relationships with parents, siblings, peers, grandparents, neighbours and the like can be a

Attachment

'The strong, affectionate tie we have with special people in our lives that leads us to experience pleasure when we interact with them and to be comforted by their nearness during times of stress' (Berk, 2009, p. 425).

Temperament

Characteristic ways of responding to emotional events and novel situations and of regulating their actions.

FIGURE 3.5 Attachment relationships provide a resource for children.

source of great pleasure to young children. While having relationships with a number of special people can actually broaden the range of people who care about the young child, problems may arise when there are so many new faces and relationships that children become overwhelmed and confused. Such a situation could arise in an early childhood setting where, because of staff turnover or illness, children may not be able to recognise a familiar face on arrival. It is important in settings, whenever possible, to have at least one familiar face to greet young children in the morning and to farewell them at the end of the day.

UNDERSTANDING THE SELF

How children come to understand the social world has a lot to do with how they understand themselves. Very young infants do not seem to distinguish readily between themselves and others. When children start to engage in imitative play – indicating that they can imitate others – we can imply that they are developing a sense that they and others exist separately. At about the same time, children start to realise that a photo of themselves is really them and start to refer to themselves by name. Self-recognition is an integral part of children's lives and development. Children need to recognise themselves in order to form plans and to recognise the consequences of their own actions. Self-recognition is a step towards developing **self-concept**.

Over the early childhood years, children begin to realise that several personal characteristics are permanent and unchanged – for example, children remain either a boy or girl, and they remain human. Preschool children are aware of an inner self, which is made up of private thoughts and imaginings accessible only to themselves. These children are beginning to realise that reality and beliefs can differ, so that they can accept that a person might think something that is contrary to reality, or look one way and feel another. Children are also referring to mental terms and states, such as remembering, thinking and pretending, in appropriate ways in everyday conversation.

Young children often describe themselves in terms of observable characteristics (*see* Figure 3.6). For example, in response to 'Who are you?' a three-year-old may say, 'I go to preschool', or 'I help Mummy, I a big boy'. In response to the same question, a six-year-old or seven-year-old may respond, 'I am a girl. I have friends that I play with. I have long black hair. My favourite colour is red and I like to eat chips'. Rather than focusing on observable characteristics, older children refer to competencies, personality and dispositions. Older children are often very aware of social comparisons, judging themselves in relation to others.

Our understanding of ourselves is not permanent, unified or fixed. It does vary from situation to situation, from experience to experience, and from one phase of our lives to another. The developing self-concept is influenced by parents, caregivers and other family members in the early years. A mature self-concept has several aspects. These include an idea of what individuals are like (their real self) and an idea of what they would like to be like (their ideal selves). Sometimes, children's real selves and ideal selves are very similar, and sometimes there is a great difference between the two. During the early school years, children's ideal selves become more complex and often their real selves are seen in a less positive light. The beliefs we have about ourselves affect our behaviour.

Most of us think of ourselves as good at some things and as not so good at others. Children make these distinctions as well. Children who have a positive **self-esteem** are those whose definitions of themselves are essentially positive, whereas those who define themselves in mainly negative terms are said to have low self-esteem.

Self-concept
The set of attributes, abilities, attitudes and values that individuals use to define themselves.

FIGURE 3.6 Young children often define themselves in terms of observable characteristics, in this case, 'I'm two!'

Self-esteem
The evaluative dimension of self-concept.

For some time, it was assumed that self-esteem was a general feeling or judgement about the self. Now it is suggested that children make evaluative judgements about different aspects of their lives; for example, they are good at writing but not good at skipping. There is evidence that preschool children make several judgements about themselves – judgements about their learning, how they get along with friends and family and their physical capabilities (Marsh et al., 2002). These judgements are made on the basis of evaluative information that children receive from others, as well as their own evaluations of their skills, abilities and performances. Children reach decisions about themselves and the sort of people they are by observing their own actions and behaviour as well as the reactions of others. Adults convey strong messages to children – children realise when adults express love, happiness or disappointment and rejection towards them. Children pick up on these reactions (verbal and non-verbal) and incorporate these into their developing view of themselves.

Self-esteem is usually described as positive or negative, where positive is regarded as 'good' and negative as 'bad'. Children with positive self-esteem are described as confident and outgoing, while those with low self-esteem are thought to be dependent and shy. However, the reality is that these are stereotypes. Children and adults have different feelings about themselves in different situations, and probably fit between these two descriptions most often. These evaluations of self influence beliefs about **self-efficacy**. Children, and adults, are most likely to take on tasks they think are achievable, and avoid those things that are not considered achievable. Individuals have their own view of the competencies that influence the experiences they seek out or avoid (*see* Figure 3.7).

Self-efficacy

Beliefs about the ability to do specific things.

FIGURE 3.7 Identity is shaped by experience.

Understanding the self is a critical part of developing identity. Erikson's (1968) theory of psychosocial development was based on the assumption that the resolution of a series of stages throughout childhood resulted in the construction of a particular identity. At each stage, Erikson described a conflict as the child sought a resolution between qualities, expressed as opposites, such as trust vs mistrust, and autonomy vs shame and doubt. While more recent approaches acknowledge the importance of these qualities, they avoid the notion of a crisis point. For example, rather than assuming that trust or mistrust has developed with a child's first year of life, there is recognition that trust develops over time, in a range of situations and interactions with others.

The importance of identity is recognised in the EYLF, where the first learning outcome is noted as '*Children have a strong sense of identity*' (DEEWR, 2009, p. 20). The conceptualisation of identity referred to in this document goes beyond the understanding of self outlined by Erikson; indeed, it involves much more than the development of a unified, rational self often outlined in developmental psychology texts. The EYLF recognises that 'Children learn about themselves and construct their own identity within the context of their families and communities … identity is not fixed. It is shaped by experiences' (DEEWR, 2009, p. 20).

This approach to identity reflects postmodern understandings, where identities are regarded as 'dynamic and multiple, and always positioned in relation to particular discourses and the practices produced by the discourses' (Grieshaber & Cannella, 2001, p. 13). In other words, individuals can have multiple, even contradictory, identities, depending on the context, their interactions and relationships.

Changing paradigms have led to changing views of children and childhood, recognising the complex and dynamic nature of children and their worlds. For example, sociological approaches have underpinned perspectives of children as capable and competent, part of a family, but also with their own interests and challenges (James & Prout, 1997). Children have come to be recognised as members of society in their own right, and with their own rights (United Nations, 1989). Part of this revised understanding of children and childhood is that children are regarded as co-constructors of their knowledge, culture and identity (Dahlberg et al., 2007). In this way, children co-construct their identities when they build relationships with people, places and objects, and when they evaluate the responsiveness of others towards them. Developing a strong identity is underpinned by a sense of belonging – of worth and respect for who we are.

Gender

Developing a gendered identity is regarded as an essential element of establishing a sense of self. How do children develop such identities? One suggestion draws on sex-role socialisation theory, which assumes the 'biological basis of sexual difference is assumed, and the "roles" that children are taught by adults are a superficial social dressing laid over the "real" biological difference' (Davies, 1989, p. 5). In this theory, sex-role socialisation 'happens' to children; they are not actively involved in constructing, understanding and negotiating power or identity. A different perspective offered by Davies (1989, p. 12) is that 'sex and gender are at one and the same time elements of the social structure, and something created by individuals and within individuals as they learn the discursive practices through which that social structure is created and maintained'. In other words, masculinity and femininity are products of the social and cultural context of children. There are different ways of being male or female, depending on the social and cultural context. Children learn to position themselves as male or female as they establish a social identity.

Interactions with others provide the basis for the formation of identity (Mac Naughton, 2000). Children learn gender through their interactions in discourses and as they try to make sense of themselves and others. In early childhood settings, interactions between children and adults, and between children, are often based on gender and children's assumptions or expectations about gender. Children will often distinguish between 'boy toys' and 'girl toys', sometimes excluding others from interaction because they 'are a boy' or 'are a girl'. Children develop a sense of what it means to 'be a boy' or 'be a girl'.

Promoting gender equity in early childhood settings would seem to be a very reasonable aim. However, Mac Naughton (2000) notes that many myths pervade attempts to achieve this. In order to promote gender equity, she calls for critique of existing strategies and adoption of approaches that incorporate the following:

- struggling with gendered power relations
- exercising adult power for girls and against boys
- stopping sexism between children
- making children alert to adult surveillance of sexism
- increasing children's discursive repertoires
- understanding the pleasures and benefits children find in traditional gendering
- disrupting the demarcation lines between genders
- intervening in, and extending, children's storylines
- challenging category-maintenance work on less traditionally gendered children
- exercising pedagogical power with feminist intent(s).

In Mac Naughton's words, 'creating gender equity with young children is more unsettling and more complex than modelling non-sexist behaviours and encouraging boys and girls to play non-stereotypically' (2000, p. 238).

UNDERSTANDING OTHERS

> Young children experience their world as an environment of relationships, and these relationships affect virtually all aspects of their development … Relationships engage children in the human community in ways that help them define who they are, what they can become and how and why they are important to other people.

National Scientific Council on the Developing Child, p. 1, © 2009 Center on the Developing Child, Harvard University.

Programming and Planning
in Early Childhood Settings

Relationships with family – particularly parents/caregivers – provide the basis for relationships with others. Early interactions, where parents and children interact using sound and gesture, play games and enjoy each other's company, nurture developing abilities and understandings. As children interact with parents, they develop a range of skills that help them in other relationships – such as understandings of other people's reactions, perspectives and expectations.

Peer relationships

As children grow and develop and their experiences broaden away from the home, they often have opportunities to interact with peers. Interacting with peers is an important element in children's play, development and learning. However, even more important is the formation of friendships with peers. Some children find interacting with peers and forming friendships difficult; for example, some children are shy, some seem to initiate interactions with aggression and some take time to become accustomed to the context or the participants involved. These challenges do not necessarily signify problems. However, they may indicate that children need some assistance to help them navigate interactions.

We know that friends matter, even to very young children (Dunn, 2004). Friendships occur outside the family, and are different from relationships with family. Friendships can provide key emotional supports for children as well as provide a source of excitement, happiness and joy (*see* Figure 3.8). Children express concerns about their friends and will often aim to work out if something is wrong and, if so, how they can help. A number of researchers trace the beginning of moral understanding to children's interactions with friends, where children express empathy, concern and understanding.

The nature and quality of children's friendships vary. In some friendships, there seem to be an equal sense of power and engagement; in others, there is evidence of jealousy, insecurity and rejection. Not all friendships offer the same levels of support and understanding. Dunn (2004) notes that friendships do not guarantee kindness and understanding. Nevertheless, children do want to get on well with their friends, and in doing so will try to understand others and respond in ways that support them.

Children's friendships are built upon, and maintained by, many things. Some friends share play worlds – whether these be around pretend play with similar scenarios, roles and scripts, or specific skills and abilities associated with games. Still others share secrets, favourite possessions or common interests. Some children have lots of friends; others have few. Some children have friends, but seem to be happiest when they are on their own. There is no one right way to have or be a friend.

FIGURE 3.8 Friendships are important for young children.

While children's being on their own is not necessarily a concern, it can be so if children are rejected. The popularity of children has an impact on their social interactions and their social development. Generally, rejected or isolated children are thought to have fewer, or less refined, social skills. They also report being lonely more often, and not happy or comfortable in social interactions. However, some children who are thought to be unpopular still develop strong friendships, sometimes with other children regarded as unpopular.

Emotional development

Emotions are affective responses to events that are relevant to us (McDevitt & Ormrod, 2007, p. G2). Emotions prompt us to think and act in particular ways. For example, feeling happy can lead to laughter; feeling sad can lead to seeking out someone to provide comfort. As children grow and develop, they demonstrate a range of emotional reactions and increasing ability to regulate these. Increasing regulation signifies children's developing independence in social as well as personal contexts (Shonkoff & Phillips, 2000). Children have a range of ways to regulate themselves and their environments, and these change as they become more experienced. From an early age, babies use crying to signal their needs. As children become older, there is a greater emphasis on alternative strategies.

Infants are unable to describe their emotions. However, this does not mean that they neither experience nor demonstrate a range of emotions. The most researched emotions in infants have been happiness, anger, sadness and fear. As well as these basic emotions, there has been considerable research on self-conscious emotions, such as feelings of shame, pride, guilt, embarrassment and envy. Children generally demonstrate these as they start to develop a sense of self.

As well as expressing a wide range of emotions, children also start to learn to regulate or conceal some emotions. As children develop their vocabulary for emotion, they are more able to tell us about how they feel – happy, yukky, scared, mad. Young children use a range of communication strategies including gestures, movement and sounds to express feelings. Older children also use some actions to regulate emotion, such as closing their eyes when something scary is around, blocking their ears, crossing the road when they see a dog and talking to themselves. Still older children have other strategies, such as distraction and reinterpretation of events. Children tend to learn about expressing emotions by observing the emotional reactions of others. Educators can promote children's understanding of emotions by creating warm, secure and responsive environments, where children are encouraged to discuss their feelings and where there are opportunities to express feelings in appropriate ways – such as through drawing, writing, talking, music and movement.

Young children can experience a range of emotions, including happiness, pride, shame, sadness and anxiety. These feelings can influence their interactions with others as well as their general wellbeing. Educators who are aware of how children are feeling can help them develop some strategies for managing situations. For example, knowing that some children feel anxious about change can mean that educators consider how changes are introduced and how children are consulted about changes.

Some children have negative emotional experiences that can be debilitating, impacting on their quality of life. These can be ongoing experiences, or the result of disaster or trauma, including experiences of bushfires, floods and earthquakes. Children who arrive in Australia as refugees, or who seek asylum as refugees, may have experienced trauma that is unimaginable for many Australians.

Prolonged exposure to trauma can increase children's levels of stress and feelings of anxiety and impact on learning and development. Children who experience ongoing trauma can lose feelings of safety, security and trust. In some circumstances, this can result in a 'reduced sense of their worth ... increased levels of emotional stress, shame, grief, and increased destructive behaviours' (Atkinson et al., 2009, p. 136). Trauma can also be transmitted across generations, affecting whole families and communities (Duran & Duran, 1995).

Sometimes children can struggle to express emotions in acceptable ways, or experience intense emotions that may seem out of proportion to the events that triggered them. There is increasing attention to the mental health of young children, recognising that optimum development includes both physical and mental health. Kidsmatter (http://www.kidsmatter.edu. au/ec/) is a recent early childhood mental health initiative to promote the development of strong social and emotional skills among children.

TEMPERAMENT

Much recent research relating to emotional development has focused on *temperament*. We all know that some people seem to take a while to get going, others are incredibly eager, still others are withdrawn and so on. We may be able to explain some of these differences by considering temperament.

Characteristics that are associated with temperament include children's activity level, sensitivity to physical input, emotional intensity, sociability, adaptability and persistence.

Temperament does have some stability even from infancy through to adulthood – but this does not mean that it cannot change or respond to environmental conditions. In many cases, considerable differences are noted, suggesting that while temperament may have a biological base, environmental factors contribute significantly to the expression of temperament.

Cognitive development

Cognition refers to mental processes, such as reasoning, planning, problem solving, representing and remembering. Cognition leads to knowing. In early childhood education, two theories have had a major influence over the past 50 or so years – the theories of Piaget and Vygotsky.

PIAGET'S THEORY OF COGNITIVE DEVELOPMENT

According to Piaget (1962), children's thinking shows their unique way of understanding and interpreting the world. From Piaget, we get the views that:

- there are *qualitative differences* in the ways children interpret and think about the world
- children are *actively involved* in the construction of their own knowledge and understanding, through experience (*see* Figure 3.9).

Piaget proposed a 'stage' theory, where cognitive growth was described as a continuous process, beginning at birth and continuing throughout life, passing through four major stages. According to this theory, individuals pass through different stages at different ages, though it should be noted that the age association made by Piaget was meant as a general guide only. The rate at which children reached different stages varied, but the sequence of stages did not; Piaget described an invariant stage sequence. Another feature of this theory was that the developmental sequence described by Piaget was taken to be universal; that is, all children in all situations and all contexts were expected to progress through the same stages.

FIGURE 3.9 Children are actively involved in constructing knowledge through experience.

Schemes

Strategies for interaction.

Organisation

Integration of two or more schemes into a more complex, higher order scheme.

Adaptation

The process of adjusting to the environment.

Assimilation

Where the world is interpreted through current schemes.

Accommodation

Where new schemes, or modified schemes, are constructed to explain the world.

Each of Piaget's periods of cognitive development incorporate a number of associated structures. These are structures of the mind that form the framework for understanding the world. The structures develop as a result of the interactions between children and the environment. The strategies for interaction are themselves called **schemes**. Initially, children utilise schemes based on reflexes, such as sucking. Over time, these schemes come to be used in more organised and deliberate ways, based on mental representations instead of reflexes.

Piaget's theory assumes that cognition involves mental representation, so that things can be represented mentally, rather than having to be physically present. This differentiates cognition from perception, which relates to things that can be perceived in the here and now. Mental representation allows thinking about something that has not yet happened or that is not present.

Piaget described two tendencies that govern an individual's interaction with the environment: **organisation** and **adaptation**. Through these two processes, individuals modify schemes to make sense of the world. *Organisation* is the integration of two or more schemes into a more complex, higher order scheme, such as combining the scheme for grasping with seeing and reaching for an object while watching it. *Adaptation* is the process of adjusting to the environment. It is achieved through the processes of assimilation and accommodation. Both **assimilation** and **accommodation** are important in bringing about gradual change in cognition. They result in an ongoing adaptation to the environment.

The four stages of cognitive development outlined by Piaget are:

- *The sensorimotor stage.* The interactions of infants in this first stage are based on overt sensory and motor abilities, such as sucking, grasping and touching. The term 'sensorimotor' means that infants know their world by their direct actions on it. In other words, the thoughts of infants are tied to their explorations of the environment. Infants learn by acting upon the objects and people around them.

  The assumption of this period is that infants can represent objects only by the actions that they can perform on them, so a toy is something to chew on, to suck on or to throw. By the end of the sensorimotor period, infants develop abilities to maintain mental images and an idea of object permanence. This is the understanding that objects still exist even though they cannot be seen, heard, touched, smelt or tasted.

- *The preoperational stage.* The name 'preoperational' refers to Piaget's idea that this stage precedes logical thought; that is, it is prelogical. Piaget's description of this stage relates mainly to what children can not do. For example, children's egocentrism was thought to limit their abilities to see other perspectives. Children are described as unable to reason from cause to effect or to use strategies such as reversibility. Nevertheless, children are regarded as capable of symbolic functioning, particularly as seen in symbolic play and in the acquisition of language.

- *The stage of concrete operations.* Concrete operations is described as the period where children are seen to be able to organise ideas in a systematic way; that is, to perform mental operations. This means that children can mentally transform, modify or manipulate things according to some basic rules of logic, using skills such as reversibility. The limitation of this period is that these operations can only be performed on things that are concrete rather than abstract.

- *The stage of formal operations.* This is the fourth and final stage of cognitive development proposed by Piaget. It is described as the period of greatest efficiency in the acquisition of knowledge. In this stage, operations are not tied to concrete objects, and individuals can handle and manipulate abstract ideas and concepts.

Early childhood education has utilised Piaget's theory in many ways. It formed the basis of Developmentally Appropriate Practice (Bredekamp & Copple, 1997) as well as the theoretical base for several early childhood programs, such as High Scope (Schweinhart & Weikart, 1997). Piaget contributed a great deal to the study of young children, and to the recognition that children think and understand in ways that are qualitatively different from adults. However, recent advances in understanding children have challenged his theory in a number of ways. It is now known that:

- Young children are more competent than described by Piaget. Not only do young children demonstrate some of the thinking skills Piaget ascribed to older children (such as object permanence), they also do not demonstrate some of the limitations noted within the preoperational period (such as egocentrism). In addition, children in the preoperational stage can show the ability to use abstract thinking and perform tasks such as conservation (Cohen & Cashon, 2006; Donaldson, 1978).

- Children's cognitive development is not nearly as stage-like as described by Piaget (Bjorklund, 2005). While it may be possible to describe trends in development, educators are now much more aware that the nature of children's reasoning in any given situation depends on their prior knowledge and experience, as well as the specific context. As a result, children do not necessarily demonstrate consistent reasoning across contexts.

- Children's prior knowledge and experience influences their thinking and reasoning. This is in contrast to the Piagetian position that once children have developed a particular aspect of logical thought, they can apply it in any context (Halford & Andrews, 2006).

- Culture influences cognitive development. The universal stage sequence outlined by Piaget is not always evident across different cultural contexts (Miller, 1997).

A number of researchers have incorporated elements of Piaget's theory into more recent research around the area of cognitive development. Neo-Piagetians, such as Halford and Andrews (2006), combine Piaget's stage-based theory with understandings derived from

information-processing research, resulting in a theory that uses a loose approach to stages that are linked to developing competencies, but influenced by issues such as brain development and experience. In another example, Case (1985) noted that cognitive development depended, at least to some degree, on brain maturation. In particular, he indicated that the development of working memory was linked to children's developing reasoning skills.

VYGOTSKY, CULTURAL-HISTORICAL THEORY AND COGNITIVE DEVELOPMENT

Whereas Piaget stressed the role of the individual, with individual development being his primary concern, Vygotsky (1978) stressed the role of the individual as a social being, influenced by the social world and particularly by the surrounding culture. Some of the key features of this perspective are:

- As they interact with children, adults share what is important in their culture and the meanings ascribed to elements of that culture. Adults act as mediators as they explain and share elements of culture. This can occur in everyday interactions, such as conversations, but also through the more formal systems of education.
- Culture shapes cognitive development. Not only do members of the cultural group guide children towards certain experiences, they also assist children to develop culturally relevant interpretations of those experiences.
- While culture influences development, children adapt culture in ways that make sense to them.
- Thought and language are interrelated. While they start out as separate entities, over the first few years of life, they gradually become entwined, with the result that children express their thoughts when they speak, and they start to think in words. The very

FIGURE 3.10 Vygotsky described learning as a social experience.

Private speech

Self-directed speech used by children to guide their thinking and behaviour.

beginning of this is seen when children talk to themselves using **private speech**. Through private speech, children direct their thinking and actions, particularly when involved in difficult or challenging tasks. Over time, private speech becomes inner speech, as the need to say things out loud is replaced by the ability to do this mentally.

- Cognitive development has social origins. Vygotsky proposed that thinking emerges from social interactions. He described children engaging in social interactions with more knowledgeable others who provide culturally relevant interpretations of these interactions, and starting to incorporate words, meanings, symbols and strategies into their own thinking. This process is labelled **internalisation**. Private speech provides an example of an activity that starts out as a social activity – parents guiding children's actions – then moves to children providing the commentary to guide their own actions, and finally becomes internalised as inner speech.

Internalisation

The process by which social activities become mental processes.

- While social interaction with adults is important, so too is interaction with peers. Interactions in play, for example, provide opportunities for children to become aware of different roles and perspectives (*see* Figure 3.10).

Zone of proximal development

Where tasks are too difficult for a child to perform independently, but are possible with the assistance of more knowledgeable others.

- Play is one context that establishes a **zone of proximal development** (ZPD). Vygotsky described learning as occurring within the ZPD; that is, where tasks are too difficult for a child to perform independently, but are possible with the assistance of more knowledgeable others. This suggests that children learn little from tasks they can already perform independently. Rather, they are likely to learn when they are confronted by a challenging task they can complete with the assistance of others. Tasks that have already been accomplished, as well as those that are impossible, even with the help of others, are regarded as unproductive in terms of learning.

• Cognitive development is promoted when social interactions are based on **intersubjectivity**. Intersubjectivity develops when people have shared understandings of the task and their approach. Intersubjectivity allows participants to generate a common set of understandings, so that they can communicate effectively.

> **Intersubjectivity**
> Shared understandings of a task or situation.

As noted at the beginning of this chapter, cultural-historical theory has influenced our thinking about early childhood education in many ways. A number of contemporary researchers have elaborated this theory and explored its relevance for education. There has been particular attention paid to the social construction of meaning, emphasising the role adults play in helping children to attach meaning to the people, places, events and objects they encounter. In many situations, adults and children, or children and their peers, co-construct meaning. The role of others as mediators of children's cognitive development is reflected in the term **scaffolding**.

> **Scaffolding**
> The level of support provided by a more knowledgeable other as children tackle tasks within the ZPD.

Through scaffolding, those with expertise in a particular area, such as parents, teachers or peers, provide the framework or support that enables children to try out new ideas (*see* Figure 3.11). Scaffolding can be as simple as providing some verbal prompts or cues as to what might be done next, or can relate to the more general provision of a supportive learning environment that offers some of the safety and security that can be derived from the existence of such structural support.

While providing scaffolding is something that adults routinely do for children, it is sometimes harder to reduce the levels of support and allow children to create their own support. The reduction of scaffolding can also be seen as children take over the role of providing the prompts or cues; for example, when they adopt private speech and then later when this becomes internalised as thought. Scaffolding is discussed further in Chapter 9.

Much scaffolding occurs within the context of guided participation (Rogoff, 2003), where participants of varying levels of expertise engage in shared tasks. Examples include any situation where children participate in adult activities. As children participate, they acquire greater proficiency and often increased responsibility.

Both Piaget's and Vygotsky's theories have been influential in early childhood education for some time. Educators can see their influences in many of the everyday actions in both prior-to-school and school settings. Both theories recognise the importance of children encountering challenge in a supportive environment. For Piaget, cognitive development resulted from children encountering a situation they could not understand. In Vygotsky's theory, the ZPD reflected the psychological space just beyond children's capabilities, where assistance and guidance is most effective.

FIGURE 3.11 Adults provide scaffolding for children.

In contrast to Piaget's theory of universal stages, Vygotsky's theory promotes a view of cognitive development characterised by cultural variation and highlights the importance of children interacting in social and cultural contexts with more knowledgeable others. This can be linked directly to the role of educators, who can guide children's learning and development through scaffolding and participation.

Language development

Learning language is an important element of becoming a member of, and participating in, a particular culture. Many of the cultural practices used in families determine the language learned and the ways in which language (including both verbal and non-verbal elements of interaction) is used (Bowman et al., 2001).

The early learning of language seems to be a fairly robust area of development. This means that only in extreme circumstances do children not develop language skills. Generally, children

learn to use language without being specifically taught, although we do know that there are many ways in which educators can support, facilitate and encourage particular types of language learning. On the other hand, learning to read does not seem to be such an automatic or robust process. Not everyone learns to read as effectively as they learn to speak. Some form of teaching is likely to be needed for reading proficiency to emerge.

While there are clear cultural differences in what language is learned and how this is learned, there is also remarkable similarity among the early language learning of most children, regardless of cultural background. In their early babbling, infants can generally produce the range of sounds used in languages across the world. As they start to say actual words, children refine these sound elements to match those of their language context; that is, sounds that relate to languages other than those around them are lost.

From birth, infants demonstrate some of the actions and interactions that are important in communication. These include abilities such as making eye contact, looking in the same direction as others and, later, joint attention, where the focus of the interaction is the same for both child and adult. Interactions based on turn taking (such as 'peekaboo') and utilising conversational skills are enjoyed by adults and young children in the first years of life.

Developing language competence involves a wide range of difficult and complex tasks. Not only are children expected to master the words of the language (vocabulary), they are also expected to master the sounds of language (phonology), how words are combined (grammar), the different purposes and uses of language (discourse) and how language can be used to influence the behaviour of others (pragmatics) (Hendrick & Weissman, 2006).

Young children's language development is rapid and intense. From the earliest expressions of crying and later babbling, children build an extensive repertoire of words and the ability to use these in many ways. Carey (1985) has described children learning about nine new words a day, every day, from their second year of life. Even though children may not utter their first word until around one year of age (Berk, 2009), it is important to realise that their comprehension, or their understanding of language, is not tied to this. Children understand what is said well before they can produce the same words.

As well as learning vocabulary and comprehending what has been said, children learn how to put words together to form meaningful phrases and sentences. Children learn about their environment through language and also learn to respond to their environment by using language.

Early experiences with language establish some of the parameters of interaction. For example, games of 'peekaboo' set up patterns of turn taking in interaction, setting the scene for more complex conversations as children's language skills develop. Adults provide a great deal of guidance and suggestion (scaffolding) in these early interactions, gradually relinquishing control as children's skills build. When adults establish joint attention with infants – that is, when they follow what an infant may be looking at and talk about that – infants learn a great deal about their environment as well as the language that describes that environment (Berk, 2009).

As children extend their vocabulary, they also extend their functional use of language. It seems to be that, regardless of their first language, children initially use language to get access to the things they want, and to regulate their own and other people's behaviour. As children become more proficient language learners and users, they extend these functions of language to include exploring and discovering the world around them, as well as entering into imaginative functions.

Early childhood educators can promote language learning through:
- listening to children
- encouraging children to talk about things that matter or are important to them
- engaging in conversation
- facilitating opportunities for children to engage in both speaking and listening
- recognising multiple literacies
- creating language-rich environments.

LEARNING MORE THAN ONE LANGUAGE

Many children in Australia are bilingual or multilingual. Some children learn more than one language simultaneously. For these children, language development in each language tends to proceed at about the same pace as for children who are learning one language. Some children are successive bilingual learners, learning one language and then adding another. Successive bilingual learners need a strong foundation in the first language before learning the second (Siraj-Blatchford & Clarke, 2000). Therefore, it is important to support the development of the first language when children are acquiring a second language. Young children entering early childhood services or the first years of school are still developing their first language, and are still developing concepts within this language. It is crucial for children's learning that they are able to continue using their first language (Genesee & Nicoladis, 2007).

Learning more than one language is a positive experience for children when the language development is supported and encouraged by the social and cultural context. As in all language learning, supportive relationships help to make the process meaningful, relevant and purposeful. A range of research indicates that children who are supported to learn more than one language can benefit in many ways, particularly in areas of cognitive development and linguistic awareness (Berk, 2009).

Many Aboriginal and Torres Strait Islander children are bilingual or multilingual. Sometimes their first language will be Standard Australian English; other times it will be traditional language or creole. Regardless of the language, it is a reminder that:

- First languages define every child — their knowledge, identity and relationships.
- First languages (FLs) are primarily acquired from families, and have been developing from birth, shaping the way children see and describe the world. Language is a powerful communicative tool, and Aboriginal and Torres Strait Islander children are generally competent users of their developing FLs when they come to kindergarten.

Foundations for Success: Guideline for extending and enriching learning for Aboriginal and Torres Strait Islander children in the Kindergarten year, p. 3, © 2013 State of Queensland, Department of Education.

There is incredible variation in the languages spoken by Aboriginal and Torres Strait Islander children. Some languages have been generated by the interaction of English and traditional languages, resulting in pidgins or creoles. This is often the case when communities were founded around missions, bringing together many disparate language groups and when people were prohibited from speaking their traditional languages. Some of the pidgins and creoles have names, such as Yumpla Tok and Torres Strait Creole; others are named after the locations in which they are spoken, such as Cape York Creole. In some locations, families use traditional languages, such as Wik Mungkan (Queensland Department of Education and Training, 2010). Sometimes the term Aboriginal English is applied to a wide variety of languages spoken by Aboriginal and Torres Strait Islanders. This generic term tends to hide the great diversity of languages that exist.

It is important to note that even when Aboriginal and Torres Strait Islander children do not speak traditional languages, they exist within social and cultural contexts that often reflect elements of traditional language and value traditional languages. When educators acknowledge the importance of traditional languages, they also acknowledge the cultural and personal significance of language for children and families. This in turn can contribute to a strong sense of cultural identity and pride in that identity (see Figure 3.12).

FIGURE 3.12 Language variations can be acknowledged in many ways.

Language variations such as pidgin or creole are often stigmatised, being compared unfavourably with Standard Australian English. Eades (1993, p. 6) emphasises that such variations do not represent 'bad' English; nor does the use of these languages imply deficiency in Standard Australian English. Rather, she notes that children who speak the many variations of Aboriginal and Torres Strait Islander languages are 'fluent, articulate and creative users of language … Respecting, valuing and understanding Aboriginal ways of using English is [a] significant step in respecting, valuing and understanding the identity and self-esteem of these children'.

DEVELOPING LITERACY

Many children demonstrate an interest in written and visual texts from an early age (*see* Figure 3.13). They may readily identify aspects of environmental print, be able to retell their favourite book or DVD, and become familiar with their name and sometimes the names of family members and friends. Some children are eager to start writing; others are easily frustrated by the motor demands of holding a pencil or crayon and making a series of marks on paper. Some children will be competent at negotiating a computer mouse and creating words and images on screen. Other children will engage in many and varied experiences with books in their early years, and still others will be less familiar with some of the accepted procedures for handling books but may be familiar with a range of everyday texts such as street signs, food packaging and advertising catalogues. Some children will have experiences with a range of digital and electronic texts often linked to their favourite popular culture characters and narratives. In other words, young children have many diverse literacy understandings.

FIGURE 3.13 Children demonstrate an interest in visual text from an early age.

Contemporary perspectives on literacy go beyond reading and writing to include speaking and listening, viewing and creating multimodal texts, and critical thinking about texts (Makin et al., 2007). Literacy is a social practice embedded within daily events such as shopping, meaning that children experience a range of literacy practices in English and in languages other than English within many complex and dynamic communities (Barton & Hamilton, 2000). Literacy is a 'process that is interactive, dynamic and purposeful' (ACT Department of Education and Community Services & the Australian Early Childhood Association, 1999, p. vii). This view is reflected in the EYLF, particularly through the learning outcome focused on children as effective communicators. In addition to promoting children's non-verbal and verbal communication, educators are urged to engage children in experiences that reflect a range of literacies, the many purposes of literacy and the many strategies that promote it. As children move to school, the expectations for literacy reflect the areas of language (knowing about the English language), literature (understanding, appreciating, responding to, analysing and creating literature) and literacy (expanding the repertoire of English usage).

DEVELOPING NUMERACY

While many early childhood educators have embraced literacy within their everyday programs, this has not always been the case with numeracy. In part, this reluctance can be explained by the predominance of Piagetian perspectives and the hesitation to incorporate intentional teaching at the expense of children's play. However, recent research indicates not only that children are competent numeracy learners, but also that numeracy forms an integral part of their everyday experiences. In a joint statement, the Australian Association of Mathematics Teachers and Early Childhood Australia (2006, p. 1) stated that

> all children in their early childhood years are capable of accessing powerful mathematical ideas that are both relevant to their current lives and form a critical foundation to their future mathematical and other learning. Children should be given the opportunity to access these ideas through high quality child-centred activities in their homes, communities, prior-to-school settings and schools.

A range of international, as well as Australian, research has recognised that children are capable mathematical learners and thinkers (Perry & Dockett, 2008), and results from a recent survey of Australian early childhood educators concluded that young children are capable of working with mathematical ideas that can be attributed to the areas of number, algebra, geometry, measurement, data analysis and probability (Hunting et al., 2008). While these terms are not used, the importance of mathematical thinking for young children is reflected in the inclusion of a range of these same areas within the EYLF, which refers to the importance of sharing and clarifying thinking and ideas, developing understanding of measurement and numbers, experimenting with ways of expressing ideas, recognising patterns and relationships and using symbols to represent meaning (*see* Figure 3.14). Curriculum for the Foundation Year of school also reflects these areas, though it formalises them into the content strands of number and algebra, measurement and geometry, and statistics and probability (ACARA, 2010).

Children's learning

Recent critiques of early childhood education have challenged the reliance on traditional developmental approaches, which emphasise Piagetian theories and approaches, such as developmentally appropriate practice (DAP) (Bredekamp & Copple, 1997). One of the strong trends to emerge has been influenced by the elaboration of Vygostky's theories of learning and development. Vygotsky argued that learning leads development, rather than the Piagetian position that learning

FIGURE 3.14 Children demonstrate an interest in numeracy from an early age.

is dependent on development. The Piagetian approach emphasises notions of developmental readiness, suggesting that some learning is not possible unless development has already occurred. Also from Piagetian theory, there is a focus on developing environments that promote individual children's exploration and discovery learning – where children are expected to learn through interaction with the environment. These environments are often characterised by free play. Inappropriate teaching – that is, teaching that occurs before children are considered developmentally ready – is regarded as an inhibitor for children's learning.

Vygotsky's (1978) alternative view was that learning leads development. He described learning as an inherently social activity, rather than something that occurrs as children individually explore and discover their world. Following Vygotsky, researchers have argued that interactions and relationships are the core of effective learning environments and that there is a complex relationship between learning and development (for example, Eun, 2010; Hatch, 2010; Hedegaard, 2009; Rogoff, 2003).

Learning through participation

Rogoff has described the importance of learning through participation. She uses the term Intent Community Participation to emphasise the importance of children observing, listening, anticipating and joining in community endeavours as the underpinning of learning. In this approach, experiences that connect children with the activities of their communities and that involve social interactions are regarded as cornerstones of learning. Participation leads to transformation – individuals are transformed through the processes of participation, just as the experience itself is transformed by the involvement of multiple participants (Rogoff, 2003). The guidance by more experienced members of the community is important for children, as they learn not only what is happening but also their role within the community. Those more-experienced others play crucial roles as they guide the children's participation, focus on developing joint attention with the children and adjust the requirements of participation according to each child's

proficiency. In Rogoff's words 'children everywhere learn skills in the context of their use and with the aid of those around them' (2003, pp. 69–70).

Learning in the early childhood years can be described and facilitated by reference to Rogoff's concept of participation. For example, children learn to write by engaging in the process of writing. Their interest and commitment to write is increased when there is a real purpose for writing, and when they can be assisted appropriately by more experienced writers. In such situations, a didactic adult providing instruction is unlikely to be necessary. This view firmly locates learning as a social endeavour, relying on collaboration at many different levels and involving different people guiding the participation of others.

Rogoff's definition of learning is that it is a 'process of changing participation in community activities … a process of taking on new roles and responsibilities' (2003, p. 284). The focus on participation situates this view of learning in a similar space to that of 'communities of practice' (Wenger, 1998), which also emphasises the central role of engagement within a particular community in learning.

Guided participation is not one particular strategy. Rather, it can take different forms in different contexts. Regardless of the form, guided participation is underpinned by the processes described by Rogoff as mutual bridging of meanings and mutual structuring of participation. Mutual bridging of meaning occurs when, 'in bringing different perspectives, partners seek a common perspective or language through which to communicate their ideas in order to co-ordinate their efforts' (Rogoff, 2003, p. 285). Such understandings develop between people as they seek a common ground and a common agenda for participation. The toddler and adult engaging in a tea party, using both actions and telegraphic speech, provide an example of this. Mutual structuring of participation relates to the structure of situations in which children participate. Rogoff (2003, p. 287) notes that 'the structuring occurs through choice of which activities children have access to observe and engage in, as well as through in-person endeavours, including conversations, recounting of narratives, and engagement in routines and play'. These experiences are at the core of early childhood education.

Making sense of the world

It is clear by children's interactions, actions, comments and questions that they are actively trying to make sense of their world. Children use many different strategies to make meaning – for example, they use their bodies, actions, words, drawings and play to engage with others, explore, reflect and represent their understandings. These are all ways of making meaning, or learning about the world (*see* Figure 3.15).

How children learn is quite a different question from what children should be learning. Most educators would agree that learning is important. However, there are different views on how learning occurs and about what is important in learning. This discussion outlines some different views of the processes of learning. A more detailed discussion of different approaches and perspectives can be found in McInerney and McInerney (2006).

In her definition of learning, Woolfolk (2010) notes that learning always involves a change in the learner. When learning occurs, the result is a change brought about by experience. So, changes that are a result of maturation, such as growing taller, are not considered to involve learning. But changes in how individuals interact with the environment in order to accommodate their changing height could be a result of learning. The elements of change and experience are important in any study of learning. There are many different theories or explanations of learning. One of the key differences among these theories is the explanation of what sort of change is involved in learning.

FIGURE 3.15 Children often make sense of the world through drawing: 'A picture of me at school with my friends'.

Behaviourist approaches to learning focus on changes in the observable behaviour of individuals. The child who touches a hot cup of tea, for example, may learn through the experience that hot tea is to be avoided, and the result could be a change in their behaviour. In behaviourist theory, the environment experienced by individuals is considered in terms of the stimuli available to individuals. Human behaviour is explained in terms of how people react to the environment. If the environment is rewarding, chances are that the behaviour will continue. In this approach, the emphasis is on what people do (their behaviour) and the connection of this to observable stimuli in the environment. Early childhood educators rely on behaviourist approaches in some of their everyday interactions. These include offering some form of reinforcement, or positive response, for behaviour considered desirable, such as stickers, stamps or praise and positive attention. Taking away some of the desirable elements of the environment – such as using time-out strategies, or removing the toy children were fighting over – also relates to behaviourist principles.

Cognitivist perspectives of learning offer an alternative view. These focus on learning as an internal mental process that cannot be observed. Cognitivist perspectives describe the changes that occur through learning as changes in an individual's ability to respond to, or understand, a particular situation (Woolfolk, 2010). Changes in behaviour are regarded as reflections of internal changes in understanding. As a result, cognitivists focus their study on the unobservable – knowledge, meaning, intentions, feeling and so on. These perspectives assume that people actively try to make sense of the world and that they do not just react unconsciously to the environment. People are regarded as capable of directing their attention to particular aspects of the environment, and interpreting and acting upon these. The role of the individual is seen to be one of filtering out and attending to relevant information (McInerney & McInerney, 2006). According to cognitivists, people try to make sense of the environment; that is, to attach meaning to people, places and events within the environment. The result is that they engage in processes of decision making and problem solving. With growth and experience, as well as the assistance of others, children are described as developing more complex mental structures that enable them to process information and to extract meaning. This function develops over time and through experience, so we would expect children to extract deeper and more complex meanings and understandings as they grow older and interact with different people and as their experiences broaden. Early childhood educators draw on cognitivist approaches when they engage with children in problem-solving experiences, discuss possibilities, support decision making and seek explanations for events and interactions.

As with most explanations of complex phenomena, it is not simply a matter of one set of perspectives being regarded as 'more right' than others. Contemporary perspectives of children's learning recognise the contributions of both behaviourist and cognitivist approaches to our understanding of how young children learn and how educators can support and facilitate this learning. However, they are not limited to these perspectives. Contemporary perspectives recognise that the social and cultural context of children, families and communities contributes significantly to children's learning (Rogoff, 2003) and a greater appreciation of the variability of individual development and learning. There are efforts to understand early childhood settings and schools as communities of practice (Wenger, 1998) and to consider children in context, rather than as individuals existing in isolation (Hatch, 2010; Rogoff, 2003).

How do children learn?

Questions of how children learn have exercised a great many researchers over a good many years. It became clear that theories focusing on stimulus and response connections could not explain all aspects of children's learning. Piaget's work was one area that focused on understanding how children learn, describing children's learning as a process of change influenced by children's interactions with the environment and the people within it. Children's thinking and learning was described as qualitatively different from that of adults. Piaget's stages of intellectual development have come to be a core of much early childhood practice. More recent interpretations and extrapolations of Piaget's work suggest that he didn't have all the answers. For example, Donaldson's (1978) work suggested that some of the tasks used by Piaget are confusing for children, with the result that they seem to perform poorly. Her focus on the importance of communication and considering alternative points of view opened up a range of new research agendas when considering young children's learning. While a lot can be gained from observing children with Piagetian theory in mind, educators need to be wary of letting

this one theory limit what they see and how they see it. Some of the descriptions of children associated with Piaget's theory focus on the limitations of young children; for example, they are described as egocentric, lacking the ability to think logically and so on. Yet much research now suggests that young children are indeed quite capable in many ways.

Eun (2010, p. 401) describes 'social interaction among two or more people' as the greatest motivating force for development and learning. Engaging with others in collaborative activities, with shared goals negotiated through dialogue, provides the basis for learning. This view reflects the earlier research of Vygotsky (1978) and Bruner (1983), who argued that language and communication are at the core of intellectual development. This is particularly evident in Vygotsky's description of the ZPD and Bruner's description of 'scaffolding' as a strategy by which more experienced individuals can support and guide the learning of the less experienced.

Learning dispositions

Margaret Carr (2001, p. 21) has described learning dispositions as:

> situated learning strategies plus motivation – participation repertoires from which a learner recognises, selects, edits, responds to, resists, searches for, and constructs learning opportunities … being ready, willing and able to participate in various ways: a combination of inclination, sensitivity to the occasion, and the relevant skill and knowledge.

This is similar to the definition used by Katz (1988, p. 30), who referred to dispositions as 'habits of mind'. A focus on dispositions reminds educators that learning is not only about content; just as everyone learns factual information, they also learn ways of approaching tasks and experiences. Early childhood educators can often name many dispositions they would like to foster within children, including helpfulness, curiosity, creativity, generosity, responsibility, caring and independence. Children learn these dispositions largely from their interactions with others.

Aligned with each of the strands of the New Zealand early childhood curriculum, Te Whāriki (Ministry of Education 1996), is a disposition. These, in turn, align with actions and behaviours. These are outlined in Table 3.1.

TABLE 3.1 Dispositions and behaviours from Te Whāriki (Ministry of Education 1996)

Dispositions	Behaviours
Courage (and curiosity)	Taking an interest
Trust (and playfulness)	Being involved
Perseverance – to tackle and persist with difficulty and uncertainty	Persisting with difficulty or uncertainty
Confidence to express an idea, a feeling or a point of view	Communicating with others
Responsibility for justice and fairness and the disposition to take on another perspective or point of view	Taking responsibility

Learning dispositions are regarded as fundamental outcomes of early childhood education. They provide the basis for children being 'ready, willing and able' to participate in a wide range of experiences; as Carr and Claxton (2002, p. 9) argue, the purpose of education:

is not so much the transmission of particular bodies of knowledge, skill and understanding as facilitating the development of the capacity and the confidence to engage in lifelong learning. Central to this enterprise is the development of positive learning dispositions, such as resilience, playfulness and reciprocity.

Educators and learning

Recognition of the importance of social and cultural contexts for development and learning, and of the importance of guided participation and scaffolding, highlight the importance of the educator and their role in intentional teaching. This can be quite different from the role adopted in programs based on Piagetian perspectives, where the emphasis has often been on setting up a rich environment and then facilitating, rather than guiding, children's interactions and learning. In some environments, educators have been hesitant to engage with children in play, fearing that this would interrupt the play and inhibit children's exploration and discovery. It certainly is the case that some teacher interactions can stifle play, or change the direction of children's activities. However, it is also possible that with careful and thoughtful interactions, educators can enrich and expand children's experiences in positive and creative ways. Eun (2010) talks about the need for educators to stretch learners, fostering and scaffolding learning, rather than waiting for it to happen. Where educators have positive relationships with children, they can be sensitive responders to children's culture, language, individual needs and interests, as they actively guide learning.

Sensitive and compassionate educators who provide guidance that is attuned to children's current level of understanding enable them to learn concepts that were initially beyond individual comprehension (Eun, 2010, p. 403).

Educators create positive and supportive learning environments when they:

- adopt the role of learner, as well as teacher
- build positive relationships with children
- are responsive to children's social and cultural contexts
- help children connect their learning – for example, by connecting home and school learning
- recognise the situated nature of learning
- acknowledge learning as a gradual process that occurs over time and as children build on existing knowledge and experience
- promote opportunities for collaboration in learning.

How educators promote learning largely depends on their pedagogy. The EYLF (DEEWR, 2009, p. 9) defines pedagogy as 'early childhood educators' professional practice, especially those aspects that involve building and nurturing relationships, curriculum decision-making, teaching and learning'.

This definition recognises that there will be many pedagogies, and that these will be relevant for different children, in different contexts over different times (*see* Chapter 7 for details about curriculum approaches and pedagogies). Hatch (2010) calls for teachers to develop a wide repertoire of teaching strategies as part of their overall pedagogy, reflecting the diverse children, families and contexts they meet in educational contexts (*see* Chapter 9 for repertoire of teaching strategies).

There is a long history of the use of play within early childhood education (*see* Figure 3.16). Recent explorations of the role and place of play have called for reconceptualisation of play-based pedagogy, focusing on the ways in which play can be both a vehicle for children's exploration and a venue for learning.

FIGURE 3.16 A child at play.

Children's play

Play has been a central element of early childhood education for some time. However, there are many different definitions and approaches to play and many ways in which children's play varies according to individual preferences, interests, abilities, contexts and supports. Article 31 of the United Nations Convention on the Rights of the Child (United Nations, 1989) highlights children's right to play, though the ways in which this is respected and enacted vary considerably. In urbanised communities, there is particular concern that a number of pressures have impinged on children's rights and opportunities to play. These pressures include living in urban areas where there may be few connections with nature, risk-averse societies, increasing stress in family life, educational pressures (Lester & Russell, 2010; Whitebread, 2012) and greater surveillance of children and children's spaces.

While a shared definition of play remains elusive, there is consensus that play can be complex and multidimensional. In their review, Lester and Russell (2010, p. 7) argue that:

> play is a behaviour that is distinguished by specific features that represent a unique way of being: a way of perceiving, feeling and acting in the world. The act of playing, where children appropriate time and space for their own needs and desires, has value for developing a range of flexible and adaptable responses to the environment.

Educators point to the value of play across areas such as social, emotional and cognitive domains. Partly, this derives from the attention to play in the cognitive development literature, where Piaget's (1962) description of stages of play accompanied his broader stage-based theory. As a consequence, the sensorimotor stage of development is associated with **functional play**, **symbolic play** with the preoperational stage and **games with rules** with the stage of concrete operations. A similar approach was identified by Parten's (1932) attention to the social stages of play, resulting in the description of **unoccupied play**, **onlooker play**, **solitary play**, **parallel play**, **associative play** and **cooperative play**.

Types of play

Rather than referring to stages, some categorisations of play refer instead to play types. These highlight:

- physical play
- play with objects
- symbolic play
- pretend play
- sociodramatic play
- games with rules.

PHYSICAL PLAY

This involves active play such as jumping, running, playing with balls, cycling and the like as well as fine motor activities such as construction or drawing. Physical play develops as children develop a range of physical competencies. It is reported that about one fifth of the play of children in the preschool years involves gross motor physical play (Pellegrini & Smith, 1998). Two forms of physical play that have attracted a great deal of attention are rough-and-tumble play and risky play.

Rough-and-tumble play

Rough-and-tumble play is often characterised as play fighting. It usually involves activities such as wrestling, rolling around on the ground, picking each other up and/or chasing. The difference between real fighting and rough-and-tumble play is the laughing and smiling that accompanies the latter. Rough-and-tumble play can help children establish the boundaries between play and fighting, while at the same time promoting understandings of physical strengths, limits and the impact of actions on others.

Functional play

Repeated use of objects or actions.

Symbolic play

The use of symbols to represent people and objects.

Games with rules

Play according to established rules.

Unoccupied play

Children are in the vicinity of play.

Onlooker play

Children observe play, but do not seek to enter the play.

Solitary play

Playing alone.

Parallel play

Playing near others, but with no interaction.

Associative play

Group play, but without common goals.

Cooperative play

Group play working towards a shared goal.

Risky play

Risky play involves children taking physical risks in their play. It can be seen when children climb or swing as high as they can, or jump from heights. Supporters of risky play argue that some societies have become overprotective of children, recognise that it is not possible to protect children from all risks and emphasise that children learn to manage risks through engaging in risky play. Opponents highlight the very real dangers of some risky play as well as a social focus on mitigating risks (Sandseter, 2013). For children, risky play tends to include attempting something new and/or unfamiliar, pushing boundaries and overcoming fear (Stephenson, 2003).

PLAY WITH OBJECTS

This is seen as infants grasp, chew and drop objects, as well as when children incorporate objects in their play, engage in construction or actively investigate the properties of objects. Play with objects often occurs as part of other forms of play, such as pretend play or physical play.

SYMBOLIC PLAY

Children play with symbols in many ways – as they speak, sing, make music, draw, paint, read, write, count and engage with technology. Adults notice when children start to use language and play with the sounds, words and rhythms of their culture. They also notice when children start to draw numerals or groups of objects. While play around numeracy and literacy is very important, so is children's play with visual media and music.

PRETEND PLAY

Pretend play signals children's developing understandings of representation. As children engage in pretense, they start to use symbols to stand for people and objects in the real world. This use of symbols occurs at around the same time that children start to become proficient users of language. The two symbol systems – language and pretense – contribute to children's developing understandings of the world and the people, places and objects within it.

SOCIODRAMATIC PLAY

Sociodramatic play involves shared pretend play as children adopt roles and act out interactive play scripts. It can become very complex, as a range of players adopt roles, use props and act out evolving or predetermined scripts. Complex sociodramatic play can involve multiple episodes enacted over extended periods of time (Monighan Nourot, 2006).

Pretend play is also a space where children experience and exercise elements of self-regulation. This comes from applying the rules that are evident in play as well as the opportunities to experience and manage emotionally stressful events through play (Berk, Mann, & Ogan, 2006).

GAMES WITH RULES

Children are often fascinated with rules and incorporate these into their play. Sometimes, they will apply rules they have generated themselves, other times they will apply established rules to games such as skipping or hopscotch. Children can also be adept at changing the rules, depending on the circumstances of play. Part of the motivation for engaging in games with rules can be the desire to engage with other children – that is, games with rules are often the basis for social interactions.

> ## EXAMPLE 3.1
> ### Changing the rules
>
> Maurice and Eva are playing the card game *Memory*. After several turns where he cannot find a matching pair, Maurice turns over a third card and then a fourth. On the last occasion, he is able to match his original card.
>
> Eva complains that his actions are not fair. 'You're not allowed to do that!'
>
> Maurice explains, 'It's a new rule'.
>
> 'Not it's not', counters Eva.
>
> 'Yes it is. That's the way we play it at my house.'

Play and technology

Increasingly, young children's play focus involves technology. While children incorporate technology into their play, there can be a tendency for educators to ignore this element in the provisions for play (Mawson, 2011). At times, play with the virtual worlds accessed through new technologies, such as computers or tablets, is regarded as taking away from play in the real world (Yelland, 2011). Yet, recent studies indicate that children's engagement in virtual worlds does afford opportunities for play and that these often relate to play in the real world (Marsh, 2010). Rather than ignoring these opportunities, educators need to examine these, with a view to recognising both the benefits and possible limitations of these opportunities. Edwards (2013) argues that there are multiple pedagogical opportunities for educators to engage with children and their play with, through and about technology.

Play as a social experience

Much of the recent research about play draws on the work of Vygotsky and those who have revisited his initial writings about play. The resultant exploration of play using cultural-historical theory (Bodrova & Leong, 2011) outlines play as a mode of activity, particularly a form of cultural activity. This approach emphasises the nature of the activity, rather than the objects of play (van Oers, 2013). It is important to note that Vygotsky's (1978) discussions of play referred to pretend play – not necessarily to the range of play noted above. However, as already noted, pretend play can incorporate play with objects, technology and many of the other types of play noted above.

Vygotsky's writings highlighted the importance of children's pretend play – their use of symbols and representation – in the development of language and in promoting self-regulation. Essential features of such play are the creation of an imaginary situation, the adoption of roles within the play and the playing out of those roles according to social rules (Bodrova & Leong, 2011). Creating an imaginary situation requires awareness of both real and pretend contexts and adopting roles with rules involves recognition of both internal (mental) and external (physical) actions. These actions contribute to the development of higher mental functions, as well as to children's developing self-regulation. Building on Vygotsky's initial thinking, Elkonin (2005) outlined four ways that play contributes to the development of higher mental functions:

1. Children are motivated to play and through play, to consider both short-term and long-term goals. For example, to 'prepare dinner' children need to think about what is needed and what they will do, before they can achieve the desired play.
2. Play often requires children to acknowledge the perspectives of others.
3. Pretend play requires mental representation. This is linked to the development of abstract thinking and imagination.
4. Play promotes children's deliberate actions as they identify and follow the rules of play.

Play facilitates children's participation in many of the routines of social and cultural contexts. Within play, children explore and practise some of the skills that facilitate participation, as well as receiving feedback from others about the nature of that participation. Rogoff (2003) notes that children also change some of these routines and rituals through their participation. Through participation, children learn the structure and social expectations of events. For example, participating in play conversations facilitates an awareness of the nature of conversations (such as turn taking, speaking and listening) and can provide opportunities to explore the nature of conversations with children and with adults. Play conversations have the added dimension of not being 'for-real' and so do not carry sanctions or penalties for making mistakes. Children can play with the scripts of real and imagined worlds and, in doing so, develop a greater understanding of the rules and roles of those around them.

Benefits of play

The potential learning benefits of play are well documented. One of the benefits of play for cognitive development is the focus on 'means' rather than 'ends' (Pellegrini, 2009). It is argued that focusing on processes, rather than an end product, provides the freedom to explore and to 'try out new behaviours, exaggerate, modify, abbreviate or change the sequence of behaviours, [and] endlessly repeat slight variations of behaviours' (Whitebread, 2012, p. 15). Such actions are characteristic of problem-solving skills.

In addition, the development of private speech – where children seem to guide their own actions with self-commentary – supports not only play and language, but also is posited as supporting children's **metacognitive** and self-regulatory capabilities (May, 2013). Metacognitive skills allow individuals to monitor and control cognitive processes. For example, awareness of what interests us, or strategies to help us remember, influence our approaches to learning. Young children develop awareness of their own competencies as well as strategies to assist them, largely through play and playful contexts. For example, strategies are in evidence when children play the card game *Memory*, or when they recall the way a building looked in order to re-create it with blocks.

Play has a central role in learning for Vygotsky, as it almost always creates a ZPD. So, through play, children have the opportunity to expand their world. Play, then, is an extremely beneficial activity

Metacognition

Awareness, understanding and analysis of our own cognitive processes.

FIGURE 3.17 Play can take many forms.

FIGURE 3.18 Play with peers provides opportunities for development and learning across many areas.

FIGURE 3.19 There are many opportunities for problem solving within play.

where children are learning through their interactions, as well as adopting and working through the rules and values of their own cultural group (*see* Figures 3.17, 3.18 and 3.19).

Play for children with special needs

The potential benefits of play are noted for all children – including those with special needs. In planning for play when children have special needs, it is important for educators to consider the range of resources available and the ways in which environments can support or limit play. Research with adolescents suggests that environmental factors – such as limited wheelchair access to some play areas – influence play opportunities, as do psychosocial factors, such as feelings of belonging and confidence. Positive approaches to play for these young people include a focus on changing the environment – rather than interventions designed to 'fix' a problem with the individuals themselves; it also focuses on recognition of the social element of play, with children with special needs – like most others – seeking and enjoying the company of others, and the provision of opportunities to engage in play (Pollock, et al. 1997). The same elements would seem important in the provision of play opportunities for young children with special needs.

Play-based pedagogy

In recent years, the role of play in early childhood education has been challenged by:

- changing notions of play that question the developmental base underpinning it
- recognition of the diversity of ways in which children learn
- increasing demands for academic instruction
- uncertainty from educators about their role in play
- the changing nature of play as children engage with popular culture and a range of technologies
- considerable variation in the quality of provision for, and engagement in, children's play.

(adapted from Dockett, 2011)

Play-based pedagogy

Where play is characterised as a planned and purposeful activity, built around a well-resourced environment and rich interactions with adults (British Educational Research Association Early years Special Interest Group (BERA-SIG), 2003).

From this has emerged a call to articulate the rationale and purposes of play within early childhood education and clarify the roles of educators within play, particularly within the context of sociocultural understandings. One result has been discussion of **play-based pedagogy**, where play is characterised as a planned and purposeful activity, built around a well-resourced environment and rich interactions with adults (British Educational Research Association Early Years Special Interest Group (BERA-SIG), 2003). This trend can be seen in the EYLF (2009, p. 15):

> Early childhood educators take on many roles in play with children and use a range of strategies to support learning. They engage in sustained shared conversations with children to extend their thinking. They provide a balance

between child-led, child initiated and educator supported learning. They create learning environments that encourage children to explore, solve problems, create and construct … They actively support the inclusion of all children in play, help children to recognise when play is unfair and offer constructive ways to build a caring, fair and inclusive learning community.

Yet, Rogers (2011, p. 5) argues that the coupling of play and pedagogy in early childhood education is problematic for several reasons:

'first because traditionally, the concept of play has been positioned in marked opposition to its apparently more worthwhile counterpart, work (play *versus* work) … Second, theorising "play *as* work" … may obscure the ways in which play may become a technique of social control and a means of transmitting assumptions and beliefs regarding the nature and purpose of childhood … Third, the *pedagogisation* of play (Rogers 2011) has meant that play has increasingly become an instrument for learning future competencies'.

As one means to address this, Rogers (2011, p. 6) challenges educators to view play from inside perspectives – that is, to consider the perspectives of the players about play, drawing attention to 'the content, nature and dynamic of play to inform pedagogy in a reciprocal and relational way'. Such an approach prioritises relationships and the co-construction of play, focusing on the social elements of play, whether with other children or adults. It also positions play as an opportunity for children to exercise agency, demonstrate competence, engage with peers and to seek and resist interaction with adults. This approach reminds us that play is complex and multifaceted.

Reconceptualising play-based pedagogy can help us recognise the complexity, as well as the potential, of play for teaching and learning. Features of such a play-based pedagogy include:

- recognition of the complexity and diversity of play, rather than an expectation of any universality of play
- awareness that play has multiple forms and types
- acceptance that all play is neither positive nor desirable – play can be used to exclude, as well as to include, others
- willingness to critique the theoretical dimensions of play
- focus on social and cultural contexts, including power relations, and the enactment of these in play
- increased focus on the interactive roles of adults and other children in play as they engage with children to co-construct knowledge, promote challenge and support play that is socially and conceptually complex
- exploration and documentation of the links between play and learning
- generation of opportunities for educators to reflect on their pedagogies of play
- incorporation of multiple perspectives of play, including those of children, families and educators.

(adapted from Dockett, 2011)

Within this framework, it is possible to outline many ways in which educators can support and promote complex play. For example, from their base of cultural-historical theory, Bodrova and Leong (2011) advocate pedagogy that promotes:

- using toys in symbolic ways – reliance on the use of the object as representation, rather than the object itself. Adult scaffolding can encourage representation in many ways
- developing consistent and extended play sequences – not only providing the time and space to do this, but also providing the adult support and encouragement for the construction of complex and ongoing pretend scenarios
- developing and maintaining play roles and rules – adding to the complexity of play by introducing a range of roles and acknowledging the rules that accompany these.

At the beginning of this section, we referred to Article 31 of the UN Convention on the Rights of the Child. We argue that educators support children's right to play when we consider not only

what provisions we make for play, but also reflect on what we mean by play, what we value in play, what we expect from play and how we articulate this; in other words, when we examine our beliefs about play as well as our actions. In this vein, McLane (2003, p. 11) urges educators to 'know enough about play to be both its advocates and its sceptics ... [to] recognise play's potential without romanticising it and reducing it to fuzzy, simplistic slogans'.

Conclusion and reflection

As educators come to know the children with whom they work and interact, they draw on a range of knowledge, skills, understandings, expectations, beliefs and values. Many elements contribute to the ways they approach children and what they regard as important. They too are embedded within a range of social and cultural contexts that influence what is valued and of value. Reflecting on what is know about children's learning, development and play provides a basis for educator's actions. Rather than taking for granted an established theory, set of milestones or expectations about play, this book urges educators to be critically reflexive, evaluating what is known and considering what it is they do not yet know.

Questions for reflection

1. What are the theoretical approaches that underpin your approaches to working with young children and their families? Have these changed over time? If so, what has caused them to change? If not, what might cause them to change?

2. What dispositions would you like to encourage among children?

3. What do you consider to be appropriate roles for adults in children's play?

Key terms

accommodation, 84

adaptation, 84

agency, 76

assimilation, 84

associative play, 96

attachment, 78

bioecological theory, 71

context, 71

cooperative play, 96

cultural-historical theory, 73

functional play, 96

games with rules, 96

guided participation, 73

internalisation, 86

intersubjectivity, 87

metacognition, 99

onlooker play, 96

organisation, 84

parallel play, 96

person, 71

play-based learning, 69

play-based pedagogy, 100

private speech, 86

proximal processes, 71

scaffolding, 87

schemes, 84

self-concept, 79

self-efficacy, 80

self-esteem, 79

solitary play, 96

symbolic play, 96

temperament, 78

time, 71

unoccupied play, 96

zone of proximal development, 86

Online study resources

Visit http://login.cengagebrain.com and use the access code that comes with this book for 12 months access to the student resources for this text.

CourseMate Express

The CourseMate Express website contains a range of resources and study tools for this chapter, including:

- Online video activities
- Online research activities
- A revision quiz
- Matching pair exercises
- A list of key weblinks
- A chapter glossary, flashcards and crossword to help you revise terminology
- and more!

Search me! education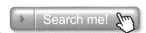

Explore **Search me! education** for articles relevant to this chapter. Fast and convenient, Search me! education is updated daily and provides you with 24-hour access to full text articles from hundreds of scholarly and popular journals, ebooks and newspapers, including *The Australian* and *The New York Times*. Log in to Search me! through http://login.cengage.com and try searching for the following key words:

- development
- learning
- cultural-historical

- bioecological
- relationships
- play.

Search tip: **Search me! education** contains information from both local and international sources. To get the greatest number of search results, try using both Australian and American spellings in your searches, e.g. 'globalisation' and 'globalization'; 'organisation' and 'organization'

Recommended resources

Department of Education, Employment and Workforce Relations (DEEWR) 2009, *Belonging, Being and Becoming: The Early Years Learning Framework for Australia*, Commonwealth of Australia, Canberra.

Rogers, S 2011 (ed), *Rethinking Play and Pedagogy in Early Childhood Education*, Routledge, London.

Rogoff, B 2003, *The Cultural Nature of Human Development*, Oxford University Press, Oxford.

Key weblinks

Australian Research Alliance for Children and Youth (ARACY): http://www.aracy.org.au

Centre for Community Child Health: http://www.rch.org.au/ccch/

Early Childhood Australia: http://earlychildhoodaustralia.org.au

Kidsmatter: http://www.kidsmatter.edu.au/ec/

National Children's Bureau: http://www.ncb.org.uk/

National Institute for Child Health and Human Development: http://www.nichd.nih.gov/

Secretariat of National Aboriginal and Islander Child Care: http://www.snaicc.asn.au

Telethon Institute: http://www.ichr.uwa.edu.au/

UNICEF: http://www.unicef.org.au

Zero to Three: http://www.zerotothree.org/

References

ACT Department of Education and Community Services & the Australian Early Childhood Association 1999, *Issues and Practices in Literacy Development*, AECA, Canberra.

Atkinson J, Nelson J & Atkinson C 2009, 'Trauma, transgenerational transfer and effects on community wellbeing' in N Purdie, P Dudgeon & R Walker (eds). *Working Together: Aboriginal and Torres Strait Islander Mental Health and Wellbeing Principles and Practice*, Canberra, Department of Health and Ageing, pp. 135–44.

Australian Association of Mathematics Teachers and Early Childhood Australia (AAMT/ECA) 2006, *Position Paper on Early Childhood Mathematics*, http://www.aamt.edu.au/Publications-and-statements/Position-statements/Alternative-formats/Early-Childhood-Position-black, accessed 3 April 2014.

Australian Curriculum, Assessment and Reporting Authority (ACARA) 2010, *Australian Curriculum*, http://www.australiancurriculum.edu.au/Home, accessed 3 April 2014.

Barton, D & Hamilton, M 2000, 'Literacy practices', in D Barton, M Hamilton & R Ivanic (eds), *Situated Literacies: Reading and Writing in Context*, Routledge, London, pp. 7–15.

Berk, L 2009, *Child Development*, 8th edn., Allyn & Bacon, Boston, MA.

Berk, L, Mann, T & Ogan, A 2006, 'Make-believe play: Wellspring for development of self-regulation', in D Singer, R Golinkoff & K Hirsh-Pasek (eds.), *Play = Learning: How Play Motivates and Enhances Children's Cognitive and Social-Emotional Growth*, Oxford University Press, Oxford, pp. 74–100.

Bjorklund, DF 2005, *Children's Thinking: Cognitive Development and Individual Differences*, 4th edn., Wadsworth, Belmont, CA.

Bodrova, E, & Leong, D 2011, 'Revisiting Vygotskian perspectives on play', in S Rogers (ed.), *Rethinking Play and Pedagogy in Early Childhood Education*, Routledge, London, pp. 60-72.

Bowman, BT, Donovan, MS & Burns, MS (eds) 2001, *Eager to Learn: Educating our Preschoolers*, National Academy Press, Washington, DC.

Bredekamp, S & Copple, C 1997, *Developmentally Appropriate Practice in Early Childhood Programs Serving Children from Birth through Age 8*, NAEYC, Washington, DC.

British Educational Research Association Early Years Special Interest Group (BERA-SIG) 2003, *Early Years Research: Pedagogy Curriculum and Adult Roles, Training and Professionalism*, http://www.bera.ac.uk/files/reviews/beraearlyyearsreview31may03.pdf accessed 15 July 2014.

Bronfenbrenner, U 1979, *The Ecology of Human Development*, Harvard University Press, Cambridge, MA.

Bronfenbrenner, U & Morris, PA 2006, 'The bioecological model of human development', in RM Lerner (ed.), *Vol. 1 of Handbook of Child Psychology: Theoretical Models of Human Development*, 6th edn., Wiley, Hoboken, NJ, pp. 793–828.

Bruner, J 1983, *Child's Talk*, Norton, New York.

Carey, S 1985, *Conceptual Change in Childhood*, MIT Press, Cambridge, MA.

Carlson, F 2009, 'Rough and tumble play 101', *Exchange*, July/August, pp. 70–73.

Carr, M 2001, *Assessment in Early Childhood Settings*, London, Paul Chapman.

Carr, M, & Claxton, G 2002, 'Tracking the development of learning dispositions', *Assessment in Education*, vol. 9, no.1, pp. 9–37.

Case, R 1985, *Intellectual Development: Birth to Adulthood*, Academic Press, Orlando, FL.

Cohen, LB & Cashon, CH 2006, 'Infant cognition', in D Kuhn & R Siegler (eds), *Handbook of Child Psychology: Vol 2. Cognition, Perception and Language*, 6th edn., Wiley Hoboken, NJ, pp. 214–51.

Dahlberg, G, Moss, P & Pence, A 2007, *Beyond Quality in Early Childhood Education and Care: Postmodern Perspectives*, Falmer Press, London.

Davies, B 1989, *Frogs and Snails and Feminist Tales: Preschool Children and Gender*, Allen & Unwin, Sydney.

Degotardi, S 2013, '"I think-I can": Acknowledging and promoting agency during educator-infant play', in O Lillemyr, S Dockett & B Perry (eds), *Varied Perspectives on Play and Learning*, Charlotte NC, Information Age, pp. 75–90.

Dockett, S 2011, 'The challenge of play for early childhood educators', in S Rogers (ed.), *Rethinking Play and Pedagogy in Early Childhood Education: Concepts, Contexts and Cultures*, Routledge, London, pp. 32–47.

Donaldson, M 1978, *Children's Minds*, Norton, New York.

Dunn, J 2004, *Children's Friendships: The Beginnings of Intimacy*, Blackwell, Oxford.

Duran E & Duran B 1995, *Native American Post-colonial Psychology*, Plenum Press, Albany.

Eades, D 1993, *Aboriginal English, PEN 93*, Primary English Teaching Association, Marrickville, NSW, http://www.petaa.edu.au/resources/petaa-papers/pen-93, accessed 15 July 2014.

Edwards, S 2013, 'Digital play in the early years: A contextual response to the problem of integrating technologies and play-based pedagogies in the early childhood curriculum', *European Early Childhood Education Research Journal*, vol. 21, no. 2, pp. 199–212.

Elder, GH 1998, 'The life course as developmental theory', *Child Development*, vol. 69, no. 1, pp. 1–12.

Elkonin, D 2005, 'The psychology of play: Chapter 1', *Journal of Russian and East European Psychology*, vol. 43, no. 1, pp. 22–48. (Original work published 1978).

Erikson, EH 1968, *Identity, Youth, and Crisis*, Norton, New York.

Eun, B. 2010, 'From learning to development: A sociocultural approach to instruction', *Cambridge Journal of Education*, vol. 40, no. 4, pp. 401–18.

Fleer, M, Anning, A & Cullen, J (eds) 2004, *Early Childhood Education: Society and Culture*, Sage, London.

Genesee, F & Nicoladis, E 2007, 'Bilingual first language acquisition', in E Hoff & M Shatz (eds), *Blackwell Handbook of Language Development*, Blackwell, Malden, MA, pp. 324–42.

Grieshaber, S & Cannella, G (eds) 2001, *Embracing Identities in Early Childhood Education: Diversity and Possibilities*, Teachers College Press, New York.

Halford, GS & Andrews, G 2006, 'Reasoning and problem solving', in D Kuhn & R Siegler (eds), *Handbook of Child Psychology: Vol 2. Cognition, Perception and Language*, 6th edn., Wiley, Hoboken, NJ, pp. 557–608.

Hatch, JA 2010, 'Rethinking the relationship between learning and development: teaching for learning in early childhood classrooms', *The Educational Forum*, vol. 74, pp. 258–68.

Hedegaard, M 2009, 'Children's development from a cultural-historical approach: Children's activity in everyday local settings as foundation for their development', *Mind, Culture and Society*, vol. 16, no. 1, pp. 64–82.

Hendrick, J & Weissman P 2006, *The Whole Child*, 8th edn., Pearson, Upper Saddle River, NJ.

Hunting, R, Bobis, J, Doig, B, English, L, Mousley, J, Mulligan, J, Papic, M, Pearn, C, Perry, B, Robbins, J, Wright, R & Young-Loveridge, J 2008, *Mathematical Thinking of Preschool Children in Rural and Regional Australia: Research and Practice*, La Trobe University, Bendigo.

James, A & Prout, A 1997, *Constructing and Reconstructing Childhood: Contemporary Issues in the Sociological Study of Childhood*, 2nd edn., Falmer Press, London.

Katz, L 1988, 'What should young children be learning?', *American Educator*, Summer, pp. 29–45.

Lester, S & Russell, W 2010, *Children's Right to Play: An Examination of the Importance of Play in the Lives of Children Worldwide*. Bernard van Leer Foundation, The Hague, The Netherlands. http://www.bernardvanleer.org/Childrens-right-to-play-An-examination-of-the-importance-of-play-in-the-lives-of-children-worldwide, accessed 3 April 2014.

Mac Naughton, G 2000, *Rethinking Gender in Early Childhood Education*, Allen & Unwin, Sydney.

Mac Naughton, G 2004, 'The politics of logic in early childhood research: A case of the brain, hard facts, trees and rhizomes', *Australian Educational Researcher*, vol. 31, no. 3, pp. 87–104.

Makin, L, Jones Diaz, C & McLachlan, C (eds) 2007, *Literacies in Early Childhood: Changing Views, Challenging Practices*, Elsevier, Sydney.

Marsh, HW, Ellis, LA & Craven, R 2002, 'How do preschool children feel about themselves? Unravelling measurement and multidimensional self-concept structure', *Developmental Psychology*, vol. 38, no. 3, pp. 376–93.

Marsh, J 2010, 'Young children's play in online virtual worlds', *Journal of Early Childhood Research*, vol. 8, no.1, pp. 23–39.

Mawson, B 2011 'Technological funds of knowledge in children's play: Implications for early childhood educators', *Australasian Journal of Early Childhood*, vol. 36, no. 1, pp. 30–35.

May, P 2013, *The Thinking Child: Laying the Foundations of Understanding and Competence*, Routledge, Abingdon, Oxon.

McDevitt, TM & Ormrod, JE 2007, *Child Development and Education*, 3rd edn., Pearson, Upper Saddle River, NJ.

McInerney, D & McInerney, V 2006, *Educational Psychology: Constructing Learning*, 4th edn., Pearson, Sydney.

McLane, J 2003, *"Does not". "Does too". Thinking about Play in the Early Childhood Classroom*. Erikson Institute Occasional Paper Number 4. www.erikson.edu/wp-content/uploads/OP_mclane.pdf, accessed 3 April 2014.

Miller, JG 1997, 'Cultural influences on the development of conceptual differentiation in person description', *British Journal of Developmental Psychology*, vol. 5, no. 4, pp. 309–19.

Ministry of Education 1996, *Te Whāriki*, http://www.educate.ece.govt.nz/~/media/Educate/Files/Reference%20Downloads/whariki.pdf, accessed 3 April 2014.

Monighan Nourot, P 2006, 'Sociodramatic play: Pretending together', in DP Fromberg, & D Bergin (eds.), *Play from Birth to Twelve*, 2nd edn., Routledge, New York, pp. 87–101.

National Scientific Council on the Developing Child 2009, *Young Children Develop in an Environment of Relationships*, Working paper no. 1, http://developingchild.harvard.edu/index.php/resources/reports_and_working_papers/working_papers/wp1/, accessed 3 April 2014.

Parten, M 1932, 'Social participation among preschool children', *Journal of Abnormal and Social Psychology*, vol. 27, pp. 243–69.

Pellegrini, A 2009, *The Role of Play in Human Development*, Oxford, Oxford University Press.

Pellegrini, A & Smith, P 1998, 'Physical activity play: the nature and function of a neglected aspect of play', *Child Development*, vol. 69, no. 3, pp. 577–98.

Perry, B & Dockett, S 2008 'Young children's access to powerful mathematical ideas', in L English (ed.), *Handbook of International Research in Mathematics Education*, 2nd edn., Routledge, New York, pp. 75–108.

Piaget, J 1962, *Play, Dreams and Imitation in Childhood*, Norton, New York.

Pollock, N, Stewart, D, Law, M, Sahagian-Whalen, S, Harvey, S & Toal, C 1997 'The meaning of play for young people with physical disabilities', *Canadian Journal of Occupational Therapy*, vol. 64, no. 1, pp. 25–31.

Queensland Department of Education and Training 2010, *Language Perspectives*, http://www.languageperspectives.org.au, accessed 3 April 2014.

Queensland Department of Education, Training and the Arts 2007, *Foundations for Success: Guidelines for an Early Learning Program in Aboriginal and Torres Strait communities*, Queensland Government, Brisbane, Qld.

Rogers, S 2011 'Play and pedagogy: A conflict of interests?', in S Rogers (ed.), *Rethinking Play and Pedagogy in Early Childhood Education*, Routledge, London, pp. 5–18.

Rogoff, B 2003, *The Cultural Nature of Human Development*, Oxford University Press, Oxford.

Sandseter, EBH 2103, 'Learning risk management through play', in OF Lillemyr, S Dockett & B Perry (eds.), *Varied Perspectives on Play and Learning*. Information Age, Charlotte, NC, pp. 141–57.

Schweder, RA, Goodnow, JJ, Hatano, G, LeVine, RA, Markus, HR & Miller, P 1998, 'The cultural psychology of development: One mind, many mentalities', in W Damon (ed.), *Handbook of Child Psychology, Vol. 1, Theoretical Models of Human Development*. John Wiley & Sons, New York, pp. 865–937.

Schweinhart, LJ & Weikart, DP 1997, 'The High/Scope Preschool Curriculum Comparison Study through age 23', *Early Childhood Research Quarterly*, vol. 12, pp. 117–43.

Shonkoff, J & Phillips, D (eds) 2000, *From Neurons to Neighborhoods: The Science of Early Childhood Development*, National Academy Press, Washington, DC.

Siraj-Blatchford, I & Clarke, P 2000, *Supporting Identity, Diversity and Language in the Early Years*, Open University Press, Buckingham.

Stephenson, A 2003, 'Physical risk-taking: Dangerous or endangered?', *Early Years*, vol. 23, no. 1, pp. 35–43.

Twardosz, S 2012, 'Effects of experience on the brain: The role of neuroscience in early education and development', *Early Education and Development*, vol. 23, pp. 96–119.

United Nations 1989, *Convention on the Rights of the Child*, http://www.unicef.org/crc/, accessed 3 April 2014.

van Oers, D 2013, 'Is it play? Towards a reconceptualisation of role play from an activity theory perspective', *European Early Childhood Education Research Journal*, vol. 21, no. 2, pp. 185–98.

Vygotsky, L 1978, *Mind in Society: The Development of Higher Psychological Processes*, Harvard University Press, Cambridge, MA.

Wenger, E 1998, *Communities of Practice: Learning, Meaning and Identity*, Cambridge University Press, Cambridge.

Whitebread, D 2012, *The Importance of Play*, http://www.importanceofplay.eu/IMG/pdf/dr_david_whitebread_-_the_importance_of_play.pdf, accessed 3 April 2014.

Woolfolk, A 2010, *Educational Psychology*, 11th edn., Allyn & Bacon, Boston, MA.

Yelland, N 2011, 'Reconceptualising play and learning in the lives of young children', *Australasian Journal of Early Childhood*, vol. 36, no. 2, pp. 4–12.

CHAPTER FOUR

EVALUATING AND REFLECTING TO STRENGTHEN PROGRAMS

Chapter learning focus

This chapter will investigate:

- concepts of evaluation and reflection to strengthen programs
- principles for evaluation and reflection
- evaluation tools and processes
- reflection tools and processes
- strategic planning
- strengthening programs to extend all children's learning.

Introduction

As investigated in other chapters, the planning process involves many phases; for example, developing philosophies, understanding the setting and evaluating and reflecting upon the program. This chapter will assist educators to use the principles, processes and tools of evaluation and reflection to analyse gathered information to recommend program improvements. The underlying vision is to extend learning for all children through strengthening the program.

Selecting useful tools and processes for evaluation and reflection begins with recognising the theoretical perspectives, beliefs and values embedded in the setting/school philosophy. Although **evaluation** and reflection often involve **assessment** of children's learning, this chapter investigates evaluation and reflection concerning the program, while assessment is examined in Chapter 8. When reading this chapter, educators and education students in early childhood settings and schools can draw on their own experiences of evaluation and reflection and consider how improving programs extends learning for all children.

This chapter outlines the purpose of evaluation and reflection and then investigates some principles, tools and processes for evaluation and reflection. Collaborating with **partners** is a significant dimension in many of these principles and processes. Setting/school-based strategic planning can provide clarity and focus for holistic long-term planning through evaluation and reflection that continually strengthen programs.

What has been your experience of evaluation in your life and work? Who was involved? How did evaluation improve the situation? Why? Why not?

Evaluation

Occurs when educators, families, children, community members and policymakers purposefully collect evidence, analyse and judge the information, and make recommendations that improve the program.

Assessment

Takes place when educators, families, children, community members and policymakers make sense of all children's learning over time across differing contexts and purposes in order to extend their learning.

Partners

The people involved in the setting/school with whom educators work, including children, families, managers, policy makers and community members.

Reflection and evaluation to strengthen programs

Source: KU Hebersham Preschool, 2014

FIGURE 4.1 Evaluation involves educators, families and children in strengthening the program.

This section of the chapter investigates the nature, rationale and contexts for evaluation and reflection. Participating in program evaluation is one of the mandatory responsibilities for educators in early childhood settings and schools. In early childhood settings, program evaluation for quality is the focus of the National Standard (ACECQA, 2011; 2013), including the implementation of *Belonging, Being and Becoming: The Early Years Learning Framework* (EYLF) (DEEWR, 2009, p.8). This aims to ensure the realisation of that 'all children experience learning that is engaging and builds success for life' (DEEWR, 2009, p.7). Similarly, one of the aims of program evaluation in schools is to judge the implementation of the *Melbourne Declaration on Educational Goals for Young Australians*, that 'All young Australians become successful learners, confident and creative individuals and active and informed citizens' (MCEETYA, 2009, p. 3).

What is evaluation?

Everyday educators gather and analyse evidence, and judge and make decisions about theory, philosophy, ethics and practice. Their judgements may be tacit or considered (DEEWR, 2010, p. 3) concerning philosophy, curriculum approaches, pedagogies, learning environments, documentation methods, family collaboration, staff rosters or professional learning. Educators constantly investigate the success of what was planned, and often what was not planned. All aspects of the program can be evaluated: relationships, inclusion of all children and families, the indoor/outdoor environment, grouping strategies, assessment processes, power relations among partners, resources and educator interactions with children and families, as well as the overall program. This involves gathering evidence from a number of sources; for example, conversations with partners, observing the program and examining documents (surveys, photographs, wall displays, questionnaires, daily diaries and meeting minutes). This evidence is organised and analysed to make judgements about the current program, and to recommend future program improvements that extend children's learning (DEEWR, 2009; Australian Institute for Teaching and School Leadership (AITSL), 2011). These judgements are based on the values of the setting/school, as well as current theory and research. Analysing the collected evidence helps educators make decisions about what has happened and why, and what they believe should happen next. The focus on meaningfulness in evaluation distinguishes itself from standardised measures of 'quality' (Dahlberg et al., 2007).

What is reflection?

Reflection involves thinking about ideas and examining the underlying relationships to theoretical perspectives, philosophy, ethics and practice. When educators mindfully approach evaluation decisions, they investigate questions independently and with others as they link to big ideas to strengthen the program for all children's wellbeing and learning (DEEWR, 2010). Professional learning occurs in **reflective practice** where educators continually investigate and construct new understandings about ways to enhance children's wellbeing and learning. Where educators draw on diverse viewpoints to increase understandings of practice, they participate

Reflection

Involves educators, families, children, community members and/or policymakers in thinking about some puzzling aspect of theory and practice that develops new understandings and new ways to strengthen practice.

Reflective practice

Occurs when educators and partners regularly examine aspects of practice and theory that puzzle them as they reconsider ideas and construct new understandings of, and the connections between, theoretical perspectives, philosophy, ethics and practice.

in **critically reflective practice**, as they construct new understandings about theoretical perspectives, philosophy, ethics and practice.

Rationale for evaluation and reflection

Realistic understanding of each setting or school is essential (*see* Chapter 6), since there are many influences affecting program decision making and evaluation. The complexities of the values underlying the setting/school philosophy, curriculum approaches and understandings of partners may impact on the program in positive or negative ways. These influences support or impede the two-way communication, relationship building, democratic participatory processes, decision making, evaluation and the following implementation. The challenges are for educators to respond innovatively and positively to situational factors. The potentials, contradictions and conflicts can be investigated, or current perceptions of these can be investigated. Then educators can analyse, judge, recommend and implement recommendations for daily practice. Whatever is evaluated can be reflected upon. Even though every day may be hectic, incorporating reflection into daily practice is beneficial for educators. Thinking about what happened, why and what is next – evaluation – leads to considering what else could be happening, how else the program could be stronger and how children's learning could be extended further.

Educators need to decide the effectiveness of the program and the possibilities for moving forward, as they cannot rely on anyone else to do this for them. The ability to interweave the educational, political, ethical, financial, emotional and regulatory aspects of evaluation shapes this work. Working powerfully with change occurs when educators evaluate and reflect on their philosophy and practice. Change is everywhere – theories, research, policies and diverse life experiences for children, families and educators, as noted in this book – and this offers opportunities and challenges for all programs. If educators do not evaluate and reflect with the aim of program improvement, they may be tempted to accept evaluations from elsewhere.

Evaluation and reflection support educators to clarify their values and construct new knowledge by offering advice about past practices and identifying future directions for curriculum with partners. Such practices extend theory and practice. This work may establish 'living standards of judgement' (Whitehead, 2005, p. 2) as educators evaluate and reflect on their work. When educators and partners understand the meaning of the work through evaluation and reflection they define theory and practice within their local context. Malaguzzi regarded this work as very important.

> Teachers … feel the need to grow … competences; they want to transform experiences into thoughts, thoughts into reflections, and reflections into new thoughts and new actions. They also feel the need to make predictions, to try things out, and then interpret them. The act of interpretation is most important.

C Edwards, L Gandini and G Forman, *The Hundred Languages of Children*, p. 73, © 1998 Ablex Publishing Corporation.

He emphasised that interpreting action *in progress* is more useful than doing it later.

Through experience and necessity, educators plan and evaluate on multiple philosophical and program levels. For example, they may focus on analysing the effectiveness of the outdoor learning environment, family participation or administrative tasks from daily management to yearly strategic planning. Just as important is evaluating and reflecting on our own career journey (*see* Chapter 11), as well as self evaluating in annual work reports. Ultimately

Critical reflective practice

Reflective practice becomes critically reflective practice when educators continually inspect practice from diverse viewpoints to construct new understandings of, and the connections between, theoretical perspectives, philosophy, ethics and practice.

Why might evaluation and reflection be useful for children, families, educators and managers?

FIGURE 4.2 Conversations can promote professional learning. Asking colleagues how things went often promotes evaluation and sometimes reflection as they explain their practice reflecting their philosophy.

the philosophy and program decisions that are taken direct the evaluation. These decisions may be about family collaboration, philosophy, curriculum approaches, pedagogies, documentation methods, learning environments, resources, learning experiences, grouping, staff rosters and professional learning (concepts which are extensively covered in Chapters 5, 7, 8, 9 and 10).

Reflection deepens educator understandings of the early childhood setting/school philosophy and practice, as well as maintaining their focus on, and enthusiasm for, the profession. Researchers believe that reflecting *in* our practice and *on* our practice as well as '*reflecting upon our reflections*' (Schon 1983; 1987) is vital for all professionals (O'Connor & Diggins, 2002; Miller, Cable & Devereux, 2005) (*see* Chapter 11). If everyone is to grow as professionals, they must think about what they do and why they do it. Despite their initial teacher education and ongoing professional learning, educators find situations they have not expected. Reflection guides everyone to better examine what is happening and the possibilities for moving forward.

Reflection can enhance flexibility and articulation when educators share information and perspectives with partners. Reflection can also guide how changing demands, strengths, needs, potentials and constraints are met. Being able to articulate and validate the philosophy and practice of the setting/school is important should the individual setting's/school's expectations conflict with what is commonly understood as 'best practice'. As 'best practice' is contested, consideration of *wise* validation in its own context is advised. Educators are warned about the 'universal and stultifying "best practice", to be evaluated through the concept of *quality*' (Dahlberg et al., 2007, p. vii) (emphasis added) since 'quality' is defined by the beholder, as discussed later.

Reflective educators strive to accommodate community perceptions of the importance of early years learning with diverse family practices and shifting economic and political climates. This occurs within contexts of local, national and global changes across sociocultural and natural environments. Because of this, making sense of theoretical and research developments is an essential element of reflection. Families and communities seek optimal conditions for their children, and governments influence accountability expectations for children's outcomes in educational settings/schools. That said, expectations vary across families and educators. For example, understandings often vary about children's cooperative or competitive relationships with others, or children's learning through collaborative problem solving or individual adult predetermined maths and literacy experiences.

Balancing accountability demands with *relationship building* and *meaning making* is essential for providing strong programs, but it is also challenging. Educators need to monitor their practice; for example, 'Are we spending more time documenting what we do or what children do, rather than extending children's learning? Are we documenting things that may not directly help us with teaching this group of children?' Effective time allocation and documentation/evaluation methods ensure that precious time working with children is not sacrificed to excessive record keeping and administration. Educators are highly accountable to *children* and *families* as well as *government organisations* and *ourselves*.

The Reggio Emilia experience reveals that children's learning needs to be the focus in philosophy and practice. When Gunilla Dahlberg asked educators why they established early childhood centres based on children's perspectives, the city mayor explained:

> The fascist experience had taught them that people who conformed and obeyed were dangerous, and that in building the new society it was imperative to safeguard and communicate that lesson and maintain a vision of children who can think and act for themselves.

> G Dahlberg, P Moss and A Pence, *Beyond Quality in Early Childhood Education and Care:*
> *Postmodern Perspectives*, p12, © 1999, 2007 Falmer Press.

Reflecting and critiquing their own histories and experiences led families and educators to clarify the rationale for their philosophy and practice in the setting.

Contexts for reflection and evaluation

Australian government departments as well as public and private organisations have increased their focus on the prior-to-school sector as well as the early years of school, generating possibilities and resources to improve programs for all children. In this context, the relentless drive of some globalised, nationalised and politicised accountability and achievement measures puzzle many educators as well as many families. However, policymakers and constructors of national learning curricula, and 'quality' measures, signal the need for educators to address the complexity of learning and diverse contexts for all Australian children. Understanding these discourses alerts us to opportunities and challenges to implement the setting/school philosophy in the program. Reflection and evaluation provide educators with essential tools to continually improve programs for children and their families.

Over the past 20 years the notion of accountability and continual improvement has emerged in community, media and political discussions, as well as continuing in early childhood and school settings. While it is important for educators to appreciate their accountability to children, families and themselves, they are also answerable to the wider community, as providers of community services that attract considerable public funding. Educators need to be sure that they are working well to implement the philosophy that extends children's learning. Evaluation would seem a reasonable and commonsensical way to do so. However, when the evaluations come from outside the setting context, they may include useful foci, but these may not be so relevant to children with diverse abilities, cultures and funds of knowledge (Moll, Amanti, Neff & Gonzalez, 1992), their learning and educational work in the setting.

The values and philosophy embedded in each evaluation reflect what findings are likely to be established and how timely and useful that analysed information is for immediate program improvement for the current children and educators. For example, examining the EYLF and its relevance to Aboriginal and Torres Strait Islander (ATSI) settings led educators to recognise the great vision and diversity of practice reflected in the EYLF (DEEWR, 2009). But Goodwin (2009) 'identifies a major concern that Aboriginal and Torres Strait Islander children and families have not been recognised properly in the EYLF document. Both ways of teaching (learning through both traditional language and culture, as well as contemporary learning) was not explored or clearly defined' (p. 10). This critique identifies implications for all programs in all Australian educational settings (*see* Chapter 11).

National mandatory program evaluations are now being implemented to increase quality and promote constant improvement. One of these is the *National Quality Framework* (NQF) (Early Childhood Development Steering Committee & Council of Australian Governments, 2009). This includes the *National Quality Standard for Early Childhood Education and Care and School Aged Care*, known as *National Quality Standard* (NQS) (ACECQA, 2013), a national quality rating and assessment process and national regulations. The NQS for all early childhood settings and school aged care aims to offer services information, licensing and quality assurance for programs that support children's growth and development so the best 'quality' care and education for families and their children can be offered. Enforced from January 2012, the NQF aims to provide information so that families can distinguish different quality levels in services such as long day care, family day care, preschool and outside school hours care, based on the setting's Self Assessment and Quality Improvement Plan (QIP) process. This process involves rating the following seven areas:

- educational program and practice
- children's health and safety
- physical environment
- staffing arrangements (including the number who look after children)
- relationships with children
- collaborative partnerships with families and communities
- leadership and service management.

ACECQA, 2013, p.9

The Australian Children's Education and Care Quality Authority (ACECQA) oversees the implementation of the NQF and has responsibility for establishing consistent, effective and efficient procedures for the operation of the new system. For details, consult the ACECQA website (http://acecqa.gov.au > National Quality Framework). Reports are generated quarterly regarding setting achievements of the quality standards. Similarly in schools, evaluation and review of the Australian Curriculum currently being gradually implemented is important (ACARA, n.d., 2013a). For current developments, see the ACARA and AITSL sites (http://www.acara.edu.au/default.asp; http://aitsl.edu.au).

Settings are required to undertake a self-assessment process and a QIP (ACECQA, 2011) to guide their work towards meeting criteria for NQF and associated legislation (ACECQA, 2013a; 2013b) (Framework & Quality Areas). This is followed by a site visit by the state organisation charged with the responsibility for following up. Similarly, the Australian Curriculum (ACARA; n,d, 2013a; 2012) is being progressively implemented in schools and program reviews will occur. Through implementing and evaluating new curriculum frameworks, educators are likely to extend their professional knowledge, skills and competence (DEEWR, 2009) and so the program should be continually strengthening to extend all children's learning.

Why are ethical evaluations essential in daily practice with children, educators and families?

However, due to the complexity and the timing of the implementation of the NQF and the Australian Curriculum, it is advisable that educators continue with their own strategic planning (*see* later in this chapter) and plans of action so that program renewal occurs independently and can also add positively to these formal evaluation guides.

Ethical guidance provides another form of evaluation useful to all educators. For example, the Early Childhood Australia's *Code of Ethics* (Early Childhood Australia, 2006), developed by early childhood educators with lengthy field consultation, guides educators to make informed fair decisions in their daily work, reflecting responsible ways of working with all children, families, colleagues and managers. This does not mean all decisions are easy, but that the collective wisdom of many experienced and reflective educators offers helpful ethical guidance. Ethical practice with families, colleagues and community members is similarly expected for school educators, as identified in *The National Professional Standards for Teachers* (AITSL, 2011, p.19).

Participating in strategic planning, annual reporting to families and managers, annual work reports, action research and self-study projects engages educators in more forms of evaluation. These onsite evaluations, mainly designed by educators in the setting, provoke collegiality, professional learning and clarification from insider perspectives of what is happening across the setting/school philosophy and program. These evaluations are considered later in this chapter.

In many places there are efforts to evaluate programs as educators' work through assessing children's learning alone. These often grade learning achievement in predetermined ways with little consideration of children's diverse abilities and funds of knowledge, disabilities or complex learning contexts (Moll et al, 1992; Thompson, 2002) or educators' working conditions (Bill and Melinda Gates Foundation, 2010). Current national curriculum documents in Australia draw attention to diversity of children (DEEWR, 2009; ACARA, 2013b). US research, the Measure of Effective Teaching, involved educators, researchers and philanthropists using multiple sources to investigate educator effectiveness that extends all children's learning (Bill and Melinda Gates Foundation, 2010). Sources included achievement from various standardised test results, children's perceptions, classroom observations and educator reflections, and educators' understandings of pedagogical knowledge and their working conditions. Findings identified that pedagogical relationships – focusing on care, respect, challenge, conferring and captivating student participation – and constructive feedback to all children appeared to make a difference. These features reflect aspects of productive pedagogies and new basics – and also a narrow foci and short-term learning in lessons – rather than prolonged learning periods. This research validated the beliefs of many: the negative influences of limited opportunities for educators' professional learning and limited curriculum that overlooks children's diversity and funds of knowledge, as well as ignores the complexity of promoting lasting learning.

Principles for evaluation and reflection

This section introduces some principles for evaluation and reflection. These include continuity of values across philosophy and practice and principles for involving partners.

Values continuity

The consistency of values across philosophy and the program provides unity. Where evaluation and reflection are considered as part of the setting/school curriculum process, it is most likely that evaluation and reflection will mirror the setting/school values, philosophy, curriculum approaches and pedagogies. For example, if educators believe that the most important indicator of the strength of early childhood and school programs are reciprocal relationships between children, families and educators, they will evaluate aspects of the program in terms of respectful social interactions for children and adults, meaningfulness, participation and inclusion of all partners, especially children and families, as well as curriculum experiences and resources reflecting family and community. If educators believe that children learn well through constructivist approaches, then they may evaluate aspects of the program – for example, partner collaboration, learning environment, resources, learning experiences – for how these extend children's active learning.

Why is including and clarifying values held by different partners important in evaluation and reflection?

Values lie at the heart of all evaluations and reflections. Everyone needs to be sensitive and proactive in identifying values since potentials, dilemmas and conflicts may be encountered in evaluation and reflection. One parent or educator may value a constructivist-based learning environment while another may prefer a direct instruction learning environment. Some families and educators may value happiness, friends and agency for children in the program while others may value children's cognitive, creative or critiquing achievements. Just as people sometimes have difficulty in deciding and agreeing about values, so also do organisations and educational systems (Prendergast, 1994). However, values inclusion and clarification is important in evaluation and reflection as educators seek to integrate values into their living practices (McNiff & Whitehead, 2005). Reflection is important to reach deeper understandings of what is meaningful about the big ideas for all partners. This process emphasises the importance of philosophy development and its continual evaluation with current partners.

Evaluations and reflections in early childhood education respect the value of meaningfulness in children's learning, as identified in documentation of children's learning by Dahlberg et al. (2007). Program design and evaluation also rests on this principle as it acknowledges the learning context, the values and assumptions of the partners and their subjectivities, as well as the uncertainties and the provisional nature of learning. This chapter examines various ways to evaluate program components as well as whole programs, as in strategic planning. Just as understanding children's learning draws over time on shared interpretations from children, educators, and families (*see* Chapter 8), understanding how programs deepen children's learning requires shared interpretations from these partners in evaluation.

Critiques of formal evaluations – for example, standardised procedures constructed outside the setting – state that 'quality is a social construct and should not be defined and measured in a defined way' (Fenech, 2006, p. 52), since 'quality' lies in the eye of the beholder. Care needs to be taken as such evaluations proclaiming that standards have been met are not always evidence that strong programs actually operate. There was criticism of the superseded Quality Improvement and Accreditation System (National Childcare Accreditation Council, 2006) as being often too narrowly defined once criteria becomes standardised to a list of specific practices. Although these standardised evaluations are organised around what some educators view as principles of 'quality', implementing the evaluation does not always work out that way. So although these guides are useful to extend programs for children, in practice there are always possibilities

for improvement in the guide. They serve a purpose, but educators need to maintain their own evaluations of how the program is improving. Educators seem to be always challenging and revising the guides themselves, as well as continually refining how their practice embodies the setting/school philosophy.

Involving partners

Children, educators, families, management bodies, government departments and other agencies have much to contribute to the evaluations and reflections, since everyone's views and understandings widen the scope. Extra information, alternative explanations and perspectives can be gained with partner involvement. Diverse understandings help strengthen evaluation and reflection. While involving all partners cannot be achieved at each stage of every evaluation/ reflection, it is possible to involve more participants in various aspects to gain richer insights (*see* the example of children's evaluation in Table 4.2). Until partners are involved, educators don't know their perceptions. Critical friends, partners or mentors can support educator evaluation and reflection on programs and provide encouragement during challenging times.

Tools and processes for evaluation

There are many evaluation tools or guides available to educators and organisations. All evaluation guides – whether ethical, informal, formal or mandatory – are constructed by people or organisations, reflecting differing philosophies, values and perspectives. These ultimately shape each evaluation and its purpose. Ethical evaluations reflect fair perspectives; for example, the Early Childhood Australia *Code of Ethics* (Early Childhood Australia, 2006). Some evaluations aim to discriminate statistically, some aim to diagnose and provide feedback and some reflect legislation or performance goals. Examples of informal guides are found throughout this book, while more formal and moral guides are found within government accountability systems and legislation, professional standards such as the *Professional National Standards for Teachers*, *National Quality Standard*, *Melbourne Declaration of Educational Goals of Young Australians* and the Australian curriculum, and state adaptations of those where relevant.

Which evaluation tools and processes are used in a setting/school that you know? How well do these work to strengthen the program for all children?

Educators and organisations need to design or select the tools that suit the evaluation purpose and focus they have in mind. There is no one external measure agreed upon by all people that can be used in evaluation. This situation could tempt educators and organisations with apparently easy answers; for example, using standardised tests to attempt to determine whether the program ensures children are literate and numerate and perhaps, by implication, whether educators teach effectively. In some circumstances educators may seek standards; for example, using a building code to evaluate the safety and accessibility of ramps in the environment. If educators believe that children's learning is dynamic and occurs over time then they tend to make judgements about how well the program – the philosophy and practice, including the pedagogies of intentional teaching, resources, environments and groupings as well as the documentation itself – extend children's learning. Then they identify further directions.

There are formal evaluations designed by people outside the setting based on one-use templates that reflect 'predetermined norms and setting out criteria for their measurement' (Dahlberg et al., 2007, p. ix). These may include checklists, rating scales, standardised procedures or detailed audit checks that aim to measure a snapshot of practice in terms of the idealised practice. These usually ignore the learners' contexts and operate from outside the setting. The worth of any evaluation is the credibility of the tool, the evaluators, the information and its interpretation that leads to direct improvement of the program, so educators need to consider the purpose and usefulness of any evaluation.

Some self-improvement evaluations keep us mindful of aspects of the big picture. For example, the Early Childhood Environmental Rating Scale-Extension (ECERS-E) (Sylva et al., 2006), when used to observe the learning environment, may predict children's achievement based on particular understandings of children's literacy, mathematics and scientific thinking. However, observing environments with the Early Childhood Environmental Rating Scale-Revised

(ECERS-R) (Harms et al., 1998) may help predict children's social interaction and cooperative behaviours (Sylva et al., 2006). Because these trends result from these instruments, researchers advise using both scales.

What is deemed as *quality* in programs varies, Sylva et al. (2006) suggest that quality does not appear a universal or fixed concept as it reflects national curricula and cultural policy, which in itself is subject to change and reflects the policymakers and politicians as well as the constructors. Evaluation tools as standardised measures reflect various ideas about what counts as quality and this again changes. From experience with the ECERS-R (Harms et al., 1980; 1998), the fact that these scales have been modified by educators in several countries and significantly in some places – for example in Tamil Nadu (Isley, 2000) – provides evidence that educators demand that local cultural contexts for children need to be recognised (Sylva et al., 2006). The Early Childhood Environmental Rating Scale (Harms et al., 1998), initially developed in 1980 in the United States, drew on prevailing views of developmental understandings for research, self-study and supervision. Over time, changing understandings of children's development, curriculum and learning and teaching progressively appear in this scale for observing and rating curriculum, pedagogy and resources. In slightly differing cultural contexts – for example, in Germany, England and Portugal – researchers and educators have slightly modified the tool (Tietze et al., 1996; Sylva et al., 1999); or, in Australia, constructed a literacy component of the tool (Makin et al., 1999); and in Tamil Nadu, reconstructed the tool (Sylva et al., 2006). A scale refinement in the UK – for example, Early Childhood Environmental Rating Scale-Extension (Sylva et al., 2003; 2006) – pays attention to children's literacy, numeracy and scientific learning, as well as children's cultural and intellectual diversity. This tool was adapted for the purpose and focus of researching curriculum and pedagogy in settings in England. While these tools may remind educators of some aspects important in their work, they may also overlook some aspects. So everyone should be aware of potential issues with standardised measures – like us, they are not perfect! It is not easy to design standardised diagnostic evaluation tools; they are always works in progress.

Process for evaluation

Evaluations in the setting/school are best established from a well-informed and collaborative base. If the focus, purpose and nature of methods are refined, educators save time and energy finding out what they need to know to strengthen the program. If the purpose and focus are clarified, educators might better select strategies, involve partners, analyse and reflect on collected information, make judgements and recommend future directions. Evaluation operates in an ongoing manner through various stages so everyone needs to be alert and flexible to make 'best fit' and timely decisions. Considering the following stages of the process (Table 4.1) assists in making informed decisions by involving relevant educators, management and families. Each stage is considered in what follows.

TABLE 4.1   Process of evaluation.

Purpose (why)	Deciding on the reason for or the focus of the evaluation
Focus (what)	Deciding what is to be evaluated
Methods (how)	Deciding appropriate strategies, time frame and how partners might participate Gathering the relevant information
Analysis (What does the information mean?)	Analysing the information with partners Analysing information in relation to theory and research Making judgements and recommendations
Action (What changes are we implementing? How will we do it?)	Using the recommendations in future planning and action Planning evaluation of the implementation of the action plan

WHY? THE PURPOSE

Any evaluation needs to have a reason; that is, educators need to know why they are evaluating. For example:

- They need to understand their interactions with all children and all families to strengthen the program.
- They need to investigate what happens for children in the outdoor learning environment/ playground.
- They need to know how well they use intentional teaching pedagogies to extend all children's sustained shared thinking.

As part of this purpose, the audience of the evaluation needs consideration; that is, who will use this information and who will the information be shared with – children, families, educators, professionals from other organisations, government organisations or the early childhood profession – and how the recommendations could be implemented. This may influence how the information is gathered and recorded; in other words, how educators spend time and effort.

WHAT? THE FOCUS

Clear focus means decision making about which aspect educators are examining. The focus varies with each evaluation; for example, 'We investigate how we plan interactions with children and families in the setting or school', or 'How well we support children's sustained shared thinking in small groups'. The focus reflects the setting/school philosophy and curriculum approaches (*see* Chapters 5 and 7).

HOW? METHODS AND IMPLEMENTATION

Making decisions about appropriate strategies, time frames and responsibilities of partners occurs next. Only the most useful and practical strategies that gather relevant information for the purpose and focus are needed, and predicting the amount of time and energy involved for educators and partners is necessary. These ideas are important for implementing a plan of action, as explored throughout this book.

Strategies for collecting data

Information can be collected in various ways; for example, informal, formal, standardised, mandated, moral or professional evaluation. Strategies include:

- standardised evaluations
- observations
- conversations
- photographs
- interviews
- mind maps
- focus group discussions
- document analysis
- surveys
- questionnaires
- rating scales
- checklists.

Standardised evaluations, such as environmental rating scales, can be used to guide educators observations of the program. Alternatively, educators can set their own focus for observation; for example, documenting interactions between educators and children and families over a week, or documenting their intentional teaching with children over two weeks. Interviews are useful to find out what different partners may think about aspects of the program; for example, asking children, families, educators and visiting educators how the outdoor environment promotes collaborative behaviours and inclusive relationships among children. Educators can make notes on conversations between children and educators, photograph children's learning experiences and the environment, and collect samples of children's work. Team or room journals, maintained by colleagues, enhance the process of revisiting both interactions and the overall philosophy and program. This presents an opportunity for all educators to contribute to evaluation of the day or week (short term), month or year (long term). When the whole team is engaged, evaluations and reflections grow richer with each entry, resulting in deeper understandings. Team members who feel uncertain about their evaluations and reflections can use each other's entries as a springboard for their own.

Collecting information

This can be done in timely and practical ways when partners are involved. Recording information should be easy and not cause distractions from working with the children. Combining information from different collection strategies increases the comprehensiveness of information for analysis and improves the usefulness of recommendations.

- *Observations* of many aspects of the program can be examined to see how well it is working and for whom, provided a focus and time period has been set for observing. Educators may make brief notes or tallies on the evaluation focus; for example, the effectiveness of the outdoor environment/playground for children's learning as some children keenly play outdoors while others are reluctant to go outdoors. They may observe several children each day for two weeks while outdoors or on duty. Information from conversations with children and families can extend these observations.

- *Conversations with partners* can inform the evaluation about what they think, feel and believe about a particular aspect of the program. Team members can talk with colleagues, children, family, community members and managers and their rationale for their views. Conversations can be brief or lengthy, spontaneous or considered, so offer a flexible and productive way to gather information from all partners, especially when conversation notes are combined with other strategies. Questions can be open and general or targeted to aspects upon which specific insights are sought; for example, what children think of the outdoors/playground, how educators feel and think about their interactions with children and families, and what children and educators think about engaging in sustained shared thinking about topics.

- *Photographs* taken by partners provide visual evidence of what happens in the program, as well as revealing what the photographer decides to take. Photographs are useful for engaging all partners in recalling what happened and what they expected to happen. Photographs are a cost- and time-effective means of recording the program and can be used to refocus partners' examinations and interpretations at the next part of the evaluative process. Photographs can easily be included in computer-generated documentation to share. Photographs inspire much spontaneous evaluation, as in visual displays for an annual setting meeting. Children can photograph their favourite and least favourite parts of the outdoors or playgrounds, families can photograph literacy practices at home, and educators can photograph interactions and sustained shared thinking. However, it is important to remember that photographs – on their own – can be interpreted in many ways. Sometimes, it is the conversations around the selected photographs that provide the most relevant evidence for the evaluation.

- *Interviews* with a short set of prepared questions can provide educators with concise information concerning the selected part of the program being evaluated. Questions may be open-ended or closed and specific, depending on the focus and purpose. Colleagues, children, family members and managers can be interviewed at a previously arranged time and place, over the phone or by email. Face-to-face interviews may be recorded in written notes or audio-taped for later note taking of relevant aspects. Flexibility enables more partners to participate.

- *Mind maps or webbing* can be drawn by individuals or in groups concerning the evaluation focus. Understandings and values about the topic can be documented. Educators might draw their own map on a topic; for example, their interactions with children and families over a week about inclusiveness. They could share this at a staff meeting for feedback and with children and families to include further interpretations.

- *Focus group discussions* are useful where educators decide to evaluate an aspect of the program in detail; for example, the philosophy (*see* Chapter 5), family collaboration or pedagogies for promoting sustained shared thinking. Invited partners participate

in the discussion on a topic for a set time, maybe 1–2 hours, during the day or evening. Interruptions need to be avoided, so a quiet location with appropriate furniture and refreshments is needed. Discussion can be facilitated by inviting participants to respond to approximately five to seven questions. A support person takes notes and helps in various ways. The word-processed notes are analysed.

- *Surveys/open-ended questionnaires* gather information from various partners and may be face to face, written or electronic. Partners express their ideas with no limits on their response to the open-ended how, what and why questions. This strategy is useful for many partners to evaluate an aspect of the program; for example, the effectiveness of setting–family two-way communications.

- *Rating scales* may be standardised tools, such as the ECERS-R (Harms et al., 1998) and ECERS-E (Sylva et al., 2006), designed to examine learning environments, or they can be constructed by setting educators. Rating scales offer a snapshot of specific dimensions of the program at one particular time. Given the discussion elsewhere in this chapter on the variability and change in standardised evaluations, it's worth noting that they still provide a useful tool for examining the learning environment and making recommendations. Scales typically list components of the learning environment, supported by graded descriptive criteria. Observers examine the environment, and select the 'best-fit' description. Alternatively, educators and partners can rate areas in their learning environment on a floor plan according to given criteria and their knowledge of the program in action. For example, see Curtis and Carter (2003, pp. 223–7) for examples of rating scales of setting learning environments that enable evaluations from the perspectives of children, families and educators.

- *Artefact collection* involves educators and partners in collecting artefacts relevant to the evaluation focus. Artefacts include many different items; for example, learning resources, posters, photographs, program documentation, journals, reflective journals, communication emails, books, newsletters, posters and so on. They reflect various meanings, providing insights for the evaluation. For example, partners might gather artefacts related to family communication and collaboration with a focus on their effectiveness for all families. In another example, partners might collect artefacts related to children's literacy and maths learning resources to evaluate how well these reflect all children's funds of knowledge. Educators may want to evaluate the usefulness of their program documentation processes, so they gather the daily schedule, project books, daily journal, children's records, family communication records and weekly slideshow for analysis.

Sometimes what is collected is still sketchy and lacking sufficient detail for any reliable interpretation, so more information is needed. At other times there is so much information that analysing it is an overwhelming task that everyone will want to avoid. So decisions need to be made about how much information is needed. Pragmatic decisions are necessary regarding data collection strategies and resources. Clear identification of the most productive strategies is wise so everyone's time and energy is invested in gathering useful information.

Sometimes it is useful to write down all possible options and predicted outcomes from using various strategies. By taking 15 minutes exploring the options on paper – considering who is involved, how and when the information is gathered and thinking about likely outcomes – making mistakes with people and time can be avoided. Opportunities can then be pinpointed as well as any constraints concerning the focus, purpose and selected methods chosen. This information can refine important decisions on paper about designing the evaluation as well as the criteria and then make the best of its features – namely the expertise and time of the people involved.

Partners in data collection

Everyone, including children, can participate in evaluations. Often, involved educators are the most informed implementers of the evaluation recommendations. Where a team approach to gathering information occurs, the workload reduces considerably for everyone. More importantly, interpreting and sharing can become professional learning times. In school classrooms, where educators evaluate their own practices, involving a colleague in observations and analysis provides new perspectives and reflective benefits for both.

Children can evaluate: they can express their ideas and feelings (and their rationales) about their learning environment, experiences, resources and documentation. In a local project, children in the first year of school were asked to evaluate their school environment, specifically what they did or did not like about their school (Dockett et al., 2007). Using text and drawings, children indicated a range of preferences, including playing, being outside, recess and lunch, as well as some academic tasks, such as reading (*see* Figure 4.3). They also emphasised the importance of friends and being with friends at school. They did not like 'mean teachers', 'really hard work' or 'missing out on play'.

Involving families in evaluations draws on their understanding of the setting and program, especially as to how this assists their child's learning, and reveals the program qualities they value. Through participating in evaluations, families can also increase their understanding of the complex workings of the setting or school, the program and the managing organisation. Once families are aware of the program, and why things are done the way they are, they often become articulate in the community, advocating support for educators, settings and schools. They can constructively suggest possibilities for the program.

Source: Dockett et al., 2007

FIGURE 4.3 'At school I like playing tennis. I don't like playing football because I'm not used to it.'

Time frames for data collection

Schedules should be relevant and cost-effective for each evaluation purpose. With limited human resources and time, decisions are essential about the timing of the evaluation and the conciseness of the documentation. A major concern in program decision making involves balancing short-term and long-term evaluation, so deciding clear priorities in these areas is useful. A short-term example over one week could be 'we evaluate information exchange with a new family to support the child's immediate wellbeing', while a long-term example over a year is 'evaluating our own cultural competence in maintaining two-way communications with all families to inform the program'.

Using formative and summative evaluation assists educators in timely ways. Data are gathered on a regular formative basis in the short term. It may be more time effective if brief evaluative notes about technologies in the learning environment are made during the day, before a break or at the end of the day. Often brief criteria assist educators to guide and integrate evaluation into the day. These involve short sets of questions that prompt identification of information for analysis from multiple perspectives. For example, questions for evaluating on the effectiveness of educator interactions with families over the first month may include:

- What are our effective interactions with families?
- Which ways work best, for whom and why?
- What doesn't appear to work well, for whom and why?
- What next?

However, over time further details may be useful, as in the following:

- Which family members do I know by name?
- Have I identified any shared interests among families and educators?
- How have I shared some of my interests and experiences with families?
- Which ways of communicating with families have been most useful?
- What opportunities have I offered families for collaborating on useful activities that they feel comfortable with?
- What spontaneous things happened that helped me interact with families?
- What do I know about families' home and community literacy practices?
- What do I know about children's funds of knowledge? What else do I need to know?
- What should I do next to promote all parents' interactions in the setting?

Educators use their formative evaluations to develop their summative evaluation at the end of a time period to direct future planning. For example, formative daily/weekly evaluations may include analysis of educator interactions with children and families, and children's interactions in the outdoor learning environment/playground. At the end of the

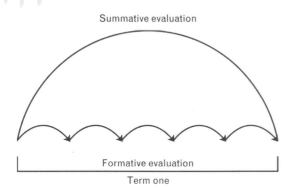

FIGURE 4.4 Links between formative and summative evaluation.

month, these formative evaluations inform summative evaluations, which provide future planning directions. In another example, weekly formative evaluations in Term one of children's inclusionary behaviours in the classroom and playground can be drawn upon to form a summative evaluation that informs the Term two program. Summative evaluations at the end of the month, term, year or project, without formative evaluation, will often be less helpful for planning. These connections are seen in Figure 4.4.

ANALYSIS: WHAT DOES THIS INFORMATION MEAN? MAKING JUDGEMENTS AND DECISIONS

Once the information is gathered, the broad patterns are analysed to make sense of the information. Analysing may mean partners examine the data; for example, in evaluating educator interaction, partners may interpret children's, families' and educators' mind maps of interactions over a week; or in evaluating outdoors/playground, partners may interpret interviews with children and the photographs children and educators took over two weeks to understand what happens for children in that location. In evaluating intentional teaching, partners may share and examine daily diary entries or daily planning about sustained shared thinking experiences. Using more than one source of information and involving partners makes information stronger for analysis. Identifying consistent and/or paradoxical patterns and critical readings in the area may help deepen the analysis.

Criteria can be designed for analysing the gathered information that draw on understandings of theory, research and practice. Constructing sets of questions when designing the evaluation draws attention to what is important in robust programs that extend children's learning. Questions also keep the evaluation focus sharp and do-able. But unexpected joys and issues can arise in practice, which can strengthen the evaluation and ultimately the program. For example, when the space, time and resources in the indoor/outdoor learning environment are regularly evaluated, the following questions may be very useful:

- How welcoming is the indoor/outdoor space for all families and children? What is the evidence?
- How visible and accessible is children's current learning? How can children extend their learning?
- How does the space and experiences offered invite children's decision making and movement around and beyond the indoor environment?
- How does the space support quiet, active, collaborative and creative/construction experiences?
- How does the space promote small group interaction as well as larger group interactions?
- How does resource storage promote children's independence for accessing and returning resources?
- How do resources reflect children's range of interests, abilities, curiosities, cultures, languages and family experiences?
- How open-ended are resources to support problem solving and creativity?
- How are digital resources integrated with books, paper, pencils, paints and brushes in learning centres?
- How suitable are resources for the current program focus?
- How do the daily schedule and time blocks promote children's engagement in experiences and avoid queuing?

(adapted from Briggs & Potter, 1999)

The criteria depend on the setting/school philosophy, approaches to curriculum and pedagogies. There are many aspects that can be evaluated, including communicating with families, intentional teaching strategies, inclusivity, grouping, documentation systems, assessment systems, professional learning practices, use of learning and curriculum documents. Whenever programs are evaluated with appropriate criteria, program improvement becomes more possible.

WHAT ACTION? DESIGNING, IMPLEMENTING AND EVALUATING CHANGE

After shared analysis of data, educators make judgements and recommendations for future program directions. Smith (2006) suggests all judgements need to make sense and respect the work of all the people involved. Decisions are made about integrating recommendations into the program and developing an **action plan** (*see* Table 4.2, where partners decide to improve interaction and learning in the outdoors/playground).

Action plan

This plan results from an evaluation. It lists the decision and recommendations/ goals, as well as the details of the planned action. This includes the new action, timing, people involved and evaluation criteria

TABLE 4.2   Evaluation – Plan of action: Improving interactions in the outdoors/playground learning environment.

Decision

The outdoors/playground offers some children interesting experiences, while some children find little of interest to do, especially those who do not like running around. Families commented on the hard paving, uninviting plantings and limited resources. Educators need to see children for safety reasons. Readings (Reid at al., 2010) suggest that all environments can create a sense of connection and belonging.

Recommendations

- Plan with children, families and team for learning experiences in the outdoors/playground.
- Consider possibilities for a new sandpit.
- Consider possibilities for a new garden patch.

WHAT?	WHEN?	HOW?	WHO?	HOW DO WE KNOW WHEN WE GET THERE?
Involve children in resource selection.	Daily class/group meetings and conversations so resources are relevant to children's learning.	Identify and list with children all possible resources for outside learning experiences. Children decide and check off list of what is needed.	Educators facilitate class/group meetings.	Children being selective with resources. Children engaged with resources. Children prolonging their experiences.
Plan a gardening patch with interested children and families.	Daily communication for discussing ideas with families and children.	Use newsletter and class/group meetings. Webbing to plan for all to add to in ongoing way. Place web and marker in visible and accessible location.	All educators and interested children and families.	Children and families identify preferred options for garden patch. Children, families and educators consider how to use what is grown in the garden.
Investigate: • What is important for children's learning? • How do sandpits support children's learning? • What is the cost? • What are desirable design features?	Report back in three months time.	Educators and families explore with children? What do you like to do in sandpit? What else would you like to do when playing in the sandpit? Educators investigate readings from a range of sources. Educators and families and children individually share insights and photos from sandpit building in other settings. Talk with other educators at settings re. any design/landscaping problems	All educators and interested children and families.	Children, families and educators share their findings and display documentation on the notice board. Director reports on budget possibilities.

Educators, children and families can recommend ways to improve the learning environment. At a children's centre, partners suggested making storage space mobile, extending shade areas and establishing a kitchen and flower garden. This extended the educators' analysis and shaped the recommendations. However, the flower garden at the front of the centre failed because the watering (and supervision) proved difficult. Later, when it was moved to the outdoor environment, children took responsibility for watering the garden, which became part of the program. Further family participation eventuated as their ideas were acknowledged and acted upon. In terms of teamwork, time is needed to communicate more frequently with all partners. Evaluations do not have neat and tidy endings; rather, they identify future possibilities for program improvement.

Reflective tools and processes

> What do you think about the reflective processes and tools used in a setting/school that you know? How have these strengthened the program?

Reflection often resides with evaluation. This process draws educators deeper into things, searching for the big ideas and expanding the possibilities for understandings and practice. Many reflection tools support investigating the setting/school philosophy, theory and practices to clarify values, beliefs and practices and to break new ground. When reflecting, it is essential to move beyond merely describing events to identify and examine values and ideas and to investigate how different theoretical perspectives and research could strengthen practice. Educators can then re-evaluate their learning in explaining to partners and developing new understandings that may lead to changing their values and beliefs, which then can be translated into practice.

Tools for reflection

Inconsistencies between our philosophy and practice can be more readily examined with reflective tools. These include informal and formal conversations, using journals individually and collaboratively, constructing visual displays of the program, critical reading, writing and discussing, deconstructing and reconstructing, as well as participating in professional networks and research activity. These tools scaffold the reflective process, which generates possibilities for program improvement.

REFLECTIVE CONVERSATIONS

In moments of practice, educators may suddenly perceive a different meaning to something that is happening with the environment, resources or children's learning. *Informal* and *formal reflective conversations* with families, educators and children provide valuable opportunities to develop understanding through 'the discourse of making meaning [which] involves deep and sustained dialogue regarding the philosophy and goals of the school and the work of the children' (Fu et al., 2002, p. 74). For example, formal questions for critical reflection can invite conversations leading to program improvement as in the following:

- How might educators rethink gender and culture in our practices for equity?
- What are the ways educators might consider the gender equity in Aboriginal issues in both indigenous and non-indigenous children's centres and schools?
- How might educators engage these complexities of gender and culture with families?

(Adapted from Giugni & Mundine, 2010, p.78)

Children's responses to experiences and interactions provide educators with opportunities to involve children in reflecting on the environment or the day that may contribute insights to strengthen the program. Children reflect, especially on matters affecting them, for example projects, experiences, outdoor environment/playground and expectations at settings and school.

With many families, *informal reflections* occur in arrival and departure conversations, or perhaps with a prescheduled telephone or email conversation. Formal meetings between family members and educators can supplement these interactions or be the primary method of collaborative reflection. The agenda for these interactions will optimally be set by the family; however, sensitivity to family expectations and comfort will at times require the educator to initiate the process and support family members in expressing their thoughts, feelings, observations and vision for their children.

Reflection with colleagues often happens during the day at lunch breaks, transitions and quiet times. Malaguzzi (1998) encourages educators to move forward from previous isolated and unrecorded patterns of reflection and discover how to document children's evolving learning experiences. Non-contact time set aside each week is one way to ensure that more *formal conversations* and documentation between colleagues and families become a routine component of the program as 'designating a portion of staff meetings to share observations and reflections … as teachers share their reflections, it is important that others listen and share their insights' (Helm et al., 1998, p. 128).

Formal reflection with colleagues often occurs in meetings; for example, when considering new initiatives or revisions to philosophy and practice. See Tables 4.3a and 4.3b, where educators reflect individually and collaboratively on current practice towards EYLF outcomes and consider further directions.

More formal reflective conversations with partners can focus on a particular topic, such as approaches to literacy learning and teaching, transition to school, collaborating with families or examining 'school readiness', where educators and families share their views. This can initiate ongoing conversations that lead to further investigations and meetings as well as implementing changes in particular aspects of the program. It is important to remember that:

> A good conversation is neither a fight nor a contest. Circular in form, cooperative in manner and constructive in intent, it is an interchange of ideas by those who see themselves not as adversaries but as human beings come together to talk and listen and learn from one another.

K Roskos, V Risko and C Vukelich, *Reading Research Quarterly*, Vol. 33 (2): 228–239, © 1998 International Reading Association.

Whether educators agree or not with colleagues or families, dialogue can open up possibilities for values clarification through investigation and inclusion of diverse perspectives that can lead to program improvement.

O'Connor and Diggins (2002) suggest *reflective conversations* as a means of exploring incidents and examining them in terms of different viewpoints and theoretical perspectives. In this way different insights are brought to bear on analysing the situation. O'Connor and Diggins (2002, pp. 28–9) suggest asking questions such as:

- Why do you think this event occurred in this way? *or* What did I/we do to contribute to this situation?
- What could have been done differently? *or* What should I/we do differently next time?
- What other factors contributed to the situation? How were my/our practices appropriate?

Often ordinary observations and conversations become reflective when educators and partners take time to talk. In the following Example 4.1, Jackie Staudinger reflected on an incident at departure time that challenged her assumptions about family practices. This conversation offered the educator and the parent the time and space to freely narrate their experience (Cozoluo & Sprokay, 2006) and the educator to decide future action.

TABLE 4.3a   PSC WA matrix for EYLF reflections.

EYLF Reflections

Outcome 3: Children have a strong sense of wellbeing
• Children become strong in their social and emotional wellbeing

REFLECTIVE QUESTION	CURRENT PRACTICE/ STRENGTHS	ACTIONS FOR CONTINUOUS IMPROVEMENT
How do you work collaboratively with children when recording their achievements through documentation (observations, planning and evaluation)?	*E.g. Our observations are written as learning stories and we read them to the children and ask them how they want to extend their learning.*	*E.g. We could ask for children's feedback when we are evaluating experiences.*
Are children and parents actively involved in the documentation process on a daily basis? How do you see this happening in your service?		
How do children contribute to shared projects and experiences? Is it possible for projects to extend over weeks or months?		

Source: PSC WA, 2013

TABLE 4.3b   PSC WA matrix for EYLF reflections.

EYLF Reflections

Outcome 3: Children have a strong sense of wellbeing
• Children take increasing responsibility for their own health and physical wellbeing

REFLECTIVE QUESTION	CURRENT PRACTICE/ STRENGTHS	ACTIONS FOR CONTINUOUS IMPROVEMENT
How often are your services educators confident and enthusiastic to participate in energetic physical activity with children? How do educators incorporate dance, drama, movement and physical games into their daily program?		
What opportunities are there throughout the day for children to discuss and learn about their own personal hygiene?		
Is there a range of active and restful experiences provided throughout the day, and can children make their own decision to participate or not? What is your view on the participation of children for group times?	*E.g. Children always have a choice if they want to participate; we have other experiences available.*	*E.g. We need to work on children having the choice to rest or not.*

Source: PSC WA, 2013

EXAMPLE 4.1
Reflecting in practice and on practice

Family practices

After I put the daily program reflection in the foyer for families to read, I noticed that Michelle, the mother of William and Tia, placed the reflection in her bag. I was curious as to why she was taking the reflection so asked her was she going to read it later. To my surprise Michelle answered 'I always take one home so we can read what the kids have done at preschool at dinner time'. I then went on to tell her how wonderful it was that not only their family sat for dinner together, but they also revisited the children's day at preschool and the importance of the family dinner time discussion. We talked about how this would scaffold and build on the children's expressive and receptive language as both children have mild language delays. Michelle talked about group time and how much William loves stories and how he comes home each day and tells his parents what story was read at preschool. I raised the importance of borrowing books from the KU ELLI library and rereading the stories. Michelle said the children love the KU ELLI library and borrow books all the time and that the family have even bought the children's favourite stories.

Now I make sure there are extra copies of the refection available for all parents to take home. Our next newsletter will also talk about the daily reflection for parents.

Source: Jackie Staudinger KU Children's Services Educator, 2012

JOURNALS

A personal *reflective journal* maintained by individual educators enhances their process of evaluating and reflecting all aspects of the program. This daily record of events and reflection on these often focuses on adult–child/ren, child–child, educator–family or educator–educator interactions. These complex relationships, attitudes, feelings and values provoke honest reflection and action.

A journal also enables recording personal feelings of competence in new or challenging situations, and to reflect upon the strategies/resources that were used. Recognising personal growth is understanding ourselves within these situations, at times identifying areas for professional learning or affirming newly developed skills. Holly (2003, p. 5) explains journals as documenting 'impressions set in a context of description of circumstances, others, the self, motives, thoughts and feelings'. She sees that they can become 'a tool for analysis and introspection. It is a chronicle of events as they happen, a dialogue with the facts (objective) and interpretations (subjective), and perhaps most importantly it develops a basis for developing an awareness of the difference between facts and interpretations'. She recommends returning to reflect on selected journal entries, thus reflecting on our previous thinking. This heightens understandings and appreciation of patterns between seemingly separate events.

FIGURE 4.5 Critical and ethical reflections: ethical responsibilities still apply to reflecting in conversations and journals; for example, avoiding being defamatory to others. Reflections need to avoid personal attacks and work to investigate the reasons why people perceive and act in particular ways and so lead to positive thinking and future actions.

Working out future directions for oneself is vital, as shown in Example 4.2, a reflection written by Christy, a beginning educator faced with dilemmas that helped refine her philosophy and identities as an educator. She explains: 'Looking through my reflective journal that I've kept (sporadically) over the last four years of my beginning teaching career, I've identified several pivotal experiences that provoked my professional growth. Following is one of those, what this meant for me, students, families or education and some links to big ideas that are important to me'.

EXAMPLE 4.2

Reflecting on reflections – recognising my assumptions

At the start of a year, I am always thrown by students with intellectual additional needs. I have very high expectations of all of my students and when faced with a student working well above stage expectations I am inspired by the challenge of extending them, often with the success of trophies or successful attempts at obtaining OC class positions. However, when faced with a student like Nikolche, who has a diagnosed intellectual disability, I am immediately daunted by the aspect of helping them reach my expectations.

The crux of the problem is my expectations. I knew from the first week that something wasn't right with Nikolche; he just wasn't understanding anything in class and had some physical peculiarities that were causing concern. I arranged a meeting with his parents and they reluctantly informed me that they'd had to change schools because his teacher didn't want to teach him in a mainstream public school and recommended a 'special' school for Nikolche. They were appalled at the prospect, although on paper, Nikolche was suited to a school or class for students with additional needs. I chose to support their decision and work with them to keep Nikolche in my class. Fortunately, and this is indeed rare, Nikolche's mother was a very highly educated woman with two other children who were considered academically 'gifted' and she was able to offer substantial amounts of her time in support of Nikolche's additional needs. It was the first time I had witnessed such an ability. After each day, Nikolche's mother would reteach the maths lessons that I had taught, which she purchased herself from the same company from which the school purchased them. Each night, she would not only read with Nikolche, but she would discuss the book, understanding that he could decode the words but had no ability to retain meaning. For hours she would get him to practise his spelling words from his homework and not just so he could spell them but understand and discuss the meaning of each word. The results of her efforts were unbelievable.

The results of this inspired me. I had given up hope on Nikolche when I'd found out about his additional needs. My expectations were immediately lowered and had his mother not shown me how capable her child was, I would have reduced him to doing below stage work and achieving nothing. Further meetings with his mother were crucial to my supporting her efforts. I learned the prompts that she used to get him to focus and pay attention. I learned from her his physical needs to get him to enjoy the lessons and learn the content. I learned to praise him the same as I praised the other students for his successes and to include him in everything regardless of what the result might be. But most of all, I learned that my preconceived expectations of students, although still high, need to have flexibility and need to be able to adjust for each student. At the end of the year, I had to take a term off for the unexpected early birth of my son. My supervisor recognised Nikolche's achievements by giving him one of the five awards given at a big ceremony at the local RSL. Nikolche's mother cried and cried and thanked me but I really hadn't done anything by comparison.

I had learned more from her and her fantastic son than I could ever repay. I will never forget her tearful face and how much she credited to me when it was her efforts and the nature of her son who deserved the recognition.

Source: Christie Roe, 2011

VISUAL DISPLAYS

Reflective conversations between all partners can be inspired by visual displays of children's work that document assessment of learning, interests, concepts and relationships (*see* Chapter 8). These displays reflecting the philosophy and practices of the setting can inform partners' reflective dialogue. Hoyuelos believes that Malaguzzi saw documentation as a transparent way for the setting to promote practice, democracy and reflection. He explained, 'Documentation in all its forms also represents an extraordinary tool for dialogue, for exchange, for sharing. For Malaguzzi it means the possibility to discuss and dialogue "everything with everyone"' (Hoyuelos, 2004, p. 7 in Dahlberg et al., 2007, p. 7). At one centre, in preparing for their annual meeting with families, educators constructed a visual display showcasing the current practices of the setting. The process of creating the display prompted team evaluation and reflection on their philosophy and practices. During its creation, differences in philosophy and curriculum approaches became visible, providing a launch pad for future discussion.

This display provoked critical dialogue between colleagues, educators, children and families, as well as educators and management. Finally, educators bound the display into a flipbook for explaining the program to new children, families and educators.

CRITICAL READING, WRITING, DISCUSSING AND IMPLEMENTING

Another tool for evaluating and reflecting on philosophy, theory and practice engages educators in preparing readings for sharing with colleagues (*see* Figure 4.6). Research reports of practices in other settings are often read, but links are not made to setting practices. When educators deliberately investigate their thinking with colleagues, possibilities arise for applying research or renewing practice. Preparing a reading, then reading again with colleagues to discuss significant parts, is useful for mindfulness and collaboration that promote learning (Russell, n.d.).

DECONSTRUCTING AND RECONSTRUCTING

This tool can assist educators to see the parts that make up a whole or examine the conditions that led to a particular event. Once an event or idea has been deconstructed, then educators can 'apply the skills of reflection to put these deconstructed pieces back together in ways that help you configure new meanings and reach new understandings', as suggested by O'Connor and Diggins (2002, p. 16). In other words educators can *reconstruct* by integrating multiple perspectives and new meanings. Mac Naughton and Williams (2009) signal that deconstructing as a complex critical process draws heavily on how language constructs, but also limits meaning. Deconstruction enables partners to perceive these restrictions and identify whose interests these represent prior to reconstructing new and fairer meanings.

FIGURE 4.6 Critical discussion of readings with colleagues can lead to further discussions about philosophy and practice with families.

The reflective tools examined in this section have the potential to enhance how educators use the reflective process. Some complexities in the process are outlined in what follows.

Reflective process

Schon (1983; 1987) saw reflection as occurring in two time frames: *reflection in action* and *reflection on action*. Most educators engage in *reflection in action* – constantly reflecting when making decisions on the floor about how to respond to children and how to implement spontaneous experiences. *Reflection on action* can occur before an experience as part of the planning process or after an experience or event; for example, at a staff meeting or after a family meeting. Therein lies the challenge: how to placehold *reflections in practice* for future use and how to share reflections with colleagues because *reflecting on reflections* assists everyone to take fresh perspectives over time.

When educators, especially student educators, grapple with challenging aspects of philosophy, theory and practice, *deep reflective process* may assist them to work innovatively with those aspects to reach some new awareness. The need for further learning and reconsidering connections between theory and practice can be identified through reflection (O'Connor & Diggins, 2002). The following box provides a guide for a deep reflective process.

O'Connor and Diggins (2002) highlight the importance of recognising how the values, beliefs and assumptions held by educators shape their reflections. Holding particular values that make it difficult to accept some practices or regulatory requirements, or holding certain assumptions or understandings, may influence the ways educators respond in certain situations. Others may be judged negatively. This happens with issues; for example, expectations of children's behaviour and processes for guiding behaviour. Many assumptions are culturally specific and based on personal experiences. It is important to be aware of personal values and assumptions and to recognise that others may hold different, and equally valid, beliefs and values. O'Connor and Diggins (2002, p. 26) suggest that 'reflective practice helps you to catch your own assumptions and explore them rather than take them for granted', as seen in samples of reflective practice questions (Abbey & Maclean, 2010; Giugni & Mundine, 2010). In Example 4.3, Patty, an education student on professional experience, examines her own and others' assumptions.

Reflective process

Describe a particularly significant aspect of your practice – this could be the way you interact with a particular child or group of children, family or educator, the way you organise the environment, document children's learning, etc. Write about the selected significant practice in detail regarding actions, conversations, ideas, resources, environment, etc.

- How do you feel about this practice? What do you see as your emerging values and beliefs?
- Which aspects of theoretical perspectives, philosophy and research might explain your practice?
- What have you learnt from clarifying your ideas about theoretical perspectives, philosophy, values and practice through conversations with educators, families, children, university advisers, and peer and communities of practice circles?
- How are you changing your thinking? What does this mean for changing your practices? Or how does your practice change your thinking?
- Based on this reflection, where are you going with your thinking and practice, especially in relation to connections and gaps? How does this link to your goals for professional learning?

EXAMPLE 4.3

Reflecting in practice and on practice – recognising diversity in self and others

The setting for my prac is different. I can sense the type of relationships that the educators have with each of the parents. They seem to have developed close relationships with those parents who have similar backgrounds to themselves.

One morning when a parent came to drop off her child, I heard a conversation between the parent and an educator. The parent was talking about a gifted boy who she saw on television: 'Isn't this boy's parent lucky that they have a boy that is intelligent and educated'. Louise (educator) said, 'But how about this boy's social skills … he probably doesn't have any friends because he doesn't have any people skills'. The parent continued, 'That doesn't matter because if you have brains you can do anything'. Louise responded, 'I don't agree with you on that'. It was from this conversation that I evaluated my own thinking. What did I think about this issue? Who did I agree with? Where do my values come from?

I continued thinking about this throughout the day. I could not decide on whose conversation I agreed with. I could understand both viewpoints, but it was just so hard to decide which I agreed with more. I then realised this was because I was brought up in Australia influenced by both Australian and Korean cultures. It was my family and community 'funds of knowledge' that gave me these conflicting views about this issue. I could understand both sides of the argument and why each party had those views. But as a student educator I believe I need to show that difference among children and families is valued and accepted by others and myself at the preschool. This is because knowledge is actively constructed by interpreting and building on what one already knows in their social context (Fleer & Robbins, 2006). Hence, we need to understand why and how people learn through their social participation in the practices of specific groups and cultures (Cairney, 2002). It is through this understanding of families and children that I can ensure experiences cater for all children to engage in purposeful and meaningful ways.

I feel that differing values, experiences and expectations of parents and educators about children's learning are not building on children's literacy understandings. My aim in my project is for educators, parents and student teachers to strengthen their relationships with one another through understanding of different views.

Source: Patty Yun, University of Western Sydney, 2006

Where reflective practice is thoughtfully integrated into regular staff meetings, participation and professional learning can be enhanced to strengthen philosophy to practice connections. Sharing reflections and questions about the program can deepen reflections for the group. See Barnes (2013) for case studies of settings where educators restructured staff meeting by reflecting on strengths and areas for improvement in their program. Many of these educators enhanced their expectations for meeting NQS, National Regulations and ECA Code of Ethics expectations and clarifying focus for their QIPs.

Critical reflection occurs as educators deepen their reflection to include different viewpoints of events and experiences in the program (DEEWR, 2009; Cartmel, Mac Farlene & Casley, 2012). Developing overarching questions and contributing questions guide educators to progressively deepen their investigation. See the following questions:

- What are my understandings of each child?
- What theories, philosophies and understandings shape and assist my work?
- Who is advantaged when I work this way? Who is disadvantaged?

- What questions do I have about my work? What am I challenged by? What am I curious about? What am I confronted by?
- What aspects of my work are not helped by the theories and guidance that I usually draw on to make sense of what I do?
- Are there other theories or knowledge that could help me understand best what I have observed or experienced? What are they? How might those theories and that knowledge affect my practice?

DEEWR, 2009, p.13

Critical reflection significantly makes topics visible that strengthen the program, which, when overlooked, limit children's learning opportunities. Approaching these topics involves children, educators and families in deepening their understandings of the community they live in and working towards fairer participation and learning outcomes. Some topics include Aboriginality, whiteness, gender sexualities, ethnicity/language, abilities, spirituality/religion and refugees (Giugni and Mundine, 2010). For example, some questions guiding critical reflection around Aboriginality/whiteness may include:

- How can we act together to resist dominant culture and its effects?
- How can we act to stand proud as one?
- How can we act to ensure that all people are given equal opportunities to participate in society?

M Giugni & K Mundine, 2010, p.21, *Talkin' Up and Speakin' Out: Aboriginal and Multicultural Voices in Early Childhood*, Castle Hill, Pademelon Press.

Finally it is important to continually draw on professional knowledge of practice along with theoretical perspectives, philosophy and ethics whenever reflecting. Participating in *strategic planning*, *quality improvement plans* and *research projects* engages partners in articulating and reflecting on philosophy, theory and practice, as discussed in the following section and in Chapter 11.

Strategic planning

Strategic planning
Describes the goals of the organisation and the strategies that will be used to achieve these goals (Kearns, 2007).

The term **strategic planning** has long been associated with long-term and short-term planning and evaluation within organisations, including settings and schools. It is now often linked to developing and evaluating the business plan for the setting/school.

What is strategic planning?

There are many definitions of strategic planning. Consider the following:

A strategic plan describes the goals of the organisation and the strategies that will be used to achieve these goals. It is a useful tool in assisting the organisation to work towards desired goals and to assist in decision making and the implementation of change.

K Kearns, *The Business of Child Care*, p 2, © 2007 Pearson Australia Group Pty Ltd.

These definitions suggest that strategic planning is a staged approach to planning and evaluation that will help any organisation, including settings and schools, to make fundamental decisions and produce actions that define what it does and why. In other words, this form of planning balances both broad long-term planning (philosophy and goals) and short-term planning (action, strategies, resources and formative evaluation).

Strategic planning in early childhood and school settings can:

- assist settings and schools to manage current and future challenges
- assist managers and educators to respond to change; for example, unpredictable resources, shifting community and government expectations, societal movements and economic climates
- maintain the vision for the setting/school
- support the leadership to build on organisational strengths and take advantage of opportunities, while minimising constraints and pressures on the organisation.

The benefits of using strategic planning are identified as providing clarity of work for everyone: 'the staff team will have an understanding of the goals to be achieved; and the service will have strategies for achieving a vision, which will generate a sense of community as people will want to get involved in achieving greater quality for the children and families of the service' (Community Child Care, 2004, S15.1).

Strategic planning (and evaluation) is one way of ensuring that families, children and the community are continually provided with a strong program. Educators have a responsibility to lead and guide their workplaces, local communities, profession and governments. By understanding strategic planning concepts, educators can better understand the direction their own and associated organisations are taking. Most organisations, such as children's services, schools, professional organisations, local councils, state and regional departments of school education, and local, state and federal government departments, as well as major corporations and businesses, develop strategic plans to guide their practice. See, for example, the strategic plan for Early Childhood Australia (Early Childhood Australia, 2008). Schools typically would have their own management plans reflecting aspects of the larger plan of their organisation and the Australian Curriculum.

In each work environment, strategic planning will improve the team's ability to achieve its goals and ensure that all partners are involved in the setting/school's planning process. The strategic planning process can assist in fulfilling many criteria related to mandates, or guidelines for settings/ schools (as detailed previously in this chapter). Finally, as team members, educators are empowered and, as a result, become more productive when participating in strategic planning.

When regular reflection and evaluation is integrated into the setting/school strategic plan, it can be used to respond to the service's unique strengths, potentials, challenges and resources. Strategic planning is a means of ensuring that the decisions made about the organisation will help to achieve the goals developed within the setting/school, and those developed by management and government bodies. The plan for each organisation will be different, but the steps in developing that plan may be reasonably similar; that is, the concepts, procedures and tools within the strategic planning process can be applied to any organisation.

Strategic planning can be undertaken in concise and direct ways as suggested by Kearns (2007) (*see* Table 4.4). Kearns emphasises that involving all partners in some way, as well as allocating resources to the plan, often shape its likely success.

The general steps involved in strategic planning are outlined in detail in Table 4.5. Any planning process needs to have direction – this comes from the philosophy. As illustrated here, the first step in the process is to consider what type of setting/school is desired, identifying the setting/school philosophy and mission/statement of purpose. The next step is to identify what is likely to have an impact upon implementing that philosophy; that is, to identify the mandates/ requirements and carry out the setting analysis. The setting philosophy/vision/statement of purpose will provide the broad direction for the setting. However, the goals that provide clear direction for the setting will also reflect the mandates and situational analysis. The steps, strategies, actions and resources should provide more details about how the setting will achieve its goals.

TABLE 4.4   Strategic planning.

DEVELOPMENT AND STATEMENT OF SETTING PHILOSOPHY AND VALUES
Description of who we are and what we do (organisation, financial situation and services offered to the community)   Analysis of description with Strengths, Weaknesses, Opportunities and Threats (SWOT)
Goals and rationales (What we want to achieve? Why?)   Long term (2–5 years)   Short term (12 months)
Action Plan including evaluation   How? When? Where? Why? Who? How will we know when we get there?

Source: adapted from K Kearns, *The Business of Child Care*, © 2007 Pearson Education Australia.

Whether the setting is achieving what it set out to in the philosophy, or whether it can be improved, is analysed through evaluation and reflection. This process may look linear in Tables 4.4 and 4.5; however, in practice, evaluation and reflection occur at each stage of the process (formative evaluation), while the process is reflected upon at the end of the regular time period (summative evaluation). Therefore, planning, evaluation and reflection on the strategic planning process involve:

- a vision of what is wanted
- knowledge and understanding of the strengths, needs and hopes of partners
- an analysis of available resources
- responsiveness to the existing constraints and freedoms
- accountability in terms of responsibility for future directions
- negotiation with major interest groups about desired outcomes and the means and resources to achieve them.

As both Table 4.4 and Table 4.5 illustrate, strategies, actions and resources used in the setting will be influenced by all factors within the strategic planning process, and by those who are involved in developing a strategic plan.

TABLE 4.5 Strategic planning process in action.

	STRATEGIC PLANNING IN ACTION
Philosophy	*The values underlying the process*: • What are the values of the society and community that drive the organisation/community? • How is the setting multicultural, bicultural or monocultural? • How is there a focus on equity of opportunity, specific religious beliefs or specific educational philosophies or approaches (e.g. High Scope, Steiner, Montessori, Reggio Emilia)? • What is the purpose of the organisation (e.g. charitable, family support or meeting changes in society, schooling)? • What is the value of individual/group strengths/interests?
Philosophical/ mission statements/ statement of purpose	*The ideal outcome (based on these values)*: • From the philosophy, what is the ideal that this organisation/setting has for itself? • If it could be the 'ideal setting', what features would it have? • Would it value all cultures; i.e. all people? • Would it encourage boys and girls equally? All children with diverse funds of knowledge? All children with diverse capabilities? • Would it provide positive discrimination to minorities? • Which educational ideas would it value? • What would justify its existence as a service?
Mandates – formal and informal	*What is allowed/required by outside factors*: • What is the setting obliged to do? • What rules, regulations or mandates must it follow? (National Quality Standard; Early Years Learning Framework; QIP; Melbourne Declaration on educational goals for young Australians; Australian Curriculum; NPST) • What does the community demand that it is ethically bound to follow? • What does the profession believe is important? • What are the standards (e.g. NQF, NPST, QIP)? • What does the management body/sponsor demand?

Situational analysis/ Understanding the setting	*The existing situation*: • Which stage is the setting at now? • What are its strengths, challenges and needs? • What opportunities exist for changes in funding, enrolments, grants, assistance and resources? • What are the constraints and potentials? • Who are the partners? How is current participation? • What external threats to its operation can we identify? • How different is it at present from the 'ideal setting' described in the philosophy/mission statement/statement of intent?
Goals	*The changes needed to move from the existing situation towards the philosophy/ mission*: • What are the changes we need to make to move our organisation/setting from what it is now to what we want it to be? • Are there any priorities?
Steps (short-term objectives)	*The steps to take in reaching the goals*: • For each goal, what steps can we take to begin making that change? • How long will it take? What is next? Are the steps in the best order? Are there alternatives if we have problems?
Strategies	*How to take these steps (major actions to achieve steps)*: • How can we take each step? • What barriers exist, and how can we overcome or learn to live with those barriers? • What resource potentials and problems are there (funds, time, educators, appropriate training and so on)? • What practical alternatives exist? • How will we evaluate our progress towards our goal? • What areas of policy development and professional learning might be appropriate?
Action/ Resources	*Actions and resources needed to undertake each strategy*: • When, where and how will the strategy be undertaken? • When, where and who will put the agreed strategies in place? • Which resources will help? • Do we have these resources or do we need new resources?
Evaluation	*Looking at what happened, and using those insights to contribute to future planning*: • How well did we achieve our change? • Is it achievable? • How far did we go towards it? • What is the next goal/step/strategy? • Do we need to rethink the philosophy or situation, goals, strategies/actions or resources?

Source: adapted S Farmer, *Policy Development in Early Childhood Services*, © 1995, Community Child Care Co-operative; originally developed by Leo Prendergast, UTS Child Care, 1994.

Annual reports, which can form part of accountability to funding bodies or management committees, are formal ways to gather information from colleagues and management, and reflect on and set work plans for the next year. This report process is an example of strategic planning in action. Reflection upon the previous year may be constrained by rigid guidelines. In NSW, annual reports from schools are available to school communities and head office. However, it is often not

the end product that is of most value, but the process shared as all stakeholders are involved in compiling the document. Directors/managers/principals must resist the urge to 'just do it' and, instead, facilitate a collaborative process with adequate time where team members enhance their evaluative perspectives of the program. See Example 4.4 for the collaborative process for strategic planning and evaluating at Rainbow Children's Centre, as explained to families (complete details are found in Chapter 5, Chapter 6 and Chapter 7 for approaches). Following this is the director's insightful outline of the evaluation and reflection undertaken by the team (*see* Example 4.5).

EXAMPLE 4.4
Strategic planning at Rainbow Children's Centre

Rainbow Children's Centre Inc. including Ballina Early Intervention

Annual Centre Planning
Report to committee from Leo Prendergast
Monday, 7 June 2012

I have prepared this discussion paper setting out the Annual Centre Plan for 2010. I am sorry it has taken so far into the year for it to be presented, but the Enterprise Agreement and some staffing issues took my focus away from the plan for some time.

This year's plan is different to previous years. There have been many matters discussed and decisions made by the Committee over the last year. The plan seeks to place those policy, financial and procedural decisions into a coherent and unified format. The planning process is an important tool to assist all families and staff to understand and appreciate the aims of the centre and how and why operational and management decisions are made. As well, the staff, at evening staff meetings and Jackie and myself in particular collating all the ideas put forward by staff, have looked at what we are trying to achieve – what values and principles we are utilising in creating an effective and appropriate learning environment for children. The process has completely reviewed the philosophy, mission and vision to better clarify what we are on about in today's Rainbow.

As well, we have had a significant change in our operations over the past five years, and will face further changes again in the next five. We have developed new OOSHC services, changed hours operation, changed the number of childcare places and amalgamated with BEI. As well our external environment has changed, with new Government Regulations and expected outcomes for all early childhood services and the new *Early Years Learning Framework* setting out the expected curriculum for ECE. Society as a whole and Government has told Rainbow it wants a review of the operation of all ECE services across Australia, including Rainbow, and a fundamental re-evaluation of what services should be available in our children's centres. I believe this document reflects those changes.

We have added a section to our planning format from previous plans. It is a 'vision' for Rainbow. It has become more apparent to staff in a number of ways that Rainbow operates in ways that are not the same as many other ECE services. Following staff discussions, staff training and in-service, recruitment of staff with experiences at other centres plus visits by Rainbow staff to other centres, it is clear that we operate under some planning principles that are unique to our centre. Our 'vision' is an attempt to outline those special features of Rainbow as a Children's Service that define the way we work. While many parents and committee members will be familiar with the ideas of emergent curriculum and mixed age grouping, this vision is far broader than that as it embraces child choice, child directed programs, play based curriculum, natural play environments etc.

The format used for the report is:

Centre philosophy	setting out **our agreed basic beliefs and values** as an organisation
Centre mission	setting out **our agreed vision** of what the centre is broadly trying to achieve
Centre vision	setting out the **broad principles** under which we operate the centre and its services to enable us to fulfil our mission. It defines what our organisation and its services will look like and how it will operate so we can meet our mission and operate within our philosophy
Situational analysis	setting out **our agreed understanding of where the centre is at the moment** and an evaluation of what we have achieved in 2009
Centre objectives	setting out the **agreed main strategies we will undertake in 2010** to enable us to progress during the year so that hopefully the centre is closer to our agreed vision by the end of 2010. It will be important that during 2010, when we are making decisions, we look to see how each decision will assist us in moving closer to that vision

I hope that members do not see this as a merely theoretical process. As a group we need to know where we want to get to and we need to make sure our decisions assist us in that journey. In particular we need to consider:

- Are you in agreement that the philosophy reflects the beliefs we should have?
- Are you happy that the Mission and Vision succinctly sets out what we want to do at this centre?
- Are you prepared to endorse the aims set out for Rainbow Children's Centre for 2010?

Source: Rainbow Children's Centre Inc., *Report to Committee*, 7 June 2010, p. 1

The process for implementing strategic planning undertaken at each service needs planning that offers clarity, opportunities for participation and adequate resources, especially time. Example 4.5 illustrates how strategic planning investigates and builds on current philosophy and practice before examining the mandatory EYLF requirements as assessed by NQF.

EXAMPLE 4.5
Process for strategic planning at Rainbow Children's Centre

In considering the EYLF, the centre first obtained sufficient copies of the EYLF documentation and over a 4–6 week period copies were left on the staff room table, staff read them and there were numerous conversations among staff to familiarise themselves with the EYLF documentation.

1. We then held an evening staff planning meeting with all staff present. We normally hold such meetings each six months. The first thing we discussed was a philosophical issue. Why do we want and how should we use an external curriculum document?

a. Do we implement a high quality ECE program for our children because an external body says we should do so? If so then that external curriculum (e.g., NQS or NCAC or NSW Curriculum Framework) should be our starting point and everything we do starts from and stems from one of those documents. They set the standard and we follow as we are required to. We respect them as the 'authority' re. ECE curriculum and want to implement whatever standards have been set out by their experts about what constitutes high quality ECE.

b. Or do we implement a high quality program because we (the staff and families at our service and in our community) believe it is important for the children in our care? If so, then our program planning should start from a statement of our beliefs and our expectations and our knowledge.

c. We as a group of staff clearly agreed that we want to implement a high-quality ECE program, due to our beliefs in the rights of the children in our care. As such it was important that in designing, implementing and evaluating our program, we did so on our terms and based on our philosophy and our beliefs. As such our program is the Rainbow program and it is unique to our centre. Having done so, if we are then required by an external body to prove that our program also meets their standards, so be it. However, that process becomes a secondary and not a primary motivation for what we do and how we do it.

2. All staff had been asked to come to the evening staff meeting with up to five things they liked about our program and felt were important. We collected all the ideas and spent the meeting discussing them and where there were overlaps and coming up with a list of 29 features – important, valued, desired and respected features of our Rainbow program. The 29 included obvious matters such as mixed age grouping, child initiated learning and emergent curriculum as well as less obvious matters such as that staff support the emotional stability of each child, staff assist children in creating inviting and colourful spaces, and children and parents are encouraged to value the aesthetics of the centre and its surrounds.

3. We then looked at these 29 program features to see if they were in line with our statement of centre philosophy. We were pleased to see that they were generally in line but it highlighted a couple of important areas not covered by the centre philosophy. We subsequently raised this with the parent committee and it resulted in a review of the philosophy and some changes where the families agreed there should be more emphasis on the rights of children to a high quality learning experience and to an inspiring living/learning environment. Our philosophy moved from one which emphasised the aspirations and beliefs of staff and parents to one which expressed more clearly the rights of all our children to high quality education and care.

4. We (staff and families) agreed we would call these the 29 'Principles of our learning environment'. It was agreed that in our programming and our evaluation we should test what we do each day and each week to see that the program we are actually providing is in line with those principles and is therefore contributing to our ensuring the centre program is in line with our agreed Rainbow philosophy.

5. Our next step was to map how these 29 principles compared against the EYLF principles. At another evening a few months later, we found – much to our joy – that our principles did fit very well with the EYLF and that our 29 principles did indeed reflect most of the EYLF agenda. It was easy to categorise our 29 learning environment principles within the five EYLF principles (or depending on how you look at it, how the five EYLF principles fitted into our

learning environment principles) Hence all staff could see how our 29 principles then would lead us to the same outcomes for children as required by the EYLF. We recognised that much of what they were already doing was in line with the EYLF requirements.

6. As such our next evening staff meeting would focus on developing a recording and evaluation process that allowed us to continue with our agreed learning environment principles, but to record the program evaluations in such a way that an outsider coming in (such as an NQS assessor) would be able to see how the NQS was being implemented in our centre using our learning environment principles.

Source: Leo Prendergast, Rainbow Children's Centre, Ballina, 2011

Strategic planning is just as important in schools; for example, Robert Townson Public School, NSW Department Education and Communities, as shown in Example 4.6. Note the revised plan showing the focus for the school and the professional learning for educators from participating in federal government partnerships, as part of the MEECDYA strategic plan 2009–2012. This shows the adaptability and responsiveness of educators to changing circumstances and opportunities.

EXAMPLE 4.6
Strategic planning at Robert Townson Public School

ROBERT TOWNSON PUBLIC SCHOOL
SCHOOL PLAN FOR 2009–2011

School context

Robert Townson Public School is situated near Campbelltown. School based decisions are made in the best interests of students. At Robert Townson we are committed to maximising learning outcomes for all with a philosophy that reflects our school motto 'Aim High'. The school has an enrolment of 585 students (220 K-2 and 365 3-6). There are 22 students (3.5%) from indigenous backgrounds and 179 (30.5%) NESB students. The school numbers are stable. The staff comprises a mix of experienced and early career teachers as well as permanent and temporary teachers. A number of teachers are working in a part time capacity. Students are supported by a learning support team, a school counsellor (.6), a reading recovery program and an allocation of 1.3 STLA and 1.0 ESL. Aboriginal education has become an area of increasing focus with an increase in indigenous students and an appointment of an indigenous classroom teacher. Literacy and numeracy have both been priority areas for the last 3 years in an attempt to improve student achievement. The Jolly Phonics program was introduced into Early Stage One in 2008 and the Jolly Grammar program for Year One in 2009. In 2008 the school successfully completed a Writing Curriculum Project that focussed on the writing of quality sentences. This program has been evaluated and recommendations have resulted in the development of a consistent stage based writing criteria and editing checklist. This year the school has had the support of regional consultants in implementing Count Me in Too and Counting On programs as well as involvement in the Working Mathematically Project.

School priority areas (3-year horizon)	Target
1. Improved literacy with a focus on Reading outcomes for all students	1.1 To decrease the proportion of Year 3 students at or below national minimum standard (lowest two bands) in Reading to 12.5% 1.2 To decrease the proportion of Year 5 students at or below national minimum standard (lowest two bands) in Reading to 19.5% (meeting the required 2.5%) 1.3 To increase the proportion of Year 3 students at state proficiency standard (top two bands) in Reading to 41.5% (exceeding the required 1.5%) 1.4 To increase the proportion of Year 5 students at state proficiency standard (top two bands) in Reading to 32% (exceeding the required 1.5%) 1.5 To increase the proportion of students achieving expected minimum growth in Reading to 79.6% by 2011
2. Improved numeracy outcomes for all students	2.1 To decrease the proportion of Year 3 and Year 5 students at or below national minimum standard (lowest two bands) in Numeracy to 5.5% Year 3 and 24.5% Year 5 2.2 To increase the proportion of Year 3 students at state proficiency standard (top two bands) in Numeracy to 34% and Year 5 students to 30% (exceeding the required 1.5%) 2.3 To increase the proportion of students achieving expected minimum growth in Numeracy to 77% in 2011 2.4 To improve the diagnostic assessment of numeracy in Kindergarten 2.5 The implementation of a rigorous continuum of learning in numeracy K-6
3. Improved levels of student engagement	3.1 Quality teaching strategies are evident in class programs and classroom practice 3.2 Improved internal and external performance data regarding student achievement 3.3 Increased use of technology in classroom practice as evidenced through surveys, discussions and observations 3.4 Diminished gap between aboriginal students and non aboriginal students

THE PLAN HAS BEEN ENDORSED AND IMPROVED BY:			
Principal:	Date:	School Education Director:	Date:

REVISED SCHOOL PLAN AS AT 8.12.09			

School priority area: Improved literacy with a focus on reading outcomes for all students

Intended outcomes:

1.6 To decrease the proportion of Year 3 students at or below national minimum standard (lowest band) in Reading by 2.5%

1.7 To decrease the proportion of Year 5 students at or below national minimum standard (lowest band) in Reading by 2.5%

1.8 To increase the proportion of Year 3 students at state proficiency standard (top two bands) in Reading by 1.5%

1.9 To increase the proportion of Year 5 students at state proficiency standard (top two bands) in Reading by 1.5%

1.10 To increase the proport ion of students achieving expected minimum growth in Reading to 75% by 2011

Intended outcomes	Target 2009	Target 2010	Target 2011
1.1 To decrease the proportion of Year 3 students at or below national minimum standard (lowest band) in Reading by 2.5%	**1.1** To decrease the proportion of Year 3 students at or below national minimum standard (lowest two bands) in Reading from 20% in 2008 to 17.5%	**1.1** To decrease the proportion of Year 3 students at or below national minimum standard (lowest two bands) in Reading to 15%	**1.1** To decrease the proportion of Year 3 students at or below national minimum standard (lowest two bands) in Reading to 12.5%
1.2 To decrease the proportion of Year 5 students at or below national minimum standard (lowest band) in Reading by 2.5%	**1.2** To decrease the proportion of Year 5 students at or below national minimum standard (lowest two bands) in Reading from 27% in 2008 to 24.5%	**1.2** To decrease the proportion of Year 5 students at or below national minimum standard (lowest two bands) in Reading to 22%	**1.2** To decrease the proportion of Year 5 students at or below national minimum standard (lowest two bands) in Reading to 19.5%
1.3 To increase the proportion of Year 3 students at state proficiency standard (top two bands) in Reading by 1.5%	**1.3** To increase the proportion of Year 3 students at state proficiency standard (top two bands) in Reading from 37% in 2008 to 38.5%	**1.3** To increase the proportion of Year 3 students at state proficiency standard (top two bands) in Reading to 40%	**1.3** To increase the proportion of Year 3 students at state proficiency standard (top two bands) in Reading to 41.5%
1.4 To increase the proportion of Year 5 students at state proficiency standard (top two bands) in Reading by 1.5%	**1.4** To increase the proportion of Year 5 students at state proficiency standard (top two bands) in Reading from 14% in 2008 to 28% (exceeding 1.5%)	**1.4** To increase the proportion of Year 5 students at state proficiency standard (top two bands) in Reading to 30% (exceeding 1.5%)	**1.4** To increase the proportion of Year 5 students at state proficiency standard (top two bands) in Reading to 32% (exceeding 1.5%)

1.5 To increase the proportion of students achieving expected minimum growth in Reading to 75% by 2011	**1.5** To increase the proportion of students achieving expected minimum standard from 45.6% in 2008 to 69.7% in Reading	**1.5** To increase the proportion of students achieving expected minimum standard to 74.6% in Reading	**1.5** To increase the proportion of students achieving expected minimum standard to 79.6% in Reading

Source: Robert Townson Public School, 2011

Programs for extending all children's learning

Ongoing evaluation and reflection provide catalysts to continually strengthen programs. Responding to and managing change is more complex than simply being aware of what is or what might be happening. For example, many educators are 'aware' of new standards and learning and curriculum documents, but this may mean only knowing the abbreviation of the title. Everyone faces challenges on a daily basis, making sense of the flood of changing mandates, understandings, legislation and research, as well as census surveys, general surveys, funding applications and general information that materialise. Texts are rarely neutral (Knobel & Healy, 1998), so critical reflection is imperative. To ensure that setting/school programs continually strengthen to extend all children's learning, educators must use evaluation and reflection in meaningful ways.

Whole-setting/school evaluations, such as strategic planning or quality improvement plans, focus on the total program for all partners in the setting. This form of evaluation is important since it helps systematic consideration of many aspects of the program. Initially this long-term evaluation may seem unnecessary and redundant since evaluation is part and parcel of daily planning and the more irregular special-purpose evaluations. However, unless educators *stop*, *evaluate* and *reflect* on what makes up the total program, they may focus on their own interests, those aspects of the program with which they feel comfortable or that which urgently demands attention. In addition, becoming easily sidetracked into daily program tasks or responding to the latest wave of changes can take priority. The National Standard, Strategic Planning and Annual Reports are examples of this form of evaluation. These present an opportunity for educators, families, children, managers and community members to participate in shared reflection and evaluation of many elements of the program as well as gain feedback from critical friends.

Evaluating using a comprehensive but focused guide, such as one constructed at the setting/school or adapting a standardised evaluation (keeping in mind the purpose and nature of the instrument), should help identify strong consistencies and paradoxes in the setting/school. Evaluation can provide a representation of the program, as well as offer constructive feedback that acknowledges and further extends what is being done well. Importantly, it identifies areas where improvement is needed. This kind of constructive feedback process should enhance team competence as curriculum decision makers and problem solvers – skills, abilities and dispositions needed in responding to change in the wider world. From the recommendations, a plan of action guiding future practice can be developed.

Whole-setting evaluation and reflection involves planning and evaluation decisions across the whole program for the long term, taking into account many of the aspects below. Effective and meaningful evaluation and reflection can occur every time educators strengthen the following aspects:

- the theoretical perspectives, philosophies and values that are appreciated
- understandings of the community, families and setting

- curriculum approaches that are most consistent with the theoretical perspectives, philosophy, values and the individual setting/school
- issues of equity and social justice, participation and democratic dialogue in the program
- educator interactions and communications with families, colleagues, other professionals and community members
- processes of assessing and sharing children's learning
- experiences and projects that are planned and implemented
- educator interactions with children and children's interactions with each other
- pedagogies used to extend children's learning
- methods of program evaluation and reflection that would be most appropriate in these circumstances.

As already mentioned, the general aim of evaluation and reflection is to continually improve programs in early childhood and schools for children and families. It is important to remember that there is no one definitive set of quality practices. Dahlberg et al. (2007), among others, dispute any universal framework of quality in settings and schools.

Conclusion and reflection

Evaluation and reflection form an essential part of the planning process as outlined in this chapter. Some concepts and examples of principles, processes and tools of evaluation and reflection were identified that educators can use to strengthen programs to extend learning for all children. When evaluation and reflection align with the theoretical perspectives, beliefs and values embedded in the setting/school philosophy, philosophy and practice connections will be enhanced. Gathering information from and with partners about aspects of the program broadens the information for analysis and enriches the recommendations for improving the program. Evaluation and reflection are integral to programs achieving quality identified by the mandatory NQF (ACEQA, 2013), which includes the NQS, national regulations and quality assurance for early childhood settings. Similarly the Australian Curriculum will undergo continual monitoring, evaluation and review with yearly reports to the ACARA board (ACARA, 2012).

Questions for reflection

1. How are practices at a setting/school you are familiar with moving closer towards the philosophy? How do you know? Where is the evidence? What is the next step? Who is involved on a regular basis? Who is not involved? How could informal and formal participation be increased?

2. Which aspects of the program cause joy or concern for children, families, educators and yourself? When did partners last gather and analyse information about this aspect before recommending a change to practice. How did this change strengthen practice?

3. How have educators or yourself used evaluation and reflection in the program this week? How did it help strengthen the program? How did it influence children's learning? How might educators or yourself use critical reflection?

Key terms

action plan 121
assessment, 107
critical reflective practice, 109
evaluation, 107
partners, 107
reflection, 108
reflective practice, 108
strategic planning 130

Online study resources

Visit http://login.cengagebrain.com and use the access code that comes with this book for 12 months access to the student resources for this text.

CourseMate Express  CourseMateExpress

The CourseMate Express website contains a range of resources and study tools for this chapter, including:

- Online video activities
- Online research activities
- A revision quiz
- Matching pair exercises
- A list of key weblinks
- A chapter glossary, flashcards and crossword to help you revise terminology
- and more!

Search me! education ▶ Search me!

Explore **Search me! education** for articles relevant to this chapter. Fast and convenient, Search me! education is updated daily and provides you with 24-hour access to full text articles from hundreds of scholarly and popular journals, ebooks and newspapers, including *The Australian* and *The New York Times*. Log in to Search me! through http://login.cengage.com and try searching for the following key words:

- critical reflective practice
- collaborating
- criteria
- evaluating
- meaning based evaluation
- partners
- quality
- reflecting
- reflection journals
- reflective practice
- standardised evaluation
- strategic planning
- values.

Search tip: **Search me! education** contains information from both local and international sources. To get the greatest number of search results, try using both Australian and American spellings in your searches, e.g. 'globalisation' and 'globalization'; 'organisation' and 'organization'

Recommended resources

Abbey, B & MacLean, P 2010, *What is Reflective Practice and What Does it Mean for You?*,
http://www.psctas.org.au/wp-content/uploads/2011/02/reflective-practice-self-questions.pdf , accessed 9 March 2011.

Australian Curriculum, Assessment and reporting Authority (ACARA), nd, *The Australian Curriculum*,
http://www.australiancurriculum.edu.au/, accessed 19 February 2014.

Australian Curriculum Assessment and Reporting Authority (ACARA) 2012, *Assessment and Reporting: Improving Student Performance.*
ACARA, Sydney, http://www.acara.edu.au/verve/_resources/Assessment__Reporting__Improving_Student_Performance.pdf, accessed
15 February 2014.

Barnes, H 2013, *Critical Reflection as a Tool for Change: Stories about Quality Improvement.* Early Childhood Australia, Deakin West.

Cartmel, J, MacFarlene, K & Casley, M 2012, *Reflection as a Tool for Quality: Working with the National Quality Standard*, Early Childhood
Australia, Deakin West.

Department of Education, Employment and Workplace Relations (DEEWR) 2009, *Belonging, Being and Becoming: The Early Years Learning
Framework for Australia*, Commonwealth of Australia, Canberra.

Malaguzzi, L 1998, 'History, ideas and basic philosophy', in C Edwards, L Gandini & G Forman (eds), *The Hundred Languages of Children*,
2nd edn., Ablex, NJ, pp. 49–97.

O'Connor, A & Diggins, C 2002, *On Reflection: Reflective Practice for Early Childhood Educators*, Open Mind Publishing, Lower Hutt, New Zealand.

Russell, A n.d., *Child Care Staff: Learning and Growing through Professional Development*, Professional Support Coordinator Alliance, South
Australia.

Key weblinks

The Australian Curriculum Design and Development, http://www.acara.edu.au/curriculum/curriculum_design_and_development.html
Australian Curriculum, http://www.acara.edu.au/default.asp
Code of Ethics, http://earlychildhoodaustralia.org.au/pdf/code_of_ethics/code_of_ethics_web.pdf
Code of ethics literature review, http://www.earlychildhoodaustralia.org.au/code_of_ethics/code_of_ethics_literature_review.html
National Assessment Program Literacy and Numeracy: NAPLAN, http://www.naplan.edu.au
National Curriculum, http://www.australiancurriculum.edu.au/Home
Towards a National Agenda for Early Childhood Policy,
http://www.earlychildhoodaustralia.org.au/early_childhood_news/submissions/towards_a_national_agenda_for_early_childhood.html
National Early Years Learning Framework and National Curriculum, http://education.gov.au/early-years-learning-framework
National Professional Standards for Teachers,
http://www.aitsl.edu.au/verve/_resources/AITSL_National_Professional_Standards_for_Teachers.pdf
National Teaching Standards, http://www.teacherstandards.aitsl.edu.au/Standards/
National Quality Standard, http://acecqa.gov.au/national-quality-framework/the-national-quality-standard
National Quality Standard Quality Areas, http://www.acecqa.gov.au/quality-areas
Professional Support Co-ordinator, Western Australia, https://www.facebook.com/PSCWA
Research in practice, http://www.earlychildhoodaustralia.org.au/research_in_practice_series/about_rips.html

References

Australian Curriculum Assessment and Reporting Authority (ACARA), nd, *Australian Curriculum*,
http://www.acara.edu.au/curriculum/curriculum_design_and_development.html, accessed 15 February 2014.

Australian Curriculum Assessment and Reporting Authority (ACARA), 2013a, *The Shape of the Australian Curriculum October 2012*,
http://www.acara.edu.au/verve/_resources/The_Shape_of_the_Australian_Curriculum_v4.pdf, accessed 15 February 2014.

Australian Curriculum Assessment and Reporting Authority (ACARA), 2013b; *Student Diversity and the Australian Curriculum*, ACARA,
Sydney, http://www.australiancurriculum.edu.au/StudentDiversity/Pdf/StudentDiversity, accessed 15 February, 2014.

Australian Curriculum Assessment and Reporting Authority (ACARA), 2012, *Curriculum Development Process Version 6*,
http://acara.edu.au/verve/_resources/ACARA_Curriculum_Development_Process_Version_6.0_-_04_April_2012_-_FINAL_COPY.pdf,
accessed 15 February 2014.

Australian Children's Education and Care Quality Authority (ACECQA), October 2011, *Guide to Developing a Quality Improvement Plan.*
ACECQA.

Australian Children's Education and Care Quality Authority (ACECQA) 2013, *Guide to the National Quality Standard*,
http://files.acecqa.gov.au/files/National-Quality-Framework-Resources-Kit/NQF03-Guide-to-NQS-130902.pdf, accessed 15 January 2014.

Australian Institute for Teaching and School Leadership 2011, *Professional National Standards for Teachers*,
http://www.aitsl.edu.au/verve/_resources/AITSL_National_Professional_Standards_for_Teachers.pdf, accessed 16 February 2014.

Barnes, H 2013, *Critical Reflection as a Tool for Change: Stories about Quality Improvement.* Early Childhood Australia, Deakin West.

Briggs, F & Potter, G 1999, *The Early Years of School*, Longmans, South Melbourne.

Cairney, T, 2002, 'Bridging home and school literacy: In search of transformative approaches to curriculum', *Early Child Development and
Care*, vol. 172, no. 2, pp.153–72.

Cartmel, J, MacFarlene, K & Casley, M 2012, *Reflection as a Tool for Quality: Working with the National Quality Standard*, Early Childhood
Australia, Deakin West.

Community Child Care 2004, *Managing a Child Care Service: A Hands on Guide for Service Providers*, Community Child Care, Sydney.

Cozolino, L & Sprokay, S 2006, 'Neuroscience and adult learning', in S Johnson & K Taylor (eds), *The Neuroscience of Adult Learning: New
Directions for Adult and Continuing Education*, no. 110, Summer, Jossey-Bass, San Francisco, pp. 11–20.

Curtis, D & Carter, M 2003, *Designs for Living and Learning*, Redleaf Press, St Paul, MN.

Dahlberg, G, Moss, P & Pence, A 1999/2007, *Beyond Quality in Early Childhood Education and Care: Postmodern Perspectives*, 1st/2nd edn.,
Falmer Press, London.

Department of Education, Employment and Workplace Relations 2010, *Educators, Belonging, Being and Becoming: Educators Guide to The Early Years Learning Framework for Australia*, DEEWR, Barton.

Dockett, S, Perry, B, Campbell, H, Hard, L, Kearney, E, Taffe, R & Greenhill, J 2007, *Early Years Curriculum Continuity for Learning Project: Final Report*, South Australian Department of Education and Children's Services, Adelaide.

Early Childhood Australia 2006, *Early Childhood Australia Code of Ethics*, Early Childhood Australia, Canberra.

Early Childhood Australia 2008, *Strategic Directions January 2009 December 2011*, http://www.earlychildhoodaustralia.org.au/pdf/submissions/eca_strategic_directions_2009_11.pdf, accessed 12 September 2011.

Farmer, S 1995, *Policy Development in Early Childhood Services*, Community Child Care Cooperative, Sydney.

Fenech, M 2006, 'The impact of regulatory environments on early childhood professional practice and job satisfaction', *Australian Journal of Early Childhood*, vol. 31, no. 2, June, pp. 49–57.

Fleer, M & Robbins, J 2006, 'Diversity in the context of universal early childhood education: Family involvement or family exclusion?', in M. Fleer et al. (eds), *Early Childhood Learning Communities: Sociocultural Research in Practice*, Pearson Education Australia, Frenchs Forest, NSW, pp. 57–69.

Fu, V, Stremmel, A & Hill, L (eds) 2002, *Teaching and Learning: Collaborative Exploration of the Reggio Emilia Approach*, Pearson Education, Upper Saddle River, NJ.

Goodwin, J 2009, 'Interview with Jo Goodwin', *Every Child*, vol. 15, no. 4, Early Childhood Australia, Deakin, ACT.

Greenway, C , 2013, '"Look, it's me!" The power of critical reflection in a teacher's journey', *Challenge*, November, pp. 28–33.

Harms, T, Clifford, R & Cryer, D 1980/1998, *Early Childhood Environment Rating Scale*, Teachers College Press, New York.

Helm, J, Beneke S & Steinheimer, K 1998, *Windows on Learning: Documenting Young Children's Work*, Teachers College Press, New York.

Holly, M 2003/1987, *Keeping a Personal-professional Journal*, 2nd edn., University of New South Wales Press, Sydney & Deakin University, Melbourne.

Isley, BJ 2000, *Tamil Nadu Early Childhood Environment Rating Scale*, MS Swaminathan Research Foundation, Madras.

Kearns, K 2007, *The Business of Child Care*, Pearson Education Australia, Frenchs Forest.

Knobel, M & Healy, A (eds) 1998, *Critical Literacies in the Primary Classroom*, Primary English Teaching Association, Newtown.

Mac Naughton, G & Williams, G 2009, *Techniques for Teaching Young Children*, 3rd edn., Pearson Education Australia, Frenchs Forest.

Makin, L, Hayden, J, Holland, A, Arthur, L, Beecher, B, Jones Diaz, C, et al., 1999, *Mapping Literacy Practices in Early Childhood Services*, NSW Department of Education and Training and NSW Department of Community Services, Sydney.

McNiff, J & Whitehead, J 2005, 'Teachers as educational theorists: Transforming epistemological hegemonies', paper presented at the British Educational Research Association Annual Conference, University of Glamorgan, 16 September, 2005.

Miller, L, Cable, C & Devereux, J 2005, *Developing Early Years Practice*, The Open University, London.

Ministerial Council for Education, Early Childhood Development and Youth Affairs 2009, *MCEECDYA Four Year plan*, http://www.mceecdya.edu.au/mceecdya/action_plan,25966.html, accessed 17 February 2014.

Moll, L, Amanti, C, Neff, D & Gonzalez, N 1992, 'Funds of knowledge for teaching: Using a qualitative approach to connect homes and classrooms', *Theory into Practice*, vol. 31, no. 2, pp. 132–41.

National Childcare Accreditation Council 2006, *Quality Improvement and Accreditation System Handbook*, 4th edn., National Childcare Accreditation Council, Surry Hills.

O'Connor, A & Diggins, C 2002, *On Reflection: Reflective Practice for Early Childhood Educators*, Open Mind Publishing, Lower Hutt, New Zealand.

Prendergast, L 1994, *Early Childhood Environments 4*, unpublished lecture, University of Western Sydney, Macarthur.

Reid, M, Farmer, S & Mawson M 2010, *Journeys of Inclusion*, Lifeline Communitycare Queensland & UnitingCare Queensland.

Roskos, K, Risko, V & Vukelich, C 1998, 'Head start and the practice of literacy pedagogy', *Reading Research Quarterly*, vol. 3, no. 2, pp. 228–39.

Schon, D 1983, *The Reflective Practitioner: How Professionals Think in Action*, Basic Books, New York.

Schon, D 1987, *Educating the Reflective Practitioner Towards a New Design for Teaching and Learning in the Professions*, Jossey Bass, San Francisco, CA.

Smith, MK 2001/2006, '"Evaluation" in the encyclopaedia of informal education', http://www.infed.org/biblio/b-eval.htm, accessed 8 February 2007.

Sylva, K, Siraj-Blatchford, I, Melhuish, E, Sammons, P, Taggart, B, Evans, E et al., 1999, *The Effective Provision of Pre-school Education Project (EPPE)*, Technical Paper 6, Characteristics of the centres in the EPPE Sample: Observational profiles, DfES/Institute of Education, University of London.

Sylva, K, Siraj-Blatchford, I & Taggart, B 2003/2006, *Assessing Quality in the Early Years: Early Childhood Environment Rating Scale – Extension (ECERS-E) Four curricular subscales*, Trentham Books, Oakhill.

Tietze, W, Cryer, D, Bairrao, J, Palacios, J & Wetzel, G 1996, 'Comparisons of observed process quality in early child care and education programs in five countries', *Early Childhood Research Quarterly*, vol. 11, no. 4, pp. 447–75.

Whitehead, J 2005, 'Living inclusional values in educational standards of practice and judgement', *Ontario Action Researcher*, vol. 8, no. 2.1, pp. 1–29, www.nipissingu.ca/oar/PDFS/V821E.pdf, assessed 28 March 2011.

· CHAPTER FIVE ·

DEVELOPING PHILOSOPHIES

Chapter learning focus

This chapter will investigate:

- the importance of developing a personal/ professional and setting philosophy

- processes of philosophy development

- documenting a philosophy

- implementing and evaluating a philosophy through reflective practice.

Introduction

As explored in Chapter 4, the starting points in any planning process for early childhood settings and schools are to understand why strategic planning is an integral part of all educational settings (Waniganayake, Cheeseman, Fenech, Hadley & Shepherd, 2012) and how this might be put into practice. This requires much evaluation of what early childhood educators have done in the past, awareness of how theoretical perspectives influence the beliefs and values educators hold about children and families and reflections on changing perspectives on curriculum processes and quality standards.

Central to developing new practices, responding to change and rethinking our relationships with children and families are beliefs and values – that is, our philosophy. As suggested by Waniganayake et al. (2012, p. 83) 'underpinning any future plans for an early childhood setting are the guiding beliefs and values that give the organisation a purpose'. These beliefs and values derive from different theories as well as experience. Educators generally draw on a range of theories – such as developmental, sociocultural and post-structural theories – and related theorists – such as Piaget, Vygotsky and Foucault – to provide different lenses to assist in analysing and responding to complex issues (CSU Early Years Learning Framework Consortium, 2009).

A philosophy provides a vision or set of principles which underpin practice (Broinowski, 2002; DEEWR, 2009; Farmer, 1995; Mac Naughton & Williams, 2009). An effectively developed and documented philosophy shapes a sense of identity within a setting and creates a culture of ongoing reflection and continual improvement.

This chapter considers processes for developing both a personal and shared philosophy and provides a range of examples of philosophies in early childhood settings and schools. What educators understand, value and believe to be important in their work with children and families will largely determine their practices. To bring about a change in understanding and practice (as explored in Chapters 1 and 11) or implement practices which reflect the theoretical perspectives, beliefs and values that are important in any setting, educators, families and managers need to work together to identify these perspectives and beliefs so that pedagogical practices are aligned with philosophical guidelines (Widger & Schofield, 2012).

What is a philosophy?

A **philosophy** interprets the theoretical perspectives, beliefs and values that underpin practices. It may be called a philosophy, but often terms such as 'beliefs' or '**values**' will be used as alternatives. When undertaking a strategic planning process, some organisations and settings will not only develop a philosophy but also a **mission** and a **vision** for that service or organisation (as explored in Chapter 4). Carter and Curtis (2010) outline the differences between the ideas of a mission and a vision:

> A mission statement is usually about purpose, but it is seldom about a dream. Typically, a mission statement tries to address a problem with a statement of services. A vision … goes beyond how things are to describe how we would like them to be.

M Carter & D Curtis, *The Visionary Director*, pp. 21–2 © 2010 Redleaf Press, a division of Think Small.

Each stakeholder, whether an educator or family member, has a particular vision – with knowledge, beliefs, assumptions and values – about education. These beliefs and values are reflected in what he/she does each day. These are the core ideals or dreams at the centre of daily practices. Sometimes these ideals are clearly articulated and visible.

At other times, educators are not aware of their perspectives, vision or philosophy, or its patterns, inconsistencies or paradoxes, and how they influence their behaviour and expectations. It is important to remember that even though a philosophy may not be formalised and recorded, it still exists and is reflected in the practices that an individual implements. As Conner (2011, p.1) identified, the *Early Years Learning Framework* (EYLF) (DEEWR, 2009a) does not define 'philosophy'. Rather, beliefs about young children and learning are inherent in the '3 Bs' – belonging, being, becoming – and its values are embodied in the five *principles* that underpin *practice*.

Making the theoretical perspectives and philosophy of a setting explicit through discussion and documentation provides educators and families with a set of reference points or a framework for informed decision making; for example, how to behave and act. Being aware of the setting's philosophy can also guide educators as they reflect critically on theories and practices, and plan to make changes based on these reflections.

As each early childhood setting and school is unique, there is no 'one' philosophy that is suitable for everywhere. The vision of one group of stakeholders, or any one member of any group, is not the same as that of any other. When developing a philosophy, it would be easy to access many documented philosophies from other services or schools or from the Internet; however, these are not reflective of each individual context.

It is essential that each setting and school engage in the processes of philosophy development. The stages that need to be addressed in the process of developing a philosophy are outlined in Figure 5.1 and are discussed in the remainder of this chapter.

Consider any educational settings you have been involved in. How did the practices reflect the educators' and families' shared theoretical perspectives and philosophical foundations?

A process for philosophy development

Step 1: Discuss what a philosophy is and why it is important

It is essential that all **stakeholders** understand the purpose of a shared vision and what constitutes a philosophy. Having a vision of the program educators want to develop is a good starting point. Without it they may be making decisions that do not achieve the type of program and service that reflects the strengths and interests of those involved. The *National Quality Framework* (ACECQA, 2013) and *Belonging, Being, Becoming: The Early Years Learning*

FIGURE 5.1 A process of philosophy development.

Framework for Australia (DEEWR, 2009) clearly highlight the importance of having a vision, which Goodfellow (2009) likens to a river of thought running through the framework. The three interwoven concepts – belonging, being, becoming – provide a clear vision that can be drawn on as educators examine their philosophy and practice.

While some aspects of a philosophy or vision may seem like a 'pie in the sky', it is essential to provide a clear direction for all those working in, and associated with, the early childhood service or school. It is necessary to develop a philosophy before any of the other steps of a planning process to ensure that there is an ideal to aim towards. Our beliefs and values are 'the deepest expression of our ideals and principles' and underlie why educators do what they do in practice (Waniganayake et al., 2012, p. 83). This ideal will be based on much reflection and discussion, both on an educators own personal perceptions and values, as well as on those involved in any group process. If an educator starts to worry about the constraints of the setting at this stage, they may not create a vision of a quality program, but one that maintains the status quo. It is very easy to fall into the habit of saying 'I'd like to do this … but I can't because …', rather than clarifying ideals first and then working towards those ideals within our given situation. In other words, if educators lack ideals, they will not find ways around constraints or be able to harness the potential that exists in their setting. If educators are to continually improve their program, and maintain a direction for this improvement, they must develop a philosophy.

Step 2: Decide on who should be involved and how

As identified in Figure 5.1, making decisions about who should be involved (stakeholders) in the process of developing a philosophy in any setting or organisation is central to, and influences, every aspect of the process.

All of those who will be influenced by the philosophy and who will have an impact on its implementation should be involved in some way in its development (*see* Figure 5.2). Some of these stakeholders may be:

- families
- educators and other staff
- children
- communities
- management bodies
- government organisations.

FIGURE 5.2 The display of the philosophy in this service reflects a collaborative project which involved families, staff and children in creating a puzzle piece to form the philosophy. All stakeholders were able to create a piece to reflect their beliefs and values.

Involvement in the process of philosophy development is a worthwhile personal and professional development experience and encourages partnerships among families and staff.

Where staff and families have contributed to philosophy development, they are more able to translate aspects of the philosophy into daily practice, identify inconsistencies and conflicts in daily experiences and work to meet particular philosophical ideals in a sound and consistent manner. Once the setting or school philosophy is clarified, decision making for ongoing planning becomes much easier. As a result of participating in team philosophy development, some families will gain a better insight into the importance of components of high-quality programs, while other families will contribute significantly to ideals espoused in the philosophy. Through this participation, the setting or school will be more able to draw on the strengths offered by families.

The local community, management groups and government organisations also play an important part in the development of a philosophy. If the early childhood setting or school is to reflect the needs and strengths of the community and take policies into account that may affect implementation, there should be some consideration of the issues affecting the community and representation from the community.

In addition, the strengths, interests and experiences of the children in the setting or school will have an impact on the philosophy and should be included. If children's agency is to be taken into account in decisions that affect their lives, then it is important that they have input into the setting's philosophy.

Involving all stakeholders in philosophy development may be viewed by some as a daunting task, but it need not be. How different groups will be involved in sharing ideas and formulating the philosophy will vary. It could mean that stakeholders are represented on committees when a philosophy is being developed. In addition to this representation, other strategies to elicit the ideas and interests of all groups, including children, should be addressed. There are many ways to engage with and incorporate children's perspectives in discussions about the philosophy of services. These are explored in a wide range of research, focused on young children's perspectives of their learning environments (Clark, 2010; Dunphy & Farrell, 2011), spaces for play (Clark & Moss, 2005) and early childhood settings (Einarsdóttir, 2003; Fleet & Britt, 2011). Some specific strategies include:

- drawing on pedagogical documentation 'as content is material which records what the children are saying and doing ... process involves the use of that material as a means to reflect' (Dahlberg, Moss & Pence, 1999, p. 147)

- involving children in exploring and discussing their experiences within the setting. Questions may include: What do you like doing at … (the setting/school)? What would you change about …? What would you keep the same? What would you like more time to do?
- providing opportunities for children to use their many languages to express their perspectives and experiences. These could include drawing, construction, conversations, photography, writing and other representational methods
- connecting with families and reflecting on their stories about their children's experience, using a range of artefacts as prompts, listening seriously to children's ideas and advocating on their behalf.

However, more important than the actual strategies or methods to engage with children is the rationale for doing so. Educators who approach children's participation in tasks such as the development of philosophy with a belief in their competence and rights to be involved are much more likely to regard children's contributions as valuable and insightful than educators who seek children's involvement as a means to illustrate what has already been decided (Dockett, Einarsdóttir, & Perry, 2011).

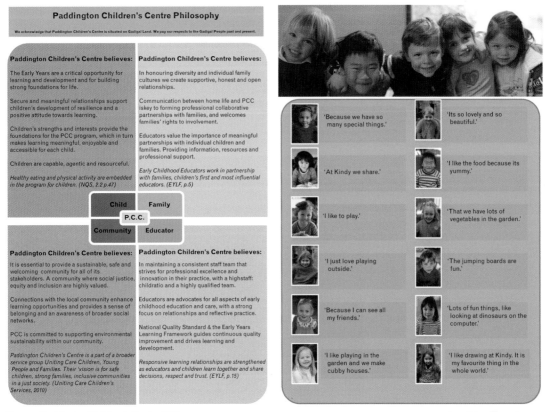

Source: Paddington Children's Centre 2013

FIGURE 5.3 Paddington Children's Centre philosophy is reflective of a variety of stakeholders involved in the setting. It includes the voices of children within the setting through their comments and images.

Involvement of stakeholders is often possible through the establishment of subcommittees with diverse representation that can feed back into the larger group. For example, a subcommittee may include one or two staff and family members, as well as representatives from management groups and community and government organisations where appropriate. This subcommittee may take on the tasks of gathering information from the larger group, collating all ideas and drafting the final document. This smaller

Using the *Talking about Practice: Revising a Service Philosophy* video, available at http://www.earlychildhoodaustralia.org.au/nqsplp > e-Learning videos > Talking about practice > Revising a Service Philosophy, consider the discussion questions with respect to a setting you have been involved in.

group would involve the wider group of stakeholders in discussion and brainstorming, seeking feedback on draft documents and ongoing evaluation.

Practical ideas for philosophy development are outlined in the following sections of this chapter, as well as in the boxed feature below. A useful website for considering different approaches to developing or revising setting philosophy is http://www.earlychildhoodaustralia .org.au/nqsplp > e-Learning video, which includes a regular newsletter and *Talking about Practice* videos.

A practical example of a process for developing a philosophy

1. *Discuss the necessity of a philosophy* for the setting or school with staff, families and management. This could be at a meeting, and may be introduced as a result of a perceived need for a philosophy, a review of the existing philosophy, changing curriculum or learning frameworks, quality assurance processes or a professional development exercise.

2. *Identify relevant strategies that involve all stakeholders* in the process of developing the setting or school philosophy. This may be a combination of subcommittee work and open meetings.

3. *Implement strategies that enable individual stakeholders* to identify what is important in early childhood education – that is, their values, beliefs or visions. Individuals could form small groups to brainstorm and share their ideas. This process may be effective at an open meeting, and the ideas should be documented. Remember to gather children's contributions to the philosophy at this stage. Following the initial gathering of ideas, individuals or groups may choose to explore some ideas further; for example, read more about a particular educational philosophy or learning framework.

4. *Categorise or organise ideas into focus areas* that are linked and arrange the material in a format that is clear and relevant to all stakeholders at the setting, including families. This task may be undertaken by a subcommittee and will reflect the unique ideas of each service and its stakeholders.

5. *Display this representation of ideas in a communal area* of the setting or school, such as the foyer, for several weeks and invite all group members to add what they think is important under the various headings/areas. Staff could encourage others to provide input. An alternative approach, where appropriate, may be to use a newsletter or email contact with families, members of the community and management to gather feedback.

6. *Collate the ideas as a subcommittee.* These ideas can then be taken to an open forum for discussion. This process of refining, clarifying and discussing ideas may occur several times until agreement is reached.

7. *Develop a draft philosophy as a subcommittee.* This document can then be displayed in a communal area, sent via email or given to individual stakeholders for any further comment or modifications.

8. *Finalise the philosophy.* The final document should be officially adopted or ratified by management (for example, committee, management organisation or council).

9. *Communicate the philosophy appropriately* to relevant groups through displays in the setting, newsletters, setting or school handbooks and other appropriate methods. This may also mean providing translations of the philosophy as appropriate and developing a version appropriate for sharing with children.

Step 3: Identify what is important: values and beliefs

There are many factors that influence what each stakeholder considers to be important for children, families, educators and communities. Each educator's knowledge is drawn from a range of sources, such as reading, reflection on different **theoretical perspectives**, membership of various professional organisations and awareness of associated documents such as the Early Childhood Australia (2006) *Code of Ethics*, understanding of guidelines for quality assurance, curriculum and learning framework documents, attendance at courses or seminars and discussions with a network of peers. Early childhood educators need to be continually involved in professional learning to remain open to possibilities for innovation and change.

Educators' beliefs and values may also be influenced by specific theorists and **educational philosophies**, such as Montessori or Steiner, or learnings from educational approaches, such as HighScope. For example, perceptions and images of children may be drawn from Piagetian developmental theory or from Vygotskian sociocultural theory. The way educators view children influences what they believe is important about children's learning and how they interact with them.

Educators may identify with particular components of others' philosophies, such as those of Malaguzzi and others from Reggio Emilia centres in Italy. In these centres there is a commitment to the creation of conditions for learning that will enhance and facilitate children's construction of their own powers of thinking through the synthesis of all expressive, communicative and cognitive languages (Edwards et al., 1998).

However, it is important to resist the temptation just to transpose someone else's philosophy to our own setting. The philosophy of Reggio Emilia, for example, is relevant to a particular region of Italy. While educators may draw on the ideas of others, it is essential that each educator develop an individual philosophy that is relevant to their own understandings and context. This means taking into account the views of the local community, families and educators, and the unique circumstances of each educational setting or school (*see* Figure 5.4).

Educators may draw on a range of theoretical perspectives in their personal and/or setting philosophy. For example, Widger and Schofield (2012) found individual educators who drew on five distinct educational philosophies – Rudolf Steiner, Maria Montessori, Magda Gerba, Playcentre and Reggio Emilia – were able to effectively integrate these perspectives in practice when their beliefs both reflected their philosophical base and the context of the setting they were involved in. The EYLF encourages educators to reflect on the theories they draw on in their work and to consider which other theories may be of use as they analyse issues and consider alternate views and practices (DEEWR, 2009).

Specific theoretical perspectives and educational philosophies, the sociocultural context of the local community and the beliefs and values of stakeholders are evident in Example 5.1.

Theoretical perspectives

A set of principles or propositions drawing on research to explain a particular experience or fact. There may be different perspectives based on different theories.

Educational philosophies

A specific vision of education that examines the goals and meaning of education.

FIGURE 5.4 Kingscliff Mini School creatively involves families and community in making relevant signs and mosaics to share their philosophy and reflect community spirit.

► ## EXAMPLE 5.1
The philosophy, mission and vision of Cape Byron Rudolf Steiner School

Rudolf Steiner's educational philosophy springs out of the spiritual science he named Anthroposophy that offers new insights into the nature of man (anthropos), the earth and the universe, and new pathways of self awareness and self consciousness. It forms the philosophical foundation stone of the Cape Byron Rudolf Steiner School and is the base upon which our educational, administrative and social community continues to grow.

Our School, one of a world-wide network of fully independent Steiner Schools, encourages creativity and free thinking. It recognises the individuality of each child and the unique gifts each has. Rather than moulding the child into a form preconceived by society and its particular needs, the school nurtures, protects and develops the intelligence of the true child in order to bring out their individuality.

To achieve this, the School has created a nurturing educational environment that acknowledges the sanctity of childhood and its specific developmental phases, and provides a creative and balanced learning program in which the academic, artistic and social aspects of the curriculum are wholly integrated for the needs of the developing child.

Our hope is that when they leave this school, each student will be able to step into the world ready to make a contribution that is uniquely theirs; they will be able to step out confidently with a sense of purpose and direction which springs from their own initiative and awareness of their own inner spiritual qualities.

'Receive the child in reverence, Educate him in love, Let him go forth in freedom'

Rudolf Steiner

Our mission
The aim of the Cape Byron Rudolf Steiner School is to provide a learning environment that mirrors the needs of the developing human being and is enlivening to their soul forces of thinking, feeling and willing, so that each individual develops the skills and abilities to realise their potential and contribute to the life of the local and wider community.

Our vision
To support this aim we will:

- Strive to put into practice Rudolf Steiner's indications for understanding child development – through study, observation and collaborative working between teachers and parents
- Develop and implement a curriculum that supports and nurtures the physical, emotional, social and intellectual growth of the child and young person – inspired by our understanding of child development, and in accordance with the requirements of the Federal and State Governments
- Continue to invest in the professional development of our teachers enabling them to deliver to all our students a holistic education that is as much about building our students spirit as it is transferring skills, knowledge and the thirst for learning
- Create a place of goodness, beauty and truth that inspires teaching and learning
- Nurture and preserve the natural environment and take care of the resources the School provides for our use
- Encourage creative expression and enthusiastic participation in all aspects of community life – in our school and beyond

- Welcome, encourage, guide and support all members of our community by embracing the universal shared values of freedom, equality, democracy, peace, human rights, responsibility, pluralism, diversity, mutual respect, human dignity and individual worth
- Create and celebrate social occasions to ensure a balance between conscientious working and light-hearted enjoyment.

Source: Cape Byron Rudolf Steiner School, http://www.capebyronsteiner.nsw.edu.au/, 2014

Step 4: Clarify personal philosophy and beliefs

A critical element of any philosophy development involves clarifying our personal philosophy, values and beliefs. When developing a team or shared philosophy, each stakeholder's ability to clearly articulate what is important to them and why is fundamental to the group process.

Sometimes when we are trying to identify what to incorporate into our personal philosophy we find it hard to get started, although once we get started it is hard to stop! The two boxes that follow provide some thinking points as a guide to help individuals to reflect and brainstorm ideas as they establish a personal philosophy.

Questions to ask yourself when developing a personal philosophy

When beginning to reflect on your ideals and values for early childhood education, think about what your ideal setting might look like. What would be happening? What is your vision?

Ask yourself the following questions:

- What do I believe is the purpose of the setting/school? Why does it exist?
- What would I like the atmosphere to be when I enter the setting/school?
- What would the children be doing?
- What would the educators be doing?
- What role would the families play? Where are they in my picture?
- What would the day be like – e.g. the atmosphere, flexibility, use of time? What is most important about the day for the children, families and educators?
- What would the environment look like? How would the space be used?
- What would the children be learning? What would their role be in this learning? What would the educator's role be?
- How would I make others aware of this learning?
- How would the staff interact with each other?
- What is most important to me? Why do I come to the setting each day?
- Which theoretical perspectives best explain my ideals and values about children's learning?

 Some areas to reflect on when developing a personal philosophy

What do I think is important in early childhood education?

Stakeholders can use these ideas to help them think about, and write down, what they believe is important about early childhood education. While these ideas are embedded within the EYLF, they are key to early childhood education across different settings. By making these ideas explicit in the reflection questions, this allows families and those beginning their career in early childhood education to focus their reflections. Key phrases or words are sufficient to provide a basis for future discussion.

What do I believe is important about the following:

- relationships with children
- partnerships with families, colleagues and support professionals
- expectations, equity and inclusive practices
- diverse family practices, values and beliefs
- educators' ongoing learning and reflective practice
- learning environments
- interactions
- transitions
- assessment.

What do I mean by:

- holistic approaches
- responsiveness to children
- learning through play-based experiences
- intentional teaching
- cultural competence.

Thinking points:

- What practices have I seen in other settings – positive and negative? Reflect on these (that is: Would I do this? Why? Why not? What would I do instead? Why?)
- What can different *theoretical perspectives* and philosophies of education add to my thinking? What new/additional research and reading could I do to challenge or extend my thinking?
- How do policies, and documents – such as the Early Childhood Australia (2006) *Code of Ethics, Belonging, Being, Becoming: The Early Years Learning Framework for Australia* (DEEWR, 2009) or the Australian Curriculum F–10 and F–12 documents – impact on my beliefs?

Educators may also use the principles and practices of the EYLF to reflect on how these principles and practices relate to their values and beliefs and to their educational setting.

Clarifying a personal educational philosophy usually takes place as educators refine the theoretical perspectives, knowledge, values and assumptions they consider important to early childhood education and to their particular setting or school. This means that educators need to be aware of their own personal philosophy before they articulate it to other members of the team and before they work with other staff, management, families and community members to develop a setting philosophy. Each educator's vision will affect many aspects of their work, including perceptions of the role of the educator, the way environments are organised and the way children's learning is documented. This vision will also influence how children participate in decision making about the environment, experiences, resources and learning they wish to be involved in; that is, their sense of agency.

Many influences shape a personal philosophy including perceptions of the roles of others – staff, families, children, communities and management – and why, how and what is evaluated. Other influences include different kinds of knowledge; the individual's role in the team; understandings, values and views of the world; qualifications, disposition, skills, expectations and experiences; and understandings of philosophies, policies, practices and expectations from outside organisations (for example, the management body and local, state and federal government departments). Theoretical perspectives are one of the influences on individual philosophical perspectives and one of the reasons philosophies change over time as educators engage with further professional learning and experience different educational settings (Kennedy, 2012). Each educator's philosophy will differ by the very nature of being individual. It is useful for each educator to document his/her philosophy as a guide for future practice, and as a helpful tool for further development of a team philosophy. Personal educational philosophies will not only reflect the individual's beliefs and vision, but many factors such as individual learning styles and preferred modes of expression. Example 5.2 is an early childhood educator named Melinda Casey's personal philosophy of early childhood education.

Melinda reflects on her personal thinking and documentation processes when developing her educational philosophy:

> When asked to think about what was important in creating my own personal philosophy in early childhood education, my initial reflection led me to eight key stakeholders who are essential to an early childhood setting. I then reflected on which area I considered the most important. I came to the conclusion that ALL stakeholders were integral to my philosophy and if any one of the stakeholders was missing, was not considered or communicated to, then the care and education of children would not be effective or would be incomplete as a result. Hence, the jigsaw puzzle which is not complete unless ALL pieces are interlinked.

Melinda Casey, 2010

EXAMPLE 5.2
A personal education philosophy

Staff

The role of staff in early childhood education is of critical importance. To provide high quality care it is essential staff display the skills necessary to provide a cohesive, harmonious environment. Kind, respectful interactions with children and peers, collaborative relationships with families, colleagues and the community, knowledge of the ECA *Code of Ethics*, relevant quality assurance, curriculum frameworks and the willingness to continue to learn and constantly develop their pedagogy are vital skills for any early childhood educator. Ongoing evaluation of practice and undertaking professional development is integral to providing quality education.

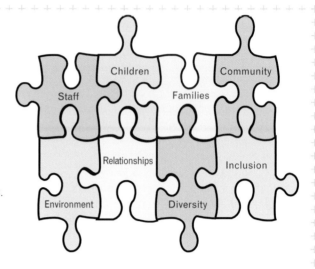

Children

Children are unique and special beings. Each and every child has the right to be safe, loved, nurtured, respected and valued. Fostering self worth, self-esteem and freedom of expression are imperative in a child's development. Encouraging children to learn through developmentally appropriate play experiences at their own pace is crucial. Children need time to explore, experiment, learn and create. Recognising and supporting each child's individuality and varying abilities will strengthen relationships with peers, educators and the wider community.

Families

The key characteristic in providing quality education and care is meeting the individual needs of children and their families. Effective communication with families will support this process. Understanding the families' viewpoint on issues and their values and concerns for their children will aid staff in implementing strategies that will support best practice for children and families and demonstrate the partnership that is crucial in forging a consistent, collaborative environment for children and families.

Community

Acknowledging and connecting with the local community demonstrates to children and families a sense of belonging. Exploring the diversity and culture of the community, networking with services and sharing resources supports and strengthens the partnership we share with the wider community, children and families. As early childhood educators we must promote an awareness and knowledge of the need and value of quality care and advocate the rights and wellbeing of each child.

Environment

Providing a safe, healthy, positive, nurturing environment is an important element in quality teaching and learning. Children learn most effectively in secure and responsive environments. Ensuring there are adequate resources, materials and sufficient space (indoor and outdoor) caters for children's interests, development and challenges their abilities. Encouraging parents and children's contributions and ideas provides opportunity to build a stimulating child-focused learning environment.

Relationships

Building positive, trusting relationships with children, families, community and work colleagues strengthens the partnership we have with these key stakeholders. When early childhood educators and families can openly discuss and negotiate ideas, views, concerns and questions this partnership is strengthened and decisions can be made reflecting the genuine needs and interests of the child. Maintaining relationships based on trust, honesty, respect and professionalism with work colleagues ensures an effective team who work together to provide quality practices and leadership within the learning environment.

Diversity

Promoting diversity in the child care environment demonstrates respect and assists children in developing positive attitudes towards similarities and difference. It is the responsibility of staff to provide opportunities and experiences that will help children develop attitudes, knowledge and skills needed to live in an increasingly complex and diverse world.

Inclusion

Inclusion is the right of every child regardless of their diverse needs. Diversity and inclusion is respected, valued and appreciated by encouraging children, families, staff and the wider community to support each individual child's needs/abilities and utilise resources and services to enhance learning and share knowledge and skills collaboratively.

Source: Melinda Casey, Early Childhood Educator

CourseMateExpress

This reflection is explored in detail in Online Example 5.1, which can be found online with CourseMate Express.

While a broad educational philosophy is a key element of any planning process, there are other areas of early childhood practice where a personal philosophy may be valuable. As part of her lifelong learning process and professional development, Lynette Funnell, an early childhood educator, reflects on the role of leadership in early childhood education.

With time and experience one might reflect on a personal philosophy – is it still relevant? After further study and experience, Lynette reflected on how her leadership philosophy impacted on her practice of leadership and its relevance to her current beliefs and values.

Step 5: Develop a team philosophy

Once each stakeholder has clarified his/her personal philosophy, it is important to work together to develop an overall team philosophy. Educators, families, children, management and community members may have diverse beliefs about children, education and early childhood programs based upon different values, perspectives and experiences. There are likely to be some similar and some different views about what is important. Members of the different stakeholder groups in each setting/school need to work together and discuss what they consider to be important as a basis for the setting's philosophy.

Acknowledging personal values and biases assists in promoting acceptance of other's beliefs and values. Developing a shared vision of the values to be encouraged in our service is one of the first steps towards achieving a philosophy (Lifeline Community Care Queensland, 2010). Promoting and making explicit these shared values within our setting and the community through appropriate resources is a worthwhile practice (*see* Figure 5.5).

If teamwork is valued, then actively encouraging others to contribute to the philosophy is important. For example, if an educator believes in family participation, they will find authentic and meaningful ways to involve families. If they believe in the importance of children's agency, they will find a way to include children's voices. Through participating in philosophy development, all members of the team are more likely to understand and be committed to the philosophy and to put it into practice.

After reading Online Example 5.1 consider what your initial beliefs about early childhood education were when you entered your course/ the early childhood workforce? How have these changed over time? What influenced these changes? How have these shifts in theoretical perspectives and philosophy been reflected in your practice?

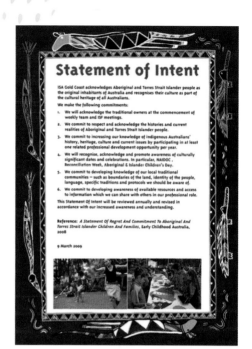

FIGURE 5.5 Shared values and statement of intent.

It is possible to gain a consensus on a philosophy as well as broaden perspectives through group brainstorming sessions, open discussion and rationalising of ideas, opening the program to others for evaluation and professional learning through in-service courses and visiting other settings. In addition, making sure everyone has an opportunity to express and share concerns through effective meeting strategies and clear decision-making procedures will make the process more productive.

Imagine yourself as different stakeholders within your service (for example, different staff members, parents, children and management committee members). What would be important to you about the setting? Are these values represented in the philosophy of the setting? Which theoretical perspectives are these linked to?

Step 6: Document the philosophy

By this stage in the process the philosophy for the setting/school will have been established. However, it is important to consolidate these ideas and provide a focus within the philosophy.

A philosophical statement or documented philosophy should reflect the focus of the beliefs of all stakeholders in a concise manner. Many values and issues raised within the philosophy discussion can often be expressed in a brief statement. Succinctly documenting the setting's philosophy is important for many reasons, including:

- to be included in information booklets and websites for various groups (for example, new and current users of a service or school, and student educators)
- to be used to recruit staff and for marketing *to different audiences*
- to be accountable to government bodies and for quality assurance measures
- to give direction for planning
- for evaluation purposes.

There is no one correct way to document a philosophy. Much will depend on members of the group, the target audience and the purposes for the written philosophy. Sometimes a philosophy will be written to include a mission and/or vision for large organisations, as a short rationale or even as a statement or concept.

When developing a written philosophy, it is important to start with the ideas already raised and collated (as individuals and in groups) to provide an idea of how the setting or school philosophy might be presented; for example, there may be several focus areas that have become clear, such as relationships, diversity and creativity. This may lead to statements centring on these issues across all groups within a setting – that is, children, families and educators. On the other hand, it may become clear that various categories are evident, such as partnerships with families, children's learning, the program, links with communities and teamwork. This will lead to statements with a focus on these categories.

Each philosophy will differ because of the unique beliefs within that setting or school. Particular beliefs may become evident for a setting – such as environmental awareness, equity or the use of media and technology – that may not be as relevant in other contexts. Philosophies will also look different as they are written in varying styles for different purposes and audiences (*see* Figures 5.3 and 5.4, and Examples 5.2, 5.5, 5.6, 5.7, 5.8 and 5.9).

EXAMPLE 5.3
An example of the philosophy of a work-based early childhood setting (long day care and occasional care) attached to a university

Tigger's Honeypot Philosophy

At Tigger's Honeypot we provide high quality care and education for children and their families. We do this by:

- building a strong sense of community
- recognising and celebrating diversity within society
- respecting and working in partnership with all families
- encouraging peer relationships
- providing stimulating learning environments
- connecting with natural surroundings
- nurturing secure attachments between children and educators
- celebrating our educators as experts in early childhood
- utilising the National *Early Years Learning Framework* as the guiding document for developing our curriculum.

At Tigger's Honeypot we strive to build a strong sense of community which is nurtured through understanding and respectful relationships. Tigger's Honeypot is a part of the UNSW community both of whom strive for excellence in education.

We also recognise that Indigenous communities have lived and learned on this land for 40 000 years. We acknowledge the original custodians of the land on which we are situated. We are honoured to continue their traditions of teaching, learning, and respecting the environment. We actively seek engagement and consultation with this community.

We embrace diversity within society and engage in discussions and experiences with children that challenge stereotypes and biases. Through our connections with families, the university and the wider community, we provide children with a range of social and cultural experiences. We actively work to break down biases, and address diversity in all its forms including family type, abilities, gender, race and culture. We support children to develop resilience and become advocates for their own rights and the rights of others.

We respect families as the primary caregiver of their child and value the diversity of families and individuals that form our community. We complement the role of the family in a child's life by encouraging family partnership through consultation and collaboration.

As a community we connect with the land on which we are situated and beyond the centre boundaries. We grow connections between children and their natural surroundings. We work, teach, and play with respect for the natural environment.

We know that through play children are able to construct knowledge, build new understandings and extend their inherent curiosity and capabilities. We provide stimulating learning environments to further encourage children's explorations and learning. The early years are a time of significant growth in a person's life and a time of setting important foundations for future development and journeys of lifelong learning. We plan for children to have fun learning, to enjoy their early years and to build strong peer relationships.

Secure attachments and relationships with responsive educators are the foundations to learning. These relationships enable children to contribute to their world now and thereafter. The educators in the centre play a significant role in scaffolding children's learning – expanding

upon existing learning to take children to a new level of understanding. The educators do this through interactions that extend and challenge children's knowledge and desire to learn.

We recognise the educators in our service as experts in the early childhood profession. This expertise is maintained with ongoing professional development, meetings and discussions. We employ educators with diverse backgrounds, experiences and skills who are willing to reflect on practice and grow. The centre draws upon staff diversity and knowledge to help develop curriculum and centre operations. Our educators commit to creating a unified team.

Communities continually evolve and research into early childhood development and education is ongoing. Therefore at Tigger's Honeypot ongoing reflection and evaluation is integral to maintaining a responsive service that is dedicated to high quality care and education for children, and for their families.

Source: developed in conjunction with families, staff and management at Tigger's Honeypot , University of New South Wales (reviewed January 2012)

In Example 5.4, Leo Prendergast, an early childhood educator and director, reflects on his service's approach to developing the setting's philosophy, mission and vision.

EXAMPLE 5.4
Reflection on developing a setting's philosophy, mission and vision

'In developing our services planning system we agreed to have three separate aspects to our philosophy. We saw that many organisations combine their philosophy and vision. However, we believed that we could have the same underlying principles or beliefs (philosophy) as another organisation – for example, support for families, empowering children, reconciliation, cultural competence, environment, caring for others and so on – but have a very different vision of what we would want our service to be. Our vision is our expression of an ideal children's service but within the context of our community, our location, our resources and building, and many other influences. We could then use our vision as our reference point when we do a situational analysis of our service each year – setting annual objectives to move us closer to that vision. Both of these, however, must be measured against our reality. In setting up our mission we wanted a plain statement that would guide each major decision we make. We believed we must balance our service quality of education and care against accessibility and affordability for families and responsiveness to our local community. Many services proudly say they aim for the highest standards of education and care for children – but what about if that standard is not affordable to parents and reduces accessibility for the families in our community? Hence we developed a philosophy, a mission and a vision as separate statements – each with a different, although interconnected, purpose.'

Leo Prendergast, Rainbow Children's Centre, 2010

This centre's philosophy, mission and vision are documented in Example 5.5.

▶ EXAMPLE 5.5
An example of the philosophy, mission and vision of a multi-purpose early childhood setting

Rainbow Children's Centre Inc

1. Centre philosophy

   a. We acknowledge that each person's life journey is unique, and that support needs can vary from person to person. We respect each child as an individual with personal rights and the programs provided by Rainbow should create an environment which supports and encourages the potential of each child.

   b. We prioritise the best interests of children, but also recognise that we must look at the best interest of families, community and staff in determining the best interests of children.

   c. We respect families as the primary carers of their children with the centre and its staff supporting families in caring for and educating their children. Rainbow recognises the value of open and trusting communication between the centre and the child's home and family.

   d. We hold the values of respect, care, justice, unity and service to be central to our culture and believe in demonstrating them in creative responsiveness to the family needs of our community. We foster in each child the values of respect and consideration for others.

   e. We believe in offering services that recognise and honour the whole person: body, mind, heart and spirit.

   f. We believe a learning environment that combines the warmth and nurturing of a home with the stimulus of an early childhood educational setting encourages optimal development of each child.

   g. We value the natural environment, both within the centre and in the wider community and we encourage children to respect and nurture the environment.

   h. We recognise the diversity of Australian culture and will encourage respect for that diversity and will reflect and celebrate diversity within the centre. In particular Rainbow recognises this region as being home to many Indigenous Australians and that Rainbow services will operate in ways to respect and value that aspect of Australian culture.

   i. We believe in responsible stewardship: placing high value on our human resources, while promoting rigorous attention to the financial, structural and material.

2. **Mission** – It is the mission of Rainbow Children's Centre to:

   a. In relation to its Education and Care and OOSH services

      i. provide high quality education and care for children; and

      ii. maintain affordable fees for families; and

      iii. provide services which are suitable for and responsive to the members of the local community.

   b. In relation to its early childhood intervention services

      i. provide an educational service which maximises the learning and development of each child; and

      ii. support and empower families in accessing appropriate support and specialist services; and

      iii. provide family friendly experiences and opportunities to support the child's everyday learning environments; and

iv.   strengthen the capacity of other early childhood services in Ballina Shire to meet the needs of children through inclusive programs.

3. Vision

Our vision of an ideal Rainbow Children's Centre features:

a. **Our organisation**

i.   We should be collaborating with other organisations that share our values to better benefit the community we serve. We should be open and alert to the views of other organisations in the community to understand how our services complement and supplement those organisations in the best interests of the community.

ii.   We would recognise the valuable community facility we manage and maximise its functioning to the benefit of the community. We would develop the uses of the centre premises in both a functional and qualitative way to improve the overall centre's program and environment for children, families, staff and the community in general.

iii. We would see Rainbow in turn acknowledged by the community as a high quality place of learning for young children. It would be well recognised and respected by the community as an early childhood centre nurturing the growth and best interests of young children.

iv.   We would ensure appropriate knowledge at management and committee level, to ensure Rainbow is aware of and can address all its managerial, legal and ethical responsibilities as required.

v.   We would acknowledge the importance of Rainbow's services continuing to operate into the future and as such implement adequate and effective management and administration that ensures sufficient income to operate, efficient expenditure to ensure we have the resources we need and sensible stewardship of the annual budget to ensure our organisation remains financially viable.

vi.   We would know that each family comes to the centre with their own identity and rights and the centre would acknowledge and respect each one's life outside the centre. The rights of children, staff and families would all be respected and acknowledged. Hence, children, staff and families would have a right to be involved in planning and implementing any change in their centre as an inclusive gradual process. The centre would also recognise that at times the rights of two or more individuals may cut across each other. The centre would strive to find the right balance between those conflicting rights.

b. **Our human resources**

i.   We would recognise the importance to our centre, of our staff, our volunteers and our committee members as the most important resource we have.

ii.   We would be providing working conditions that support our staff's capacity to operate our services.

iii. We would recognise the value of consistency among our team and be working to support the continued employment of each staff member.

iv.   We would be providing staff and committee with the opportunity to gain new skills, to undertake further training.

v.   We would acknowledge the value of a pleasant and fulfilling work environment and commit to creating and maintaining such an environment.

vi. We would acknowledge that staff have needs, interests and wants as individuals and as staff team members and the centre would acknowledge, value and respond to each staff member.

c. **Our educational programs:** We will implement high quality early childhood educational programs.

    i. **Education and care program.** While the program is informed by external documents such as the *National Quality Framework* and the *Early Years Learning Framework*, our program will be based on approaches to the education of young children that have been developed by the centre staff and families including:

      1. The service would have a friendly home like environment within which children can feel 'at home' and hence be supported to learn.

      2. There would be an emphasis on the outdoors as a learning environment in addition to indoor playrooms. Our external play spaces would include many natural features and children would have extended opportunities to interact with the natural world.

      3. Children would be organised during the day in groups where children's learning could occurs within groups containing peers of a variety of ages, siblings and children with similar interests.

      4. Each child would be able to choose to be involved and also choose not to be involved as they wish and children would be able to play in ways they choose and follow the ideas that are of interest to them.

      5. Our program would feature extended periods of free choice time encouraging and allowing children opportunities to build social relationships and interact with peers. Learning experiences available each day would be based on the interests and expressed wishes of the children.

      6. The learning experiences available to children would support being, belonging and becoming.

      7. Recognising the values of the Aboriginal community, which forms such a high proportion of the Ballina community, the program would reflect those values in all aspects of its care and education of all children.

      8. Services would be inclusive for all children, and would ensure children with additional needs felt as much a part of the service as any other child. Families of children with additional needs would feel respected and listened to in regard to all aspects of the services.

      9. The service would be operating on all levels as much as possible in a sustainable way and all major decisions to be made within the service would be made after consideration of the sustainability implications of any outcome.

    ii. Our OOSHC program would be:

      1. Providing high quality programs for children. We would recognise that while some children attend our programs on an ongoing basis over the year, others only attend on a spasmodic basis attending just a few days of vacation care over the year. We would balance what we provide to encompass the best interests of all groups. We would be encouraging children in the development of self belief and personal initiative and allowing the interest of children to guide the program. It would provide a balance of fun and play based learning experiences. Children would feel

at home at Rainbow with rights to determine their program, balanced by the knowledge of staff and families about children's best interests.

2. Operating from a variety of premises and locations in the Shire that allowed as many families as possible to access Rainbow. The premises would provide a safe, fun, stimulating and challenging learning environment, with facilities that allowed staff to meet children's and families needs.

3. Regularly evaluated to ensure they matched the needs of the Ballina community, and balancing the capacity to provide all types of care for OOSHC with the need to ensure all services are financially sustainable.

4. Ensuring fees would be as affordable to families as possible, and staff would be informed and alert to all funding opportunities to assist families.

5. Inclusive for all children, and would ensure children with additional needs felt as much a part of the service as any other child. Families of children with additional needs would feel respected and listened to in regard to all aspects of the services.

6. Respectful of the cultures of all families, including Aboriginal families and would ensure children from all cultures felt as much a part of the service as any other child. Families of children from various cultures would feel welcome to share aspects of their culture within the program.

7. Ensuring a staff team that was well qualified with a strong skill base in caring for school aged children and they would be provided with training opportunities to ensure they felt encouraged to maintain high level work skills. They would be employed under reasonable wages and other working conditions.

8. Meeting all accountabilities and requirements of the *National Quality Standard* and the *My Time, Our Place* framework. We would be balancing the expectations of families and children, with the need to address those external requirements of an educational basis, by providing a program based on child initiated play incorporating appropriate educational learning experiences.

9. Ensuring all services operated within a culture of sustainability, and were implementing a variety of sustainable practices.

iii. **Our early intervention program:** While the service is required to meet the NSW Disability Services Standards for funding requirements, it will also be influenced by the *National Quality Framework* (early childhood services) and the *Early Years Learning Framework*. Our service will also be influenced by the Early Childhood Australia and Early Childhood Intervention Australia Position Statement on the Inclusion of children with a disability in Early Childhood Education and Care.

1. Our service would keep aware of the early childhood intervention sector and recognise the recommendations of research and current best practice principles in determining an optimum program.

2. The service would recognise the child as part of a family and emphasise a sense of belonging first to a family, then to the wider community. The service would promote inclusive practice to enhance this sense of belonging. Our programs would emphasise learning to participate fully and actively in society.

3. Each child would have their strengths and challenges acknowledged as part of the program and individualised educational plans would reflect the diversity of each child's learning and development within their everyday learning environment, at home and in services within their community.

4. Planning would be ongoing and dynamic with realistic goals developed with the family and documented within Individualised Family Service Plans and Individualised Educational Plans. Families would be respected, supported and involved in all decisions affecting their child. We have a vision of families being agents of positive social change and would empower families to advocate on behalf of their child and by providing information to understand systems supporting people with a disability and strengthening their understanding of their rights.

5. Early intervention educators would respect parent's feelings and recognise that many will be coming to terms with their child's disability. We would communicate honestly and sensitively with families and work with other professionals to assist the child and family as appropriate.

6. The service would have links with community organisations and early intervention educators would collaborate and share information with relevant agencies and encourage families to share ideas and contribute to these partnerships.

7. The service would recognise the importance of a well qualified and experienced staff team and ensure ongoing professional development so that evidence based practice is reflected in the programs provided to children.

8. Early intervention educators would share knowledge, information and expertise on inclusive practice with educators of mainstream early childhood settings for children under eight years of age to enable those settings to ensure children have equitable access and appropriate inclusive programs.

9. The service would ensure that each family, including their child, is supported with the many transitions experienced in the early childhood years. Clear processes would be in place to support families with the transitions from home to early childhood setting and into school.

10. Recognising the values of inclusion, cultural competence and a strengths based approach, the service would reflect the values of the diverse Ballina community including the Aboriginal community, which forms a high proportion of the Ballina community. We would use strategies which focused on building the capacity of each family.

11. Meeting all accountabilities and requirements of the NSW Disability Standards as well as various funding accountabilities, we would balance the expectations of families and children, with the need to address those external requirements by providing programs based on evidence based practice which reflect educational practices for supporting the learning and development of children with disabilities and inclusive practice.

Source: Rainbow Children's Centre Inc, a community managed multipurpose children's service, January 2014

Large organisations, such as children's service organisations, often document the organisational philosophy as part of a strategic plan (*see* Chapter 4). This may mean the documentation includes a mission statement and goals for the entire organisation, as well as detailed information about the process on a website. Example 5.6 provides an overview of KU Children's Services' vision, philosophical basis and family feedback, while the *Strategic Plan: Making the KU Difference* and *Play Discover Learn: Our Play-based Learning Philosophy* and other relevant support documents can be accessed on the website.

EXAMPLE 5.6
KU Children's Services, 2013

KU vision:

Every family is able to access high quality, early childhood education and care for their children.

KU philosophy

Our play-based learning philosophy

The early years are a special time in a child's life: an exciting period of discovery and learning. KU has a strong play-based learning philosophy and our qualified early childhood staff create programs based on current research and practice plus decades of experience.

KU views young children as capable and strong learners rather than as dependant and needing to be 'filled up'. Our high quality play-based programs are designed to give children a wide range of active and meaningful experiences, building on the children's own strengths and interests.

In play-based programs children are learning all the time. The learning that occurs is often informal, gained as children interact, explore and try out different ways of doing things that our staff have intentionally planned. Through play, children develop skills, knowledge, feelings and dispositions that provide a solid foundation for lifelong learning.

At KU all children are viewed as individuals whilst learning to interact positively within a group. This helps develop relationships, social skills and tolerance of others and their environment.

For those children who are approaching school age, we place a strong emphasis on programs which challenge and extend their abilities and confidence, aiding their transition to school.

Source: KU Children's Services, http://www.ku.com.au

Step 7: Implement, reflect on and evaluate the philosophy

In order to implement a philosophy, stakeholders within the service will need to explore how to put these beliefs into practice. Example 5.7 provides an example of a teacher's resource developed by UnitingCare Paddington Children's Centre, a long day care centre in a major city. This resource has made detailed links between the philosophy and practice to ensure beliefs are always evident in implementation (*see* Chapters 6 and 7 for further clarification of this process).

EXAMPLE 5.7

Paddington Children's Centre teachers resource – 2013

Image of a child

WE BELIEVE THAT …	OUR PRACTICES REFLECT …
1. Children are capable, agentic and resourceful. They are valued as learners and teachers.	1. Experiences/provisions provided will be open ended and will facilitate choice. Children will be involved in evaluating programs.
2. Children are individuals within a broader community (socio-cultural).	2. Children will be involved in brainstorming of ideas. Our inclusive program caters for individual strengths and diverse abilities. Children's self- extension and 'risk taking' is enabled by supportive educators.
3. Children are collaborative learners and are active adventurers, explorers, creators and inventers.	3. Information regarding individual family cultures is gathered through enrolment forms, two-way communication in journals, informal conversations and planned meetings and is reflected in the daily program.
4. Children are powerful, resilient and successful, with emerging abilities and skills.	4. Educators provide environments and provisions that are conducive to collaboration and independent exploration. Children are encouraged to work together to solve problems and explore possibilities.
5. Children are trustworthy and are able to make choices which are reflective of their developing self regulation skills.	5. Interactions respect different ideas and opinions. Individuality is encouraged and self expression is valued. Positive language is used to communicate expectations. Children are involved in decision-making processes.
6. Children experience a range of feelings.	6. Educators support children's self expression and foster their ability to recognize and accept their feelings and the feelings of others. Educators provide appropriate strategies for children to express themselves.
7. Children learn about themselves and construct their own identity within the context of their families and communities. (EYLF p. 20)	7. Educators are provided opportunities to feel successful and celebrate individual strengths.
8. Children are our future sustainability leaders.	8. Educators promote an environmental awareness and embed sustainable practices in the daily routine. Children are involved in meaningful ways, e.g. hanging out washing, eco monitors, recycling, care of our plants, worm farm.
9. Health and nutrition play a key role in the development and well being of a child.	9. Educators promote healthy eating practices; provide information about health and nutrition to children and families. The service is dedicated to the provision of a balanced, nutritious and culturally diverse diet. Physical activity and rest times are an important part of the daily program.
10. Children are active communicators.	10. Children are listened to and their ideas and opinions are valued. Educators are in tune with children's varying ways of communicating at all ages. Communication is role modeled and encouraged in all forms such as visual cues, Makaton (sign language), oral and written language, drama, movement and singing.

WE BELIEVE THAT ...

Image of an educator

1. Educators are intentional teachers and facilitators of learning and exploration, working collaboratively with children, families and community.

2. Educators support children to make different choices when challenging behaviours arise. Educators foster the development of pro-social behaviours.

3. Educators value the development of self regulation as a life skill.

4. Educators provide unique perspectives and experiences linking communities and relationships.

5. Educators are committed to continuous professional growth and development. Critical reflection is ongoing.

6. Educators support children to develop positive attitudes towards learning, intrinsic motivation and a positive self-concept.

7. Educators are committed to building collaborative partnerships with families.

8. Educators are creative, spontaneous and resourceful, capitalising on teachable moments.

OUR PRACTICES REFLECT ...

1. Educators use technology, learning journals, observation, interaction, webs, information sheets and surveys to gather valuable information from children and families which contribute to the program. Staff utilise our immediate community for excursions, incursions, information, fundraising events and program support. Staff seek support from external agencies to support individual children's diverse abilities.

2. Expectations will be clear and consistent. Environments will be set up to promote positive behaviours. Children are involved and empowered to solve problems that arise, developing conflict resolution skills. Children are involved in setting limits to ensure safe play agreements. Teachers use child choice not time out. Teachers have age appropriate expectations. Individual behaviour strategies will be developed when necessary in conjunction with families.

3. Educators value the emotional health of children and employ strategies to reduce cortisol levels (e.g. reflecting on group sizes, relaxation opportunities, smooth transitions)

4. Staff contribute unique experiences from their own personal cultures and family backgrounds providing resources and diversity to the service.

5. Staff participate in regular in-service training, workshops and Tertiary education. Staff support and communicate with other services and professionals. Staff meetings are used for professional sharing and reflection. Staff have regular opportunities to liaise with the Director and Educational Leader to reflect and evaluate their professional development. Staff have a thorough knowledge and understanding of child development. A planning cycle incorporates EYLF outcomes, developmental milestones and current early childhood theories.

6. Staff are respectful and supportive to children's emotional well being. Educators provide positive feedback and support for children's efforts without the use of rewards, encouraging intrinsic motivation. Educators are welcoming and approachable. Journals are used as a two way communication tool. Families are invited to participate in the program. Educators engage in daily informal conversations and meetings with families. Social events provide opportunities to enhance professional relationships. Programs are displayed visibly and shared with families. Educators make themselves available and open to sharing information and support to meet all families' needs.

7. Educators seek out information and observe interests and skills of individuals and the group to ensure that learning is exciting, engaging and empowering. Educators communicate and interact with children at their level.

WE BELIEVE THAT …	OUR PRACTICES REFLECT …
Places and spaces for childhood	
1. Environments reflect interests, providing choice and ownership to children.	1. Provisions are based on current interests and projects. Rooms are child friendly e.g. Low shelves and furniture. Children are active participants in creating play spaces, and room agreements give them ownership over their environments. Children are involved in regular evaluation of the program.
2. Learning environments value family and community cultures, creating safe and welcoming spaces.	2. Resources from home are incorporated into the environment, creating links between home and the centre, such as family photos. Cross cultural resources are included in the environment. Family and community celebrations are meaningfully and appropriately reflected in the program.
3. Consistent play spaces foster and encourage involvement and self extension.	3. Environments and equipment are added to, rather than changed. Consistent play spaces allow for opportunities to practice and master skills and further extend.
4. Environments are open ended, evolving and celebrate emerging interests.	4. Programs promote creative expression and exploration. Unstructured experiences allow for experimentation and success. The emergent curriculum enables children's interests and ideas to be extended upon meaningfully. Programs/projects reflect children's current interests.
5. Environments provide for the opportunity of freedom of self expression, promoting interactions and the development of relationships.	5. Creativity and self expression are encouraged and embraced. Sensory experiences, art, music, drama and movement are integrated into the program. Children's creations and individuality are celebrated. Working on projects and interaction during the day encourage children to be active members of a team/ community.
6. Environments support the development of aesthetic awareness and respectful attitudes towards the environment.	6. Rooms are visually stimulating and welcoming. All areas in the indoor and outdoor environment are utilized and valued as possible areas for learning and enjoyment. Children are supported to respect their environments. The use of natural and renewable resources, such as wooden furniture and toys.
7. Connections with nature provide valuable learning experiences and enhances emotional wellbeing.	7. Our outdoor environment provides sensory opportunities with natural provisions. The outdoor environment is valued as an opportunity for learning (e.g. gardening, recycling). The wider community provides access to larger natural spaces and for bush connections.
8. Routines are flexible and child focused.	8. Routines provide for predictability and security, but appreciate that limited interruptions to play allow time for exploration and flow. Children contribute to daily routines such as lunch, set up and packing away. Independence and self help skills are encouraged through relaxed transitions, progressive routines and flexibility. Individual needs are respected and allowed for within the daily routine.

WE BELIEVE THAT …	OUR PRACTICES REFLECT …
The language of relationships	
1. We honor diversity and create supportive, honest and open interactions. The needs of others are valued and respected.	1. Diversity is reflected in the program and physical environments. Educators are open and honest with families about their day and experiences. Support is provided to both children and families by Educators. Educators are aware of family contexts providing understanding and support. Educator's role model respect and empathy during their interactions. Children are encouraged and supported to develop an appreciation for difference and individuality.
2. Children's relationships within their family cultures are acknowledged and respected within the centre.	2. Educators recognize family relationships as important and crucial in a child's life. Individual family cultures are acknowledged and respected through inclusive practices. All family types are recognized by celebrating diversity within the program. Indigenous culture is acknowledged within the service
3. The development of positive conflict resolution and relationship skills, support children to become respectful members of their community.	3. Conflict resolution is role modeled with support and guidance for all children, providing age appropriate language and strategies to resolve conflict. Children are given space and time to solve problems independently with peers. Adult support is available if needed.
4. Families are a valuable resource for teaching and learning.	4. Families are respected as the child's primary care and support network. Families are encouraged to contribute from their wealth of knowledge. Individual programming is done in collaboration with families. Families are welcomed to participate within the daily program. Family feedback is valued and utilized during program and policy review.
5. Relationships are the foundation for learning, as children learn in a social context. Friendships are fostered and supported.	5. Our environments are set up to encourage social interaction. Respectful interactions are modeled and encouraged by Educators. A sense of teamwork is created by staff actively developing a strong sense of social justice, through group and individual discussions. Providing a respectful and accepting environment will ensure that children are able to take safe risks and express their individuality.
6. The EYLF supports a sense of belonging, being and becoming for each individual child.	6. Educators have a thorough commitment to the principles and practices of the EYLF. Outcomes guide individual programming and learning.
7. Relationships with families are developed through effective communication methods, which provide for individual needs.	7. Varieties of communication approaches are used to ensure all families are informed and involved (newsletter, notices, individual room email addresses, Family Feedback Surveys, Individual Learning Journals, parent/teacher meetings and informal chats).

WE BELIEVE THAT …	OUR PRACTICES REFLECT …
The learning journey	
1. Each Child's learning journey is celebrated and shared between families and educators.	1. Individual journals celebrate learning, providing opportunities for two way communication and information sharing. Journals include photographs, observations, learning stories, Curriculum in Action, room and individual programming (clear planning cycle, learning outcomes, summative assessment), work samples, artwork, project information, articles, developmental information, routines and entries from families and educators.
2. Documentation provides insights and understanding of individuals learning, development and interests.	2. A variety of media is used to document children's experiences, such as webs, brainstorming, photographs, learning stories, observations and evaluations. Educators ask open ended questions to encourage enquiry and critical thinking.
3. Programs are individualised, based on emerging interests and skills.	3. Time is provided for one to one interaction (supported by high staff–child ratios) to enable educators to develop a positive rapport with each individual. Educators focus on the child's strengths and abilities. Using the children's interests as the basis for programming ensures that learning is relevant. Planning is shared with educators, families and learners.
4. Projects are driven by children and provide opportunities for in-depth learning. Through collaborative investigation, children make meaningful discoveries.	4. Projects are documented and displayed in rooms and in learning journals. Educators support children to be resourceful and investigate ideas, rather than just providing answers. There is a focus on the process of investigation through hands on collaborative involvement and the use of technology to access information.
5. Through critical thinking and discussion, children are able to consider other points of view.	5. We encourage children to question and explore their worlds. Ideas and opinions are captured through documentation. Children are encouraged to consider alternative possibilities. Small and large group work is a part of the daily program. Critical literacy is explored and stereotypes are challenged.
6. Exploring projects and emerging interests, provides opportunities for children to develop in all of the learning outcomes.	6. Learning is driven by children and supported by educators. Areas which are explored within projects and interests include: relationships, environmental and cultural awareness, acquisition of knowledge and information, academic and social skills, physical and language.
7. Play motivates children to learn and extends upon strengths and interests.	7. Play is valued and supported by staff. Interaction with peers is valued as an important learning opportunity. The environment is organised to encourage play experiences based on children's interests. Open ended resources promote creativity and individuality.
8. EYLF and NQS drives our programming and practices.	8. EYLF and NQS documents are used to guide decision making, the curriculum and critical reflection.

Source: Paddington Children's Centre, 2013

By making the setting's documented philosophy explicit, different groups – staff, families, students, future clients of the service and visitors – become aware of the direction of the setting's program and are able to question or make comments on it (*see* Figures 5.3–5.7 and Example 5.8). In Example 5.8, Ballina Public School outlines the philosophy that guides the school's practice in *Our School*, which supports families in making decsions about the choice of school for their children.

It is important that, once documented, the philosophy remains relevant to the setting. While the philosophy is less likely to change dramatically than perhaps are goals and practices in the short term, it is necessary to evaluate this at regular intervals or whenever there is substantial change within the setting. For example, over time, research raises new and different perspectives on early childhood education. Changing state and federal government policy, initiatives and curriculum frameworks will require settings to revisit their philosophy and mission. Societal values will also change as well as individual experiences and beliefs. These changes should lead to regular reviews of individual and group philosophies.

Source: Rainbow Children's Centre Inc.

FIGURE 5.6 When philosophies are available for all stakeholders and visitors to read, families, children and visitors are aware of the educational setting's beliefs and values.

FIGURE 5.7 Displaying the setting philosophy, along with images of the management committee and their children, assists all stakeholders and visitors to become aware of the theoretical perspectives, beliefs and values of the setting, as well as some of the stakeholders involved in the community managed structure. Note: For detail re philosophy and mission see text in Example 5.5.

EXAMPLE 5.8
Ballina Public School

Our school

Our school provides opportunities for students to participate in quality learning while building meaningful relationships that meet individual needs. We encourage each child to develop a positive and confident identity in a caring environment.

Through the school's curriculum, our students develop a love of learning. This is demonstrated in their own work as individuals as well as their active contribution to the school and the wider community. We foster the importance of developing personal beliefs, sharing our diverse cultural heritage and pride in being Australian within a world community.

Professional and highly skilled staff is the key to building success in our students. They ensure a cohesive whole school approach in a safe and happy environment as well as productive classrooms with high quality outcomes-based learning.

We acknowledge that parents are of prime importance in the education of their children. Parents and caregivers are seen as partners in education and we foster strong links between home and school.

Source: http://www.ballina-p.schools.nsw.edu.au/our-school, 2014

When *Belonging, Being, Becoming: The Early Years Learning Framework for Australia* was introduced many stakeholders were encouraged to reflect on their philosophical basis. Reflection is a positive strategy to start to review existing philosophies or to develop a philosophy for the first time. It may mean changing existing philosophy documents, or reflecting on how a current philosophy relates to the vision and principles of current theory and practice.

In Example 5.9 Natalie Cordukes, the Director of UnitingCare Paddington Children's Centre, reflects on the process of revisiting the centre philosophy which resulted in the changes evident in Figure 5.3 from earlier in the chapter.

EXAMPLE 5.9
Paddington Children's Centre Quality Improvement Plan

As part of our Quality Improvement Plan (QIP) review it was identified that our philosophy was due for an update to reflect the achievements made from the previous year. During a development day the whole staff team came together to review our QIP, and the following areas were discussed as missing in our philosophy:

- Our commitment to sustainability and the environment
- Reflecting the implementation of the EYLF and NQS in our daily practices
- Our high staff to child ratios and our highly qualified staff
- Children's voices
- Indigenous acknowledgement
- Our strong focus on health and nutrition.

Representatives from each room, the Director and the Educational Leader created a draft philosophy based on discussions at the staff development day. The philosophy draft was distributed to all staff, families and Board of Management for feedback. Children of all ages at the Centre were interviewed to gather children's points of view of the service and a variety of quotes were selected to represent a broad range of children. Following many drafts we finally came to a philosophy that reflects our current beliefs with all stakeholders represented. A pop-up banner with the new philosophy was produced to display in our foyer and at our Annual General Meeting.

Source: Natalie Cordukes, Director of UnitingCare Paddington Children's Centre, 2014

The philosophy may also need to be reviewed if there are changes within the setting; for example, how relevant is the philosophy if many of the stakeholders who participated in developing it are no longer involved with the setting? Evaluation is necessary to ensure not only that the philosophy is relevant but also that it is reflected in the everyday practices of the setting. Sylvia Turner, Director of Tigger's Honeypot Children's Centres, reflects on the importance of continually reflecting on and reviewing the setting's philosophy in Example 5.10.

EXAMPLE 5.10
Reflection process: Philosophy of Tigger's Honeypot Children's Centres

Working in the one service for a number of years brings with it so many benefits. One interesting opportunity is looking back over the centre's philosophy and it's development and reviews over the years. Tracking back in time to what was missing or what was of particular interest each time we reviewed our philosophy is evident when looking at the past editions of the philosophy as well as the review process and questions of each. Each review has seen us have a different focal point or reflecting on a different framework. In the past we focused strongly on social justice and feel that it is well embedded within the philosophy and remains one of the centres' commitments.

With our current philosophy we reflected on how our philosophy fitted with the *Early Years Learning Framework* and the *National Quality Framework*. We also included a focus on the natural environment to reflect our large attached garden, which, due to regulation changes, has now been able to become a part of our daily experiences with children.

As the director of Tigger's Place for 12 years there is an attachment to this centre's philosophy, having been involved in its evolution. The centre also has a number of long-term staff and families equally attached. Letting go of this attachment and acknowledging new perspectives is critical if all staff and families are to be able to live and breathe the philosophy. Making sure everyone's voice is heard takes time and a variety of strategies. We understand this and are patient with our reviews.

Our philosophy is something that we are proud of and something that is shared with prospective new families on tours of the centre and again with families during their induction prior to commencement at the centre. Families choose to accept a position at this centre or not based on our philosophy. Our strong articulation of our focus on social justice and risk taking is important so that families are able to make an informed decision as to whether our centre fits their families goals for their child.

The educators within the centre are all able to clearly express their commitment and enthusiasm to our philosophy, it is discussed regularly in staff meetings and when tricky situations arise it is our tool to rethink our practices. Our community committee is also instrumental in supporting us to review our practices. The committee is made up of staff and families, the manager of UNSW Early Years Services and centre director.

When we review the centres' philosophy we do so through family meetings, committee meetings, emails with staff and families, and discussions with children.

The following questions were used to support families, staff and children during the reflection process.

Families reflected on the following questions using our previous philosophy and information about the *Early Years Learning Framework*:

1. What role does this service play in your child's and your family life?
2. List three things that you feel are the most important things we can provide for your child while they are enrolled at the centre.
3. List three things that you feel are the most important things we can provide for your family while they are enrolled at the centre.
4. How does the current philosophy reflect your family's needs and expectations?
5. What is missing from our philosophy that you would like to see represented?
6. How does our philosophy respect and reflect your expectations?

Staff reflected on the following questions:

1. How does the centre philosophy reflect or contradict your personal philosophy?
2. Does the philosophy reflect the Early Years Learning Framework – in what ways? What is missing?

Children were asked:

- What do you enjoy about Tigger's Honeypot?
- What would you like to do more?
- What don't you like?
- What's your favourite thing about Tigger's Honeypot?
- What makes Tigger's Honeypot special?

The input from these discussions and emails were collated and used as a springboard for further conversations at our philosophy night.

All of the above assisted us in the development of our current philosophy. Reviewing the philosophy is a wonderful time for team building and collaborating with families. I find our team's 'anything is possible' attitude and commitment to collaborations helps us work towards our dream, which is our philosophy.

Our centre acknowledges the traditional custodians of the land on which we now teach, play and learn and pay our respect to elders both past, present and future.

Source: Sylvia Turner, Director of Tigger's Honeypot Children's Centre, 2013

Where staff clearly identify the process used within the setting to develop and evaluate the philosophy, they create awareness of this process by providing this information to families, staff and management. This process encourages stakeholders' input into the evaluation process.

Conclusion and reflection

The process of philosophy development for a setting can take a long time, sometimes up to a year if the process has not been in place previously. Reviewing a philosophy does not tend to take as long, particularly if some group members participated in the process before and they have evaluated the current perspectives and philosophy as an ongoing process. By taking this time initially, turning ideals into reality will be a much clearer task.

Questions for reflection

1. How do your values influence your work as an early childhood educator? What importance do you place on working in an early childhood setting or school where stakeholders have the same philosophical basis as yours? How would you respond to situations where practices appeared to be in conflict with the stated philosophy of a service?

2. Within the community a number of different early childhood settings with differing philosophies exist. For example:

   a. a community-managed early childhood education centre with strong beliefs about community involvement, reflection of the daily lives of children within the centre program and the reflection of the diversity of children through encouraging children of different ages to play.

   b. a large for-profit early childhood education centre where children learn in groups based on ages with individual educators, a program which reflects a structured approach to learning in various curriculum areas, and works towards supporting children in the preparation for school.

   Place yourself in either of the settings. What assumptions can you make about the following:

   - perspectives and theories on which the philosophy is based
   - understandings of how children learn and the underlying perspectives
   - the role of families, educators and children in the learning environment
   - the role of play in learning.

3. Think about three situations when you said, 'I'd like to do … but I can't because …'. Explore how you might bring about a change to work towards these ideals.

4. What process is in place in your setting for developing and evaluating a setting philosophy? Are all voices heard? What strategies could be put in place to have stakeholders' voices represented?

Key terms

educational philosophies, 151

mission, 146

philosophy, 146

values, 146

vision, 146

stakeholders, 146

theoretical perspectives, 151

Online study resources

Visit http://login.cengagebrain.com and use the access code that comes with this book for 12 months access to the student resources for this text.

CourseMate Express

The CourseMate Express website contains a range of resources and study tools for this chapter, including:

- Online video activities
- Online research activities
- A revision quiz
- Matching pair exercises
- A list of key weblinks
- A chapter glossary, flashcards and crossword to help you revise terminology
- and more!

Search me! education

Explore **Search me! education** for articles relevant to this chapter. Fast and convenient, Search me! education is updated daily and provides you with 24-hour access to full text articles from hundreds of scholarly and popular journals, ebooks and newspapers, including *The Australian* and *The New York Times*. Log in to Search me! through http://login.cengage.com and try searching for the following key words:

- theoretical perspective
- educational philosophy
- mission statement
- vision statement
- collective or team philosophy
- developing a philosophy
- stakeholder
- documenting philosophy
- implementing and evaluating philosophy
- reflective planning process.

Search tip: **Search me! education** contains information from both local and international sources. To get the greatest number of search results, try using both Australian and American spellings in your searches, e.g. 'globalisation' and 'globalization'; 'organisation' and 'organization'

Recommended resources

Carter, M & Curtis, D 2010, *The Visionary Director*, Redleaf Press, USA.

Department of Education, Employment and Workplace relations (DEEWR) 2009, *Belonging, Being, Becoming: The Early Years Learning Framework for Australia*, Commonwealth of Australia, Canberra.

Giugni, M 2011, *Inclusion Support Facilitators Encountering the Early Years Learning Framework*, Australian Government Inclusion and Professional Support Program.

Mac Naughton, G & Williams, G 2009, *Techniques for Teaching Young Children: Choices for Theory and Practice*, Pearson Education, French's Forest, NSW.

Patterson, C & Fleet, A 2011, 'Planning in the context of the EYLF: Powerful, practical and pedagogically sound', *Research in Practice Series*, vol. 18, no. 2.

Key weblinks

DEEWR, http://www.deewr.gov.au

Early Childhood Australia, http://www.earlychildhoodaustralia.org.au/

Professional Learning program, http://www.earlychildhoodaustralia.org.au/nqsplp/

Secretariat of National Aboriginal and islander Child care, http://www.snaicc.org.au/

Australian Children's education and Care Quality Authority, http://www.acecqa.gov.au/

References

Australian Children's Education and Care Quality Authority October 2011, *Guide to Developing a Quality Improvement Plan*. ACECQA, Sydney.

Australian Children's Education and Care Quality Authority 2013, *Guide to the National Quality Standard*, http://files.acecqa.gov.au/files/National-Quality-Framework-Resources-Kit/NQF03-Guide-to-NQS-130902.pdf, accessed 15 January 2014, ACECQA, Sydney.

Broinowski, I 2002, *Creative Childcare Practice: Program Design in Early Childhood*, Pearson Education, Sydney.

Buoy, L 2007, 'Reflections on Leadership', *Reflections Magazine*, vol. 28, Spring, Gowrie Australia, Qld.

Clark, A. 2010, *Transforming Children's Spaces*, Routledge, London.

Clark, A & Moss, P. 2005, *Spaces to Play*, National Children's Bureau, London

Dahlberg, G, Moss, P & Pence, A 1999, *Beyond Quality in Early Childhood Education and Care: Languages of Evaluation*, Routledge, London.

Dahlberg, G, Moss, P & Pence, A 2007, *Beyond Quality in Early Childhood Education and Care: Languages of Evaluation*, 2nd edn., Routledge, London.

De Jean, W 2010, taped conversation with Louise Hard from Charles Sturt University, Australia, accessed via supplied DVD with Subject EEB423.

Dockett, S & Einarsdottir, J and Perry, B 2011, 'Balancing methodologies and methods in researching with young children', in D Harcourt, B Perry & T Waller (Eds), *Researching Young Children's Perspectives* (pp. 68–80), Routledge, London.

Dunphy, L & Farrell, T 2011, 'Eliciting young children's perspectives on indoor play provision in their classroom', in D Harcourt, B Perry & T Waller (Eds), *Researching Young Children's Perspectives* (pp. 128–42), Routledge, London.

Early Childhood Australia 2006, *Early Childhood Australia's Code of Ethics*, http://www.communities.wa.gov.au/education-and-care/nqfgb/Documents/code_of_ethics.pdf, accessed 6 February 2014.

Ebbeck, M & Waniganayaka, M 2004, 'Early childhood professionals leading today and tomorrow', *Every Child Magazine*, vol. 10, no. 1, pp. 29–30, http://80-search.informit.com.au.ezproxy.csu.edu.au/fullText, accessed 12 August 2010.

Edwards, C, Gandini, L & Forman, G (eds) 1998, *The Hundred Languages of Children*, 2nd edn., Ablex, Greenwich, CN.

Einarsdottir, J. 2003. '"When the bell rings we have to go inside": Pre-school children's views on the Primary school', *European Early Childhood Education Research Association Themed Monograph 1*, 35–50.

Elliot, A 2008, 'Mentoring for professional growth', *Every Child Magazine*, vol. 14, no. 3, Early Childhood Australia, Canberra.

Farmer, S 1995, *Policy Development in Early Childhood Services*, Community Child Care Cooperative, Sydney.

Fleet, A, Patterson, C & Robertson, J (eds) 2006, *Insights: Behind Early Childhood Pedagogical Documentation*, Pademelon Press, Castle Hill, NSW.

Fleet, A & Britt, C. 2010, 'Seeing spaces, inhabiting places: Hearing school beginners', in D Harcourt, B Perry & T Waller (Eds), *Researching Young Children's Perspectives* (pp. 143–62), Routledge, London.

Giugni, M 2008, *Exploring Multiculturalism, Anti Bias and Social Justice in Children's Services*, Children's Services Central, Sydney.

Goodfellow, J 2009, 'The Early Years Learning Framework: Getting started', *Research in Practice Series*, vol. 16, no. 4.

Hard, L 2004, 'How is leadership understood in early childhood education and care?', *Journal of Australian Research in Early Childhood Education*, vol. 11, no. 1, pp. 123–32.

Kennedy, A 2012, 'What do theories have to do with it?', *National Quality Standard Professional Learning Program*, Newsletter No. 31, http://www.earlychildhoodaustralia.org.au/nqsplp/e-newsletters/newsletters-31-35/newsletter-31/, accessed 11 April 2014.

Lifeline Community Care 2010, *Journeys of Inclusion*, Lifeline Community Care, Qld.

Press, F 2010, taped conversation with Louise Hard from Charles Sturt University, Australia, accessed via supplied DVD with Subject EEB423.

Sidoti, C 2008, 'Rights and advocacy', *Every Child Magazine*, vol. 14, no. 4, Early Childhood Australia, Canberra.

Vygotsky, L 1978, *Mind in Society: The Development of Higher Psychological Processes*, Harvard University Press, Cambridge, MA.

Waniganayake, M, Cheeseman, S, Fenech, M, Hadley, F & Shepherd, W 2012, *Leadership: Contexts and Complexities in Early Childhood Education*, Oxford University Press, South Melbourne, Victoria.

Waniganayake, M, Morda, R & Kapsalakis, A 2000, 'Leadership in child care centres: Is it just another job?', *Australian Journal of Early Childhood*, vol. 25, no. 1, pp. 13–20.

Widger, S and Schofield, A 2012, 'Interaction or interruption? Five child-centred philosophical perspectives', *Australian Journal of Early Childhood Education*, vol. 37, no. 4, pp. 29–32.

CHAPTER SIX

UNDERSTANDING THE SETTING

Chapter learning focus

This chapter will investigate:

- the importance of understanding the setting

- identifying relevant information

- analysing information

- developing future directions

- developing a team plan of action

- reflecting on and evaluating goals.

Introduction

This chapter will assist educators, families and other stakeholders to develop a program reflecting both the early childhood setting or school's philosophical basis and the potentials and challenges existing within a particular setting. *Early childhood setting* refers to a range of services including early childhood education and care centres, preschools, outside school hours' care, family day care and early intervention services.

As explored in Chapters 4 and 5, processes of evaluation and strategic planning assist the setting or school to make the transition from its ideals (philosophy) to the realities (the practices). Once a philosophy or vision has been developed – a direction – stakeholders (educators, children, families and community members) need to engage in further investigation to identify the unique characteristics of the setting. Having identified and analysed this information, stakeholders can then identify a range of ways to work more effectively with the potentials and challenges within the setting. A situational analysis is also a useful process for student educators to engage in during professional experience placements, as it enables them to identify key aspects of the setting. This analysis helps students to link their professional learning goals to the potentials and constraints of the setting as well as to their own personal learning strengths and needs.

In some cases, issues will be specific to only one setting; in other cases they will be similar across settings. Some challenges, such as the lack of suitable resources for infants, may be easy to overcome. Others, such as developing staff skills in the use of contemporary pedagogical approaches, will require negotiation with team members and the instigation of a plan of action for improvement within the setting that continues over a longer time frame. It is important to keep these issues in mind, but also to be clear about what the setting's bottom line is for achievement of a program and practices that reflect the setting's philosophy. With this in mind, a firm but gradual direction for improvements can be followed based on the setting's philosophy.

The importance of understanding the setting

As identified in Chapter 1, there have been many new directions in early childhood education that have challenged the authors, and many early childhood educators, to reconceptualise their understandings of planning and programming, curriculum and documentation of children's learning. In the context of multiple changes, it is important to outline what is important within a specific setting as well as the approaches to planning that are used to support these. **Situational analysis** is a tool useful in this process.

Situational analysis

Collecting and analysing information about an organisation to identify strengths and directions for future planning and implementation.

While philosophy development provides the broad direction for the setting, other aspects of the setting also need to be investigated on a regular basis. This is often known as an environmental or situational analysis (Arthur et al., 2008; Kearns, 2010). A situational analysis provides clear directions for practice. Carter and Curtis (2010, p. 25) identify this process as a core element to creating a vision, when they state that 'leaders create management systems and structures to support a visionary organizational culture'.

Without an analysis of current practices it would be difficult to implement change or undertake any reflective processes. Investigating what is occurring is central to ongoing improvement in practice in any early childhood setting or school and is the focus of reflective practice, which is a key feature of the *National Quality Framework* for Early Childhood Education and Care (DEEWR, 2010b). Undertaking a situational analysis 'begins the process of transforming the ideas embodied in the philosophy into practice' (Kearns, 2010, p. 6), and is the next step towards planning for ongoing quality improvement and change in each service (Carter & Curtis, 2010; Community Child Care, 2009; Jorde Bloom, 2005).

Gap analysis

Identifying the steps that need to be taken in order to move from actual practice to desired practice based on the gap between ideal and reality.

This process is also identified in some organisations as a **gap analysis** and can be used to support the development of a setting's Quality Improvement Plan (QIP) for the Australian Children's Education and Care Quality Authority (ACECQA, 2012).

All educators tend to undertake a situational analysis, often in an informal way. For example, whenever an educator starts a job, they take time to find out how that setting operates, who the children and families are, what role each staff member plays, how the program is implemented and what management structures exist. They make sense of this information before they attempt to implement any changes. As with philosophy development, investigating the situation is a worthwhile collaborative effort, and analysing and documenting this information in a workable process and format helps to develop a clear understanding about the setting.

A situational analysis helps all those involved in the setting to become familiar with, and understand more about, the setting in terms of human and material resources, policies and legal and funding guidelines. Investigation of the setting also provides a clear understanding about the sociocultural context of families and children attending the setting so that the curriculum can be culturally responsive. Irrespective of the type of setting, documentation of a situational analysis provides a concise overview and analysis of collected and analysed information that will assist educators and other stakeholders to develop a plan of action for change in the setting. It is expected that additional, more detailed information and documentation, such as policies and documentation of children's learning, will be available on file to support the situational analysis. Ongoing investigation of the setting will ensure that the situational analysis remains a current and useful document. Dating information as it is added helps to give a clear picture of changes over time. Identifying when changes are achieved and new goals are developed is crucial to any quality improvement plan.

FIGURE 6.1 A team approach to collecting and analysing information about the setting enables stakeholders to develop an effective plan for ongoing improvement.

A team approach to situational analysis enables all stakeholders to have a clear understanding of the setting and contribute to planning goals. Encouraging the involvement of different groups in the processes of the situational analysis is vital to a collaborative approach (Patterson, 2006) and will make the task more manageable. This includes the collection, collation and analysis of information and the resultant decision making. Any planning process must allow for team members to investigate possible requirements, constraints and potentials within the setting, and should enable them to develop a program that reflects their ideals in response to these issues. The experience of being involved in the process of situational analysis establishes trustworthy understandings of the setting and develops the skills needed for informed curriculum and management decisions. Collaborative management processes are also a core requirement of most quality assurance measures. Further, any decisions made as a result of a collaborative situational analysis process will reflect multiple perceptions of a situation and therefore be inclusive of a range of voices within the setting.

> What opportunities exist for collaborative situational analysis in your setting? What strategies are used to analyse the information that is produced?

Identifying relevant information

When beginning to gather data about a setting, the sort of information that may be useful to collect could focus on three main sections: community and families, setting and children (as outlined in Table 6.1). Organising the information in this way enables the handling of information

TABLE 6.1 Investigating the situation: useful information for collection

COMMUNITY AND FAMILIES	SETTING	CHILDREN
• Ethnic, language, religious and socio-economic groups in local community, including Aboriginal and Torres Strait Islander groups • Ethnic, language and socio-economic groups of families using setting, including Aboriginal and Torres Strait Islander families • Features of the local community environment • Families' values, beliefs, experiences and expectations • Family and community experiences and expertise • Family and community participation in the setting and daily program • Family and community resources • Relationships and communication practices between families and educators • Role of families and communities in setting management and curriculum decision making	• Management model • Relevant history • Human resources – staff (full-time, part-time) and specialist advisors; skills, strengths and interests; qualifications and experience; professional development, etc. • Organisational culture and climate of the setting • Material resources – building (space and design), equipment, environment (indoor/outdoor) • Policies (documented and unwritten) • Mandates – regulations and standards, funding guidelines, quality assurance, departmental policy, legal requirements • Philosophy • Existing practices in planning and documentation • Quality assurance process – e.g. *National Quality Standard* • Curriculum guidelines • Size of group, nature of groups, distribution of children throughout the whole group or setting • Funding arrangements • Access to support services • Links to other settings/schools	• Sociocultural contexts – languages, family and community practices, faiths • Funds of knowledge based on children's experiences within their families and communities • Strengths, interests, emerging development • Relationships – with peers and adults within the setting • Prior experiences before commencing at the setting • Diversity of children attending; e.g. ethnicity, additional needs, languages

in meaningful components as well as facilitating ease of documentation; however, there is no 'blanket format' that is required to be used to gather information. Jorde Bloom (2005, p. 6) identifies the social systems within any organisation under the key components of external environment, people, structure, processes, culture and outcomes, stressing the interrelated parts of this system when looking at change. Whatever method is relevant to the setting is appropriate, as long as it is manageable, not overly time-consuming and provides useful program directions.

It is likely that student educators and educators in early childhood settings and schools will document using different levels of detail at different stages of their career and in response to different government initiatives. For example, schools may use the process of a situational analysis to provide the information required to apply for specific funding designed to extend the learning of children from communities of socio-economic disadvantage.

Some useful information to be collected relates to the mandates (legal requirements), constraints and potentials the setting works within. **Mandates** refer to what a service is required to do, or not do, by external authorities. These requirements are likely to be codified in laws, ordinances, articles of incorporation or charters. Early childhood services and schools also face informal mandates or requirements, often found in the norms within the society and profession (Farmer, 1995; Kearns, 2010).

As well as mandates that apply to all settings, relevant information as it relates specifically to the individual setting needs to be collected, documented and then analysed. The range of information that can be collected is outlined in Table 6.1. These are suggestions only and can be adapted to suit particular settings; however, they can provide a starting point for collecting relevant information.

Mandates

What a service is required to do, or not do, by external authorities.

Sample questions to guide information gathering

Information about the local community and families

- Which languages, religions and ethnic groups are represented in the community?
- Do children and families from each of these groups attend this setting?
- What information is available to explain why this is the case?
- Do families have the opportunity and/or the need to learn English?
- Among the community, what support is there for maintenance of home language/s?
- What are important general child-rearing practices in families in the community?
- What is the socio-economic status (SES) of the community and the families using the setting?
- What are the strengths of the community?
- Which community services are accessible to families?
- Which interests do families spend time and energy on; e.g. study, sport, travel, house and garden, community events?
- What are important experiences or challenges for families; e.g. migration, unemployment, study, health status, transport and housing concerns?
- What funds of knowledge can families share; e.g. expertise with gardening, music, languages, etc.?
- What particular values do families regard highly; e.g. 'clean' play, challenging gender stereotypes, kinship and importance of family?
- What sort of time, energy, talent and presence can families contribute towards the setting?

- What resources are available in the community; e.g. parks, other early childhood education and care settings, senior citizens centres, disability services, resource centres, transport?
- What roles do the community and families play in the management of the setting?
- How are the community and families involved in the setting and curriculum decision making?
- Which communication practices are used between educators and families? Educators and community?

Setting

- Which management model (sponsor, government, community, for-profit, corporate) relates to the setting? What is the history of the setting? Have there been any major changes to the service operation and development?
- Which staff members are available – full-time, part-time, occasional?
- What commitments are there to professional development?
- What experiences, talents and interests do staff members have?
- What is the nature of the building/s?
- What is the indoor/outdoor environment like?
- How is the setting resourced with equipment?
- What consumable resources are available? How is sustainable practice supported?
- Which policies are important to the setting? Which are documented?
- What are the relevant laws, regulations, quality assurance requirements and funding guidelines for the setting?
- What specific funding is available for children with additional needs?
- What quality assurance standard does the setting have and what are they working towards?
- What resource and support services does the setting have access to?
- What is the current documented philosophy?
- What are the existing practices for documenting children's learning and experiences?
- What is the size of the total group?
- How are smaller groups distributed throughout the setting?
- How are smaller groups used throughout the day?

Children

- What diversity exists within the group – e.g., ethnicity, additional needs, age, interests?
- Which language/s or dialect/s does each child speak at home?
- Which literacy materials are available in the home and in which language/s?
- What are children's family and community experiences?
- What are parent expectations for their children?
- What are the groups' strengths, interests and emerging development?
- What are the interests shared by small groups of children?
- What strategies are used to get to know about children's strengths and interests?

Analysing information

Identifying relevant information about an early childhood setting is the starting point for transforming the values and beliefs embodied in the setting philosophy into practice (Kearns, 2010b) within each setting. Analysing what that information might mean is a vital step in the process. This includes the analysis of constraints and potentials.

Constraints

Features that present obstacles to, or negative influences on, practices.

Potentials

Features that can facilitate or support the implementation of our philosophy and practices.

Constraints are considered to be any features that present obstacles to, or negative influences on, practices. An example of a constraint may be a lack of resources or a lack of opportunities for professional development. While many factors may be seen as obstacles to implementing our philosophy by some, others are often viewed as positive and can assist the implementation of our philosophy. **Potentials** are features that can facilitate or support the implementation of our philosophy and practices. An example of a potential may be a highly qualified and experienced staff team.

Mandates, constraints and potentials may be classified as internal (related to the specific setting) or external (may influence other settings and be seen as an outside influence, such as government mandates or lack of funding); that is, some may be specific to an individual setting, while others will be similar across settings. Mandates, constraints and potentials may either support or impede the implementation of philosophical ideals.

Depending on our perspectives, what one person may see as a constraint may be seen by someone else as a potential. For example, mandates such as government legislation may be perceived from some perspectives to be restrictive and costly to implement, while other sections of the early childhood profession may recognise these requirements as a support to strengthening the quality of a children's service. Fenech et al. (2006) report, in a study based on working in a regulatory environment, that some early childhood professionals saw regulations as a 'double-edged sword' that can either enhance or impede potentials within a setting.

Some examples of constraints and potentials are identified in Tables 6.2 and 6.3. Different perspectives can be seen when the analysis is compared in Tables 6.2 and 6.3, where similar factors are viewed from different viewpoints and thus are included as both a constraint and a potential.

TABLE 6.2 Possible constraints

INTERNAL CONSTRAINTS	EXTERNAL CONSTRAINTS

• Building design, e.g.:
  – renovated factory/house
  – limited purpose-built design re. outdoor and indoor environments
  – school building on different levels
• Staffing difficulties, e.g.:
  – lack of availability of qualified or experienced staff
  – high staff turnover
  – limited professional learning opportunities
  – negative organisational climate
• Limited resources/inappropriate resources
• Limited time for team meetings
• Diverse expectations and needs of families, community, staff and management
• Children's diverse strengths and challenges
• Diverse languages and ethnic backgrounds of community and families
• Hours of operation
• Diverse attendance patterns
	• *National Quality Standard:*
	  – different interpretations of standards
	• Quality assurance measures:
	  – time consuming and prescriptive
	• Mandatory curriculum in schools
	• Mandatory learning outcomes in prior to school settings
	• Mandatory standardised assessment of children's learning, e.g. NAPLAN
	• Funding issues:
	  – limited funding
	  – different funding guidelines and demands for accountability measures
	  – dealing with different government departments for funding
	• Management organisations:
	  – limited understanding of children's services
	  – centralised systems
	  – bureaucracy

TABLE 6.3 Possible potentials

INTERNAL POTENTIALS	EXTERNAL POTENTIALS

• Building design, e.g.:
   – purpose-built with flexible space and amenities indoors and outdoors
   – school on one level
   – access for people with additional needs
 • Staffing, e.g.:
   – stable staff
   – experienced and qualified staff
   – effective teamwork
   – continued professional learning opportunities
   – strong organisational climate
 • Wide range of resources including technologies
 • Time available during work for team meetings and planning
 • Diversity within families, children, community, staff and management
	• *National Quality Standard:*
	   – cohesive system across Australia maintains appropriate level of quality for all Australian children
	 • Quality assurance:
	   – encourages self-evaluation, improvement and reporting to families and managers
	 • Funding issues:
	   – adequate levels of funding
	   – availability of additional funding for specific purposes
	   – funding for professional learning
	 • Management organisations:
	   – supportive management
	   – additional resources to draw on
	 • Government policy, legislation and funding:
	   – support for children's services and education
	   – maintaining safe environments for children, staff and families

Once potentials and constraints are identified, it is much easier to solve any problems and to work around these to implement the setting's philosophy. Rather than view a constraint as an excuse for inaction, those involved can work towards finding a creative solution to the challenge. Fenech (2006) suggests that using **critical reflexivity** – that is an active, not passive, response to a situation – along with a commitment to quality is one way of tackling these challenges. Where such reflection identifies constraints that are detrimental to the service, and those involved in it, Fenech identifies a range of resistance strategies that support educators' professional judgements, rather than educators having to shape 'their practices to fit regulatory requirements that are not always perceived to promote quality standards' (Fenech, 2006, p. 18).

These strategies include:

- utilising complaint mechanisms
- proactively developing collaborative, respectful relationships with children's services advisors (or equivalent representatives of government regulatory bodies)
- strategically deciding when to acquiesce and when to 'fight'
- confidently knowing and articulating the theoretical, value and knowledge bases of your practice
- mobilising collective resistance
- openly resisting interpretations (of government and regulatory requirements) when you perceive conflict with the interests of children in the service.

M Fenech, *Working in a Regulatory Environment: Challenges and Opportunities*, p 19, © 2006.

Critical reflexivity

Thinking critically about the impact of our assumptions, values and actions on others in order to develop a more collaborative, responsive and ethical response.

Another way of looking at identifying constraints and potentials within an early childhood setting or school is to undertake a SWOT analysis (Community Child Care, 2009; Kearns, 2010). This process involves exploring the strengths, weaknesses, opportunities and threats within an organisation to identify all possible impacts and future planning needed to reduce these impacts.

Gathering perspectives about possible constraints and potentials from stakeholders, undertaking a SWOT analysis at a meeting or seeking feedback from a range of perspectives can be effective ways to collect different views. An example of a simple way to gather views is provided in the box below. This could be used at a parent, management or staff meeting, or given to individuals for written ideas.

Format for investigating constraints and potentials within a setting

Constraints are considered to be any features that present obstacles to, or negative influences on, practices.

Potentials are features that can facilitate or support the implementation of the setting's philosophy and practices.

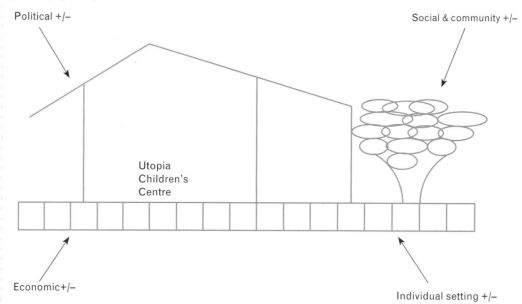

What constraints (−) or potentials (+) are faced in early childhood settings?

Source: Developed by S Farmer, H Meredith & R Watson for a workshop, Australian Early Childhood Association Conference, 1999; adapted S Farmer, 2011

The Quality Improvement Plan tool used as part of the *National Quality Framework* (ACECQA, 2011) draws on this idea of constraints and potentials by including the areas of identified strengths (potentials) and key improvement areas (constraints) to be worked on as part of the quality improvement process.

In addition to the analysis of mandates, constraints and potentials, the box below suggests possible questions to guide the analysis of information that has been collected and its meaning for the setting or for student educators.

Sample questions to guide information analysis

Analysing information about the local community and families

- To what extent does the setting reflect the different language, religious and ethnic groups represented in the local community?
- Which languages, religious and ethnic groups in the local community attend or don't attend this setting? Why might this happen?
- How are family and community values and resources reflected in the practice within the setting?
- How accessible are basic services and community support services for families?
- How does the program reflect family interests and funds of knowledge; e.g. study, sport, travel, house and garden, community events?
- How does the setting respond to diverse family values; e.g. 'clean' play, challenging stereotypes ('race', gender, ability), kinship and importance of family?
- How do the setting's communication, management and curriculum practices cater for varying family contributions to the setting program; e.g. time, energy, talent and presence? How are families supported to participate?
- How are/might community resources be utilised in the setting; e.g. parks, shopping centres, transport, public art galleries, libraries and museums?
- What roles do community and families play in management and curriculum development?

Analysing information about the setting

- How does the management model (sponsor, government, community, for profit, corporate) influence the setting program?
- What does staff availability mean for the program?
- How are experiences, talents and interests of current staff members integrated in to the program?
- How does management support each educator's professional learning?
- How are specialist educators used to support children with additional needs and other educators?
- What collaborations are supported among educators in different settings?
- How does the built environment influence the program?
- How does the indoor/outdoor environment influence the program?
- How do major equipment resources support the program?
- How do consumable resources extend the program?
- How is sustainable practice reflected in the program and the environment?
- How do resources reflect families, children and communities; e.g. cultures, languages, etc.?
- Which important policies influence the program? How?
- Which relevant laws, regulations, quality assurance requirements and funding guidelines impact on setting practices?

- How is funding for children with additional needs used to support an inclusive environment?
- To what extent is the setting's philosophy reflected in practice?
- How does the size of the total group and grouping strategies influence the daily program?

Analysing information about the children

- To what extent are children's interests, experiences and strengths included in the program?
- To what extent are children's language/s or dialect/s extended in daily programs and resources?
- To what extent are children's current friendships and interests extended by the program?
- To what extent is diversity within the group of children used to support an inclusive program?

Developing future directions

Collecting and analysing information about the setting assists in the move from existing practices to improved future practices. Analysis of the extent to which the current setting practices reflect the setting philosophy and appropriate quality standards provides a springboard for future change – that is, moving towards the setting's ideals. If the setting has developed a vision (as well as a philosophy), this can provide a further guide for future directions (*see* Chapter 5). While the philosophy identifies what is valued and why, future directions identify how these beliefs can be put into practice and help identify goals for the setting.

The value of a situational analysis can be best demonstrated by looking at two examples and predicting some future directions for planning. These examples focus on settings for young children – one for children aged from birth to five years and the other for children in the early years of school.

Tables 6.4 and 6.5 illustrate the procedure of adjusting the notion of situational analysis to the individual setting, and of identifying and analysing significant information and drawing out future directions for planning that will be used to formulate a plan of action for practice. This is relevant to the Self Assessment and Quality Improvement Planning process, which is part of the *National Quality Framework* (ACECQA, 2011). Early childhood education and care settings that are part of this process will develop a Quality Improvement Plan (QIP) as a result of self-assessment and consultation and review steps, thus indicating the worthwhile practice of undertaking a situational analysis.

When a situational analysis is conducted by a student teacher, the future directions for planning are likely to relate to future directions for the student in the professional experience placement and these future directions can then link to specific student goals.

TABLE 6.4 An example of a situational analysis for a setting for children from birth to five years

Community and families

INFORMATION	ANALYSIS (WHAT DOES THIS INFORMATION MEAN?)	FUTURE DIRECTIONS
• Local community is diverse with many Greek, Lebanese and Vietnamese families.	• As there is a range of languages within the community, the setting needs to consider how it will communicate effectively with families and the community.	• Use interpreters to translate and assist in improving and extending family and community communication.
• Most families using the centre are from Greek, Lebanese and Vietnamese backgrounds.	• As there is a range of languages, cultures and beliefs within the community and families, the setting should explore ways of including these in the program.	• Provide visual displays – posters, photos and so on – to communicate aspects of the program to families and community members.
• Most families speak their first language at home.		• Interview parents (where time and languages permit) about important practices, values and beliefs within their family.
• Approximately 5 per cent of families in the community are from Aboriginal and Torres Strait Islander backgrounds.	• As there is a diverse community, the setting should draw on families to assist in developing a program that reflects diversity and social justice issues.	• Include diverse cultural practices and lifestyles of families within the total program in collaboration with staff and families.
• There are no families of Aboriginal and Torres Strait Islander backgrounds currently enrolled in the setting.	• As there are currently no families from Aboriginal and Torres Strait Islander backgrounds enrolled, the setting should investigate ways of encouraging connections with families in the community.	• Encourage interested families to share aspects of their family culture with the children.
• Local community is predominantly low to middle socio-economic status.		• Include the diverse languages of families and the local community in the centre; e.g. by including menus from local restaurants, photographs of shop signs and bilingual books and posters.
• Most families are from a low socio-economic group; some families are from a middle socio-economic group.		• Make connections with Aboriginal and Torres Strait Islander community organisations and groups.
• Many parents have recently migrated to Australia; other parents migrated as children.	• As the local environment is densely populated and may be exposed to noise and air pollution, the setting should take this into account when preparing the environment, and in developing appropriate policies.	• Explore practices that would appropriately reflect Aboriginal and Torres Strait Islander culture within the setting.
• A range of beliefs – Buddhism, Islam, Taoism, Christian and humanist – are held by parents.	• As most of the families are working, the setting needs to take this into account when planning any family participation and in providing a relevant service to them.	• Organise brief informal family meetings that are social and informative, and fit in with parents' working days.
• There is a range of child-rearing practices.		• Develop an environmental policy to reflect environmental awareness issues within the program; e.g. limit the use of toxic products, and reuse and recycle materials where possible.
• They are mostly two-parent families with both parents working. Some families are sole-parent families and there are a number of lesbian families.		
• Parents are engaged in factory, retail, restaurant and office work.		
• Local community is highly urbanised and is in a light industrial area with many busy roads and a few small parks.		
• There are mini-supermarkets, restaurants and takeaway food stores representing the local cultures.		

TABLE 6.4   An example of a situational analysis for a setting for children from birth to five years

INFORMATION	ANALYSIS (WHAT DOES THIS INFORMATION MEAN?)	FUTURE DIRECTIONS
• Most parents live close to work and close to the centre. • There are various levels of family participation in the centre, but all families show support in some way. • There are a number of communication methods within the setting; e.g. noticeboards, written documentation journals and some translated information.	• As communication methods are dominated by written text, the effectiveness of these need to be evaluated.	• Implement a balance of outdoor and indoor experiences. • Gather feedback from families as to most effective forms of communication including use of technology through email, facebook and SMS texting.
Setting		
• Open 7.00 a.m. to 6.00 p.m. • The centre has been open for 20 years. Centre extended hours three years ago to meet needs of community. Currently exploring centre demand for higher numbers of babies. • Centre managed by the local council. • Human resources: – one director/teacher (4-year qualification) working in the centre for three years, with an interest in children with additional needs – one teacher: newly graduated (previously held a Diploma qualification), bilingual (Vietnamese and English) – three Diploma staff: one interested in diversity issues and one working closely with families – and one with an interest in health and safety policy issues – two staff members with Certificate III, new to early childhood field but interested in further education – one untrained staff member: upgrading qualifications to Certificate III, strong musical talents – one cook: Arabic-speaking, currently completing a nutrition course	• As the setting is managed by the local council, the range of available resources and support should be explored. • As the setting was built to suit the needs of the community 20 years ago, staff and management should constantly investigate current community needs, as well as how contemporary curriculum approaches might be implemented within the setting. • As there is a range of experience, training, skills, strengths, cultures and languages within the staff, the centre can make use of these throughout the program. • As several staff wish to continue their education, supports for this within the organisation should be investigated. • As there is a range of resources within the setting, staff should evaluate the use of these resources, and how the issue of environmental awareness and sustainability may affect this area.	• Provide families with relevant information about council's role in the setting and resources that are available through council. • Undertake yearly surveys of community needs with the support of council. • Explore diverse planning methods, such as focusing on children's interests and different ways to involve children and families in documenting children's learning. • Provide staff with support to evaluate the program and investigate how *The Early Years Learning Framework* might be reflected further in the setting philosophy and practice. • Promote staff professional learning in the area of new approaches to documentation and planning with identified funding support for seminars and workshops, professional reading, networking with other settings, and sharing of existing skills and knowledge among staff. • Utilise staff skills and interests more effectively within the program; e.g. through use of staff languages with children and professional development by specialist staff for all staff.

- one administrative assistant: bilingual (Cantonese and English)
- one cleaner: interested in gardening
- one teacher (Masters qualification for working with children with additional needs) two days a week
- one inclusion support staff member working with two children with additional needs across five days.

• Support agencies:
- The setting has contact with the local early intervention service and draws on the Inclusion Support Agency for funding and support.

• Material resources:
- purpose-built centre 20 years old
- lawn and trees; some shady patches where lawn does not grow, no garden, small sandpit
- range of play equipment and consumable resources.

• Setting philosophy revised in 2012
• Currently rated as meeting Quality Standards of *National Quality Framework.*
• Planning:
- children age-grouped (birth to three-, three to five-year-olds)
- staff currently working in set groups and documenting and planning individually in set rooms with particular groups of children
- developmental approach to planning and documentation currently used.

• As the setting has not reviewed the philosophy for two years, evaluation should occur.
• As the setting is working towards their Quality Improvement Plan this process can be used to identify issues and future directions.
• As two staff with specific skills in working with children with additional needs are employed, the setting should investigate the most appropriate way to share these skills across the setting.
• As the setting has access to agencies supporting children with additional needs, the services that can be provided need to be fully investigated.
• As staff currently plan in isolation, the effectiveness of this approach should be investigated.
• As staff currently only use developmental approaches as a basis for documenting children's learning and for planning experiences, evaluation of the relevance of one approach to understanding children's learning is necessary in light of current research and contemporary practice.
• As the children are grouped in two large, age-related groupings, staff need to explore how the building may be more effectively used to meet the needs and challenges of different children.

• Evaluate the current use of resources, including wastage of any resources and recycling possibilities.
• Evaluate and update the philosophy.
• Evaluate resources – books, posters, art prints, dramatic play accessories, music and musical instruments – in light of families' and children's cultures, family structure, beliefs and languages. Landscape outdoor areas and make plans to use these more effectively.
• Investigate the possible use of planning time for small teams within the program so that staff can explore how a stronger team approach to planning and documentation within the centre might be developed.
• Gather information from support agencies about what can be provided to the setting for support of children with additional needs.
• Provide staff with professional learning opportunities in order to explore varied theories and approaches to children's learning.
• Involve staff and families in discussions around the possibility of using a combination of family or mixed grouping, and same language and interest-based groups.

TABLE 6.4   An example of a situational analysis for a setting for children from birth to five years

INFORMATION	ANALYSIS (WHAT DOES THIS INFORMATION MEAN?)	FUTURE DIRECTIONS
Children		

• 60 children (40 in attendance on any day):
  – 20 Anglo-Australian
  – seven Greek-Australian
  – nine Lebanese-Australian
  – 16 Vietnamese-Australian
  – two Malay-Australian
  – five Chinese-Australian
  – one Sudanese (refugee).
• Two children have been identified as on the Autistic Spectrum.
• Age groups:
  – five infants (0–18 months)
  – 15 toddlers (2–3 years)
  – 20 preschoolers (3–5 years).
• Experiences and interests:
  – Many children eat and shop in local community, thus experiencing a range of community languages.
  – All children have television (some with cable), and most have DVD player and computer access. Children's favourite programs are *Play School, Dora the Explorer, Octonauts* and *Peppa Pig.* Popular culture characters are frequently part of children's play and artwork. Favourite music is *The Wiggles* and *Hi-5.*
  – Many children exhibit gendered roles in their play and interactions.
	• As there are a range of ages and cultural, religious, family structure and language backgrounds, the program needs to reflect this diversity in different program elements, such as routines, planning, experiences and grouping.
	• As the children have different life experiences, these need to be supported and reflected within the program.
	• As two children have identified additional needs, educators may require specific training or resources in the area of additional needs.
	• As there are a number of children transitioning to school in the following year, this needs to be taken into account when developing the program.
	• As children are familiar with local shops and restaurants, stronger connections could be built with these community resources.
	• As many children are interested in popular media culture, ways of including children's favourite programs, characters and music in the program could be investigated.
	• As many children exhibit gender bias, this needs to be addressed in the setting's program.
		• Encourage staff, children and families to use their home languages within the program.
		• Provide information to families on the importance of maintenance of children's home language and the development of literacy in the home language.
		• Incorporate resources that reflect children's life experiences.
		• Gather information about Autistic Spectrum Disorder from relevant support agencies.
		• Develop strategies to support the inclusion of all children with additional needs.
		• Include strategies to support the transition to school process, e.g. visits to local schools and support social and emotional skills.
		• Build collaborations with schools and other early childhood settings to support a range of transition practices.
		• Include print in children's home languages; e.g. restaurant menus, food packaging, newspapers and magazines.
		• Observe and analyse children's play and interactions for examples of gendered roles and children's exercise of power.
		• Intervene to challenge gender stereotypes and unequal power relations.

TABLE 6.5   Situational analysis in a school setting

Community and families

INFORMATION	WHAT DOES THIS INFORMATION MEAN?	FUTURE DIRECTIONS FOR TEACHER'S PLANNING	FUTURE DIRECTIONS FOR STUDENT EDUCATOR'S PROFESSIONAL EXPERIENCE
• Local community has some private areas and a large area of renewed public housing, well-maintained community gardens and is culturally diverse. • There are several Aboriginal families, a large active Tongan group and several Indian and Spanish families in the community. There is a Tongan cultural group and Spanish and Indian communities in nearby areas. • School community is made up of Anglo-Australian families with some Aboriginal, Tongan-Australian, Indian-Australian and Spanish-Australian families. • Aboriginal families speak Aboriginal English and use Standard Australian English to varying degrees. • Tongan-Australian, Indian-Australian and Spanish-Australian families speak their first language at home, including Tongan, Urdu and Spanish. Adults have different degrees of English competency. • Families are mostly from low socio-economic groups, while others are from middle socio-economic groups. • Range of sole, two-parent families, extended families with grandparents, aunts and uncles.	• As the families are from one majority and four minority language/cultural groups, communication should be promoted within and across groups to reflect the diversity within Australian society. • As there is diversity in the community, possible partnerships of community members and school members should be explored. • As some families work at home, some flexible participation in the school may be possible. • As many family incomes are low, financial requests need monitoring (e.g. the number and cost of excursions and resources). • As families' work hours vary, these constraints need consideration when planning meetings and functions. • As there are several children's centres in the community, establishing contact and two-way communication would strengthen transition programs.	• Organise translation of newsletters into Urdu, Tongan and Spanish. • Utilise a range of visual communication methods to cater for varying levels of English language literacy proficiency. • Include Aboriginal, Spanish and Tongan resources that reflect everyday life in the classroom. • Include Aboriginal, Indian, Spanish and Tongan musicians and dancers from the local community in the program. • Keep requests for families to pay cost of 'extras' to a minimum. • Encourage interested family and community members to be involved in daily experiences within the school/classroom. • Provide informal social gatherings that may appeal to some families' levels of participation.	• Consider ways that connections can be made to the local community while on placement and ways of bringing local community resources into the classroom; e.g. photos of the local community, local community newspapers, menus from local restaurants.

TABLE 6.5   Situational analysis in a school setting

INFORMATION	WHAT DOES THIS INFORMATION MEAN?	FUTURE DIRECTIONS FOR TEACHER'S PLANNING	FUTURE DIRECTIONS FOR STUDENT EDUCATOR'S PROFESSIONAL EXPERIENCE
• Families live in a mixture of public and private housing. They use playgrounds, parks, sporting fields, the regional centre and botanical gardens. • Some parents work in manufacturing, building and retail positions at a nearby regional centre. Some parents work from home and others are between jobs. • Some parents are interested in participating in the classroom. A few parents have shown interest in parent meetings, especially social events.		• Build partnerships with local community organisations, e.g. Aboriginal, Torres Strait Islander groups, health professionals, local Early Childhood Education and Care centres (ECEC), family support centres.	
School			
• Staff resources: – 20 classroom educators including three who speak Spanish, Arabic and Italian – one teacher librarian – two part-time English as a second language (ESL) educators and two part-time Learning Assistance Support Teachers (LASTs) who work with small groups – one relief from face to face (RFF) teacher who takes children for creative arts. • Material resources: – built in 1970s, classrooms have sliding doors onto verhandahs and courtyards, library and new assembly hall	• As the staff are experienced and have a range of skills and interests, these should be utilised in classroom and school programs to promote program effectiveness and job satisfaction. • As there are several staff with languages other than English, this expertise should be drawn upon across classrooms and in translating communications to families. • As there is additional staffing, team teaching is possible in classrooms.	• Consult teacher librarian regarding possibilities for team teaching. • Borrow and make bilingual resources, and resources that incorporate Aboriginal English. • Evaluate current use of outdoor environment, and involve children, community members and educators in planning for further developments. • Consider the possibilities for buddy classes.	• Investigate outdoor areas as possible spaces for some learning experiences. • Check the resources available in the school library.

– large concrete and grass playground – landscaped and bush tucker garden developed with community members – extensive children's literature resources – many maths and literacy resources in early years classrooms – three computers and one printer, digital camera, iPads, one television/DVD player in each classroom, interactive white board (IWB) in each classroom – range of ICT software.	• As classrooms have IWBs, educators able to link to web resources. • As the school has large outdoor areas, possibilities for developing the environment should be explored.	• Practice using IWB on field visits; link to web resources where relevant. • Check how to use IT resources; locate computer software and iPad apps that would extend planned focus in experiences.

Kindergarten classroom

• Human resources:
  – one class educator with four years' experience, trained in early childhood and interested in sociocultural and constructivist approaches.
  – ESL educator – ½ hour per week × 5 days
  – two parents – 2 × ½ hour per week in the classroom
  – librarian – 1 × ½ hour per week
• Material resources:
  – classroom with verandah and courtyard access
  – range of equipment and resources
  – range of open-ended resources in shelving, accessible to children.
	• As teacher has interest and expertise in English, Mathematics, History and Science and can involve extra human resources; possibilities may exist for team teaching with small groups.
	• As classroom has a verandah, some extension of learning environment may be possible.
	• As teacher is experienced and interested in English, Mathematics, History and Science, and constructivist learning, and there are many authentic resources, possibilities of investigating sessions to begin each day can be explored.
		• Plan and implement sociocultural, constructivist and new basics approaches through various pedagogies, including active experiences, relevant resources and learning centres.
		• Integrate children's shared popular culture interests and IT resources into learning centres.
		• Utilise the verandah and courtyard to extend the classroom when implementing small groups.
		• Share ideas about diverse planning and documentation pedagogies with other staff.
		• Consult with the teacher regarding roles and responsibilities and how to incorporate ESL teacher, librarian and parents into planning.
		• Negotiate pedagogies that are relevant to the classroom and consistent with professional experience expectations and personal philosophy.
		• Develop a method for planning and evaluating all learning experiences that reflect the teacher's two-week planning cycle.

TABLE 6.5   Situational analysis in a school setting

INFORMATION	WHAT DOES THIS INFORMATION MEAN?	FUTURE DIRECTIONS FOR TEACHER'S PLANNING	FUTURE DIRECTIONS FOR STUDENT EDUCATOR'S PROFESSIONAL EXPERIENCE

• Teaching and learning:
  – map outcomes and learning focus in curriculum areas for each coming two-week period
  – organise resources for each two-week period in advance.
	• Need workable process for collecting observations and learning samples of 20 children.
	• Organisation of educator and children for implementation.
		• Document children's learning, locate progress towards learning achievements and outcomes in: intentional teaching; small groups; complex rich tasks and project work in History and Science sessions.
		• Utilise photos of children's learning in monthly family communication in slideshows, identifying outcomes and learning achievements; include all children each term.
		• Establish and extend family relationships with social meetings – lunches, afternoon teas – for regular sharing of children's learning.
		• Use weekly observation schedule and grids; involve ESL teacher and parents in small group independent experiences.
			• Develop a workable process for observing and documenting children's learning during professional experience and share this with the teacher and with families.

Children			

• 20 children:
  – 10 Anglo-Australian
  – four Aboriginal, speak Aboriginal English at home, families interested in language revival
  – two Tongan-Australian, speak mainly Tongan at home
  – two Spanish-Australian: one speak Spanish only at home, one speak Spanish and English
	• Some children are confident in using their first language/dialect. Most children experienced with various popular culture narratives; e.g. *Angelina Ballerina, Yo Gabba Gabba!, High 5, The Wiggles*. Some children are very knowledgeable about DVDs and television narratives.	• Utilise family and community members, and bilingual resources to support children's languages and dialects.
		• Locate/order bilingual resources.
		• Structure predictable routines to promote children's confidence in starting the school day and promote children's decision making at all times.
		• Investigate research and practices re. starting school; contact network colleagues.
			• Prepare some useful phrases in children's languages.
			• Use relevant language and culture songs, poems, narratives and music for transitions and to introduce and extend experiences.

- two Indian-Australian children speaking Urdu at home.
- most children attended a prior-to-school setting.
• Children's dispositions and learning:
  - most children confidently arrive each morning. Caroline, Jett and Toni sometimes anxious about separation. A few children (Jaxon, Allan, Sean and Tami) take time to decide which learning centres to work at.
  - most children interact confidently with each other. Some Spanish-Australians (John and Maria) and Tongan-Australians (Tomara and Junior) use their first language with confidence, and often discuss the experiences quietly with peers.
  - children have diverse home literacy experiences – in community languages and in English. Many children know narratives through television and DVDs. Some children have books. All children interested in popular culture and IT.
  - most children interested in and able to sort and classify objects, beginning to problem solve, predict and reason.

• Most children are confident with the classroom situation, but some find family separation or school transition uncomfortable.
• A few children are overwhelmed by choosing learning centres.
• As most children attended prior to school settings, make contact with these settings to strengthen transition experience for children.

• Set up literacy and maths learning centres with computers and resources from family and community experiences (e.g. McDonald's, pizza place, doctor's surgery or supermarket), available during day and English and Mathematics sessions.
• Chat with parents of children uneasy re. transitions.
• Establish contact with local prior to school settings.
• Begin the day with Investigating Session independent small group experiences – observe and collect samples with ESL educator.
• English and Maths – open-ended independent small group experiences for peer scaffolding, sustained conversations and language/maths learning.
• Work with a different small group daily for intentional teaching and document children's learning.
• Support children to stay with independent small group experiences and have resources available.
• Integrate narratives and characters from familiar popular culture into independent English and Maths experiences; use community language resources, especially IT resources.
• Model open-ended questions, prediction, problem solving and confirmation in discussions.

• Extend all experiences – with local community resources newspapers, magazines, music. Invite children to bring in home resources for sustained silent reading time.
• Consult with teacher re. family members interested in sharing their talents and experiences in the program; e.g. music, gardening, recycling, story telling, fitness activities.
• Plan learning centres with students' interests in mind, especially those who are learning to settle into the daily program.
• Invite Aboriginal, Indian, Spanish and Tongan children and families to share with the class some community language resources.
• Link some learning experiences to children's favourite popular culture narratives.
• Develop useful language to model conceptual language in learning experiences and to promote problem-solving and extended conversations.

The situational analyses in Tables 6.4 and 6.5 reflect the different areas of focus in different settings. Table 6.4 illustrates an investigation and analysis of a long day care centre, with an emphasis on the setting as a whole and links to future directions for planning. In this example, aspects of the setting program are explored in detail. The section related to children is not presented in as much detail, as more information about each child would be provided in separate documentation about children's learning and development. This is not a reflection of the value of children within the total program or specific approaches to planning. This is a reflection of the fact that this method of documentation and planning is a key feature in this type of early childhood education and care setting, and often a requirement of various government bodies and quality assurance.

Table 6.5, a situational analysis in a school setting, shows a variation with the inclusion of another section of information: the classroom. In this example of a suburban school most of the detail is found in the classroom and children's sections, as well as in the corresponding sections for future directions, as most planning takes place within the classroom context. One of the resources that may be available in a school context is a school-based situational analysis developed by the staff as part of a strategic plan, related to community, families and resources (human and material) for the school as a whole.

One way of looking at the different emphases between the two contexts is to consider the similarities and differences. Both examples contain similar sections: community and families, setting (setting/school and classroom) and children, with the focus on analysis (what does this information mean?) and future directions for planning. In the setting for children from birth to five years of age the future directions for planning refer to the way the total program will operate – that is, for all children, families and staff in the setting. Future directions for planning in the school setting pertain mainly to the classroom context, and reflect priorities in the school plan. This example also includes future directions for a student educator's professional experience to illustrate the possibilities that may be implemented within such a context.

There is a range of ways to document the situational analysis process, depending on the purpose and experience of those stakeholders involved in this process. The detailed examples in Tables 6.4 and 6.5 demonstrate one method of documentation. Different group members can collect information in a way they feel comfortable with and then bring this information to the group. For example, as well as gathering existing documentation that is available within the setting, such as policies and planning documentation, photographs can be used to provide a visual image, as in Figure 6.2. While the photograph may be an important part of the documentation, analysis is also required. A collection of photographs with little analysis can provide a useful illustration, but will probably not contribute a great deal to future planning. Analysis is just as important when using visual data as it is for verbal or text-based data.

School settings also undertake detailed situational analysis reports as part of long-term planning processes, as can be seen at the URL for Curran Public School (http://www.curran-p .schoolwebsites.com.au > National Partnerships > Situational Analysis.).

CourseMateExpress

A further example of a detailed situational analysis undertaking a different approach within a multipurpose early childhood education and care setting can be found in the Rainbow Children's Centre Situational Analysis in Online Example 6.1 on the textbook's website.

The outdoor area reflects the strong philosophy of community and families towards environmental awareness and nature.

The local school reflects the Aboriginal and Torres Strait Islander community and supports the transition process from preschool to school.

The entrance to the preschool includes a painting completed by a local Aboriginal artist and tells the story of the local Bundjalung people and the trip from Mt Warning to the coast.

The setting has a focus on environmental sustainability with the use of water tanks, gardens and vegetable patches, composting, solar energy and recycled water.

The entrance area to the setting provides a welcoming area for families and children.

The environment encourages the children to investigate their interests and is linked to the library area for access to resources.

The library area was designed and created by staff and families. It reflects the link to nature that the service promotes.

Source: Kingscliff Mini School

The sand and water play area uses recycled water and reflects a natural environment.

FIGURE 6.2 Photographs can be a useful tool for gathering information for a situational analysis.

Irrespective of the documentation method used, the main aspects in the process are making the link between the existing practice and current information about the setting, and what that means for improving future practice.

Leo Prendergast, the director of a multipurpose early childhood education and care centre, reflects on the importance of undertaking a situational analysis as part of the organisational planning process:

> How would you as an individual stakeholder within a setting encourage collaborative involvement in undertaking a situational analysis?

> As part of our planning with children we all acknowledge the need to observe the child and answer 'what happened, what does it mean, where next?' I apply the same logic to the service as a whole. Observe it. Record what has happened this year and what is happening now. What does it mean for the quality of our education and care? Where to next in working towards our mission as an organisation? I also find the situational analysis process to be invaluable in forcing myself and others to sit back from the everyday workload for a while and allow myself and other staff and Committee members to look at the big picture.

L Prendergast, Director, Rainbow Children's Centre, north coast NSW

Developing a team plan of action

In order to develop a plan of action for changes to assist the setting in moving from its philosophical base (ideals) to practices that reflect this philosophy, those involved in the setting should use enhanced understandings of current practice gleaned from the situational analysis. Each setting will have different journeys of change, as demonstrated in Chapter 11. In some settings, the team will feel that many changes are required to reach their ideals, while in others the team may feel there are only some areas that should be altered. Engaging in the change process is the most important step in evaluation and reflection, no matter how long that journey takes. Taking small steps towards any change and making that change manageable will help promote the continuation of reflective practice.

In any plan of action it is important that everyone is working towards shared goals in order to provide for consistency and cohesion. It is essential to have the support and participation of families, staff, children and other groups, such as management, to achieve these goals. If goals are not fully understood or are resisted by any of these groups, it is generally very difficult to achieve successful implementation.

Goal

A specific statement and measureable accomplishment to be achieved within a specified time and under specified resource constraints.

A **goal** is a statement of broad direction (or purpose) based on identified challenges, strengths and values within a situation.

While goals may still be idealistic and rather general, they are statements that establish a clearer and more realistic direction for the setting than the philosophy. Goals should be achievable within the nominated time frame.

Group goals are important, and teamwork is an effective way of working towards meeting goals. A goal needs to be desired by enough group members so that the group will work towards its achievement. Formulating goals helps us to clarify our principles and confirm what is valued by the individual or group; therefore, group goals should be developed through group processes similar to those of philosophy development.

Goals help to:

- transform the philosophy into concrete practices
- respond to issues raised in the situational analysis
- provide manageable steps towards achieving the philosophy in practice
- set priorities
- provide the direction for any changes
- inform our program evaluation and ongoing reflection.

Formulating goals for the setting

After the development of a philosophy and analysis of the situation, goals can be developed by looking at the future directions formulated for the setting, and linking these to the documented philosophy – that is, what steps are needed to take to move towards our philosophy?

The process of developing goals should involve input from all the groups connected with the setting. This may be a lengthy and time-consuming process, involving much discussion and some negotiation, but it is essential if all the interests of the group are to be considered. Involving everyone in the process of developing goals for the setting helps to ensure that there is a commitment from all to work towards those goals.

It is essential when developing goals to be realistic about the situation and the resources that are available. Ambitious plans will fail without adequate resources or sufficient time for changes in practices to occur. When formulating goals, it is important to take into account staffing, time and financial constraints, as well as the impact that these decisions may have on staff, children, families and the local community, including other early childhood educational settings. This is why it is vital not only to formulate goals based upon the philosophy (ideals), but also to use the future directions for planning from the analysis so that the goals are achievable.

The following steps may assist in the development and documentation of goal setting:

1. Identify the issue – this may be identified as a result of a difference between the philosophy and what is happening in practice. There may be several main issues derived from the investigation of the setting and the philosophy. These may be prioritised and worked through over a designated time frame.
2. Identify the current situation – this should be evident from the situational analysis.
3. Identify what the ideal would look like in regard to this issue – based on the setting philosophy.
4. Identify what must be done to take the first step from current practice (identified in Step 2) to work towards ideal practice (identified in Step 3). This is a goal.
5. Identify the main issues derived from the situational analysis and the philosophy, and work through Steps 2–4.
6. Formulate a plan of action, as shown in Table 6.6, based on the goals identified from Steps 1–4.

TABLE 6.6 Steps for developing goals and a plan of action for change based on the philosophy and situational analysis

ISSUE	CURRENT SITUATION	IDEAL	GOAL	ACTION
Grouping	There is limited use of small groups; most groups include 20 children and relate to adult initiated language and music experiences.	Diversity of grouping methods should be used such as child and adult initiated, mixed ages, interest based, same language groups and small groups for transitions and routines.	To investigate different grouping strategies including the benefits and possibilities for future implementation within the setting.	• Provide reading material on grouping methods for staff. • Visit other settings to see different grouping strategies in action. • Explore current methods of grouping used within the setting. What are the disadvantages? Are there any advantages? Observe children's involvement in current grouping methods. • Survey families to find out what type of group experiences they would like to see in practice within the centre for their children. • Collate information gathered. • Meet with staff and families to share collated ideas with all stakeholders. • Brainstorm possible changes based on current practice and ideas explored about alternative grouping methods. • Develop an implementation plan for changes to grouping. • Trial changes, and evaluate and modify as needed.

A brief example of these steps in action, as a guide, is outlined in Table 6.6. This example outlines Steps 1–4 in detail. Each setting's plan of action will be different, depending on where that setting is headed in terms of its philosophy, what its current situation is and what resources it has available for implementing a plan of action. Chapter 7 provides a further reflection on the link between philosophy, approaches and pedagogies.

Setting priorities

Goals alone are not enough. Priorities also need to be set. It may be more productive to focus on one or two areas at a time, rather than attempting to work on every goal at once. If energies are spread over too many areas at the same time, it may not be possible to achieve any of the goals. The stakeholders in each setting will need to decide on what basis priorities will be identified. Sometimes the basis for setting priorities is urgency or legal requirements, quality assurance and philosophical ideas, or even resources available in a given time period. An important factor to remember is that it would be difficult to effectively implement all aspects of the philosophy and goals simultaneously.

Developing a time frame for implementation of various aspects of the philosophy and goals can make this procedure clearer and more manageable. The box below identifies a timeline for implementing one goal for a plan of action in steps.

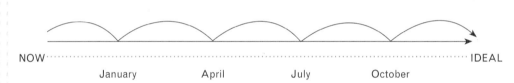

Developing a realistic timeline for the implementation of goals

Steps

NOW ⋯⋯ January ⋯ April ⋯ July ⋯ October ⋯ IDEAL

In January

Currently, children's learning is mainly documented and assessed according to developmental domains.

By April

Gather information about dispositions and learning processes and different methods of documentation that go beyond development. Undertake professional learning through reading, attendance at workshops and visits to settings implementing different approaches to documentation and planning that incorporate *The Early Years Learning Framework*. Delegate different team members to undertake research on different areas.

By July

Share ideas and examples of methods of documentation and assessment that incorporate dispositions and learning processes with staff and families. Discuss alternatives and brainstorm possible implementation strategies. Identify some methods for trialling.

By October

Trial and evaluate meaningful documentation and assessment methods that reflect new learning in this area. Make modifications as necessary.

Ideal

Implement methods of documentation and assessment of children's learning and planning of learning environments based on understandings of dispositions and learning processes and the practices and pedagogies of the *Early Years Learning Framework* that involve staff, children and families (original goal).

The challenges of time, staff energy and the possible stress of change for all team members should be firmly acknowledged, but also balanced to allow for establishing and working through priorities. There are always aspects of philosophy and goals to be seriously considered later in the year as well as the following year!

Taking action

Once goals have been developed and prioritised, perhaps through a subcommittee with representation from all stakeholders, they should be shared and discussed with all those involved in the setting. This can be accomplished in a variety of ways, including both spoken and written means of communication, such as photos, booklets for family and community members, or workshops presented by staff for management and families. Once this is achieved, it is important that the goals are used as a basis for planning.

Planning this translation from philosophy and goals into practice can be done with educators and other team members in brainstorming sessions. It is important to have the opportunity for the team to explore all potential implementations of a goal as team members can participate in evaluation and reflective processes related to the goals to strengthen their own practice. This approach might also be valuable for those settings that are required to develop goals and a plan of action for quality assurance purposes.

To achieve goals, it is necessary to devise strategies to enable the goals to be reflected in practice and to be achievable. Identifying the evidence that will show the goal has been achieved is an important step in developing strategies. When strategies have been outlined, a reasonable time frame for achieving each goal should be worked out and tasks delegated to particular people or teams to make the implementation of each goal more manageable. In addition, all members of the planning team should reflect constantly on the progress towards meeting these goals. As part of the *National Quality Framework*, settings are required to undertake this process as part of self assessment against the *National Quality Standard* by completing a QIP. In completing the QIP, stakeholders in each setting acknowledge what they are doing well and identify areas that require improvement.

> Using the *Talking about practice* self-assessment, reflective practice and quality improvement processes video, consider a setting you have been involved in. Reflect on the strengths of the setting and what quality areas may have needed improvement plans.
> Video Link: http://www.earlychildhoodaustralia.org.au > National Quality Standard PLP > e_Learning videos > Talking about practice > Self-assessment, reflective practice and quality improvement processes

Reflecting on and evaluating goals

Ongoing critical evaluation of progress towards meeting goals is needed. To assist in the management of the evaluation process, it is useful to evaluate the strategies implemented to reach goals on a regular basis. By identifying the target goals, briefly outlining the practical ways the setting is implementing these goals and providing a brief evaluation of the implementation – for example, on a monthly or two-monthly basis – the task of evaluation is not so daunting. This evaluation may be

undertaken by a variety of team members. At the end of the year or at other regular intervals, this formative evaluation can be used to create a summative evaluation and provide direction for long-term planning. It is important to use a method such as this so that the team realises its achievements towards the goals and philosophy, as well as where to focus attention next.

To continually work towards the implementation of a setting philosophy, educators should first evaluate the philosophy or long-term plan with respect to contemporary knowledge and research. Keeping up to date with journals, accessing professional respected websites, attending workshops, conferences and seminars, networking with others through meetings or electronic forums and maintaining subscriptions and membership to professional organisations will provide relevant and practical ideas that can be implemented. Second, longstanding approaches to curriculum planning (Patterson & Fleet, 2003), which may have become entrenched in our practice without us even realising, should be challenged. Third, there is a need to evaluate for future action. This includes making recommendations for forward planning – this is an ongoing process that examines how modifications and changes occur; and then the development process commences again. This means continually reassessing the information and analysis of the setting (*see* Chapter 4 for further ideas on reflection, evaluation and dynamic programs).

Undertaking this process is not time-consuming in the long run. By putting in the initial time and effort, educators can gather and analyse important information for future planning which can be used in many formats and for different purposes, such as accountability, quality assurance, submissions and quality improvement. Team approaches to clarifying and developing planning within a specific setting, from philosophy development to collating and analysing information to putting it into practice, are essential to rethinking staff practices, professional learning and the direction the setting is taking. This form of planning assists settings in working towards ongoing improvements as highlighted in quality assurance.

Conclusion and reflection

Participating in the processes outlined in this chapter, as well as in Chapter 5, will ensure that each setting develops unique approaches to forward planning that clearly implement the beliefs and values of those involved, and encourage innovative and dynamic practice. Undertaking a situational analysis should end with clear goals and a roadmap of ways to achieve them rather than being surprised by new information. This process enables all involved to direct change in a mindful way.

Questions for reflection

1. As a student teacher, what does your analysis of your professional experience setting mean for your professional experience placement? How can you reflect the socio-cultural context of the setting in your curriculum planning? What professional learning goals would be relevant for you in this professional experience setting?

2. As an educator, based on your current situational analysis, what factors do you need to take into account to make the transition from the current situation to the ideals outlined in your philosophy?

   a. How close are your practices to your philosophy? Which aspects might you focus on first in bridging the gap? How might you collaborate in this process inside the setting and beyond the setting (i.e. mentors and support groups)?

   b. What are the identified strengths within your educational setting? What are the key improvements sought? What steps and timeline is appropriate to work towards these improvements? A useful resource to support this reflective task is *The really simple guide to … writing a quality improvement plan*, March 2013, Community Child Cooperative NSW, http://ccccnsw.org.au/wp-content/uploads/simple-guide-QIP.pdf.

Key terms

constraints, 184

gap analysis, 180

critical reflexivity, 185

goal, 200

mandates, 182

potentials, 184

situational analysis, 180

Online study resources

Visit http://login.cengagebrain.com and use the access code that comes with this book for 12 months access to the student resources for this text.

CourseMate Express  CourseMateExpress

The CourseMate Express website contains a range of resources and study tools for this chapter, including:

- Online video activities
- Online research activities
- A revision quiz
- Matching pair exercises
- A list of key weblinks
- A chapter glossary, flashcards and crossword to help you revise terminology
- and more!

Search me! education ▶ Search me! 🖑

Explore **Search me! education** for articles relevant to this chapter. Fast and convenient, Search me! education is updated daily and provides you with 24-hour access to full text articles from hundreds of scholarly and popular journals, ebooks and newspapers, including *The Australian* and *The New York Times*. Log in to Search me! through http://login.cengage.com and try searching for the following key words:

- philosophy into practice
- strategic planning
- SWOT analysis
- plan of action
- situational analysis
- investigating the situation
- mandates and legal requirements
- constraints and potentials
- accountability
- critical reflexivity
- analysis
- documentation of a situational analysis
- evaluation and reflection
- formulating goals
- setting priorities

- goals into practice
- planning for change
- quality improvement plans
- collaborating
- gap analysis.

Search tip: **Search me! education** contains information from both local and international sources. To get the greatest number of search results, try using both Australian and American spellings in your searches, e.g. 'globalisation' and 'globalization'; 'organisation' and 'organization'

Recommended resources

Australian Children's Education and Care Quality Authority (ACECQA) 2012, *Guide to Developing a Quality Improvement Plan*, http://www.acecqa.gov.au

Carter, M & Curtis, D 2010, *The visionary director*, Redleaf Press, USA.

Department of Education, Employment and Workplace relations (DEEWR) 2009, *Belonging, Being and Becoming: The Early Years Learning Framework for Australia*, Commonwealth of Australia, Canberra, ACT.

Department of Education, Employment and Workplace relations (DEEWR) 2010, *Educators Belonging, Being and Becoming: Educators Guide to Early Years Learning Framework for Australia*, Commonwealth of Australia, Canberra, ACT.

Kearns, K 2010, *The Big Picture*, 2nd edn. Pearson, Frenchs Forest, NSW.

Key weblinks

Australian Children's Education and Care Quality Authority, http://www.acecqa.gov.au/

ACT Professional Support Coordinator, http://www.actpsc.com.au/

Children's Services Central, http://www.cscentral.org.au/

Early Childhood Australia, http://www.earlychildhoodaustralia.org.au/

Professional Learning program, http://www.earlychildhoodaustralia.org.au/nqsplp/

Professional Support Coordinator Northern Territory, http://www.childaustralia.org.au

Professional Support Coordinator Queensland, http://www.workforce.org.au/initiatives/professional-support-coordinator-queensland.aspx

Professional Support Coordinator South Australia, http://www.pscsa.org.au/cms/

Professional Support Coordinator Tasmania, http://www.psctas.org.au/

Professional Support Coordinator Victoria, http://www.gowrievictoria.org.au/PSC.aspx

Professional Support Coordinator Western Australia, http://www.childaustralia.org.au

The Indigenous Professional Support Unit, http://www.ipsu.com.au/

The Indigenous Professional Support Unit NSW & ACT, http://www.ipsunswact.com.au/

The Indigenous Professional Support Unit South Australia, http://www.ipsusa.org.au/

The Indigenous Professional Support Unit Western Australia, http://www.ipsuwa.org.au/

References

Australian Children's Education and Care Quality Authority (ACECQA) 2011, *Guide to the National Quality Standard*, http://www.acecqa.gov.au, accessed 2 April 2014.

Australian Children's Education and Care Quality Authority (ACECQA) 2012, *Guide to Developing a Quality Improvement Plan*, http://www.acecqa.gov.au, accessed 2 April 2014.

Carter, M & Curtis, D 2010, *The Visionary Director*, Redleaf Press, USA.

Community Child Care 2009, *The Manual: Managing a Children's Service*, Community Child Care, Marrickville, NSW.

Farmer, S 1995, *Policy Development in Early Childhood Services*, Community Child Care Cooperative, Sydney.

Farmer, S, Meredith, H & Watson, R 1999, 'Looking forward – the future of planning in early childhood settings', paper presented at Australian Early Childhood Association Conference, Darwin, 1999.

Fenech, M 2006, 'Working in a regulatory environment: Challenges and opportunities', *Bedrock*, vol. 11, no. 3, November, pp. 18–19.

Fenech, M, Sumsion, J & Goodfellow, J 2006, 'The regulatory environment in long day care: A double-edged sword for early childhood professional practice', *Australian Journal of Early Childhood*, vol. 31, no. 3, pp. 49–58.

Jones, E & Nimmo, J 1994, *Emergent Curriculum*, National Association for the Education of Young Children, Washington, DC.

Jorde Bloom, P 2005, *Blueprint for Action: Achieving Center-based Change through Staff Development*, 2nd edn. New Horizons, Lake Forest, IL.

Kearns, K 2010, *The Business of Child Care*, 2nd edn. Pearson, Frenchs Forest, NSW.

Malaguzzi, L 1998, 'History, ideas and basic philosophy', in C Edwards, L Gandini & G Forman (eds), *The Hundred Languages of Children*, Ablex, Norwood, NJ.

Patterson, C 2006, *Professional Decision Making for Guided Experience ECHP 324*, Macquarie University, Sydney.

Patterson, C & Fleet, A 2003, 'Meaningful planning: Rethinking teaching and learning relationships', *Research in Practice Series*, vol. 10, no. 1, Australian Early Childhood Association, Canberra

CHAPTER SEVEN

CURRICULUM APPROACHES AND PEDAGOGIES

Chapter learning focus

This chapter will investigate:

- the concepts of curriculum, curriculum approaches and pedagogies

- processes for selecting curriculum approaches to support the philosophy

- matching pedagogies to selected approaches

- translating philosophy into practice.

Introduction

The planning process involves many phases, as examined in the previous two chapters, *Developing philosophies* and *Understanding the setting*. This chapter will assist educators to make decisions about their approaches to curriculum and relevant pedagogies that may most suitably translate their philosophy in practice. Selecting appropriate curriculum approaches and pedagogies begins with recognising the theoretical perspectives, beliefs and values embedded in this philosophy. Educators can enhance alignment between the setting philosophy and practice by selecting relevant curriculum approaches and pedagogies.

The chapter firstly outlines some curriculum approaches and discusses some of their potentials and challenges. An examination of some pedagogies then follows. Finally, attention is drawn to evaluating and reflecting on existing approaches and pedagogies – in other words, identifying current strengths as well as areas for improvement as philosophy is translated into practice, before making any change.

How might you identify the differences between curriculum, curriculum approaches and pedagogies? How are these notions similar and how do they differ? Why might it be useful to appreciate the difference between these notions?

Clarifying curriculum, curriculum approaches and pedagogies

In this first section the meaning of the terms *curriculum*, *curriculum approaches* and *pedagogies* is explored. Educators make decisions about curriculum approaches and the pedagogies that best support their preferred approaches to curriculum as they put their philosophy into practice.

Curriculum

Constitutes everything that happens across the day in the setting/ school.

The term **curriculum** refers to everything that happens throughout the day (Nuttall & Edwards, 2007; New Zealand Ministry of Education, 1996; DEEWR, 2009a). It includes what is planned or intended to be the curriculum each day, but also includes unplanned, spontaneous interactions and experiences, as well as routines and transitions; that is, the curriculum is what actually happens each day. This notion of curriculum differs from a curriculum framework or a learning framework. Learning frameworks, such as *Belonging, Being and Becoming: The Early Years Learning Framework for Australia* (DEEWR, 2009b), provide educators with underpinning principles to guide practice and, in the case of the EYLF, broad long-term outcomes for children's learning. How educators work with these principles and learning outcomes – that is, the approaches to curriculum and the pedagogies that they use – will differ depending on the context. Learning frameworks also provide educators with shared goals and visions for children (Alvestad & Duncan, 2006) and a shared language to use with families to explain their curriculum decisions (Nuttall & Edwards, 2007), which supports family and community understandings of the work of early childhood educators.

The EYLF and The Australian Curriculum documents, respectively, specify particular learning outcomes or continuing sequences of learning across learning areas, general capabilities and cross-curricular priorities to which educators must refer when assessing children's learning and documenting their program. The EYLF does not specify curriculum content, instead focusing on dispositions, emerging development, learning processes, attitudes and values. This enables educators to plan content that is relevant to their local context and to respond to children's interests and ideas, while still working towards the broad learning outcomes. While the 'Australian Curriculum is aligned with the EYLF and builds on its key learning outcomes in schools' (ACARA, 2013a, p. 10), it draws on 'a three dimension design – discipline-based learning areas, general capabilities as essential 21st century skills and contemporary cross-curriculum priorities' (ACARA, 2013a, p. 15). It promotes planning for student diversity as 'All students are entitled to rigorous, relevant and engaging learning programs drawn from a challenging curriculum that addresses their individual learning needs' (ACARA, 2013b, p. 4) and educators are able to build on children's 'interests, strengths, goals and learning needs' (ACARA, 2013b, p. 4).

Curriculum approaches

Stances towards curriculum that reflect the stakeholders' beliefs about how children learn and how families, communities and educators support children's learning, as well as what is important for children now and in the future.

Educators in both prior-to-school and school contexts are able to implement a range of approaches and pedagogies to support learning for children with diverse experiences. Curriculum approaches and pedagogies form the focus of this chapter.

Curriculum approaches

This chapter examines a number of different **curriculum approaches**. Each stance reflects significant ideas about the setting/school stakeholders – the children, families, educators and communities – and the relationships between these stakeholders, meaning that carefully selected approaches can support the setting/school's philosophy. The selected approaches to curriculum reflect stakeholders' visions for children and society. Some approaches may be instrumentalist, focused on learners acquiring the skills and subject content knowledge necessary to participate in the workforce and to conform to the status quo (Mac Naughton, 2003; Vickers, 2007). Other approaches are more future-oriented and see the potential of curriculum to support the sorts of learning processes and knowledge necessary to participate productively in a rapidly changing world and to transform society (Mac Naughton, 2003).

Approaches to curriculum are rarely fixed and straightforward. Rather, educators can see them as the many points along continuums, which they use flexibly to guide the program in any moment of practice. As well, many approaches complement each other and, although some may at first appear to be similar, they have distinctive features. Many approaches have something to offer. Working to achieve a balance in emphasis across approaches that are relevant for the setting/school is a challenge addressed in this chapter. Children's learning across the day also demands differing emphasis at different times, so a range of approaches are likely to be used, as well as differing continuum points within approaches at different times with different children (*see* Figure 7.1).

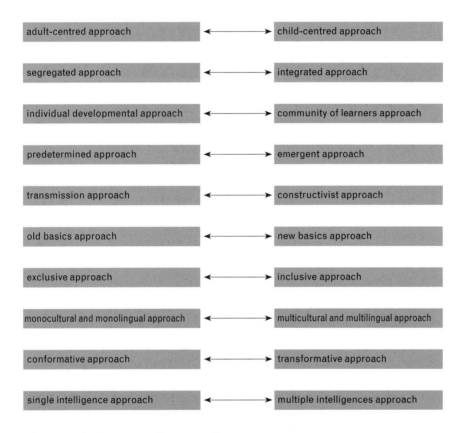

FIGURE 7.1 Some curriculum approaches as continuums.

Pedagogies

All the deliberate actions and processes that educators organise and implement to translate philosophy and approaches to curriculum into practice can be seen as **pedagogies**. These include family communication and relationships, interactions with children, intentional teaching strategies, documentation of learning, design of learning experiences and the organisation of learning environments. As explained by Siraj-Blatchford et al. (2002, pp. 27–8), pedagogies include the 'instructional techniques and strategies which enable learning to take place and provide opportunities for the acquisition of knowledge, skills, attitudes and dispositions within a particular social and material context'. The nature of interactions and relationships between children, educators, families and the learning community largely determine the pedagogies used (Siraj-Blatchford et al., 2002). It follows that educators use a flexible range of pedagogies, or in other words the many strategies that enable teaching and learning, to support their combined approaches.

Pedagogies

All the actions and processes that educators use to translate philosophy and curriculum approaches into practice.

SELECTING AND REVIEWING APPROACHES AND PEDAGOGIES

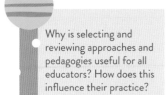

Why is selecting and reviewing approaches and pedagogies useful for all educators? How does this influence their practice?

The approaches to curriculum and the aligned pedagogies that educators select should be consistent with the setting/school's philosophy and responsive to government and educational policy changes. This means that approaches and pedagogies will differ from one setting to another, taking into account educator and family beliefs and values as reflected in the setting/school's philosophy, the analysis of the setting/school's potentials and challenges, explanatory theoretical perspectives and the preferred ways of working throughout the day. The boxes that follow provide some broad illustrations of how some different theoretical perspectives, as discussed in Chapter 1, influence understandings of children's learning, approaches to curriculum and pedagogies which shape the curriculum. Over time, educators review and adjust perspectives, approaches and pedagogies as they move daily practice closer to their philosophy, as seen in Chapter 5, Example 5.1. As educators refine their setting/school philosophy, so they plan, evaluate and review their selected approaches and pedagogies.

Theoretical perspectives

Theoretical perspectives

Theoretical perspectives are major philosophical directions that shape educator understandings of various theories, explaining many aspects of phenomena and human activity. Philosophical directions influence theories of children's learning and are represented by the values and beliefs embedded in the setting philosophy.

Modern developmental perspectives

Modern developmental perspectives are a defined set of knowledge established through scientific observation of specific groups of children, with implications being drawn for all children and all times. Knowledge generally identifies predetermined stages in developmental areas of learning with simplistic foci and sets expectations that children progress through these stages in a linear fashion.

Modern behaviourist perspectives

Modern behaviourist perspectives encompass a defined set of knowledge established through scientific observation of specific groups or individuals in controlled contexts, with general implications being drawn for the behaviours of all children at all times. Knowledge identifies that teacher initiated and directed learning experiences influence the learning of groups of children, especially when extrinsic stimulation and rewards are utilised. Practitioners often use simplistic closed experiences to focus the learner on the intended learning outcome.

Sociocultural perspectives

Sociocultural perspectives have expanded the body of knowledge established from observation of groups of various people, establishing families and communities as the place and time where children collaboratively learn their ways of interacting and behaving, using language and literacy, initiating their concepts, understandings and values. Children's learning differs according to their diverse family and community experiences.

Poststructural, postmodern and critical theoretical perspectives

Expanding bodies of knowledge identify complexity in the changes in society (postmodern) as well as changes in individuals throughout their lives (poststructural). Poststructuralism and postmodernism acknowledge children's unique, active and differing learning with their family and community in a culturally diverse world. Critical theory recognises the role of examination of power, control and social justice as educational settings privilege some social practices over others.

Philosophy, approaches and pedagogics influenced by modern developmental theoretical perspectives

Philosophy on children's learning

- Image of child as 'becoming' an adult
- Children learn through acting on their environment through play
- Focus on individuals reaching developmental milestones in a linear fashion
- Learning areas identified and influenced by traditional developmental theories

Approaches to curriculum

- Individualistic developmental approach
- Child-centred
- Constructivist

Pedagogies

- Individual observations and interpretations that focus on development – may use checklists, anecdotes, work and time samples, running records
- Focus child system – different children observed and planned for each week
- Discrete developmental areas become the focus of observations, interpretations and experiences
- Individual records organised in developmental areas
- Planned experiences based on individual developmental objectives
- Planning format organised around developmental and/or curriculum areas – often planned in 'boxes'; experiences often change daily
- Educator-determined curriculum planned in advance, but may still be flexible to respond to children's interests
- Teaching strategies mostly non-interventionist; e.g. facilitating, modelling and supporting
- Individual and small group experiences with some whole group experiences
- Focus of documentation and analysis/assessment on whether each child met objective

Philosophy, approaches and pedagogies influenced by modern behaviourist theoretical perspectives

Philosophy on children's learning

- Image of child as needy
- Set body of knowledge children need to learn
- Extrinsic motivation needed by children to learn
- Children's learning shows in their demonstrated behaviour

Approaches to curriculum

- Old basics
- Segregated
- Adult-centred
- Fixed
- Conformative
- Transmission
- Single intelligence

Pedagogies

- Teacher-determined goals and curriculum content
- Focus on content
- Curriculum areas often taught separately
- Whole class/whole group teaching with some small group and individual work
- Use of commercial materials such as textbooks, curriculum support documents and blackline masters/stencils
- Mostly closed rather than open-ended materials
- Focus of teaching strategies on whole class demonstrations
- Teacher as expert
- Documentation and analysis/assessment of individual children according to demonstrated discrete curriculum outcomes
- Play activities only when children have finished work
- Reward systems and student awards to motivate student learning towards educator-identified outcomes

Philosophy, approaches and pedagogies influenced by sociocultural theoretical perspectives

Philosophy on children's learning

- Children learn through being active in sociocultural contexts, especially with their family
- Image of child, family and community as strong and capable and always learning
- Importance of relationships between children, families, communities and educators
- Social relationships and interactions influence children's learning
- Zone of proximal development and scaffolding significant for learning

Approaches to curriculum

- Emergent
- Multiple intelligences

- Multilingual and multicultural
- Communities of learners
- Inclusive
- Integrated
- Constructivist

Pedagogies

- Documentation and analysis of groups of children; e.g. narratives, samples, photographs of representations and group projects and transcripts of children's conversations
- Focus of documentation and analysis/assessment on social interactions, relationships, group dynamics, dispositions and learning processes, changing understandings and children's questions
- Child's family context, experiences, interests, relationships, dispositions, attitudes and values documented in individual portfolios, which include input from families, children and staff
- Intentional teaching and mediated learning; e.g. sustained shared thinking, scaffolding, co-construction
- Opportunities for children to investigate their own questions and big ideas and represent their understandings through conversations, drawings, constructions, movement, drama, poetry, play, literacy, mathematics, etc.
- Flexible planning intentions rather than fixed objective or outcome; e.g. educator follows children's interests, questions and ideas through their investigation, problem-solving, representation and sharing
- Long-term projects that integrate curriculum, create connections across experiences, and include families and communities
- Stable environment with resources added or changed to extend interests and learning focus
- Accessible, open-ended and culturally responsive resources
- Spaces for small groups, meeting places and art studio provided
- Flexible daily routine with large blocks of time, workshops, learning agreements, projects
- Open-ended planning formats and retrospective and mixed media documentation; e.g. in journals, project books, digital portfolios
- Educator as colearner
- Different teaching strategies for different children in different contexts
- Reflective and responsive practice – using reflections and evaluations to extend children's learning and educators' understandings

Philosophies, approaches to curriculum and pedagogies change over time, although at differing rates and according to what is most relevant for children in the setting/school for different parts of the program. As the philosophy and practice is evaluated and refined, educators seek better-suited approaches and align their pedagogies to put their philosophy into practice. When educators draw on their experiences in different settings they can consider how philosophies (especially understandings of children's learning), approaches to curriculum and pedagogies shape curriculum decisions for particular moments of practice. Their decisions vary across the day as well as in the long term, reflecting shifts along continuums in the approaches to curriculum and relevant pedagogies as to what appears most useful to transform philosophy into practice.

Philosophy, approaches and pedagogies influenced by poststructural, postmodern and critical theoretical perspectives

Philosophy on children's learning

- Importance of children's sociocultural worlds and analysis of how gender, ethnicity and class influence children's identity construction
- Image of children as active agents in their own learning
- View of world and knowledge as complex, multifaceted and dynamic
- Importance of processes of critical thinking and reconstructing understandings

Approaches to curriculum

- Transformative
- New basics
- Community of learners
- Multilingual and multicultural
- Inclusive
- Constructivist
- Integrated

Pedagogies

- Documentation and analysis/assessment of children's interactions, conversations and understandings of identity and power relations
- Analysis, critique and renewal of power relations
- Intentional teaching strategies; e.g. sustained shared thinking, scaffolding, co-construction
- Resources that reflect diversity and open up new possibilities for identity construction
- Environments that empower children as responsible decision makers and meaning makers for now and in their future lives
- Rich, complex experiences
- Educator as colearner
- Interactions between children and educators that challenge dominant discourses and power relationships, and raise issues of equity and social justice
- Ideas, texts and images collaboratively deconstructed and reconstructed by educators and children
- Ongoing critical reflection engaged in by educators and children

Selecting curriculum approaches that support our philosophy

Why is it a useful team process for educators to share and clarify their understanding of various approaches?

Despite approaches not being mutually exclusive, they provide educators with a useful tool for examining and implementing different curriculum approaches. Figure 7.1 provides a list of approaches represented on continuums. It is acknowledged that this list is not definitive and that approaches may overlap.

In what follows, each approach to curriculum will be described in reference to a continuum, with analysis and comment regarding children's learning. It is likely that across a day, educators and student educators in any setting will use a range of continuum positions regarding their selected set of approaches. The pattern reflected in their implemented continuum points indicates the significant approaches that translate philosophy into practice. The clustering of approaches that are selected may open up or close down learning opportunities available to all children.

Adult-centred approach ↔ child-centred approach

In any setting the curriculum approach operating is likely to reflect largely **child-centred** or **adult-centred positions** on a continuum. Alternatively, this could be named a learner-centred/teacher-centred continuum. A child-centred position takes into account each child's strengths, interests and experiences as well as their needs. Children frequently initiate and direct experiences, and educators provide resources and support.

In contrast, at the other end of the continuum, an adult-centred stance is one where educators decide what and how children will learn. Educators plan in linear ways with little account of children's interests, sociocultural practices, diverse learning styles or their engagement with the topic. They preselect and presequence lessons or experiences to reflect the agenda of the educational setting (Jones, Evans & Renken, 2001). There is a set body of knowledge that they believe every child needs to learn and that is transmitted from them to the children. The focus is on 'getting the content across', creating a predetermined product or covering the curriculum. Teaching and learning are controlled by the educator and are often standardised so the diversity of learners' experiences and understandings may be viewed as a problem (Jones, Evans & Renken, 2001).

Segregated approach ↔ thematic approach ↔ integrated approach

An **integrated approach** to curriculum occurs when educators combine two or more areas of curriculum. For example, they may promote children's investigation and representation of understandings of caterpillars, integrating science, literacy (English curriculum) and the creative arts. They might provide magnifying glasses for observing caterpillars in the outdoor environment/playground and offer books, posters and the Internet to extend children's knowledge and identification skills, as well as providing resources such as paper, pencils, paints, cameras and computers to support children's multi-modal representations of their learning. Integrated curriculum has the potential to extend children's knowledge (information, concepts, relations and meaning), skills (e.g. literacy and numeracy, scientific and technical skills, social skills and personal relationships), dispositions (habits of mind such as curiosity, approaches to work such as persistence, and preferences such as cooperative or solitary learning) and feelings (such as feelings of competence) (Katz & Chard, 1989/2000). Some features of this approach are also consistent with constructivist, multiple intelligences and emergent approaches.

Child-centred approach

This approach occurs when educators consider each child's strengths, interests and experiences as well as their needs. Children learn through frequently initiating and directing experiences, and educators provide resources and support.

Adult-centred approach

This approach occurs when the educator decides what, how and when children will learn in relation to the agenda of the educational setting. There is little consideration for the children's experiences, interests, sociocultural practices or ways of learning.

Integrated approach

In this approach educators organise learning experiences across combined curriculum learning areas and across various areas in the learning environment. This enables children to learn in ways that are meaningful to themselves as they draw on various curriculum learning areas, knowledge, skills, dispositions, feelings and general capacities.

Source: Our Lady of Lourdes Catholic School,
Seven Hills

FIGURE 7.2 When small groups of
children use open-ended resources,
such as paper and paint, they
can investigate and represent
their collaborative and individual
understandings relating to the
integrated areas of narrative, social
worlds, art and mathematics.

Integrated curriculum offers children genuine opportunities to
investigate and connect across different curriculum areas. As Bredekamp
(1987, p. 3) states, 'children's learning does not occur in narrowly defined
subject areas'. Where children make choices as they deeply investigate
events and phenomena in their communities they 'create meaning through
interactions with the physical and social worlds' (Chen et al., 1998, p. 30).
The traditions of educational philosophers, including Piaget (1963) and
Dewey (1902, 1916, 1958) as part of the progressive education movement
in the United Kingdom and the USA in the 1960s, advocated that children
investigate to learn. During the 1980s and 1990s reports of programs in
Reggio Emilia, Italy, renewed interest in integrated learning. The EYLF
(DEEWR, 2009a) advocates a holistic/integrated approach to teaching and
learning. The five learning outcomes in the framework integrate curriculum
and learning areas to focus on identity, wellbeing, community, processes of
learning and communication.

Integrated curriculum encourages children to be confident and involved
learners, effective communicators and to build learning relationships and a
sense of connection to the broader community, as outlined in the learning
outcomes of the EYLF (DEEWR, 2009). The Australian Curriculum identifies
the significance of students achieving general capabilities across the
knowledge, skills, behaviours and dispositions in the learning areas as well as
in the cross curriculum perspectives (ACARA, 2013a; 2013c). This supports
students to draw on their essential skills of 'literacy, numeracy, information and
communication technology, thinking, creativity, teamwork and communication
to enhance their identity and wellbeing, connect socially, and act responsibly
and ethically in local, community and global contexts' (ACARA, 2013c, p. 3).
Such capabilities support students to reach the *Educational Goals for Young
Australians* (Ministerial Council for Education, Early Childhood Development
and Youth Affairs (MCEECDYA) 2009) so they live and work well in a complex and changing world.
Learning through integrated curriculum can expand children's ways of learning. For example,
many practices are considered in 'habits of mind' (http://www.habits-of-mind.net/; *see* Costa &
Kallick, 2000a; 2000b; 2009) or 'dispositions' (*see* Carr, 2001; DEEWR, 2009b; Arthur, 2010). Habits
of mind proponents Costa and Kallick (2000a; 2000b; 2009) investigate how children construct
knowledge as they reason, persist, create and craft in order to solve complex challenges, and
know how to use the knowledge in situ. Habits of mind include managing impulsivity, listening
with understanding and empathy, aiming for precision, raising questions and identifying
problems, using all senses, locating humour, thinking collaboratively and learning all the time
(*see* http://www.habits-of-mind.net/ for all 16 habits and see http://www.kingswood.vic.edu.au
> Facilities and programs > Habits of mind, the website of Kingswood Primary School, Dingley
Village to read how a school promotes diverse ways of thinking and learning). Confident learners
draw on these dispositions to resource their own learning and to transfer knowledge and
understandings from a known to a new context (DEEWR, 2009a).

Integrated curriculum enables children to explore 'big ideas'. Big ideas involve essential
knowledge, social improvements, shared values and so on. Some examples include ecological
sustainability, inclusion, global communities, diversity, living with change and ambiguity, justice,
rights and responsibilities, intercultural understandings, democratic processes and social
responsibility.

In recent years, perhaps due to national curriculum developments and accountability
practices, including the standardised National Assessment Program of Literacy and Numeracy
(NAPLAN) testing, educators in some school have reduced their focus on integrated curriculum.
This is despite strong evidence that this approach enables children to inquire and construct their
own learning. Figure 7.3 reflects an integrated approach where children investigate plants in
their lives. This could contribute to integrated curriculum where children examine many aspects
concerning plants.

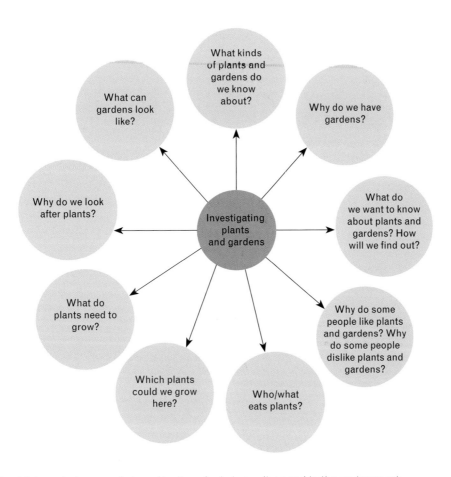

FIGURE 7.3 Integrated approach: investigating plants in our lives and in the environment.

Sometimes integrated curriculum is confused with a **thematic approach** that reflects the educator's intended focus for children's learning. For example, the theme of rabbits may be used as an organiser across the curriculum areas of mathematics, English and environmental science, but in a superficial way that does not engage children in deep, meaningful learning. The differences between *integrated* and *thematic* approaches to curriculum are illustrated in Figures 7.3 and 7.4.

At the other end of the continuum, a **segregated approach** divides the curriculum into specific sets of knowledge and skills that are viewed by children, families and educators as being separate. In prior-to-school settings a segregated approach may occur if the environment is organised into separate areas such as the Book Area and Science Centre, if literacy is only planned for group time or if children are asked not to move resources across areas. The Perry Preschool Curriculum/HighScope Curriculum (HighScope, n.d.) organises the environment with designated areas for creative arts, construction and literacy, which reflects a segregated approach to learning, although it does also provide for some flexibility by allowing children to move resources from one area to another.

In a school context, a segregated approach may mean educators maintain clear boundaries between knowledge areas by teaching discrete aspects of content areas such as phonics or writing at different times. This may be appropriate at times, but an isolated approach does not encourage learners to make connections and problem-solve, for example by learning phonemic patterns through writing. If curriculum areas, such as Mathematics or English, are broken into parts, such as counting, mathematical problem solving, spelling, reading, phonics and writing, educators teach and assess these aspects separately and may miss children's demonstrations of their understandings. On the other hand, children can integrate mathematical problem-solving

Thematic approach
This approach occurs when the educator decides the topic for children's learning through organising topic-based activities across various curriculum areas of mathematics, language, environmental science or music. Usually these activities do not engage children in deep and meaningful learning as they complete activities about the topic.

Segregated approach
If educators understand the curriculum as separate components with clear boundaries, for example separate sets of knowledge and skills, the focus is limited to these aspects, so there may be little flexibility or meaningfulness available for learners. Children may be expected to limit their learning to these boundaries related to curriculum areas, timetable and areas of the setting.

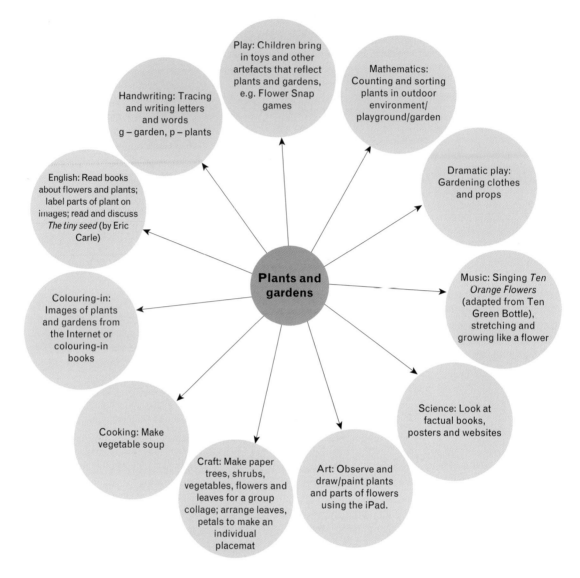

FIGURE 7.4 Segregated and thematic approach: let's make a garden.

and narratives with content that makes sense to them as well as show evidence of their learning in spelling, writing, reading and phonics.

Often educators emphasise a focus on skills in isolation because of a focus on 'school readiness' or some assessment practices. Sometimes there is anticipation of accountability requirements such as future national literacy and numeracy tests.

While some educators may see the links and purpose in segregated curriculum, these are often forced and not always evident to children, nor do they extend children's learning. Children may do various activities, but may not understand the connections between ideas or learn the processes of locating and examining information to accomplish a purpose or function. Stonehouse and Gonzalez-Mena (2007) note that themes can become more important to educators than children's ideas and the rationale for doing something becomes whether it fits the theme or draws on available resources rather than whether it is a meaningful experience for children.

Individual developmental approach ↔ community of learners approach

The contexts of families, peers and communities in children's learning are reflected in the **community of learners approach**. This features strongly in current sociocultural theories of learning, which encourage educators to take account of the social and cultural contexts of children's learning and to move the emphasis from individuals to communities of learners (Lave & Wenger, 1991). *Belonging, Being and Becoming: The Early Years Learning Framework for Australia* (DEEWR, 2009a) promotes a vision of educators extending children's learning in partnerships with families. Family collaboration and understandings of family practices strengthen educators' capacity to construct curriculum that extends children's learning. For example, when educators understand that children know many fairytales, folktales and superheroes from exchanging information with families about their literacy practices, particularly DVD viewing, they are able to expand children's learning (Beecher, 2010).

Respecting and engaging the community of learners among children and families provides a productive context for learning (Studans, 2003) and encourages educators to observe and reflect on interactions among children and to consider the role of social interactions in children's learning. It is essential that all children and families are included in the community of learners. Children from some families, such as itinerant seasonal workers, are sometimes overlooked as part of the local community by educators and denied learning opportunities (Henderson, 2005).

The philosophy and practices of Loris Malaguzzi (1998), the founder of the community-managed schools and infant-toddler centres in the city of Reggio Emilia in the Emilia Romagna region of northern Italy after the Second World War, provide insights into the community of learners approach. Malaguzzi's philosophy builds on that of John Dewey and has antecedents in the work of Pestalozzi and Froebel. Reggio philosophy and practices are relevant to a particular area of Italy and cannot be picked up and transported to another country. Yet, many underlying ideas – for example, the proposal that relationships constitute the centre of the curriculum – provide useful inspiration for many educators. Collaborative learning communities mean strong partnerships between educators, children, families and the local community, and an emphasis on children participating in shared problem solving and projects in small groups and pairs. In a community of learners approach, educators are also seen as colearners alongside children and families.

Towards the other end of the continuum, an **individualistic developmental approach** traditionally emphasises children's learning as individuals without reference to the learning that occurs in their groups of peers or in their family and community contexts. When educators use this approach they focus on analysing children's learning based on generalised developmental patterns established from dated research of particular populations of children. This research, not having accounted for sociocultural practices known by the current children in the setting/school, may offer limited insights into their learning. With this approach educators observe individual children's actions to identify their learning across developmental stages and domains, including sensory, physical, social, emotional, language and cognitive, and then plan 'developmentally appropriate' experiences. Usually the focus shifts onto the next developmental milestone in one domain, additionally reflecting segregated and adult-centred approaches.

Progressively over the last 30 years, concepts of 'developmentally appropriate practice' (DAP) have changed. During the 1980s in the United States, developmental approaches led to DAP. This term, developed by Bredekamp and the American National Association for the Education of Young Children (Bredekamp, 1987), focused on child development and curriculum that was perceived to be appropriate for children at different ages and developmental stages. DAP provided general guidelines as to the types of experiences, resources and interactions that are appropriate for children of different ages. Fleer (1995, p. 12) suggests that in a DAP approach 'program planning … predominately follows rather than leads children's development, and hence cognition'. There were two dimensions of DAP: age appropriateness and individual appropriateness. The concept of 'age appropriateness' suggests that there are universal patterns of development across all domains of learning. 'Individual appropriateness' suggests that there are individual differences among children from their social and cultural contexts, individual personality and learning style.

Community of learners approach

This approach recognises the significance of the sociocultural contexts of families, peers and communities for children's learning. The emphasis is on children participating as a member of the community of learners, rather than as an individual. Educators organise experiences to extend children's learning.

Individualistic developmental approach

Children's learning is emphasised as individuals, with little reference to their family, peers and community contexts. Educators may analyse their learning and link to generalised developmental patterns established from dated research of particular populations, offering little understanding of their learning.

The revised concept of DAP (Bredekamp & Copple, 1997; Copple & Bredekamp, 2009; National Association for the Education of Young Children, 2009) reflects more of the *community of learners* approach to curriculum. These revisions urge educators to consider the changing issues shaping children's sociocultural contexts that influence their development and learning, the significance of families and communities in children's learning and the shifts in society that narrow and crowd curriculum in the name of accountability. Understandings of general patterns of growth and development, along with awareness of the diversity of particular children's experiences within families and communities, can assist educators to provide a program that is developmentally as well as culturally appropriate. The third edition (Copple & Bredekamp, 2009) restates the focus on excellence and equity in programs for learning and development so all children with diverse experiences reach realistic and relevant goals.

DAP has been criticised as being prescriptive and limiting (Dahlberg et al., 2007). This does not necessarily mean that it should be abandoned; rather, that educator understandings and practices should be analysed. As suggested in Chapter 1, educator knowledge of changing social and cultural contexts for learning and multiple pathways of learning for children can broaden their critical understandings of development and developmentally appropriate practice that supports every child's learning. The current position statement (Copple & Bredekamp, 2009) recognises that educators need professional learning to work on the achievement gaps between children from different demographic groups, while at the same time withstanding the downward pressure from the accountability climate and standardised testing in schools. This revision states that curriculum needs to address all aspects of all children's development and learning, interests and abilities in holistic ways across social, cognitive, emotional and physical domains, although each child's learning pathway is individual. Educators' intentional interactions critically extend children's learning in child-led and teacher-led experiences.

Predetermined approach ↔ emergent approach

Emergent curriculum (Jones, Evans & Renken, 2001; Jones & Nimmo, 1994) focuses on children's learning in the potential curriculum and retrospective documentation of what happens during the day, rather than on preplanning experiences. This does not mean that there is no planning but that 'plans are place holders to get things responsibly started' and 'the planning is shared with the learners' (Jones, Evans & Renken, 2001, p. 154). An emergent curriculum 'responds to, expands, and builds upon the ideas and interests of the children in the group, collectively and individually' (Hume-Thoren, in Julovich & Heyob, 1998, p. 120). Then again, emergent curriculum is not totally dependent on children's interests – rather it draws on negotiation and collaboration between children, educators and families. This approach resembles the communities-of-learners approach as children, families, communities and educators investigate, explore, create and learn collaboratively. Families and communities are highly involved in children's learning through children's excursions in the community, by bringing the community into the setting, and through ideas and resources that families and community members may provide as in Figure 7.5.

In an emergent approach the sources of curriculum may include:

- children's interests – e.g. insects, cars, popular media culture
- educators' interests – e.g. gardening, cooking, music, fitness
- developmental activities – i.e. responding to children's development and learning
- objects in the physical environment – including manufactured and natural resources and serendipitous events

> **Emergent curriculum**
>
> This approach emphasises and supports children's learning in the potential curriculum by responding to, and extending on, their individual and group interests and questions. Educators document retrospectively what happens, rather than preplanning experiences, as they negotiate the collaboration between children, families and themselves to extend learning.

Source: KU Macquarie Fields Preschool

FIGURE 7.5 Family days involve children sharing their learning with families while educators and specialist staff can exchange information with families.

- people and relationships in the social environment – children, educators, families and community
- family, community and setting/school values and concerns – e.g. sustainability, human rights, inclusion
- resource materials that can be adapted – e.g. books, Internet resources, DVDs.

Children's interests, passions and questions are taken seriously in this approach. Educators focus on children learning about concepts and developing positive dispositions towards learning through engaging with experiences and projects that build on their interests (*see* Figure 7.6). They provide children with varied choices so that there are 'many hooks to catch the widely varying interests and skills of the children in a class' (Jones, Evans & Renken, 2001, p. 27). In this way emergent curriculum is consistent with integrated, children-centred and community of learners approaches to curriculum.

The **predetermined approach** occurs when educators take a permanent and non-responsive approach to curriculum for a particular group of children. In this approach educators may draw on last year's program, available resources from a website or, more commonly in school settings, the predetermined learning content and preplanned units from curriculum documents. Since assessment and planning, as well as NAPLAN testing in schools, are closely connected to learning focus, this fixed approach is common practice in many schools.

FIGURE 7.6 Children engage deeply with things that interest them. Understanding how to extend children's learning through their interests guides many educators.

Where educators make few connections between children and the learning experiences and allow little consideration for their strengths and current capabilities, children may complete activities but take little interest, make few advances in their learning and learn to take little responsibility for their learning. This may promote rote learning and extrinsic motivation because the curriculum is not meaningful to the children.

The *Melbourne Declaration of Educational Goals for Young Australians* (MCEECDYA, 2009, p. 3) sets the expectation that 'all young Australians become successful learners, confident and creative individuals and active and informed citizens'. It follows, then, that educators can personalise the curriculum for all children to learn: 'Teachers will use the Australian Curriculum to develop teaching and learning programs that build on students' interests, strengths, goals and learning needs, and address the cognitive, affective, physical, social and aesthetic needs of all students' (ACARA, 2013b, p. 4). With the strong recognition of the diversity of school students, educators can make the curriculum meaningful to students by paying attention to current levels of learning of individual students and the different rates at which students develop, as well as their 'needs, interests and the school and community contexts' (ACARA, 2013a, p. 26). For instance, educators could draw on the different curriculum dimensions across the learning areas, general capabilities and/or cross curriculum perspectives in various ways to support student learning. This could involve different levels in English and Science learning areas, together with general capabilities, such as literacy, intercultural understanding and personal and social capability, as well as cross curriculum priorities, which includes sustainability, the histories and cultures of Aboriginal and Torres Strait islanders, and Asia and Australia's engagement with Asia (ACARA, 2013a).

Predetermined approach

When educators take a non-responsive approach to curriculum for a particular group of children, they make few connections between the children and the intended learning, concerning children's strengths, interests, capabilities and experiences. Children may complete activities but with little interest and responsibility as they find activities not meaningful.

Transmission approach ↔ constructivist approach

Constructivist approach

In this approach educators recognise 'active learning' or 'play-based learning' where children learn across emotional, social, physical and cognitive areas. Children as active learners participate in integrated hands on experiences with open-ended materials as they construct new meanings.

The **constructivist approach** to curriculum, or what may be also called 'active learning' or 'play-based learning', draws on how children learn across emotional, social, physical and cognitive areas (Hohmann & Wekart, 1995; Kostelnik et al., 2007), particularly as engaged learners (Schwartz & Copeland, 2010).

The HighScope program, first developed in the United States in Ypsilanti, Michigan in the 1970s by David Weikart, and trialled in Australia by a small group of settings in 2007 (*see* Connor, 2008 for more details of the Australian trial), takes a constructivist approach by emphasising the importance of hands-on 'active and participatory learning' (HighScope, n.d.) with stimulating, open-ended materials that encourage manipulation and transformation (Connor, 2008). In the HighScope curriculum, 'children choose materials and play partners, change and build on their play ideas, and plan activities according to their interests and needs' (Connor, 2008, p. 3). Adult–child interactions encourage children to communicate their thinking and challenge children to accommodate new ideas and engage in problem solving and conflict resolution (Connor, 2008). Understandings of children's active learning originate with Dewey (1902; 1938/1963), Genishi (1992), Koplow (1996), Piaget and Inhelder (1969) and Vygotsky (1978). Active learning builds on children's strengths, interests and known experiences and offers learning potentials for children of all ages and abilities (Brock, 2009; Bruce & Ockleford, 2010; Cologon & McNaught, 2014; Dodds, 2009; Doherty et al., 2009; Wilson & Wing Jan, 2009).

Play enables children to develop their dispositions and to transfer current understandings to new contexts that extend learning. Importantly, it supports children to build relationships and establish concepts as well as a sense of wellbeing, which is vital to the learning process (DEEWR, 2009a). Similarly, general capabilities enable children at school to transfer their learning to new contexts and to build relationships, for example, personal and social capability, ethical behaviour and intercultural understanding (ACARA, 2013c, p. 2).

Not all play is pleasurable, however; Mac Naughton (1999) warns of instances where children exclude others and cause discomfort and harm. There is a critical role for educators to engage children in discussions of power relationships and fair and unfair behaviour, as explored in the following discussions of transformative curriculum and interactions with children.

Play-based curriculum enables children to draw on their family and community experiences and funds of knowledge (Moll et al., 1992). This scaffolds children's understandings of symbol systems such as literacy and numeracy (Bruce & Ockleford, 2010). When children take on different roles in play contexts or playful experiences, literacy and numeracy become embedded in their play in the same way that they function in the social worlds of children's families and communities and children are able to connect their knowledge of their social worlds with school literacies (Kenner, 2003) (*see* Example 7.1 and Figure 7.7).

Increasingly, school educators adopting a constructivist approach offer children investigating sessions with choices of open-ended experiences integrating science, mathematics, history and English as ACARA recommends 'integrated approaches where appropriate' (ACARA, 2013a, p. 26). Examples of children's learning through prolonged investigation and representation, reflecting a constructivist approach, may be seen in the South Australian Learning to Learn project (http://www.learningtolearn.sa.edu.au).

Transmission approach

In this approach children participate in activities involving direct instruction, followed by practice as individuals and in small groups to increase their skills and content knowledge (Schwartz & Copeland, 2010). Educators may also hold behavioural understandings of learning as they use sequenced activities and standardised assessment to provide evidence of how children have learnt the skills taught by educators.

Where the focus is primarily on educators delivering curriculum content in didactic ways to children, this can be seen as a **transmission approach** to curriculum (Kalantzis & Cope, 2008). In this approach educators are active, with children listening or *absorbing* and then demonstrating their growing understandings with individual or small group activities in response to educator requests. Often the educators and textbooks provide the authority for particular knowledge, which may be seen as fixed, rather than starting from children's current understandings and reflecting on shifting truths and diverse perspectives about knowledge. Children are passive in rote learning; they seldom ask questions apart from 'what do I have to do?' Usually there is little time for children to pose questions or construct their own understandings as the educator's focus is on covering the content and then assessing children's learning – with the assumption that assessment tasks reveal how effectively the content was transmitted.

▶ EXAMPLE 7.1
Harrison and Max make their own iPads

Play-based environments enable children to collaboratively draw on their understandings of literacy in personally meaningful ways. Educators can assess what children already know so they can extend their learning.

Max and Harrison make their own iPads

Monday 22/7/13

Harrison said, *'We made iPads for a game'*.

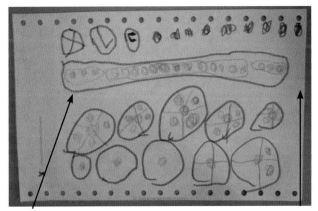 

'Those are lights that flash. It signals when there's a bad guy. We have to go and fight them. The guys transform in the game'.

Margaret asked, 'Tell me about those three circles with shapes'.

'Those are weapon things'.

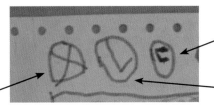

'That is Bumble Bee. That one makes auto-bot parts'.

'This one kills the bad guy powers. If they try to get us we shoot in the middle of them. If they don't have it (power) they can't get any more power'.

Harrison asked Margaret, *'Do you know what the game is called?*
Transformers. Max has heaps of the toys of them. Even more than me'.

Harrison was very ordered and organised in his drawing of his iPad. He shows his

 observations and knowledge of lines of icons, of regular sizes and regular spacing.

Harrison created two rows of five large buttons. Each one was divided into quarters with a circle in each quadrant and one in the centre of the circle. Harrison showed great persistence and self control as he positioned and completed his detailed work. Remarkable work Harrison!

'… art becomes a tool for thinking. Children draw to learn as opposed to merely learn to draw. Children are revising their theories, not simply revising the accuracy of a copy'.George Foreman

▶ *'Children use play to participate in their culture, to develop the literacy of their culture'*,
EYLF Educators' Guide p. 30

> *'Harrison did this top bit.*
> *These are some games too'*.

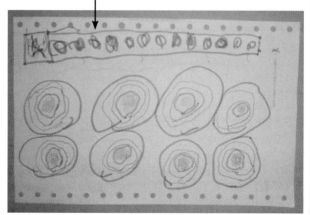

'I made an iPad and Harrison did the top bit. I did the circle bits and the yellow lines.
These are just games. Power rangers, Sonic Sega, Skylanders, Plane drawings, Angry Birds,
Space Angry Birds. I wanted to do interesting things that grownups do' said Max.

Max drew two rows of four identical circles with a red coloured-in circle in the middle and concentric rings of brown, purple, lime green and olive green.

Each of the circles was within a square grid drawn in yellow. This yellow grid is very hard to see. Max also shows attention to order and organisation. He drew a circle around each of the dot holes lining the length of the paper.

Max showed great determination as he circled each of the 34 dots along the edge and maintained the correct order of colours in his game buttons. Most impressive Max!

'Spatial sense, structure and pattern, number, measurement, data argumentation, connections and exploring the world mathematically are the powerful mathematical ideas children need to become numerate.' EYLF p. 38.

EYLF Outcome 1: Children have a strong sense of identity
- Children develop their emerging autonomy, inter dependence, resilience and sense of agency.

EYLF Outcome 4: Children are confident and involved learners
- Children develop dispositions for learning such as curiosity, cooperation, confidence, creativity, commitment, enthusiasm, persistence, imagination and reflexivity.
- Children resource their own learning through connecting with people, place, technologies and natural and processed materials.

EYLF Outcome 5: Children are effective communicators
- Children begin to understand how symbols and pattern systems work.

Source: Keiraville Community Preschool, 2013

The transmission approach stems from understandings of learning which advocate that direct instruction followed by practice as individuals or in small groups can increase children's skills and content knowledge (Schwartz & Copeland, 2010). Educators may draw on behavioural understandings of learning and use sequenced activities and standardised assessment to provide evidence of how children have learnt the skills educators taught. Educators may choose this approach because it is easy to document what has been presented to children and identify how this relates to current standards for English and mathematics syllabi areas. The challenge is that children may learn in the short term, but they are likely to lose interest and the successes are unlikely to be sustainable (Schwartz & Copeland, 2010).

Transmission approaches to curriculum often feature in popular culture movies and television programs, influencing the images of learning and teaching held by many families (Kalantzis & Cope, 2008). This approach is also evident if educators select textbooks to help manage their curriculum planning, with an extreme example of this approach being reflected by DISTAR textbooks. (DISTAR is an acronym for Direct Instruction System for Teaching Arithmetic and Reading). In some situations a transmission approach may be warranted; for example, adult-centred and directed transactions may be needed when preparing children for emergency evacuation procedures or implementing urgent health and safety practices. Other situations where it may be useful for limited times include drawing attention to cultural meanings in situ; for example, when we visit the temple we need to cover our arms and legs, demonstrating how to use tools and technologies to support children's creativity or when working with children with additional needs.

Old basics approach ↔ new basics approach

The **new basics approach** to curriculum recognises the complexity of life and learning as well as economic, sociocultural and technological changes in the world. It supports children's participation now and in the future in a flexible knowledge-based society and teaches how to respond productively, both personally and professionally. Such understandings are reflected in the Australian Curriculum (2013a, p.30), 'to equip young Australians with the knowledge, understanding and skills that will enable them to engage effectively with, and prosper in, society, to compete in a globalised world and to thrive in the information-rich workplaces of the future.'

This has led to rethinking the curriculum across broader areas rather than only within the traditional segregated key learning areas as previously discussed (ACARA, 2013a). The Australian Curriculum also recognises the 'current levels of learning of individual students and the different rates at which students develop' (ACARA, 2013a, p. 28). This can be seen as 'multileveled' and 'multiperspectival', which acknowledges the 'overlapping, simultaneous and synchronous contexts of curriculum – itself a reconceptualisation (Bernstein, 1996) of human discourse, knowledge and practice' (Luke, 2008, p. 146). This approach also aligns with integrated, child-centred and community of learners approaches.

New basics in early childhood have been inspired by programs in Scandinavia (*see* the Stockholm Project, Dahlberg et. al., 2007) and Reggio Emilia and the Te Whāriki national curriculum in Aotearoa/New Zealand (New Zealand Ministry of Education, 1996). The Te Whāriki and the associated learning stories (Carr, 2001) included a shift from a developmental focus to a greater consideration of learning dispositions. Dispositions and learning processes also form a strong component of the EYLF (DEEWR, 2009a) for prior-to-school settings. Rather than divide children's learning into developmental or curriculum areas, the EYLF encompasses broad and integrated learning outcomes that are consistent with the Australian goals for schooling (Ministerial Council on Education, Employment, Training and Youth Affairs, 2008) and relevant to lifelong learning. Similarly, the Australian Curriculum broadens the focus for learning – learning areas, general capacities and cross-curriculum priorities as explained elsewhere in this chapter (ACARA, 2013a, p. 15).

New basics approach

In this approach educators recognise complexity in life and learning as well as change in the world so they support children's participation now and in the future in a flexible knowledge-based society. Children learn how to respond productively, both personally and professionally.

Source: Our Lady of Lourdes Catholic School, Seven Hills

FIGURE 7.7 Well-resourced investigating sessions at school enable children to actively show educators what they know and can do. Educators and parents then can extend children's construction of new learnings.

In schools, the new basics draw on the educational philosophies of Vygotsky, Dewey and Freire. This approach reaches beyond the old basics of the 3 Rs (reading, [w]riting and [a]rithmetic) to complex and authentic new basics. These include life pathways and social futures, multiliteracies and communication media, active citizenship and environments and technologies (Education Queensland, 2004). Similarly, the seven capabilities noted in the Australian Curriculum identify 'knowledge, skills, behaviours and dispositions that, together with curriculum content in each learning area and the cross-curriculum priorities, will assist students to live and to work successfully in the twenty-first century', which extend on the outcomes of the EYLF (ACARA, 2013c, p. 3) and include:

- literacy
- numeracy
- information and communication technology (ICT) capability
- critical and creative thinking
- personal and social capability
- ethical behaviour
- intercultural understanding.

ACARA, 2013, p. 3

Educators integrate curriculum content, pedagogy and assessment. The EYLF and the Australian Curriculum recognise the changing and diverse sociocultural contexts of children's learning, as stated by ACARA in the following: 'The design of the curriculum assumes that schools are best able to decide how to deliver the curriculum and will, for example, apply integrated approaches where appropriate and use pedagogical approaches that account for students' needs, interests and the school and community context' (ACARA, 2013a, p. 15). For example, recent reconceptualisations of literacy encompass the notion of multiliteracies, expanding understandings of literacy to include a broad range of texts and social practices that reflect social and technological changes for families in society (Healy, 2004; Jones Diaz et al., 2001; Jones Diaz, 2007; Kalantzis & Cope, 2008; Arthur, Ashton & Beecher, 2014).

Many national curriculum documents identify dimensions of teaching and learning that are linked to improved achievement standards. These dimensions promote high levels of intellectual quality and high-quality learning environments and create significance through connecting children with the intellectual challenge of their learning; as noted by ACARA, 'All students are entitled to rigorous, relevant and engaging learning programs drawn from a challenging curriculum that addresses their individual learning needs' (ACARA, 2013b, p. 5). Children's engagement in learning experiences is recommended through educators including children's interests, background knowledge and cultural understandings and negotiating experiences. 'Teachers will use the Australian Curriculum to develop teaching and learning programs that build on student interests, strengths, goals and learning needs, and address the cognitive, affective, social and aesthetic needs of all students' (ACARA, 2013b, p. 5).

The new basics approach emphasises children's deep engagement, higher order thinking and integration of learning across the curriculum (Ewing, 2010; Watt, 2006). There is a focus on broad knowledge, and the development of the skills and personal qualities that enable people to live well in a fluid, multidimensional and information-rich world. The futures that students will establish need to be sustainable, innovative and have a strong sociocultural community base. To explain, living in the twenty-first century, as noted by the Melbourne Declaration, implies learners who 'can manage their own wellbeing, relate well to others, make informed decisions about their lives, become citizens who behave with ethical integrity, relate to and communicate across cultures, work for the common good and act with responsibly at local, regional and global levels' (ACARA, 2013c, p. 3).

The **old basics approach** to curriculum can be understood as what is commonly interpreted by the public, families and the media as the traditional 3 Rs. For children attending early childhood settings, old basics tend to involve narrow developmental views of children's learning. Using this approach, educators focus on how children grow and develop according to fixed

Old basics approach

In this approach, commonly interpreted as the traditional 3 Rs, educators may focus on narrow developmental views of children's learning according to fixed patterns at early childhood settings and then focus on the next step. In schools educators may emphasise 'academic' learning areas, or the fragmentation of literacy into phonics, dictation and so on.

patterns as they use rigid developmental checklists to understand children's learning and plot the next step in each separate domain. Knowing primary colours, counting and self-help skills are some of the pointers that educators may consider important as learning and indicators of 'school readiness'.

In school settings, old basics may be reflected in an emphasis on 'academic' learning areas or subjects, or the fragmentation of literacy into phonics, dictation, writing, handwriting, vocabulary extension, sights words and so on, with little attention to how children use literacy in integrated ways in everyday life. There are times when a clear focus on aspects of literacy – for example, spelling patterns in words, sound/letter correspondences or text structures/genres – is appropriate in order to explicitly draw children's attention to language features. But a narrow focus can result in unintended experiences, such as that of a six-year-old child who reported that at school she wrote 'mostly sentences with full stops at the end', illustrating that she paid little or no attention to any personal meanings in these texts (Vickers, 2007).

Economic and industrial restructuring, resulting in increased levels of unemployment, has fuelled the 'back to (old) basics' movement and the consequent emphasis on literacy and numeracy tests, which has led to literacy and numeracy dominating the curriculum in some schools (Vickers, 2007). When what children are asked to do in literacy and numeracy tests is compared with rich tasks used in new basics to assess children's learning, the differences along the continuum of approaches stand out. Evaluation and assessment are further examined in Chapters 4 and 9.

Exclusive approach ↔ inclusive approach

Inclusive approach

Educators embrace diversity and difference and actively work to reflect the diversity among children, families and communities in the curriculum. Children's learning reflects the importance of understanding and working with diversity and difference in a globalised world.

Disadvantage

Includes people's 'personal capabilities, their family circumstances; the community where they live (and the opportunities it offers); life experiences; and the broader economic and social environment' (McLachlan, Gilfillan & Gordon, 2013, p. 2).

Where educators take an **inclusive approach** they recognise and embrace diversity and difference and actively work to reflect the diversity among children, families and communities in the curriculum. Understandings reflected in this approach include the importance of understanding and working with diversity and difference in a globalised world (Kalantzis and Cope, 2008; Robinson & Jones Diaz, 2006; Wilson & Murdoch, 2008). The vision for the EYLF advocates that all children have opportunities to experience engaged learning that builds success for life (DEEWR, 2009a). Likewise the Australian Curriculum reflects the policy framework of the National Educational Goals, that 'All young Australians become successful learners, confident and creative individuals and active and informed citizens' (Ministerial Council for Education, Early Childhood Development and Youth Affairs (MCEECDYA), 2009, p. 3). Children can only belong, be and become where they and their experiences are respected and included in the curriculum and their contributions are taken seriously. This includes recognition of the strengths of children with additional needs (Reid et al., 2010, p. 15). The Australian Curriculum also recognises the importance of educator flexibility in personalising learning, as follows: 'The three-dimensional design of the Australian Curriculum, comprising learning areas, general capabilities and cross-curriculum priorities, provides teachers with flexibility to cater for the diverse needs of students across Australia and to personalise their learning' (ACARA, 2013a, p. 20). Ewing (2010, p. 95) advocates that 'curriculum needs to be selected and organised in a way that is meaningful for all students'.

Respecting diversity means working with different cultures, including diverse abilities, languages, ethnicities, learning styles, socio-economic resources, classes, genders, sexuality and family structures. Social inclusion policies and practices work towards ensuring 'all people are able to participate socially and economically with dignity in their community' (Ewing, 2010, p. 82)

Disadvantage, for children is shaped by compounding interrelated factors rather than the single indicator of low income, and occurs for a significant number of Australian families and their children. Definitions and numbers are difficult to establish as few longitudinal studies have occurred. Disadvantage includes people's 'personal capabilities, their family circumstances; the community where they live (and the opportunities it offers); life experiences; and the broader economic and social environment' (McLachlan, Gilfillan & Gordon, 2013, p. 2). Early childhood and school education are two determining periods for children's successful learning and life outcomes, including developing positive relationships, as well as continuing their education and training beyond school and gaining employment. Families who are likely to experience disadvantage include sole parents, Aboriginal and Torres Strait Islanders and those parents with chronic health issues, disabilities and limited educational success. These families often rent public housing and work infrequently (McLachlan et al., 2013). The concept of disadvantage and the implications are of concern, especially given that the Program for International Student Assessment identified Australian education as high quality, but low equity for students (Organisation for Economic Co-operation and Development, 2009); the first goal of *The Melbourne Declaration on Educational Goals for Young Australians* (MCEETYA, 2009, p. 3) is that 'Australian schooling promotes equity and excellence'.

One approach to addressing the educational support of children from families with low socio-economic resources is to provide children and their families in the community with access to targeted resources and early intervention services. Specifically targeted services are also provided to address the needs of children with additional needs and Aboriginal and Torres Strait Islander learners. While there are arguments that these targeted services are best able to cater for specific learning needs, there are also arguments for the universal provision of more integrated child and family services. A more inclusive approach to addressing issues of access and equity is to provide early childhood services to all children and families. The Australian government's early childhood agenda, currently undergoing implementation, provides universal access to a year of early childhood education in the year prior to formal schooling.

An inclusive approach also argues that children with additional needs should be included in mainstream educational settings rather than segregated in 'special' settings, albeit with relevant funding and suitability qualified and interested educators (Reid et al., 2010). An inclusive approach is consistent with many other approaches; for example, emergent, integrated and constructivist approaches can readily incorporate children's diversity into the curriculum as the hook for extending children's learning. On the other hand, an **exclusive curriculum approach** lacks inclusivity as it ignores children's diversity or treats it as a problem.

Monocultural and monolingual approach ↔ multicultural and multilingual approach

Alongside an inclusive approach to curriculum, a **multicultural and multilingual approach** to curriculum integrates the diverse cultures and languages of children and families into the program. If educators are resourceful and knowledgeable about the cultures and languages that children bring from their family and community contexts into the setting, the interactions, resources and experiences can reflect children's everyday family and community experiences. Most people in the world are bilinguals or multilinguals, speaking more than one language in daily life. This practice enables them to gather social capital and status within their own community (Singh, 2002).

Approximately 3.7 million Australians, including children, speak one or more language other than English or more than one dialect of English (ABS, 2011). With families speaking almost 400 languages, including nearly 200 Aboriginal languages, at home (ABS, 2010), this diversity produces a valuable and enriching cultural and language resource to be extended in children's settings and schools. Increasingly, languages are being introduced to monolingual as well as bilingual students as part of primary and secondary education as desirable curriculum. In early childhood settings and schools educators can make curriculum decisions so that young bilingual/multilingual children retain, rather than lose, their home language as they learn English, and all children can learn to appreciate the diversity of languages. Maintaining their home language can influence the child's relationships with their family, as well as their sense of wellbeing and their successful learning and life opportunities.

Siraj-Blatchford and Clarke (2000, p. 36) suggest that 'a bilingual program aims to maintain and develop the home languages of children, to introduce all children to second or additional

Exclusive approach

Educators overlook or ignore diversity and difference among children, families and communities in the curriculum; sometimes diversity and difference is seen as a problem.

Multicultural and multilingual approach

This occurs when the diverse cultures and languages of children and families are integrated into the program. Educators are knowledgeable about children's languages and cultures and the interactions, resources and experiences reflect children's everyday family and community experiences, and children learn to respect and understand their own languages and cultures as well as those of others.

language learning, to facilitate fluency in language development, to promote a strong self-concept with positive feelings about ethnic identity and to cultivate multicultural or pluralist perspectives'. Children's home languages and cultures are incorporated into the setting when educators include both oral and written language resources in the daily program. Bilingual educators may be employed to assist in the maintenance and further development of children's home languages and to strengthen communication with families. Children's social and cultural identities, bilingual practices and literacies need strong extension from early childhood educators to continue their learning (Jones Diaz & Harvey, 2007; Beecher & Jones Diaz, 2014) on the pathways to becoming bilinguals.

A multilingual and multicultural approach to curriculum is just as important for monolingual and monocultural children as it is for bilingual and multilingual children. It is just as crucial for monolingual and monocultural children to be alert to and learn about different cultures and languages as it is for bilingual children to maintain and extend their language at the setting. This approach supports monolingual children and families to establish positive attitudes towards and improved understandings of different languages and cultures, sociocultural histories and, most importantly, of bilingual children and families.

Monolingual and monocultural approaches relate to curriculum based on a single language and culture. This may occur where children and educators are from the same linguistic and cultural group, or it may occur where children are from diverse language and cultural groups, but the educators are from a single sociocultural group that reflects the dominant language and culture. The situation may also occur where educators enact the dominant views in society and believe that all children should speak English and that home languages do not need to be maintained. Monolingual and monocultural approaches to curriculum also occur when educators unconditionally accept families' requests for an English-only curriculum without presenting families with information based on current research and recommended practices that may challenge these views. Educators may also choose a monolingual and monocultural curriculum because they believe that they cannot access linguistic or cultural resources to support bilingual children and families.

Where monolingual and monocultural approaches operate, this reduces learning opportunities for all children to develop understandings about the use of languages and cultural practices in local and global contexts. Bilingual and multilingual children are marginalised when their family and community languages and practices are not included in the curriculum, reflecting also the exclusive approach to curriculum and contributing towards disadvantage (McLachlan, et al. 2013). A monocultural and monolingual approach goes against the tide in times of increasing globalism of cultures, languages, ideas, economic and productivity measures through education, work, migration, information technology and the Internet, as explained in Chapter 1.

Conforming approach ↔ reforming ↔ transforming approach

Mac Naughton (2003) proposes a continuum of approaches to curriculum that spans transforming, reforming and conforming. The **transforming or transformative approach** to curriculum, based on the work of educational theorists such as Freire (1972; 1985), Giroux (1990) and Delpit (1995), aims to transform or fundamentally change existing curriculum practices to achieve greater equity and social justice for all children. Current traditions are analysed and existing power structures and dominant discourses are critiqued. Education systems in particular are analysed in terms of who has access to the 'culture of power' (Delpit, 1995). Success in mainstream culture is dependent on acquisition of the culture of power, which includes ways of talking, writing, dressing and interacting. While the powerless are very aware of the existence of power, those in positions of power are often unaware of equity issues or are unwilling to acknowledge that they have power. Delpit (1995) argues that issues of power are enacted in classrooms and that power bases include the power of educators over children and the power of dominant world views in the classroom.

Monocultural and monolingual approach

This occurs when the program is based on a single language and culture. Children and educators may be from one linguistic and cultural group, or the children and families may be from diverse language and cultural groups, but the educators are from a single sociocultural group reflecting the dominant culture and language.

Transforming or transformative approach

This occurs when the existing curriculum practices are transformed to achieve greater equity and social justice for all children. Educators engage children in the critique and reconfiguration of dominant discourses so they may learn to operate within the culture of power in mainstream society. This involves explicit teaching of the expected ways of talking and being to gain acceptance (Mac Naughton, 2003).

A transformative approach points out that there are codes or rules for participating in power and that these rules reflect the culture of the dominant group. Some children learn how to operate in the culture of power at home and bring this expertise to the educational setting. Other children learn other ways of being and doing that have cultural capital in their families and communities but not in the educational setting. Educational settings may reinforce the culture of the dominant group, thus many children from minority communities are marginalised from learning opportunities in educational settings.

In a transformative approach educators go beyond active learning, inclusive and multicultural/multilingual approaches to engage children in the critique and reconfiguration of dominant discourses because this assists all children to learn to operate within the culture of power. This approach argues for explicitness through intentional teaching of the ways of talking and being that are expected in order to gain acceptance in mainstream society. It is argued that learning the rules and learning about the arbitrariness of codes and the power relationships they represent makes acquiring power easier. The focus involves challenging sociopolitical and economic structures such as democracy, race, class and gender, especially as seen in unfair social relations between people. Mac Naughton (2003, p. 184) points out that 'critical educators are concerned with discrimination, oppression, marginalization; their diminishing effect on our possibilities of becoming; and the role that critical knowledge can play in challenging them'.

The anti-bias approach is another expression of a transformative approach. The anti-bias curriculum (Creaser & Dau, 1995; Dau, 2001; Derman-Sparks, 1989) was first developed for children in the birth to eight-year-old age group in the USA. Derman-Sparks (1989) argued that young children notice diversity, that they make evaluative judgements about differences and that they develop biases from a young age. The anti-bias approach aims to promote positive attitudes towards diversity and to counter stereotypes and discrimination.

At the other end of the continuum, a **conforming approach** to curriculum reinforces the status quo by focusing on the skills needed to achieve national economic, social and political goals and the values and practices that enable society to reproduce itself (Mac Naughton, 2003). In the middle of the continuum is the **reforming approach**, which Mac Naughton (2003) defines as reforming the individual from a dependant and developing child to a self-realised autonomous adult and free thinker; and reforming society so that there is a greater emphasis on freedom, truth and justice.

Conforming approach

This approach occurs when the program reinforces the status quo by focusing on the skills needed to achieve national, economic, social and political goals, and the values and practices that enable society to reproduce itself (Mac Naughton, 2003).

Reforming approach

This occurs when the individual child moves from a dependant and developing child to a self-realised autonomous adult and free thinker; and reforming society reflects a greater emphasis on freedom, truth and justice (Mac Naughton, 2003).

Single intelligence/s approach ↔ multiple intelligences approach

The **multiple intelligences approach** (Gardner, 1983/1993a; 1993b; 2003) espouses the view that children learn in different ways as there are many ways that intelligence manifests in different individuals and across different cultures. Gardner originally identified seven intelligences to which he later added naturalist and existential intelligences (Gardner, 1998b):

- *Logico-mathematical intelligence* – the ability to detect patterns, reason deductively and think logically. This intelligence is most often associated with scientific and mathematical thinking.
- *Linguistic intelligence* – the mastery of language. This intelligence includes the ability to effectively manipulate language to express oneself and to communicate with others.
- *Spatial intelligence* – the ability to manipulate and create mental images in order to solve problems. This intelligence is often connected, but not limited, to visual domains.
- *Musical intelligence* – the capability to recognise and compose musical pitches, tones and rhythms.
- *Bodily-kinaesthetic intelligence* – the ability to use one's mental abilities to coordinate one's own bodily movements.
- *Interpersonal intelligence* – the ability to understand the feelings and intentions of others.
- *Intrapersonal intelligence* – the ability to understand one's own feelings and motivations.

Multiple intelligences approach

This approach acknowledges that children learn in different ways, and there are at least seven to nine different ways that intelligence manifests in different individuals and across different cultures (Gardner, 1983/1993a; 1993b;1998b; 2003).

- *Naturalist intelligence* – added in 1998 and characterised by a fascination with the natural environment.
- *Existential intelligence* – the possibility of a new intelligence, which Gardner calls 'the intelligence of big questions'.

Additional intelligences, including emotional, spiritual and moral intelligence, have been proposed by Gardner and others (*see* Goleman, 1995; Harrison, 2000; Mayer & contributors, 2007; Roberts, 2006), but are not included by Gardner in his Multiple Intelligences pedagogy (Gardner, 2003). Given that linguistic and logico-mathematical intelligences are the ones that are privileged in educational settings, a diverse intelligences or MI approach seeks to expand the range of children's intelligences that are catered for in classrooms. MI fits within the non-universal theory of Feldman (1980/1994), who argues (1998, p. 10) that, contrary to the theory of Piaget and other universalist theories, 'there are many "domains" of activity that are *not* common to all individuals and groups, and that bring with them *no* guarantee of success'. Non-universal theory and MI highlight the need for a variety of learning experiences and pedagogies that provide opportunities for children to reach their potential through different domains of learning. Sonawat and Toshniwal (2009) suggest that combining ideas about MI and learning styles may inspire us to expand our pedagogies to offer children more learning opportunities.

When children's MI are supported in educational settings, they recognise that they are all good at something and begin to experience success and to feel valued (Chen et al., 1998). The research conducted by Chen and her colleagues further suggests that children who may not have strengths in academic areas such as linguistic and logico-mathematical domains are able to demonstrate competencies in different areas such as the interpersonal when educators adopt this approach. This can assist in strengthening academic learning by 'using children's experiences in their area of strength as pathways into other learning areas and academic performance' (Chen et al., 1998, p. 61). Increased confidence can lead to risk taking in new areas; for example, the use of strengths such as music can extend to new areas of counting and rhyming. Refer to the box on page 234 for a task that enables children at school to select and use their multiple intelligences in learning.

Single or restricted intelligences approach

The use of this approach occurs when educators consider only a limited number of intelligences, which reduces children's learning opportunities. Programs and assessment procedures in schools have traditionally reflected linguistic and logico-mathematical intelligences while overlooking the many others.

The use of the **single or restricted intelligences approach** in the curriculum occurs when educators take a limited number of intelligences into account; this reduces learning opportunities. Traditionally, many schools and their assessment procedures have highlighted linguistic and logico-mathematical intelligences while overlooking the many others. The emphasis on behavioural and psychometric testing has influenced many children and families by reducing children's opportunities to learn, to experience success and to feel competent at school and in life. In addition, the notion of single intelligences can label children and influence their learning opportunities. For example, an emphasis on English language competencies or reading test achievements may mean a child is labelled as 'bright' or 'delayed' and placed in a certain 'ability' group within a certain class where they may remain. With literacy and mathematics taking up most of the school day, children may be grouped in limited ways for considerable time. Following on, if segregated and exclusive approaches heavily influence our program, children may not be able to use their strengths and interests to reach their learning potentials.

This section has outlined some possibilities in approaches to curriculum. Pedagogies that relate to each of these approaches are introduced in the following section.

Matching pedagogies to selected approaches

Educators select pedagogies to put their approaches to curriculum into practice; in other words, to translate philosophy into practice. Pedagogies involve the 'early childhood educator's professional practice, especially those aspects that involve building and nurturing relationships, curriculum decision-making, teaching and learning' (DEEWR, 2009a, p. 9). Pedagogies are functional things

Learning experience extending multiple intelligences

Zoo animal experiences

Name: _____

You need to choose one experience from each column and negotiate your choices and the dates for starting and finishing with the teacher before starting the experience. You must choose and complete three experiences. If you decide, you can design and negotiate one experience that is not on the lists. **All your experiences need to show what you have learnt about zoo animals and the purpose of zoos in our community.**

EXPERIENCES								
ENVIRONMENT	VISUAL/WORD	MATHS	MUSIC	LANGUAGE & LITERACY	SELF	GROUP	ART	KINAESTHETIC
• Build a diorama of some animals in their natural environment. • Construct models of some animals that live in a similar environment.	• Design and make a card game that shows what you know about how people care for zoo animals. • Design and make a factual picture book about what you know zoos are doing with endangered animals.	• Investigate the budget needed to supply food for zoo animals for a week. • Examine the current zoo map. From your excursion notes and photographs, estimate numbers of animals in enclosures. Check your prediction with zoo workers.	• Compose a song or piece of music about animals in the wild. • Compose a rap about ways to support endangered animals in the wild.	• Build a crossword that focuses on fascinating facts about your favourite animals. • Create an information pamphlet on the zoo for young children.	• Reflect on what you have learnt about the needs of animals at the local zoo. Document this in your learning journal. • Consider how and why you might work with animals later.	• Design and create a group slideshow that reports on why zoos are needed. • Create three clay sculptures of animals and their habitats.	• Create a drawing, painting or collage that shows what you understand about the relationships between animals, people and the environment. • Design and print cards that convey important meanings about endangered animals.	• Create a dance that depicts the movements of one of the animals.

educators decide, organise and do in the centre/classroom to implement their approaches. Educators draw on a range of pedagogies to support implementation of each selected approach or the cluster of approaches and to suit the moment of practice. The cumulative effect of congruent pedagogies may have an energising influence on children's learning. The Australian Curriculum supports educators and schools making their own decisions about their teaching and learning practices; however, the Australian Curriculum strongly signals that educators need to make learning meaningful for students so that all Australian students are successful learners.

> Schools are able to decide how best to deliver the curriculum, drawing on integrated approaches where appropriate and using pedagogical approaches that account for students' needs, interests and the school and community context. School authorities will be able to offer curriculum beyond that specified in the Australian Curriculum.

ACARA, 2013a, p. 15

What do you consider as the most important pedagogies that educators use? Why? What does this reflect about the values and beliefs embedded in your own philosophy?

When implementing approaches to curriculum educators need to investigate and make decisions about the pedagogies that will be most useful in supporting their selected approaches in daily practices. These include but are not restricted to:

- communication with families
- interactions with children, including intentional teaching strategies
- documentation and assessment of children's learning
- learning experiences
- learning environments.

Exchanging information with families

Some approaches to curriculum put a greater emphasis on communicating with families than others. For example, multicultural/multilingual, inclusive and community-of-learner approaches encourage educators to build effective two-way communications, leading to partnerships with families, in order to best support children's sense of belonging at the setting and to extend their learning. If educators work with these approaches, they recognise the value of finding out about and building on information from home as well as sharing information about the child's experiences at the setting with all families. Understanding families' practices provides guidance as to which languages/dialects, modes, strategies and resources may be most suitable for effective cross-cultural communication. Pedagogies may include focused conversations at arrival and departure times, informal or formal meetings on site or at other locations, social functions, regular slideshows of children's experiences, setting information and policies displayed at the setting and accessible on the Internet, paper and regular communication via email newsletters and/or websites. Reflecting on what parents pay attention to in the setting can promote educators to learn more from parents.

The way that the environment is organised gives messages to children and families about the setting's philosophy. An environment that is aesthetically pleasing, culturally respectful and includes places for educators and families to sit and meet sets the scene for positive interaction, communication and relationships between educators, children and families (*see* Figure 7.8). Where features of the overall environment appeal visually and emotionally to families and children, they quickly understand that they are welcome and valued (Henniger, 2002).

Relationships are central to curriculum construction in many approaches, such as multicultural/multilingual, children-centred, community of learners and emergent curriculum. As noted in the EYLF (DEEWR, 2009a), relationships between educators, children and families are significant in children's learning. See Chapter 2 for more information on communication with families.

Source: KU Hebersham Preschool

FIGURE 7.8 Educators create welcoming environments when they provide items of interest to families as well as reflect their cultures and languages.

Interactions with children

The way that educators interact with children also varies across approaches. Child-centred, constructivist, community of learners and emergent approaches to curriculum emphasise educators listening to children's ideas and engaging in conversations with individuals and small groups. More adult-centred, transmission and old basics approaches prioritise adults delivering content to children and overlook interactions. At the more child-centred end of the continuum, adult–child interactions are always sensitive to children's interests and intentions, which enable children to stay in control of the learning. When educators are responsive to children's ideas they are able to build on children's thinking. The views of Vygotsky highlight the critical role of educators in supporting and extending children's active learning through the way that they interact with children to scaffold learning or engage in what HighScope (Connor, 2008) and the EYLF (DEEWR, 2009a) term 'intentional teaching'. Intentional teaching supports many approaches to curriculum.

Educators will often move to different points along a continuum of interactions or teaching strategies as different strategies will be appropriate at different times. At times they may choose to step back and observe children's play and learning, and at other times step in and interact with the children in ways that challenge and extend their learning. Less interventionist pedagogies, such as facilitating, acknowledging children's learning and modelling behaviours and practices, often support developmental approaches to curriculum. Pedagogies emphasising mediating interactions, such as scaffolding and co-constructing children's learning, are more consistent with a community of learners approach as well as emergent, integrated and new basics approaches.

Interaction and communication between educators and children constitute the core of relationships and learning contexts. Where trust, mutual respect and fairness characterise interactions, relationships develop and children are in a position to extend their wellbeing and achieve their learning potential. Intentional teaching becomes a powerful pedagogy to enhance learning. Intentional teaching and the range of teaching strategies are outlined further in Chapter 9.

When educators focus on deconstructing and reconstructing texts and supporting critical thinking and critical literacy in their interactions with children, they use pedagogies that support transformative approaches to curriculum. According to Mac Naughton and Williams (2009, p. 268), deconstruction 'is a form of critical thinking about social relationships that involves questioning the meanings of words or concepts that normally go unquestioned'. To deconstruct something is to take it apart and critically examine the parts. This encourages children to analyse power relationships, to question taken-for-granted assumptions and to construct and examine alternative perspectives (*see* Example 7.2).

▶ EXAMPLE 7.2
Children deconstructing and reconstructing gender, 'race', class or ability

Educators reflect on beginning the deconstruction of some aspects of gender and families with children

Not getting married was something we looked into. Children wanted the happy ending. Girls getting rescued and there was a wedding. In *The Paper Bag Princess*, the princess was left on her own and she lived happily ever after. There are lots of single parents in the group and they appear happy. We did explore different perspectives; for example, girls rescuing boys, not being married and being happy, girls not being useless and thinking for themselves. We are clear that things don't have to be like that (as in fairytales). We provide choice for children and families don't have to be 2 parents and 2.2 kids.

Children deconstructing gender later in their fairytale play – Jack resisting the assumed prince role

Keira: I want to be Cinderella.

Jack wears a prince crown and reads a fairytale book with Harry who points out illustrations of Cinderella and the prince marrying.

Harry: You have to kiss Cinderella!

Jack: I'm not marrying her!

Jack takes off the crown.

Jack: I'm not pretending.

Jack leaves the play.

Educator reflects on some children reconstructing gender in their play

Gilly and Jack appeared to critique and express expanded gender positionings. Gilly was the only girl to engage in sword-fighting. She didn't seek 'the look' of a cape like many boys, she sought 'the action'. Awkwardly she began sword-fighting, maybe drawing on *The Paper Bag Princess* for textual authority where clothing was unimportant but courage and physical prowess were vital. After developing physical competence, she often sword-fought and ran with the boys and engaged them in fairytale narratives. Jack played a prince with many actions, including marrying/ not marrying, sword-fighting, not sword-fighting, caring for others and investigating mermaids.

Source: Cherry Tree Pre-school Kindergarten, 2005.

Children and educators can deconstruct and reconstruct texts, including images. As an example, educators and children can critically examine every-day texts such as advertisements for the images and messages. Contradictions between advertising texts and real life can be the catalyst for a discussion on the ways that males and females are portrayed in the media and the ways that texts are used to promote commercial interests (Arthur, 2001). Alternative texts and images can be reconstructed to reflect a range of alternative perspectives that reflect children's new learning, as in re-creating a toy catalogue that addresses the interests of children in the group.

Documentation and assessment of children's learning

Educators record and assess children's learning in different ways, with the methods of documentation and focus of analysis that are selected reflecting their chosen approaches to curriculum. If they value a developmental approach, anecdotes, checklists, rating scales and running records would be appropriate methods to record and assess individual children's development. Summaries of children's development would generally be organised in separate developmental domains; for example, physical, cognitive, social/emotional and language/literacy learning. If educators take more of a sociocultural perspective – which is reflected in approaches such as communities of learners and emergent curriculum – they are likely to focus on collecting information from families to gain insights into what children are able to do in their homes and communities and to use observations of interactions, samples and photographs of children's representations that show children's progress over time. They may support this with transcripts of conversations and lists of children's questions to identify relationships, learning processes and dispositions. An emphasis on the constructivist/active learning approach would include documentation of children engaged in play-based experiences and a focus on collection of children's changing understandings and processes through their questions, investigations, constructions, drawings, writings and photographs of their participating in active learning across the day.

If educators take a community of learners approach, they may organise analysed observations into *portfolios* or *journals* that include annotated photographs of children's engagement in experiences or projects and in conversations with peers, analysed samples of work and narratives of learning. They may seek contributions from children and family members to these forms of open documentation so the focus remains on children within the contexts of family, peers, community and educators. This documentation offers rich storytelling that connects children, families and educators with literacy learning, provokes meaningful curriculum in the setting and extends collaborative relationships (Hatherly, 2006). If educators adopt a new basics and/or integrated approach, the focus would be on documentation of complex integrated experiences or what are sometimes known as 'rich tasks' (see below for further discussion). With a transformative approach, there may be documentation of children's questions and conversations, and analysis of power relations between children, and children and educators.

Emergent curriculum, integrated, community of learners and child-centred approaches encourage educators to display children's learning in order to make their learning processes, dispositions and understandings visible to others and to provoke educators, children and families to revisit and 'reflect on the processes and issues associated with children's learning around a particular event' (Mac Naughton & Williams, 2009, p. 300). This stimulates many possibilities for families to follow up with children and educators about children's experiences and learning, and provides insights into the program. Displays of work encourage children to further investigate and deepen their understandings of a topic (Katz & Chard, 1989/2000), as a regular feature of the learning environment (*see* Figure 7.9).

Adult-centred, transmission and old basics approaches to curriculum often result in a focus on content and learning outcomes in documentation and assessment, and often highlight what children are not able to do. In contrast, child-centred, new basics, transformative and integrated approaches focus on educators using documentation and assessment to plan experiences that extend children's deep learning of significant ideas and knowledge, and their engagement in substantive conversations and inclusive actions.

Learning experiences

Educators design and implement learning experiences to support their selected approaches to curriculum. In child-centred, community of learners and emergent approaches to curriculum the planning is provisional and responsive to family information about children's 'funds of knowledge' (Moll et al., 1992) or 'virtual school bags' (Thompson, 2002), observations of children's ideas, and current events or serendipitous moments that provoke children's curiosity and interest. Flexible educators are always 'seeing possibilities, being thoughtful about opportunities, and looking at possibilities in the unorthodox' (NSW DoCS, 2002, p. 111). They use conversations with children to find out more about children's ideas and to negotiate the curriculum. While some experiences are planned in open-ended ways, other experiences are spontaneous in response to children's questions and ideas. Planned and spontaneous experiences are explored in Chapters 9 and 10.

Source: Summer Hill Children's Centre

FIGURE 7.9 Displays of children's work makes their learning visible to everyone. Children can access the project documentation to revisit, evaluate and reflect on their learning with other children, family and educators.

In contrast, experiences and lessons in adult-centred and transmission approaches to curriculum tend to be preplanned and not open to negotiation. These experiences are increasingly planned based on national curriculum, whole school plans in learning areas, sample units of work and/or ideas in commercially available texts where an activity or underlying idea is the focus. Educators can work with more child-centred, integrated and/or new basics approaches in adapting these sources to make the experiences more meaningful and relevant to children's family and community contexts and to extend children's learning as noted previously in this chapter by ACARA (2013a; 2013b).

PROJECTS

Children's interests can be extended through a series of integrated connected experiences when they investigate a topic related to their interests over a number of days, weeks or even months (Helm & Katz, 2011). The catalyst for a project can be an incident at the setting such as children discovering a bird's nest, a shared interest among the children such as lizards, a shared story or DVD, an excursion or a visitor to the setting. Projects often relate to children's everyday experiences. When the project topic is something that is familiar to children they are able to draw on their existing knowledge to generate their own questions, take on leadership in planning and assume responsibility for their own learning (Katz, 1994).

Projects involve small group cooperative investigations, child choice and child initiation. The combination of extended periods of time and access to a range of resources facilitates children's exploration and encourages them to represent ideas and understandings through a range of media, including drawing, writing, construction and dramatic play. Children may engage in small group interactions where the construction of a product is a culminating part of a project. With younger children the focus is on the investigation rather than on the representation of ideas (Helm & Katz, 2011).

In projects, children engage deeply and direct the investigation with their questions and personal interests. Projects differ from themes; in a theme, educators preplan the content and direct children's learning. Projects develop organically, building on what children already know, and directions often change in response to children's interests as they investigate their questions and the available resources. Projects support many approaches, including emergent, community of learners, child-centred, integrated, new basics and multiple intelligences.

UNITS OF WORK

Units of work (sometimes called integrated units, integrated inquiry units or modules) are used in school settings and consist of a series of lessons or experiences based on a topic that

Source: Keiraville Community Preschool 2013

FIGURE 7.10 When educators notice children's diverse interests and then follow up with further experiences, projects can develop.

the teacher, school or department has chosen to support children's learning towards selected outcomes/indicators over a period of time. The unit may integrate learning areas, capabilities and cross curriculum perspectives. Educators can develop their own units, adapt published units to suit their context or use units that are published in support documents and educational texts.

Units of work are preplanned, as educators set the focus, sometimes in negotiation with children, and generally in relation to knowledge, skills, dispositions and attitudes across learning areas, capabilities and cross curriculum perspectives. The degree of child/educator negotiation regarding focus and resources results from the unit model chosen and the degree of adaptation. In most cases units are more adult-centred and more prescriptive than projects. A unit can extend children's understandings of significant concepts as well as processes such as investigation, problem solving, negotiation, collaboration and reflection (Hamston & Murdoch, 2004). With this pedagogy, educators can support new basics and integrated approaches to curriculum as well as multiple intelligences.

Unit work may occur daily or weekly. Within units of work, learners use general and specialised knowledge as well as research processes to examine questions or ideas. They experience the complexities of knowledge and differing real world investigations as they unify knowledge to establish generalisations and concepts (Wilson & Wing Jan, 2009).

Inquiry-based units of work can extend children's learning of meaningful English (literacy)/ History and Science understandings through robust investigative processes (Wilson & Murdoch, 2008; Wilson & Wing Jan, 2009). Integrated units enable learners to meaningfully integrate aspects of different disciplines into a holistic entity. When English is integrated with History, Science and/or Maths, for example, children are able to utilise meaningful literacy and inquiry processes with significant curriculum. See the Online Example 7.1 for this chapter for an integrated unit based on this process, adapted from Hamston and Murdoch (2004) and Murdoch and Hornsby (1997). Unit processes include:

1. *negotiating the unit* – with children; and considering relevant curriculum content, general capabilities and cross-curriculum priorities across learning areas in relation to expected achievement standards
2. *tuning in* – experiences aimed at finding out what children already know and what they would like to know

CourseMateExpress

See Online Example 7.1, which can be found online with CourseMate Express.

3. *investigating* – experiences and resources that enable students to access new information
4. *making sense of investigations* – opportunities for students to make sense of their investigations
5. *documenting* – what educators know and what else they need to know
6. *investigating further* – experiences to extend children's learning
7. *making conclusions* – making generalisations, clarifying values, assessing understandings
8. *taking action* – looking at what can be done
9. *sharing, discussing and reflecting* – opportunities to share individual/small group projects with a larger group and to reflect on learning
10. *assessing* – children's learning towards curriculum content, general capabilities and cross-curriculum priorities across learning areas in relation to expected achievement standards
11. *evaluating* – the unit, resources and relevant pedagogies.

RICH TASKS

Rich tasks are designed to be integrated, sequential, open-ended, authentic and complex, reflecting the real world. The work of Dewey and Freire inspired this pedagogy, where students are supported to problem-solve and think freely about concepts, ideas and issues as well as their learning. Risk tasks provide the visible signs of children's participation in the new basics and are used to assess and report student learning (Education Queensland, 2004). These developments by Education Queensland contributed to deepening awareness of how the new basics, integrated and constructivist approaches may use rich tasks as pedagogies for learning and assessment that are 'rich in cognitive, developmental and intellectual depth and breadth' (Education Queensland, 2001, p. 5). Although no longer policy in Queensland, this work stimulated further initiatives in Australia, such as Quality Teaching initiatives (NSW Department of Education, 2003a) and National Professional Standards for Teachers (AITSL, 2011).

Educators working with a new basics approach in schools have begun to sketch the big picture; for example, mapping the sequences of transitional outcomes for various stages that connect to each other and to the transformational outcomes, or achievement standards, across learning areas, capabilities and cross-cultural perspectives (ACARA, 2013a). The renewed clarity and connections across curriculum, pedagogy, assessment and the inspirational outcomes utilises rich complex tasks as a vehicle for children to reach the achievement standards.

Learners generally engage deeply in rich tasks, which integrate new basics areas with their world. Rich tasks are designed to reflect culmination of work over a significant period, and may include a 'culminating performance, or demonstration, or product' (Education Queensland, 2001, p. 5). These tasks reflect learning qualities deemed important in quality teaching frameworks (NSW Department of Education, 2003a).

Often students participate in designing the assessment criteria for such tasks, so they clarify the concepts of the assessment task and the significant processes involved. They draft their responses and manage their time as well as reflect on and analyse their learning, which, as identified by Ewing (2010), suggests aspects of Bloom's taxonomy (1956), De Bono's thinking skills (1970) and Gardner's multiple intelligences (1983; 1993).

WEBBING

Webbing can support educators to plan and record rich tasks, projects and units of work. A web is a tentative diagram that suggests possible directions. It is rather like a giant brainstorm with connections across ideas (*see* Figure 7.11). It can be used for a range of purposes, including planning possibilities and documenting actual investigations and learning, as well evaluating and reflecting on the planning for rich tasks, projects or units of work.

Webs can also be useful in mapping children's current understandings as well as the ideas and questions they would like to investigate. Educators and children can add to a web on a daily basis, thus showing how ideas are developed and connected to each other. At the end of a project, unit or rich task, webs can also be a useful way to document and understand children's learning and reflections – for example, what did we learn? How did we learn this? And how do we think, act and feel differently now? This pedagogy is useful for many approaches to curriculum that negotiate content with the learner in mind, including emergent, multiple intelligences and new basics approaches.

EXAMPLE 7.3
Webbing

The following is progressive documentation about children's learning about mice and was initiated when a parent regularly shared pets and expertise with the children.

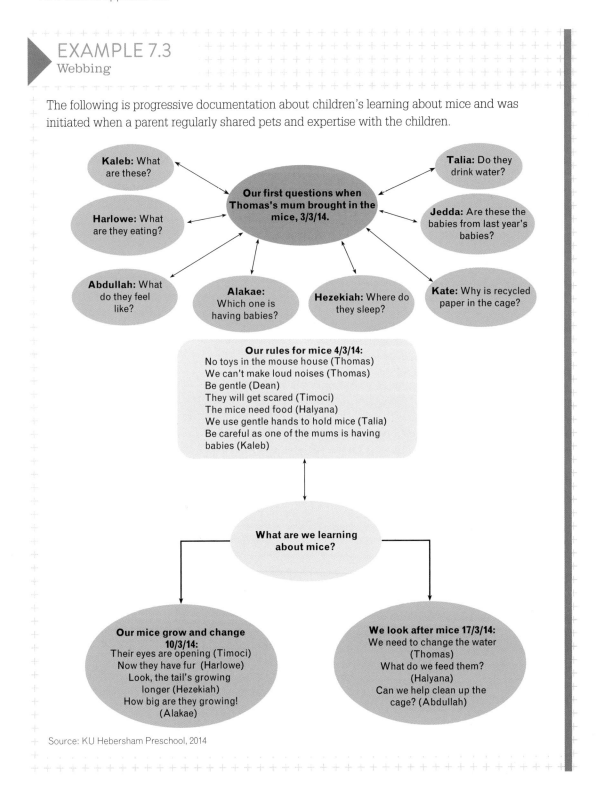

Source: KU Hebersham Preschool, 2014

Learning environments

This section examines the links between approaches to curriculum and pedagogies related to how educators organise learning environments, including space, resources, grouping and time. See Chapter 9 and Chapter 10 for more information on grouping, time, space and resources.

SPACE

When organising space, educators are required to think about environments, the approaches to curriculum and the understandings of learning that they support. Different environments, as well as the different spaces within, can promote different responses, behaviours, interactions and relationships among children, families and educators. When the design of learning environments is more open-ended and flexible, educators provide more possibilities for collaborative small groups, interactions, relationships and learning. Redesigning traditional classrooms with specialised spaces for expression and small group gatherings, and accessible storage space for resources, can open up and connect spaces for democratic communities of learners.

Educators inspired by programs in Reggio Emilia advocate consistency in the environment, with an emphasis on interactions and the use of basic open-ended resources to explore ideas and represent understandings. This means that environments do not need to change every day, but rather basic open-ended resources can be added to and extended in response to children's interests. Pedagogies such as projects demand space in learning environments where children can readily access resources and engage in projects that can be left safely for several days or weeks so that children can return, reflect on and continue to add to their work.

A flexible learning environment, where children flow from one physical space to another and from one experience to another, facilitates children's investigation of open-ended and moveable resources and experiences, reflecting learner-centred, constructivist, new basics and emergent approaches. Predictable and flexible learning environments respond to diverse interests, abilities and rates of learning, promote independent learning and responsibility and support positive social behaviours, (Briggs & Potter, 1999) and therefore support inclusive and multilingual approaches.

RESOURCES

The types of resources used in early childhood settings and schools should reflect the selected approaches to curriculum. Resources vary along a continuum from open-ended to closed, and can be purchased, freely available, home-made, recycled or reused materials (*see* Figure 7.11).

Open-ended, flexible resources support children as competent and capable learners who direct their own learning. Open-ended resources include natural materials such as sand, water and leaves, authentic artefacts and tools such as computers, paints and clay, as well as recyclable materials such as magazines, maps, food packages, fabrics, clothing, plastic jugs and hosing. These types of materials offer many opportunities for children to explore, investigate and problem-solve while constructing and representing their changing understandings. Open-ended resources support many approaches, including child/learner-centred, emergent, community of learners, integrated, inclusive and new basics (*see* Figures 7.12 and 7.13).

Many resources are freely and commercially available such as books, DVDs, computer programs or on the Internet. They may include curriculum documents, books of drills and skills, blackline masters or stencils, workbooks, Internet sites, software and books of novelty craft ideas. National curriculum documents, such as curriculum content, general capabilities, cross-curriculum priorities, scope and sequence charts, achievement standards and so on are open-ended as educators can use them flexibly to respond to the diversity of students in their group. Commercial texts may seem to offer a sense of security in that materials have been used and tested and can save preparation time. However, there may be disadvantages for children's learning since these texts and materials are not responsive to diverse contexts or the circumstances of individual learners and they offer children closed rather than open-

Source: Cringila Public School

FIGURE 7.11 The open-ended resources of the permaculture garden enable children to investigate sustainability and nutrition as they grow vegetables and herbs. Children, educators and an educator/permaculturalist maintain the garden.

ended learning opportunities. These types of resources may be useful as a beginning point and educators can adapt them to take account of different contexts and children. However, where there is little chance for children to build on their funds of knowledge, current learning and few opportunities for active learning, there may also be little chance that deep and sustained learning will occur. Reliance on these types of texts and materials reflects adult/teacher-centred, transmission, exclusive, segregated, fixed or old basics approaches to curriculum, and may signal the need for professional learning and support for educators to move towards more learner-centred approaches.

Constant use of commercial materials often focuses on keeping children busy, rather than extending children's learning. Where educators consistently use commercial products and 'gimmicky' materials – for example, stickers or glitter – they may inadvertently focus on the end product, rather than strengthening children's learning. Activities chosen from a book, or selected to decorate the classroom and perhaps to please parents, may lead to the 'egg carton' curriculum (Stonehouse, 1988) where the resource dominates curriculum decision making and children's learning is overlooked. Usually the products displayed seem identical and fail to reflect children's self-expressions of learning.

Resources reflecting diversity support children's learning about their own and other peoples' lives. The diversity of children's families

Source: Summer Hill Children's Centre

FIGURE 7.12 Open-ended resources support children to examine and problem-solve collaboratively.

Source: Summer Hill Children's Centre

FIGURE 7.13 Everyday culturally relevant artefacts strengthen connections between families, communities and the educational setting. These resources encourage all children to investigate diversity.

and the wider community can feature in classrooms as children's books, DVDs, software, musical instruments, dress-up clothes, food packaging, posters, writing materials, calendars and so on. Inclusion of these culturally relevant resources in the learning environment assists children to connect to their social worlds and examine everyday family practices, including literacies (Beecher, 2010). As well as material resources, human resources, including bilingual educators and community language workers, support children's appreciation of diverse languages, as well as the maintenance of home languages for bilingual children. Culturally responsive human and material resources support many approaches, including child/learner-centred, inclusive, community of learners, multicultural and multilingual, and new basics (*see* Figure 7.14).

Source: Cringila Public School

FIGURE 7.14 Where families and educators collaborate to display cultural resources at the setting, they honour the diversity of the children and families.

How educators integrate diversity into the program can support or detract from children's learning. Where experiences and resources reflect the diversity of the children, families and local community and are integrated meaningfully and consistently into the program, they are likely to extend children's learning. On the other hand, if random and spasmodic experiences and resources are labelled as multicultural and different, the program may appear tokenistic and little happens to support children's learning, their sense of wellbeing and capabilities.

GROUPING CHILDREN

Different sizes and types of groups can be used by educators to implement their approaches to curriculum. The grouping pedagogies selected reflect understandings of children's learning and visions for the future. For example, if educators attach importance to open, sociable children who show empathy and accept and value others different to themselves, they will use a range of groupings including diverse and same languages, developmental levels, ages and interests. These forms of grouping reflect community of learners, child-centred, emergent, inclusive, integrated, multicultural/multilingual and multiple intelligences approaches. Where educators focus on defined experiences, set bodies of understandings at certain stages and understand learning as rote, drill and practice, they are likely to base groups on perceived similarities – for example, age and ability – and to use many whole group experiences. These groupings usually reflect fixed, segregated, individual developmental and adult-centred approaches to curriculum.

Small groups enable children to work collaboratively on shared interests and experiences, to scaffold each others' learning and enhance participation and problem solving, as in Figure 7.15. Where small groups are always based on same-ability or same-developmental stages, the above benefits may not always eventuate.

Small groups are relevant to several approaches, including new basics, child/learner-centred, constructivist, emergent, multiple intelligences, community of learners and integrated. A community of learners approach to curriculum purposefully plans ways of grouping children to promote learning. Because interactions between children often lead to shared experiences, questioning, sustained conversations and collaborative constructions that extend learning, the provision of opportunities for small groups is very important. Where these groups include differing ages, cultures and languages, the dynamics for interaction and relationships bring about learning through lively zones of proximal development, as children challenge and extend each other's learning across different domains or curriculum dimensions. Flexibly using a range of groupings across the program each day enables children to interact with different children at different times, including younger and older children, children with similar and different cultural and language backgrounds, children with differing understandings, strengths and skills or those with similar interests. Same language groups can be an effective way of supporting children's home language maintenance, while mixed language groups can support second language learning. When working with bilingual children it is important to ensure that there is a mixture of same language and different language groupings to support learning in both languages. Using grouping flexibly, rather than restricting the forms of grouping in the program, opens up many learning opportunities.

TIMETABLES/DAILY ROUTINES

The structure of the day will differ depending on the approaches to curriculum. Adult-centred, fixed and segregated approaches encourage the use of a timetable or daily routine that is broken into small periods. Approaches such as emergent, integrated, new basics and child/learner-centred promote longer blocks of time, minimal transitions and flexible routines. Adjustable, overlapping time blocks where learning experiences can be integrated into routines, which form a substantial part of the day, are especially important for very young children (Greenman et al., 2008).

Children need blocks of time of at least 60 minutes to engage in the meaningful investigation and learning advocated by constructivist, emergent, integrated and new basics approaches (Helm & Katz, 2001). Large time blocks mean the need for packing away is minimised so educators can spend more time participating in meaningful interactions with children. Other pedagogies, including integrated units, workshops and projects, help limit the number of transitions as curriculum content is integrated and daily experiences do not stop and start constantly, as when the time is broken into small blocks. In a school context, where time with children as a class is limited by many regular out-of-class

Source: Summer Hill Children's Centre

FIGURE 7.15 Small groups enable children to work collaboratively on shared interests as they scaffold each other's learning.

sessions during the week, including library, physical education, assemblies and shared grade experiences, allocating blocks of time for investigation sessions and integrated units may offer a way to maximise learning opportunities.

Children and families develop a sense of comfort and familiarity with what is likely to happen when they understand the predictable and flexible structure of the day. The HighScope approach to curriculum places a strong emphasis on consistent routines that enable children to predict what will happen next. The daily routine incorporates plan–do–review (HighScope, n.d.), which includes a time for children and educators to discuss and negotiate what they will do in the play-based sessions, extended periods of time in which to engage in play-based experiences and then a group time where children share their experiences.

WORKSHOP SESSIONS

Workshops can be used by school educators to manage learning experiences for many children over large blocks of time. They might start with a brief whole group experience – for example, a demonstration and discussion – then offer a range of small group experiences from which children choose. This pedagogy enables educators to interact closely with small groups and individuals and to observe, teach intentionally and to conference with children. Meanwhile the other children engage independently in small group learning experiences. Towards the end of the session, a sharing time enables children to briefly report on their learning. Approaches to curriculum such as constructivist, child-centred, integrated, multicultural/multilingual, inclusive and new basics can be supported by this pedagogy.

To be effective, workshops require a large block of time; for example, a session from recess until lunch. Workshops use several other pedagogies, such as learning centres and contracts. The establishment of learning centres with children – such as project areas, investigating areas and representation areas – means that children quickly know where to go for experiences and resources.

Most workshop time is allocated to small group experiences. Often, educators design a pool of compulsory and elective experiences from which children choose. Children may then contract to complete the compulsory experiences and a number of elective experiences over a week, or educators may allocate children to different experiences each day. The elective experiences are likely to be ones with which children are familiar and which they can undertake without adult assistance. Additional adults – support teachers and aides or volunteers such as parents, grandparents or community members – may assist during workshops by supporting children in small group experiences. Buddies from different classrooms can also guide small groups on a regular basis. This additional support is very useful in the early years of school.

Workshops can focus on one curriculum content area such as English, or several integrated areas, such as Science, History and English. Variations depend on different combinations of grouping, learning experiences and sharing times. The types of experiences planned within a workshop, the methods of grouping and the teaching strategies used will be different depending on the educator's approaches to curriculum.

The box below is an example of an English workshop for a Year 2 class. The small group experiences planned for the week are all related to the big book that is shared with the children on Monday and revisited during the week. Children go to a different experience each day. Each day the educator works with a different group of children in guided reading, where each child in the group is reading the same book and the educator focuses on scaffolding reading strategies. At the end of the workshop small groups share their experiences with another small group or with the whole class.

LEARNING CENTRES

Learning centres, alternatively called learning areas and resource work stations, present collections of resources for possible learning experiences for extended blocks of time that support children's different learning styles and multiple intelligences. A learning centre can become a regular part of the timetable and the room; for example, workshop sessions with centres for dramatic play, project work or investigating. Resources may include commercially produced, handmade, online or recycled materials. These learning areas can always be available for children to access as required

English/Science workshop for a Stage 2 class

Transition from playground

Science/English quiet time (15 minutes)

Individual and small group

Everyone, including the educator, reads/views/draws/writes. Children choose from resources on animal habitats in dry and wet environments. Resources are from the classroom shelves or children's homes or the school/community libraries (picture books, photograph albums, postcard collections, alphabet books, factual books, digital books/software, brochures, community papers, magazines, shopping catalogues). The area includes a range of texts that appeal to children's interests related to this unit and cater for various literacy levels.

Demonstration (10 minutes)

Whole group

Shared reading – the educator involves children in discussing reading strategies (ACELY 1659) as the whole class has a shared reading of a known big book central to the topic; for example, *Where the forest meets the sea* (Baker, 1987).

Learning experiences (50 minutes concurrent)

Small groups of five children.

1. **Guided reading with educator** with multiple copies of *Two summers* (Heffernan, 2003). Educator documents progress towards English content description.

   a. *Read* supportive texts using developing phrasing, fluency, contextual, semantic, grammatical and phonic knowledge and emerging text processing strategies; for example, prediction, monitoring meaning and rereading (ACELY1659). See http://www.australiancurriculum.edu.au > Foundation to Year 10 Curriculum > 2.

   b. *Investigation centre* – computer software and Internet sites related to environments and habits for animals and people. Children draw and write about main ideas and any further questions in their learning journals.

   c. *Factual books on lizards and their habitats* – children read in pairs, decide on significant needs of lizards for their habitats related to people's actions and record ideas and diagrams for sharing and any further questions in their learning journals.

   d. *DVD on Aboriginal animals in local region* – view and record significant needs of animals related to people's actions and any further questions in their learning journals. Investigation of local Aboriginal language for these animals.

   e. *Learning centre with backyard/balcony/park animals* – worm farm, insect collection and lizard, factual books, brochures and local council information on keeping animals and worm farms. Children draw and write their observations of the activities and needs of these animals and any further questions in their learning journals.

   f. *Construction* – children use junk materials to construct an animal and its habitat selected from the local area, using the resources of posters, diagrams, books and models, sketch their work and write in their learning journals.

> ### Sharing time (10 minutes)
>
> Small groups share their learning with another small group or with the whole class. Children share some of their further questions, which are added to the webbing on the noticeboard.
>
> **Transition to recess**

or unpacked daily from materials stored in a box. In some cases, learning centres are available only at certain times, such as the investigating session at the beginning of each day or when children have finished set experiences (e.g. in an early years of school classroom). In early childhood settings they may be accessible to children at all times. Where learning centres are permanently set up, educators and children frequently change or extend resources, based on children's responses, questions and interests.

Learning centres can focus on a singular curriculum content area, such as music or science. The science centre might focus on mechanics and construction, and include old computers and clocks for children to pull apart, as well as construction materials such as blocks and Lego. Learning centres may also be set up based on multiple intelligences (Chen et al., 1998), such as a dramatic play area to support interpersonal and intrapersonal intelligences and a visual arts centre to support spatial intelligence. A movement learning centre with music, scarves and handbells could support bodily-kinaesthetic intelligence, and a music learning centre with percussion instruments, sound-making materials and a sound system could support musical intelligence.

Learning areas can be based on children's interests and productively integrate curriculum content areas. For example, a learning centre could be organised around children's interest in sharks and include books, posters, Internet sites, iPads with relevant apps and plastic sea creatures as well as musical instruments and drawing and writing materials.

Generally, a number of learning centres are set up in a classroom, allowing for several small group experiences. Children may choose to go to different learning centres, be directed to a particular centre by an educator or, in a school classroom, enter into a contract or learning agreement to complete experiences at a certain number of learning centres in a set time (see Figures 7.16 and 7.17).

In schools, learning centres or resource work stations often incorporate a play-based or hands-on approach to curriculum within integrated or segregated approaches. For example, they provide experiences that enhance children's learning in learning areas of English and Maths, as well as their general capabilities of literacy and numeracy. A dramatic play post office learning centre can promote children's purposeful writing, understanding of money and awareness of community experiences. Learning centres can also support other pedagogies; for example, projects and integrated units, as well as mixed ability, culture and language groups. A number of different experiences can be organised in learning centres that are all related to the children's current learning.

Contracts, learning agreement boards or menu boards are often used alongside learning centres and involve children moving their name to their selected experience from the available options. Contracts allow for child choice while ensuring that children experience a range of learning centres or learning experiences. Contracts or learning agreements are often used in a school setting where educators may plan a number of small group or individual experiences from which children choose. Children then decide on a contract with the educator to complete certain experiences within a fixed time period. Variations on this type of pedagogy are often useful for children with additional needs. These can include pictorial representations of available experiences of parts of the daily program. In this way, children can initiate and direct their learning while the educator focuses on intentional teaching with small groups.

PRODUCTIVE PEDAGOGIES

New basics promotes the use of 'productive pedagogies', where the emphasis rests on educators constructing curriculum so active learners engage in problem solving and social action. Educators

Source: Werrington TAFE Children's Centre

FIGURE 7.16 This learning centre supports children to actively learn as they examine plants and how they grow.

are encouraged to use a range of pedagogies, including structured pedagogies when appropriate, to enhance children's learning (Education Queensland, 2001). This is seen as particularly important for 'at-risk learners' such as those from culturally, linguistically and socially diverse backgrounds.

Initially identified by a group of educators (Lingard et al., 1998), productive pedagogies is a set of complex ideas about teaching and learning characterising the new basics approach to curriculum in Queensland (Education Queensland, 1999). These pedagogies involve many learning and teaching decisions that enable educators to work productively with all groups of children, especially reflecting their family and community contexts. Teaching focuses on supporting children to actively construct understandings and engage in higher order thinking and actions as they engage with real world contexts, knowledge and problems. These pedagogies reflect various approaches to curriculum, including community of learners, emergent, children/learner-centred, inclusive, multiple intelligences, multicultural and multilingual as well as new basics.

Four themes feature in productive pedagogies, including the intellectual quality of the learning experiences, connectedness between learners and the learning, supportive learning environment and recognition of diversity (Education Queensland, 2004). Despite no longer being policy in Queensland, these initiatives promoted developments elsewhere in Australia. The productive pedagogies supported features of learning, as further expanded in the following with significant aspects italicised.

- *Intellectual quality* – in a world where knowledge is constantly changing, intellectual quality ensures that learners have opportunities to use information and ideas in ways that transform meanings. It encourages *higher order thinking* and *deep knowledge* where learners

Source: Our Lady of Lourdes Catholic School, Seven Hills

FIGURE 7.17 Predictable but flexible menu board and weekly programs assist children to develop a sense of security and competence with what they are doing. They can make choices and plan their learning.

are involved with key concepts and *substantial understandings*. *Problematic knowledge* fosters critical thinking where learners are encouraged to read critically and to question taken-for-granted world views and discourses. *Metalanguage* provides educators and learners with a language for talking about language use in classrooms.

- *Connectedness* – in a connected classroom learners are actively engaged in *meaningful problem-solving* that *connects to children's background knowledge and everyday life*, that *integrates curriculum areas* and that connects to the learners' prior knowledge. Engagement and *connectedness to real-world experiences* are essential for effective learning.
- *Supportive classroom environment* – a supportive classroom environment encourages *student control* and *engagement* and ensures that learners are aware of the educator's expectations through *explicit criteria*. High expectations and respect provide *social support* which encourages learners to take risks and to *self-regulate* their own learning.
- *Recognition of difference* – recognition of difference encourages *inclusion* and respect for *cultural knowledge*. All cultures, languages, beliefs, practices and ways of knowing are valued in the classroom. Appreciation of difference creates positive relationships and helps to develop a sense of community through recognising and working with children's *narratives*, *group identity* and development of *citizenship*.

Similarly, the New South Wales Model of Pedagogy (NSW DET, 2003b) promotes related principles and aims to strengthen educators' classroom practices for all learners from kindergarten to Year 12. This model articulates three dimensions of pedagogy including intellectual quality, quality learning environments and significance of learning for students. These dimensions include the following elements:

- Intellectual quality:
  - deep knowledge
  - deep understanding
  - problematic knowledge
  - higher order thinking
  - metalanguage
  - substantive communication.
- Quality learning environment:
  - explicit quality criteria
  - engagement
  - high expectations
  - social support
  - student self-regulation
  - student direction.
- Significance:
  - background knowledge
  - cultural knowledge
  - knowledge integration

- inclusivity
- connectedness
- narrative.

Similarly, the *Fair Go Project*, conducted by researchers from the University of Western Sydney in collaboration with teachers in schools in low socio-economic (SES) areas in New South Wales, highlights the importance of relevant learning experiences of high intellectual quality in raising the educational outcomes for learners from low SES communities (NSW Department of Education and Training, 2006; Munns et al., 2011).

When productive pedagogies are combined with inspirational or transitional outcomes, children are likely to engage in challenging and compelling investigations and learning experiences.

Strengthening philosophy in practice

There is a range of approaches and pedagogies from which educators can select. What is important is that the pedagogies selected are consistent with the setting/school's philosophy and chosen approaches to curriculum. Educators benefit from clarifying their philosophy and underlying theoretical perspectives, beliefs and values before deciding their approaches to curriculum and associated pedagogies. Whatever the setting, ongoing evaluation and critical reflection is essential to strengthen how the philosophy is translated into practice.

Conclusion and reflection

This chapter outlined the phase in the planning process concerning selecting curriculum approaches and pedagogies that implement the philosophy. This begins with identifying the embedded theoretical perspectives, beliefs and values in the setting/school philosophy prior to selecting a cluster of approaches that guide the selection of pedagogies.

A number of curriculum approaches were discussed in relation to their foci. Their directions were considered in terms of their potentials and challenges in promoting children's learning. This was followed by an examination of some pedagogies that would enable educators to implement these approaches. Understanding the nature of continuity, approaches and pedagogies assists educators to refine their philosophy to practice connections. As with all change, educators benefit from evaluating their current philosophy and practice for strengths and areas for improvement prior to initiating any change.

Questions for reflection

1. Which values, beliefs and understandings of the world, learning and teaching are embedded in the philosophy for a setting or school that you know? Which theoretical perspectives are suggested in the philosophy? How well do these explain how children, families and educators that you know live and learn?

2. What are the main curriculum approaches in a setting/school that you are familiar with? How well do these support the philosophy? Which additional curriculum approach/es could shift practice closer to the philosophy? Which additional relevant pedagogies could be useful to strengthen children's learning?

3. Reflecting on a session, identify the approaches you observed or used. How well did this cluster of approaches and aligned pedagogies extend all children's learning? How might you adjust across the continuums of approaches? How might the pedagogies be refined?

Key terms

adult-centred approach, 215
child-centred approach, 215
community of learners approach, 219
conforming approach, 231
constructivist approach, 222
curriculum, 208
curriculum approaches, 208
disadvantage, 228
emergent curriculum, 220
exclusive approach, 229
inclusive approach, 228
individualistic developmental approach, 219
integrated approach, 215

monocultural and monolingual approach, 230
multicultural and multilingual approach, 229
multiple intelligences approach, 231
new basics approach, 227
old basics approach, 229
pedagogies, 209
predetermined approach, 221
reforming approach, 231
segregated approach, 217
single or restricted intelligences approach, 232
thematic approach, 217
transforming or transformative approach, 230
transmission approach, 222

Online study resources

Visit http://login.cengagebrain.com and use the access code that comes with this book for 12 months access to the student resources for this text.

CourseMate Express

The CourseMate Express website contains a range of resources and study tools for this chapter, including:

- Online video activities
- Online research activities
- A revision quiz
- Matching pair exercises
- A list of key weblinks
- A chapter glossary, flashcards and crossword to help you revise terminology
- and more!

Search me! education

Explore **Search me! education** for articles relevant to this chapter. Fast and convenient, Search me! education is updated daily and provides you with 24-hour access to full text articles from hundreds of scholarly and popular journals, ebooks and newspapers, including *The Australian* and *The New York Times*. Log in to Search me! through http://login.cengage.com and try searching for the following key words:

- educational philosophy
- theoretical perspectives
- curriculum
- curriculum approach
- pedagogy
- play-based learning
- active learning
- intentional teaching

- relationships
- inquiry learning
- constructivist learning
- transformational curriculum.

Search tip: **Search me! education** contains information from both local and international sources. To get the greatest number of search results, try using both Australian and American spellings in your searches, e.g. 'globalisation' and 'globalization'; 'organisation' and 'organization'

Recommended resources

Arthur, L, Ashton, J & Beecher, B (eds) 2014, *Diverse Literacies in Early Childhood: A Social Justice Approach*, Australian Council for Educational Research, Melbourne.
Ewing, R 2010, *Curriculum and Assessment: A Narrative Approach*, Oxford University Press, South Melbourne.
McLachlan, C, Fleer, M & Edwards, S 2010, *Early Childhood Curriculum. Planning; Assessment and Implementation.* Cambridge University Press, New York.
Mac Naughton, G & Williams, G 2009, *Techniques for Teaching Young Children: Choices for Theory and Practice*, 3rd edn., Pearson Education Australia, Frenchs Forest.
Wilson, J & Wing Jan, L 2009, *Focus on Inquiry: A Practical Approach to Integrated Curriculum Planning*, 2nd edn., Curriculum Corporation, Carlton South.

Key weblinks

Early Childhood Research and Practice (ECRP), http://ecrp.uiuc.edu
Ministry of Education New Zealand, Te Kete Ipurangi, http://www.tki.org.nz/
Australian Curriculum, http://www.australiancurriculum.edu.au
Australian Curriculum Assessment and Reporting Authority (ACARA), http://www.acara.edu.au
The Australian Curriculum, http://www.australiancurriculum.edu.au
South Australian Learning to Learn project, http://www.learningtolearn.sa.edu.au
The Institute for Habits of Mind, http://www.habits-of-mind.net
The Project Approach, http://www.projectapproach.org

References

ABS, *see* Australian Bureau of Statistics
ACARA, *see* Australian Curriculum, Assessment and Reporting Authority.
Alvestad, M & Duncan, J 2006, 'The value is enormous – It's priceless I think: New Zealand preschool teachers' understandings of the early childhood curriculum in New Zealand – a comparative perspective', *International Journal of Education*, vol. 38, no. 1, pp. 31–45.
Arthur, L 2001, 'Young children as critical consumers', *Australian Journal of Language and Literacy*, vol. 24, no. 3, pp. 182–94.
Arthur, L 2010, *The Early Years Learning Framework: Building Confident Learners*, Australian Early Childhood Association, Watson, ACT.
Australian Bureau of Statistics (ABS) 2010, *Year Book Australia 2009–2010*, http://www.abs.gov.au/AUSSTATS/abs@.nsf/Latestproducts/1301.0Feature%20Article7012009%E2%80%9310?opendocument&tabname=Summary&prodno=1301.0&issue=2009%E2%80%9310&num=&view=,accessed 12 September 2011.
Australian Bureau of Statistics (ABS) 2011, *Community Census Profile*, http://www.censusdata.abs.gov.au/census_services/getproduct/census/2011/communityprofi le/0?opendocument&navpos=230, accessed 29 June 2012.
Australian Curriculum Assessment and Reporting Authority 2013a, *The Shape of the Australian Curriculum October 2012*, ACARA, Sydney.
Australian Curriculum Assessment and Reporting Authority 2013b, *Student Diversity and the Australian Curriculum: Advice for Principals, Schools and Teachers*, ACARA, Sydney,
Australian Curriculum Assessment and Reporting Authority 2013c, *General Capabilities in the Australian Curriculum*, ACARA, Sydney.
Baker, J 1987, *Where the Forest Meets the Sea*, MacRae, Sydney.
Beecher, B 2010, 'No I won't marry you! Critiquing gender in multiliteracies fairytale play', *Canadian Children*, vol. 35, no. 2, Fall, pp. 15–24.
Beecher, B & Jones Diaz, C 2014, 'Extending children's literacies through partnerships', in L Arthur, J Ashton & B Beecher (eds.), *Diverse Literacies in Early Childhood: A Social Justice Approach* (pp.41–64), Australian Council for Educational Research, Melbourne.
Berstein, B 2006, *Pedagogy, Symbolic Control and Identity: Theory, Research and Critique*, Taylor & Francis, London.
Bloom, BS (ed.) 1956, *Taxonomy of Educational Objectives Handbook 1*, Longman, Green & Co, New York.
Brady, L & Kennedy, K 2010, *Curriculum Construction*, 4th edn., Pearson Australia, Frenchs Forest, NSW.
Bredekamp, S 1987, *Developmentally Appropriate Practice in Early Childhood Programs Serving Children from Birth through Age 8*, National Association for the Education of Young Children, Washington, DC.
Bredekamp, S & Copple, C 1997, *Developmentally Appropriate Practice in Early Childhood Programs Serving Children from Birth through Age 8*, National Association for the Education of Young Children, Washington, DC.
Briggs, F & Potter, G 1999, *The Early Years of School: Teaching and Learning*, 2nd edn., Longman, Melbourne.
Brock, A 2009, 'Curriculum and pedagogy of play: A multitude of perspectives', in A Brock, S Dodds, P Jarvis & Y Olusoga (eds), *Perspectives on Play: Learning for Life* (pp. 67–93), Pearson Australia, Harlow.

Bruce, T & Ockleford, A 2010, 'Understanding symbolic development', in T Bruce (ed.), *Early Childhood: A Guide for Students* (pp. 105–18), 2nd edn., Sage Publications, London.

Carr, M 2001, *Assessment in Early Childhood: Learning Stories*, Paul Chapman, London.

Chard, S 1998/1999/2000/2001, *Project Approach in Early Childhood and Elementary Education*, http://www.project-approach.com/definition.htm, accessed 25 March 2004.

Chen, J, Krechevsky, M & Viens, J with Isberg, E 1998/2000, *Building on Children's Strengths: The Experience of Project Spectrum*, Teachers College Press, New York.

Cologon, M & McNaught, M 2014, 'Early intervention for literacy learning', in L Arthur, J Ashton & B Beecher (eds.) 2014, *Diverse Literacies in Early Childhood: A Social Justice Approach* (pp. 146–65), Australian Council of Educational Research, Melbourne.

Connell, R, White, V & Johnson, K 1992, *Measuring Up: Assessment, Evaluation and Educational Disadvantage*, Australian Curriculum Studies Association, Belconnen, ACT.

Connor, J 2008, *Learnings from HighScope: Enriching Everyday Practice*, Australian Early Childhood Association, Watson, ACT.

Copple, C & Bredekamp, S 2009, *Developmentally Appropriate Practice in Early Childhood Programs Serving Children from Birth through Age 8*, National Association for the Education of Young Children, Washington, DC.

Corson, D 1998, *Changing Education for Diversity*, Open University Press, Buckingham.

Costa, A & Kallick, B 2000a, *Habits of Mind: A Developmental Series*, Association for Supervision and Curriculum Development, Alexandria, VA.

Costa, A & Kallick, B 2000b, 'Describing 16 habits of mind', http://www.habits-of-mind.net/, accessed 13 February 2007.

Costa, A & Kallick, B (eds) 2009, *Habits of Mind Across the Curriculum: Practical and Creative Strategies for Teachers*, Association for Supervision and Curriculum Development, Alexandria, VA.

Creaser, B & Dau, E (eds) 1995, *The Anti-bias Approach in Early Childhood*, Harper Educational, Sydney.

Dahlberg, G, Moss, P & Pence, A 2007, *Beyond Quality in Early Childhood Education and Care: Postmodern Perspectives*, 2nd edn., Routledge, London.

Dau, E (ed.) 2001, *The Anti-bias Approach in Early Childhood*, Pearson, Sydney.

De Bono, E 1970, *Thinking Laterally*, Harper Row, New York.

DEEWR, *see* Department of Education, Employment and Workplace Relations.

Department of Education, Employment and Workplace Relations 2009a, *Belonging, Being and Becoming: The Early Years Learning Framework for Australia*, Australian Government Department of Education, Employment and Workplace Relations, Canberra.

Department of Education, Employment and Workplace Relations 2009b, *National Quality Framework for Early Childhood Education and Care*, http://www.deewr.gov.au/earlychildhood/policy_agenda/quality/pages/home.aspx, accessed 12 September 2011.

Delpit, L 1995, *Other People's Children: Cultural Conflict in the Classroom*, The New Press, New York.

Derman-Sparks, L & The Anti-bias Taskforce 1989, *The Anti-bias Curriculum: Tools for Empowering Young Children*, National Association for the Education of Young Children, Washington, DC.

Dewey, J 1902, *The Child and the Curriculum and the School and Society*, University of Chicago Press, Chicago.

Dewey, J 1916, *Democracy and Education*, Macmillan Company, New York.

Dewey, J 1938/1963, *Experience and Education*, Collier, New York.

Dewey, J 1958, *Experience and Education*, Macmillan Company, New York.

Dodds, A 2009, *The Shape of Things*, Candlewick Press, Cambridge.

Doherty, J, Brock, A, Brock, J & Jarvis, P 2009, 'Born to play: Babies and toddlers playing', in A Brock, S Dodds, P Jarvis & Y Olusoga (eds), *Perspectives on Play: Learning for Life* (pp. 94–119), Pearson Education, Harlow.

Education Queensland 1999/2010, *Queensland State Education: A Future Strategy*, Education Queensland, Brisbane.

Education Queensland 2001, *New Basics: The What, Why, When and How of Rich Tasks*, Education Queensland, Brisbane.

Education Queensland 2004, *New Basics Project*, http://education.qld.gov.au/corporate/newbasics/html/, accessed 24 March 2004.

Education Queensland, *Queensland School Reform Longitudinal Study*, Productive Pedagogies Characteristics, http://education.qld.gov.au/public_media/reports/curriculum-framework/qsrls/html/abt_ppc.html, accessed 13 February 2007.

Edwards, C, Gandini, L & Foreman, G (eds) 1998, *The Hundred Languages of Children*, 2nd edn., Ablex, Norwood, NJ.

Edwards, C, Gandini, L & Foreman, G 1998, 'Introduction', in C Edwards, L Gandini & G Forman (eds), *The Hundred Languages of Children*, 2nd edn., Ablex, Norwood, NJ.

Feldman, D 1980/1994, *Beyond Universals in Cognitive Development*, Ablex, Norwood, NJ.

Feldman, D 1998, 'How Spectrum began', in J Chen, M Krechevsky & J Viens (eds), *Building on Children's Strengths: The Experiences of Project Spectrum*, Teachers College Press, New York.

Fleer, M 1995, 'Does cognition lead development, or does development lead cognition?', in M Fleer (ed.), *DAPCentrism: Challenging Developmentally Appropriate Practice*, Australian Early Childhood Association, Canberra.

Fogarty, R & Stoehr, J 2008, (eds), *Integrating Curricula with Multiple Intelligences*, 2nd edn., Skylight Professional Development, Arlington Heights.

Freire, P 1972, *Pedagogy of the Oppressed*, Penguin Books, Harmondsworth, Middlesex.

Freire, P 1985, *The Politics of Education, Culture, Power and Liberation*, Macmillan, Basingstoke.

Gardner, H 1983/1993a, *Frames of Mind: The Theory of Multiple Intelligences*, Basic Books, New York.

Gardner, H 1993b, *Multiple Intelligences: The Theory in Practice*, Basic Books, New York.

Gardner, H 1998a, 'Foreword: Complementary perspectives', in C Edwards, L Gandini & G Forman (eds.), *The Hundred Languages of Children*, 2nd edn., Ablex, Norwood, NJ.

Gardner, H 1998b, 'Are there additional intelligences?', in J Kane (ed.), *Education, Information and Transformation*, Prentice Hall, Englewood Cliffs, NJ.

Gardner, H 2003, 'Multiple intelligences after twenty years', paper presented at the American Educational Research Association, Illinois, 21 April 2003, http://www.pz.harvard.edu/Pls/HG, accessed 24 March 2004.

Genishi, C (ed) 1992, *Ways of Assessing Children and Curriculum: Stories of Early Childhood Practice*, Teachers College Press, New York.

Giroux, H 1990, *Curriculum Discourse as Postmodern Practice*, Deakin University, Melbourne.

Goleman, D 1995, *Emotional Intelligence: Why it Matters more than IQ*, Bloomsbury, London.

Greenman, J, Stonehouse, A & Schweikert, G 2008, *Prime Times: A Handbook for Excellence in Infant and Toddler Programs*, 2nd edn., Readleaf Press, St Paul, MN.

Hamston, J & Murdoch, K 1996/2004, *Integrating Socially: Planning Integrated Units of Work for Social Education*, Eleanor Curtain, Melbourne.

Harrison, C 2000, 'Out of the mouths of babes', *Advanced Development Journal*, vol. 2, pp. 31–43.

Hatherly, A 2006, 'The stories we share: Using narrative assessment to build communities of practice of literacy participants in early childhood settings', *Australian Journal of Early Childhood*, vol. 31, no. 1, pp. 27–34.

Healy, A 2004, 'The critical heart of multiliteracies: Four resources, multimodal texts and classroom practice', in A Healy & E Honan (eds.), *Text next* (pp. 19–35), Primary English Teaching Association, Newtown, NSW.

Heffernan, J & Blackwood, F 2003, *Two Summers*, Scholastic Press, Linfield.

Helm, J & Katz, L, 2011, *Young Investigators: The Project Approach in the Early Years*, 2nd edn., Teachers College Press, New York.

Henderson, R 2005, *The Social and Discursive Construction of Itinerant Farm Workers Children as Literacy Learners*, unpublished doctoral manuscript, James Cook University, Townville.

Henniger, ML 2002, *Teaching Young Children*, 2nd edn., Merrill/ Prentice Hall, Upper Saddle River, NJ.

HighScope (n.d.), *HighScope Curriculum for Preschool, Infants, Toddlers and Early Elementary*, http://www.highscope.org, accessed 23 May 2011.

Hohmann, M & Wekart, D 1995, *Educating Young Children: Active Learning Activities in Preschool and Child Care Programs*, High Scope Press, Ypsilanti, MI.

Jones Diaz, C 2007, 'Literacy as social practice', in L Makin, C Jones Diaz, & C McLachlan (eds.), *Literacies in Early Childhood: Changing Views, Challenging Practices* (pp. 31–42), Elsevier Australia, Sydney.

Jones Diaz, C, Beecher, B, Arthur, L, Ashton, J, Hayden, J, McNaught, M & Clugston, L 2001, *Literacies, Communities and Under 5s*, NSW Department of Education and NSW Department of Community Services, Sydney.

Jones Diaz, C & Harvey, N 2007, 'Other words, other worlds: bilingual identities and literacy', in L Makin, C Jones Diaz & C McLachlan (eds.), *Literacies in Early Childhood: Changing Views, Challenging Practices* (pp. 203–16), Elsevier Australia, Sydney.

Jones, E, Evans, K & Renken, KS 2001, *The Lively Kindergarten: Emergent Curriculum in Action*, National Association for the Education of Young Children, Washington, DC.

Jones, E & Nimmo, J 1994, *Emergent Curriculum*, National Association for the Education of Young Children, Washington, DC.

Julovich, B & Heyob, T 1998, 'Emergent curriculum', in E Tertell, S Klein & J Jewett (eds.), *When Teachers Reflect: Journeys Towards Effective, Inclusive Practice*, National Association for the Education of Young Children, Washington, DC.

Kalantzis, M & Cope, B 2008, *New Learning*, Cambridge University Press, Port Melbourne.

Katz, L 1994, *The Project Approach*, ERIC Clearinghouse on Elementary and Early Childhood Education, Champaign, IL.

Katz, L 1998, 'What can we learn from Reggio Emilia', in C Edwards, L Gandini & G Forman (eds.), *The Hundred Languages of Children*, 2nd edn., Ablex Norwood, NJ.

Katz, L & Chard, S 1989/2000, *Engaging Children's Minds: The Project Approach*, Ablex, Stamford, CT.

Kenner, C 2003, 'Literacy benefits', *Literacy Today*, December.

Koplow, L (ed.) 1996, *Unsmiling Faces: How Preschools can Heal*, Teachers College Press, New York.

Kostelnik, M, Soderman, A & Whiren, A 2007, *Developmentally Appropriate Curriculum: Best Practices in Early Childhood Education*, 4th edn., Pearson Education, Upper Saddle River, NJ.

Lave, J & Wenger, W 1991, *Situated Learning: Legitimate Peripheral Participation*, University of Cambridge Press, Cambridge.

Lingard, B, Ladwig, J, Mills, M, Bahr, M, Chant, D, Warry, M, Ailwood, J, Capeness, R, Christie, P, Gore, J, Hayes, D, & Luke, A 2001, *Queensland School Reform Longitudinal Study: Final Report*, vol. 1, report prepared for Education Queensland by the School of Education, The University of Queensland, Brisbane.

Luke, A 2008, 'Curriculum in context', in M Connelly, M He Fang & J Phillion (eds.), *Sage Handbook on Curriculum and Instruction*, Sage, Thousand Oaks.

Mac Naughton, G 1999, 'Even pink tents have glass ceilings: Cross the gender boundaries in pretend play', in E Dau (ed.), *Childs' Play: Revisiting Play in Early Childhood Settings* (pp. 81–96), Maclennan and Petty, Sydney.

Mac Naughton, G 2003, *Shaping Early Childhood: Learners, Curriculum and Contexts*, Open University Press, Maidenhead, Berkshire.

Mac Naughton, G & Williams, G 2009, *Techniques for Teaching Young Children: Choices for Theory and Practice*, 3rd edn., Longman, Melbourne.

Malaguzzi, L 1998, 'History, ideas and basic philosophy', in C Edwards, L Gandini & G Forman (eds.), *The Hundred Languages of Children*, 2nd edn., Ablex, Norwood, NJ.

Marsh, J & Millard, E 2000, *Literacy and Popular Culture: Using Children's Culture in The Classroom*, Paul Chapman Publishing Limited, London.

Mayer, JD & contributors 2007, *Emotional intelligence information*, http://www.unh.edu/emotional_intelligence/ei%20Site/ei%20site%20 2005%20home%20page.htm, accessed 13 February 2007.

McLachlan, R, Gilfillan, G & Gordon, J 2013, *Deep and Persistent Disadvantage in Australia*, rev., Productivity Commission Staff Working Paper, Commonwealth of Australia, Canberra.

Ministerial Council for Education, Early Childhood Development and Youth Affairs 2009, *MCEECDYA Four Year plan*, http://www.mceecdya. edu.au/mceecdya/action_plan,25966.html, accessed 17 February 2014.

Moll, L, Amanti, C, Neff, D & Gonzalez, N 1992, 'Funds of knowledge for teaching: Using a qualitative approach to connect homes and classrooms', *Theory into Practice*, vol. 31, no. 2, pp. 132–41.

Moll, L & Arnot-Hopffer, E 2005, 'Sociocultural competence in teacher education', *Journal of Teacher Education*, vol. 56, no. 3, pp. 242–7.

Munns, G, Arthur, L, Hertzberg, M, Sawyer, W & Zammit, K 2011, 'A fair go for students in poverty', in T Wrigley, P Thomson & R Lingard (eds.), *Changing Schools: Alternative Ways to Make a World of Difference*, Routledge, London.

Murdoch, K & Hornsby, D 1998, *Planning Curriculum Connections: Whole School Planning for Integrated Curriculum*, Eleanor Curtain, Melbourne.

Murdoch, K & Wilson, J 2008, *Helping Your Pupils to Work Co-operatively*, Taylor and Francis, London.

National Association for the Education of Young Children (NAEYC) 2009, 'Developmentally appropriate practice in early childhood programs serving children from birth to age 8', http://www.naeyc.org/positionstatements/dap, accessed 23 May 2011.

New South Wales Department of Community Services (DoCS) 2002, *New South Wales Curriculum Framework for Children's Services: The Practice of Relationships, Essential Provisions for Children's Services*, NSW Department of Community Services, Sydney.

New South Wales Department of Education and Training (DET) 2003a, *Quality Teaching*, NSW Department of Education and Training, Sydney.

New South Wales Department of Education and Training (DET) 2003b, *Quality Teaching in NSW Public Schools: A Classroom Practice Guide*, NSW Department of Education and Training, Sydney.

New Zealand Ministry of Education 1996, *Te Whāriki*, Learning Media, Wellington.

NSW DET, *see* New South Wales Department of Education and Training

NSW DoCS, *see* New South Wales Department of Community Services

Nuttall, J & Edwards, S 2007, 'Theory, policy and practice: Three contexts for the development of Australasia's early childhood curriculum documents', in L Keesing-Styles & H Hedges (eds.), *Theorising Early Childhood Practice: Emerging Dialogue* (pp. 3–26), Pademelon Press, Castle Hill.

Organisation for Economic Co-operation and Development (OECD), *Program for International Student Assessment (PISA) results*, http://www.oecd.org/document/61/0,3343,en_2649_35845621_46567613_1_1_1_1,00.html, accessed 10 June 2011.

Piaget, J 1963, *The Origins of Intelligence in Children*, WW Norton, New York.

Piaget, J & Inhelder, B 1969, *The Psychology of the Child*, Basic Books, New York.

Reid, J, Farmer, S & Mawson, M 2010, *Journeys of Inclusion*, Lifeline Communitycare Queensland and UnitingCare Queensland.

Roberts, M 2006, 'Spirituality with a broad brush', *Every Child*, vol. 12, no. 4, http://www.earlychildhoodaustralia.org.au/every_child_magazine/every_child_index/spirituality_with_a_broad_brush.html, accessed 13 February 2007.

Robinson, K & Jones Diaz, C 2006, *Diversity and Difference in Early Childhood Education: Issues for Theory and Practice*, Oxford University Press, Maidenhead.

Schwartz, SL & Copeland, SM 2010, *Connecting Emergent Curriculum and Standards in the Early Childhood Classroom*, Teachers College Press, New York.

Singh, MG 2002, *The Sustainability of the Earth's People and their Cultures: Risks and Opportunities: The Multilingual Knowledge Economy*, paper presented to RMIT, 12 September.

Siraj-Blatchford, I & Clarke, P 2000, *Supporting Identity, Diversity and Language in the Early Years*, Open University Press, Buckingham.

Siraj-Blatchford, I, Sylva, K, Muttock, K, Gilden, R, Bell, D 2002, *Researching Effective Pedagogy in the Early Years*, The Queens Printer, Norwich.

Stonehouse, A 1988, *Trusting Toddlers*, Australian Early Childhood Association, Canberra.

Stonehouse, A & Gonzalez-Mena, J 2007, *Making Links: A Collaborative Approach to Planning and Practice in Early Childhood Services*, 2nd edn., Pademelon Press, Sydney.

Studans, L 2003, 'Developing learning communities in the first years of school', *PEN 139*, Primary English Teaching Association, Newtown.

Thompson, P 2002, *Schooling the Rustbelt Kids: Making the Difference in Changing Times*, Allen & Unwin, Sydney.

Vickers, M 2007, 'Youth transition', in R Connell, C Campbell, M Vickers, A Welch, D Foley & N Bagnall, *Education, Change and Society* (pp. 51–69), Oxford University Press, South Melbourne.

Vygotsky, L 1978, *Mind in Society*, Prentice Hall, Cambridge, MA, NJ.

Watt, M 2006, 'Looking at curriculum change in Tasmania: Will essential learnings promote successful reform?', *Curriculum Leadership*, vol. 4, no. 3.

Wilson, J & Wing Jan, L 2008, *Focusing on a Practical Approach to Curriculum Planning*, Curriculum Corporation, Carlton South.

CHAPTER EIGHT

ASSESSING AND PLANNING FOR CHILDREN'S LEARNING

Chapter learning focus

This chapter will investigate:

- purposes of assessment

- shared understandings about assessment

- contemporary perspectives on assessment

- processes of documenting children's learning

- analysing documentation

- methods of documentation and analysis

- collating information from multiple sources

- linking documentation and analysis to planning

- documenting experiences, investigations and projects.

Introduction

Assessment is a key component of the curriculum planning process. It involves gathering information about children (documenting learning), reflecting on what this information means and then using it to plan for future learning. In the Reggio Emilia centres and schools, as well as many Scandinavian settings and more recently in Australia, the term 'pedagogical documentation' is used to highlight the importance of reflection and analysis and the links to future planning for learning. In this chapter the term 'assessment' is used in this sense.

This chapter includes an overview of contemporary approaches to assessment, which reflect sociocultural and critical theories. This includes contemporary methods of documentation, such as Learning Stories, and analysis that draws on sociocultural and critical approaches as well as theories of development. There is a strong focus on collaborative approaches to assessment that involve children and families as well as educators in documenting, analysing and reflecting on learning and planning for future learning.

Assessment

Involves gathering information, reflecting on its meaning and using this analysis to inform future planning.

Purposes of assessment

The Early Years Learning Framework (EYLF) (DEEWR, 2009) includes three purposes for assessment: assessment *for* learning, assessment *of* learning and assessment *as* learning. Assessment for learning is one of the framework's pedagogical principles. Assessment for learning involves a cyclical process of documenting and analysing information about children and using this information to make decisions about future planning so that the types of experiences educators plan and the way that they interact with children in these experiences supports and extends children's learning.

Assessment *for* learning is formative.

> [It] refers to the process of gathering and analysing information as evidence about what children know, can do and understand. It is part of an ongoing cycle that includes planning, documenting and evaluating children's learning.
>
> DEEWR, 2009, p. 17

Assessment for learning enables educators to make informed decisions that result in a clear purpose for learning and **intentional teaching** (DEEWR, 2009).

Assessment *of* learning typically occurs at the end of a set period of time, such as the end of term or at the end of a project or a series of experiences, and is summative in nature. Assessment of learning can be used to establish the differences in learning at the beginning and end of a period of learning. Assessment of learning may also occur when children need a specific assessment by a specialist or may need to be referred for additional assessment.

Asssessment *as* learning focuses on children learning about the processes of learning and developing understandings of themselves as learners. It respects children's agency in their own learning. Children can be actively involved in documenting their own learning and reflecting on group interactions and learning processes.

Assessment involves gathering and analysing information about children from a range of different contexts and sources and includes written, pictorial and/or audio documentation of children's interactions with others, works in progress and their questions and ideas. Children, as well as families and educators, can be actively involved in the processes of documenting and analysing this information. Documentation in this sense is often referred to as **pedagogical documentation**.

Pedagogical documentation is a process that helps educators, families, children and communities to understand and value children's learning. It helps to make children's learning processes visible and therefore accessible to children, families, educators and other stakeholders. When documentation is accessible to children they are able to revisit and reflect on their own learning, which deepens their understandings and develops metacognitive awareness (Malaguzzi, 1998; Mac Naughton & Williams, 2009).

As well as revealing what children are experiencing and learning, pedagogical documentation also reveals what educators are learning about teaching (Helm et al., 2007). This documentation provides detailed records that encourage educators and families to reflect on teaching and learning practices in the setting (Mac Naughton & Williams, 2009).

Assessment is more than just collecting samples of work, photographs and anecdotes. It involves making meaning from the observations that are documented; that is, interpreting or analysing the observations. Educators use their knowledge of dispositions, learning processes and child development, along with a range of learning continua and learning outcomes, to support their analysis of children's learning and to plan future directions to extend learning.

Documentation of learning provides a 'catalyst for discussion' (Podmore & Carr, 1999, p. 5). These shared conversations with staff, families and children enable multiple perspectives to be brought to the analysis of children's learning and help educators to reflect on documentation and reinterpret it in the light of new understandings. This collaboration encourages different hypotheses, questions and provocations (Fleet et al., 2011). Educators are then able to construct meanings and make informed decisions about curriculum.

Intentional teaching

Involves deliberate planning of experiences and pedagogies with a clear learning focus.

Pedagogical documentation

Provides a record of children's experiences and learning that facilitates discussion among children, families and educators and analysis of children's learning from diverse perspectives.

Developing shared understandings about assessment

Educators within any early childhood setting or school can work best together when they have shared understandings about children's learning and agreed-upon approaches to curriculum.

Dunphy (2010, p. 42) notes it is essential that there is coherence between 'the curriculum and the assessment of the learning that the curriculum seeks to promote'. In the case of the EYLF the learning outcomes indicate 'the types of learners it is hoped children will become as a result of their participation in prior to school early years childhood programs' (Barnes, 2012, p. 9). In addition, each educator and early childhood setting will have other ideals that should also be reflected in their approaches to assessment.

When teams have developed a shared philosophy, discussion will focus on the practicalities of putting the ideals into reality, as the principles that underpin the program will already be clearly articulated. At Integricare Children's Centre Homebush–Kurralcc, for example, educators in each room come together in weekly team meetings to discuss their vision, ideals and strategies that support staff to put these ideas into practice. Where teams are yet to develop a shared philosophy, discussion will be more complicated as educators may be grounding their practice in differing philosophies. In some schools where shared philosophies, approaches and pedagogies may be less evident, locating colleagues at the setting or within personal networks with shared perceptions is important (Jones et al., 2001).

It is essential that teams reflect on and critically evaluate the extent to which their current methods of assessment are consistent with their beliefs about children's learning. Educators are often so entwined within our practice that seeing 'the discrepancies between one's theory and one's practice' is almost impossible in isolation (Jones et al., 2001, p. 8). To help educators move towards critiquing their practice, Jones and her colleagues suggest 'growing thinking teachers who are full of dialogue about children and their learning and about curriculum' (2001, p. 8). Exposing ourselves as practitioners to the opinions of fellow educators, as well as children, families and educational consultants, allows opportunities for others to either affirm or challenge our practices and philosophy.

> What methods do you use to assess children's learning? Why do you use these methods? What other methods could you use that might provide different types of information about children's learning?

When dialogue is encouraged, supportive environments will have:

- staff rooms full of lively and constructive conversations
- philosophical debate in staff meetings
- staff enthusiasm for participation in further professional learning opportunities
- a stimulating, challenging and collegial environment.

How pedagogical leaders facilitate thinking educators will not only be influenced by individuals' willingness to challenge themselves, but also by the leader's ability to provide a safe environment for educators to express their beliefs, feelings, values and attitudes. This may be achieved through a variety of longer-term strategies, including personal growth and team-building exercises, modelling of open and honest communication and fair and clearly identified grievance procedures. An important short-term strategy is the chairperson's role in setting clear guidelines in meetings to promote positive discussion. This can be established if the chair clearly articulates that:

- decision making will be democratic
- everyone is doing their personal best with the information currently at their disposal
- everyone has a right for their opinions to be respected
- everyone has a right to receive uninterrupted time to express their opinions and be heard.

Dispositions

Habits of mind
or tendencies to
respond to situations
in similar ways.
Some dispositions
include creativity,
persistence and
confidence.

The following questions provide a starting point for encouraging discussion about documentation of children's relationships, **dispositions** and learning that may help staff to reflect on current methods:

- Why do we document and plan in the way we do?
- Are our methods of assessment consistent with our beliefs about children and their processes of learning?
- Are our methods of assessment workable?
- How do we ensure that children are active players in the assessment process?
- How do families have a voice in the assessment of children's learning?
- Is our documentation accessible to children and families?
- Do our assessment methods give enough information about children's relationships, dispositions and learning so that they inform future planning?

These questions encourage reflection and planning for changes that can work towards improvements in assessment methods. It is important to note here that previous experience and practice can only enhance understanding of children's learning. It would be unwise to suggest that what was done in the past is wrong, but it is also unwise to suggest that in a diverse and changing world, old approaches are the only approaches. Challenging pre-existing understandings of children's learning results in an increase in the depth of knowledge and understanding, practices that are more culturally relevant and an enhanced ability to clearly articulate individual and setting philosophy and practices to children, families and significant others. When educators work together with families to explore contemporary approaches to assessment, shared understandings facilitate stronger connections between children's homes and the educational setting. Educators who critically reflect upon their practices and are open to new or different approaches will continually evaluate and make changes to the methods they utilise to assess children's learning.

Contemporary perspectives on assessment

The terminology used to talk about processes of documentation and assessment has changed. In the past the term 'observation' was often used in early childhood contexts and the term 'assessment' was used more in schools. However, the term 'observation', for some, promotes images of formal observation rooms, test-like environments, assessment of children's 'deficits', checklists, developmental records and requirements from funding bodies. Traditionally, early childhood observations have been strongly focused on recording individual development and categorising children's behaviour into developmental stages. There has been an emphasis on the objective and scientific study of children with the use of formal, preplanned observation methods designed to observe particular aspects of growth such as fine motor, language or cognitive development. This way of observing divides the child into separate developmental domains and encourages educators to follow children around making sure that they get a 'language observation' and a 'gross motor observation' – and often missing lots of learning in the process.

Traditional developmentalist perspectives have encouraged the use of checklists to record what children are able to do and what they 'can't do'. Observations were often used to 'find a gap in children's learning' so that educators could target 'problem areas' perceived as not developing to 'normative' standards. This approach gave educators guidance for 'deficit' programming, but left many baffled about how to program for a child who does not have a perceived priority area of 'need'.

More contemporary understandings of children view children as active co-constructors of knowledge, as reflected in Reggio Emilia centres (Edwards et al., 1993/1998), *Te Whāriki* in New Zealand (Ministry of Education, New Zealand, 1996) and in *Belonging, Being and Becoming: The Early Years Learning Framework for Australia* (DEEWR, 2009). The EYLF presents an image of children as 'active participants and decision-makers' who 'construct their own understandings and contribute to others' learning' (DEEWR, 2009, p. 9). Other countries such as Canada have also moved from a developmental perspective to postmodern theories and practices that recognise diverse ways of being and becoming and acknowledge children's learning as complex and embedded within social and cultural contexts (Pacini-Ketchabaw & Pence, 2011).

These contemporary images of children as competent and capable and with diverse strengths and interests have challenged educators to look critically at traditional approaches to observation and to consider broader approaches to assessing children's learning. As one University of Western Sydney (UWS) student, who had moved from a developmentalist to a sociocultural approach, commented:

> I used to be a vivisectionist. I cut the child up into little pieces. I knew how the child held a pencil and walked along a balance beam. But I didn't really understand the child. Now (with a sociocultural focus) I understand the whole child, including their family and community experiences and funds of knowledge.
>
> Samira Tokalic, UWS student, 2006

There has been a shift towards using the term 'documentation' or 'pedagogical documentation' rather than 'observation' as a way of moving away from the notion of observations as reflecting *objective* and *scientific truth* about children towards more open-ended and collaborative forms of documentation that focus on dispositions and processes of learning and that acknowledge that all observations are subjective. Contemporary methods of documentation recognise the importance of the social and cultural contexts of learning by including group dynamics and interactions between adults and children and between children (*see*, for example, Fleer et al., 2006; Fleer, 2010). They move away from standardised assessment in the form of checklists and tests towards methods of documentation that 'value depth and context' and 'acknowledge cultural and linguistic diversity' (Pacini-Ketchabaw & Pence, 2011, p. 4).

Contemporary approaches to documentation involve educators, children and families in the recording of learning and the shared celebration of children's achievements. The use of methods such as photographs, videos, samples of drawings, sketches of constructions and audiotapes of conversations have helped to make children's learning 'concrete and visible (or audible)' (Dahlberg et al., 2007, p. 148). When children are viewed as capable and competent rather than as needy, educators focus on children's interests and strengths and their emerging understandings and critical points of learning. There is also a strong focus in contemporary methods of documentation on reflective practice in collaboration with children, families and all staff members, and the use of these reflections to analyse what is happening and to inform planning. This focus on reflection and analysis is what distinguishes pedagogical documentation from observation (Fleet et al., 2011). At the same time, planning has shifted in focus from prescriptive behavioural objectives to long-term outcomes and related short-term goals that incorporate children's strengths and interests and to experiences that challenge children's thinking and complicate their learning.

To what extent do your methods of assessment include the voices of children and families? What strategies could you use to provide more opportunities for children and families to have input into all stages of assessment and planning?

In summary, contemporary approaches to documentation:

- highlight children's competencies
- consider the whole child – reflecting the holistic way children learn
- include groups of children – acknowledging the collaborative nature of learning
- are accessible to families and children as well as to staff with a range of qualifications
- document children's ideas and questions
- acknowledge the different modes of representation that children use, such as drama, music and visual arts
- provide insights into children's interests, dispositions and learning processes
- focus on social aspects of learning – friendships, relationships, social interactions and collaboration
- include the voices of children and families
- document power relations
- are concerned with issues of social justice.

Recognition of the social and cultural contexts of learning, collaborative approaches to curriculum, understandings of dispositions of learning and recognition of power relations have

resulted in changing approaches to observation and documentation. Each of these will be discussed in further detail below.

Sociocultural contexts of learning

Chapter 3 emphasised the interactive nature of learning and development and the significant impact of family and community contexts on learning. A sociocultural view focuses on what children are beginning to be able to do and what they are able to do with the assistance of peers or an adult. This reflects what actual children are doing and their capabilities at different points of time and in different contexts.

While individual milestones may tell us something about learning and development, they do not tap into the social and cultural domains to provide information about how individuals operate within particular contexts. Documentation of children's learning within their families and communities and acknowledgement of the **'funds of knowledge'** (Moll et al., 1992) or 'virtual school bags' (Thompson, 2002) that children bring from home to early childhood settings and schools can assist educators to build on children's existing expertise. In addition, documentation of children's involvement in learning experiences and group interactions at the early childhood setting or school can capture the processes of learning and the role of adults and peers in the mediation of learning.

Funds of knowledge

The skills, understandings, interests and expertise that children acquire as they participate in family and community life.

If a group of children is playing in the sand, for example, rather than observing one child digging and building, the educator can observe how the group of children play and build together and how they share ideas, negotiate, collaborate and resolve conflicts. In this way shared interests, friendships, group interactions and cooperative behaviours can be documented as well as what children are able to do in a supportive environment. This approach to documentation results in examples of children's learning that are 'far more vibrant, reflective and complex' than a traditional developmental approach (Fleer & Robbins, 2003, p. 15). Fleer and Surman (2006, p. 146) found that when educators documented the learning of groups of children rather than individuals, they were better able to note the 'interactional patterns of peers and the clear reciprocity of learning that was taking place in these contexts'. A sociocultural approach to documentation focuses on 'the dynamic interplay of pairs or groups of children, or children and adults, noting the scaffolding, supporting, extending, leading and following … that occurs in any activity in which children participate' (Fleer & Robbins, 2003, p. 15).

One example of a sociocultural framework for documenting young children's learning has been developed by Fleer and her colleagues (Fleer & Richardson, 2003; Fleer & Robbins, 2003). This framework draws on Rogoff's (1998; 2003) three planes of analysis: the personal (individual), interpersonal and community/institutional. An example of this framework in use can be seen in Example 8.1.

Drawing on the information in Example 8.1, if the focus is on the individual, it would be possible to note that Henry was unable to write his name. From a sociocultural perspective, using Rogoff's three planes of analysis, as suggested by Fleer and Robbins (2003), the following comments could be made about Henry:

- *Personal plane:* Henry is hesitant to write his name, but does write the letter 'H'.
- *Interpersonal plane:* Henry is very aware of what the other boys are doing and seems keen to follow their lead. He is quick to confirm that he is the same as Alex, when he notes that he is also unable to write his name. He is happy to observe the teacher and note what she is doing. When all the other boys resume the activity, he does so as well.
- *Contextual plane:* Contextual information is provided by Henry's mother in the communication book when she shares her surprise at Henry's apparent lack of desire to be perceived as different from the other children. This communication between Henry's mother and the teacher can start a conversation that moves to creating spaces within the child care setting where Henry is challenged to demonstrate his understanding and skills in ways that are valued by himself and his peers.

There are several positive effects of observing in this way, including:

- greater focus on what children can do, both on their own and with assistance, rather than on what they cannot do, in collaboration with families

- greater recognition of the social nature and contexts of development and learning
- an enhanced role for educators within documentation of learning and teaching situations, as the mediation role of adults impacts on the experience
- rich data that takes account of complex situations and interactions, rather than focusing on fixed attributes.

EXAMPLE 8.1
Henry's writing

Context: Henry is a four-year-old who has been attending child care for two years. He enjoys being with the staff and children. His main activities at child care involve gross motor experiences, and he is particularly keen on playing soccer with other four-year-old boys.

Observation

One afternoon, Henry's mother arrived early. Henry was sitting at a table with some other boys. They were writing their names on small blackboards. Henry was hesitant, writing 'H' and then putting down the blackboard and chalk. He looked over at the other boys. Some had written letters, others had made patterns and some had covered as much of the blackboard as possible with scribbles.

Henry's mum watched and then asked what he was doing. 'Nothing', was the reply.
Sam, sitting next to Henry, said, 'We were making names, but now we're just drawing'.
Alex added, 'I can't write my name. This is boring. Let's go and play'.
Henry commented, 'Na, neither can I'.
Henry's mum expressed surprise, and said, 'Yes you can'.

An educator was nearby. She approached the group and started writing her own name on a blackboard. The boys watched her and started to clean their own blackboards. Some then started to copy the teacher's name, and others drew lines and squiggles.

This activity continued for some time. The children displayed interest in the experience as the educator discussed what she was doing and modelled writing letters and names.

Henry's mum commented later in the communication book that she was surprised at Henry's reluctance to write his name, and indicated that he is confident in writing his own name in many home situations.

Collaborative approaches to assessment

The setting philosophy will influence not only what is assessed but also who is involved in collating and analysing data. When the setting philosophy supports a collaborative approach to assessment, children, family members, educators and other professionals, such as speech therapists and Inclusion Support Staff (ISS), are all involved in the collection and interpretation of information that provides insights into children's learning. These collaborative processes give all participants a voice in assessment and facilitate the sharing of power. All educators bring diverse experiences, qualifications, values and attitudes to their team. Respect for multiple perspectives in philosophical discussion and input enables educators to reflect upon and challenge their own values and attitudes.

Children are important partners in the documentation process. When given the opportunity to be heard, children will inform adults of their interests, at the same time revealing their emerging capabilities and social expectations, as evident in Example 8.2. Opportunities for children to express themselves openly and confidently will provide invaluable information.

▶ EXAMPLE 8.2
Documenting children's ideas: what do princesses eat?

Context: Several children are eating lunch together. Ana, the educator, joins the table, initiating conversation with a comment about a Disney princess on the packaging for Hanna's yoghurt.

Observation

Ana:	I wonder why there is a princess on the yoghurt container.
Hanna:	Because children like princesses.
Jack:	Maybe that's what kids like.
Ana:	Do princesses eat yoghurt?
	Children laughed a lot
Ana:	Why are you laughing?
Child:	Princesses don't eat yoghurt.
Martin:	They don't go to the shops!
Keira:	Yes, they do!
Martin:	No they don't! They don't have a car!
Keira:	They drive the royal car!
Ana:	Which princess goes in the car?
Keira:	The queen.
Ana:	Well, what about Princess Mary? She's having a baby, isn't she? Do you think she eats yoghurt?
Several children:	Yes!!
Keira:	Princess Mary is having her baby in October after my mum's birthday.
Ana:	Why would Princess Mary eat yoghurt but not the other princesses?
Mitchell:	Because they're not real.
Ana:	I don't understand. What do you mean?
Martin:	The other princesses are only stories but Princess Mary is real.
Ana:	Do princesses in stories eat?
Martin:	No, you have to be 'real'.

Analysis

From a brief two-minute lunchtime conversation, the children conveyed clear understandings of the difference between real and story worlds. Martin expressed the view that only real people go to the shops and eat. He understood that while Princess Mary could eat yoghurt, the idea of Disney princesses eating was funny and fiction. Keira drew on her funds of knowledge about real princesses and the 'royal car', her mum's birthday and Mary's expected delivery date.

Source: Bronwyn Beecher, 2010 (unreported data)

It is important to balance ways that children's voices can be included in documentation while at the same time respecting their right to privacy and their agency in their own learning (Cheeseman & Robertson, 2006). The sociology of childhood (*see* Chapter 1) argues that children are active constructors of their own learning and are citizens with rights, and therefore should be active participants in documentation. In *The mosaic approach* (2001), Clark and Moss argue that children are experts in their own lives and skilful communicators and meaning makers. They emphasise the importance of educators listening to children and co-constructing knowledge – what is known as the pedagogy of listening (Dahlberg & Moss, 2005).

Children can be involved in self-evaluation about how they responded in various experiences, and how they felt about them. Photographs are particularly useful in involving younger children in documentation of and reflection on their own learning (Mac Naughton & Williams, 2009; Salamon, 2011). Older children can evaluate their experiences using learning journals and self-assessment. Children and families can be involved in many aspects of the documentation of children's learning such as contributing artefacts to portfolios and documenting Learning Stories. Munns and Woodward (2006) and Munns, Woodward and Koletti (2006) report on school children, from kindergarten to Year 6, reflecting on their feelings, thoughts and actions in learning and their view of themselves as a learner. Munns and Woodward advocate that where children participate in self and collective peer assessment, this offers educators information concerning student engagement in learning. Through involvement in their own assessment, children become aware of the outcomes, goals and wider perspectives they are moving towards (Munns & Woodward, 2006).

Advocates of children's rights, including Mac Naughton (2003), Clark and Moss (2001), Cheeseman and Robertson (2006) and Harcourt, Perry and Waller (2011), argue that truly collaborative documentation respects children's agency, which means that educators:

- engage in critical reflections regarding the power relationships between children and educators and take steps to develop more equal power relationships
- offer children explanations of what they are documenting and why
- offer children the right to refuse to participate at any point and respect their decision
- involve children as documenters – for example children as photographers
- include children in decisions about what documentation is displayed and what is included in their portfolios
- are alert and responsive to subtle cues indicating that children are not comfortable with being observed
- document children's learning in naturalistic environments where children can choose to be active participants in the documentation process
- use multiple methods of documentation to provide all children with opportunities to express their ideas
- respect children's ownership of their ideas
- provide children with opportunities to engage in dialogue about the meaning of documentation
- include children's self-reflections in documentation on their learning.

When educators and children engage in conversations about learning they are involved in negotiation and the exchange of ideas and joint decision making.

This type of dialogue is equally important for families. Families are also key players in the documentation of children's learning as they can provide intimate knowledge of the understandings that children have acquired through their family and community experiences and can bring new perspectives to the analysis of the meaning of children's voices. Information about children's family and community influences and expertise, as well as their learning styles, interests, fears and routines, can be gained through respectful partnerships with families, as outlined in Chapter 2. Family members see their child in different contexts from those of educators and therefore will often observe different strengths, interests, abilities and emerging development from those observed by educators. These observations should be included in the assessment of children's learning and considered in future planning so that assessment reflects all the child's experiences and abilities.

When educators understand family practices and values they are better able to understand that there are no universal ways of doing things and can provide the scaffolding children need to support their transition from home to centre practices. Drawing on the work of Vygotsky (1978) and Hedegaard (2009), Fleer (2010) argues that these transitions from home to the educational setting provide opportunities for children's development to follow multiple trajectories.

Ongoing dialogue between educators and families increases the opportunities for children to use their existing understandings in new contexts (Carr & Lee, 2012) and supports the construction of curriculum that is 'relevant to children in their local context' (DEEWR, 2009, p. 11).

Source: Integricare Children's Centre Homebush – Kurralee

FIGURE 8.1 A daily diary or journal in an accessible area with comfortable furniture encourages children, families and staff to find out about, revisit and reflect on children's learning.

Families are more likely to contribute to assessment of children's learning 'when the request to engage in the dialogue is respectful and sensitive ... and when families see a reflection of their thoughts and impressions in the documentation' (Fleet et al., 2011, p. 10). Chapter 2 provides suggestions for collaborating with families.

When documentation of children's learning is displayed, families are able to look at, read and comment on this (*see* Figure 8.1). The placement of daily diaries and project books in a comfortable and family-friendly area provides opportunities for families, staff and children to spend time revisiting and discussing previous experiences. These displays are more indicative of the growth in children's learning when they include examples of different stages of projects and works in progress as well as end products. Three-dimensional products such as sculptures and models should also be displayed as well as photographs and samples of drawing, painting and writing at various stages. Displays are more reflective of children's work if children are involved in selecting items for display and in composing narratives to accompany samples and photographs. Annotations that identify children's learning assist family members to understand the significance of what is displayed (Helm et al., 2007).

Dispositions

Lillian Katz's (Katz & Chard, 1989/2000) focus on the importance of dispositions of learning, such as curiosity and creatitivy, encouraged a debate about what is valued in early childhood curriculum. Carr (2001) built on the notion that dispositions are tendencies to respond to situations in particular ways, describing dispositions as an 'accumulation of motivation, situation and skill' (p. 9). Disposition is taken to refer to habits of mind, such as preferred ways or strategies of approaching situations (Katz & Chard, 1989/2000) and 'encouraging or constraining the exploration and construction of new knowledge or ideas' (Carr & Lee, 2012, p. 15). Carr and Lee (2012) point out that the outcomes in the New Zealand school curriculum are dispositional. It could also be argued that the learning outcomes in the EYLF are dispositional. Dispositional outcomes, according to Carr and Lee, require the use of narrative forms of assessment and samples of work.

Carr (2001) uses Bourdieu's (1984/1993) term 'habitus' as 'it can refer to participation repertoires that have become attached to a community' (p. 10). Hence, in the focus on dispositions, Carr emphasises the strategies children have and use, and their willingness to use these, as well as the assumptions and expectations about what are appropriate participation repertoires for particular contexts, such as early childhood settings.

Dispositions are a key element of many early childhood curriculum documents – for example the *Te Whāriki* curriculum in New Zealand (New Zealand Ministry of Education, 1996), *Belonging, Being and Becoming: The Early Years Learning Framework for Australia* (DEEWR, 2009) and *The Statutory Framework for the Early Years Foundation Stage in England* (Department for Children, Schools and Families, 2008). Dispositions are also reflected in the *General Capabilities* in the Australian Curriculum, including personal and social capability, critical and creative thinking and ethical understanding (ACARA, http://www.acara.edu.au/> Curriculum > General capabilities). Dispositions such as curiosity, flexibility and persistence are important for all learners, particularly in a world that is rapidly changing (Arthur, 2010). When children explore and ask questions, and are open to and try new ideas, they are more likely to be confident and actively engaged in learning (DEEWR, 2009).

Power relations

Children's play is sometimes influenced by power relations evident in the wider society. Sometimes play can be unfair and unjust. Children can exclude others from play on the basis of criteria such as gender, skin colour, English-language proficiency, age, ethnicity and sexuality, as well as other criteria. Documentation of children's learning should not ignore these power relations as they are an important influence on what children learn and how they all approach learning (Mac Naughton & Williams, 2009). Video and audio transcripts of children's play can provide educators with useful information to help them understand the power dynamics and unfair behaviour that sometimes appears in children's play and lead to planning that promotes social justice, equity and fairness and the inclusion of all children. A focus on power relations is consistent with anti-bias and inclusive approaches to curriculum (*see* Chapter 7) that aim to challenge negative stereotypes and unfair behaviour and to promote inclusive practices.

Processes of documenting and assessing children's learning

Professionalism

Confidential and ethical behaviour is critical when documenting information about children. This means ensuring that families and children are comfortable with the processes of observation and documentation being used, that children can make decisions about what is documented and how, and that families can access information collected on their child and contribute new information at any time.

The use of technologies such as photography and video recording produce new challenges in terms of ethics and confidentiality (Dockett & Perry, 2011; Harcourt et al., 2011). While most families are happy for photographs of their children to be included in documentation, some families may be reluctant to give permission for their child's photograph to be taken or displayed. Ethical documentation also requires that children are asked if they want to be photographed and if they are happy to have their photograph shared with others. To date, very little consideration has been afforded to the ethical issues of the storage and continued use of photographs or other images. For example, can we predict how children will feel if they see images of themselves some years after their (and the parents') permission to use them was obtained? What obligations do we have to ensure that all are represented favourably? Can the use of stereotypical images add to the marginalisation of some children and/or groups? (Holm, 2008)

The documentation of group interactions also raises issues of children's rights to participate or not, who has access to information about a child and how and where group observations can be shared. These are issues that educators need to negotiate carefully with children and families while respecting each participant's views. When families give written permission for a service to document information about their child and the family, how that documentation is to be completed, used and shared with others (within the early childhood setting or school) should be detailed. For example, if a portfolio process is used and children and families are given access to their portfolio, families should be able to decide whether they would like this to be open access or whether they prefer to have documentation stored more privately and only accessed by asking a staff member. Children should also have the options of participating in documentation or not, and be able to participate in decisions about what is displayed.

There are concerns that visual documentation has the potential to increase adult surveillance of children (Lindgren, 2012). Lindgren enourages educators to reflect on whether visual documentation positions children as passive objects to be viewed by others, thus reinforcing the power of the adult, or as active agents able to document and reflect on their own learning. When children are able to document and assess their own learning, their agency is recognised and valued.

Managing time and resources

Pedagogical documentation takes time. It is important to think about how to make the most effective use of time and resources to produce meaningful documentation. This means making decisions about what to document and the best methods to collect and record that information. It means thinking about how technologies can assist with documentation and how one piece of documentation can be used for multiple purposes. It also means inviting children, families and all members of staff to be involved in documentation so that multiple perspectives can be included.

As educators have many demands on their time, it is important to balance documentation methods that provide rich, detailed descriptions with other methods that are less time-consuming. Many methods of documentation – such as collecting samples of work, making jottings and taking photographs – are quick and efficient, can occur as educators are interacting with children and can involve children and families in the documentation process. Narrative methods, such as Learning Stories and detailed transcripts of conversations, require more time but provide useful, rich and descriptive data.

One time-management strategy is the inclusion of a number of children in the one observation. This process also highlights the social aspects of children's learning and enables educators to focus on group interests and relationships. These observations can be included in individual children's portfolios as well as the documentation of the group's investigations. Selected individual and group narratives can be word-processed and then used in many different ways. Multiple copies of narratives, children's conversations, drawings and webs can be used in individual and group documentation. The one piece of information can be included as part of a child's record in a portfolio or journal, in the daily diary for families and in the documentation of a project. Examples of children's learning can also be emailed to families and placed on the setting's website (when this section of the website is confidential and not accessible to others or where permission has been obtained).

Technologies such as digital cameras and audio and video recorders can assist educators, families and children to record, analyse and share children's learning. Digital recorders, such as those found on tablets and phones, can assist in making recordings unobtrusive and user friendly. Children's play, conversations, constructions in progress, dramatic play and excursions can be recorded for later reflection and analysis. Children can also make their own audio and video recordings. These may include children's musical creations or dramatic performances. When audio and video recordings are shared with families and children, further insights can be gained and children are encouraged to revisit and reflect on their learning.

Cameras can be used to take photographs of excursions, children's play and works in progress for sharing and reflecting on with staff, children and families. Photographs provide much useful information to families about the setting's program. Digital images can be uploaded into children's portfolios or journals, project books, the centre's journal or daily diary, or can be printed and placed in individual and group documentation. In this way one well-selected photograph can be used several times across different forms of documentation. Photographs can also be used to create slide shows for families and children. These can be on display in the foyer area – while always maintaining confidentiality issues as identified earlier – encouraging families, educators and children to share in the children's experiences. The photos remind children about aspects of their day that then act as a trigger for rich conversations.

It is important to remember, however, that when educators do not have access to these technologies other methods can be used to capture children's learning. Where educators do not have access to cameras, or where the budget for printing photographs is limited, educators and children can make drawings and diagrams of children's constructions and include samples of children's work in documentation.

Another way to manage time is to include documentation as part of the everyday routine and to involve children in processes of documentation. Rather than being something that is done away from the children, often in the educator's own time, documentation can occur in the classroom. Children can be actively involved in co-constructing the narrative with educators and reflecting on what it means, so assessment becomes a learning process – assessment *as* learning. When children also have access to their own folders or working portfolios they can add their own samples and photographs to these. For example, children can save drawing and writing completed on the interactive whiteboard or a laptop directly to their own folder, they can upload photos or video recordings to their own file or they can place hard copies of drawing or writing into their paper portfolio.

What additional strategies could you use in your setting to make assessment processes more manageable?

Educators also need time away from face-to-face work with children to engage in conversations about documentation and collaborate about future planning. Structuring the day so that educators are able to plan in pairs or small groups enhances the documentation processes.

Authentic assessment

To be meaningful and authentic records of children's learning, assessment should be part of children's daily experiences and be 'embedded into the whole curriculum' (Siraj-Blatchford & Clarke, 2000, p. 112) rather than something that occurs in isolation. As Hart (1994, p. 9, in Fleet & Torr, 2007, p. 186) notes, 'an assessment is authentic when it involves students in tasks that are worthwhile, significant and meaningful'. Authentic assessment occurs in a 'context of meaningful, supportive and respectful interactions' between educators and children (DEEWR, 2010, p. 39) and involves children interacting naturally with each other and the environment (Fraser & Gestwicki, 2001), rather than being asked to do unusual tasks or to do things in staged or isolated ways, as in a testing situation. Authentic assessment offers analysis of descriptive information regarding children's learning, strengths and interests within familiar contexts.

Authentic and ethical assessment uses a range of methods of documentation, collects information over time and includes children in self-reflection and self-assessment (DEEWR, 2009). This provides opportunities for all children to confidently demonstrate their capabilities and focus on future potential as well as current understandings (DEEWR, 2009).

In contrast, standardised tests measure children against a standard or 'norm'. As discussed in Chapter 1, all children starting school are now assessed for literacy and numeracy using standardised assessment tools. Assessing learning in the first term of school using standardised assessment tools for English literacy and numeracy may provide educators with a snapshot of each child's understandings that can be used to plan future learning. However, ongoing observations of children engaged in literacy and numeracy experiences, interviewing children about how they and their family write, read or view texts or use numbers at home, and intentionally teaching children in small groups and documenting children's learning are needed to build rich pictures of all children's learning, and to appreciate the depth and breadth of this learning for children with diverse abilities and capital. With this rich documentation educators can create programs that cater for individual children.

The National Assessment Programs for Literacy and Numeracy (NAPLAN), and similar standardised tests, generally do not provide an accurate measure of what children know, do not recognise the different learning that occurs in children's diverse social and cultural contexts and do not provide information that is relevant to children's ongoing learning (Fleet & Torr, 2007). It is important to remember that young children's abilities are emerging, not fixed. Evaluation at any one point may present a distorted view of capabilities (Bowman et al., 2001). In general, reliance on norm-referenced standardised tests is problematic in relation to young children (National Association of Early Childhood Specialists in State Departments of Education, 2000). Many standardised assessments do not recognise that young children can demonstrate learnings, skills and abilities in many different ways, and are not particularly sensitive to cultural and linguistic diversity (Bowman et al., 2001), nor meaningful to children with diverse experiences.

Similar concerns are stated by the National Council of Teachers of English (2004). This professional body rejects the singular use of standardised tests and recommends that educators assess literacy learning within regular program experiences so they can concentrate on strengths, areas for improvement and goals leading to changes to be implemented. This organisation argues that 'literacy assessments are only valid to the extent that they help students learn' (National Council of Teachers of English, 2004, p. 4) and recommends that all people – educators, families and students as well as the wider community – who use test information need to be wise to what the data actually means, and does not mean, about children's literacy learning. This body advocates that educators develop expertise and insights into a range of assessment tools, often involving families and children in tool development and lobbying community education concerning standardised instruments.

In contrast to standardised tests, assessment in a naturalistic context provides children with opportunities to represent their understandings in a variety of different ways. It is important to document children's interactions in a range of social and learning contexts. This includes social situations with family members, groups of children and with staff as well as individual situations, in different play areas indoors and outdoors and in child- and adult-initiated experiences.

Children who are bilingual should be assessed in their home language as well as in English. Bilingual staff, family members or community language teachers can assist in building a profile of the child's experiences and competencies in the home language. It is essential that judgements are not made about children's language and cognitive proficiencies based only on their use of the English language. It is vital that assessment procedures are equitable. This means taking account of the culture and languages of children's homes and communities.

Similarly, children with additional needs should be assessed with reference to their strengths and interests as well as their needs, if the assessment seeks to identify their learning. For example, children with low vision or visual impairments may be able to complete experiences that involve kinaesethetic and tactile resources, movement, conversations and so on, as well as with Braille materials.

Analysing documentation

Documenting children's learning is more than just collecting samples of work, photographs, transcripts and narratives. These documents need to be analysed for meaning and this analysis used to inform future planning. Educators draw on a range of theories and information about children's learning when interpreting documentation, including comprehensive knowledge of early learning and development and the diversity of children's learning paths and the learning outcomes in the EYLF (DEEWR, 2009).

Educators should also document, reflect on and analyse their own pedagogical principles and practices and the extent to which these support children's belonging, being and becoming. Reflection and evaluation of learning environments and pedagogies is included in Chapter 4.

When analysing documentation of children's experiences, educators ask questions such as:

- What does the photograph/transcript/sample/narrative tell us about the children's interests, knowledge and dispositions?
- How are children progressing towards meeting the learning outcomes outlined in the EYLF? What examples illustrate this learning?
- What questions or problems are children encountering or designing and how are they responding to these; for example, persisting at a task, seeking assistance?
- What learning processes are evident; for example, problem solving or co-construction of learning?
- What does the photograph/transcript/sample/narrative indicate about group dynamics and social interactions?
- What does it tell us about power relations and equity issues?
- What does it tell us about the effectiveness of our teaching strategies?
- What does it tell us about the classroom environment?

(adapted from Curtis & Carter, 2000; Helm, Beneke & Steinheimer, 2007; Mac Naughton, 2003)

Example 8.3 has been developed by staff at an early childhood centre to assist with the documentation and analysis of children's learning. The questions provide useful prompts for staff when they are documenting children's learning and for the director and staff team when they are identifying children's strengths and interests and planning possible future directions.

EXAMPLE 8.3
Observation, study and planning

Observation/narrative/noticing the details of children belonging, being and becoming

Provide an introduction
- Note if this reflection is a follow-up to prior suggested Future Intentions
- Record if you introduced something into the environment and why

As you observe and take notes, strive to:
- Describe what was happening in the play noting specifics about what children said to one another; recording direct quotes and conversations
- Describe the children's reactions to modifications to the environment or something new
- Capture the mood noting down: tones of voice, body language, facial expressions, hand gestures

When you take photos, strive to:
- Capture the action, rather than arranging a posed picture
- Get up close to capture expressions or the child's handwork.

Before moving to the planning stage answer the following questions:
- Who was involved in the play? What materials did the children work with? Do they typically play in this area or in this way?
- What did the children specifically do?
- Who was coming up with the ideas; Who was leading the play and who was following?

Early Years Learning Framework learning outcomes, key learning and developmental areas

- EYLF Five Learning Outcomes
- Key Learning Areas including: visual arts, drama, literacy, mathematics, science etc
- Developmental areas

Studying observation notes: finding big ideas

Answer the questions
- What behaviour suggests that the child/ren is/are belonging, being and becoming?
- Who or what is helping the child/ren to belong, be and become?
- What are the children's strengths and interests?
- What are the children curious about?
- What are the children wondering?
- What knowledge are the children drawing on?
- What theory are they testing?

- What personal experiences are they drawing upon?
- Are the children reflecting any family values?
- How is the setting and circumstance influencing the children's behaviour?
- Do the children have any loosely formed ideas or theories that need more explanation?
- What do you want the children to learn more about?
- What is your hypothesis about the underlying meaning of this play?
- What are the children learning or getting out of the play?
- What goals and values come up for you about the children's play situation?

Planning the next step

Thinking about your hypothesis, what is the next step

- What can we do to support the child/ren belonging, being and becoming?
- What changes can you make to the environment?
- What materials or provocations can you add to the environment?
- How could you participate in the children's play?
- How could you invite the children to use other language to deepen their thinking?
- How will you use your observations to revisit and extend on the children's play?
- How will you discuss this exploration with families, inviting their reflections and insights?

Source: Mary Bailey House, 2014

How educators analyse documentation will depend on their philosophy and approaches to curriculum. These philosophies and approaches draw on different theoretical perspectives, such as developmental, sociocultural and critical theories. These theories bring different lenses to the interpretation of documentation.

Traditionally, observations often focused on a particular area of development, such as language or fine motor skills, and were interpreted in terms of what children could and couldn't do in the selected area. Contemporary theories have encouraged educators to move beyond this level of analysis to consider broader issues and multiple perspectives. This does not mean that there is no room for a developmental focus, but that consideration also needs to be given to issues such as dispositions, group dynamics and power relations, as well as a more holistic perspective of development, as in Example 8.3. It is important to see how aspects of development influence the child and his/her relationships, understandings and experience.

Educators with a sociocultural perspective will analyse the dispositions that are evident in pieces of documentation as well as interactions, relationships and processes of learning, as in Example 8.4. A sociocultural perspective also encourages the involvement of different members of the team in analysing documentation, ensuring that diverse perspectives are brought to the making of meaning. It is important to remember that 'interpretation is a very subjective process that is strongly influenced by our cultural values and beliefs, and by those cultural values and beliefs that are dominant in our society' (Mac Naughton & Williams, 2009, p. 305). A team approach to documentation and analysis helps counteract these biases. Educators at Mary Bailey House, for example, use the reflective questions in Example 8.3 in collaborative discussions of children's experiences and learning.

The inclusion of family information, as in the example with Henry's writing in Example 8.1, can also add new insights to the meaning of documentation, and encourage educators to further explore opportunities for children to draw on and display the expertise developed with their families and communities in the educational setting. A sociocultural perspective will also encourage families and children to be involved in the reflection on documentation and analysis of meaning and future planning.

EXAMPLE 8.4
Documenting children's learning

Date: 10th April 2013

Context: As a follow up on the children's interest in writing, this morning we set up some pens and writing paper outside on the collage table. Mariam (an educator) reminded the children of their previous experiences engaged in writing and invited some of them to the table.

Observation

Tiana, Summer and Rose approached and sat down to do some writing. They all picked up their pens and began to write. Tiana wrote something onto the paper and Mariam asked her what she wrote. Tiana replied, 'Mariam'. Mariam then asked her, 'Are you writing my name?' and Tiana responded, 'Yes'. After a short while Tiana wrote another thing on the paper above Mariam's 'name'. When asked what she wrote, Tiana said, 'Mona's name'. Tiana then drew a large circle around both 'names' as she said, 'Round and round'. Tiana picked up another paper and said, 'Another paper' and then continued to write.

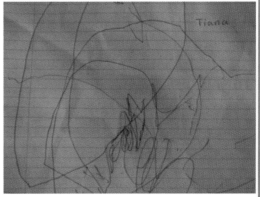

Summer was also very busy writing and before she started she said, 'Write mummy'. Mariam asked her if she was writing 'mummy' and Summer replied, 'Mummy, daddy and nanna'. Summer later said that she was writing 'cars'. Mariam wrote Summer's name onto the paper and Summer pointed to her name and said, 'Me'.

Rose picked up her pen and started to write in small writing on top of her page as she said, 'Rose ... Rosy is Bella ...' Rose then started to draw large circles at the bottom of her page whilst saying to Alessia, 'It's Thomas, it's your brother'. Tiana continued to write and then used a yellow texta to write over her work. Summer went up to Mariam and started to write on Mariam's paper (which had children's comments). Summer looked up at Mariam and smiled as she wrote onto Mariam's paper.

Study of the observation

Tiana, Rose and Summer continue to explore this interest in writing. They have been observed on numerous occasions writing using the pen and paper. They appear to enjoy having an educator sit by their side who engages them in conversation through open questioning. This also helps the children develop a longer concentration and attention span. The children are drawing upon their knowledge of writing and appear to be imitating the adults in their environments. Do the children enjoy writing because they observe their educators write or have they observed this in other contexts such as their home setting? Summer mentioned that she was writing the word 'car'. Did she remember the previous time where she was engaged in playing with the cars and when Mariam mentioned to her that she was writing about her playing with the car? Could she be writing her own reflections?

The children also appear to be more interested in writing on their educator's paper than writing on their own. This has been observed on numerous occasions where the children attempt to write on the real eat/sleep charts and the observation papers despite being provided a photocopy of their own. Why is that? Is it because they want to be involved in the real thing? For instance, writing on the real eat/sleep chart provides them with a greater sense of authenticity.

Planning the next step

- Incorporate some of the daily reflections into the writing area and see how the children respond to this material. Perhaps the children might use this to inspire their writing.
- Could we ask the parents about whether the children engage in writing at home and what things they enjoy writing about?

Source: Lily Pilly Gully (Toddlers' Room), Mary Bailey House, April 2013

Educators with a critical perspective focus their analysis on power relationships and issues of social justice, as in Example 8.5. This means exploring aspects such as:

- the equity dynamics within specific groups of children
- the equity implications of what is being seen
- the multiple ways of seeing what has been found
- the possibilities for transformational action through what has been learnt.

G Mac Naughton, *Shaping Early Childhood: Learners, Curriculum and Contexts*, pp. 203–4, © 2003 Open University Press.

This may mean analysing observations in terms of the language used as well as practices, such as which children are playing together and how they are interacting. Educators can ask questions that investigate if particular groups of children are marginalised by being excluded from play. Mac Naughton (2003) suggests asking questions such as:

- Are boys excluding girls from play?
- Do children with English as a second language interact with children who have English as a first language?
- Are children who have a disability able to successfully access play situations with children who are not disabled?
- Do some children have more power than others? How do they exercise this power and to what effect?

EXAMPLE 8.5
Critical analysis of a language transcript

Mardi:	Batman has all black …
Eleanor:	… well Barbie has pink. Forever!
Mardi:	But she [Barbie] doesn't have …
Colm:	… and she [Barbie] doesn't have the black suit like Batman.
Lucinda:	No, because she's pink.
Eleanor:	Yeah, she's *just pink*!

This argumentative agreement exposes the apparent conceptions of power between these children. Both Mardi and Colm express what Barbie does *not* have. Clearly, Colm is articulating reasons why Barbie is different from Batman and not powerful through her lack of a 'black' suit. This lack represents the received construction of gender: by what it is not. Lucinda's statement of Barbie's *pinkness* appears to be a direct inscription on Barbie's body, in contrast to Colm's identification of the addition of the 'black suit'. The power negotiations between these children suggest that the symbolic power invested in Barbie's metaphysical 'pinkness' is worth less cultural currency in contrast to the 'black' Batman economy used as capital in this market. The friction in their agreement highlights the discursive binary power struggle on a macro political level where blackness, perhaps a signifier of patriarchy, is dominant and pinkness is subordinate. However, Lucinda's use of the word 'no', as the point of agreement, reveals her desire to maintain power while attempting to resist the power Colm espouses through the 'black' suit. Eleanor's apparent agreement reiterates the pink position these girls assume. The children's argument is 'coloured' by desire, their desire to perform gender through received and chosen images of femininity and masculinity. Consequently, these images are available to the children through popular cultural characters and commodities that appear to be powerful and desirable ways of performing gender (Alloway, 1995; Mac Naughton, 2000).

Source: Giugni, 2003

Methods of documentation and assessment

There is a range of methods of documentation that support different curriculum approaches and that assist in the collection of information for different purposes and for different audiences. These can be grouped into narratives, samples, language transcripts, visual records and checklists. Decisions about methods of documentation to be used should be based on the

setting's philosophy and approaches to curriculum and the purposes of the documentation. The format for recording information about children and the level of detail may vary according to experience (a student engaged in professional experience, a beginning educator or an experienced educator) as well as the purpose of the documentation and the audience (e.g. families, children, licensing bodies, community).

Narratives

Narratives are descriptive accounts of an event or experience. They can document the experiences of one child or a group of children. These methods of documentation are open-ended, enabling educators to record all behaviours, not just specific aspects of development (Martin, 2010). Narratives include running records (also called descriptive narratives), Learning Stories, anecdotes and jottings. Descriptive narratives, anecdotes and jottings require different levels of detail, with running records having more detail than jottings.

When documenting narratives it is important to include as much detail as possible about the context, such as what happened before the experience that is being documented, who was present and what happened afterwards. Careful observation also requires the use of specific language to describe children's actions. Dunphy (2010, p. 51) cites Bruner's (1999) caution that narratives are not an end in themselves but 'tools for reflection', and as with all documentation, they need to be reflected on and shared with others to identify possible meanings.

RUNNING RECORDS

Running records are the most detailed narratives. They are written while an event or an interaction is occurring and include rich descriptive details, as in Example 8.6. The observer should record exactly what the child does and says as it happens. Running records are traditionally focused on one child although they can also document the interactions of a group of children. Running records provide much useful information, but should be balanced with other methods as they are time-consuming and also make it difficult for the educator to interact with the children while observing.

ANECDOTES

An anecdote records a 'snapshot' of a child or children. Anecdotes are written after the event, meaning that the educator can participate in the program and record anecdotes at the end of the day or during a child-free time during the day.

An anecdote tells a narrative or story: 'Anecdotal records can be seen as 'word pictures' of incidents, behaviour or events that occur in certain circumstances' (Briggs & Potter, 1999, p. 145). Anecdotes can focus on everyday events and behaviours of a child or group of children, or on unusual events and milestones in a child's understandings.

As anecdotes are written after the event, they are often short and focused (Bentzen, 2000), although they may be longer and more detailed. Anecdotes will therefore provide the observer with as much or as little information about the individual or the group as the observer chooses to record. Martin (2010) notes that anecdotes rely on memory, requiring the educator to be skilled in recording contextual details as well as the actual event.

Anecdotes can be used to support various philosophical approaches. They can focus on an individual child's development, on the social interactions and relationships of a group of children or on power relationships, as illustrated in Examples 8.7, 8.8 and 8.9.

EXAMPLE 8.6
An example of a running record

Name: Krishna **Date:** 30/5/14 **Time:** 4.15 pm–4.20 pm

Setting: Krishna was sitting in the block area, building a tower with another child, Danielle.

TIME	OBSERVATION	ANALYSIS OF LEARNING	FUTURE PLANNING
4.15 pm	Krishna is holding a long, rectangular block in her hand. She places it on the floor next to the house that she and Danielle have built. '*This is the road*,' she says. She takes a shorter rectangular block and places it in front of the first one. '*It's going to be a long road. Here Danielle, you help me. Make the road to the end of the room*.' Krishna gets more blocks and she and Danielle continue to build the road with one long block and then one short block.	Krishna is able to initiate play experiences that draw on her own ideas and experiences (EYLF Outcome 4). Krishna is engaged in a shared learning experience with Danielle and there is evidence of cooperative play as they use the blocks to build a tower and road (EYLF Outcome 2). Krishna is able to preplan to achieve her goal (EYLF Outcome 4).	Plan further experiences in the area of construction, join in the play and engage children in conversations that encourage them to exchange ideas and work towards a shared goal. Model mathematical language including 'longer', 'shorter' and 'higher', and reasoning and predicting language, e.g. '*We need to build a bridge here so that the road can go across the train track*'.
4.17 pm	Krishna looks at Danielle, who is still building the tower. She says, '*It's too high. It will fall down*.' Danielle looks at the tower and then takes a cylindrical block and carefully *places it on top* of the tower. Krishna claps her hands and says, '*It's very high now*.'	She is able to create a pattern (EYLF Outcome 5) and uses visual discrimination to select appropriate-sized blocks. She is beginning to understand mathematical concepts such as size.	
4.19 pm	Krishna adds another cylindrical block to the tower. Danielle says, '*Now it needs a roof*.' Krishna takes a short rectangular block and tries to put it across the top of the tower, but it is too short. She puts this block down and takes a longer rectangular block, and then carefully places this across the top.	Krishna initiates conversation with a peer and communicates with purpose and confidence. She uses language to report what she is doing, to direct others, to predict what will happen and to plan, showing that she is using language for a number of different purposes (EYLF Outcome 5).	

 EXAMPLE 8.7

Anecdotes can support a developmental approach

Child: Maya

Date: 21/3/14

Context: This observation took place in the art area. The resources available were paint, magazines, scissors and coloured paper. Other children present were Sarah, Hamien and Jackson. Staff member present was Naomi.

Observation

Maya was sitting at the table with a piece of coloured paper in front of her. She picked up a paintbrush in her right hand and held it with all of her fingers wrapped around the brush. She placed some paint on the paper and then spread it around with the brush. Then she picked up a magazine and turned the pages.

She said, 'Look. Buzz.'

Hamien said, 'I've got Buzz at home.'

Maya said, 'Me too. I've got the video.'

She then picked up a pair of scissors in her right hand and held the scissors with her thumb and two fingers. She started cutting out a picture of Buzz Lightyear. She cut around his legs and then started to cut his body and moved up to his head. She had difficulty cutting when she got to his head as she started to twist her hand around rather than turning the paper. The paper started to tear. Maya put the scissors down and continued to tear the paper so that part of Buzz's head was torn off. She then used both her hands to stick the picture on to the paper.

She then said to Naomi, 'This is Buzz. Write Buzz.'

Analysis of learning

Maya shows preference for her right hand. She uses palmer grasp to hold a paintbrush. She is beginning to develop control of paintbrush and scissors. She uses language to interact with peers. She demonstrates conversational skills – initiating and responding and staying focused on the topic. She uses reporting language. She is beginning to understand the purpose of print and that words can be written down.

 EXAMPLE 8.8

Anecdotes can support sociocultural theories

Children: Angus, Ben, Charlie, Robbie

Date: 21/4/14

Context: Block construction with cars, trucks and road signs. There is a train station near the centre and Ben and Robbie both travel to the centre by train. The station has recently been redesigned and now includes lifts and ramps.

Observation

Angus and Ben went to the block construction area. They took down some blocks.

Angus said, 'Let's make a road'.

Ben said, 'Okay'. They laid some long blocks on the floor.

Angus said, 'We need more long ones'. Ben got more long blocks and placed them on the floor so that they joined together. Ben pushed a car along the road. Charlie and Robbie came over and started to build a tower. They pushed some of Angus and Ben's blocks out of the way.

Angus said, 'We were here first'.

Charlie and Robbie said, 'There's no room'.

After much discussion the boys decided to work together to build a road. Charlie started to get some cylindrical blocks off the shelf and to stack them on top of each other.

He said, 'This is the shops'.

'Put them over there', said Angus, pointing to the other side of the road.

Charlie and Robbie got more cylindrical blocks and built more shops. Ben said they needed a train station. Ben, Charlie and Angus built a station. Often the pieces fell down and they would pick them up and start again. Robbie put some cars on the road and pushed them around. Robbie said that the station needed a ramp for people in wheelchairs and babies in strollers. He tried to make a ramp with a rectangular block.

Angus said, 'You need a slopey one, like this', and put the block in place.

Charlie then decided that they needed some train track and a train and so he went to the wooden train set and took out some pieces of train track, an engine and some carriages. Robbie said they needed the ticket machine and a sign for the station. He got some cardboard from the craft trolley and asked Alex (educator) how to write 'station'. He wrote the letters on the cardboard: 2TaTion. The boys continued building the train track and station until it was time for lunch.

Analysis of learning

Angus initiated the building of the road and worked cooperatively with Ben. Charlie and Robbie initiated their own construction alongside and interrupted the play. The boys managed to negotiate and find a shared goal and then cooperated to build the road and the train station and train track (Outcome 2). They were actively engaged in the experience, able to persist with the task when faced with difficulties and were able to communicate with each other to share ideas, indicating they are developing dispositions such as persistence (Outcome 4). They are drawing on their real-world knowledge of roads and train stations and understand the purposes of environmental print, indicating that they understand that we use print for a range of purposes (Outcome 5).

EXAMPLE 8.9
Anecdotes can support critical theories

Children: Rhiannan, Susie, Mineka, Gabriel and Sam
Date: 14/2/14
Context: Pack-away time at the end of the day.

Observation

The girls – Rhiannan, Susie and Mineka – were playing in the dramatic play area. Gabriel and Sam walked in and said, 'We're Power Rangers'. They started leaping about and kicking at the furniture and the girls.

Susie said, 'Get out! This is the house! You can't come in here'.

Mineka and Rhiannan said, 'Yeah! Get out!'

The boys walked off. One minute later they came back and said, 'We're world championship wrestlers! We're the dads!' They started wrestling each other on the floor.

Mineka said, 'The dads have to go to work. We're staying home to look after the babies'.

The boys left and went over to the block area and started kicking at the block constructions that Brendan and Luke were building.

Analysis of learning

Gender relations – the children are re-enacting dominant discourses of what it is to be a girl/boy. The dialogue demonstrates the influence of popular media culture on children's identity construction.

Power relations – the girls are excluding the boys from play. The boys try to find an appropriate way to join in the play by being the 'dads', but at the same time are exerting power by being Power Rangers and then world championship wrestlers.

LEARNING STORIES

Postmodern and critical theorists have encouraged educators to rethink the ways in which they observe and document children's learning. They argue that observations are subjective and that power relations influence what educators see and know about a child (Mac Naughton, 2003). They also assert that there is no singular 'truth' about a child and that multiple perspectives, including those of children and families, as well as different members of staff and reflective conversations provide different pieces to the puzzle that makes up the full picture of the child (Karlsdottir & Gardarsdottir, 2010).

Learning Stories (*see* Examples 8.4, 8.10 and 8.18) are one means of achieving this. Carr (2001) and Carr and Lee (2012) have documented the Learning Stories approach to observation and assessment that has been used to great effect in New Zealand and Australia and has now spread to all parts of the world. This approach focuses on children's strengths within a social and cultural context. Learning Stories are narratives that detail children's everyday experiences, highlighting the 'significant points', rather than attempting to record minute details, and making 'feelings and interpretations visible' (Hatherly, 2006, p. 20). The format has evolved since they were introduced in 2001 and Learning Stories now generally include digital photographs to support the narrative or are digital or video stories (Carr & Lee, 2012).

Part of the significance of Learning Stories is the move from a deficit model of observing and recording what children can't do, and using this as the basis for planning, to a credit model, where it is possible to document situations when children show interest, when they stay with a task even if they are finding it difficult or where they make various attempts to communicate with peers or adults. The focus on children's strengths, identities, interests and dispositions promotes a positive focus on children's learning. Learning Stories help to make children's competencies 'more explicit and transparent' (Hatherly, 2006, p. 33). Hatherly's research, for instance, suggests that Learning Stories assist many families to see the literacy that is embedded in everyday experiences within the early childhood setting.

Learning Stories also provide many and varied opportunities for families and children to have input into the processes of documentation and 'enhance reciprocal, respectful relationships with families' (Hatherly, 2006, p. 29) and democratic processes. Families can contribute stories that provide insights into children's experiences at home and in their community, and can comment on and add to educator's and children's stories. Children can also contribute their own stories and make suggestions as to what should be included. Learning Stories can be co-authored with children, with educators doing the writing and children contributing the words, possibly accompanied by drawings or photographs, and children can contribute to the analysis and the future planning.

Digital technologies provide enhanced opportunities for involvement in all stages of Learning Stories, from documentation to analysis and future planning. Carr and Lee (2012, p. 42) also found that Learning Stories can become 'a jointly owned tool for sustained shared thinking' – the type of conversations that extend learning. They note that this type of dialogue helps children to reflect on and understand their learning, and to make connections between past and present experiences, thus providing continuity of learning.

EXAMPLE 8.10
Learning story – sorting buttons

Bree and Anna, thanks for your help in sorting through these buttons. When you started, they were all mixed up in one tin, but when you were finished, they buttons were sorted by colour and size, into a storage container with several compartments.

I could see that you enjoyed running your fingers through the buttons to start with! Then you started to put buttons into groups. Mostly, these were colour groups, but as you talked about what you were doing, you explained that you were making some interesting choices.

You told me about the white buttons, and how there was a group of plain white buttons, as well as a group of shiny white buttons. Then there were some pink buttons, but also some that were very pale pink, so you placed those in between the pink and the white groups. You had one group of big buttons and another group of buttons that were to be sewn from the back.

I liked the way you explained what you were doing. I could see how you placed buttons next to the groups to see if they matched on colour and you said that when you were not sure, you left the buttons between groups while you checked to see if there were any others like it. Sometimes, you decided to add to the main group; other times you made a new group.

When you had some very large groups, you looked at ways to break these into two smaller groups; when you had a very small group, you made decisions about which other buttons these could be grouped with. At the end, you made sure there was exactly the right number of groups for the number of compartments. You ended up with two groups of black buttons – one of flat buttons and the other sewn from the back; the same for white buttons; light pink, dark pink and red groups; a group of flat green buttons, and a group of other shaped green buttons; a group of yellow; a group of multicoloured buttons we decided to call 'tortoiseshell'; a mixed group of silver and multi-coloured buttons; a group of gold buttons; as well as groups of clear, grey, blue and brown buttons.

While you were sorting the buttons, I could tell that you were making lots of decisions about grouping. Sometimes, you could make a decision very quickly; other times you thought about your decision and tried out some different possibilities before making a decision.

What learning is happening here?

You both showed me how much you know about sorting and classification as you organised these buttons. You used many of the strategies that are important in data representation and interpretation. You were classifying data according to a range of variables – notably colour and size as well as the ways in which the buttons were to be sewn. As well, you were demonstrating principles of data reduction when you combined groups.

Opportunities and possibilities

It will be interesting to follow up your skills in working with data by exploring ways of recording this, for example using pictorial formats, such as charts or graphs.

JOTTINGS

Jottings are short notes about significant aspects or characteristics of a behaviour or event (McAfee & Leong, 2011). McAfee and Leong note that jottings are less time-consuming than anecdotes while still preserving significant details. Jottings may include words that children used in interactions, a description of the processes that a group of children engaged in as they constructed something or an explanation of how a child created a painting or drawing. Jottings can provide contextual details to support other observations, such as participation charts and work samples (McAfee & Leong, 2011). A series of jottings can be documented for a child or group of children as illustrated in Example 8.11.

DIARY OR JOURNAL

A diary or journal is also a type of narrative and can be a useful method for recording observations of a group of children or an individual child and educator's self-reflections. Families and children, as well as educators, can contribute entries to a child's diary or the setting's or classroom's diary, thus encouraging family involvement and partnerships. Stories of the day, or daily diaries, are a valuable medium for sharing children's learning with families. Families are aware that at the close of a child's day at the service, educators are not always free to engage with parents and/or carers in lengthy

EXAMPLE 8.11
A series of jottings for a group of children

2/9/14	Sebastian, Hiro and Mitchell have been very interested in the pirate books that we have put out. Their favourite is *I wish I had a pirate suit*. Sebastian is able to read some of this himself by using the pictures and his knowledge of the story.
4/9/14	Sebastian wanted to make a pirate's hat today, like the one in the book *I wish I had a pirate suit*. Lots of the children were interested – mostly boys but some of the girls also wanted to make hats. There was lots of discussion about whether girls could also be pirates. We looked up some of our books and found that there were women pirates. The children wore their hats for most of the day and there was lots of pirate play.
5/9/14	The children were pretending that the climbing structure was a pirate ship. The balance board was the plank! We found some rope to use to tie up the ship. Hiro said that they needed a pirate flag. We looked up some of our books to find out what a pirate flag looks like. Hiro, Mitchell, Kenya and Viktor worked together to make a large flag to fly on the pirate ship. Some of the other children – Sebastian, Lola, Alice and Amelia – made their own smaller flags.
6/9/14	Today the children continued with the pirate play. They used some empty fruit boxes as treasure chests.
9/9/14	The pirate play continued. Some of the children – Hiro, Ken and Sebastian – wanted to make swords. We discussed whether this was a good idea. Kenya and Lola said we shouldn't have swords because people would get hurt. Hiro said that the pirates needed swords to defend their treasure. We talked about this and decided that children could have swords if they were not used to hurt other children. We looked at our pirate books to find out what sorts of swords pirates had.

Analysis of learning

Sebastian, Hiro, Mitchell, Ken, Lola, Kenya, Viktor, Alice and Amelia are showing dispositions such as creativity, enthusiasm, persistence, imagination and cooperation. They are able to initiate and sustain their own play (EYLF Outcome 4). They are able to cooperate and negotiate with others and are beginning to consider others' perspectives, to critique dominant discourses of gender and to understand what is fair and unfair (EYLF Outcomes 1 and 2). They use verbal language to communicate their ideas and use books to investigate information as well as for pleasure (EYLF Outcome 5).

Sebastian is demonstrating an interest in books and stories and is beginning to understand the processes involved in reading (EYLF Outcome 5).

Ideas for future planning

Continue to provide resources that encourage children to investigate their interest in pirates. Include a range of art materials such as paper and paint, collage materials and boxes that will encourage children to represent their understandings using a range of media. Provide a range of texts including factual books and narratives about pirates, maps and treasure to extend children's learning. Continue to engage in conversations with children that challenge stereotypical views of gender roles and discourses of power and violence. Continue to encourage collaboration and negotiation and cooperative learning.

descriptions due to their responsibilities to the remaining children. However, written and visual information about the day will stimulate family collaboration in children's learning through discussion, research and possible provision of resources to extend on particular concepts or ideas. A story of the day accompanied by photographs and/or samples of work can make children's learning immediately visible in conjunction with progressive documentation over a period of time. The story of the day can be written in the room's daily diary or on a whiteboard.

The story of the day, or daily diary or journal, can provide a narrative, supported by visual documentation, of key moments in children's learning throughout the day, as illustrated in Figure 8.2. Documentation may include:

- transcripts of children's conversations
- photos of constructions, interactions or special events
- educators' commentary on the day's events
- children's and families' comments.

CHILDREN'S SELF-REFLECTIONS

Children's reflections on their own learnings are also narratives. Self-reflections provide children with opportunities to think critically about their learning, dispositions and engagement (Helm et al., 2007) and this contributes to their identities as learners (Carr, 2011). Reflections on learning support children to clarify and articulate their ideas, particularly when they are engaged in conversations with educators that scaffold and extend their thinking (Carr, 2011). When children's self-reflections are documented they provoke children to expand on and extend their earlier works (Helm et al., 2007).

Children's self-reflections can occur at the end of a project or unit of work when they are encouraged to remember and reflect on learning processes, group interactions and the way that their knowledge and understanding increased. Children's personal reflections can be oral, pictorial and/or written. Educators can assist young children to express their ideas by writing down their words alongside their own drawings or photographs of experiences. Children's participation in the documentation of their own learning also encourages self-reflection. Older children can be involved in self-assessing their own learning individually, by recording in a learning journal, or can be involved in group discussions or written documentation where group processes and learning are reflected on, as in Example 8.12.

Source: Integricare Children's Centre Homebush - Kurralee

FIGURE 8.2 An example of a daily diary.

EXAMPLE 8.12
Reflecting on learning

Context: Shanthi, Fatima and Mustaf were building in the block area. Emma (the educator) asked them if she could make a drawing of their building and if they could tell her about it so she could write it down. The children agreed.

> **Observation**
>
> Emma: So can you tell me how you created this building?
> Shanthi: We used some little blocks at the bottom but it fell down.
> Emma: So then what did you do?
> Shanthi: It kept falling down.
> Emma: So how did you solve the problem of the blocks falling down?
> Mustaf: We got bigger blocks.
> Emma: So where did you put the big blocks Mustaf?
> Mustaf: At the bottom.
> Emma: That's good problem solving. The big blocks at the bottom make the building more stable, don't they? It's stronger.
> Emma: Can you tell me about this bit at the top here Fatima?
> Shanthi: That's the offices.
> Emma: And how did you get those pieces to balance on top?
> Shanthi: We put this one here and then that one on top.
> Emma: That's a good strategy. The big blocks make a stable base for the smaller blocks on top.
> Mustaf: It's tall.
> Emma: Yes you made a tall building.
>
> The following day Emma showed the children the drawings she had made of their construction and talked with them about their building and the strategies they used. The children were keen to rebuild their ideas from yesterday and went straight to the block area. They recalled the strategies they had used the day before and began with large blocks at the base of their building. This time they extended the play by adding wooden people and cars at the base of the building and role played people going to work in their tower. Emma asked the children if she could take some photos and whether the children would like to share these at small group time with the other children and then display them for their parents to see.

Accessible documentation of children's work in progress and final pieces of work in portfolios and on wall displays, with still and or moving images, encourages conversations and reflections on learning amongst children and between children and families and children and educators.

Educators' questions and comments can encourage children's self-reflections. Some prompts for self-reflection include:

- Tell me (or show me) how you …?
- Can you explain how you did this part?
- Did you have any problems doing this? What did you do to solve them?
- How do you feel about this painting/sculpture …?
- How did you work as a group to …?
- What would you do differently if you were to do this again?
- Why do you want this included in the centre display/your portfolio?
- What do you think you have learned from doing this?

(Source: adapted from McAfee & Leong, 1997, p. 107.)

Research conducted by Carr (2011) found that conversations between educators and groups of children were effective, with the strategy of inviting children to explain to another child or group of children how they did something being particularly useful in eliciting detailed responses. When children engage regularly in these types of interactions and educators model the language used to talk about learning, children and educators develop a 'shared and situated learning language' (Carr, 2011, p. 264) and children begin to use this in their own talk.

Samples

Sampling observations include gathering examples of children's work, time samples and event samples. Some types of sampling, such as the collection of artefacts/work samples, give children and families a voice in the documentation of their experiences and learning as they are able to select artefacts for inclusion. Other types of samples, such as event samples, only include the educator's perspective. Time samples traditionally only include the educator's perspective, although they can be extended to be more inclusive of children's voices and more accessible to families; for example, with the addition of photographs taken by children or children's drawings of their day.

SAMPLES OF WORK /ARTEFACTS

Samples of work can include children's drawings, paintings, collages, constructions, sewing and weaving, maps and diagrams, writing and use of numbers. These can be individual or group samples, and may include children's words as they describe the processes involved or reflect on the end product. Families as well as educators can be involved in the collection of artefacts and children can be involved in decisions regarding which samples should be included in their portfolios. Some samples of work are included in Figure 8.3.

When samples are collected and dated they can provide insights into children's progress over time. Examples of works in progress, and first and final drafts of pieces of writing for older children, can also provide insights into the processes involved in the creation of artefacts. Collecting the most 'perfect' samples may not be so useful in identifying critical learning moments for children. When children select their own samples to add to the portfolio their choice also informs educators about their perceptions of learning and their self-assessment.

Samples on their own do not provide as much information as when the context and the processes are also documented. The circumstances leading up to, and surrounding, the production of a piece of work provide useful information as to the catalyst for the work and insights into the child's thinking. Descriptive notes or jottings of what occurred, who else was there and any conversations that occurred among children or between children and educators provide useful information as to how the artefact was produced.

TIME SAMPLES

Time samples are often used to support a developmental approach by observing particular behaviours or aspects of development and quantifying behaviours. They can also provide more qualitative information about the experiences of a child or group of children when the focus is on documenting narratives at regular intervals throughout the day or documenting the day in photographs.

Time samples can be useful for mapping a child's or a group's experiences for the whole day or part of the day. A time sample can record group dynamics and social interactions, experiences children engage with and their experience of routine times. In this way relationships, gender dynamics and friendship patterns can be observed (Mac Naughton, 2003).

FIGURE 8.3 Some samples of children's claywork, sewing, drawing and writing.

Different periods of time can be sampled, such as the outdoor play time, routine times or the whole day. The frequency of sampling will depend on the time period. It may be once every five minutes if the sample is for one hour of outdoor play, or once every hour if the sample is across the whole day. If routines are being observed, the sample would be taken during routines such as nappy change, meal times and rest times. Educators need to be careful not to draw conclusions about a child's experiences, friendships or interests based on a sample of one day. Time samples of a number of different days need to be completed before a picture of the child's day can be formed.

Time samples can be made more accessible to families and children with the inclusion of photographs or video footage to illustrate the group's day or a child's experiences. Time samples can include children's voices through children's involvement in taking the photographs and the inclusion of children's narratives to support the photographs. Annotated samples of children's work completed during the day can also be added to the time samples to further include children's thoughts.

Families' voices can be included when families document the child's day in the home environment. Just as educators document the child's day, families can be provided with a simple format that allows them to briefly document what their child/ren are involved in every 30 to 60 minutes in the home environment. Depending on each family, they may choose to add photographs or more detail as they feel comfortable. This can be particularly useful when a child is new to the service or with a very young child, as it allows the staff to ease the transition from home to centre and encourages connections between the families' child-rearing practices and the program within the service.

EVENT SAMPLES

Event sampling generally targets the particular behaviours of one child, but can also be used to observe a group of children. This type of observation may be useful for analysis of the cause and effect of behaviours, such as challenging behaviours. This information can then be used to make changes to the program. Event samples generally aim to analyse patterns of behaviour, triggers for certain behaviours and responses to particular behaviours. One useful format is the use of ABC (Martin, 2010). This involves the recording of:

A   the Antecedent event – what was happening just before the behaviour occurred that seemed to trigger it

B   the Behaviour – that is, exactly what the child does

C   the Consequent event – what occurred after the behaviour; that is: What did the adults do? What did the other children do? What happened in the environment?

Collecting this information through observation can help the educator identify why the behaviour might have occurred, what strategies are being used and what happens when these are used. It can also indicate whether it is necessary to collect more information before making any interpretations. It is important that educators do not make judgements about children's behaviours. These observations can encourage staff to make changes to the environment or the strategies in use to encourage children's social competence.

Language transcripts

Observations that record children's words are inclusive of children's voices and perspectives. These methods of observation support sociocultural and poststructuralist approaches to curriculum because they focus on interactions and the ways in which children work through and express their understandings of the world through language. As Mac Naughton (2003, p. 202) notes:

> Poststructuralist educators are interested in how language influences and structures children's understandings of the world. They observe children to discover how the discourses expressed in their language facilitate some ways of being and preclude others.

WORD LISTS

For very young children it is important to document the words that they are using. When family members and educators collaborate in compiling a list of words that a child is using and examples of these words used in context, as in Example 8.13, both parties are able to support the child's emerging language. For bilingual children it is essential to document words in the language/s that children speak at home as well as words that the child may be learning in English. Collaboration with families and bilingual staff to record the words that a bilingual child is familiar with at home can assist the staff to help the child feel comfortable in the new setting as well as supporting maintenance of the home language.

EXAMPLE 8.13

Toby's words (compiled by parent and educators)

WORD	EXAMPLE
Dog	Points to dogs when out walking and says 'dog'.
Duck	Points to a bird in a book and says 'duck'.
Go	Standing at the door and he says 'Go' (Let's go).
Dropped	Throws object from high chair, looks down and says 'Oh. Dropped'. Is walking outside and falls over and says 'dropped'. Looking at a picture book with Humpty Dumpty, gets to the part where Humpty fell off the wall and says 'dropped'.
Hat	'Oooh, hat!' Telling staff that his hat fell in the water trough.
Dat	Points to objects and says 'dat' = I want that.
Dat?	Points and says 'dat?' or 'what's dat?'
Door	Stands at door and says 'door' = open door/shut door.
Lo	Arrives in the morning and says 'lo' (hello) to staff.
Car, truck	Points to car driving past and says 'car'. Same for truck.

Lists can also be used with older children to represent what they know about a topic or the questions they want to investigate. When educators record children's words in this way children can see their words written down and use them in their own writing. Completion of word lists at the beginning and end of a project or unit of work highlights the growth in the complexity of children's understandings.

WEBS

Webs can be another means of recording children's words, as seen in Figure 8.4. Like lists, webs record children's ideas but represent them in a more connected way. Webs can be a useful way of recording children's growth in understanding and vocabulary during a project. Adding drawings and photographs to webs on display assists children to make meaning (Helm & Katz, 2001; Helm, 2011). Displaying these webs encourages children to reflect on and extend their learning.

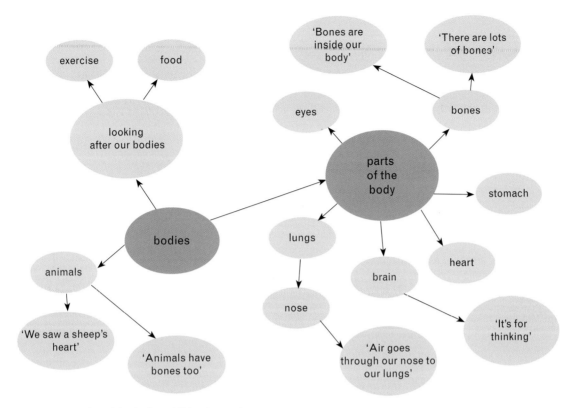

FIGURE 8.4 A web including children's words.

TRANSCRIPTS OF CONVERSATIONS

For older children, transcripts of conversations among children and between children and educators can provide many insights into children's thinking and uses of language. The recording of conversations in a range of social and learning contexts such as play, the sharing of news and the group discussion of a project enable the educator to document the ways that children use language for a variety of purposes, as illustrated in Example 8.14. Technologies such as audio or video recording can assist in the documentation of children's words as recordings can be replayed and excerpts of language transcribed.

EXAMPLE 8.14
Language transcript

Date: 16/5/13

Context: The children in the toddlers' room have been interested in reading Disney books about princesses. Ashlee's Mum said that Ashlee enjoys watching a program about 'Princess Sofia' with her sister. Not having heard of this show, Kathy (educator) did a search on the Internet for some images and engaged in a conversation with Ashlee and some other children about these. Some children then wanted to dress up as princesses using the Centre's dress-up clothes. Ashlee found a pink dress and said it was a princess dress.

Transcript of conversation:

Ashlee: I need a crown for my head (*as she looks through the baskets*).

Kathy: What else do you need to dress up as a princess?

Ashlee: Step-shoes (*high heels*)

Kathy asked if the children if they would like to have a look at the Disney princesses on the computer to get some ideas and they were very excited.

Kathy: What do you need to add to the dress ups?

Rose: Maybe more dress-ups, more dresses.

Kathy: What colours?

Amelia: Purple.

Then Kathy and the children looked and discussed what accessories the princesses were wearing like gloves, hair-bands, crowns and necklaces.

Kathy: What else do we need?

Rose: We need a torch.

Kathy: Why do we need a torch?

Rose: We need a torch to go in the cave like Sofia does.

Amelia: Can you put this on me? (*holding a crown*)

Rose: You're the royal princess! (*to Amelia*)

Rose: We have to kiss a prince.

Kathy: Why?

Rose: Because we have to get married.

Kathy then put on a clip of Beauty and the Beast dancing to a song and the children began to dance around, some of them holding hands. Rose was trying to get Amelia to kiss her as they danced.

Kathy: Who's the prince and who's the princess?

Rose: She's the prince. (*Pointing to Amelia*).

Amelia: No, I'm a princess.

Rose: Why do princes wear crowns?

After the clip had finished, most of the children went over to the dress-up area and began to put on more dress-ups, particularly the high-heeled shoes.

Rose: Bow to me when you speak to me! (*to Kathy*)

Kathy: Who says that?

Rose: Snow White.

Kathy: Snow White says that or someone in Snow White?

Rose: Oh yeah, the wicked witch says that.

Kathy: Why do I have to bow too?

Rose: Cause we're the fairy godmother.

Marcus put on a crown and was dancing around too.

Rose: He's the prince.

Kathy: Why does he have a tiara?

Study of the observation

Rose appears to be quite interested in the differences in the roles and 'outfits' of the princes and princesses. Why is this? Is she trying to get the details of the stories and character's right? Is she trying to encourage others to as well? The children appeared to be more interested in getting dress-ups on after looking at the pictures and watching the video clip. Did this give them ideas about what they could dress in or act out? If there were more gender specific princess and prince dress-ups, what would the children choose to use?

Planning the next step

- Add some different styles of crowns and dress-ups and observe what the children choose to use and how they use them.
- Engage in more critical literacy discussions, asking questions that challenge children's assumptions about gender roles.

Source: Mary Bailey House, 2013

It is not possible or necessary to record every conversation with children, and educators become very adept at identifying the essence of conversations with children. Educators can also work in pairs to engage in conversations with children and record their words. Digital recorders, MP3 players and tablet computers are useful for recording coversations for later analysis. When educators explain to children what they are doing and why they want to record their words, children can be involved in the documentation process by assisting educators to remember and record what they and others have said in discussions. The display of these conversations, along with artefacts that children have produced and photographs of them involved in play, enable children to revisit their discussions and clarify their ideas. As Jones and Reynolds (1992, p. 69) note, 'scribed representations of children's play can stimulate a debriefing process in which children and adults encounter each other on the shared turf of mutual curiosity'.

INTERVIEWS

'Interviews with children can provide great insight into how they perceive their world' (Puckett & Diffily, 1999, p. 135) and can be useful to obtain information about children's dispositions and the affective domains of learning (Dunphy, 2010). When people think of interviews they think of a formal and structured process, but interviews may be informal conversations as well as more formal discussions with preset questions. Informal conversations occur when an educator sits with a child or group of children and talks with them about what they are doing. More formal interviews may involve asking a child or group of children what they think about a subject such as maths, what they do when they read or how they feel about starting school, as in Example 8.15. It is important that interviews involve 'reciprocity and mutual turn-taking' (Dunphy, 2010, p. 49) so that children have agency in the process.

EXAMPLE 8.15
Interview with children

Context: Four preschool children (aged about four) and an interviewer (Sue) are sitting together in the drawing area of the preschool. The children have all chosen some paper and drawing materials and have agreed to draw and talk about what they think school will be like.

Sue: Ok, let me just check. Are you still happy to talk to me about what you think school will be like?

Ali: Yeah. I know what it will be like, 'cause I go there every day with my brother.

James: OK.

Maria: Yes. I do good drawings.

Sue: What about you, Marley? Do you want to draw and talk with me about school?

Marley: Mm. I don't know about school. I haven't been there yet.

Sue:	That's OK. You can still talk and draw if you like. But if you want to leave, just let me know and that will be OK too. So, you are all going to go to school soon – what do you think it will be like?
Ali:	I know there will be homework, 'cause I see my brother's homework every day!
Maria:	I think there will be numbers.
Marley:	And reading …
Sue:	Is there anything you need to know when you go to school?
James:	You need to know the rules.
Sue:	What sorts of rules?
Maria:	No pushing. No running. No hitting. No being silly.
Ali:	And you have to put your hand up … and talk when the teacher says.
James:	And sit down when the teacher says.
Marley:	Look out for big kids.

Source: Dockett & Perry, 2014.

Using informal interviews or discussion is also a positive approach to helping gather children's thoughts about emotions and feelings. For example, talking with children about what makes them angry, suggesting they draw or document this feeling in some way, and then exploring their options of how to deal with these feelings is an effective way to gather information and help children develop positive conflict resolution and problem-solving skills.

TRANSCRIPTS OF READING AND RETELLING TEXTS

Transcripts of young children's readings or retellings of familiar narratives or factual texts as well as transcripts of their own narratives, poems and songs and retellings of factual events (or 'news') can provide a great deal of information about their uses of language and understandings of literacy. In Example 8.16 it can be seen that Rose is able to use the pictures as well as her familiarity with the text and her knowledge of the world and language to make meaning of the text *The very hungry caterpillar*.

EXAMPLE 8.16
Reading transcript

Context: Yesterday during the morning, some of the children, including Rose and Harriet, were engaged in reading books to each other.

Note: The actual book text is added in italics

Rose has 'The Very Hungry Caterpillar' and begins turning the pages and reading to Harriet.

Observation

Rose: 'He ate through four blueberries.' (*On Thursday he ate through four strawberries, but he was still hungry*)

Rose turns the pages.

Rose: 'On Saturday he ate through one watermelon, one cupcake, one lollypop, one pickle and one ice cream.' (*On Saturday he ate through one piece of chocolate cake, one ice cream cone, one pickle, one slice of Swiss cheese, one slice of salami, one lolly pop, one piece of cherry pie, one sausage, one cupcake and one slice of watermelon. That night he had a stomach ache.*)

Rose: 'And then he was a big butt ...' Rose turns the page and sees the caterpillar picture, elongates the word she is saying and quickly turns the page to the butterfly picture ...

Rose: '... terfly! The end.' (*Then he nibbled a hole in the cocoon, pushed his way out and he was a beautiful butterfly.*)

Source: Mary Bailey House

Book source: Eric Carle, *The Very Hungry Caterpillar*

JOINTLY CONSTRUCTED TEXTS

Educators and children can jointly construct texts, as can be seen in Example 8.17. These collaborative texts may be poems or songs, narratives, notes to parents recounting the day's events or letters to the local newspaper or council expressing a point of view.

EXAMPLE 8.17
Collaborative story telling

13th September 2013

Rose asked if she could continue her story about Princess Ellen. She went outside and retrieved her book and came to sit down at the computer. Rose looked through her book and then said, 'Actually, I want to write another story. It will still be about a princess but her name won't be Ellen. Actually, I want to have lots of princesses'. Rose asked if she could type up her story in pink font. Mariam then set up the keyboard for Rose and Rose began to type as she narrated her story. Mariam questioned her about different aspects of her story to also prompt her to extend upon her ideas. During Rose's story telling she decided to invite Marcus and Li Ya to contributed to her story as she said, 'Li Ya, you're in my story! Come!' Rose decided to use them as characters for her story and asked them questions about what they were doing in her story. Rose incorporated their responses as part of her story.

Please note: Everything written in italics isn't part of the story; it describes what the children were doing.

Rose's story with Marcus and Li Ya as co-authors

Once upon a time there were five princesses. They were called Ariel, Cinderella, Mulan, Snow White and Jasmine. They went out for dinner at a Chinese restaurant. They ate plain pasta at the restaurant. The princesses went home after they ate and went in a Hello Kitty car. They decided to go back to the restaurant as they said, 'Oh let's stay here for longer'. Then something set on fire! The whole glass fell down and it cut Princess Jasmine's finger. She had a little cut and it was bleeding. The other princesses helped Princess Jasmine get up because she fell off the chair. The doctor came and laid her down onto the blanket and put a bandage on her finger. Jasmine was feeling better and she sat back on the chair. They were stuck in the restaurant and Mariam was there and she was a princess. The princesses went back to the Hello Kitty car and went to the ball and they left both their shoes at the ball. They went back to the restaurant and Marcus came out and put out the fire and David came.

Marcus then quickly went to the locker room and picked up his fire truck and brought it over to Rose. Marcus then continued Rose's story as he said: 'Marcus's fire truck then went nee naww neee naww neeee nawww'.

Rose then continued the story: 'Marcus put out the fire with Mariam. Marcus was Mariam's mummy. Jasmine's finger was better and she took off the bandage'.

Marcus then said: 'Make the fire engine put out the fire!' *Marcus then uses the fire hose. Rose then continues:* 'Mariam was still out there and was helping Marcus put out the fire. Lyne was there too and Li Ya was there'.

Rose then called Li Ya over and asked Li Ya what she was doing in the story. Mariam then told Li Ya what Rose's story is about and told her that she is currently in a restaurant as a character in the story. Li Ya then continued the story as Rose repeated what Li Ya said and typed it onto the keyboard.

Li Ya said: 'Li Ya was outside as she was playing and she was picking sticks. She had a pink stick and she was blowing bubbles. The big bubble fell to the ground'.

Rose then continued: 'And there was a king'.

Li Ya then continued: 'Li Ya's dad was the king'.

Rose then continued: 'The king made the fire because he was at the restaurant to be mean and he was a bad king'.

Li Ya then said that the king wasn't bad and altered the story to make the king a good king. Li Ya continued the story: 'The king was making food. He was making bread and he needs egg and some butter. The king is a good cook because he knows how to cook. He ate all the food by himself'.

Rose then altered Li Ya's last sentence as she added: 'He didn't eat the food, he gave it to the people at the restaurant. And then he fell down and he hurt his head'.

Li Ya continued: 'He went home and that's the end'.

Rose then added: 'That's not the end'.

Li Ya continued: 'And he did some drawing'.

Rose then added: 'He was drawing and he put a washer on his head'.

Li Ya and Rose then had to get ready for lunch and they agreed that the story wasn't yet finished and needed to be continued … **To be continued**

Key learning areas

- Developing skills in communicating effectively
- Developing listening skills
- Engaging in oral storytelling
- Enhancing awareness of story structure and narratives
- The children are taking turns in conversations
- Developing receptive and expressive language skills
- The children are widening their vocabulary
- Developing creative expression
- Developing skills in forming sentences
- Developing confidence in speaking
- Developing an ability to create an original story
- Exploring diverse genres through story telling.

Reflections

- When educators document children's stories, children are developing an awareness of how written language can represent their thoughts.
- The children are developing a sense of community and belonging as they are freely invited to contribute to the story
- The children are exploring a diverse range of expressions including character dialogue
- By asking questions to prompt parts of the story, educators are assisting children to build knowledge of the elements of a story- the start, the characters, an event, an ending etc.

Study of the observation

The children are continuing to display confidence in telling their stories to their peers and educator. The children are adding more detail and description to their stories and we are inviting them to add some character dialogue by asking open-ended questions such as, 'Did the princess say anything?' 'Does he/she talk?' 'What did they say?' That way the children are encouraged to explore a wider range of roles in storytelling such as being the narrator or being the character within the story.

Rose skilfully used questioning to invite her peers to contribute to the story. She informed her peers that she included them in the story and then went ahead by asking them open-ended questions about what they were doing in her story. Rose incorporated all the children's suggestions into the story and was incorporating their dialogue in the form of a story by typing this onto the computer. Rose decided to use a Chinese restaurant as the setting for her story. She appears to be drawing upon her own previous experiences when she went out to dinner at a Chinese restaurant not long ago. When Li Ya and Rose were storytelling together, they had different opinions and ideas about what the characters were doing. However, both Rose and Li Ya were able to negotiate their ideas in the story and both appeared happy to accept amendments made to the story. This indicates that the children enjoy storytelling together and that they respect each other's ideas and value each other's suggestions. The children appear to thoroughly enjoy the idea of collaborative storytelling and this is a wonderful way to connect with peers and allows children to develop a sense of belonging.

Planning the next step

- To invite Li Ya and Rose to continue the story
- To continue to involve the children in group and collaborative storytelling
- Rose asked if she could get some pictures to add to her story – we will invite her to do this
- To determine how children's life experiences influence their stories.

Visual representations

Visual representations include photographs, video and digital recordings, diagrams and visual diaries. These methods vary from observations that are quick and easy to use, such as photographs, to methods that are more time-consuming but which provide a wealth of information, such as video recordings. Photographs and videos can also be added to narrative observations, such as anecdotes and Learning Stories.

Visual representations assist educators to share children's learning with families in easily accessible ways. Walters (2006), an early childhood educator, found that digital photographs supported families' understandings of play-based learning and children's role in negotiating curriculum with educators and peers. Parents 'became more involved, asked questions and thus found they had a role to play in the development of the curriculum' (Walters, 2006, p. 1).

The use of visual representations should support and extend educators' understanding of children's learning and development as well as provide opportunities for sharing this learning in a meaningful way with others. The overuse of these methods can lead to many images with no link to the contexts of children's learning and may lead to the children themselves becoming dependent on the taking of a photograph of their experience to validate their learning (Farmer, 2009).

PHOTOGRAPHS

Photographs can be particularly useful in capturing children's engagement in experiences, group processes, the stages in children's creations and constructions, and group projects. As Martin (2010) notes, the purpose is to capture children in action. It is important therefore that photographs are natural, not staged. Children understand when educators taking photographs are valuing their learning in contrast to 'smiley' and 'cute' photographs. Children can also use cameras and tablet computers to record their own learning and to create their own stories as in Example 8.18.

EXAMPLE 8.18

Children as photographers

Date: 9 October 2013

Mariam (educator) asked Summer if she wanted to use toys to tell a story. Summer liked this idea and so Mariam offered her a basket of toys and she selected the ones that she wanted to be her characters. Summer then took the toys to the computer and stood them on the table. Mariam then asked her open-ended questions to prompt her to storytell about the characters. As Summer was storytelling, Mariam asked her if she wanted to take photos of the characters and she thoroughly enjoyed getting the opportunity to use the camera. Summer was very efficient at handling the camera and took great close up shots of her characters!

Summer takes photographs that she later uses to tell a story.

Source: Mary Bailey House

Careful thought should be given to the purposes of each photograph taken and how it contributes to the understanding of the child or group of children. As with samples of work, documentation of the context in which the photograph was taken and a jotting describing the processes in which the child or children were engaged provides information that adds meaning to the photograph. If the setting's image of the child is one of a competent and capable child, then children will also be given the opportunity to be the photographer, to make decisions about which photographs are displayed and to add commentary to photographs.

The complexity of a construction completed by a child or group of children can be captured effectively through photographs. Photographs of the construction in different stages can provide insights into the problem-solving and group-negotiation skills used to make the construction. Puckett and Diffily (2004) suggest that photographs of children's block constructions can be displayed in the block area and can also be compiled into a block book that children can subsequently revisit and draw on.

VIDEO/DVD RECORDINGS

Video/DVD recordings are useful for capturing the complexity of children's play and interactions, as well as the creation of products over time. A video recording can capture movement, interactions and language. Videos/DVDs can be particularly valuable for recording children's creative expressions through forms such as song, dance and dramatic play. As with still photography, children can also be actively involved in filming, selecting excerpts to be shared with others and giving meaning to what is captured on film.

One of the benefits of video/DVD recordings is that they allow children, families and educators to revisit, discuss and reflect on what is happening. Recordings of works in progress and excursions enable children to recall past experiences and to notice things they may have missed at the time (Helm et al., 2007).

The revisiting of video or DVD footage with children also promotes children's reflective thinking and extends their learning, particularly when they are able to immediately revisit their actions. Hong and Broderick (2003) have demonstrated how reviewing video footage with children assists children to engage in conflict resolution and also to strengthen their understandings of narrative construction. Videos and DVDs also allow educators the opportunity to revisit, review and discuss events, thus assisting in the process of analysis as well as sharpening their observation and analysing processes (Forman & Hall, 2005).

DIAGRAMS AND SKETCHES

Educators do not need to have access to a camera to document children's learning. Diagrams and sketches can be effective ways of recording products that cannot be saved, such as children's constructions, as well as fostering children's understandings of multiple modes of representation. As with photographs, diagrams and sketches can record stages in the creation of a product. Diagrams such as the one in Example 8.19 provide a useful way of sharing children's constructions with families and encouraging children to reflect on

their learning. Jones and Reynolds (1992, p. 61) point out that 'reminding children of their interesting play encourages them to repeat it, to understand and elaborate it more fully'.

EXAMPLE 8.19
An educator's diagram of children's block construction

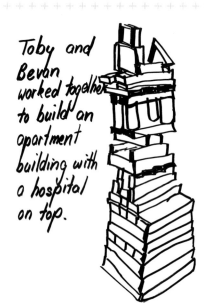

Toby and Bevan worked together to build an apartment building with a hospital on top.

Source: Summer Hill Children's and Community Centre

Analysis

The children worked collaboratively by working towards a shared goal, negotiating ideas, problem solving (EYLF Outcome 2) and developing stories to accompany their construction (Outcome 5).

Diagrams and sketches are a quick method of recording and can be completed while interacting with children. They are also a positive way to include all staff, irrespective of literacy levels or English language skills, in collecting information about children. When educators draw diagrams and display examples of diagrams, plans and maps, children are encouraged to use these forms of representation to draw their own creations or to plan for constructions, as demonstrated in Example 8.20. The addition of a narrative to accompany diagrams can provide more information about the context and processes involved in the construction. As Jones and Reynolds (1992) note, these diagrams and narratives become literacy artefacts. When educators share their diagrams and written observations with children, they can foster children's language and literacy learning, and also encourage appreciation of the way that play can be represented.

EXAMPLE 8.20
Children can draw their own plans for construction

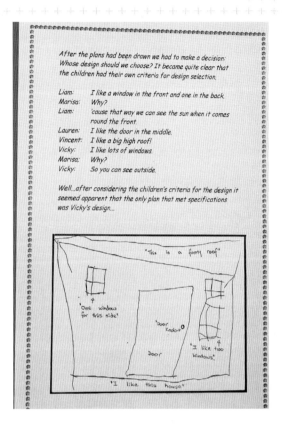

Context

As part of a project on houses the children visited houses, looked at photos and architects' plans of houses and then drew their own plans for a house to be constructed in the outdoor environment.

Analysis

The children have a strong understanding of the process of planning and constructing a house. Vicky has a strong understanding of the purposes of plans and is able to represent her ideas using 2D shapes. She is drawing on her previous experiences to include fine details representing many understandings about houses and plans.

Source: Earlwood Children's Centre

VISUAL DIARIES

Visual diaries are a quick way of recording children's engagement in experiences over a period of time. A visual diary is generally completed for one child and, if conducted over a number of days, can provide insights into a child's interests and friendships. Figure 8.5 provides an example of a visual diary.

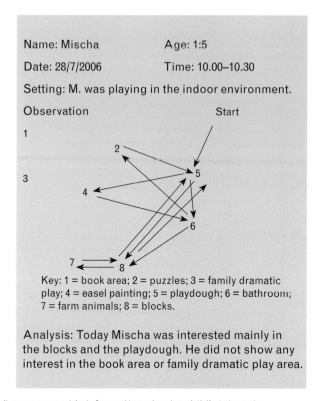

Name: Mischa   Age: 1:5

Date: 28/7/2006   Time: 10.00–10.30

Setting: M. was playing in the indoor environment.

Observation   Start

Key: 1 = book area; 2 = puzzles; 3 = family dramatic
play; 4 = easel painting; 5 = playdough; 6 = bathroom;
7 = farm animals; 8 = blocks.

Analysis: Today Mischa was interested mainly in
the blocks and the playdough. He did not show any
interest in the book area or family dramatic play area.

FIGURE 8.5 A visual diary can provide information about a child's interests.

Checklists and rating scales

Checklists are quick and easy to use and can provide a summary of children's development, but provide little information that is useful for future planning. Checklists are a closed method of observation, providing no contextual details. As Briggs and Potter (1999, p. 140) note, checklists 'do not necessarily indicate the quality of the work or the level of understanding'. Without any details, educators are also not able to understand children's perspectives or their intent (Dunphy, 2010).

McAfee and Leong (2011) argue checklists have a tendency to oversimplify the complexity of children's learning. They only focus on what a child can/can't do and are often attached to developmental milestones that are set against an age standard. These were often developed for children with additional needs as a way of assessing children's development and first appeared early last century, along with IQ testing.

Checklists have a narrow focus in that they are only concerned with measuring development and generally in narrowly defined areas of skill, such as the ability to use a pincer grip or to use three or more words in an utterance. The purpose of these developmental checklists is to tick an observable behaviour, such as balancing on one leg. In some cases experiences are set up with the specific purpose of observing children in particular areas so that these items can then be ticked on the checklist. The assessor is then meant to identify what this assessment may mean for the child, such as issues with balance, coordination or confidence, and then support the child to develop in these areas. There has been a tendency to use the assessment results to *teach the next step* on the list, which may be a skill such as hopping on one leg or cutting along a straight line, rather than encourage the underlying development and understandings behind these skills. With large groups of children, checklists may be useful for educators to see the overall patterns in what all children are currently doing, but they need to be supported by additional documents – such as anecdotes, interviews, reading running records and so on – that provide relevant details about interactions, relationships and processes of learning. Checklists are not useful as the only form of documentation.

Rating scales are similar to checklists in that they focus on development, but rather than using a simple yes or no, they rate the child's level of competence. The scale is often from one to five, with one being 'poor' and five being 'highly defined'. As with checklists, rating scales have a narrow focus on developmental skills and do not offer any contextual information. They require the observer to make qualitative judgements about a child's behaviour that is not validated with detailed observations (Martin, 2010).

Collating information from multiple sources

Educators integrate information gathered from a range of sources to facilitate collaborative analysis and planning. Regular summaries of shared understandings of a child's learning, development and interests will provide information for families, children and staff to revisit. Summaries of children's learning may be recorded in a number of different ways. They may focus on development and record the child's progress over time in each developmental area, they may focus on learning outcomes or they may be organised more holistically. Example 8.21 shows a summary of learning for a child. This example was shared with the child's family in a parent-teacher interview where the family expressed their desires for their child's learning, which was recorded by the teacher and incorporated into the planning as illustrated in Example 8.22. Planning in this way and sharing the plans with families enables them to see the way that literacy and numeracy are incorporated into every day routines and play-based experiences.

EXAMPLE 8.21
Summary of learning for Aayan, aged three years

Mid-year summary – July 2013

Dear Aayan

I am writing to you and your family to share what you have been doing at Kurralee so far this year.

You are interested in interacting with preferred peers in a variety of experiences and activities. Here you take on diverse roles of decision making to ensure all peers are respected and you have equal relations with children engaging in your learning.

You show strengths in developing secure attachments with educators and peers in the environment. This reflects your sense of identity. You collaborate and listen to ideas and suggestions of others. You have been observed engaging in apects of role play such as cooking, feeding dolls and pretending to work in an office. This is part of you exploring your identity. When working in partnership with your peers you explain your decisions. For example you say: 'There is no space in the tunnel' and you then call your peer when a space is available. This is part of your ability to self regulate. This is linked to how you connect to and contribute to your world. As part of your connection to your world you actively seek preferred peers to play with. Here you are challenged to be inclusive of all children who want to engage with you. At this stage you are only able to associate and play with one child. In relation to your wellbeing you show an ability to persevere at tasks, supporting your ongoing learning. You use complex gross and fine motor movement to achieve patterns of activity, for example dancing. You show you have a well developed sense of spatial awareness that supports you to orient yourself and move around confidently and safely. This allows you to increase opportunities for learning in activities. At this stage of the year the images you represent are in the symbolic stage. You experiment with colour and strokes. You state the name of an image you have created or say the word 'finished'. In general you show yourself as confident and involved in learning. You willingly participate in planned and spontaneous experiences. You ask questions to inquire about experiences. You show satisfaction in tasks by your comments such as 'I did it'. In your play you explore mathematical thinking, e.g. sorting.

You use objects to role play ideas. In regards to your ability to be an effective communicator you show well developed expressive and receptive language. You show an interest in exploring various print and letters.

You have been interested in learning about mathematical concepts, fundamental movement, spatial awareness, being social and being able to negotiate play.

When you play in the indoor environment you love to dance to music. Is this about your movement, creativity and exploration of your imagination? You spend a lot of time at playdough and in the homecorner. Is this reflective of your identity and wellbeing?

When you play outdoors you are observed creating and developing ideas with peers in the sandpit. Here you enjoy social interaction as part of your learning. As you manipulate the equipment you sing songs or rhymes, or you ask peers to catch you.

You like playing with Jayashri and Nera. You are developing an ability to be fair and inclusive of both children in your play.

In conclusion you show through your ability to follow routines and engage in play where you are independent and you can follow instructions. This was part of your parent input from a survey they completed about your learning.

From Carla

Source: Integricare Children's Centre Homebush – Kurralee; Proforma developed by Jenny Green; Summary completed by Carla Paszti

EXAMPLE 8.22
Family input into planning

After meeting with Aayan's parents to discuss the summary of his learning, the educator and family collaboratively developed goals for Aayan's learning and strategies to progress these.

Name: Aayan

FAMILY OBJECTIVE	STRATEGIES TO SUPPORT OBJECTIVES	IN PRACTICE	DATES FOR INCLUSION
Familiarising self with letters	Literacy in the environment. Recognising his name and what his name starts with. Looking at letters on signs, posters etc. Reading books – asking questions such as: • What do you think the picture in the book represents? • What letter does this word start with? Playing with magnetic letters.	Planning to incorporate a literacy area that reflects Aayan's engagement and interests. Incorporating literacy at transition times, e.g. If your name starts with … A … wash your hands. Clapping syllables in names. Writing your name on artwork. Talking about the letters in your name.	Intentional planning Week 9/9/13

FAMILY OBJECTIVE	STRATEGIES TO SUPPORT OBJECTIVES	IN PRACTICE	DATES FOR INCLUSION
Knowing numbers	Numeracy in the environment Recognising numbers Incorporating numbers with interests – e.g. cooking.	Discuss numbers: E.g. I wonder what this number is? Using stories or counting songs and rhymes, e.g. ten fat sausages.	Intentional Planning Week 9/9/13

Source: Integricare Children's Centre Homebush – Kurralee; Proforma developed by Jenny Green; Summary completed by Carla Paszti

Portfolios

A portfolio is a way of bringing together and organising information collected over time. The content of a portfolio will be determined by the educator's philosophy, approaches and frameworks, as well as the intended audience and purpose. Audiences for portfolios may be the child and family, a new educational setting (e.g. school) and/or other professionals (e.g. early intervention staff).

Portfolios provide evidence of children's learning and progress, often towards meeting curriculum goals or learning outcomes. Narratives, samples, transcripts and photographs can be gathered together in an individual or group portfolio. In this way a portfolio can document not only children's end-products, but also works in progress. As Martin (2010) notes, a portfolio considers the whole child. Portfolios capture many dimensions of a child's learning and include many examples of a child's strengths and approximations as they refine their learning. They include summaries of learning, family input, the child's interactions in experiences, analysis and reflections on learning, as in the excerpts from Aayan's portfolio in Examples 8.21, 8.22 and 8.24.

Portfolios take many forms, such as a scrapbook, display book, loose-leaf folder or collection box. Some settings use a digital camera to record children's experiences, word-process narratives and scan samples of children's work to create an electronic portfolio. All children have their own digital file on the setting's computer and receive a copy of the portfolio on USB or by email at the middle and end of the year.

Families and children can contribute to portfolios in a number of ways. Children can select items to be included in their portfolios or in the documentation of projects as evident in Example 8.23. Families may periodically take their child's portfolio home to read and comment on entries and to add new information, or they may read and add to the portfolio at the setting.

There may be concurrent portfolios with separate portfolios for ongoing, current and permanently kept work (Helm et al., 2007). When portfolios regularly go home with children and families, educators may need to consider the use of a working portfolio or file at the setting that enables them to maintain children's records.

EXAMPLE 8.23
Children contribute to the documentation of their learning

Context: The toddlers' room. This morning Rose, Alessia, Kevin, Caitlin and Alexander were engaged in reading stories to themselves and one another. Rose and Alessia decided to sit on the lounge and read some stories. They chose a book each and began to story tell. Kevin and Alexander stood by and listened to the children's stories:

Transcript:

Rose: That's Iggle Piggle

Alessia: And who's that?

Rose: Upsy daisy

Alessia: Iggle Piggle went to the farm

Alessia: Upsy Daisy got some flowers

Rose: Look what happened to my piggy

Alessia: What happened to your finger? Is it from the sandpit? (*Alessia notices a bandage on Rose*)

Rose: Yes

Alessia: Is it still bleeding?

Rose: No. Can you get another book for me?

Rose: Want me to read it?

Kevin: Yes.

Rose: Sit.

Rose: That's duck. Ducky. Do you know what baby means?

Kevin: Yeah.

Rose: I like that one.

Kevin: Quack

Rose: In the lake, on the lakey, on the lake.

Image selected by Rose   Image selected by Alessia   Image selected by Kevin

Children can select photos for inclusion in their portfolios or project documentation.

Source: Mary Bailey House

Linking assessment and planning

The documentation, analysis and collation of children's family contexts, friendships, strengths and interests assist educators to plan and implement appropriate learning experiences. Experiences may be planned based on the interests and questions of a group of children and result in a series of interest-based investigations or a long-term project. At other times the educator may spontaneously respond to the interests of a child or group of children by providing additional resources, making comments that challenge and complicate thinking or asking questions that encourage further investigation. This interest may be sustained over a period of time and lead to a longer-term, planned investigation or project or the children may move on to a new interest.

EXAMPLE 8.24
Excerpt of planning for Aayan, taking into account family goals

Intention for Aayan's learning

To follow up engagement in mathematically rich experiences to support mathematical concepts and associated language.

Observations for learning

8/10/13
Here you sat with Sienna, Bradley and Jayshri to explore blocks.

As you explore blocks you make the following comments. 'It square', holding up a square shaped block.

Finding an image of a house on a block you say 'it mummy's house'

When a peer knocks over someone's building you say 'go around'

You use words 'long' and 'wide' when talking about your structures.

Part of Aayan's portfolio

Source: Carla Paszti, Integricare Children's Centre Homebush – Kurralee

Links can be made from individual and group documentation to suggestions for planning. These are possible ideas for further experiences and suggestions for teaching strategies that can inform educators in their decision making regarding planned experiences and long-term projects, and in their spontaneous interactions and responses to children's ideas. For further discussion of planned and spontaneous experiences, see Chapter 10.

Example 8.25 illustrates how educators at one early childhood centre plan and evaluate using a project approach.

EXAMPLE 8.25
Weekly project investigation

Date: 12 June 2013 **Room:** Lilly Pilly Gully, Mary Bailey House

PROJECT TITLE: STORYTELLING WITH TODDLERS

Research question	Focus teacher	Intentional teaching	Strategies	Meeting the research question
Does the familiarity and subject of books determine the children's choice in reading them? What types of books motivate children to engage in reading? What influences the manner in which the children read to others?	Kathy, Lyne & Mariam	To support the children's ability to create stories from their favourite popular culture characters and picture books	• To use popular culture stories and characters as a scaffold to write stories • To show the children clips and images of popular culture characters • To note down what is attracting individual interests in books and stories • To write down the children's stories • To read the stories back to children • To invite the children illustrate their stories	The children have been creating stories that have come from images of popular culture and also from their engagement with the computer; typing, Google images. The children enjoyed looking through Google images to illustrate their stories. In most instances the children were invited to tell a story that was prompted by educators and the reading of Rose's story. The children listened to Rose's story and then created their own story drawing upon some of Rose's story and also family members; naming characters as family members. The strategy of inviting the children to 'type' their story seemed to support the process of story construction. Is this because they didn't feel pressured to tell a story? And the typing distracted the focus from them? We'll continue to use this strategy where possible to engage the children in the process. As some children seemed overwhelmed by the vast number of images on Google we could possibly print off a select number of images to use in their stories. Illustrations will be aligned with the text in the coming week and then personal stories will be read to peers and we'll observe how the group reacts. The project is presently engaging most of the older children. Is this because they have the expressive language skills to construct a story? How then can we support the younger children in telling stories? Could we use images from familiar books and popular culture characters to prompt story telling?

Mary Bailey House. 2014.

Documenting experiences, investigations and projects

Documentation of children's work, ideas and responses assists educators to guide projects (Helm & Beneke, 2003). Daily documentation of experiences and projects provides feedback on children's responses and suggests additional resources or strategies. A range of methods can be used to document children's learning in investigations and projects. These may include:

- collections of children's writing, drawing and painting with supporting narratives
- transcripts of conversations, as in Example 8.26
- narratives of children's play, such as Learning Stories
- videos of play and works in progress
- group observations of play, cooperative work, dramatic play and joint constructions
- photographs or diagrams of constructions – with clay, blocks, boxes and so on – in progress as well as the end product
- transcripts of children's recounts of events such as excursions and the processes involved in their creations
- displays of children's work with accompanying narrative of processes involved
- videotapes and texts of children's creations of music, dance and song
- webs of children's ideas, questions and changing understandings
- word lists of what children know about the topic under investigation
- children's self-reflections on their learning, engagement, dispositions and group processes.

When drawings, webs, word lists and transcripts of conversations are documented at the beginning and end of a project they can indicate the development of children's conceptual understandings and their detailed knowledge of the area under investigation. Example 8.26 shows an excerpt from a conversation at the end of a project about insects.

These types of open-ended, flexible and inclusive methods of documenting experiences and projects can assist educators to:

- analyse children's understandings, dispositions and interests
- pay attention to children's progress
- share children's experiences and learning with others – children, families, educators and community
- make children's learning visible and accessible to families and educators
- facilitate the exchange of information between families and educators
- provide opportunities for children to revisit and reflect on their experiences and learning
- provide opportunities for educator self-reflections
- record what is happening so that children and educators can reflect on it and use these reflections to make future plans
- meet accountability requirements.

For more information on documenting planned and spontaneous experiences, see Chapter 10.

▶ EXAMPLE 8.26
An excerpt from documentation of a project about insects

17.2.14

Anecdote: Today when we entered the BBY, I noticed a group of children excitedly gathered around on the barkchip, pointing at something I approached with interest, and keen to ensure not only to build on their curiosity but assess safety as well.

It turned out to be a CICADA!!!

After so many weeks of finding SO many cicada shells on the trees in the yard, we had a real live cicada to look at. Mandela recalled when we found the Green Grocer, in our first week back at Kurralee this year. This one that we found today was a Black Prince. He was not very well ...

Georgia: What happened to it?
Mandela: I think it fell down
Owen: Maybe a bird tried to eat it
Georgia: Does it fly?
Mandela: Yeah, look at its wings
Aditya: Cicada wings are long and beautiful,
Tanvi: Look I found a shell. Did it come out of this oner?
Aaron: Sophia, (action for sleep and pointing to cicada)
Sophia: Yes, the cicada is a bit sleepy, and a bit sick
Mandela: If it is sick, put it at the tree, and it can be safe

Source: Integricare Children's Centre Homebush – Kurralee, documentation by Carla Paszti

Conclusion and reflection

This chapter highlighted the importance of ongoing formative assessment as a key component of curriculum planning. Pedagogical documentation and assessment of the learning that is evident in this documentation supports informed decisions about curriculum that provides meaningful links to children's current understandings and interests, and supports and extends learning.

Questions for reflection

1. Examine the methods of documentation and assessment used in your setting. Who/what has determined that these be used? What are the advantages and disadvantages of using these methods? What interesting information is generated through these methods? What other methods of documentation might give you additional insights into children's experiences and learning?

2. What part do children and families play in initiating, contributing to and analysing documentation? Why is this? How could you strengthen children's participation in documentation processes?

3. What theories do you draw on in your documentation and assessment of children's learning? What other theories might provide insights into aspects such as processes of learning, power relations and dispositions?

Key terms

assessment, 257

dispositions, 260

funds of knowledge, 262

intentional teaching, 258

pedagogical documentation, 258

Online study resources

Visit http://login.cengagebrain.com and use the access code that comes with this book for 12 months access to the student resources for this text.

CourseMate Express

The CourseMate Express website contains a range of resources and study tools for this chapter, including:

- Online video activities
- Online research activities
- A revision quiz
- Matching pair exercises
- A list of key weblinks
- A chapter glossary, flashcards and crossword to help you revise terminology
- and more!

Search me! education ▶ Search me! 🖱

Explore **Search me! education** for articles relevant to this chapter. Fast and convenient, Search me! education is updated daily and provides you with 24-hour access to full text articles from hundreds of scholarly and popular journals, ebooks and newspapers, including *The Australian* and *The New York Times*. Log in to Search me! through http://login.cengage.com and try searching for the following key words:

- **documenting children's learning**
- **dispositions**
- **Learning Stories.**

Search tip: **Search me! education** contains information from both local and international sources. To get the greatest number of search results, try using both Australian and American spellings in your searches, e.g. 'globalisation' and 'globalization'; 'organisation' and 'organization'

Recommended resources

Barnes, S 2012, *Provocations on Assessment in Early Childhood Education*, Children's Services Central, http://www.cscentral.org.au/Resources/provocations-on-assessment-in-ece-web.pdf

Australian Government Department of Education, Employment and Workplace Relations (DEEWR) 2010, *Educators Belonging Being and Becoming: Educators Guide to the Early Years Learning Framework for Australia*, DEEWR, Canberra, http://files.acecqa.gov.au/files/National-Quality-Framework-Resources-Kit/educators_guide_to_the_early_years_learning_framework_for_australia.pdf

Farmer, S 2009, *Collaborative Documentation and Planning*, Department of Education and Training, TAFE NSW Training and Education Support, Industry Skills Unit, Meadowbank, NSW.

Fleer, M, Edwards, S, Hammer, M, Kennedy, A, Ridgway, A, Robbins, J & Surman, L 2006, *Early Childhood Learning Communities: Sociocultural Research in Practice*, Pearson, Sydney.

Fleet, A, Honig, T, Robertson, J, Semann, A & Shepherd, W 2011, *What's Pedagogy Anyway: Using Pedagogical Documentation to Engage With the Early Years Learning Framework*, Children's Services Central, http://www.cscentral.org.au/Resources/what-is-pedagogy-anyway-.pdf

Key weblinks

Australian Children's Education and Care Quality Authority (ACECQA), http://acecqa.gov.au/
Early Childhood Australia, http://www.earlychildhoodaustralia.org.au/
Early Childhood Research in Practice Journal, http://ecrp.uiuc.edu/
Project Approach, http://www.project-approach.com

References

Alloway, N 1995, *Foundation Stones: The Construction of Gender in Early Childhood*, Curriculum Corporation, Carlton, Victoria.
Arthur, L 2010, *The Early Years Learning Framework: Building Confident Learners*, Early Childhood Australia, Canberra.
Barnes, S 2012, *Provocations on Assessment in Early Childhood Education*, Children's Services Central, http://www.cscentral.org.au/Resources/provocations-on-assessment-in-ece-web.pdf, accessed 28 February 2014.
Bentzen, W 2000, *Seeing Young Children: A Guide to Observing and Recording Behaviour*, 3rd edn., Delmar, Albany, NY.
Bourdieu, P 1984/1993, *Sociology in Question*, English trans. by R Nice, Sage, London.
Bowman, B, Donovan, MS & Burns, MS (eds) 2001, *Eager to Learn: Educating Our Preschoolers*, National Academy Press, Washington, DC.
Briggs, F & Potter, G 1999, *The Early Years of School: Teaching and Learning*, 2nd edn., Longman, Melbourne.
Carr, M, Cowie, B, Gerrity, R, Jones, C, Lee, W & Pohio, L 2001, 'Democratic learning and teaching communities in early childhood: Can assessment play a role?', paper presented at the conference on Early Childhood Education for a Democratic Society, Wellington, New Zealand, October.
Carr, M, 2011, *Young Children Reflecting on their Learning: Teachers' Conversation Strategies*, Early Years, vol. 31, no. 3, pp. 257–70.
Carr, M & Lee, W 2012, *Learning Stories: Constructing Learner Identities in Early Education*, Sage Publications Ltd.
Cheeseman, S & Robertson, J 2006, 'Unsure: Private conversations publicly recorded', in A Fleet, C Patterson & J Robertson (eds), *Insights: Behind Early Childhood Pedagogical Documentation*, Pademelon Press, Castle Hill, NSW.
Children's Services Branch, ACT Department of Education, Youth and Family Services & Mac Naughton, G, Smith, K & Lawrence, H (n.d.), *Hearing Young Children's Voices*, ACT Department of Education, Youth and Family Services, Canberra, http://www.children.act.gov.au/pdf/under5report.pdf, accessed 15 July 2006.
Clark, A & Moss, P 2001, *Listening to Young Children: The Mosaic Approach*, National Children's Bureau, London.
Curtis, D & Carter, M 2000, *The Art of Awareness: How Observation Can Transform Your Teaching*, Redleaf Press, St Paul, MN.
Dahlberg, G & Moss, P 2005, *Ethics and Politics in Early Childhood Education*, Routledge Falmer, London.
Dahlberg, G, Moss, P & Pence, A 2007, *Beyond Quality in Early Childhood Education and Care: Postmodern Perspectives*, Falmer Press, London.
DEEWR, *see* Department of Education, Employment and Workplace Relations.
Department for Children, Schools and Families 2008, *The Statutory Framework for the Early Years Foundation Stage in England*, Department of Children, Schools and Families, UK.
Department of Education, Employment and Workplace Relations 2009, *Belonging, Being and Becoming: The Early Years Learning Framework for Australia*, Australian Government Department of Education, Employment and Workplace Relations, Canberra.
Dockett, S & Perry, B 2011, 'Researching with young children: Seeking assent', *Child Indicators Research*, vol. 4, no. 2, pp. 231–47.
Dunphy, E 2010, 'Assessing early learning through formative assessment: Key issues and considerations', *Irish Educational Studies*, vol. 29, no. 1, pp. 41–56.
Fleer, M 2010, *Early Learning and Development: Cultural-Historical Concepts in Play*, Cambridge University Press, Melbourne.
Fleer, M & Richardson, C 2003, 'Collective mediated assessment: Moving towards a sociocultural approach to assessing children's learning', *Journal of Australian Research in Early Childhood Education*, vol. 10, no. 1, pp. 41–55.
Fleer, M & Robbins, J 2003, 'Beyond ticking boxes: From individual developmental domains to a sociocultural framework for observing young children', paper presented at the 2003 New Zealand Early Childhood Research VII Annual Symposium, Auckland, New Zealand, November.
Fleer, M & Surman, L 2006, 'A sociocultural approach to observing and assessing', in M Fleer, S Edwards, M Hammer, A Kennedy, A Ridgway, J Robbins & L Surman, *Early Childhood Learning Communities: Sociocultural Research in Practice*, Pearson, Sydney.
Fleet, A & Torr, J 2007, 'Literacy assessment: Understanding and recording meaningful data', in L Makin, C Jones Diaz & C McLachlan (eds), *Literacies in Childhood: Changing Views, Challenging Practice*, Elsevier, Sydney.
Fleet, A, Honig, T, Robertson, J, Semann, A & Shepherd, W 2011, *What's Pedagogy Anyway: Using Pedagogical Documentation to Engage with the Early Years Learning Framework*, Children's Services Central, http://www.cscentral.org.au/Resources/what-is-pedagogy-anyway-.pdf, accessed 28 February 2014.
Forman, G & Hall, E 2005, 'Wondering with children: The importance of observation in early education', *Early Childhood Research and Practice*, vol. 7, no. 2, Fall, http://www.ecrp.uiuc.edu/v7n2/forman.html, accessed 15 June 2011.
Giugni, M 2003, *Secret Children's Business: The Black Market of Identity Work*, unpublished Honours thesis, University of Western Sydney.
Harcourt D, Perry, B & Waller, T 2011, *Researching Young Children's Perspectives: Debating the Ethics and Dilemmas of Educational Research with Children*, Routledge, London.
Hatherly, A 2006, 'The stories we share: Using narratives to build communities of literacy participants in early childhood centres', *Australian Journal of Early Childhood*, vol. 31, no. 1, pp. 27–34.
Hedegaard, M, 2009, 'Children's development from a cultural-historical approach: Children's activity in everyday local settings as foundation for their development', *Mind, Culture and Activity*, vol. 16, pp. 64–81.
Helm, J & Beneke, S (eds) 2003, *The Power of Projects: Meeting Contemporary Challenges in Early Childhood Classrooms – Strategies and Solutions*, Teachers College Press, New York.
Helm, J, Beneke, S & Steinheimer, K 1998, *Teacher Materials for Documenting Children's Work*, Teachers College Press, New York.
Helm, J, Beneke S & Steinheimer, K 2007, *Windows on Learning: Documenting Young Children's Work*, Teachers College Press, New York.
Helm, J & Katz, L 2011, *Young Investigators: The Project Approach in the Early Years*, Teachers College Press, New York.
Holm, G 2008, 'Visual research methods: Where are we and where are we going?', in S Hesse-Biber & P Leavy (eds), *Handbook of Emergent Methods*, Guildford, New York.

Jones, E, Evans, K & Renken, KS 2001, *The Lively Kindergarten: Emergent Curriculum in Action*, National Association for the Education of Young Children, Washington, DC.

Jones, E & Reynolds, G 1992, *The Play's the Thing: Teachers' Roles in Children's Play*, Teachers College Press, New York.

Karlsdottir, K & Gardarsdottir, B 2010, 'Exploring children's learning stories as an assessment method for research and practice', *Early Years*, vol. 310, no. 3, pp. 255–66.

Katz, L & Chard, S 1989/2000, *Engaging Children's Minds: The Project Approach*, Ablex, Stamford, CT.

Lee, W & Carr, M 2012, *Learning Stories: Constructing Learner Identities in Early Education*, Sage, London.

Lindgren, A 2012, 'Ethical issues in pedagogical documentation: Representations of children through digital technology', *IJEC*, vol. 44, pp. 327–40.

Mac Naughton, G 2000, *Rethinking Gender in Early Childhood Education*, Allen & Unwin, Sydney.

Mac Naughton, G 2003, *Shaping Early Childhood: Learners, Curriculum and Contexts*, Open University Press, Maidenhead, Berkshire.

Mac Naughton, G & Williams, G 2009, *Techniques for Teaching Young Children: Choices for Theory and Practice*, 3rd edn., Pearson, Frenchs Forest, NSW.

Malaguzzi, L 1998, 'History, ideas and basic philosophy', in C Edwards, L Gandini & G Forman (eds), *The Hundred Languages of Children*, 2nd edn., Ablex, Norwood, NJ.

Martin, S 2010, *Take a Look: Observation and Portfolio Assessment in Early Childhood*, 5th edn., Pearson/Addison Wesley, Toronto, Ont.

McAfee, O & Leong, D 1997/2011, *Assessing and Guiding Young Children's Development and Learning*, Allyn & Bacon, Boston, MA.

Moll, L, Amanti, C, Neff, D & Gonzalez, N 1992, 'Funds of knowledge for teaching: Using a qualitative approach to connect homes and classrooms', *Theory into Practice*, vol. 31, no. 2, pp. 132–41.

Munns, G & Woodward, H 2006, 'The REAL Framework: Student engagement and student self assessment', *PEN 155*, Primary English Teaching Association, Marrickville.

Munns, G, Woodward, H & Kolctti, J (Eds.) 2006, 'Engagement and student self assessment in NSW DET & University of Western Sydney', in *School is for me: Pathways to Student Engagement*. Fair Go Project, Editors, Sydney, pp. 15–24.

National Association of Early Childhood Specialists in State Departments of Education 2000, *STILL Unacceptable Trends in Kindergarten Entry and Placement*, http://www.naeyc.org/files/naeyc/file/positions/Psunacc.pdf accessed 6 June 2011.

National Council of Teachers of English 2004, *Framing Statements on Assessment*, http://www.ncte.org/positions/statements/assessmentframingst accessed 5 June 2011.

New Zealand Ministry of Education 1996, *Te Whāriki: He Whāriki Matauranga monga Mokopuna o Aotearoa – Early Childhood Curriculum*, Learning Media Limited, Wellington.

Pacini-Ketchabaw, V & Pence, A 2011, 'The postmodern curriculum: Making space for historically and politically situated understandings', *Australasian Journal of Early Childhood*, vol. 36, no. 1, pp. 4–8.

Perry B & Dockett, S 2008, *Voices of Children in Transition to School: Report Prepared for the Wollongong Transition to School Network*, http://www.transitiontoschool.com.au/downloads/research/Voices%20of%20children%20in%20starting%20school%20-%20Bob%20Perry%20and%20Sue%20Dockett.pdf accessed 1 December 2011.

Perry, B, Dockett, S & Harley, E 2007, *Learning Stories and Children's Powerful Mathematics*, Early Childhood Research and Practice, http://ecrp.uiuc.edu/v9n2/perry.html, accessed 17 January 2014.

Podmore, V & Carr, M 1999, *Learning and Teaching Stories: New Approaches to Assessment and Evaluation*, http://www.aare.edu.au/99pap/pod99298.htm, accessed 26 May 2011.

Puckett, M & Diffily, D 1999/2004, *Teaching Young Children: An Introduction to the Early Childhood Profession*, Harcourt Brace, Fort Worth, TX.

Rogoff, B 1998, 'Cognition as a collaborative process', in W Damon (chief ed.), D Kuhn & R Siegler (vol. eds.), *Handbook of Child Psychology: Cognitions, Perceptions and Language*, 5th edn., John Wiley & Sons, New York, pp. 679–744.

Rogoff, B 2003, *The Cultural Nature of Human Development*, Oxford University Press, Oxford.

Salamon, A 2011, 'How the early years learning framework can help shift pervasive beliefs of the social and emotional capabilities of infants and toddlers', *Contemporary Issues in Early Childhood*, vol. 12, no. 1, pp. 4–10.

Siraj-Blatchford, I & Clarke, P 2000, *Supporting Identity, Diversity and Language in the Early Years*, Open University Press, Buckingham.

Thompson, P 2002, *Schooling the Rustbelt Kids: Making the Difference in Changing Times*, Allen & Unwin, Sydney.

Vygotsky, L, 1978, *Mind in Society*, Harvard University Press, Cambridge, MA.

Walters, K 2006, *Capture the Moment: Using Digital Photography in Early Childhood Settings*, Early Childhood Australia, Canberra.

• CHAPTER NINE •

RELATIONSHIPS AND INTERACTIONS IN CHILDREN'S LEARNING

Chapter learning focus

This chapter will investigate:

- the importance of relationships and interactions for children's learning

- effective pedagogy

- teaching strategies that support children's learning, notably scaffolding and sustained shared thinking

- promoting interactions through grouping

- promoting positive interactions.

Introduction

Relationships between children, and between adults and children, provide contexts that support and encourage children's development and learning. This chapter focuses on strategies that can be used by educators to promote positive relationships. Positive relationships are at the heart of effective pedagogies and effective teaching strategies. The second part of this chapter explores teaching strategies that support children's learning and contribute to positive learning environments.

Positive relationships

'Establishing successful relationships with adults and other children provides a foundation of capacities that children will use for a lifetime' (National Scientific Council on the Developing Child, 2009, p. 1). The same emphasis on positive relationships is seen in the *Early Years Learning Framework* (EYLF) (DEEWR, 2009, pp. 20–1), where the first learning outcome highlights relationships with people, places and things in promoting children's development of a strong sense of identity. Elements of this learning outcome are that:

- children feel safe, secure and supported
- children develop their emerging autonomy, interdependence, resilience and sense of agency
- children develop knowledgeable and confident self-identities
- children learn to interact in relation to others with care, empathy and respect.

Strong, positive relationships are also the basis of effective teaching in the early years. In listing the principles underpinning effective early childhood pedagogy, the EYLF emphasises the role of secure, respectful and reciprocal relationships in promoting the wellbeing, learning and development of young children.

According to Shonkoff and Phillips (2000, p. 264), 'relationships are amongst the most significant influences on healthy growth and psychological wellbeing'. Early relationships provide a context for development and learning, and are key elements of the lives of young children. The significance of caring relationships is well established in attachment literature (Berk, 2009). Caring relationships are those where adults care *about* children, as well as care *for* them. Through these relationships, children build a sense of their own identity and their ability to influence the world around them.

There are many variations in early relationships – for example, children's relationships with a parent and an educator will be different – and also in the cultural context of relationships. Through relationships, children become a part of their social and cultural contexts. Children's development and learning is promoted when children experience relationships underpinned by:

a.   reliable support that establishes children's feelings of confident security in the adult

b.   responsiveness that strengthens children's sense of agency and self-efficacy

c.   protection from harms that children fear and the threats of which they may be unaware

d.   affection, which promotes young children's development of self-esteem

e.   opportunities to experience and resolve human conflict cooperatively

f.   support for the growth of new skills and capabilities that are within children's reach

g.   reciprocal interaction by which children learn the mutual give-and-take of positive sociability

h.   the experience of being respected by others and respecting them as human beings.

J Shonkoff & D Phillips, *From Neurons to Neighborhoods: The Science of Early Childhood Development*, pp. 264–5, © 2000 National Academy Press.

In a well-reported adage, Bronfenbrenner (1992) summed up the importance of positive relationships for children in his statement that 'every child needs someone who is crazy about [them]'.

Recent Australian research has emphasised the importance of relationships for children's wellbeing and the provision of high-quality early childhood education. The Department of Education and Children's Services (DECS) (2008, p. 9) has promoted a focus on 'three R's' (Reflect, Respect, Relate) through the development of materials and approaches that call for 'reflective practice … respectful connections and relationships between educators, families and children'. Reflective practice is also a core feature of the EYLF, which encourages educators to move beyond things that have become taken-for-granted and to question their own perspectives, roles and understandings as they engage with children, families and communities.

'Respect' is another term that appears regularly in discussions of the principles underpinning quality early childhood programs. The EYLF highlights respect for diversity as one of its core principles. This incorporates not only respect for the individual differences among children, but also for the diversity among families and communities. Diversity is discussed in detail in Chapter 2. The elements of respect noted by DECS (2008, p. 11) are:

- respect for families and communities – their diversity, their richness and the aspirations they hold for their children
- respect for children – their capacities and interests, their right to worthwhile learning experiences and their innate eagerness to learn and to socialise
- respect for educators – their professional standing, their complex roles as teachers, carers and learners and their contribution to new understandings.

Relationships are recognised as the core of learning and development. When based on reflection and respect, relationships are dynamic – changing over time in response to different contexts and circumstances. For example, relationships change as children grow, develop and learn: we relate differently to a child when they are a baby and when they become a preschooler. Circumstances change too – as a primary carer of a child, educators form particular relationships. When children start school, these relationships change – but hopefully, are not lost.

> How do your relationships with children change over time? Do you ever see a child who has left your setting to start school, or left your class at school? How do you both react?

The importance of relationships and interactions for learning

One of the major trends in understanding children's development and learning has been the recognition that children learn a great deal from talking and interacting with others. The work of Vygotsky (1978) and more recent researchers (*see*, for example, Bodrova & Leong, 2007; Rogoff, 1990; 2003) has emphasised the social nature of learning among young children.

Vygotsky's theory has been labelled sociocultural because it argues that 'participation in social life guides and energises the child's mastery of new, culturally adaptive skills' (Berk, 2001, p. 30). Interactions between children and more knowledgeable members of their society, who can include peers as well as adults, underpin the acquisition of the ways of thinking and being that are crucial to engaging in that society. Such interactions can generate a zone of proximal development (ZPD), the zone in which Vygotsky concluded that learning occurs. As outlined in Chapter 3, the ZPD is defined as the distance between what a child can actually do on his/her own and the child's potential development, indicated by what the child can achieve in collaboration with others (Vygotsky, 1978). Berk (2001, p. 41) describes this as 'the dynamic region in which new capacities form as children tackle culturally meaningful tasks with a mentor's assistance'.

As children participate in culturally meaningful experiences with more knowledgeable others – be they adults or children – there are opportunities to internalise the language and understandings used. For Vygotsky, understanding children's development required an understanding of social context and interactions. Higher forms of thinking appear first in social interactions, between the child and others, before being internalised by the child (Berk, 2001).

For children to internalise something they have encountered in social interactions, there must be a sense of shared understanding and focus in these interactions. For example, if two people are talking about different things, or even have a focus on different aspects of the same situation,

a genuine sharing of ideas is unlikely to occur. For shared understanding – intersubjectivity – to occur, there needs to be a real attempt by each participant to understand the perspective of the other participants.

If learning is considered to be a social endeavour, then communication is essential. Vygotsky's work regarded language as a critical element in learning, as language 'enables thought, and produces meaning in interaction with others' (Reid, 2002, p. 18). From a very early age, infants engage in communicative practices that encourage social interactions. With very young children, much of the responsibility for sustaining interactions comes from adults. This continues in various ways as children develop, practise and refine their range of communicative competencies and as their understandings of social and cultural practices expand. As children become proficient language users, the scope for interactions, and for achieving intersubjectivity, broadens.

Children's relationships with adults

One of the key determinants of quality in early childhood settings is the nature of the relationship between children and adults (Burchinal & Cryer, 2003). A secure and close relationship between children and educators is characterised by sensitivity, whereby educators get to know each child, establish intersubjectivity and, through this, become adept at perceiving and responding to the child's signals. Acknowledging and responding appropriately to children's signals helps children to develop trust and confidence that the adult will be available and supportive. Positive relationships help children feel safe and cared for. Both parents and educators highlight the importance of emotional responsiveness from adults as central to positive relationships (Ebbeck & Yin, 2009).

Sensitivity and responsiveness is particularly important in relationships with infants. In high-quality settings, routine interactions such as mealtime, changing and sleeping can be times of sensitive engagement with children (Degotardi, 2010). Such interactions are most likely to be achieved when there are low adult–child ratios and where adults and children have sufficient time to develop close relationships. It is also important to note that individual differences among children and adults influence relationships, meaning that some children will prefer to be with some educators rather than others. Regardless of this, it remains important that educators work to establish positive relationships.

The quality of the relationships and interactions between educators and children has an impact both on what children learn while in early childhood settings and on their future interactions with educators in different settings, including school. Where relationships between educators and children are positive, children tend to interact more positively with their peers and regard the school/early childhood setting positively, hence making more of the educational opportunities they meet (Bowman et al., 2001).

While relationships between individual educators and children are important, so too is the overall atmosphere of the setting. The climate of a setting is created by all involved – children and adults. They can range on a continuum from 'positive, pro-social environments characterised by close adult–child relationships, intricate pretend play scenarios, and little disruptive behaviour to angry, hostile environments characterised by conflictual child–teacher relationships, angry disruptive children, and little constructive peer play or collaborative learning' (Bowman et al., 2001, p. 50).

FIGURE 9.1 Educators' positive relationships with children support children's learning.

Educators need to be aware of the role they play in generating positive climates in early childhood settings. When children feel valued and respected, they are likely to seek out challenges, knowing they will receive appropriate feedback and continued encouragement. Educators who engage with children in mutually reciprocal relationships are caring, responsive and emotionally warm (*see* Figure 9.1). These types of interactions promote children's feelings of competence and self-efficacy and encourage children to take risks in solving problems (Landy, 2002). Children are supported to develop social competence when educators provide them with an environment that is appropriately challenging, where emotions and social interactions are discussed and where there are clear and appropriate expectations (Katz & McClellan, 1997; Landy, 2002).

Adult relationships in early childhood settings and schools

There is often a great deal of talk describing partnerships between families and educators and the importance of recognising parents as children's first educators. For genuine partnership and collaboration to occur, more than talk is needed. The interactions between families and educators have a major impact on the climate of the early childhood setting or school. Where adults are supportive and have trusting and respectful relationships, positive social and emotional climates are likely. Where adult interactions (whether between educators and families, families and other families or within the team of educators) are characterised by conflict and tension, this will impact on children and on the quality of the educational setting. Effective early childhood education is built on positive, respectful and caring relationships among the adults who care for children.

Baker and Manfredi/Petitt (2004) suggest that there are many benefits to be derived from positive relationships between parents and educators. These include:

- Encouraging positive relationships between educators and children – when children observe their parents in trusting and respectful relationships with educators, they too are likely to engage in positive relationships with those educators.
- Effective communication – when positive relationships exist, parents and educators can share information, with the aim of developing a greater understanding of the child and the contexts within which they exist.
- Recognition – both parents and educators can feel the positive effects of having their work recognised when relationships value the contribution each makes.
- A sense of comfort – parents are likely to feel comfortable and relaxed when they trust the educators who work with their children.

Working collaboratively with parents is a critical element of early childhood education. So too is teamwork and working collaboratively with other early childhood educators. Positive relationships among staff promote the following benefits (Baker & Manfredi/Petitt, 2004):

- Staff are more responsive to children – when educators feel that they are a valued member of a team, they are likely to treat others in the same way. 'Successful … teams share the workload along with the responsibilities … Children in turn feel safe, secure, and surrounded by a sense of belonging' (p. 23).
- Children see positive role models – when children see adults cooperating and engaging in respectful and enjoyable relationships, they observe strategies for promoting teamwork as well as managing conflict, and the pleasure that can come from being a member of such a team.
- Families feel included – positive relationships among staff extend to families. Strong staff relationships demonstrate to families that the focus of the setting is the wellbeing of the children.
- Educators enjoy their work and feel successful in their endeavours – being a valued member of an effective team can be a major incentive to stay in a workplace.

Relationships between adults that are secure, respectful and reciprocal are built on:

- Social respect – acknowledgement that many people are involved in children's education and respect for the contribution of each of these stakeholders – including children, families, educators and community members.
- Personal regard – seen in the willingness of participants to create and maintain a climate of openness, to listen and to share information, and to engage in genuine discussion.
- Competence – where each is regarded as competent in their roles. This involves recognition of the competence of parents and families, as well as the competence of educators to promote sound outcomes for all children.
- Perceived integrity – where all involved are consistent in what they say and do.

(adapted from Bryk and Schneider, 2003)

Family engagement

Much has been written about the importance of family involvement in education. Henderson and Mapp (2002) emphasise the importance of family involvement for children of all ages and through all phases of education. Essentially, the more families and educators work together, the more likely children are to engage with education and to achieve positive educational outcomes. Family involvement can take many forms and it is critical that educators recognise the various ways and means of family engagement. Family involvement is influenced by many factors including parent and family characteristics, cultural and linguistic diversity, community expectations and resources. The extent of family involvement cannot be measured by the number of times a parent or family member spends time in the setting. Sometimes, the focus on family involvement centres on what families do to support the educational goals of the school or setting. An alternative focus is to emphasise family engagement (rather than involvement) as a dynamic process that is influenced by many factors, including parents' own experiences of school or early childhood settings, resources and opportunities (Barton et al., 2004). Attitudes and beliefs influence the nature and extent of family engagement. On the one hand, parents who feel confident and regard themselves as effective parents tend to engage in their children's educational settings more than parents who do not feel confident and effective. On the other hand, educators' beliefs about family engagement determine the opportunities open to families and the nature of that engagement. For family engagement to be effective, educators need to take responsibility for making meaningful and ongoing connections with families. The importance of family engagement is discussed in detail in Chapter 2.

Children's relationships with peers

Children's relationships and interactions with other children are often complex. From an early age, children display a range of skills and understandings as they communicate with other children, help others, play, establish friendships and work to maintain them, and seek to resolve conflicts. Interactions with peers influence children's learning and development (Bowman et al., 2001, p. 53).

In one example of how understandings of child development have changed over the past decades, educators are more aware of the complexities of interactions and relationships among children from an early age. Rather than suggesting that toddlers are incapable of forming friendships, it is now recognised that some deep and lasting friendships are forged during the early years of life (Dunn, 2004). While children are often capable of forming friendships and interacting with others in many different ways, educators cannot assume that this is necessarily an easy process, without challenges and pitfalls.

Adults, who have much greater social experience than young children, often need to provide some guidance, suggestions and possibly interventions in order to help children engage in social interactions such as play and conflict resolution. Some children tend to be shy or reticent in their interactions with peers, while others tend to be very outgoing and sometimes unaware of some of the subtleties of interactions. Others respond differently in different contexts (*see* Figure 9.2).

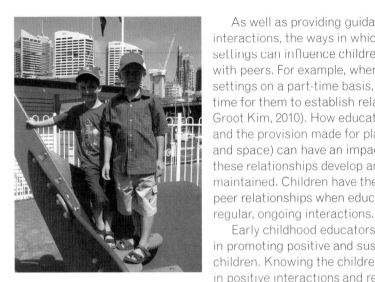

FIGURE 9.2 Friends matter.

As well as providing guidance in social interactions, the ways in which adults organise settings can influence children's interactions with peers. For example, when children attend settings on a part-time basis, it can take some time for them to establish relationships (de Groot Kim, 2010). How educators group children and the provision made for play (including time and space) can have an impact on how well these relationships develop and whether or not they are maintained. Children have the potential to develop strong peer relationships when educators provide opportunities for regular, ongoing interactions.

Early childhood educators have an important role to play in promoting positive and sustained interactions among children. Knowing the children well and engaging them in positive interactions and relationships are important elements in this expectation. This means being aware of, and being able to use, a range of teaching strategies to support children's learning.

> Consider how policies and practices in your setting support or limit children's opportunities to make friends.

Effective pedagogy

Several recent studies have explored the nature of effective pedagogy in early childhood education. The *Effective Provision of Pre-school Education* (EPPE) project (Sylva et al., 2010) has had a substantial influence on what constitutes effective pedagogy. From this study, effective early childhood pedagogy is defined as promoting:

- a balance of child-initiated and teacher-initiated activities
- regard for play as a potentially instructive activity
- complementary focus on social and cognitive outcomes
- educators with a good understanding of curriculum areas and content
- a strong focus on educators planning and initiating group work
- educators providing feedback to learners
- educators drawing on a repertoire of pedagogical practices as appropriate
- social and behaviour policies focused on conflict resolution.

In other words, effective pedagogy requires educators to know, understand and use a wide repertoire of approaches to promote teaching and learning. It also requires educators to plan, support and interact with children in multiple ways within learning environments as they demonstrate sensitivity to the nature of learning tasks, the content of what is to be taught and children's own learning and development – including their ZPD – as well as their own expertise (Siraj-Blatchford & Sylva, 2004).

There is a great deal of balance required in order to promote effective early childhood pedagogy. As well as a balance between teacher-led and child-initiated interactions, there needs to be a balance between what educators do and the provisions they make for learning and development. For example, it is not enough for educators to set up the environment and then not interact with children, nor is it sufficient for educators to focus only on interactions, without consideration for resources and planning. In other words, educators need to focus on setting up a learning environment as well as active involvement with children as they engage within that environment. Teaching strategies are the focus of this chapter, while planning and setting up learning environments are explored in Chapter 10.

Teaching strategies that support children's learning

Differences between educational settings have often been reported in terms of philosophical and pedagogical bases. For example, some comparisons of schools and early childhood settings have used the descriptors *play-based* or *constructivist* learning versus *teacher directed learning* or a *transmission approach* to describe the respective settings. Such a clear dichotomy is often misleading. Educators in different contexts will promote learning in different ways. As outlined in Chapter 7, educators will draw on pedagogies and approaches according to their contexts, the type of experience being implemented and their expectations and understandings of children's learning. As a consequence, educators will select different teaching strategies at different times to support their approaches to curriculum. Hatch (2010) calls for educators to develop a wide repertoire of teaching strategies, as part of their overall pedagogy, reflecting the diversity of children, families and educational contexts.

In past decades, the dominant discourse in early childhood education has been Developmentally Appropriate Practice (DAP), a position clearly documented in the USA by the National Association for the Education of Young Children (Bredekamp, 1987), revised in 1997 (Bredekamp & Copple, 1997) and elaborated in 2006 and 2009 (Copple & Bredekamp, 2006; 2009). This approach is based on Piaget's (1962) theories of development in which children's actions in child-initiated play are perceived as the primary source of learning. Piaget's work has resulted in the image of the child as a solitary thinker, working to make sense of the world. DAP emphasises a 'child-centred' approach to learning. This is generally interpreted by educators to mean that their role is to observe and wait for children to take the initiative in learning or to display signs of *developmental readiness* and to provide children with experiences that match their current level of development (Raban & Ure, 1998). Copple and Bredekamp (2006) have described the two basic aims of DAP as to 'meet children where they are' and 'help each child reach challenging and achievable goals' (p. 3). They emphasise that achieving these aims does not happen by chance: educators need to be proactive and intentional in their actions.

Current cultural-historical theories recognise that children actively construct their own knowledge while at the same time advocating the importance of social and cultural forces. Dominant developmentalist discourse has been challenged by the co-constructivist approach of Vygotsky (1978), and the notion of scaffolding put forward by Wood, Bruner and Ross (1976). The social interactionist theory of Vygotsky (1978) argues that the greatest learning occurs within the ZPD, where children are operating at the upper edge of their competencies. This places the focus on potential rather than current understandings and on the role of the educator in mediating learning.

Rather than be restricted by traditional roles, or their perceptions of these, all educators need to develop a repertoire of teaching strategies that enable them to switch between roles of observer, mediator and leader of children's learning in different contexts and with different children. No one set of pedagogical practices is suitable for all children or all learning contexts. As Comber (2001) has argued, it is essential that educators question the effects of different pedagogical practices for different children. Ongoing critical reflection and analysis of taken-for-granted early childhood pedagogies is needed. For example, the work of educators in Reggio Emilia suggests that there is a role for educators in complicating children's play (Edwards et al., 1998). More recently, Rogers (2011) and Wood (2009), among others, have encouraged educators to reconceptualise pedagogies of play and the role and place of play within early childhood curricula and pedagogy. The basis for reconceptualising play is outlined in Chapter 3.

Effective educators draw on a repertoire of pedagogical practices (Sylva et al., 2010). This means that educators are thoughtful and intentional in the pedagogies that they choose. Epstein (2007) uses the term 'intentional teaching' to highlight educators as active and purposeful in selecting pedagogies that are the most appropriate when planning learning environments, responding to spontaneous learning opportunities and interacting with children during routines and transitions. According to Epstein (2007, p. 1):

> intentional teaching means teachers act with specific outcomes or goals in mind for children's development and learning. Teachers must know when to use a given strategy to accommodate the different ways that individual children learn and the specific content they are learning.

Epstein (2007) advocates a balance of child-guided and adult-guided experiences. Adult guidance does not mean that educators only implement experiences that are adult-initiated and directed; rather, the intent is that they join in children's play and take active roles in guiding children's learning. This guidance is particularly important when new resources are introduced, when children may need their attention drawn to resources that are available or to capitalise on a serendipitous moment. Guidance is also important when children need support in creating 'systems of knowledge' such as understandings of literacy concepts, when they do not engage with something they need for future learning and when they seek help (Epstein, 2009, p. 46).

Furthermore, intentional teaching requires a strong understanding of curriculum content so that educators are able to 'weave content information' (Schiller, 2009, p. 57) into play experiences and model vocabulary that supports children's understandings of concepts. In planning learning environments 'the daily structure also prompts teachers to think about content broadly so they can include the full range of cognitive domains (introducing different subjects across activities) and social components (altering group size and composition; creating communities of shared interests and experiences) over the course of the day' (Epstein, 2007, p. 13).

The EYLF (DEEWR, 2009, p. 15) includes intentional teaching as one pedagogical practice and suggests that intentional teachers are 'deliberate, purposeful and thoughtful in their decisions and actions'. This refers to the ways in which they plan learning environments and their interactions with children. The framework encourages educators to draw on a repertoire of strategies to 'extend children's learning and thinking' (p. 15).

Table 9.1 illustrates a range of strategies that educators might use. These range from low levels of interaction, such as acknowledging children's learning, to mediating strategies, such as scaffolding, and then to more proactive and explicit strategies such as demonstrating and directing (Bredekamp & Rosegrant, 1992; Mac Naughton & Williams, 2009). At the low interaction end of the continuum, educators provide resources, comment on children's learning, and model language and actions, but children 'make connections on their own or through interactions with peers' in what Epstein (2007) calls 'child-guided learning'. In 'adult-guided' learning (Epstein, 2007) educators take a more active role in children's play and experiences to mediate learning and, when appropriate, engage in explicit teaching through demonstration and by providing directions.

TABLE 9.1 Continuum of teaching strategies.

LOW INTERACTION	MEDIATING	EXPLICIT
Acknowledging	Supporting	Demonstrating
Modelling	Co-constructing/sustained shared thinking	Directing
Facilitating	Scaffolding	
	Reflecting	
	Critiquing	

Low interaction strategies

ACKNOWLEDGING

At the least interactive end of the continuum, educators are onlookers (Roskos & Neuman, 1993) and may acknowledge children's play and learning. Acknowledgement occurs when educators take notice of and comment on children's behaviours and practices. At times, acknowledgement consists of empty comments or praise such as 'That's a beautiful painting'. Kostelnik, Soderman and Whiren (2004) suggest that more meaningful comments take account of children's efforts and feelings, indicate the progress children have made and comment on specific elements of children's creations. The educator may comment on the way that a child used colour and line in a painting, for example. Educators can also acknowledge children's behaviours; for example, by giving positive feedback on the way that a group of children worked collaboratively to construct a spaceship. Intentional teaching requires educators to think carefully about the comments they make and the impact their comments have on children's learning. Acknowledging recognises children's actions or interaction, but offers no way to extend them.

MODELLING

Modelling also involves low levels of interaction. In modelling, children learn by watching others. Educators can model dispositions such as playfulness and curiosity, learning processes such as problem solving and practices such as reading, as well as non-gendered behaviours and cooperation with others. Educators are powerful models for children so it is important to think about the messages that children are getting from educators' actions as well as their words. Intentional teaching requires thinking about the intended and unintended messages educators are providing to children through their words and actions.

Educators may be models by playing parallel to children while using similar materials (Dockett & Fleer, 1999). This may mean, for example, sitting next to children in the sandpit and making comments that model spatial and positional language or using specific arts vocabulary to describe elements and aspects such as colour, line, beat and rhythm when children are engaged in creative arts experiences (Arthur et al., 2010). Pickett (1998) found that when adults played alongside children in a literacy-enriched construction area, children's literacy behaviours increased markedly. The children incorporated literacy into their play by making signs, writing notes and consulting books after these practices were modelled by the educator. When educators join in children's play and carefully observe what is happening, they are able to offer models that are responsive to children's interests and play directions and support learning,

Dockett and Fleer (1999) indicate that modelling can provide important cues to children who are seeking to enter play but unsure of how to do this. Children who are unfamiliar with a particular environment may need some assistance in 'reading' the situation. Modelling provides a means of providing such cues.

FACILITATING

Mac Naughton and Williams (2009, p. 81) describe facilitating as a 'process of making children's learning easier'. As such, it includes actions such as 'scheduling, selecting materials, organising space and interacting verbally and non-verbally. Intentional teaching includes planning learning environments and interacting with children in ways that facilitate learning. Educators can facilitate learning by providing experiences that are appropriately challenging and by giving sufficient space, time and resources to promote children's engagement (see Figure 9.3). Higher level processes such as problem solving and critical thinking can be facilitated with the

FIGURE 9.3 Educators can facilitate children's learning through the provision of resources and organisation of the environment.

provision of open-ended resources and a climate that encourages divergent thinking (Mac Naughton & Williams, 2009). The educator may become what Jones and Reynolds (2011) term 'a stage manager', providing experiences and resources that will extend children's interests, making props, organising the set and making script suggestions. The educator may add some bus tickets and writing materials to the dramatic play area where a group of children are using chairs to make a bus and pretending to give out tickets, for example. The addition of literacy materials encourages the children to make bus signs and bus tickets, thus facilitating the inclusion of literacy practices in the children's play. Reynolds and Jones (1997) note that when educators add something new to facilitate what children are interested in doing, they are using their power to support the children's purposes, not taking power away from the children.

Mac Naughton and Williams (2009, p. 81) argue that facilitation on its own is not enough to promote learning. When educators set up environments and are reluctant to interact with children it is difficult to build relationships and to extend learning. Low intervention strategies such as facilitation are also 'implicated in sexist and racist relationships between peers' as they do not challenge such relationships or prompt alternatives.

Mediating strategies

Moving towards the middle of the continuum, there are several strategies that mediate children's learning. These include strategies such as supporting, scaffolding and co-constructing. Mediation requires educators to observe and interpret children's actions and interactions on the spot in order to be able to respond in a way that is sensitive to children's perspectives and that assists children's learning (Dockett & Fleer, 1999). The work of educators in Reggio Emilia suggests that educator mediation is vital as a means of sustaining and complicating children's play (Edwards et al., 1998).

SUPPORTING

Educators can support children's learning by being available to give assistance when needed and providing physical or verbal support. This may mean supporting a child as they attempt to write or assisting a child to join in play with others. For example, 'supportive adult participation' in literacy-enriched play results in gains in children's 'knowledge of environmental print and print concepts' (Morrow & Schickedanz, 2006, p. 278). Educators can support children's learning by providing clear, specific feedback. Feedback goes beyond acknowledging what children are doing to focus on the learning that is occurring and 'describes what the child is doing rather than placing a value judgement on it' (Mac Naughton & Williams, 2009, p. 94). Comments such as 'Abby, all your collage materials stayed on this time because you used the strong glue and the stapler' provide more useful support for learning than 'That's great' or 'Good girl'. To make effective use of supporting strategies, educators need to be careful observers, sensitive to children's ideas and intentions.

Educators can also use feedback to support children's sense of belonging and wellbeing and the development of relationships. At times educators may need to intervene to support children to resolve conflicts or to promote equity (Dockett & Fleer, 1999; Mac Naughton & Williams, 2009).

CO-CONSTRUCTING

Co-construction occurs when the educator and child or children are jointly involved in an activity such as building a tower with blocks, writing or retelling a narrative or working together to solve a problem (see Figure 9.4). The most powerful form of co-construction involves the co-construction of meaning as children and adults together build knowledge about their world. In this sense, knowledge refers to the understandings and interpretations educators attribute to specific events and actions, rather than an accumulation of facts (Mac Naughton & Williams, 2009)

The EPPE project refers to co-construction as **sustained shared thinking**. This is a process whereby educators and children are mutually involved in cognitive co-construction as 'each party engages with the understanding of the other and learning is achieved through a process of reflexive co-construction' (Siraj-Blatchford & Sylva, 2004, p. 720). Sustained shared thinking involves educators and children (or children together) working in an intellectual way to

Sustained shared thinking

Educators and children are mutually involved in cognitive constructions.

FIGURE 9.4 Adults can engage in co-construction with children through play.

work through an issue, solve a problem or clarify understandings. It is not a one-sided intervention, with the adult prompting all the interaction and providing all the guidance. Rather it is a mutual interaction where both parties contribute to the interaction and the thinking involved. Sustained shared thinking can only happen when there are responsive trusting relationships between adults and children. Sustained shared thinking is explored in more detail later in this chapter.

SCAFFOLDING

Scaffolding is a mediating strategy that involves educators guiding learning through interactions that assist children to achieve something they would not be able to do on their own. Rogoff (1990) uses the term 'guided participation' to highlight the way in which interactions assist children to build a bridge from current to new understandings.

Through interactions that are targeted at a child's ZPD, adults can promote challenge and complexity in children's interactions and understandings. Scaffolding is explored in more detail later in this chapter.

REFLECTING

Reflecting on learning is another mediating strategy (Wood & Attfield, 1996/2005). Educators engage in reflective practice when they think about how they teach, analyse events from different perspectives and identify and try out changes in practices. Reflection is one of the key components of professional practice outlined in the EYLF (DEEWR, 2009). By reflecting on their practices, educators can analyse the effectiveness of strategies in supporting children's learning and make informed decisions about any changes to be made.

Educators who engage in regular reflection with children model these active learning practices. Educators can encourage children to reflect by recording interactions and conversations and by taking photographs and then discussing these artefacts with children. Jones and Reynolds (2011) provide examples of educators representing children's play pictorially and in writing, and sharing these with children to encourage reflections on learning. Dockett and Perry (2007) have encouraged children to reflect on their first year at school, utilising drawings and photographs as well as comments about their experiences. Wood and Attfield (1996, p. 105) suggest that 'skilled educators encourage conscious reflection on action to promote consolidation, confidence and mastery'. This is a powerful way of focusing children's thoughts so they are able to reflect on their learning.

CRITIQUING

Educator mediation can support children to engage in critical thinking or critiquing of issues of gender, ethnicity, language, ability and class and to challenge 'stereotypical knowledge and understanding' (Siraj-Blatchford, 2009, p. 153). For example, educators can scaffold children's critique of the ways that texts such as children's books and movies are constructed to represent particular world views, reproduce disadvantage, marginalise minority groups and encourage consumerism (Buckingham, 2000). Young children have demonstrated that with educators' guidance they are able to engage in critical thinking about texts (Barratt-Pugh et al., 2006; Beecher, 2010). A critical perspective encourages children to go beneath the surface of texts to examine meanings and actively interrogate and challenge the ways people are presented and to critique the ways that texts position us to accept dominant world views. Critical literacy encourages readers to challenge and deconstruct the taken-for-granted assumptions of texts (Arthur, 2001; Comber, 2001).

Harwood (2008, p. 7) also suggests that 'the narratives that evolve from children's imaginative play may provide interesting social dilemmas for educators and groups of children to deconstruct and analyse using questions such as, "Why do only girls play in the doll corner?" or "What makes an action hero a hero?"'. Educators can encourage children to engage in critical thinking and to examine issues such as the interconnections between power, discourse and identities. As Dyson (1998, p. 400) notes, sensitive educators work to 'help children to raise their questions about the assumptions authors make about their ideological worlds' rather than imposing their views on children. This ensures that children's voices are heard and promotes the empowerment of children to take action around social and environmental issues of concern to them, such as gender identity or the pollution of the local river. An essential part of supporting children's critical thinking is the way in which educators themselves engage in such thinking.

Explicit teaching strategies

DEMONSTRATING

Demonstrating is at the more proactive end of the teaching continuum. There are times when educators need to provide clear demonstrations to children. Demonstrations can be very effective when introducing a new technique or skill or when children have forgotten how to do something (Mac Naughton & Williams, 2009). This may involve showing children how to use a particular piece of equipment or the demonstration of a particular technique that is useful when working with clay or when drawing (for example, Arthur et al., 2010; Kolbe, 2005).

There are times when adults may need to become involved in children's play as play leaders. Play leaders deliberately take steps to structure children's play, while at the same time remaining sensitive to the direction of play. Roskos and Neuman (1993) see the play leader as a coach who provides demonstrations and explicit directions. For example, playing with blocks could lead to a demonstration of balance and symmetry, as well as providing encouragement for children to build as high as they can.

In the area of literacy, critical theorists argue that children need clear demonstrations or explicit teaching. 'Explicit teaching' is a term that has been used to describe the 'uncovering, or laying bare, [of] tacit assumptions that operate in classrooms – assumptions about what the teacher wants and expects, about what the students are supposed to be doing and expecting of themselves, and about what concepts and skills are necessary in order to complete a task successfully' (Reid, 2002, p. 17). The focus on explicit teaching recognises the importance of helping children identify what they are expected to do and why, rather than assuming that all children can work out the connections for themselves.

It is important to recognise that some children come to early childhood settings or schools without having experienced the ways of thinking, behaving or talking that predominate in the setting or school. Schools and early childhood settings can seem very strange to children who do not have much experience in these contexts. In these situations, it can be very important for educators to talk about what they are doing and why, what is expected of children and educators and how to participate appropriately (Reid, 2002).

This is particularly the case for children from minority groups who do not necessarily learn the culture of school and the language of power merely by being surrounded by language. For example, Delpit (1995, p. 31) reports that many children of colour in the USA experience a culture of power in the classroom that excludes them: 'If such explicitness is not provided to students, what it feels like to people who are old enough to judge is that there are secrets being kept, that time is being wasted, that the teacher is abdicating his or her duty to teach'. In Australia, several states have endorsed approaches to teaching literacy that include 'explicit teaching' of literacy skills within meaningful contexts.

Demonstrations need to be carefully matched to individual or small group understandings, to be authentic and 'do-able' in order for children to engage with them (Geekie, Cambourne & Fitzsimmons, 1999). Demonstrations are most effective when they occur within a meaningful experience, such as the guided reading of a text or small group construction of a text, rather than in an isolated lesson, followed by opportunities for children to try these ideas for themselves.

Wood and Attfield (1996, p. 105) suggest that appropriate demonstrations provide children with access to concepts and processes that can be utilised in play, assisting 'internalisation and organisation'. Relevant demonstrations for younger children may involve showing a child how to write a particular letter or how English is read from top to bottom and left to right. For older children, educators may provide explicit demonstrations of writing conventions such as punctuation. Mac Naughton and Williams (2009) note the importance of demonstrating within a teacher's repertoire, but also caution that an over-reliance on this strategy can result in a diminishing of children's willingness to innovate and explore things for themselves.

DIRECTING

Directing, or explicit instruction, is most appropriate when children are introduced to something for the first time. It is also necessary when there are safety issues and the educator is required to intervene and remind children of procedures or rules. When educators are directing children's learning or play, the control of the experience is with the educator rather than the children. This may only be for a short period of time and then control of the situation is handed back to the children.

Sometimes when educators have very specific objectives planned for experiences, or lessons that are focused on meeting particular outcomes, the result is that educators interrupt children's play and interactions to teach particular vocabulary or concepts (Jones & Reynolds, 2011). If teacher talk dominates, Mac Naughton and Williams (2009) caution that children can become passive learners. They suggest that children should be encouraged to question, reflect and explore so that educators are able to engage in conversations that extend learning.

Selecting appropriate strategies

Effective teaching strategies consider children's home and community experiences and interaction styles as well as the child's learning in the setting (Beecher & Arthur, 2001). Burns and Casbergue (1992) have noted that a child who is used to directive strategies at home may be frustrated by a teacher who has a more indirect approach, and vice versa. Educators should investigate the strategies children are familiar with at home and in contexts such as Saturday school and begin with these, and then extend to new strategies (Beecher & Arthur, 2001).

Reflect on what you think are the main teaching strategies you use in a day. Compare this with a record of the strategies you actually use over a day. Do you use mainly low interaction, mediating or explicit strategies? Is this what you expected?

Educators' roles are dynamic and flexible, with most educators moving in and out of different roles within one learning experience or teaching session. While the strategies outlined above have been discussed separately, the reality is that educators use many of these at the same time. For example, when scaffolding a child's understandings an educator may provide a demonstration, offer support and then provide feedback by acknowledging the child's efforts. Of course, educators also need to remember that children can be engaging in complex play and learning without an adult being present at all! As the work of Vygotsky (1978) suggested, play itself scaffolds children's learning as it provides a supportive environment that encourages children to try out ideas and re-enact practices they have observed in the social worlds of their families and communities. Children can also support and scaffold each other's learning, provide each other with demonstrations and direct each other's learning.

Contemporary early childhood curriculum documents highlight the role of the educator in mediating children's learning with the use of strategies such as sustained shared thinking and scaffolding. These strategies are explored in more detail below.

Sustained shared thinking

Outcomes of the EPPE project (Siraj-Blatchford, 2005) detail a range of strategies to support children's sustained shared thinking:

- tuning in – listening and observing carefully, noting verbal and non-verbal language as children engage in experiences

- showing genuine interest – focusing attention on the child and their actions, responding appropriately
- respecting children's own decisions and choices – following children's leads
- inviting children to elaborate – seeking extra information and detail
- recapping – indicating that you have listened and understood what has been said
- offering your own expertise – adding detail that extends the interaction
- clarifying ideas – reporting your own understanding and seeking additional detail
- suggesting – offering your own input
- reminding – referring back to previous comments or intentions
- using encouragement to further thinking – acknowledging the thinking that has occurred, pointing out any contradictions, thinking out loud about what might be meant, or might happen
- offering an alternative viewpoint – provoking thinking in a different direction
- speculating – asking children to think about what might happen and why
- reciprocating – contributing to the interaction by referring to your own experiences or views
- asking open questions – considering many 'right' answers
- modelling thinking – describing your own thought processes (metacognition).

Some, rather than all, of these strategies are evident when children and adults are engaged in sustained shared thinking, as noted in Example 9.1 from Botany Downs Kindergarten in New Zealand. The processes that were involved in promoting sustained shared thinking were recorded in a Learning Story. In this example, a child's interest in towers was sparked by the gift of a key ring with a small model of the Eiffel Tower. Educators *tuned in* to this and *showed genuine interest* as they noted Madison's ongoing fascination with the topic and supported this by *contributing resources*, inviting Madison to *elaborate* and *clarify* her ideas, while also suggesting opportunities to *extend the thinking by offering input and alternative viewpoints*. Resources enabled Madison to construct her own Eiffel Tower and provided a context for *provoking thinking* and *clarifying ideas*. Extension also occurred when Madison was *reminded* of the poster comparing the height of towers around the world, and she was encouraged to make comparisons with the tower in her local environment. The addition of input from the director's overseas trip not only confirmed that she had *noticed and was interested* in Madison's topic, but also involved *reciprocal* sharing of information. This sustained interaction over a considerable period of time provides a useful example of the ways in which educators and children can engage in deep learning experiences.

EXAMPLE 9.1
The Eiffel Tower

It all started with a key ring – an Eiffel Tower key ring, a gift from Madison's Aunty from her European adventures.

For a week afterwards, Madison and her sister Georgia played games where their Eiffel towers 'talked' to each other and went on adventures. It was a few days later that Madison arrived at kindergarten asking if a picture of the Eiffel Tower could be printed out for her. Madison's Mum googled and printed a picture for her, only to be told that she needed an Eiffel Tower with four feet, just like the key ring.

A different picture was found and printed for Madison. Half an hour later Madison walked through the office door holding her Eiffel Tower, complete with four feet. It was

Glowonconcept/iStockphoto

Eiffel Tower key ring.

Madison's Eiffel Tower model.

made of paddle-pop sticks, glued together with a glue gun, and had four legs, each with a small cap attached that allowed the tower to stand up. The process of construction was documented, later becoming a Learning Story.

After looking at her Eiffel Tower and the printed photograph, Madison realised that she had forgotten to make a flag for the top. So she added one. Karen [staff member] showed Madison the pictures of the Eiffel Tower on her office wall and got out her own portfolio to show Madison the photographs of when she visited the Eiffel Tower.

Stefanie thought that Madison's Eiffel Tower was just the best: 'I want to make one like that'. With Madison's assistance, drawing on her own experience, a second Eiffel Tower was completed.

When asked what she knew about the Eiffel Tower, Madison replied, 'It's in France. It looks like the Sky Tower, except that it has different types of legs. It's thin and kind of a blackish colour. It's bigger than the Sky Tower. I like it because it is big and you can go up to the top and see the whole world'.

Eiffel Tower compared to other tall buildings.

To explore the towers of the world more closely, we found our poster picturing the sequence of heights of the towers of the world. The Eiffel Tower and the Sky Tower are certainly not the biggest in the world. When we looked more closely, we realised that we needed to update our towers chart. There are so many more towers in the world now.

It just so happened that Bronwyn [Director] was travelling to Paris on her way to a conference. She visited the Eiffel Tower and sent a postcard to Madison. She also found some additional resources about the Eiffel Tower, including a model that needed to be constructed. When the model was pieced together, some of the children chose to carry it around.

The Eiffel Tower encouraged stunning drawings and served as a provocation for many children. For example, Jacob was one of the many children who used their knowledge to replicate the tower with the building blocks. Overall, there was a growing interest in building towers.

Madison continued her fascination with the Eiffel Tower. We [staff] asked ourselves how we would be able to deepen her understanding. As we explored the intricacy of the 18 038 pieces of steel that

Eiffel Tower puzzle.

make up the Eiffel Tower we came across a digital puzzle that allowed Madison to build the tower on the computer. Madison not only had to build the tower, but she also had to come to grips with the challenges of a laptop mouse. Her initial response was one of panic; however, true to her disposition to persist, she continued with just a little support. Within minutes Madison had this new skill under control and chose to complete the puzzle over and over again.

We need to recognise children's interests and intentions and to respond in ways that support and deepen their learning. It would be interesting to find out where you can see the Sky Tower from near kindergarten. Perhaps we could take a trip to the Sky Tower?

Source: Botany Downs Kindergarten, New Zealand.

The Sky Tower.

Interactions that promote sustained shared thinking are most likely to occur within a context of responsive and trusting relationships. Where educators enjoy their interactions with children, know the children well, trust children's competencies and interests, and engage in reflective practice, the scene is set for some fascinating sustained shared thinking.

Sustained shared thinking is not the same as scaffolding, although there may at times be similarities in the way educators approach these. In sustained shared thinking, each partner contributes to the thinking and the extension of the understandings developed. This may mean that the educator can enter an interaction without knowing where it will lead, but draws on their knowledge of curriculum content and learning processes to guide the learning towards the broad learning outcomes that are appropriate for each child. In scaffolding, the adult, or more experienced person, tends to know how to compete the task at hand, and can guide the other participant through the processes needed to achieve mastery. There is often a clear goal and the educator may well have planned clearly defined steps along the way, withdrawing support as the child moves towards mastery of the task.

Intentional teaching highlights the importance of educators encouraging children to engage in experiences that they may not choose on their own, or that they may not be confident about engaging with on their own. When educators join in experiences and engage in co-construction, children often develop confidence in themselves as learners as well as developing new understandings.

Scaffolding

Supporting children as they engage in situations that take them into their ZPD is an important role for early childhood educators. The metaphor of **scaffolding** has been used to describe the process of providing support in these situations (Wood et al., 1976). When describing the early use of this metaphor, Bruner (1978) referred to a process of instruction, whereby an adult structured the interaction in such a way as to help the child reach a defined goal.

This original description is often not the way in which the term 'scaffolding' is now used (Lambert & Clyde, 2000). More recent uses of the term suggest scaffolding is the 'process of providing temporary guidance and support to children moving from one level of competence to another' (Mac Naughton & Williams, 2009, p. 370), or situations in which 'the adult provides just enough but not too much support, matching the amount of support to the skill level the

Scaffolding

A process of providing temporary guidance and support to children moving from one level of competence to another (Mac Naughton & Williams, 2009, p. 370).

child displays, providing more support if the child falters and decreasing support just enough to challenge the child to move ahead' (Bowman et al., 2001, p. 220).

It is important to emphasise here that the concept of scaffolding was not the one described by Vygotsky in his original work, nor does the current usage of the term match Bruner's (1978) original description, which relied on much more stringent adult control, allowing children access only to those aspects of the task where they had demonstrated competence (Lambert & Clyde, 2000). Nevertheless, as a concept, scaffolding is used often in educational contexts to describe interactions that occur within the ZPD as children are assisted to develop new competencies.

Scaffolding can occur at different levels. Dansie (2001) describes macro-scaffolding, which includes program planning and sequencing of experiences for a group of learners, and micro-scaffolding, which focuses on more spontaneous, individually responsive scaffolding. Macro-scaffolding could include a unit of work in the early years of school that has built-in supports as children and educators engage in teaching and learning. This could include a sequencing of tasks based on knowledge of what children can do. Within this unit of work, or within specific tasks, the responsiveness to individuals constitutes micro-scaffolding. This could involve conversations with children, demonstrations or any other individually responsive interaction. Dansie (2001) describes micro-scaffolding as contingent, so that the nature and extent of scaffolding varies for different children and in different situations. While this individual scaffolding is what most educators think of as scaffolding, Dansie argues that without the broader macro-scaffolding, micro-scaffolding may well be limited. For example, if the teaching and learning plan is not based on children's interests or strengths, if it is irrelevant to their experiences or it is just inappropriate in expectations, lots of individual support will not overcome this.

Effective scaffolding provides varied assistance depending on the children's actual grasp of the task. With novel tasks for young children, scaffolding may commence with a physical demonstration, usually accompanied by a verbal explanation. For example: nine-month-old James is sitting on the floor. His father gives him a mirror. James turns the mirror over several times and notices the shifting light. His father holds the mirror in front of James and exclaims, 'Wow! I can see a baby!'

As children get older and more articulate, the verbal element of scaffolding tends to increase. The adult may ask questions, provide prompts, model strategies, encourage risk taking, confirm children's thinking and give feedback (Mac Naughton & Williams, 2009).

Berk (2001) describes the goals of effective scaffolding as:

- joint problem solving aimed at keeping the child in the ZPD
- self-regulation
- warmth, responsiveness and engagement.

Consider these goals within the following examples in this section. In Example 9.2, five-year-old Will is completing a complex puzzle with his dad. The puzzle is a 200-piece picture of Ireland. It is a gift from a special friend and Will is keen to complete it. The puzzle has been completed before, so Will has a sense of what it looks like. Some puzzle pieces are placed on the table and others remain in the box. In Example 9.3, Angus is encouraged to try his developing skill of crawling and reaching, with support from his mother. In Example 9.4, Ellie's participation in social play is scaffolded by her preschool teacher, Amy. In each example, the elements described by Berk (2001) are evident.

▶ EXAMPLE 9.2
The puzzle

'Where do we start?' asks Dad

'Over here in the corner. There's some of these pieces, and I found two already,' replies Will.

'What about corner pieces. Have you seen any of them?'

'Well, yes, I suppose so. But I'm looking for these bits; you can find the corner pieces.'

They continue sifting through the pieces. Dad finds and places some corner pieces in appropriate places. He then asks, 'Can you help me find a bit with yellow on one corner and some black on the other side?'

'Mmm,' says Will. 'OK. I'm looking.'

'Thanks, remember it's yellow and black.'

'Yes, yellow and black … yellow and black, yellow and black. Here's one!'

'Can you see if it fits? Maybe you'll need to turn it around a few times. Hey, wow, you've got a piece. Now we need another piece here. What do you think it might have on it?'

'I don't know,' replies Will.

'Is there anywhere you could find out?'

'Well, let me look at the picture [on the box]. I think that should be Dublin there, so maybe it's something with a D or something on it?'

'That would make sense,' replies Dad. 'Can you see anything like that?'

After looking for a few minutes Will cries, 'Ohhh! No! I just can't find anything like that.'

'Well,' says Dad, 'how about we sort these pieces out, so all the blue ones are over here, the ones with writing can go over there …'

'Look, here's one. I think this one fits,' calls Will.

'How did you work that one out? That was a good one to look for,' says Dad.

'I just looked for some black letters and some green on the side and there it was,' says Will, grinning.

EXAMPLE 9.3
Angus is crawling

Angus, at eight months of age, was almost crawling. As he lay on his tummy on the floor, his mother placed a favourite toy nearby. Angus looked at it and swung his hand and arm towards it. He could not reach it. He looked to his mother, who had not noticed his action. Once again, he reached towards the toy. This time, his mother saw him and said, 'Wow Angus, you can almost reach that!' She moved it a little closer to him. Angus smiled as he looked again at the toy and his mother. He arched his back, and proceeded to raise himself almost to his knees. His mother clapped and cheered as he did so. Now on his knees and with his arms in a crawling position, Angus balanced himself in such a way that he could move one arm and leg forward – his first crawl. He reached the toy, and as he grasped it, lost his balance and fell back onto his tummy. With a big grin on his face, he brought the toy to his mouth and looked at his mother.

EXAMPLE 9.4
Is this a restaurant?

Ellie is four years old and attends preschool one day each week. She tends to engage in onlooker play, but seems keen to join in with the other children. Amy, the teacher, has noticed this and aims to help Ellie become more involved in social play. This morning, Ellie has been watching a group of girls set up a restaurant in the family corner. Amy moves to the area and knocks.

'Can I come in? Is this a restaurant?'

'Yes, you can come in and eat,' replies Mandy.

'My friend has just arrived. Can she come too?' asks Amy. She motions to Ellie to join her. Together they sit at a table. Amy opens her arms as if looking at the menu.

'What would you like to eat, Ellie? Do you think the pasta, or the fish and chips?'

After a few minutes, Ellie says, 'The pasta.'

'OK, can we have two pastas, please?' Amy asks Mandy.

Mandy replies, 'OK two pastas coming right up.' Mandy pretends to write on a notepad, and then tells Janine the order.

Mandy moves back to the table and asks Ellie, 'Would you like anything to drink?'

Ellie looks up and says, 'Yes please. Can I have a nice cold drink of water?'

'Coming right up,' says Mandy.

In a few minutes, Mandy and Janine serve their customers. Amy and Ellie pretend to eat.

Amy looks at Ellie and says, 'I've got to go, there's an emergency at home. You stay for dessert.' Ellie replies, 'OK.'

Mandy and Ellie then discuss what Ellie would like for dessert. They continue some conversation when dessert arrives and then when the bill arrives.

Joint problem solving aimed at keeping the child in the zone of proximal development

Effective scaffolding requires a focus on a specific task or situation. Together, those involved work jointly to reach a solution or conclusion. The adult (or more experienced peer) needs to make judgements about the progress of the task. If the child is becoming frustrated, changing the nature of the task, breaking it into manageable bits or re-examining what is required may be advisable to maintain the task within the child's ZPD. At different times, the assistance provided by the adult might be quite specific or quite general. A critical element of effective scaffolding is that it is adapted to the situation (*see* Figure 9.5). The amount and nature of assistance required by each child varies. What is appropriate for the same child varies as the context, the task and the expectations change.

FIGURE 9.5 Friends can provide scaffolding.

Self-regulation

Berk (2001) describes the promotion of self-regulation – the capacity to use thought to guide behaviour – as one of the goals of effective scaffolding. Scaffolding can encourage children to think before they act, facilitating planning to meet particular goals and encouraging children to be in control of their own learning. Self-regulation develops through scaffolding as children have access to a range of strategies to work towards a given goal, and control is ceded to the children as they become more proficient in the task. Helping children to realise a range of possible strategies and passing control of the task to children encourages thinking about the task and planning – essential characteristics of self-regulation.

Warmth, responsiveness and engagement

As discussed earlier in this chapter, warm, supportive relationships between adults and children are important in promoting learning. Effective scaffolding is also based on such relationships. Adults who are responsive and warm in their interactions with children tend to offer explanations for their expectations. They offer encouragement as well as challenge and engage in discussions related to expectations. Children know what is expected and feel certain that they can rely on support and encouragement. The same elements in scaffolding that promote warmth, responsiveness and engagement have been linked to authoritative parenting (Berk, 2001).

Scaffolding occurs in many contexts and in many interactions. It has an inherently instructional purpose and tends to be directed towards a specified goal. It is not essential that scaffolding be planned – some of the most interesting and exciting instances of scaffolding can be spontaneous. However, there is often a strong element of planned learning and teaching related to scaffolding. Using Dansie's (2001) descriptions of macro- and micro-scaffolding, much macro-scaffolding can be planned. It is based on knowing the children in a particular group and planning experiences that reflect their understandings and interests as well as providing challenges. Micro-scaffolding may be planned in a general sense (for example, making sure that there is plenty of time to talk with children about a task or experience), but the specific nature of micro-scaffolding will depend on the individual child and her/his interactions. In other words, it is difficult to plan exactly what you might say when you interact with the child.

Recall that children can also provide scaffolding for their peers in many contexts. Example 9.5 describes scaffolding between two school-aged children who were working on a joint project.

EXAMPLE 9.5
Making a PowerPoint presentation

Annabel and Jade have a joint school project to complete. They have the option of completing a paper copy of their work or making a PowerPoint presentation. Annabel has never made a PowerPoint presentation before. Jade has access to her parents' computer and has made several PowerPoint presentations. They work together on a project about Pinocchio.

Jade opens up the program and sets up a new page. She describes what she is doing: 'I'll just get a new page, and here it is. What sort of background do you think would be good? Do you think a colour, or maybe just a pattern?'

'Let's have red,' suggests Annabel.

Jade fills the background red, but then changes it to green. The girls laugh. After changing the background to blue, yellow and orange, Annabel says, 'Can I have a turn?'

Jade hands her the mouse and Annabel chooses various shades of blue and green before they settle for a red background.

'OK, what's the first question?' asks Jade.

Annabel looks at the questions they need to answer and reads it out.

Jade types in the question and asks, 'What do you think we should say?'

Annabel suggests a response and Jade types it into the computer. Jade talks out loud as she does this, describing the font size and where the text is to be placed. At one point, Annabel suggests that a different font should be used, and the girls explore a range of possibilities.

The girls complete the first two questions. Then Annabel says, 'My turn to type', as she takes control of the keyboard and the mouse. She types in the question and waits for Jade to suggest an answer.

The girls continue to work on the project until they have completed a 10-page presentation.

Conversations

There are many unplanned experiences in which children and adults engage that promote learning. Berk (2001) describes the power of conversations, highlighting their 'free-ranging' nature and the existence of conversations in everyday activities and events. The narratives of conversation assist children as they try to make sense of their personal experiences and as they seek to organise and interpret these experiences. Through narratives, children become aware of the perspectives and expectations of others, as well as developing their own awareness of self and deepening their understandings of the world around them.

Adult–child conversations provide many informal opportunities for children to develop understanding (Reid, 2002). Within early childhood settings and schools, as at home, there are many opportunities for conversations about routine tasks or events, as well as discussions about novel occurrences or interests. The time adults spend in conversation with children can be incredibly rich in learning opportunities as well as emotional warmth. Berk (2001, p. 74) notes the crucial role of adults interacting with children: 'Through dialogues with children, adults play a formative role in the development of children's self-concept, sensitivity to others, cognition, academic knowledge, morality, social skills, and capacity to use language and gain control over thought and behaviour'.

Engaging in conversations with children is one of the most effective teaching strategies educators can use. Some adult–child interactions are controlled by the adult, often through direct questioning, resulting in a one-sided interaction that can feel like an interrogation, often following the initiation/response/evaluation pattern. These are clearly not conversations! A more positive alternative is the spontaneous conversation, generated from an interest, event or relationship, which is meaningful and enjoyable for all involved. These conversations often consist of statements that extend and confirm children's ideas and interests, and some open-ended questions to challenge and extend thinking. Such conversations can be initiated by children or adults. Often the most enlightening conversations develop from child initiations and interests. Conversations can help build positive relationships between children and adults as well as act to sustain them. Throughout the day educators will engage in many conversations – with individuals, small groups, large groups or a whole class group (*see* Figure 9.6).

Promoting interactions through grouping

Just as educators will draw on a range of teaching strategies, they will also utilise a range of grouping strategies. The use of particular grouping strategies will depend on many things, including the context, the age and other characteristics of the children, the nature of experiences planned, children's interests and disposition.

While many decisions about grouping reflect educators' beliefs, plans or preferences, as well as setting policies and practices, it is important to consider what those decisions feel like for the children who experience them. For example, Jones (2008, p. 34) describes three-year-old Jeanna who was just beginning to play beside Lori, a new friend, when 'the teacher calls the children inside for class meeting time … Jeanna tries to sit beside Lori, but the teacher directs her to an assigned spot … After the group time, she tries to join her new friend in the play kitchen, but now it's her turn to do an art project'.

Considering what it feels like to be grouped, and to be part of some groups and not others, may help educators reflect on some of the unintended consequences of the strategies they use.

Group size

Large group conversations may well occur at the beginning or the end of the day, and could include story times, sharing times and whole group discussions. Small group and whole class conversations can be used to introduce topics, find out what children know or have experienced about a particular issue, or set the scene for the day ahead. They can be interesting sessions where children plan their experiences or report their experiences of the day. The work of educators in Reggio Emilia suggests that educators can lead the learning of a group of children through strategies such as writing down what children say and then involving them in reflection on their words, searching for insights that will 'stimulate a "spark"' (Edwards, 1994).

Small groups are an important teaching and learning strategy in both prior-to-school and school settings (*see* Figure 9.7). While Reid (2002, p.13) describes the use of small groups in school settings as 'central to all curriculum planning', she also notes that effective use of small groups requires more than setting up a cluster of desks or seating children together. The benefits of small group organisation in school classrooms include flexible classroom organisation, increased opportunities for students and teachers to build relationships and enhanced learning opportunities for students as they engage in situations drawing on different discourses and functions (Reid, 2002). However, these benefits are not attained without a strong teacher commitment to small group organisation, as well as an understanding that group structures and processes take some time to develop.

Arguments for small group size do not necessarily mean that the best grouping strategy is one educator with a small group of children in a room or space on their own. There are benefits in two or more educators working together with a larger group of children, at least for part of the day. This could be a group of three educators with a mixed age group of infants and toddlers, or in a school setting it may mean two or three teachers team-teaching across a grade or across a number of grades or stages. It could also mean support teachers, aides and librarians working in classrooms alongside the class teacher rather than withdrawing children for specialist classes or remedial work.

Grouping strategies

There are many different ways of grouping children, whether in long day care programs, preschools or schools. There is no 'best' method of grouping. It is useful to explore a range of possibilities rather than to continue with current practices 'because that's how we always do it' or 'because regulations say we have to'. It is important to be aware of licensing guidelines and to follow required group sizes and staff–child ratios. This does not mean, however, that only one type of grouping is possible. It is possible to meet mandatory requirements for licensing and quality assurance standards by using a number of different grouping methods. It is to be expected that the pedagogical

FIGURE 9.6 Adult–child conversations provide many opportunities for co-construction.

FIGURE 9.7 Small group experiences provide opportunities for conversations among children as well as between children and educators.

ꞁs made by educators will result in children interacting within diverse groups over
t times of the day or year.

ꞁpings can be based on similarities across language or culture, age, ability and interest
ꞁre 9.8). Groupings based on differences include mixed culture and language groups,
mixed ability groups and mixed ages.

AGE

Age has become the major criterion for grouping children in many educational communities.
Rogoff (2003, p. 8) notes that 'with the rise of industrialisation and efforts to systematise
human services such as education … age became a measure of development and a criterion
for sorting people'. This is reflected in the organisation of many early childhood settings and in
schools.

One of the advantages of same age groups is that the environment can be planned specifically
to cater for that particular age group. This assumes, however, that all children of the same age
will be similar – for example, that a group of four–five-year-olds will have similar developmental
and learning attainments. It can be very convenient to classify children by age. However, the
reality is that individual differences may well outweigh similarities.

There can be a wide range of differences even when all children are the same age. Children
who are 18 months old, for example, will vary enormously in their use of language, their physical
prowess and their relationships. Same-age grouping works to narrow the range of possibilities
for children's behaviour and learning, and to encourage children to fit the expectations for their
age group. As Greenman, Stonehouse and Schweikert (2008) note, the tendency of caregivers to
minimise individual differences is strongest when the age range of children is narrow. There are
arguments that a wider range of behaviours is likely to be accepted in a mixed age than in a single
age classroom (Katz, Evangelou & Hartman, 1990; Porter, 2007) and that mixed age groups provide
greater opportunities for children to learn from peers than age groups (Gerard, 2005). These
support the view that **mixed age groups** facilitate attention to individuals.

Some schools utilise multi-age classes. Briggs and Potter (1999) draw the distinction between
multi-age classes and multigrade or composite classes. In multi-age classes the focus is on
children working at their own level and at their own pace. In multigrade or composite classes,
children are still divided and taught as separate grades. Multi-age classes are a philosophical
choice whereas composite classes are often a pragmatic reality. In schools where classes
are based on stages of curriculum achievement (broader than age or grade classifications),
anecdotal reports from educators focus on continual learning and little on classification of age
and grade.

Mixed age groups

When children of
different ages are
grouped together.

Advantages of mixed age grouping

Mixed age grouping is also known as family grouping, as it replicates the sorts of age spans that
are typical in many families. In some cases of mixed age grouping the same group may stay
with the one educator, or team of staff, over a number of years. For example, a team of staff and
a group of children may move through a child care centre from the 'babies' group' up to the
four–five-year-old group. This also occurs in some school contexts, where educators move with a
group of children as they progress from preschool to school. In Scotland, this process has been
described as 'looping' (Fabian & Dunlop, 2007).

When the same staff members and a group of children stay together over a number of years
there are fewer transitions for children, families and staff. In school settings this has been
found to reduce the disruption to children's learning that occurs at the beginning of the year
when children are required to adjust to a new teacher (Briggs & Potter, 1999). It also means that
educators and families have longer to get to know each other and to build strong relationships.

A further advantage of mixed age grouping/multi-age classes is that children are encouraged
to see the perspectives of different group members. Older children, in particular, learn to
consider the rights of younger children and have been found to demonstrate increased prosocial
behaviours and leadership skills (Briggs & Potter, 1999; Katz, et al., 1990). At the same time,
younger children can learn from the older children and have been found to engage in more

complex play in mixed age groups (Briggs & Potter, 1999). In multi-age classrooms gifted children can accelerate, and children who need additional assistance can be accommodated without standing out as different or needing to be withdrawn from the classroom.

A range of ages in a group means that routines may be less stressful for staff as older children are able to assist the younger children. Older children are able to provide support and scaffolding for younger children; for example, by engaging in conversations, sharing a book or assisting with a construction.

In school settings, buddy programs have been used to build connections between older, more experienced members of the school community and those starting school (Dockett & Perry, 2013). **Buddy programs** aim to help those starting school feel comfortable with the new environment and those within it, as well as providing opportunities for the older buddies to build and enact mentoring and leadership skills.

FIGURE 9.8 Mixed age groups provide scaffolding and encourage consideration of multiple perspectives.

Disadvantages of mixed age grouping

Concerns about mixed age grouping relate to younger children's safety and older children's learning. It may be difficult for staff to provide an environment that is safe for younger children but that at the same time provides suitable challenges for older children. Porter (2007) has expressed concerns that a mixed age environment may include resources that are not appropriate for younger children or that the curriculum may be 'dumbed down' for older children.

Porter (2007) also expresses concerns that mixed age groups create more work for staff to manage as they have to program and set up the environment for a wide range of interests and abilities. In addition, some staff members may not be confident working with a broad age range and may feel more able to interact with a particular age group.

In some small settings, mixed age grouping may mean that family members, who spend a great deal of time together at home, also spend time together in the setting. While this can have many benefits, it can also be difficult for children to establish their own individual identity.

Responses to concerns

Mixed age grouping does not mean that all children in an early childhood setting will spend the whole day together, or that a multi-age class will stay grouped as one class all day. Mixed age groups can be made up of a number of small groups.

It is important to remember that different forms of grouping can be used throughout the day. Children may be based in mixed age groups for part of the day and be grouped according to ages at routine times and for small group experiences, or for particular curriculum areas in a school setting. In a long day care setting, issues of safety can be addressed by providing small equipment that may pose a safety hazard for infants and toddlers while the younger children are eating and/or sleeping.

Educators can also consider the use of space so that small group learning centres are created within the mixed age environment. Resources for older children can sometimes be placed within an enclosed area that older children can access but which keeps younger children safe.

ABILITY

Children can be grouped in same ability or mixed **ability groups**. These groups may be for the whole day, such as when children are placed in a school class based on general ability. Grouping can also be flexible so that children may be in a mixed ability class and be ability-grouped for classes such as mathematics and English.

Buddy programs

Programs where older or more experienced members of a community support younger or newer members of that community. Buddy programs often operate in schools where older students are paired with those starting school, providing a friendly face and source of support in the new environment.

Ability groups

Grouping students according to achievement, skill or ability.

Advantages of ability groups

There is a wide range of abilities in any group of children, making it difficult for educators to cater for each child's potential and for children to remain motivated. The advantages of ability groups are that the curriculum can be more closely matched to children's development and learning, children are able to interact with peers at a similar level of interest and understanding and are able to challenge each other (Whitton et al., 2010). Ability grouping may well be beneficial for some children and not others. For example, Hong et al. (2012) report that homogeneous ability grouping had little effect for high-ability students, but some positive effects for other children when combined with instruction time. This study reminds us that grouping is one of many factors that influence children's learning.

Gross and Sleap (2000) argue that children who are gifted benefit from doing work at levels beyond their age rather than from enrichment at their own age level. While some educators are concerned that children who are placed in the top ability group may become conceited, Gross (1997) states that when children who are gifted are ability-grouped they realise that there are children who are more capable than they are.

Disadvantages of ability groups

Grouping children by ability can result in children being labelled with such terms as 'bright' and 'gifted' or with such terms as 'slow learner' and 'learning disabled'. Consciously or not, many staff respond to the way that children are grouped by adapting their behaviour and expectations. Educators may expect more of children who are in a high ability group and less of children in a lower ability group. It is important when using ability groups to regularly reassess children (Whitton et al., 2010).

Ability grouping may reinforce competition between children and increase the focus on success and failure. Children who are placed in lower ability groups may develop negative self-concepts and self-fulfilling prophecies, believing, for example, that 'I can't do maths' or 'I'm only on level one. I'm no good at reading'. Equally, children who are identified as gifted may have trouble living up to the high expectations placed on them and become stressed (Porter, 2005).

Decisions on how to group children may be based on a test of children's ability. These tests are often culturally biased, advantaging children from English-speaking, middle-class backgrounds. As a result, some children's strengths may not be identified. In addition, some children do not perform well in a test situation.

There are some general issues to consider regarding the assessment of young children (Dockett & Perry, 2007); these include the following:

- Young children's abilities are emerging, not fixed. Assessment at any one point may present a distorted view of capabilities (Bowman et al., 2001).
- How and where should assessment be undertaken?
- What assessment procedures are to be used?
- What decisions (for example, school entry, progression, retention, access to early intervention services, and programs for gifted children) are based on the assessment?

Responses to concerns

Ability grouping may occur for some, rather than all, parts of the day. Within these groups, 'different students can complete differentiated work that meets individual academic needs' (Whitton, 2003, p. 1). When educators plan a range of experiences with varying levels of complexity and various modes of engagement, it is possible to respond to children's differing abilities.

LANGUAGE

Children can be grouped in same language groups or in mixed language groups. Often, children will naturally form groups with others who share the same language background. These groups can draw on shared experiences that foster talk and meaning making as well as positive self-esteem and a feeling of security. Educators can also plan groups based on language. They may plan same language groups in order to support the maintenance and development of children's home languages and to build children's self-esteem. Mixed language groups may also be planned to support bilingual children's second-language learning through interactions with native speakers. Educators may also utilise grouping strategies that promote cross-cultural understandings and appreciation of linguistic diversity (*see* Figure 9.9).

Educators can encourage and support children to interact informally with same language peers. It is important to allow time for extended interactions in the home language so that children have time to be engaged in learning and develop concepts in the home language (Jones Diaz, 2001). Educators can also plan for same language groups at routine times such as mealtimes, where a group of children and an adult who speaks the same language are seated together. Other educator-initiated same language groups may occur at small group time where a bilingual worker, community language teacher or family member may share a story or song with a group of children or interact with children in play in their home language. Same language groups will generally require children to be grouped across ages and stages, meaning that older children can scaffold younger children's language learning.

Advantages of same language groups

Same language groupings provide children with opportunities to use their home language in the educational setting and give children the message that languages other than English are valued. Language is a means of maintaining group identity and solidarity and for passing on cultural heritage. Same language groups provide children with 'opportunities to use their home language in meaningful contexts that encourage sustained and active conversations' (Jones Diaz, 2001, p. 4).

FIGURE 9.9 Print materials can promote the use of home languages.

The maintenance of the home language is essential, particularly for young children. Gibbons (2002) suggests that a second language such as English should not be introduced until the child is confident in the first language. Children who have a firm foundation in the first language are in a much stronger position to develop a second language than the child who is still in the process of learning the first language (Gibbons, 2002; Siraj-Blatchford & Clarke, 2000). When the home language is not supported, children may experience subtractive bilingualism where the home language is replaced by the second language (Wong Fillmore, 1991). Subtractive bilingualism, particularly at an early age, can have a negative impact on a child's learning, social interactions and self-esteem, and can result in the child rejecting the language and culture of the home. When this occurs, children may end up fluent in neither their home language nor English and unable to communicate effectively at home or at school.

Advantages of mixed language groups

Mixed language groups expose monolingual children to the diversity of languages in the broader community, while also providing second-language learners with opportunities to hear and use the new language. Mixed language groups promote respect for different ways of speaking and different types of print.

Children growing up in a monolingual environment need to be introduced to the reality of the linguistic diversity of their broader community. The concept that there are different ways of talking needs to be consciously introduced to children (Hopson, 1990). If there is no linguistic diversity in the early childhood setting, educators need to bring it in from the surrounding community in whatever ways are possible.

For bilingual children, small child-initiated mixed language groups provide opportunities to be involved in experiences where the second language is used to describe actions, negotiate with peers, develop hypotheses and solve problems (Arthur, 2001). Mixed language play

experiences provide second-language learners with exposure to the new language in stress-free and meaningful environments that support and scaffold their second-language use in communications with others. Siraj-Blatchford and Clarke (2000) note that young children learning English as a second language need to be involved in interactive situations with other children and adults where dialogue is encouraged and their language attempts are supported.

Concerns about same language groups

Educators may express concerns that there are many different language groups in their setting or classroom and that it is not possible to support them all. There may also be concerns regarding the lack of resources to support the further development of oral and written language in children's home languages. In addition, educators may be concerned that children are not exposed to children from other language groups and do not have opportunities to interact in English if they only participate in same language groups.

Responses to concerns about same language groups

The bilingual resources in a setting and among families and the broader community can be used to support bilingualism and biliteracy. Educators can borrow community language resources from local libraries, resource centres and family members. Many resources can also be created through the collection of newspapers, magazines, menus and food packaging in relevant community languages as well as the use of photographs of shop and street signs in languages other than English. Access to the Internet also provides opportunities to locate a wide range of online resources.

Where there are bilingual staff in the setting, regardless of whether they are an educator, teaching assistant or cook, they can support children's home language development and liaise with family and community members. Bilingual staff who speak the same languages as the children can play alongside children and engage them in interactions in the home language. Where there are no staff who speak the appropriate languages, staff can often be accessed through support agencies.

Family members, community volunteers and older children can also be involved in educational settings to support children's home languages. Family and community members can participate in children's play and encourage interactions in the home language. They may also be able to share stories, songs and rhymes with children in their home language, although educators need to be sensitive to the fact that not everyone who speaks a language other than English is literate in that language. Older children can also work with younger children to support home language learning. In a school setting, for example, children from the upper primary years can participate in experiences with children in the first years of school where they use the home language to communicate. Jones Diaz (2001) suggests other types of same language groupings, including sibling groups and buddy groups.

As with any form of grouping, same language groups are not necessarily used for the whole day. It is most appropriate if bilingual learners have opportunities to engage in same language and mixed language groups (Siraj-Blatchford & Clarke, 2000).

INTERESTS

Children will often form their own groups based on shared interests (see Figure 9.10). In a preschool setting, for example, a group of children may

FIGURE 9.10 Interest-based groups encourage learning and engagement.

be interested in digging in the sandpit and exploring how deep they can dig. Another group of children may be interested in taking on roles in dramatic play where the theme is related to their interest in animals and veterinary surgeons. Yet another group of children may be interested in using writing materials and exploring print. Children will move in and out of different interest groups throughout the day.

Children's interests can form the basis of the curriculum; for example, in an emergent curriculum approach. In other cases the curriculum may be organised around mandatory curriculum or teacher-selected themes where children are permitted to make choices based on their interests.

Advantages of interest-based grouping

Where children are able to form their own interest-based groups they are often motivated to engage in in-depth learning as they investigate questions and solve problems they have generated: 'When the problems to be solved are set mainly by the teacher, the children are not necessarily motivated to search for solutions' (Helm & Katz, 2001, p. 8). Jones, Evans and Renken (2001) point out that when children are following their interests, educators are able to work with, rather than against, children's passions and concerns.

Children's family and community experiences often create shared interests that encourage talk, collaborative play and investigation. This may be an interest in the latest popular children's television program or collectable cards, or an interest that emerges from family or community experiences such as visiting the beach or playing soccer. Shared experiences at the setting, such as building construction occurring next door, the discovery of a bird's nest or a visit to Chinatown, may also spark children's interests. In other cases the experiences of one child, such as taking a sick animal to the vet, may spark the sharing of experiences and interests among a group of children (Arthur et al., 2003). These shared experiences provide many opportunities for collaborative learning.

In an emergent curriculum approach, educators are responsive to children's interests and aim to extend their understandings. Educators can provide spontaneous support for children's interests by showing an interest themselves, asking questions and providing resources. At other times the interest of a group of children can provide the catalyst for an in-depth investigation or project that requires long-term planning as well as spontaneous interactions and resourcing. The addition of relevant resources can encourage further exploration and the representation of ideas using a range of media. Projects are rich with opportunities for children to use mathematics, science and literacy in meaningful contexts and for children to develop dispositions to be curious, to solve problems and to be actively engaged in learning (Helm & Katz, 2001).

Disadvantages of interest-based grouping

Educators may be concerned with children not receiving a broad education if they only follow their interests. For example, some children may not choose to engage in any creative arts experiences, or may never visit the book area or writing centre. If children are allowed to always follow their interests, they may only ever engage in gender stereotypical play. Other concerns include the diversity of children's interests and educators' inability to follow the interests of all children. Some educators are concerned that children may be interested in areas such as popular media culture that they believe are commercially driven and ideologically unsound.

Responses to concerns

Not all children's interests need to, or can, be followed and extended in educational settings. However, where the program is open and responsive to children's interests there are possibilities for all children to make choices and to engage in meaningful learning.

Educators' interests and experiences – provided children respond to these positively – can also be the catalyst for children's investigations. Jones and her colleagues (2001) suggest that by including their own interests in the curriculum, educators model knowledge and enthusiasm. Educators' values as well as the values of the children's families and broader community also influence decisions as to what is included in the curriculum (Jones & Nimmo, 1994). Jones et al. (2001, p. 8) argue that 'in-depth curriculum emerges in the intersections between teachers' interests, kids' interests and school–community values'.

Interest-based projects are unlikely to constitute the whole of the program, whether it is in long day care, preschool or school. There will be many other learning activities that will be occurring such as creative arts, construction and literacy. However, interest-based projects can also integrate many domains of learning (Helm & Katz, 2001).

Children who may not choose to engage with reading and writing in traditional areas will often use books and computer resources to investigate an area of interest. They will also tend to integrate reading and writing into their play as the project provides a purpose for using print to represent their meanings (Helm & Katz, 2001). This may involve writing signs to accompany a block structure, creating menus in restaurant play and reading signs and posters (Beecher & Arthur, 2001).

Some interests may be based on traditional gendered roles, such as girls' interest in fairies or boys' interest in superheroes. However, educators' involvement in and extension of children's interests can help to break down gender barriers. Educators can work with children to critique gendered roles and to examine power relationships (Mac Naughton, 2000). Other interests, such as dinosaurs or The Wiggles, may cross gender divides and encourage boys and girls to collaborate.

While many educators have expressed concerns about the ideological and commercial influences of popular media culture on children's lives, and feel uneasy about including children's popular media interests in educational settings, popular media culture provides links to children's home and community experiences. Research undertaken in a British nursery school (Marsh, 2000) highlights the ways in which literacy experiences based on popular culture tap into children's lives. Marsh particularly noted that children who had not previously taken part in literacy experiences, and who did not generally engage in many verbal interactions with educators – mostly working-class boys from bilingual backgrounds – were very enthusiastic when the literacy materials linked to their popular culture interests.

Rather than dismissing popular culture as commercially driven and ideologically unsound, it can provide opportunities for critical analysis. Popular texts can be used to extend children's pleasure and at the same time assist them to examine the ways that texts are constructed to present particular ideologies (O'Brien & Comber, 2000). Educators can work with children to challenge and transform the messages of popular media and to critique the commercial nature of many popular texts. It is important, however, that the critique of texts of popular culture arises from children's issues and questions and that it is extended to all texts.

FRIENDSHIPS

Friendship groups

Groups formed on the basis of social connections or shared interests.

Children will also form their own friendship groups. **Friendship groups** are formed based on social ties and often on shared experiences and interests. These groups can be the basis of small spontaneous groupings or for groupings in more formal contexts; for example, when children are able to choose to work with friends in a classroom context. Friendships matter to children. Friendships also take effort and energy to maintain. Educators need to provide opportunities for children to make and be with friends, and sometimes to impart guidance about the responsibilities that can go with friendships.

Advantages of friendship groupings

Friendship groups encourage social interactions, language use and collaborative learning. Children are much more likely to engage in arguments – in conversations, rather than in a conflictual sense – with friends and to have a vested interest in solving arguments (Dockett & Perry, 2001). Play between friends does seem to generate more disputes; however, because of the friendship, there is great motivation to resolve these disputes in ways that maintain the relationship (Dunn, 2004).

Friendship groups provide stability and security. When children enter unfamiliar environments, such as when they start school, the presence of friends and the chance to be with friends are important (Dockett & Perry, 2007). Children make judgements about their 'belongingness' in school based on whether or not they have friends. Where children start school not knowing any of the other children, they report expecting to make friends and the chance to be with those friends for much of the school day.

Disadvantages of friendship groupings

Some children may find it difficult to form friendships and may be rejected by their peers. Rejection may be because of a child's difficult behaviour or because of perceived or actual differences. Children may be rejected because of race, culture, language or religious beliefs, because of physical attributes such as height or weight or because they do not fit expectations of gender roles. Curry and Johnson (1990) point out that peer rejection is one of the best predictors of psychosocial problems in later life.

Educators also may be concerned that children will not remain on task if they are sitting next to their friends.

Responses to concerns

Children generally feel devastated when others utter the call: 'You're not my friend and I'm not playing with you today'. To use friendship groups effectively, educators need to spend time talking with young children about the nature of friendships. They will also need to model some of the strategies that can be used to make and support friendships. These are important skills and it is not surprising that young children may need some assistance at various times. Educators have a responsibility to assist children who are experiencing difficulties with peers. Educators can assist children to gain entry to a group and encourage friendships among children. It is also the educator's responsibility to address discrimination and unfair behaviours such as bullying, racism and victimisation.

Children talking to each other and seemingly drifting off-task may be perceived by some educators as a disadvantage of friendship grouping – but it is also one of the great advantages of friendship groups. Given the importance of talk in cultural-historical approaches to learning, children need to talk with their peers. Of course, educators would be quite happy if the talk generated among friends related only to the task at hand; this is rarely the case, whether we are considering groups of children or adults. One of the challenges for educators is to encourage talk about learning experiences. Berk (2009) reminds us that children (and adults) resort to talking to themselves (and others) about a task when it is just that little bit too difficult to do automatically – in other words, when the task is located in the ZPD. She suggests that a classroom full of conversation related to the learning experiences provided is a classroom where you expect a lot of learning to take place.

GENDER

Often children will spontaneously form **same-sex groups** based on shared interests and social worlds. When children form their own groups based on gender they often engage in stereotypical experiences such as boys playing with trucks in the sandpit and girls playing with dolls in the home corner. In play contexts, in particular, children 'create and recreate their understandings of what they believe to be normal behaviour for boys and girls, women and men' (Mac Naughton, 2000, p. 119).

At times, educators may form children's groups based on gender. Educators may group children with others of the same gender at routine times, such as forming lines to move from one area of the setting to another or when asking children to complete tasks such as emptying bins or packing away. Often these groupings reinforce traditional gendered roles. Educators may also decide to group boys and girls separately for particular school curriculum areas such as mathematics or English. At other times educators may encourage boys and girls to play and work together or encourage boys and girls to engage in non-stereotypical roles and experiences.

Same-sex groups
Groups formed on the basis of sex or gender.

Advantages of same-sex groups

One response to children's gendered play is to encourage both girls and boys to experience a wide range of curriculum experiences. Children may be encouraged into non-traditional areas through strategies such as role modelling (for example, having a male teacher or parent in the home corner or a female member of staff in the block area) and through strategies such as 'girls' day' in the block area. These strategies may provide some encouragement and support for children to explore non-traditional play experiences.

Single-sex classes have been advocated by some educators as a means of addressing the poor performance of some boys in literacy and furthering boys' interest in areas such as English (House of Representatives Standing Committee on Education and Training, 2002). Martino, Mills & Lingard (2005) argue that the strategy of single-sex groups, on its own, does not necessarily produce changes in educational outcomes for boys. Rather, changes in pedagogy, in combination with the contexts in which single-sex groups occur, are associated with differentiated outcomes. One of the advantages of single-sex classes is that educators are able to select content and teaching strategies that are likely to engage boys or girls. However, this can also occur in co-educational classes.

Disadvantages of same-sex groups

Same-sex groupings such as 'girls' day' in the block area or 'boys' day in the family area, aim to provide opportunities for girls as well as boys to engage in a wide range of experiences. However, such approaches do little to explore or challenge assumptions about gendered play or to encourage children to think about the traditional discourse of masculinity or femininity (Mac Naughton, 2000).

In schools, the organisation of separate classes for boys and girls assumes that all boys learn in the same way and are interested in the same topics and that girls do the same. This ignores the diversity among groups of boys and girls and the intersections of race, class and socio-economic status with gender (Alloway & Gilbert, 2002). Same-sex classes can also work to reinforce dominant masculinities. Rather than separate classes and programs of study, curriculum and assessment that relates to children's real-world experiences and integrates out-of-school knowledge has the potential to support both boys and girls to engage in meaningful learning and to improve the motivation, engagement and socio-academic achievement of both boys and girls (Munns et al., 2006).

Responses to issues of gender

Children spend considerable time trying to work out what it is to be masculine and feminine and learning the discourses of masculinity and femininity. Educators need to understand how gendered roles are constructed and how power relations impact on children's play and their social futures. Educators can work with children to help them analyse their own play and gendered relations and to deconstruct dominant discourses. Educators can plan experiences and resources that challenge the demarcation line that often exists between boys and girls. The encouragement of new dramatic play scripts that are inclusive of boys and girls, the negotiation of roles and discussion of what is fair and unfair helps to re-create new possibilities. Educators can use instances of children crossing traditional gender boundaries as opportunities to open up discussions about the limitations of traditional gendered roles and the exploration of alternative practices.

Cultural-historical and postmodern theories argue that there is a complex interplay as gender interacts with children's linguistic, social and cultural backgrounds to influence the ways that boys and girls take up school practices such as school literacies. Identities, including what it means to be a boy or a girl, are socially constructed. As boys take up masculine ways of being they may see reading and writing as unmasculine, and as girls take up feminine ways of being they may see mechanics and construction as unfeminine. Effective teaching practices challenge boys and girls to broaden the way they see themselves as learners, the ways they relate to others and the strategies they use for learning (Beecher, 2010; Department of Education, Science and Training, 2003). Educators need to work with children and families to challenge children's preconceptions, link the curriculum to all children's family and community experiences and take a critical perspective in analysing gender roles in popular media and educational texts.

Making decisions about grouping

Effective pedagogy calls for a range of grouping strategies. A number of different strategies may be used within the one setting throughout the day.

When making decisions about grouping, staff, families and children should be involved. The following steps provide a guide to settings when investigating methods of grouping that may be appropriate to the setting:

- *Exploring alternatives* – brainstorming all of the possible grouping strategies will assist the team to explore all alternatives.
- *Examining advantages and disadvantages* – each type of grouping can be explored from the perspectives of families, staff and children. This process enables the group to examine the myths and realities associated with different types of groupings and to discuss any concerns that people might have. Ways of responding to concerns about different grouping strategies can be explored through the use of resources such as readings and videos, as well as through networking with other settings.
- *Investigating different grouping strategies for different parts of the program* – it may be useful at this stage to investigate the use of different types of grouping for different times, such as mealtimes or adult-initiated small group times.
- *Exploring human resources* – including staff, support staff such as bilingual workers, family and community members and older children, can be explored. Flexible staffing arrangements and the use of volunteers and systems such as buddying or peer mentoring can provide opportunities to implement new grouping strategies.
- *Examining constraints* – any constraints that may affect the implementation of different types of grouping should be addressed. This may include constraints regarding building or classroom design, curriculum resources, or staff knowledge and confidence with new grouping strategies.
- *Developing a plan of action* – once the possibilities and constraints have been explored, decisions can be made about grouping strategies to be implemented. The development of a plan of action can assist with the process of implementing changes.
- *Evaluating effectiveness of grouping strategies* – it is important to engage in ongoing reflection on the effectiveness of grouping strategies being utilised and progress towards implementation of the plan of action.

Communicating with families about grouping

It is essential that educators respect family values and expectations and include families in decision-making about grouping. At the same time, educators can provide families with information that outlines how the setting/school approaches children's learning and the role of grouping strategies. Ways of exploring issues with families may include:

- staff–parent interviews where individual children's experiences and learning at home and at the setting can be discussed
- meetings where the setting/school philosophy and program are discussed with families
- images of children interacting in a variety of groups such as mixed age and interest groups, with annotations to highlight children's learning
- programs displayed for parents so that they can read about what their child has been doing each day – throughout the whole day, not just at educator-initiated group time
- observations that highlight children's social interactions and prosocial behaviours available for families to read
- notes to families in communication books or diaries about what their child has been doing each day, with families encouraged to contribute comments
- articles in the newsletter and in the foyer about the benefits of particular types of grouping such as multi-age classes or same language groups
- workshops presented by staff on areas such as interest-based programming
- open door policy so that families can see first-hand how grouping strategies are working in the setting.

Promoting positive interactions

Relationships and interactions provide a context for learning. However, educators have all experienced situations when interactions are not positive and relationships seem to be based on angst rather than support. How can they encourage children to engage in positive interactions? It is not suggested in this chapter that children should not engage in conflict or disagreement. Rather, it is suggested that there are positive ways of handling these situations. Disagreement and argument, supported by explanation and justification, can be a powerful learning context. This can only happen if children are encouraged to listen to and respect the views of others, expect to justify their position and recognise that people construct different understandings based on different perspectives and experiences. Positive interactions are essential to developing a sense of identity and belonging. As explored in the EYLF (DEEWR, 2009, p. 20),

> Children learn about themselves and construct their own identity within the
> context of their families and communities. This includes their relationships
> with other people, places and things and the actions and responses of others.
> [Identity] is shaped by experience. When children have positive experiences
> they develop an understanding of themselves as significant and respected,
> and feel a sense of belonging.

Educators have a major role to play in creating the positive and supportive climate that underpins such expectations. They have a responsibility to help children develop and demonstrate their social competence; in other words, to help children develop the skills required to interact successfully with other children and adults (Landy, 2002). For example, educators may need to support children in initiating and sustaining relationships with peers, interacting cooperatively and functioning as part of a group. Some children will need assistance in learning how to approach a group, how to articulate their feelings, preferences and reasons, and how to join in play. Educators can assist children to interpret what is going on in other children's play, see the situation from others' perspectives, choose an appropriate response and carry it out (Meece & Soderman, 2010).

Prosocial behaviours

Actions to help others, without the expectation of reward.

Educators can also assist children to develop **prosocial behaviours**. Prosocial behaviours include cooperation, caring behaviours and responding with concern to others' distress.

Landy (2002) suggests five principles for fostering children's social competence and prosocial behaviours. These are:

1. modelling socially acceptable behaviours
2. helping children to see the effects of their behaviour on others and encouraging role taking and perspective taking
3. encouraging children to take on responsibilities
4. encouraging children to interact with their peers, and scaffolding strategies that will assist positive interactions
5. assisting children to develop strategies of conflict resolution and interpersonal negotiation.

Positive interactions are promoted in an environment where all participants feel valued. Just as the physical environment is instrumental in generating opportunities for interactions, so too is the verbal environment. A positive verbal environment (Kostelnik et al., 2009) helps children feel valued and respected and, through this, promotes children's self-regulation. Strategies to create positive verbal environments include showing genuine interest in children's activities, speaking courteously with children, stating expectations clearly and providing children with choices (Meece & Soderman, 2010).

Guidance instead of discipline

Many early childhood settings display sets of class or group rules. Sometimes these have been negotiated with children; other times they are the educators' rules. Rules are usually written in the negative – 'No running', 'No pushing' – suggesting that educators actually expect children to break these rules (Wein, 2004), and that the role of educators is rule enforcement. Gartrell (2012) argues that rule enforcement indicates to children that they have made mistakes, but does not help children work out what mistakes they have made. He advocates the use of guidelines, rather than rules, as well as strategies to help children use the guidelines.

Positive environments tend to reflect a guidance approach, rather than a discipline approach, to promoting prosocial behaviours (Porter, 2007). Discipline is adult-centred, focuses on obedience, tends to punish misbehaviour and reward 'good' behaviour, and relies on rules. A discipline approach relies on adults to monitor and manage children's behaviour. Gartrell (2010) differentiates between misbehaviour and mistaken behaviour and reminds us that learning self-regulation and making ethical decisions is a lifelong learning process.

In contrast to discipline, a guidance approach encourages the development of self-regulation, respect for others, joint problem solving and ethically and socially just behaviours (Gartrell, 2010). In a guidance approach, adults model language and strategies, provide private feedback rather than public humiliation and engage children in general group discussions about positive social behaviours. Wellbeing is correlated with resilience. Helping children develop the capacity to cope with day-to-day stress and challenges, as well as the disposition for perseverance when faced with unfamiliar situations, promotes self-regulation and generates opportunities for ongoing success (DEEWR, 2009).

Creating positive learning environments

The physical environment educators create has implications for children's interactions and behaviours. Learning environments that promote prosocial behaviours and collaborative learning have the following features:

- *Sufficient, open-ended and accessible resources*. Positive learning environments include resources that encourage active learning, involvement, negotiation and collaboration. Resources that are well organised, aesthetically displayed and easily accessible to children help them to be in control of their own learning and to become deeply engaged in experiences of interest. Educators who are sensitive to children's emerging social skills provide sufficient resources to alleviate disputes, while at the same time assisting children to negotiate with their peers.
- *Meaningful experiences that include appropriate levels of challenge*. Positive learning environments include experiences, learning centres and projects that facilitate in-depth investigations and promote collaborative learning. Experiences that provide appropriate levels of challenge and adult guidance promote success and build feelings of competence.
- *Large blocks of time that encourage children to engage in deep learning*. A flexible timetable with large chunks of overlapping time (Greenman et al., 2008) allows sufficient time for children to engage in deep learning and limits the frustrations associated with constantly needing to pack away and move on to a new activity. A flexible timetable with as few transitions, delays and interruptions as possible encourages a relaxed atmosphere. Effective educators acknowledge and respect children's feelings and their engagement in experiences. When young children are provided with sufficient time they are also able to complete tasks such as getting dressed independently and they develop autonomy and positive self-esteem. Even in school settings, a creative organisation of the school day can provide large chunks of time to facilitate play sessions (Dockett & Fleer, 1999).
- *Sufficient space for children to explore and to form small groups*. Well-planned spaces can promote the sorts of behaviours educators want to encourage – whether these are quiet reflection, collaboration or creativity. Environments can be organised in ways that promote small group experiences and interactions, and that balance quiet and private spaces with more active spaces, enabling children to be together or alone. Porter (2007) also suggests that a positive social environment provides sufficient space to avoid congestion and competing demands. Careful planning of spaces and resources that take account of traffic

flow and the amount of space needed for an experience can eliminate many frustrations and potential conflicts.

- *An aesthetically pleasing environment*. Environments for young children should be places of beauty (Greenman, 2005). Displays of children's work, photographs of children and their families and artefacts from children's families and communities can help create a sense of belonging and promote conversations among children.

- *A range of flexible groupings that support collaborative learning and the co-construction of knowledge*. Positive learning environments encourage small group collaborative interactions that, in turn, encourage perspective taking, negotiation, turn taking and cooperation in a realistic and meaningful context. A range of flexible grouping strategies throughout the day – including mixed age, friendship and interest groups – foster interactions and make it more likely that children are grouped at times with more socially competent children who can model prosocial behaviours and group relationships. Effective educators have realistic expectations of children and do not expect young children to sit and listen in large groups for long periods of time.

- *A community of care*. Responsive educators plan environments that respect children's competencies and emerging social skills and nurture a community of care. Greenman (2005) emphasises the importance of environments that support relationships, compassion, responsibility and a sense of community.

- *Clear expectations*. Positive environments provide children with clear expectations about their behaviour and set clear and appropriate limits when necessary. Effective teachers have clear routines and procedures that support learning (Lyons et al., 2011). Educators who effectively guide children's behaviours provide consistent, predictable interactions and are sensitive to children's perspectives. Positive social environments also require educators to engage in open communication with children and families, to negotiate guidance policies and goals and to discuss appropriate behaviours with children.

- *Meaningful feedback*. Effective educators give meaningful feedback and acknowledgement to children rather than empty praise. They model and scaffold prosocial behaviours such as alternative ways of solving problems and ways of dealing with frustrations. Educators have an important role in talking with children about their feelings, scaffolding children's problem-solving and conflict-resolution skills, and assisting children to learn to appreciate diverse interaction styles and perspectives. The sharing of literature and group discussions can assist children to project into the feelings of others and to develop problem-solving skills in a less confronting environment than the playground.

Conclusion and reflection

The basis for this chapter is that positive relationships are at the core of effective interactions with children and adults. Effective early childhood environments, be they prior-to-school settings, schools or outside school care settings, are those in which people feel valued, respected and accepted. Learning occurs within the contexts of positive relationships. Educators have a responsibility to be proactive in establishing and maintaining positive interactions with children, other professionals and families. The ways in which educators engage with children – the strategies they use – and the organisational policies and practices they implement – such as grouping strategies and approaches to guidance – are reflections of the relationships they have already established as well as the ones they wish to build.

Questions for reflection

1. Consider the rules that are evident in your setting. Who developed the rules? When did this occur? What evaluation of the rules takes place? How do rules get changed?

2. Scaffolding can be a very effective strategy to promote learning. What opportunities for scaffolding exist within your setting? Who performs the scaffolding? How do you know if scaffolding has been effective?

3. How might you promote the principles of social respect, personal regard, competence and perceived integrity in your interactions with other adults involved with your setting?

Key terms

ability groups, 337
buddy programs, 337
friendship groups, 342
mixed age groups, 336
prosocial behaviours, 346
same-scx groups, 343
scaffolding, 330
sustained shared thinking, 323

Online study resources

Visit http://login.cengagebrain.com and use the access code that comes with this book for 12 months access to the student resources for this text.

CourseMate Express

The CourseMate Express website contains a range of resources and study tools for this chapter, including:

- Online video activities
- Online research activities
- A revision quiz
- Matching pair exercises
- A list of key weblinks
- A chapter glossary, flashcards and crossword to help you revise terminology
- and more!

Search me! education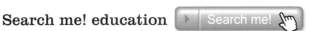

Explore **Search me! education** for articles relevant to this chapter. Fast and convenient, Search me! education is updated daily and provides you with 24-hour access to full text articles from hundreds of scholarly and popular journals, ebooks and newspapers, including *The Australian* and *The New York Times*. Log in to Search me! through http://login.cengage.com and try searching for the following key words:

- relationships
- teaching strategies
- intentional teaching
- sustained shared thinking
- scaffolding
- grouping
- positive interactions.

Search tip: **Search me! education** contains information from both local and international sources. To get the greatest number of search results, try using both Australian and American spellings in your searches, e.g. 'globalisation' and 'globalization'; 'organisation' and 'organization'

Recommended resources

Department of Education and Children's Services (DECS), South Australia 2008, *Assessing for Learning and Development in the Early Years Using Observation Scales: Reflect Respect Relate*, DECS, Adelaide.

Epstein, A 2007, *The Intentional Teacher: Choosing the Best Strategies for Young Children's Learning*, National Association for the Education of Young Children, Washington, DC.

Hatch, JA 2010, 'Rethinking the relationship between learning and development: Teaching for learning in early childhood classrooms', *The Educational Forum*, vol. 74, no. 3, pp. 258–68.

Jones, E & Reynolds, G 2011, *The Play's the Thing: Teachers' Roles in Children's Play*, 2nd edn., Teachers College Press, New York

Mac Naughton, G & Williams, G 2009, *Techniques for Teaching Young Children*, 3rd edn., Longman, Melbourne.

National Scientific Council on the Developing Child 2009, *Young Children Develop in an Environment of Relationships*, Working paper no. 1, http://developingchild.harvard.edu/index.php/activities/council/, accessed 15 July 2014.

Key weblinks

Early Childhood Australia, http://www.earlychildhoodaustralia.org.au.

Effective Pre-school and Primary Education Project, http://www.ioe.ac.uk/research/153.html.

New York University Child Study Center, http://www.aboutourkids.org.

References

Alloway, N & Gilbert, P 2002, 'Literacy and gender in early childhood contexts', in L. Makin & C Jones Diaz (eds), *Literacies in Early Childhood*, MacLennan & Petty, Sydney, pp. 251–265.

Arthur, L 2001, 'Diverse languages and dialects', in E Dau (ed.), *The Anti-Bias Approach in Early Childhood*, 2nd edn., Pearson, Sydney, pp. 95–113.

Arthur, L, Beecher, B, Harrison, C & Morandini, C 2003, 'Sharing the lived experiences of children', *Australian Journal of Early Childhood*, vol. 28, no. 2, pp. 8–13.

Arthur, L, McArdle, F & Papic, M 2010, *Stars are Made of Glass: Children as Capable and Creative Communicators*, Early Childhood Australia, Canberra.

Baker, AC & Manfredi/Petitt, LA 2004, *Relationships, the Heart of Quality Care: Creating Community Among Adults in Early Care Settings*, National Association for the Education of Young Children, Washington, DC.

Barratt-Pugh, C, Rivalland, J, Hamer, J & Adams, P 2006, *Literacy Learning in Australia: Practical Ideas for Early Childhood Educators*, Thomson/Dunmore, Melbourne.

Barton, AC, Drake, C, Perez, JG, St Louis, K & George, M 2004, 'Ecologies of parental engagement in urban education', *Educational Researcher*, vol. 33, no. 4, pp. 3–12.

Beecher, B & Arthur, L 2001, *Play and Literacy in Children's Worlds*, Primary English Teaching Association, Newtown, NSW.

Beecher, B 2010, '"No, I won't marry you!" Critiquing gender in multiliteracies fairytale play', *Canadian Children*, vol. 35, no. 2, pp. 15–24.

Berk, L 2001, *Awakening Children's Minds: How Parents and Teachers Can Make a Difference*, Oxford University Press, Oxford.

Berk, L 2009, *Child Development*, 8th edn., Allyn & Bacon, Boston, MA.

Bodrova, E & Leong, DJ 2007, *Tools of the Mind: The Vygotskian Approach to Early Childhood Education*, 2nd edn., Merrill/Prentice Hall, Columbus, OH.

Bowman, B, Donovan, MS & Burns, MS (eds) 2001, *Eager to Learn: Educating our Preschoolers*, National Academy Press, Washington, DC.

Bredekamp, S 1987, *Developmentally Appropriate Practice in Early Childhood Programs Serving Children from Birth Through Age 8*, National Association for the Education of Young Children, Washington, DC.

Bredekamp, S & Copple, C 1997, *Developmentally Appropriate Practice in Early Childhood Programs Serving Children from Birth Through Age 8*, National Association for the Education of Young Children, Washington, DC.

Bredekamp, S & Rosegrant, T 1992, *Reaching Potentials: Appropriate Curriculum and Assessment for Young Children*, National Association for the Education of Young Children, Washington, DC.

Briggs, F & Potter, G 1999, *The Early Years of School: Teaching and Learning*, 2nd edn., Longman, Melbourne.

Bronfenbrenner, U 1992, 'Ecological systems theory', in U Bronfenbrenner, *Making Human Beings Human: Biological Perspectives on Human Development*, Thousand Oaks, CA, Sage Publications, pp. 106–73.

Bruner, J 1978, 'Learning how to do things with words', in J Bruner & A Garton (eds), *Human Growth and Development*, Clarendon Press, Oxford, pp. 62-84.

Bryk, A & Schneider, B 2004, *Trust in Schools: A Core Resource for Improvement*, Russell Sage Foundation, New York.

Buckingham, D 2000, *After the Death of Childhood*, Polity Press in assoc. with Blackwell Publishers, Cambridge, UK.

Burchinal, MR, & Cryer D 2003, 'Diversity, child care quality, and developmental outcomes', *Early Childhood Research Quarterly*, vol. 18, pp. 401–26.

Burns, M & Casbergue, R 1992, 'Parent–child interaction in a letter-writing context', *Journal of Reading Behaviour*, vol. 24, no. 3.

Comber, B 2001, 'Critical literacies and local action: Teacher knowledge and a "new" research agenda', in B Comber & A Simpson (eds), *Negotiating Critical Literacies in Classrooms*, Lawrence Erlbaum Associates, Mahwah, NJ, pp. 271–282.

Copple, C & Bredekamp, S 2006, *Basics of Developmentally Appropriate Practice*, National Association for the Education of Young Children, Washington, DC.

Copple, C & Bredekamp, S (eds) 2009, *Developmentally Appropriate Practice in Early Childhood Programs Serving Children from Birth Through Age 8*, 3rd edn., National Association for the Education of Young Children, Washington, DC.

Curry, N & Johnson, C 1990, *Beyond Self-Esteem: Developing a Genuine Sense of Human Value*, National Association for the Education of Young Children, Washington, DC.

Dansie, B 2001, 'Scaffolding oral language: "The Hungry Giant"', retold in J Hammond (ed.), *Scaffolding: Teaching and Learning in Language and Literacy Interaction*, Primary English Teaching Association, Sydney.

de Groot Kim, S 2010, 'There's Elly, it must be Tuesday: Discontinuity in child care programs and its impact on the development of peer relationships in young children', *Early Childhood Education Journal*, vol. 38, pp. 153–64.

Degotardi, S 2010, 'High quality interactions with infants', *International Journal of Early Years Education*, vol. 18, pp. 27–41.

Delpit, L 1995, *Other People's Children: Cultural Conflict in the Classroom*, New Press, New York.

Department of Education, Employment and Workforce Relations (DEEWR) 2009, *Belonging, Being and Becoming: The Early Years Learning Framework for Australia*, Commonwealth of Australia, Canberra.

Department of Education, Science and Training 2003, *Educating Boys: Issues and Information*, Department of Education, Science and Training, Canberra.

Dockett, S & Fleer, M 1999, *Pedagogy and Play in Early Childhood Settings: Bending the Rules*, Harcourt, Sydney.

Dockett, S & Perry, B 2001, '"Air is a kind of wind": Argumentation and the construction of knowledge', in S Reifel & M Brown (eds), *Advances in Early Education and Day Care*, vol. 11, *Early Education and Care, and Reconceptualising Play*, Emerald Publishing, UK, pp. 227–58.

Dockett, S & Perry, B 2007, *Transitions to School: Perceptions, Expectations, Experiences*, University of New South Wales Press, Sydney.

Dockett, S & Perry B 2013, 'Siblings and buddies: Providing expert advice about starting school', *International Journal of Early Years Education*, vol. 21, no. 4, pp. 340–61.

Dunn, J 2004, *Children's Friendships: The Beginnings of Intimacy*, Blackwell, Oxford.

Dyson, A 1998, 'Folk processes and media cultures: Reflection on popular culture for literacy educators', *The Reading Teacher*, vol. 51, pp. 392–402.

Ebbeck, M & Yim HY 2009, 'Rethinking attachment: Fostering positive relationships between infants, toddlers, and their primary caregivers', *Early Child Development and Care*, vol. 179, pp. 899–909.

Edwards, C 1994, 'Partner, nurturer, and guide: The roles of the Reggio teacher in action', in Edwards, C, Gandini, L & Forman, G (Eds.), *The Hundred Languages of Children*, Ablex, Norwood, NJ, p. 154.

Edwards, C, Gandini, L & Forman, G (eds) 1998, *The Hundred Languages of Children*, 2nd edn., Ablex, Norwood, NJ.

Epstein, A 2009, 'Think before you (inter)act: What it means to be an intentional teacher', *Exchange*, December–January, pp. 46–9, http://www.earlylearningcoalitionsarasota.org/forms/2011/intentionalteaching/Beginnings%20Intentional%20Teaching.pdf, accessed 14 July 2015.

Fabian, H & Dunlop, A-W 2007, *Outcomes of Good Practice in Transition Processes for Children Entering Primary School*. Working Paper 42, Bernard van Leer Foundation. The Hague, The Netherlands.

Gartrell D 2010, *A Guidance Approach for the Encouraging Classroom*, Cengage, Belmont, CA.

Gartrell, D 2012, 'From rules to guidelines', *Young Children*, vol. 67, no. 1, pp. 56–58.

Geekie, P, Cambourne, B & Fitzsimmons, P 1999, *Understanding Literacy Development*, Trentham Books, Stoke-on-Trent, Staffordshire.

Gerard, M 2005. 'Bridging the gap: Towards an understanding of young children's thinking in multiage groups', *Journal of Research in Childhood Education*, vol. 19, no. 3, pp. 243–50.

Gibbons, P 2002, *Scaffolding Language, Scaffolding Learning: Teaching Second Language Learners in the Mainstream Classroom*, Heinemann, Portsmouth, NH.

Greenman, J 2005, 'Places for childhood in the twenty-first century: A conceptual framework', *Young Children: Beyond the Journal*, May 2005.

Greenman, J, Stonehouse, A & Schweikert, A, 2008, *Prime Times: A Handbook for Excellence in Infant and Toddler Programs*, 2nd edn., Addison Wesley Longman, Melbourne.

Gross, M 1997, 'How ability grouping turns big fish into little fish – or does it? Of optical illusions and optimal environments', *Australian Journal of Gifted Education*, vol. 6, no. 2, pp. 18–30.

Gross, M & Sleap, B 2000, 'Responding to gifted and talented students', *PEN, no. 122*, Primary English Teaching Association, Sydney.

Harwood, D 2008, 'Deconstructing and reconstructing Cinderella: Theoretical defence of critical literacy for young children', *Language and Literacy*, vol. 10, no. 2, pp. 1–13.

Helm, J & Katz, L 2001, *Young Investigators: The Project Approach in the Early Years*, Teachers College Press, New York.

Henderson, AT & Mapp, KL 2002, *A New Wave of Evidence: The Impact of School, Family and Community Connections on Student Achievement*, National Center for Family and Community Connections with Schools, Austin, TX, http://www.sedl.org/connections/resources/evidence.pdf accessed 14 July 2014.

Hong G, Corter, C, Hong, Y & Pelletier J 2012, 'Differential effects of literacy instruction time and homogeneous ability grouping in kindergarten classrooms: Who will benefit? Who will suffer?', *Educational Evaluations and Policy Analysis*, vol. 34, no. 1, pp. 69–88.

Hopson, E 1990, *Valuing Diversity: Implementing a Cross Cultural, Anti-Bias Approach in Early Childhood Programs*, Lady Gowrie Child Centre, Sydney.

House of Representatives Standing Committee on Education and Training 2002, *Boys: Getting it Right. Report into the Inquiry into the Education of Boys*, House of Representatives Standing Committee on Education and Training, Canberra.

Jones, E, Evans, K & Renken, KS 2001, *The Lively Kindergarten: Emergent Curriculum in Action*, National Association for the Education of Young Children, Washington, DC.

Jones, E & Nimmo, J 1994, *Emergent Curriculum*, National Association for the Education of Young Children, Washington, DC.

Jones, NP 2008, 'Two, 4 or 6? Grouping children to promote social and emotional development', *Young Children*, vol. 63, no. 3, pp. 34–39.

Jones Diaz, C 2001, 'Multilingual literacies in the primary classroom: Making the connections', *PEN, no. 130*, Primary English Teaching Association, Sydney.

Katz, L, Evangelou, D & Hartman, J 1990, *The Case for Mixed-Age Grouping in Early Education*, National Association for the Education of Young Children, Washington, DC.

Katz, L & McClellan, D 1997, *Fostering Children's Social Competence: The Teacher's Role*, National Association for the Education of Young Children, Washington, DC.

Kolbe, U 2005, *It's Not a Bird Yet: The Drama of Drawing*, Peppinot Press, Byron Bay, NSW.

Kostelnik, M, Soderman, A & Whiren, A 2004, *Developmentally Appropriate Curriculum: Best practices in Early Childhood Education*, 3rd edn., Prentice Hall, Upper Saddle River, NJ.

Kostelnik, MJ, Whiren AP, Soderman, AK, & Gregory, K 2009, *Guiding Children's Social Development: Theory to Practice*, 6th edn., Thomson, Clifton Park, NY.

Lambert, B & Clyde, M 2000, *Rethinking Early Childhood Theory and Practice*, Social Science Press, Katoomba, NSW.

Landy, S 2002, *Pathways to Competence: Encouraging Healthy Social and Emotional Development in Young Children*, Paul Brookes Publishing, Baltimore, MD.

Lyons, G, Ford, M & Arthur-Kelly, M 2011, *Classroom Management: Creating Positive Learning Environments*, Cengage, South Melbourne.

Mac Naughton, G 2000, *Rethinking Gender in Early Childhood Education*, Allen & Unwin, Sydney.

Marsh, J 2000, 'Teletubby tales: Popular culture in the early years language and literacy curriculum', *Contemporary Issues in Early Childhood*, vol. 1, no. 2, pp. 119–33, http://www.wwwords.co.uk/pdf/freetoview.asp?j=ciec&vol=1&issue=2&year=2000&article=marsh, accessed 15 July 2014.

Martino, W Mills, M& Lingard, B 2005, 'Interrogating single-sex classes as a strategy for addressing boys' educational and social needs', *Oxford Review of Education*, vol. 31, no. 2, pp. 237–54.

Meece D & Soderman, AK 2010, 'Positive verbal environments', *Young Children*, vol. 65, no. 5, pp. 81–86.

Morrow, L & Schickedanz, J 2006, 'The relationship between sociodramatic play and literacy development', in D Dickenson & S Neumann (eds), *The Handbook of Early Literacy Research*, vol. 2, The Guildford Press, New York, pp. 269–80.

Munns, G, Arthur, L, Downes, T, Gregson, R, Power, A, Sawyer, W, Singh, M, Steel, F & Thistleton-Martin, J 2006, *Motivation and Engagement of Boys: Evidence-Based Teaching Practices*, Department of Education, Science and Training, Canberra.

O'Brien, J & Comber, B 2000, 'Negotiating critical literacies with young children', in C Barratt-Pugh & M Rohl, *Literacy Learning in the Early Years*, Allen & Unwin, Sydney, pp. 152–71.

Piaget, J 1962, *Play, Dreams and Imitation in Childhood*, Norton, New York.

Pickett, L 1998, 'Literacy learning during block play', *Journal of Research in Childhood Education*, vol. 12, no. 2, pp. 225–30.

Porter, L 2005, *Gifted Young Children: A Guide for Teachers and Parents*, 2nd edn., Allen & Unwin, Sydney.

Porter, L 2007, *Young Children's Behaviour*, 3rd edn., MacLennan & Petty, Sydney.

Raban, B & Ure, C 1998, 'Literacy in the preschool: An Australian case study', in J Hayden (ed.), *Early Childhood Landscapes: Cross National Perspectives on Empowerment and Restraint*, Peter Lang Publishing, New York, pp. 375–390

Reid, J 2002, *Managing Small-Group Learning*, Primary English Teaching Association, Sydney.

Reynolds, G & Jones, E 1997, *Master Players: Learning from Children at Play*, Teachers College Press, New York.

Rogers, S (ed.) 2011, *Rethinking Play and Pedagogy in Early Childhood Education*, Routledge, London.

Rogoff, B 1990, *Apprenticeship in Thinking: Cognitive Development in Social Context*, Oxford University Press, New York.

Rogoff, B 2003, *The Cultural Nature of Human Development*, Oxford University Press, Oxford.

Roskos, K & Neuman, S 1993, 'Descriptive observations of adults' facilitation of literacy in play', *Early Childhood Research Quarterly*, vol. 4, pp. 225–55.

Schiller, P 2009, 'Program practices that support intentionality in teaching', *Exchange*, December–January, pp. 57–60, http://www.earlylearningcoalitionsarasota.org/forms/2011/intentionalteaching/Beginnings%20Intentional%20Teaching.pdf, accessed 15 July 2014.

Shonkoff, J & Phillips, D (eds) 2000, *From Neurons to Neighborhoods: The science of Early Childhood Development*, National Academy Press, Washington, DC.

Siraj-Blatchford, I 2005, *Quality Interactions in the Early Years*, paper presented at the TACTYC Annual Conference, Cardiff, Wales, November, http://www.tactyc.org.uk/pdfs/2005conf_siraj.pdf, accessed 15 July 2014.

Siraj-Blatchford, I & Clarke, P 2000, *Supporting Identity, Diversity and Language in the Early Years*, Open University Press, Buckingham.

Siraj-Blatchford, I & Sylva, K 2004, 'Researching pedagogy in English preschools', *British Educational Research Journal*, vol. 30, no. 5, pp. 715–30.

Siraj-Blatchford, I, 2009, 'Quality teaching in the early years', in A Anning, J Cullen & M Fleer (eds), *Early Childhood Education: Society and Culture*, 2nd edn., Sage, London, UK, pp. 147–57.

Sylva, K, Melhuish, E, Sammons, P, Siraj-Blatchford, I & Taggart, B 2010, *Early Childhood Matters: Evidence from the Effective Pre-school and Primary Education Project*, Routledge, London.

Vygotsky, L 1978, *Mind in Society: The Development of Higher Psychological Processes*, Harvard University Press, Cambridge, MA.

Wein CA 2004, 'From policing to participation: Overturning the rules and creating amiable classrooms', *Young Children*, vol. 59, no. 1, pp. 34–40.

Whitton, D 2003, 'Designing for difference: Units that work', *PEN, no. 141*, Primary English Teaching Association, Sydney.

Whitton, D, Barker, K, Nosworthy, M, Sinclair, C & Nanlohy, P 2010, *Learning for Teaching, Teaching for Learning*, 2nd edn., Cengage, South Melbourne.

Wong Fillmore, L 1991, 'When learning a second language means losing the first', *Early Childhood Research Quarterly*, vol. 6, pp. 323–46.

Wood, DJ, Bruner, J & Ross, G 1976, 'The role of tutoring in problem solving', *Journal of Child Psychology and Psychiatry*, vol. 17, pp. 89–100.

Wood, E, 2009, 'Developing a pedagogy of play', in A Anning, J Cullen & M Fleer (eds), *Early Childhood Education: Society and Culture*, Sage, London, pp. 17–30.

Wood, E & Attfield, J 1996/2005, *Play, Learning and the Early Childhood Curriculum*, Paul Chapman Publishing, London.

CHAPTER TEN

LEARNING ENVIRONMENTS

Chapter learning focus

This chapter will investigate:

- physical environments

- inclusive environments

- outdoor learning environments

- sustainable environments

- considerations for planning

- balancing planned and spontaneous experiences

- resources that promote learning.

Introduction

Learning environments are welcoming spaces when they reflect and enrich the lives and identities of children and families participating in the setting and respond to their interests and needs. Environments that support learning are vibrant and flexible spaces that are responsive to the interests and abilities of each child. They cater for different learning capacities and learning styles and invite children and families to contribute ideas, interests and questions.

DEEWR, 2009, p. 15

As described above and in Chapter 3, environments are much more than physical buildings and playgrounds. Learning environments in early childhood settings and schools have the potential to enhance or inhibit how children, families, the broader community and educators interact with space, materials and each other. Environments can welcome or alienate individuals and cultural groups, and inspire or restrict exploration and learning. The engagement of each individual will be strongly influenced by the educator's cultural competence and pedagogy. Every early childhood environment abounds with unspoken messages for each child and adult who enters the setting. When educators develop heightened awareness and purposeful management of these messages, there is increased likelihood of children and families having a positive experience of the setting.

What unspoken messages do the physical environments you have experienced give to families and children?

Physical environments

Physical environments are extremely diverse across urban, rural, remote, coastal or inland settings, as are the children, families and communities who reside there. Each unique environment may be influenced by factors such as building design and purpose, climate, culture, accessibility, infrastructure, funding and legislation.

Design and pedagogies

The educational program within a setting will be influenced by physical design and the philosophical beliefs of the educators. Some settings are purpose-built permanent early childhood spaces, where others may be designed as multi-use buildings requiring packing away each day or week.

Purpose-built early childhood buildings designed for hot, wet climates may have louvre windows fixed open for continuous airflow with open plan space. When designed for the extreme conditions of desert climates, they may have well sealed windows to minimise dust and separate spaces for ease of cooling and heating.

For example, a purpose-built setting where educators implement a Reggio Emilia inspired program may have a permanent eating space with tables and chairs for meal times (*see* Figure 10.1), classrooms designated for selected purposes such as art spaces and undisturbed areas for long-term project work. In a remote multi-use setting where family and elders are active participants, and physical structures may hinder engagement, resources including tables, chairs, cushions and floor mats may be accessible on the perimeter of an open, versatile space (*see* Figure 10.2).

Early childhood expertise and a high level of consultation with all stakeholders in the building design phase will support architects to accommodate practical, desirable and legislative requirements of educational spaces. There is no 'ultimate' design or physical environment for early childhood settings. Appropriate settings will be designed to suit the climate, children, families, pedagogies and practices of each unique community of learners.

An exceptional program may be delivered in any environment from purpose-built to multi-use . One setting may have varnished timber flooring and brick walls, while another will have concrete floors and corrugated iron walls. The program in either setting will be dependent upon the expertise and commitment of the educators to engage with children, families and communities to provide appropriate curriculum and pedagogy within their unique setting (*see* Chapter 7).

Funding and legislative restrictions are crucial considerations; however, responsive programs remain possible even when lack of funds or apparently restrictive regulations present what feel like insurmountable hurdles. Perceptions of appropriate spaces and programs vary greatly across settings and are reflective of community expectations and local environments, as well as children's experiences and funding. For

FIGURE 10.1 Urban purpose-built setting.

FIGURE 10.2 Remote multipurpose setting.

FIGURE 10.3 Urban playground.

FIGURE 10.4 Remote playground.

Two-way learning

Children and educators learn together through observing, listening to, respecting and incorporating each other's language, culture and ways of learning.

example, one setting may have artificial grass and soft surfaces (*see* Figure 10.3) while another will have red dirt and sand (*see* Figure 10.4).

The children and families in each of these settings will have vastly different life experiences and expectations of the educators and program. Each environment has the potential for rich learning experiences (*see* Figure 10.5) when philosophy and pedagogies are developed in consultation with all stakeholders.

In either space, responsive and effective educators will watch and listen. As Aboriginal elder Bob Randall states in the film *Kanyini*, educators can engage in **two-way learning**, or 'walking in each other's shoes' (2006), with the children, families and communities. When educators observe, listen, respect and learn, they are provoked to provide flexible ideas, practices, expectations and reflections.

You're in New Country (Farmer & Fasoli, 2010) is a thought provoking resource for non-indigenous early childhood professionals working with Indigenous communities in the remote community of Wadeye in the Northern Territory. It provides reflection points for us all as we step into any new setting, but particularly into a remote Indigenous community. Karrkirr Kinthari represents (see Figure 10.6) two-way learning as follows:

> This is my symbol of learning in two ways.
>
> On the left are two water holes which represent a place of life. The words around these waterholes are important things for us as Aboriginal people - our land, our dreaming, our ceremonies, our totems and our food. On the right are the circles of whitefella learning. The footprints represent the children and teachers walking to the service to learn in both-ways.

> R Farmer & L Fasoli, *You're in New Country: Advice for Non-Indigenous
> Early Childhood Mentors, Trainers and Teachers*, p. 5,
> © 2010 Commonwealth of Australia

FIGURE 10.5 Sharing learning in a remote environment.

Inappropriate preconceived or inflexible definitions of 'quality' physical environments, 'appropriate' parenting, 'acceptable levels' of adult engagement or 'required' children's attendance patterns may hinder our ability to listen to and learn from what families and communities truly desire for their children (*see* Chapter 2 and Chapter 5).

Children's and families' experiences will vary in every setting. *Belonging, Being and Becoming: The Early Years Learning Framework for Australia* (EYLF) recognises the importance of contextualised pedagogy for children and families (DEEWR, 2009). Regardless of the differences, each setting has the potential to not only reach *National Quality Standard* but exceed and strive for an Excellent rating (ACECQA, 2013).

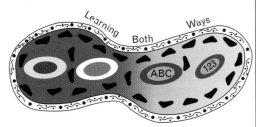

| Mi – food |
| Ku – animal |
| Kura – water |
| Tharnpa – ceremonial dance group |
| Wangka – ceremonial dance group |
| Lirrga – ceremonial dance group |
| ngakumarl – totem |
| da – country |
| nanhthi – things |
| thamul – spear |

Source: Farmer & Fasoli, 2010, *You're in New Country: Advice for Non-Indigenous Early Childhood Mentors Trainers and Teachers*, Commonwealth of Australia, Canberra, p5 © Karrkirr Kinthari 2010.

FIGURE 10.6 Learning two ways.

In Example 10.1 Hannah Scully, early childhood educator and team leader at Watiyawanu Children's Centre, reflects on the physical learning environment in a very remote Aboriginal community setting.

EXAMPLE 10.1
Watiyawanu Children's Centre

Watiyawanu (Mt Liebig) is a remote Aboriginal community situated approximately 320 kilometres west of Alice Springs, Northern Territory, within the Luritja ward of MacDonnell Shire Council. There are between 100 and 150 people residing in the community, which rests at the foot of Central Australia's West MacDonnell ranges. A number of educational, health and other services are delivered in the community, including the Budget Based Funded (BBF) early childhood education and care (ECEC) service.

This service caters for children aged birth to five years within the morning program from 8 a.m. till 12 p.m., and children aged five–twelve years in the after school program. There are currently four local Indigenous educators employed across both services who are due to begin their on-site training in Certificate III children's services.

The ECEC service strives to be a safe place for all children and families, a play-based learning environment for children and a catalyst to support parent and family education around health and wellbeing. Encouraging and emphasising the importance of early childhood education is paramount.

The transient population means the service's numbers vary greatly on a day-to-day basis, which can make programming and planning challenging. Being flexible and able to adapt concepts of knowledge is crucial in this remote environment.

Families see the ECEC service as a place for children to play and engage in new experiences and, equally as importantly, a place to have a bath, wash their clothes and mungarri palya ngalkula (eat good food).

The physical space is large and contains two main areas – an indoor play space and an outdoor play space (*see* Figure 10.4). The indoor space serves several main purposes – washing, eating, art experiences, language and social games, dramatic and imaginative play. The outdoor space facilitates physical and gross motor experiences, nature explorations and family interactions.

Logistics and the physical location of the community mean that commercial materials and resources can be difficult to source for the service. The natural environment plays a vital role in the effective delivery of a quality learning environment.

Educators, families and children utilise bush trips as a great way to collect appropriate natural resources and materials from the surrounding environment to incorporate into the program, as well as an opportunity for cultural learning.

▶ The children's interest based investigation and experimentations are enhanced by these natural resources, while increasing their connection to the land.

Children, families and community involvement

The service would not function effectively without significant involvement of the community on many levels. Children, families and community members are encouraged to be involved in program decision making, aesthetic changes and enhancements, employment of educators, provision of resources and appropriate integration of cultural learning. Regular community discussions and meetings are able to facilitate this highly valued input.

The service is a welcoming place for everyone. It is a hub for social interactions between children, their families, extended families and other members of the community. The outdoor environment invites opportunity for communications where children and families are often observed enjoying one another's company, creating a positive space for modelling as well as rich, meaningful social interactions.

English is a second and often third and fourth language for children, families and community, therefore it is imperative that learning and communication occurs in both Luritja and English to maximise the potential for children's involvement in learning. Posters can be found in the environment that contain photographs of children enrolled in the service alongside text in both Luritja and English – these often prompt collaborative language learning.

Making patterns in the sand.

Shared learning experiences.

There are several large artworks created by community members that are displayed in the service which promote the importance of culture and the connection between the service and their own culture. Many learning stories are displayed which highlight bush/cultural trips and are an avenue for families to connect to play, culture and learning. Large photographs of all children enrolled in the service as well as family photographs are displayed which prompt discussions on social connections and enhance a sense of belonging in the children and families that attend the service.

▶

▶ **The learning environment reflects the setting's philosophy**

It is pertinent that we reflect our philosophy in the learning environment as it was developed in consultation with the community. To deliver a successful early childhood program we must maintain consistent cultural integrity. The educators strive to create a stimulating and culturally significant program. They encourage participation of the community with provisions for shared learning around health and hygiene, supporting the development of children and guiding positive behaviour.

Appropriateness to the community

To ensure our service is appropriate and successful in the community it needs to be driven by the community and culturally significant. Involvement and meaningful collaborations need to occur with a range of community members if there is to be a service at all and if it is regarded as a place of importance for children. Children, families and the community are encouraged to take strong ownership of the service to increase ongoing participation and the future potential of the service.

To capture the interest of children and families in this community the service should undoubtedly retain the culture of the community. Respecting cultural values, knowledge and incorporating them into a quality program for children is of high importance.

Previous professional experiences, in predominantly Anglo-Australian middle class communities, have involved different views on social and cultural significance of the community in which the service is situated. The most critical consideration for the service to be appropriate in those communities would have been the ability to deliver a high quality educational program that sees children immersed in meaningful learning experiences. The impact and importance of family and community involvement would not have been necessarily treated as the most crucial element of a successful program.

Source: Hannah Scully, early childhood educator and team leader Watiyawanu Children's Centre, 2013.

Welcoming and aesthetic environments

Learning environments are welcoming spaces when they reflect and enrich the lives and identities of children and families participating in the setting and respond to their interests and needs.

DEEWR, 2009, p. 15

First impressions have a lasting impact on children, families and community. These impressions are often subconscious and based on our personal feeling of belonging within an environment. Children and families entering an early childhood setting or school will bring expectations of the learning environment based on their own past experiences. A parent who had negative experiences in educational settings as a child will be more apprehensive than a parent who enjoyed their schooling. Children are intuitive and will internalise their parent or carer's anxiety. To ameliorate the possible tension, thoughtful physical environments can convey positive messages about the educators, learning and care within the environment when children and families experience:
- educators to greet them
- welcoming notices and displays that clearly articulate philosophy and vision
- inviting and comfortable adult and child spaces

FIGURE 10.7 Welcoming environment.

FIGURE 10.8 Aesthetic environment

- carefully documented and displayed examples of children's learning with evidence of child, family and educator voices
- physical reflections of diversity and recognition of their own cultural heritage
- examples of thoughtful use of colour, light, design and space
- spaces that are organised and uncluttered.

Alternatively, families who enter a space to find staff too busy to provide assistance, only directive notices, no information about the settings philosophy, no comfortable space to be with their child, careless and minimal displays of children's work, mono cultural messages, poorly maintained surroundings and equipment with excessive adult clutter will have a vastly different first impression.

What makes you feel welcome in a new environment?

Families entering a setting will scan the environment for familiar faces, images and equipment. As a new child enters the environment, it is common for parents to comfort the child by sharing a familiar experience; for example, a known book or toy. If families are unable to find something familiar, they will have as much difficulty feeling at ease within the environment as will their child.

Spaces for learning

The use of space influences all aspects of the setting. Gandini (cited in Fu et al., 2002, p. 17) challenges educators to recognise the instructional power of the layout of physical space to welcome and foster relationships and encourage 'choices, problem solving and discoveries in the process of learning'.

When educators critically reflect upon the instructional power of learning spaces, they build and maintain strong pedagogical connections between theory and practice. The following questions and photographs are provocations to reflect upon the instructional power of our spaces:

- Does the environment reflect the setting's philosophy, approaches to curriculum and pedagogy? For example, does it encourage a community of learners through spaces for collaboration, interaction and relationships?
- Does the environment welcome children, families and educators and promote a sense of belonging?
- Are both indoors and outdoors utilised fully as learning spaces (e.g. traditional indoors experiences are accessible outdoors and outdoors experiences accessible indoors,

and educators are mindful of children's learning in all environments)?

- Does the environment provide quiet and private spaces for individuals and small groups (e.g. physically defined spaces where children can withdraw for quiet moments alone or with a friend; sensory spaces)?
- Does the environment provide active and shared spaces (e.g. areas where physical exertion, running, boisterous play and risk taking experiences are supported)?
- Does the environment foresee any potential challenges (e.g. there is an appropriate amount of space for block construction or space is cleared for this purpose as required)?
- Is there enough space to allow for pedestrian traffic flow and avoid walking through play spaces (e.g. areas are physically defined by movable mats or petitions with adequate access around them for children to be respectful of each other's play space)?
- Can the children make an impact on the environment (e.g. children can rearrange or setup new spaces and access resources independently)?
- Are the children's lives and the broader community reflected within the space (e.g. photos, books and resources that reflect cultural heritage, family structures and diverse abilities or a variety of implements for use at mealtimes)?
- Does the set-up encourage extended participation by families through provision of space for adults and siblings appropriate for the context (e.g. spaces that provoke storytelling or skill sharing; spaces for sitting on the floor/ ground together; drawing and painting areas with adult and child furniture)?
- Are there spaces for educators and children to meet and share dialogue (e.g. yarning spaces, lounges)?
- Are there soft spaces and furnishings?
- Has natural and artificial light been used effectively?
- Have aesthetics been considered and does the space inspire creativity and exploration?
- Is the space organised and uncluttered (e.g. the resources clearly and attractively arranged to encourage respectful use, spaces are clearly defined, tools are available to complete projects.
- Does the space include easily accessible documentation of children's learning, including descriptions of the development of their projects, thereby encouraging children, educators and families to revisit and rediscover?

The provocations above are not an exhaustive list but an initial start to the process of critically reflecting on learning spaces in educational settings.

> We value space because of its power to organise, promote pleasant relationships between children of different ages, create a handsome environment, provide changes, promote choices and activity, and its potential for sparking all kinds of social, affective and cognitive learning. All of

FIGURE 10.9 Contextually appropriate resources.

FIGURE 10.10 Soft spaces.

FIGURE 10.11 Effective use of light.

FIGURE 10.12 Attractively arranged resources.

this contributes to a sense of well-being and security in children. We also think that the space has to be a sort of aquarium that mirrors the ideas, values, attitudes, and cultures of the people who live within it.

Malaguzzi, 1984, in L Gandani, *Educational Caring Spaces*, p. 148 from C Edwards, L Gandini and G Forman, *The Hundred Languages of Children*, © 1993 Ablex, Norwood.

Some educators control the types and quantities of resources children may access at any particular time, the aim being to support objectives set for individual children through environments set up with preplanned experiences on designated tables, mats or areas. Alternatively, when children are viewed as capable, self-motivated and social learners, the environment can be seen through different eyes. When children have ready access to resources that support their interests or enhance their shared investigations without necessitating the permission or physical provision by educators, educators are planning to support children's self-motivation and opportunities for shared learning.

Environments that empower children through easy access to resources are possible with the use of open shelving, accessible storage boxes and permanently available resources. Aesthetic presentation, well maintained equipment and open environments will encourage children to care for and respect resources. When children are trusted with equipment, empowered to care for their environment and are able to access material resources as required, the depth of their explorations and creations will be enhanced.

Inclusive environments

Early childhood educators who are committed to equity believe in all children's capacities to succeed, regardless of diverse circumstances and abilities.

DEEWR, 2009, p12

Inclusion means that all children are treated as valued members of a service and participate fully in the life of that setting (Lifeline Community Care Queensland, 2010) and as such inclusive environments support children who have a wide range of physical, social, intellectual and communication abilities and cultural and life experiences. Inclusion of children with diverse circumstances and abilities enriches early childhood programs and provokes educators, children and families to 'learn both ways'.

A mindful enrolment process will enhance a positive orientation for each child and family, smoothing the transition from home into the early childhood setting. The experience and feelings of educators, children and families all interplay to support inclusive practice.

It may be the first group setting for a child experiencing learning challenges or a new cultural context. It may also be the first time other children have interacted with a child who has abilities or culture considerably different to their own. It may also be the first time an educator transitions a child with challenges to learning into their care. Some children may require specific resources, spaces and interactions to assist their transition and inclusion in the program. These may include, but are not limited to, visual communication systems, mobility and manipulative aids and auditory aids.

Meaningful outcomes are achieved when the enrolment process is a *two-way learning process* that enables information about the setting to be shared with the family and information about the child within the context of their family to be shared with the setting.

An extended orientation may suit some children and families; however, the length and pattern of orientation should be contextual for the child and family, not a prescribed time or type decided by the setting. For example, some children may require many visits to the setting with a family member or carer before they are ready to venture away from the security of close carer contact. Other children may relish the engagement with another environment, leaving their carer's side the moment they enter the setting. Concurrently, the family member or carer may require equal support from the educators to feel comfortable and safe to leave their child. It may be appropriate for some carers to always remain with their child. Educators should respect such choices. The orientation 'dance' will be dependent upon the unique partners (educators, children, families, specialists), their previous experiences and comfort in the environment's capacity to educate and care for their child.

Supporting the engagement of children with diverse abilities requires educators to work collaboratively not only with families, but also specialist early childhood services and allied health professionals. Awareness of where each person's qualification and expertise starts and finishes is an important acknowledgement for educators. Early intervention services can provide valuable specialist support for educators, families and children.

Example 10.2 provides a window into how one child's abilities are incorporated into a preschool program through the use of physical resources, visual communication aids and educator support.

FIGURE 10.13 Visual daily routine and visual prompts for group.

EXAMPLE 10.2
Inclusive resources and practices

Early intervention supports the inclusion of children with additional needs in the preschool setting through programming support and the use of communication, physical and sensory aids. The educators who work with children on the autism spectrum are encouraged to include a lot of movement in group experiences and utilise visual communication aids and sign language throughout the day. These children often require extra physical and sensory stimuli to sustain their attendance to a task or experience.

The child in the image to the right is seated on a purpose built heavy chair that is used to help some children on the autism spectrum to attend. The arms of the chair provide a secure defined space and its heavy weight is stabilising, so the child does not need to wriggle as he would in a standard chair. A scarf is tied to the chair to provide an opportunity for sensory input and supporting 'twiddle' toys would also be at hand.

Physical aids for sitting and attending.

Children on the autism spectrum are visual learners and they respond well to the use of visuals for communication to help stay on task and to support them to make choices. Anxiety may be a major issue for children with this diagnosis and visuals can help alleviate this at peak transition times such as the beginning of the day when children are arriving at Preschool.

Source: Rebecca Leacock, early childhood and early intervention educator, 2013

Educator support for sustained attendance.

FIGURE 10.14 Visual aids to assist rating personal emotions.

Is the environment reflective of the diversity of the children and families?

All children, regardless of ability, should have access to and opportunities for success in the whole early childhood environment. Simple tools such as self-opening scissors and well organised, self-accessible resources are examples of simple and naturally inclusive tools. Often resources for children with diverse abilities can be adapted for use by all children. Figure 10.14 is an example of a visual aid specifically designed for a child experiencing challenges expressing their emotions. This could also be an evaluation tool for all children to rate the menu in a long day care setting. The inclusive use of one child's learning aid *generalises* the resource and promotes interaction and acceptance from peers. Skilful educators who find opportunities to use one child's targeted resources in a generalised way can promote all children's understanding of diverse abilities and promote respectful interactions between children. In Figure 10.15 the sensory room is available for all children.

Many services incorporate sign language in their programs. This enhances the learning of all participants, not just that of the child experiencing communication challenges. In the beginning, families may question the value and appropriateness of their children learning sign language. However, the children's enjoyment, quick uptake (including very young children) and grasp of 'another language' increases support and understanding of communication challenges for everyone involved.

For children to respond to others with diverse circumstances and abilities in a respectful manner, educators must firstly 'demonstrate positive responses to diversity in their own behaviour and in conversations with children' (DEEWR, 2009, p. 27). Other children's responses to a child requiring specific resources will be strongly dependent upon the models provided by significant adults in their life. These positive interactions will support other family members and carers to embark on their own journey of acceptance of and respect for diversity. Educators have a responsibility to advocate for the rights of all children's inclusion in early childhood settings.

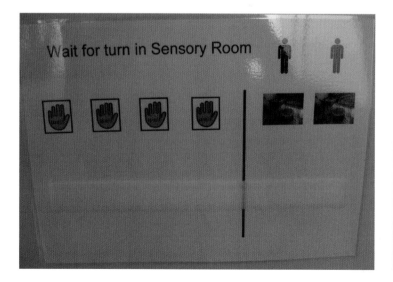

FIGURE 10.15 Visual turn taking helps maintain order in the sensory room.

Outdoor learning environments

The outdoor environment holds rich and diverse learning opportunities not always possible indoors (DEEWR, 2009). Why, then, have early childhood programs often ignored the learning potential of outdoor environments and programmed primarily for indoors? Australia's high incidence of melanoma should never be ignored; however, careful planning of shade (natural and man-made), routine application of sunscreen and appropriate clothing will ameliorate this risk.

In many urban early childhood settings and schools, artificial grass and asphalt have replaced natural grass and dirt and manufactured, fixed play equipment has replaced moveable natural resources. It is therefore imperative that educators tap into the natural community environment as part of the learning program. Local parks, community gardens and bushland are spaces where children can reconnect to the natural environment. Regular excursions have the potential to bring nature back into the daily lives of children. Natural resources can also be used in early childhood settings and schools to support children's appreciation of the natural environment. For example, pine cones, flowers and seed pods can be added to the sandpit, musical instruments can be made from natural materials and natural resources can provide inspiration for the creative arts. Ward (2011; 2013) argues that creative arts' experiences using natural materials can assist early childhood educators to support children's connections to the environment, their understanding of and appreciation of the environment and their advocacy for the environment. This is particularly effective when educators devise their own experiences, incorporating ideas, issues and resources relevant to their local community (Ward, 2011, 2013). These types of resources 'foster an appreciation of the natural environment, develop environmental awareness and provide a platform for ongoing environmental education' (DEEWR, 2009, p. 16). This approach is consistent with Davis' (2010) view that environmental education involves education *in*, *about* and *for* the environment. Education *in* the environment supports the development of appreciation for the natural world, education *about* the environment supports the development of understandings about how the natural world works and education *for* the environment focuses on advocacy and action for change. Educators, as well as children and families, have an advocacy role to argue for the adequate provision of natural environments both within early childhood settings and schools and in the local community.

The EYLF (DEEWR, 2009) includes a focus on environment education in *Learning Outcome 2: Children are connected with and contribute to their world*. This outcome includes a focus on children becoming socially responsible and showing respect for the environment. Where learning environments include natural resources such as sand, mud and water, children are encouraged to engage in 'open-ended interactions, spontaneity, risk-taking, exploration, discovery and connection with nature' (DEEWR, 2009, p. 16). Fleer (2013) also emphasises the potential of natural resources to facilitate imagination and exploration.

The use of natural resources from the local community connects the curriculum to children's social worlds. Real resources such as gardening tools, metal spades in the sandpit, camping stoves, picnic sets, child-sized camping chairs, wood-working tools and other authentic resources also provide connections to children's family and community contexts and will enhance the outdoor learning environment.

FIGURE 10.16 Children are more likely to create their own spaces in the outdoor environment when it is a familiar and safe space.

FIGURE 10.17 Resources that link to children's family experiences, e.g. camping.

FIGURE 10.18 Indoor resources in outdoor environment.

The use of everyday resources and recycled materials is appropriate in all early childhood environments and supports children's understandings about environmental sustainability. Simple resources such as a face washer and a cardboard box can become the focus of creative and sustained learning.

Natural resources can be used in the indoor as well as the outdoor environment, for example, for sorting and classifying and in visual arts experiences. Similarly, any resources that can be used indoors can also be used in the outdoor environment. This flexible use of resources not only extends learning opportunities but also provides familiar resources for children who may not be as comfortable as others in either the indoor or the outdoor environment.

> Does the program balance learning in both indoor and outdoor environments?

Sustainable environments

The United Nations General Assembly declared 2005 to 2014 the Decade of Education for Sustainable Development. Sustainability is also a cross-curriculum priority in the Australian Curriculum for Foundation to Year 10 (ACARA, n.d.). The focus on sustainability

> will allow all young Australians to develop the knowledge, skills, values and world views necessary for them to act in ways that contribute to more sustainable patterns of living. It will enable individuals and communities to reflect on ways of interpreting and engaging with the world. The sustainability priority is futures-oriented, focusing on protecting environments and creating a more ecologically and socially just world through informed action. Actions that support more sustainable patterns of living require consideration of environmental, social, cultural and economic systems and their interdependence
>
> ACARA, 2013

The EYLF also focuses on sustainability, recognising that:

> Environments and resources can also highlight our responsibilities for a sustainable future and promote children's understanding about their responsibility to care for the environment. They can foster hope, wonder and knowledge about the natural world.
>
> DEEWR, 2009, p. 16

Early childhood educators are well versed in the importance of the early years as the foundation for lifelong learning, attitudes and behaviours. Early childhood educators are in an influential position to provoke children's investigation, awareness and participation in sustainable practices.

Children's exposure to, and awareness of, the natural environment is dependent upon location, cultural context and educational setting. For some children, their days are predominantly spent in early childhood settings or school and after school care, so their contact with the natural world relies heavily upon their experiences within the program. For others, they are totally immersed in the natural environment and educators learn from children and families. For example, in remote Indigenous communities, educators and children learn from elders how to care for the land, find bush tucker and make bush medicine.

Educators have a moral responsibility to encourage children's development of respect and caring for their natural environment. In all early childhood settings, this may be achieved through many simple, ongoing strategies. A waste audit is a concrete way to identify our patterns of behaviour and impact on the environment. By identifying the items that are compostable, recyclable or landfill, sustained conversations and investigation may begin. The introduction of recycling bins into the setting will prompt awareness and proactive behaviour from both children and educators, as will the removal of unnecessary commercial cleaning products from our cupboards and the use of environmentally friendly substitutes; for example, the use of bicarbonate of soda for cleaning surfaces, soda water to clean stainless steel or vinegar to clean the dishwasher.

Integrating environmental responsibility into the program will result in projects that can certainly be considered 'real world topic(s) worthy of children's attention and effort' (Chard, 2001); for example, summer water restrictions in Australia. Media coverage will assist the educator to initiate a project on water. Webs of children's questions and understandings about water may include: How does water get into the tap? Where does it go when it goes down the sink? Why is water important? Who needs water? How can we save water? Can we make water? Can we find water?

In remote settings, elders may share their stories about water, how their ancestors found water in the desert and the importance of water for survival. The cultural competence of the educator will influence the realisation of the vast opportunities for extended two-way learning.

Following information gathering and dialogue with family, elders and each other, the children and educator may problem solve how they can save water in the setting. The results will be highly contextualised and each setting should determine appropriate strategies to suit their environment. For example:

- placing a bucket beside the water container so that unused drinking water can be used to water the garden
- only hosing early or late in the day (or during legal watering hours)
- mulching gardens
- reducing water play and placing buckets outside to catch rainwater
- sharing a map of the sewerage and plumbing of the service
- investigating and discussing the importance of dual flush toilet systems
- installing flow restrictors/timers on taps
- creating dry creek beds in the playground to capture rainwater and return to the garden
- installing a rainwater tank.

Conscious avoidance of plastic, commercial products and a focus on natural resources will not only promote softness and have aesthetic appeal in the environment, but also encourage children to appreciate their environment and non-commercial resources.

Walking with children, families and community members on a sustainability learning journey is an exciting responsibility all early childhood educators share. In the following examples, one urban children's centre describes the process involved in beginning their sustainability journey.

EXAMPLE 10.3
A case study: sustainability and change

We are a high quality service with a strong commitment to relationships, children, families, community and staffing excellence. However, when reflecting on *The Early Years Learning Framework* (EYLF) and *National Quality Standard* (NQS) documents, we identified holes in our overall program: our sustainable practices and environmental awareness. It was time to make some changes and to embark on a whole new area of learning.

We started by planting a small herb garden. This began in the early stages following the release of EYLF and NQS. I started gathering information which was then neatly filed and forgotten. At that point I thought that we had made a start and with all of the other new documents to entrench in our program that was enough.

A small number of staff also attended sustainability training, initially attempting to share findings from training, but unfortunately the rest of the team were just not ready to listen. As time went on and we be came more confident with the new Regulations and *National Quality Framework*, I realised that what I was choosing to put aside was starting to affect the overall quality of our service and needed to be embraced.

As Director, the initial hurdle was to engage myself. It all seemed foreign, too hard, time consuming, expensive and not of personal interest. I also had 28 other staff to engage and with limited initial passion I found it difficult to inspire others.

To begin I presented at a staff meeting, introducing the basics to break down the information in the *National Quality Standards* and EYLF. The team took on the information at the meeting, but things continued as before the following day.

I was feeling frustrated and disheartened, not knowing what it would take to inspire my already hard working crew in this new area of change. They were still working with the many changes we had so smoothly moved through thus far.

Realising that my lack of real commitment was holding us back, my well labelled and neatly organised pile remained sitting patiently in my office.

Strategies that worked

Months later, I attended a two day NSW Early Childhood Environmental Education Network conference which won me! I began to understand the impact on our environment of things like plastic bag usage. I was sold, engaged, inspired and shocked into action. This was timely, as it was just before our team Quality Improvement Plan review day which involved the team coming together on a Saturday to review and reflect on our practices. Each room of our 4 unit centre prepared a presentation on their selected quality area and I prepared for the remaining areas which included Quality Areas 3, 4 & 7.

This time my presentation was filled with commitment which engaged and involved the team who provided great ideas to implement change. Following our productive day I made sure that I acted quickly while the team were so open to change. The newly appointed room sustainability representatives met weekly to brainstorm and implement our collective ideas.

I also worked with our Educational Leader to actively engage staff through our monthly professional challenges.

What it looks like now

Physically our environment has a lot more green and natural elements, it is clear and visually evident to families and children that we have a new commitment to our 'environment'. This

became much more than just our little herb garden but required a review of everything: Cleaning products/approaches, menu and food selections, connections with nature, environments, toys, parent and staff library, community resources available, electricity use, paper use, waste management, baby products, worm farms, connections with local community gardens, reducing the daily dryer use and a lot more excursions into our local community to increase our community bush connections.

Emotionally – we are feeling excited, open and ready to share our new-found commitment. Once the initial hurdles were tackled and most of the team were engaged, a magical shift flowed throughout our entire program.

Community engagement – I then started to research and became a documentary addict! From my favourites I selected and added some wonderful new resources to share with staff, families and the community. Monthly movie nights will be held for the documentaries to be shared with families and the broader community. The children were of course on board immediately with the mention of worm farms, excursions and gardening opportunities. Newsletters now have a section committed to sustainability to share information and celebrate our changes.

In the future

I would hope that we will increase our connections with the wider community, share resources and information with other Centres, Students and families.

I hope families are involved and their gardens are nourished by our food waste and our worms' hard work.

Our children have many opportunities in their week to be out in the community to engage with nature, and that they are equipped with a passion and knowledge to live sustainable lives.

The greatest ongoing challenges

At the moment sustainability is consuming most of my daily hours. I am hoping that it just becomes part of my day and our sustainable practices become integrated and routine with a commitment from all team members.

Lessons learned!

- Be completely engaged before trying to engage others
- Be knowledgeable and informed to support change smoothly
- Embrace change head on, with excitement and commitment
- Change takes time. Be happy with small steps, but you need to plan and keep the steps moving.
- Reflect with your teams regularly throughout the process
- Celebrate and share the steps with families and children

Source: Natalie Cordukes, Director Paddington Children's Centre, 2013.

There are many demands on leaders and educators within the current early childhood and school professional environments (*see* Chapter 11). Regardless, the Director and team in the previous example have strived to continue their sustainability journey by critically reflecting on policy and pedagogy. The following examples provide provocation to reflect on our daily life practices and those within our early childhood settings.

In Figure 10.19 all sustainability initiatives have been mapped out and given target dates for completion.

Reducing/reuse
Paper in rooms and office
Smaller paper towels
Freecycle old items and donating to other centres
Donating unused equipment to other services

Reducing electricity
Dryer use
Air conditioning reduction
Clothes drying with children involvement

Sustainability resources for rooms (June 2013)
Puzzles
Games
Posters
Books (children, staff and families)

Increased trees/plants in the environment

Natural products in new structure/renovations 2011

Worm farm and composting (August 2013)
Share with families and communal gardens

Sustainability information included in newsletter for families

Info nights for families
Installed projector
Monthly movie nights
(Bag it; Waste not; Orbit; Story of stuff)

SUSTAINABILITY AT PCC

Apple iPads purchased to reduce paper usage

Garbage
Increased recycling options with SITA (August 2013)
Reducing waste in compost and wormfarm

Removed plastic cups and bowls (May 2013)
Containers replaced with glass
Cling wrap only used to cover cakes for blowing out candles (2012)
Plastic/melamine replaces with stainless steel and glass
Reducing plastic toy purchases

ECEEN training
Teri and Emily (2012)
Natalie – two day training
(June 2013) All staff (July 2013)

Review cleaning products and chemical use (August 2013)

Sustainability meetings (June 2013 – current)
ECO Smart audit
Room reps
ECEEN conference (July 2013)

Bush connections
Nollaig course
Increased excursions
Wet weather gear purchased

Menu review
Reducing processed foods
Seasonal fruit/ veggies

Outdoor area review
Increase natural elements in the outdoor environment

Purchase of fruit and veggies locally (2012)

Added more herbs and veggie patches (July 2013)

Source: Paddington Children's Centre

FIGURE 10.19 Sustainability web.

Modelling thoughtful, sustainable practice is a powerful educative tool. In Example 10.4, a reflection of the settings practices resulted in changes to daily practice with the development of a thorough sustainability routine. This routine will provoke sustainability conversations between educators, children and families, combined with shared child and educator action.

EXAMPLE 10.4
Sustainability routine

7.30am	Kitchen staff retain food scraps during food preparation for worm farm to reduce food waste.
	Kitchen staff review menu and where appropriate gather herbs/veggie from the patch for the days recipes. (Children to support)
	Glass, ceramics and stainless steel cups and bowls are used to reduce the use of non-biodegradable products at the service.
	Cling wrap is now only used for hygiene purposes to cover Birthday cakes and to allow a child to blow out the candles.
	Dishes are prepared just prior to being served to reduce the use of the microwave.
8.00am	Children and staff rake, sweep and water garden (environment care).
9.00am	Rooms turn off air conditioning units and unnecessary lighting when leaving rooms.
9.30am	Small groups of children gather scraps from the kitchen to feed worm farm with kitchen/staff.
10.00am	Star/Sun room children hang out washed bibs, washers and tea towels to dry in the sun to reduce dryer usage.
11.00am	Recycling bins are used to reduce paper wastage.
12.00pm	Paddington Children's Centre menu strives to utilise local produce.
	When children and staff leave the room the light/water monitors check the room to ensure lights, air conditioner and taps are turned off.
3.00pm	Spontaneous gardening experiences throughout all rooms during outdoor play.
5.00pm	Children's water bottles are emptied into plants and gardens.
	Children support packing away of the outdoor environment to care for our materials and resources for longevity of our equipment.
6.10pm	Light, air conditioners, water and electricity check on final lock up.

Source: Paddington Children's Centre

Family collaboration with environmental projects and the development of policies and procedures will strengthen the implementation process and ownership of the changes. Sharing information about new service initiatives and sustainable practice will strengthen children and family understanding and generalise new learning to the community.

> Environmental education for the early years should be based on a sense of wonder and the joy of discovery.
>
> Wilson, 1996, p. 2

Educators can nurture children's natural enthusiasm for their world through meaningful modelling of care for the immediate environment; children can be amazing catalysts for our own behaviours. When children are armed with enthusiasm and understanding of the impact their activities have on the environment, never underestimate their ability to impact on family and community attitudes and behaviour.

Considerations for planning

One of the delights and difficulties of educating children is that every day is different.

A O'Connor & C Diggins, *On Reflection: Reflective Practice for Early Childhood Educators*, p. 7, © 2002 Open Mind Publishing.

Planning is a complex and multifaceted process requiring sound knowledge of children and their developing competencies, positive relationships with children, families and colleagues, and the ability and desire to reflect on the setting's philosophy and practice.

Planning in early childhood settings involves the daily challenge of providing flexible yet secure environments with large blocks of time, provisions for relaxation during the day, supportive relationships and peaceful and respectful interactions .

Balance of flexibility and security

When planning a day for young children, security within a predictable (but flexible) routine is a key factor. Security may take many forms; for example, familiar educators, a stable physical environment, a sense of safety within and belonging to the group, a sense of ownership/independence for learning and regular events throughout the day, to name a few.

Planning secure frameworks, such as routines and schedules, provides families and educators with a sketch of the day so that each part of the day functions without prescription but maintains a secure sequence of events and flexible service delivery.

Example 10.5 is a sample of a daily routine for under three-year-old children in an urban early childhood education and care centre. In this setting, the physical location of cot-room and kitchen facilities determines that babies will be located in a separate room from older children. This routine reflects a sociocultural philosophy and regulatory policies and practices such as:

- promoting social interactions
- recognition of shared expertise: families engage in communication and shared planning to enhance their children's learning
- extended blocks of time: these minimise transitions and hurried children and enable a stronger focus on relationships and intentional teaching
- children's personal routines: these incorporate flexible eating and sleeping patterns, and nappy changing as required (arbitrary blocks of time are included, as a reminder for educators to ensure all children are monitored regularly)
- child protection procedures: rooms combine in the early morning and late afternoon, when child and educator numbers are lowest, to provide a home-like environment and to ensure that two educators maintain visual contact at all times throughout the day and educators are available to talk with families on arrival and departure
- sun safety: children are indoors between 11 a.m. and 3 p.m. during daylight saving hours, and sunscreen and hats are applied prior to sun exposure
- health and hygiene procedures: to minimise cross-infection from home to centre and vice versa on departure, parents change their child's nappy and wash their child's and their own hands on arrival.

Alongside the routine in Example 10.5, educators' shift descriptions provide detailed roster duties to ensure optimum organisation for learning, interaction and care-giving opportunities. Both these documents then work alongside the written plan for the day – this plan will incorporate planned/intentional teaching experiences and small groups as well as the opportunity to record emerging curriculum.

> ## EXAMPLE 10.5
> Sample daily routine for children birth–two years old, families and
> educators in a long day care environment

| 7.30 a.m.–9 a.m. | Children arrive, indoor/outdoor play.
Birth–two- and two–three-year-old groups combine until 8.30 a.m. shifts commence.
Children participate in the set-up of indoor environment.
Free choice of equipment and experiences guided by children's interests and requests.
Spontaneous small group times. |

Families, on arrival, please change your child's nappy, following the visual procedure displayed (to minimise cross-infection from home to centre), apply sunscreen (and hat if outdoors) and enjoy a settling experience with your child. During this time, please share any relevant updates verbally with an educator, or jot a note next to your child's name on the sign in/out sheet to advise educators of information recorded in your child's communication book. As you prepare to say goodbye, please advise an educator so that person can support your child in this transition.

8.30 a.m.	Morning tea.
9 a.m.–10.45 a.m.	Indoor/outdoor play. Children wash hands and sit for morning tea when ready, and then transition back to free-choice experiences. Free choice of equipment and experiences guided by children's interests and requests. Spontaneous and planned/intentional teaching small group times involving two–five children (based upon your child's interests these may involve investigation, music, movement, language and so on). Transition into lunchtime with group time singing or story time.

Designated nappy change at 9.30 a.m. or as required.
Sleep, morning tea and other care giving determined by children's personal routines.

10.45 a.m.	Hand washing.
11 a.m.–3 p.m.	Lunch Indoor play. Free choice of equipment and experiences guided by children's interests and requests. Spontaneous and planned/intentional teaching small group times. Staggered sleep/rest times.

Designated nappy change prior to sleep or as required.
Older children wash hands, help prepare tables and sit for lunch together.
Younger children have lunch, sleep, nappy change, bottles and other care-giving routines based upon their individual personal routines.
Sleep times and food intake recorded on the lunch/sleep record sheet and interests, interaction and learning information recorded in your child's communication book.

| 2 p.m.–5 p.m. | Afternoon tea.
Outdoor play.
Free choice of equipment and experiences guided by children's interests and planned/intentional teaching.
Spontaneous and planned/intentional teaching small group times. |

 Afternoon tea, nappy change and other care-giving routines based upon your child's personal routine.

| 5 p.m.–6 p.m. | Late afternoon snack. Indoor/outdoor play. Free choice of equipment and experiences guided by children's interests and planned/intentional teaching. Birth–two-year-old and two–three-year-old groups combine at 5.30 p.m. as shifts finish and children leave. |

Families, on departure, are welcome to change your child's nappy, following the visual procedure displayed (to minimise cross-infection from centre to home). Please share in our day by reading and perhaps making comments and/or suggestions for follow-up experiences in our story of the day, located beside the sign in/out folder. Please say goodbye to advise an educator of your departure and enable that person to farewell you and your child.

Example 10.6 reflects a more structured time frame within a school setting. Although time frames may be externally set, educators within such settings are able to focus on play-based active learning, reducing whole group transitions, balancing individual/group experiences, and the inclusion of intentional teaching as in birth-to-five settings. Educators observe children's learning throughout the day, especially during small group intentional teaching experiences. Small groups also provide opportunities for conversations with peers, where children can explore ideas and scaffold each other's learning. This example also illustrates the many ways that educators can incorporate children's interests (in this case fairies and cars) and their family experiences (e.g. visiting the doctor) throughout the school day.

▶ EXAMPLE 10.6

Sample daily routine for children five–eight years old

8.45 a.m.–9.15 a.m.	Children and families arrive. Children play in playground.
9.15 a.m.	Children move to classrooms when bell goes. Families encouraged to the classrooms to assist in settling children and join into investigating experiences. Children select small group active learning experiences – e.g. literacy-enriched dramatic play: doctor's surgery with literacy resources; block construction with toy cars and literacy resources; painting resources on the verandah with a parent; iPads with drawing and music apps; laptops and word processing software; playdough with fairytale figurines, posters and books.
9.45 a.m.	Transition to whole group, songs and rhymes.
10 a.m.	Whole group shared book experience.
10.15 a.m.	Small group and individual English experiences: writing and drawing response to shared book on paper and computer; iBooks on iPad; guided reading with teacher; individual independent reading aloud to parent; doctor's surgery dramatic play with literacy resources. Educator completes running records of children in guided reading.

10.45 a.m.	Whole class sharing. Educator documents observations of children who report on their experiences.
11 a.m.	Recess.
11.20 a.m.	Transition to classroom, counting songs and rhymes.
11.30 a.m.	Whole class demonstration of new mathematics concept.
11.45 a.m.	Small group mathematics experiences exploring new concept using hands-on materials.
12.15 p.m.	Whole class sharing and educator documents observations, transition to lunch.
12.30 p.m.	Lunch, playground experiences, library.
1.15 p.m.	Transition to classroom, Drop Everything and Read (DEAR).
1.40 p.m.	Integrated science or history unit involving collaborative small group project; continues for two weeks. Children investigate topic; small groups construct a model, diorama or poster or develop a dramatisation; culminating in small group presentations to whole the group.
2.40 p.m.	Music or drama workshops
3.15 p.m.	Home.

Photographic or other visual displays of the daily timetable can support security for children by enhancing their understanding of time and sequence. Visual prompts are an excellent resource when working with all children and, in particular, children requiring additional communication support. Children experiencing communication barriers will be more independent in their interactions with peers if they are able to support their communication of interests or desires with the aid of formal visual tools, e.g. Boardmaker. Peers will also be more able to identify positive strategies to engage with children experiencing barriers to learning – in particular communication challenges.

For children to be able to engage in investigations, extended projects and collaborative learning, it is advantageous to plan for a reduced number of whole group transitions and empower children with choices about what, when and how long they will engage in particular experiences or interactions. It also means planning for ways to limit the number of times resources need to be packed away so that children are able to continue an experience, such as block construction, across the whole day.

Where children are engaged in projects that extend over a number of days or weeks it is important to plan for a space where works may be left out and revisited. This may require flexible use of spaces, such as eating and sleeping spaces, and may mean careful negotiations with cleaners to clean around works in progress. When children are allowed increased autonomy to plan the amount of time they spend on an experience, investigation or project, they further develop the ability to self-regulate and as a result achieve greater satisfaction in their learning. When children self-regulate, there is less demand for educators to 'direct' the day, making them more available to plan with other children and scaffold their learning and interests into prolonged investigations or projects.

Some settings may have mixed age groupings for a substantial part of the day, with children moving freely between rooms and the outdoor environment. In one long day care setting for three–five-year-olds with wide verandahs, trees and shade covers, the whole day plan consists of free flow between the indoor and outdoor environments with the only large group transition being to lunch. Where services are age-grouped and spaces are shared with distinct groupings, whole group transitions may also be required to ensure each group has adequate time either indoors or outdoors.

Regulatory and safety criteria may also require planning for whole group transitions. Fxamples 10.5 and 10.6 focus on continuity of learning with minimal interruptions.

> Time is not by a clock and continuity is not interrupted by the calendar. Children's own sense of time and their personal rhythm are considered in planning.

Gandini, 2002, p. 17

Educators who are in tune with children will understand that each child will use time in her/his own unique way. In busy urban environments, many children arrive at a setting after a busy and at times hectic start to their day, rushed preparation and traffic jams. Alternatively, in remote environments, many children arrive at a setting later in the morning having firstly meandered around the community walking alongside a family member.

Simple provisions such as a relaxed breakfast on arrival, quiet spaces and familiar experiences where children can begin their day in a peaceful manner will enhance interactions and learning for the remainder of the day in either setting.

Some simple questions with which to reflect on the use of time are detailed below. Does our planned schedule:

- allow sufficient time for experiences so that children are able to actively and constructively engage in experiences and do not become frustrated by being constantly asked to pack away?
- provide a relaxed atmosphere where educators interact and build attachment (DEEWR, 2009, p. 15)?
- utilise a flexible timetable with large chunks of overlapping time (Greenman & Stonehouse, 1997)?
- minimise transitions and waiting time?
- minimise delays and interruptions?
- give warning time before transitions?
- individualise routines?
- allow time for children to do tasks both independently and cooperatively?
- allow time for prolonged interactions where educators engage in sustained shared conversations with children to extend their thinking (DEEWR, 2009, p. 15)?
- encourage both autonomy and cooperation and enable learning to occur in social contexts, acknowledging the importance of interactions and conversations for learning (DEEWR, 2009, p. 15)?
- encourage children to explore, solve problems, create and construct (DEEWR, 2009, p. 15)?

When educators are aware of the value of prolonged interactions and exploration of projects, they will plan to use time in a relaxed and flexible manner. Maintenance of appropriate educator–child ratios across the day, including educator break times, provides the necessary resources to enable educators to achieve a more relaxed, 'less hurried' environment where interactions with children take priority.

FIGURE 10.20 It is important to allow children quiet time to create.

FIGURE 10.21 Teachers and children can create together.

Relaxation as part of the day

Children and early childhood professionals are facing increased pressures and stress in a hurried society. Planning time and space for relaxation provides 'a simple, enjoyable way of bringing calm, peace and positivity to each day'

P Thomas & V Lockwood, 'Relax!...chill-out techniques for kids and carers', Rattler 66, p. 8,
Winter 2003, © 2003 Community Child Care Co-operative Ltd.

Setting aside time and space to engage in small group relaxation exercises will provide children and educators with lifelong tools to regulate stress in their lives. Whether it is a preplanned experience such as stretching or visualisation as illustrated in Figure 10.22, an alternative self-regulated experience or a quiet space for reflection, children will benefit from the calm moments of the day.

Children, like adults, will experience stressful situations on a daily basis, and the tools and skills children develop in their early years will assist them throughout their lives. One group of children and educators engaged in a dialogue to discover the different ways they could choose to calm themselves when they felt angry. Some of the children's suggestions were:

FIGURE 10.22 Children stretching in a small group relaxation experience.

- spend some time on your own
- read a book
- do some yoga
- have a drink of water
- talk about it
- take a deep breath
- work at a table by yourself
- find a quiet space
- have a lie down
- draw about your feelings.

The educators then documented this in posters, showing photos of the children and their chosen experience. Sharing their ideas led to awareness of the diversity in children's temperaments and choices, and also provided children with many different areas and methods of relaxation to investigate.

Supportive relationships and interactions

Secure and supportive relationships are essential for all children. Continuity of educators who play a powerful role in the lives of children is a pivotal factor of these relationships within early childhood settings.

Purposeful planning for supportive relationships will encourage children to develop 'strategies and skills for initiating, maintaining, and enjoying a relationship with other children – including taking turns, problem solving, negotiating, taking another's point of view, supporting others, and understanding other people's attitudes and feelings – in a variety of contexts' (New Zealand Ministry of Education, 1996, p. 70).

Greeting children and families with a familiar face each morning will assist in easing the transition from home to the early childhood setting or school. In early childhood settings this requires purposeful forward planning of rosters to minimise staff changes on early shifts and to guarantee regular replacement of educators for holidays or sick leave.

Continuity of educators over the years is another way to develop secure and meaningful connections between children, families and educators. This may occur as a result of planning for mixed age grouping, or educators transitioning with the children into a new room/environment.

When educators remain with children over more than one year, relationships, understandings and expectations are continuous rather than requiring re-establishment from year to year. This continuity will enable children to feel secure in their knowledge that familiar educators will support their learning. There is a shared understanding about the child's and family's cultural context, and without the need for 'adjustment to new relations, there is less pressure to reach certain goals, to finish the year's work with a clean break, or to start each year with a clean slate' (Gandini, 1993, p. 147).

Peaceful and respectful interactions

Promoting peaceful and respectful interactions between children, educators and families positively impacts upon each child's disposition to learning and concept of self.

> Through a widening network of secure relationships, children develop confidence and feel respected and valued. They become increasingly able to recognise and respect the feelings of others and to interact positively with them.

> DEEWR, 2009, p. 12

Conflict resolution is a lifelong tool for children and adults, and is also a large part of the routine of our day, as children develop 'a range of strategies for solving conflicts in peaceful ways, and a perception that peaceful ways are best' (New Zealand Ministry of Education, 1996, p. 70). Strategies for promoting positive interactions are explored further in Chapter 9.

Promoting peace is also about respecting diversity and advocating for social justice. Campbell et al. (2002) note that 'peace is about justice and respect for everyone's basic rights' (p. 2). The authors emphasise the importance of interactions and relationships in promoting peace. The ways in which people interact and relate to each other set up the expectations that people will be treated positively and with respect.

Traditionally, educators have acted as keepers of the peace, resolving conflict for children rather than with children. Scaffolding children's learning with positive conflict resolution language and skills is one way to support children to express their true feelings, desires and frustrations. Intentional teaching and group dialogue has the potential to empower children to jointly define the behaviours that are acceptable within the group, distinguishing the differences between individually accepted behaviours and the common good of the group. Each group and setting will identify different behaviours, and educators may find their personal values challenged in this process and require considerable self-reflection. By visually displaying children engaged in group dialogue, as in Figure 10.23, children are reminded of the possibilities. This photo is powerful in its representation of children working through conflict without an educator.

It is never too early to encourage peaceful interactions and language. Young children will become familiar with language for peace when educators model its use. Older children will begin to use language for peace if educators provide a script and emotional support for children when conflict arises; for example, providing scripted language for a child to address his discomfort at raised voices, such as 'When you yell at me I feel scared; please use a quiet voice'.

It is important that educators recognise the value of children working through their disagreements independently: 'When children are having a conflict or disagreement, the professional (educator) balances the value of children working things out themselves with getting involved' (NSW DoCS, 2002, p. 41). Dramatic play and persona dolls are valuable tools available to educators when promoting peaceful interactions. Persona dolls can be used to explore negative or positive interactions and to assist children to reflect on their behaviour and attitudes. Persona dolls play a vastly different role from other dolls in the environment. They are introduced with life stories detailing family relationships, home environments, personality traits and possibly problems to address. For example, the persona doll 'Sunjiv' is used by an educator in one setting to explore children's feelings of rejection when a common taunt of 'You're not coming to my party' or 'You can't play here; only girls can' is used to isolate a peer from a play situation.

FIGURE 10.23 Clear visual statements reinforce the idea that quiet times are positive experiences, which can be self-regulated. They can also be used to remind children of possibilities for positive social interactions.

Modelling of respectful and peaceful interactions between families and educators is critical to developing peaceful and positive relationships between children. For example, a parent with her two young children shares information with an educator on arrival. The parent explains how her younger child was teething, with two molars breaking through the gum, and really wasn't herself today. The discussion continued about the empathy for the pain associated with multiple toothaches, whether temperatures and nappy rash could be caused by teething, and so on. The children were therefore witness to modelling of two-way learning and respectful and peaceful interaction between their parent and educator. Time for such interaction can be consciously planned into the day. Typically this occurs at arrival and departure times; however, this is not always the most appropriate time and strategies to enable interaction at alternative times throughout the day may be required.

Once children develop the ability to articulate what is meaningful in their interactions, educators need to take care not to expect that knowing will result in doing. Children may be able to verbalise that it is not okay to hit your friends, but still lapse under the pressure of the moment. We all need to practise new skills to master them; they do not come automatically and educators should show patience and support children in practising strategies for peaceful interaction.

Children engaged in decisions about their behaviour have a greater chance of success if they scaffold each other's learning. Children can empower each other with shared understanding and clearly identified agreements. Dialogue between a group of four–five-year-olds and their educator about their own expected group behaviours, and why they are important, resulted in the following agreement, recorded in the children's language:

- We need to listen to the teacher and each other.
- You need to be quiet when someone is resting, reading and at group times.
- We need to use eye contact and 'I' statements.
- We can make things and choices for ourselves.
- Choose an activity and do not hurt anyone or you will move away.
- We walk inside.
- Keep activities where they belong.
- We need to pack away.
- We think of each other's feelings.
- We walk up and down the stairs.
- During group time we listen and keep our hands to ourselves.
- We use quiet voices inside.

Balancing planned and spontaneous experiences

The *Effective Pedagogy in the Early Years* project found that the most effective early years settings had a balance of child-initiated and adult-inititated experiences (Sylva et al., 2004; 2010). The EYLF also advocates 'a balance between child led, child initiated and educator supported learning' (DEEWR, 2009, p. 15).

Traditionally, only part of the day was planned; for example, indoors and group time. If only isolated parts of the day are planned, it is easy to omit a balance of movement between quiet and boisterous, active and passive, routine and discovery, and self and group. It is also easy to miss learning opportunities that incidentally occur throughout the journey of each day. Reflection, as discussed in Chapter 4, enables educators to step back and evaluate this balance and to plan for the total learning environment, including the outdoor, indoor and routines such as meal times.

Sociocultural theorists such as Rogoff (2003) emphasise the role of adult-child interactions in children's learning. One implication of this research is that educators need to be actively involved in all aspects of the program as all elements in the day have potential for learning. This means planning with an intentional learning focus and responding to child-initiated experiences with intentional teaching. When educators engage in child-initiated spontaneous experiences with children there are many opportunities for intentional teaching (Epstein, 2007, 2009). Intentional teaching is particularly important in these contexts as it enables educators to capitalise on the learning potential in a serendipitous moment and can support children to engage with the learning opportunities available (Epstein, 2007).

The *Effective Provision of Preschool Education* (EPPE) research (Siraj-Blatchord & Sylva, 2004) highlights the importance of educator–child interactions in both adult and child initiated small group and individual experiences. These experiences provide opportunities for the sustained shared thinking this research identified as a critical aspect of effective learning environments. Sustained shared thinking is a process whereby educators and children listen to and build on the ideas of each other and is discussed further in Chapter 9.

Planning is most effective when it is based on children's previously identified interests, emerging interests and development and ongoing investigations or projects. This type of planning requires educators to be highly organised but at the same time flexible and open to ideas, questions and resources suggested by children and families.

When educators are respectful of children and families they find ways to include them as partners in the processes of planning, documentation and evaluation. Educators can encourage children and families to contribute to the planning of the learning environment (DEEWR, 2009).

As discussed in Chapter 3, children's learning does not always follow a linear, predetermined path. We can equate learning with a dance, rather than a race: full of movement up, down, backwards, forwards and around, rather than starting from one point and moving in a direct line to the finish. Therefore, we are unable to plan how and where our partnership will take us – however, we can enjoy the ride!

Gandini (2002, p. 18) argues that 'it flows naturally that, to be truly respectful of children's and teachers' ideas and processes of learning, the curriculum cannot be set in advance'. While educators plan with intentions these plans are not set in concrete. Educators need to be responsive to children's questions and ideas. This requires educators to be able to change directions in the implementation of their plans, to reflect on the implications for future planning in their evaluations and to respond to spontaneous moments. Spontaneous experiences enable educators to respond to serendipitous events, local issues and children's questions and ideas and make the most effective use of ordinary, everyday moments to extend learning in meaningful ways.

Ordinary, yet extraordinary, moments

Ordinary moments are the pages in the child's diary for the day. If we could resist our temptation to record only the grand moments, we might find the authentic child living in the in-between. If we could resist our temptation to put the children on a stage, we might find the real work being done in the wings. If we understood the great value in the ordinary moments, we might be less inclined to have a marvellous finale for a long-term project. We appeal to educators everywhere to find the marvel in the mundane, to find the power of the ordinary moment.

G Forman et al., *Child Care Information Exchange*, p. 53, © 2001 Exchange Press, Inc.

Educators focused upon showcasing children's learning within their programs, or planning only for predetermined outcomes, often miss the subtle learning that occurs alongside and, at times, in spite of our planning. Educators have access to endless examples of children's learning through daily encounters with the physical and social environment. Once again, an educator's philosophy will guide whether they support these moments within their planning or allow them to pass by.

Shafer (2002, p. 185) notes that a shift in focus from always seeking big projects will enable the potential of ordinary moments to be recognised and become an integral part of our planning. An ordinary moment may simply be a child's question – for example, Thom's question: 'Does your stomach and heart grow up or do your legs grow down?', or Will's question: 'Could you have only odd numbered cars on the side with odd numbers on houses?'

When educators resist the temptation to turn either of these questions back on the child or answer with a fact, but instead provoke further investigation, they are opening the opportunity to prompt and share further inquiry, reflection and understanding. If the adult responds 'That's an interesting question; how do you think we could find out?' the opportunity for shared inquiry is established. In response to Thom's question, the inquiry may commence with a web detailing current understandings of hearts, stomachs and growth, or any other information that results from the dialogue between adult and child, child and child or child and parent. Thom's interest in the body could be further extended by educators and parents through:

- visiting the museum to explore body parts of humans and animals
- consulting books and Internet sites to find out about bodies and how they work
- inviting a doctor or veterinarian to bring a sheep's heart for children to investigate
- exploring model skeletons and body parts.

As a result of Will's question, there was discussion about numbers in general: odd numbers, even numbers and favourite numbers. Will's favourite number is 17 – he was interested in why it is called odd. Did it look odd? What made it odd? What does the word 'odd' mean? Will and his parents read a book about the history of numbers to seek some answers. Other investigations for Will and his educators and parents to further extend this interest could include:

- How can we find out about other numbers, such as even numbers and favourite numbers?
- How do numbers sound (for example, in words, rhymes and counting)?
- Do all houses and cars have numbers? Why do you think they have numbers?
- Do people have choices about the numbers on their house or their car?

Forman states:

If a child asks you a why question and you just turn it back to the child, you have a good chance of reducing the number of why questions that the child will ask in the future. After all, he did ask a question and wants some level of help. A child might enter a wondering phase with you, but he does not want to do it all by himself.

G Forman et al., *Ordinary Moments, Extraordinary Possibilities*, p. 194, from *Teaching and Learning: Collaborative Exploration of the Reggio Emilia approach*, © 1998 Pearson Education, Upper Saddle River, NJ.

Partnerships in planning

Approaches to planning that draw on sociocultural theories describe the educator's role as one of partnership with children, colleagues and families. Educators observe and listen to children, and ask questions to discover children's ideas, hypotheses and theories in order to gain an understanding of how they can resource the children's learning. Educators also invite families to contribute their insights into their child's experiences and learning at home and in the community.

Through this process educators 'recognise the connections between children, families and communities and the importance of reciprocal relationships and partnerships for learning. They see learning as a social activity and value collaborative learning and community participation' (DEEWR, 2009, p. 14).

Families may contribute information and suggestions through conversation or through written notes such as the Learning Story in Example 10.7.

EXAMPLE 10.7

A learning story from a parent

Toby has been spending lots of time at home looking at books and magazines about space and spaceships. His favourite book is *Planes and Spaceships*. He likes to find out how things work and studies the diagrams and print carefully. He is using words like engine and propellers. He was looking at a diagram of a spaceship and said, 'That's where the fire is so it can blast off!' He is interested in the fire in the fireplace as well and was asking how it worked. He said, 'I know there are gases and they get hot and this bit is orange and that other bit, it's hotter, it's red'. His favourite planet is Saturn – he likes the rings. He says he is going to go into space and catch Saturn by throwing a rope around its rings and then pull it into his spaceship and bring it back to Earth.

How the educator uses this Learning Story will determine how much information will be shared in the future. If the parent and child are supported by the educator in further investigation of Toby's interest, the learning potential will be enhanced.

Effective partnerships also require educators to keep families informed about children's learning. This can be achieved through conversations, displays of children's learning, portfolios and newsletters. In Example 10.8, an excerpt from KU Killarney Heights Preschool's newsletter, the educators provide information about children's learning for families.

EXAMPLE 10.8

An excerpt from an email to parents

News from preschool

The children at KU Killarney Heights Preschool are absolutely amazing and they very clearly define what they want the curriculum to be!

For example: In the last few weeks the children's interests have been:

- Fairies and fairy tales
- Lego construction and space play, now extending to block play
- Pirate play

- Construction sites in and out of the sandpit
- Inclines and ramps with blocks, vehicles and water
- There has been a train and station in the cubby house for about six weeks now
- Exciting play on the swings and the tyre swing in particular
- Emerging literacy skills: Writing names and words over and over and over again … this has been more evident than any year I can remember.
- Along with all the other favourite experiences: painting, puzzles, pattern blocks, manipulative equipment, home corner play (we LOVE the coffee machine and the take away cups).

Source: Jane Pethers and Kylie Kennemore, KU Killarney Heights Preschool, KU Children's Services, 2011

Attached to the newsletter in Example 10.8 was a more in-depth exploration of 'Literacy at play' (*see* Example 10.9).

EXAMPLE 10.9
Literacy at play

Literacy: in the early years literacy includes a range of modes of communication includingmusic, movement, dance, story telling, visual arts, media and drama, as well as talking, reading andwriting. (EYLF, 2009)

Writing letters, words, numbers.   Practising and mastering the complexity of writing their name.   Creating letter-like marks and symbols.

Noticing
We see the children engaged in these forms of communication everyday at Preschool but lately there has been a noticeable interest and enthusiasm for writing.

Source: Jane Pethers, Kylie Kennemore, KU Killarney Heights Preschool, KU Chidren's Services, 2011

Culturally relevant events are one example where educators, children and families can work collaboratively to plan and co-create meaningful curriculum for children. Some general examples are National Sorry Day, Ramadan and Clean Up Australia Day, and more specific events include local agricultural shows and the blessing of the fishing fleet. Each of these topics provides opportunities for families to suggest ideas and contribute resources. Knowing families, their skills and interests creates opportunities for partnerships in planning. Figure 10.24 Provides an example of how partnering with families can support children's learning by tapping into the specialist skills of a parent who is a portrait artist.

We are the Thursday *Bananas in Pyjamas* children & our ages range between 3¾ -5years. We created these self-portraits when Callum's Mum, Helen (a Portrait artist), came and visited us. We sat in front of our playroom mirror, outlined our portrait with a black marker & then we used water paints to add colour and definition to our work.

FIGURE 10.24 Self-portraits.

Organisation and planning are essential when provocation and extension of projects is a key component of the curriculum. Such projects are more meaningful when they emerge from the shared interests of children in collaboration with staff and families.

EXAMPLE 10.10
Painting our rainbow serpent

Source: Jane Pethers, Kylie Kennemore, KU Killarney Heights Preschool, KU Chidren's Services, 2011

The early years lay the critical foundations for future learning attitudes and behaviours. When introducing big ideas into the program, it is important to involve the under-three age group, have important conversations with families and promote equity.

Projects

Projects are one approach to sustained partnerships in learning. Katz and Chard (2000), assert that projects must focus on meaningful topics connected to the real world so that they are worthy of children's attention and effort. Katz and Chard (1989/2000) suggest the following phases for projects:

- Phase I – Beginning the project
- Phase II – Developing the project
- Phase III – Concluding the project.

It is important to remember that these are general guidelines providing a framework, not a prescribed format.

PHASE I: BEGINNING THE PROJECT

First of all, it is important for educators to find out what children are interested in. This may emerge in a number of ways, including from:

- an event or incident at the setting (such as the discovery of a bird's nest)
- a community event (such as the celebration of Science Week)
- a shared book or video
- the presentation of an unusual object for the children to examine and wonder about (Chard, 2001)
- information about a child's interests shared from home
- children's conversations, play and creative expressions
- an adult interest
- a topic negotiated between the children and educator/s.

Helm and Katz (2011) suggest that a few possible topics for investigation are selected and then analysed in terms of their potential value for children. Criteria for selection suggested by Helm and Katz (2011) are whether the topic will:

- help children understand their own experiences and environments more fully
- strengthen the disposition to look closely at phenomena in their environments
- encourage problem solving.

After the selection of a suitable topic, educators can web possible directions for the project. This web is a way of exploring connections across curriculum areas and investigating the possible content and learning processes that could be involved.

Helm and Katz (2011) suggest that, when planning a project, it may be useful to begin with an experience that is relevant to children's experiences and focuses children's attention on the topic. This may be a book, video, discussion, excursion or visiting expert. For example, a project on celebrations at one setting started with a visit to Chinatown for Lunar New Year. Planning also involves thinking about how families and communities may be able to be involved. Parents may be able to contribute resources such as artefacts, books or software, talk to the children or invite children to visit their workplace. For example, a project 'Our Bodies' at one setting included visits to parents who were veterinarians and doctors. Families also contributed artefacts such as plastic skeletons and X-rays as well as medical books, software related to the human body and information downloaded from the Internet. Parents were also participants in the setting's excursions. When families are involved in this way, the children, families and educators become colearners.

At this stage it can be interesting to collect ideas from the whole group and to map out what they already know about the topic from their own experience. This information can be obtained through discussions, which can be recorded, transcribed and documented with the children. Children's drawings and constructions can also be a source of information about their current knowledge (Helm, Beneke & Steinheimer, 2007; Helm & Katz, 2011). Children's current knowledge as well as their questions for further exploration can also be webbed. This provides a source for

planning as well as a means of comparing children's understandings at the beginning and end of a project.

It can also be helpful for the children to hypothesise and identify questions they would like to investigate in the course of the project (Chard, 2001). This can be done on a posted list that can be added to each day, or questions can be posted into a box that is opened at the end of Phase I for the review and discussion of the questions collected there.

The planning at this stage also involves thinking about possible resources that will stimulate children's thinking and encourage investigation. Resources may include relevant books and software, as well as artefacts, construction materials and dramatic play resources. Educators also need to plan the resources that will be available for children to represent their understandings. These may include creative arts, literacy and construction materials as well as musical instruments, iPads and computers, cameras and dramatic play materials.

Phase I involves thinking about how the project will be documented and how technologies can be used to assist with documentation and as resources for children's learning. Technologies such as cameras, computers and other media can be used by children as well as adults to assist with investigating and documenting the topic. Computers and tablets with relevant software can be useful for children to further investigate ideas and to represent understandings. Children and educators can investigate relevant websites, make signs for dramatic play and constructions, make captions and signs for displays and project books, write and draw to reflect current understandings, and communicate with children in another centre via the Internet.

PHASE II: DEVELOPING THE PROJECT

During this phase the children are engaged in investigation. Experiences may include excursions and incursions with visiting experts as well as opportunities to explore a range of resources related to the topic and to represent understandings.

One or more field trips/excursions can be arranged for which there needs to be some preparation. In preparation for fieldwork, the children can think about, discuss and record what they are likely to see, which questions they may be able to investigate, to whom they may talk and what they might bring back to the setting. Fieldwork may not necessitate leaving the setting's premises but usually involves leaving the classroom to investigate more closely some aspect of the environment. The group of children can go to a site that affords opportunities to see relevant objects, plants, animals, vehicles, events, equipment, people and processes. They take notes and make sketches of what they are most interested in and what they would most like to learn more about when they return to the setting.

As a follow-up to the excursion the children and educator/s discuss the field trip, re-create accounts of what happened, what they saw and heard and what they learned. Sketches made in the field may become the basis for detailed drawings or paintings and for the construction of models.

During this phase, information books are consulted, new questions raised and new understandings reached. Children may represent their understandings in a range of ways, including drawing, painting, constructing models, writing, creating play spaces and dramatic play. Educators, families or community members may demonstrate and scaffold new skills such as how to operate an overhead projector, use clay-modelling tools or take photographs. Educators and children can revisit the initial web/s of possible directions and questions throughout the project and analyse what the children have learned. It may be found that children have taken the project in a different direction from that originally envisioned.

Visiting experts may also be involved in this phase of the project. These are people who have first-hand experience of the topic being studied, through their work, travel or leisure pursuits. Visiting experts can be invited to the classroom to talk to the children, answer questions, engage in discussion or be interviewed.

PHASE III: CONCLUDING THE PROJECT

Helm and Katz (2011) note that in the third phase the project is drawn to a close and children's learning is summarised. Katz and Chard (1989, p. 84) stress the importance of providing opportunities at the culmination of a project for children to 'elaborate on what they have learned so that the meaning is enhanced and made personal'.

The opportunity to share children's learnings with others is an important phase of a project. Helm and Katz (2011) suggest that children can hold an exhibition, write a report, put on a play, perform music and dance or hold an open house. This sort of culminating event provides an excellent opportunity and real purpose to review and evaluate all that has been going on during the past weeks or months. Usually everything cannot be shared as there is too much, so the group has to be selective in deciding what would best tell the story of their investigation.

Chard (2001) suggests that in this phase children are also involved in personalising new knowledge. Some children need time to reflect on new knowledge in order to understand it fully in their own terms. Children vary a lot in this regard. Imaginative activity is helpful for many children. They make up their own imaginary stories and dramatic sequences to play out some of the new ideas. Fantasy and imaginative children's literature can be especially helpful for this process of making the information personally memorable.

At the conclusion of the project the educator/s should evaluate children's learning. Helm, Beneke and Steinheimer (2007) suggest that it is useful for educators to evaluate children's level of engagement in the project and to evaluate children's deepened understandings. Evaluation methods can include webbing of what children know, analysis of drawings at the beginning and end of the project, interviews and children's self-reflections. Educators are also encouraged to evaluate the appropriateness of the selected resources and the use of time and space, as well as the effectiveness of teaching strategies. Educators' self-reflections are a useful evaluation strategy.

EXAMPLE 10.11
Guide for project planning

Phase I: Beginning the project

- What general topics appear to interest the children?
- How do we know? For example:
  - children's drawings
  - transcripts of conversations
  - children's questions
  - family information.
- Choose a topic/interest to begin the process.
- What do the children want to find out about this topic?
- Would this topic be appropriate for further investigation? That is:
  - Would the topic help children to understand their world?
  - Can children engage in meaningful learning?
  - Does the topic encourage dispositions such as curiosity?
  - Are there opportunities to extend language and literacy, numeracy, problem solving, critical thinking and research skills?
  - Are there opportunities for collaborative learning involving children, educators, families and the local community?
  - Are there opportunities for children to express their ideas through various media?

- Make a web of possible directions for this project that integrate curriculum areas. How will we find out about, and document, what children already know about the topic and what else they want to know?
- What possible questions might children want to investigate?
- How will we document children's interest/s and questions?
- What are one or two possible initial experiences to focus children's thinking? For example:
  - book
  - excursion
  - video
  - artefacts – photos, objects
  - dramatic play with appropriate resources
  - visiting expert.
- How could we involve families and the local community at this stage?
- How will we document children's learning throughout the project?

Phase II: Developing the project

- What resources could be added to children's play environments to encourage further investigation of the topic, building of vocabulary and representation of ideas?
- What community resources can be brought into the setting to extend the topic?
- How can families and the local community be involved?
- How can we document children's learning?

Phase III: Concluding the project

- What evidence of children's learning have we documented? For example:
  - webs of children's beginning and final understandings of the topic
  - samples of paintings and drawings
  - samples of writing
  - photographs and diagrams of constructions
  - language transcripts
  - Learning Stories
  - anecdotes.
- How can we encourage children, staff and families to reflect on what children have learned and the processes they have engaged in?
- Is there another topic that has emerged as an interest?
- How can we share children's learning with families and the local community?
- How will educators reflect on their learning?

Source: adapted from Helm & Katz, 2011

Selecting resources that promote learning

Placing children's interests at the centre of the curriculum

If educators are to truly honour children's contributions, then they need to accept all children's ideas as being equally valid. It is very easy to be accepting of the ideas that educators are comfortable with, such as a child's interest in spiders or the body. It is more challenging when the child's interest relates to something that makes them feel uncomfortable, such as Action Man, Big Brother or World Championship Wrestling.

When an educator demonstrates approval or disapproval for a child's choice, it determines the child's willingness – or not – to further contribute to the program.

> What messages are we giving children when we accept or reject their interests and passions?

► ## EXAMPLE 10.12
Building on children's interests

One of the children in the three- to four-year-old group came in enthusiastically to show the educator her item for the interest table. The educator documented what happened next in a flip book for children and families to view and revisit. The story is detailed below.

Tuesday 14 April

Yasmin brought in a huntsman spider (in a plastic container with air holes and bark). Yasmin told everyone it was a spider they had found in their garden, and that they made the holes in the container with a fork. This then sparked a conversation about what the holes were needed for. We talked about whether the spider was dead (like our spider in its observation box) or alive; as it moved we agreed that it was alive. One of the children suggested it needed the holes for air. We then discussed whether the spider liked being in the container. Some children said yes, others no;

that it might feel frightened in there. We talked about what it might eat – grass and flies were suggested. Could the spider get grass or flies in the container? We agreed that it wasn't kind to, or respecting, the spider if we kept it in that box forever. Would we like to live in a small box all by ourselves? After we had all had a chance to look at the spider we agreed to release it. The children agreed that outside in our garden would be a good place. After quiet (rest) time the spider in its container was put on a table, so that the children who wanted to observe the spider more closely could. We remembered to keep the container on

The huntsman.

►

the table (not shaking it) and observed the spider moving around. One child commented on the spider's 'nippers'. We then talked about how spiders have fangs.

Wednesday 15 April

During a small group time after morning tea, Robert asked when we were going to let the spider go. We then decided that when we go back outside we will release the spider, which led to a discussion about where we would put the spider in the yard. Responses from the children included the bush, the grass, in a web and in the garden. One child suggested that we put the spider in a jug of water. Asked why we would do that, the child said, 'Cause'. We then talked about the fact that if we put the spider in a jug of water it wouldn't be able to breathe and the spider would die.

Investigating spider books.

When it was time to go outside, we took the spider into the yard and we had to choose where we were going to release the spider. Robert had drawn a map for where we should put the spider. Yasmin, Robert, Gabriel, Oliver and Bella walked around the yard with Catherine (adult) to find a suitable spot to release the spider. Robert suggested that we put it in the garden near the gate. Catherine then opened the container and after approximately 15 seconds the spider walked off the bark and into the garden. The watching children (including another group of children who had been playing outside) were quite eager to see what the spider would do and whether it would eat anything. We watched the spider for five minutes. It climbed onto a plant and curled into a ball. It then became quite difficult to see the spider and the children went to find other areas in which to play.

Source: Paddington Children's Centre

In Example 10.12, the discussion and investigation could have branched off into a myriad of different directions. Some of the key concepts touched upon were life and death, respiration, map drawing, food, respect for living things, feelings, venomous creatures and camouflage. The early childhood educator will influence the direction from here through discussion with the children, provision of further resources and/or documentation of the process so far. Care should be taken at this time to value the children equally with 'facts', as 'a focus on activities often means that professionals pay relatively less attention to other dimensions of the provisions (resources): interactions and relationships' (NSW DoCS, 2002, p. 111).

In contrast, at another early childhood setting, a child brings a plastic wrestling figure to the centre and shows this enthusiastically to the educator on arrival. The educator greets this item with a cursory look of disapproval, utters 'That's interesting' and quickly asks the child to place the toy in his locker until home time. What message is this child receiving about the value of their interest? In comparison to the situation and extended exploration in Example 10.12, the educator in this scenario has presumed that this child's toy has no value. Educators need to stand back and critically examine our attitudes to children's interests. Are some interests accepted and not others, and on what basis? What are our attitudes to children's popular culture interests? Are they included in the program? Why/why not? Reflecting upon our automatic responses to children's interests and ideas will assist us in valuing all children's contributions to the selection and utilisation of resources.

At KU Killarney Heights Preschool, educators include children's popular culture interests in the program and use these interests to extend learning. In Example 10.13 educators share ways they are extending children's interests with families in their preschool news email.

> ## EXAMPLE 10.13
> ### Meaningfulness in children's lives
>
> Children also have an insatiable curiosity for just about everything. It is our job as educators to find out what children's passions are and we can further their understanding and knowledge within a relevant context.
>
> For example: Fairies and Fairy Tales … what have the children been doing to extend experiences?
>
> - Drawing and painting fairies.
> - Google searching and writing the names of the various Disney fairies.
> - Recalling favourite tales … Rapunzel has been a particular favourite due to the popularity of the *Tangled* movie. We have read a few variations of the story of Rapunzel including one where Rapunzel announces quite sensibly that she hopes the next time the handsome prince comes to visit that he will just knock on the door!
> - Creating fairy gardens; inside and outside.
> - Using craft materials to make props and fairies and puppets.
>
> We support the children's experiences in an intentional way by offering space and time for the children to work. We provide materials for children to use. We are always nearby to support children's understanding and social relationships as they play and discover. We act as scribes to write the children's stories and words.
>
> Always remember that while some children are engaged in fairy experiences … others are developing interest elsewhere … there is always something exciting going on.
>
> Source: Jane Pethers and Kylie Kennemore, KU Killarney Heights Preschool, KU Children's Services, 2011

Popular culture icons such as Barbie and Spiderman and the associated texts such as Barbie magazine or Spiderman comics are an important part of many children's lives. For this reason they also have an important place in early childhood settings as they provide links to children's home and community experiences. Acceptance of children's popular culture interests means valuing the social and cultural capital that they bring from home.

When educators put aside their discomfort with popular characters and narratives and explore the learning potential of children's popular culture, there are many reasons for including it in the curriculum. In one setting that included Barbie in the curriculum, children created play scenes for Barbie including Barbie's house, car and caravan. This involved much discussion and negotiation. The addition of children's magazines encouraged children to read, draw and write about their favourite characters in another setting. There are legitimate concerns about the ideologies represented by many popular culture characters and narratives, and concerns about the focus on consumerism in many texts aimed at children. Rather than ignoring or banning popular culture, educators need to recognise it as a source of learning for children and plan experiences that extend this learning to critical thinking.

The ways that texts such as Barbie magazines and advertisements for children's toys are constructed for commercial and ideological purposes can be a focus of critical analysis with children. This could include a focus on the way that gender stereotypes are reproduced, the way that some groups such as Aboriginal and Torres Strait Islander peoples are excluded and the way that advertising texts position us as consumers. For example, educators, children and families can use advertising catalogues to discuss the way that toys aimed at boys emphasise action and aggression and bold colours, while toys aimed at girls are pink, soft and static, and whether this reflects the reality of children's lives.

Are the resources and environment reflecting the everyday lives of children and families?

Resources that stimulate

Educators can support children's explorations and their representations of their understandings in many ways. Some examples are:

- providing resources that stimulate exploration of fabric, history and purpose
- visiting local art galleries and museums
- providing resources that stimulate discussion of shape, colour, texture and form
- surrounding children with a range of art including Indigenous, classical and modern art
- exhibiting children's works with the respect they deserve.

Children's representation of their world will grow beyond our traditional expectation if they are provided with a variety of high-quality art materials, encouraged to share the responsibility of maintaining and caring for these resources, and provided with the time, space and support to explore them.

Artefacts can stimulate children's learning (see below and Example 10.14). The lead-up to this interest in masks was documented by the educator.

EXAMPLE 10.14

Exploring, researching, creating and displaying masks

At morning tea time, the children noticed the mask hanging above the lift door. What is it? Everyone wanted to know. Once identified as a mask this led to many more questions – What kind of mask was it? Where did it come from? How did they make it? Who wears masks and why? And where were we going to find the answers to all these questions?

A. suggested that her mum could take her to the library to get a book about masks. I asked if everyone would like to go to the library on a kindy day and borrow some books on masks. So we set a date for an excursion to the library.

Unfortunately we couldn't get enough grown-ups to come along for a safe excursion but luckily the children at vacation care went to the library and borrowed some books for us. We looked at these books together and got lots of information from the pictures and the teachers reading sections too.

The children began making their own masks using the materials in the drawing/writing centre. To facilitate this we included more materials – round paper pieces, shredded paper and feathers.

Looking at the mask books led to discussion about the different features on a mask. The children identified that many of the masks were like our own faces, having a mouth, two eyes and a nose.

Source: Paddington Children's Centre

Teachers have often been known to provide resources and instruct children on their use. Our current understandings of how children co-construct learning, and the value of investigating and problem solving, encourage us to provide resources and provoke problem solving, rather than provide the solution. The reliance upon adults to 'teach' can undermine the power children may experience through their shared constructing of knowledge.

Provision of a range of resources will stimulate a variety of representations of children's learning. This is clearly evidenced in Example 10.15, which began with a short collaborative story but was extended by the children's interest and careful resourcing by the educators. Pirates were represented through a variety of resources and environments.

EXAMPLE 10.15
Pirate story (by Sun Room children)

Once there were two pirates. They were girls, called Ponka and Eliza. They were driving the car to the beach to look for treasure. They walked along the sand and climbed up to the pirate ship. They sailed to a little island. The boat stopped and started to shake because crocodiles were underneath it. Eliza fell out and one crocodile ate her!

There is buried treasure in the Sun Room. Pirates have been reading treasure maps to find it. These are our stories and treasure maps.

Collaboratively and alone creating a pirate ship.

Creating props for pirate play.

Building our pirate ships indoors.

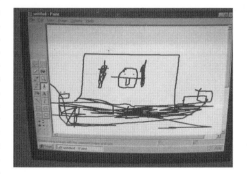

Creating computer images of pirate ships.

Creating pirate flags – the sabre was designed and then made, solving its 'wobbliness'.

Source: Paddington Children's Centre

Resources that promote a strong sense of identity

Resources either invite or isolate children and families from diverse backgrounds. As Derman-Sparks (1989) argues, children are affected as much by what is not seen as by what is seen. Resources should reflect the cultural and language backgrounds as well as family structures of the children and families using the service, plus the diversity of the broader community. It is important that resources invite all children to explore diverse cultures and practices. This is particularly important in settings where children and families are predominantly from the same cultural and language background.

It is essential that resources reflect the everyday lives of children and families rather than focus on exotic differences. See the box below for points to consider when evaluating resources. This means including items such as food packaging in relevant community languages, everyday authentic cooking utensils and eating implements in the dramatic play home area that reflect the cultures of the children, families, educators and local community. It means providing children with 'rich and diverse resources that reflect children's social worlds' (DEEWR, 2009, p. 23), such as everyday clothes from diverse cultures, or different types of hats, shoes and scarves. It is important to remember that when using these resources educators should 'talk with children in respectful ways about similarities and differences in people' (DEEWR, 2009, p. 23).

In the creative arts area, art prints, fabrics, sculptures and masks representing different cultures can affirm children's cultural identity and inspire exploration of new techniques. Similarly the inclusion of music that is relevant to children's families and communities can both support local forms of music and children's cultural heritage and identity (McLachlan, Fleer & Edwards, 2013). McArdle (2012) encourages educators to find out about Indigenous and non-Indigenous artists in the local community and investigate ways to work collaboratively with these artists. She also suggests taking children to visit local galleries or to view online gallery exhibitions.

In the construction area photographs of different types of housing and public buildings can encourage children to consider the diversity within their local context and in the broader community. Literacy materials should incorporate relevant community languages in books, posters, online resources and told stories. Literacy resources that connect to children's everyday lives within their families and communities will be different in each community but may include magazines and newspapers, food packaging and 'junk mail' in languages other than English as well as in English. It is essential to find out about the variety of literacy materials that are found in children's homes and communities and incorporate these into the setting's play resources. Resources such as bus timetables, used bus tickets, restaurant menus and advertising flyers can provide children with authentic and meaningful resources that are relevant to their everyday lives.

Culturally relevant resources support children's sense of identity and wellbeing, connect them to their local context, encourage exploration and creativity and support multimodal communication, as reflected in the EYLF learning outcomes (DEEWR, 2009). Resources that reflect diverse cultures and languages also support children's appreciation of diversity. Art in particular can be an effective way for children to develop understandings of Aboriginal and Torres Strait Islander perspectives, for example the importance of country (McArdle, 2012).

Some points to consider when selecting and evaluating resources

- Do the resources in your early childhood setting or school reflect the diversity of children, their families and the wider community?

- Are there books, puzzles and posters showing people of different physical appearance, cultures and abilities?

- Do the images represent people going about their everyday lives or are they stereotypical images that present purely exotic differences?

- Do the resources reflect people of differing lifestyles and family structures, such as sole parent families, multiracial and multi-ethnic families, and communal families?

- Are there images of people engaged in a variety of occupations, both skilled and unskilled, and resources depicting men and women in non-traditional roles?

- Are cultural, religious and social practices portrayed as universal or as some of the many ways that people engage in everyday practices?

- What values are portrayed in the choice of colours, patterns and images for furnishings and decorations? Are there earthy tones as well as bright primary colours, and patterns and images from a variety of cultural groups?

- Are there displays of artwork, such as textiles, sculpture, pottery and paintings, from a diversity of ethnic and racial groups, depicting both men and women?

- Are there images of people of mixed race and ethnic background, and paints that represent a variety of different skin tones?

- Do dolls reflect the full spectrum of skin tones, rather than just black and white? Are there dolls that are authentic representations of Aboriginal and Torres Strait Islander groups, Pacific Islanders and Vietnamese, as well as Anglo-Celtic groups? Do the dolls represent the main groups present in your centre and in Australia as a whole?

- Is there a variety of music heard by children throughout the day? Do children have the opportunity to move to music with different rhythms, and to sing and listen to songs in a variety of languages?

- Does the literature presented to children come from a variety of sources? Are there some books that are bilingual? Is there environmental print, such as labels, notices and posters, in a number of different scripts?

- Do children have the opportunity to see and hear different language systems, such as Auslan and Braille?

- Is there a selection of materials for children to manipulate and construct, including figures depicting diversity in physical appearance, ethnic group, gender and physical abilities; for example, lotto games, construction sets and block accessories? Do posters depict a variety of homes and living circumstances in urban, rural and remote communities?

Conclusion and reflection

Effective learning environments reflect children's family and community contexts and are inclusive of all children regardless of language, culture or ability. Partnerships between educators, children and families encourage environments that are responsive to the interests and ideas of children and families. Both indoor and outdoor learning environments require careful consideration of resources, including the provision of natural materials and culturally relevant resources and attention to issues of sustainability. Consideration of time and space, as well as relationships and interactions, support the provision of a secure yet flexible program. When educators are flexible and responsive in their planning and interactions they are best able to support and extend children's learning. This requires a balance of planned and spontaneous learning experiences, intentional teaching, reflective evaluations and careful consideration of future planning.

Questions for reflection

1. In what ways is the learning environment:
   - welcoming
   - flexible and secure
   - reflective and supportive of the diversity of children, families and the broader community
   - sustainable and natural
   - showcasing children's current learning and interests?
2. How does the indoor/outdoor environment encourage sustained shared thinking, interactions and collaborative learning?
3. How does the daily schedule/timetable promote small group interactions and collaborative experiences?

Key terms
two-way learning, 356

Online study resources

Visit http://login.cengagebrain.com and use the access code that comes with this book for 12 months access to the student resources for this text.

CourseMate Express

The CourseMate Express website contains a range of resources and study tools for this chapter, including:

- Online video activities
- Online research activities
- A revision quiz
- Matching pair exercises
- A list of key weblinks
- A chapter glossary, flashcards and crossword to help you revise terminology
- and more!

Search me! education

Explore **Search me! education** for articles relevant to this chapter. Fast and convenient, Search me! education is updated daily and provides you with 24-hour access to full text articles from hundreds of scholarly and popular journals, ebooks and newspapers, including *The Australian* and *The New York Times*. Log in to Search me! through http://login.cengage.com and try searching for the following key words:

- inclusion
- environments
- reflection
- projects
- relationships
- interests
- child-centred.

Search tip: **Search me! education** contains information from both local and international sources. To get the greatest number of search results, try using both Australian and American spellings in your searches, e.g. 'globalisation' and 'globalization'; 'organisation' and 'organization'

Recommended resources

Department of Education, Employment and Workforce Relations (DEEWR) 2009, *Belonging, Being and Becoming: The Early Years Learning Framework for Australia*, Commonwealth of Australia, Canberra.

Early Childhood Intervention Inclusion (ECII) 2013, *Participating and Belonging: Inclusion in Practice*, Early Childhood Intervention Inclusion, Malvern Victoria.

Farmer, R & Fasoli, L (eds) 2010, *You're in New Country: Advice for Non-Indigenous Early Childhood Mentors Trainers and Teachers*, Commonwealth of Australia, Canberra.

Helm, J & Katz, L 2011, *Young Investigators: The Project Approach in the Early Years*, Teachers College Press, New York.

Key weblinks

Children's Services Central resources, http://www.cscentral.org.au/publications/resources.html
Early Childhood Education (ECE Educate), http://www.educate.ece.govt.nz/learning/curriculumAndLearning/TeWhariki.aspx

Documentary Australia Foundation, http://www.documentaryaustralia.com.au/case_studies/details/30/kanyini
You're in a new country: Advice for non-Indigenous early childhood mentors, trainers and teachers.
http://www.csu.edu.au/special/teach-ec/RESOURCES/PDF/You%27re%20in%20new%20county-low%20res.pdf
ECIA NSW projects, http://www.ecia-nsw.org.au/projects/focus-on-inclusion-projecthttp://www.ecii.org.au/

References

Australian Curriculum and Reporting Authority (ACARA) n.d. *Cross Curriculum Priorities*,
http://www.acara.edu.au/curriculum/cross_curriculum_priorities.html, accessed 15 January 2014

Australian Children's Education and Care Quality Authority (ACECQA) 2013, *Guide to the National Quality Standard*,
http://files.acecqa.gov.au/files/National-Quality-Framework-Resources-Kit/NQF03-Guide-to-NQS-130902.pdf, accessed 15 January 2014.

Campbell, S, Castelino, T, Coady, M, Lawrence, H, Mac Naughton, G, Rolfe, S, Smith, K & Totta, J 2002, 'Our part in peace', *Research in Practice Series*, vol. 9, no. 1, Australian Early Childhood Association, Canberra.

Chard, S 1998/1999/2000/2001, *Project Approach*, http://www.project-approach.com, accessed 15 January 2014.

Davis, J M 2010, 'What is early childhood education for sustainability', in JM Davis (ed) *Young Children and Environment: Early Education for Sustainability*, Cambridge University Press, Sydney, pp. 21–42.

Derman-Sparks, L & The Anti-bias Taskforce 1989, *The Anti-Bias Curriculum: Tools for Empowering Young Children*, National Association for the Education of Young Children, Washington, DC.

Farmer, R & Fasoli, L (eds) 2010, *You're in New Country: Advice for Non-Indigenous Early Childhood Mentors Trainers and Teachers*, Commonwealth of Australia, Canberra, http://eprints.batchelor.edu.au/277/, accessed 15 January 2014

Fleer, M. 2013, *Play in the Early Years*, Cambridge University Press, Melbourne.

Forman, G 1998, 'Ordinary moments, extraordinary possibilities', in V Fu, A Stremmel & L Hill (eds), *Teaching and Learning: Collaborative Exploration of the Reggio Emilia Approach*, Pearson Education, Upper Saddle River, NJ.

Forman, G, Hall, E & Berglund, K 2001, 'The power of ordinary moments', *Child Care Information Exchange*, no. 141, pp. 52–5.

Fu, V, Stremmel, A & Hill, L (eds) 2002, *Teaching and Learning: Collaborative Exploration of the Reggio Emilia Approach*, Pearson Education, Upper Saddle River, NJ.

Gandini, L 1993, 'Educational caring spaces', in C Edwards, L Gandini & G Forman (eds), *The Hundred Languages of Children*, Ablex, NJ, pp. 135–49.

Gandini, L 2002, 'The story and foundation of the Reggio Emilia approach', in V Fu, A Stremmel & L Hill (eds), *Teaching and Learning: Collaborative Exploration of the Reggio Emilia Approach*, Pearson Education, Upper Saddle River, NJ, pp. 13–21.

Greenman, J & Stonehouse, A 1997, *Prime Times: A handbook for Excellence in Infant and Toddler Programs*, Addison Wesley Longman, Melbourne.

Helm, J, Beneke S & Steinheimer, K 2007, *Windows on Learning: Documenting Young Children's Work*, Teachers College Press, New York.

Helm, J & Katz, L 2011, *Young Investigators: The Project Approach in the Early Years*, 2nd edn., Teachers College Press, New York.

Katz, L & Chard, S 1989/2000, *Engaging Children's Minds: The Project Approach*, Ablex, Stamford, CT.

Lifeline Community Care Qld 2010, *Journeys of Inclusion*, Lifeline Community Care QLD, Gold Coast, Queensland.

McArdle, F 2012, 'The visual arts: Ways of seeing', in S. Wright (ed), *Children, Meaning Making and the Arts*, 2nd edn., Pearson, Frenches Forest, NSW, pp. 30–56.

McLachlan, C, Fleer, M & Edwards, S 2013, *Early Childhood Curriculum*, 2nd edn., Cambridge University Press, Melbourne.

New South Wales Department of Community Services (NSW DoCS) 2002, *New South Wales Curriculum Framework for Children's Services: The Practice of Relationships, Essential Provisions for Children's Services*, NSW DoCS, Sydney.

New Zealand Ministry of Education 1996, *Te Whāriki: He Whāriki Matauranga monga Mokopuna o Aotearoa – Early Childhood Curriculum*, Learning Media Limited, Wellington.

O'Connor, A & Diggins, C 2002, *On Reflection: Reflective Practice for Early Childhood Educators*, Open Mind Publishing, Lower Hutt, New Zealand.

Patterson, C & Fleet, A 2003, 'Meaningful planning: Rethinking teaching and learning relationships', *Research in Practice Series*, vol. 10, no. 1, Australian Early Childhood Association, Canberra.

Rogoff, B 2003, *The Cultural Nature of Human Development*, Oxford University Press, Oxford.

Shafer, A 2002, 'Ordinary moments, extraordinary possibilities', in V Fu, A Stremmel & L Hill (eds), *Teaching and Learning: Collaborative Exploration of the Reggio Emilia Approach*, Pearson Education, Upper Saddle River, NJ, pp. 183–96.

Siraj-Blatchford, I 2009, 'Quality teaching in the early years', in A Anning, J Cullen & M Fleer (eds), *Early Childhood Education: Society and Culture*, 2nd edn., Sage, London, pp. 147–57.

Siraj-Blatchford, I, & Sylva, K 2004, 'Researching pedagogy in English preschools', *British Educational Research Journal*, vol. 30 no. 5, pp. 713–30.

Sylva, K, Melhuish, E, Sammons, P, Siraj-Blatchford, I, & Taggart, B, 2010, *Early Childhood Matters: Evidence from the Effective Pre-school and Primary Education Project*, Routledge, London.

Sylva, K, Melhuish, E, Sammons, P, Siraj-Blatchford, I & Taggart, B 2004, *The Effective Provision of Pre-school Education [EPPE] Project: A Longitudinal Study Funded by the DfES 1997–2004*, UK.

Thomas, P & Lockwood, V 2003, 'Relax! … Chill-out techniques for kids and carers', *Rattler*, no. 66, Winter, pp. 8–11.

Ward, K 2011, *Living Curriculum: A Natural Wonder: Enhancing the Ways in Which Early Childhood Educators Scaffold Young Children's Learning About the Environment by Using Self-generated Creative Arts Experiences as a Core Component of the Early Childhood Program.* (Doctor of Philosophy Multi Media), University of Western Sydney, Sydney.

Ward, K, 2013, 'Creative arts-based pedagogies in early childhood Education for Sustainability (EfS): Challenges and possibilities', *Journal of Environmental Education*, vol. 29, no. 2, pp. 165–181.

Wilson, R 1996, 'Starting early: Environmental education during the early childhood years', *ERIC Digest*, ED402147.

CHAPTER ELEVEN

JOURNEYS OF CHANGE

Chapter learning focus

This chapter will investigate:

- professional continuums of change
- organisational culture and change
- leadership and change
- faces of change
- frameworks for change
- evaluating and modifying change.

Introduction

Change is a natural and necessary phenomenon, and one of the few certainties in all aspects of human life.

J Rodd, *Leadership in Early Childhood*, Ch. 10, © 2013 Allen and Unwin.

The early childhood profession in Australia has been on a continuum of change for many years. The publication of the Australian Government's *National Early Childhood Development Strategy, Investing in the Early Years* (COAG, 2009) commenced the most significant change for the early childhood profession since the 1980s.

In recent years this strategy has resulted in the development of the *Early Childhood National Quality Framework* incorporating the *National Quality Standard*, *Belonging, Being and Becoming: The Early Years Learning Framework for Australia* (EYLF) and the *Outside School Hours Care My Time, Our Place – Framework for School Aged Care in Australia*. Within a similar timeframe, the Australian Curriculum is being developed and implemented for the first year of school (Foundation) to Year 10.

This chapter explores the dynamic nature of early childhood education historically, culturally and within the current reform agenda through the stories and reflections of early childhood educators, managers and advocates. It does this in recognition that:

> Reflective practice is a form of ongoing learning that involves engaging with questions of philosophy, ethics and practice. Its intention is to gather information and gain insights that support, inform and enrich decision making about children's wellbeing and development.
>
> As professionals, educators examine what happens in their settings and reflect on what they might change. Critical reflection involves closely examining all aspects of events and experiences from different perspectives.

DEEWR, 2010, p. 11

Professional continuums of change

> Early childhood (education) continues to experience acute and chronic change where pressures for rapid and extensive adaptation, innovation and transformation have occurred over an extended period of time.
>
> J Rodd, *Leadership in Early Childhood*, Ch. 10, © 2013 Allen and Unwin.

Each educator's journey within this environment of change is unique, reflecting the diversity within the early childhood profession. The following interviews document the personal journeys of two educators and their unique settings, perspectives and experiences.

In Example 11.1, Tonia Godhard shares her experiences and opinions on change within the profession. Tonia is a Member of the Order of Australia, appointed by the NSW Minister for Education to the Australian Children's and Education and Care Quality Authority (ACECQA) board, an early childhood consultant and advocate. Tonia's experience spans teaching, directing, academic and senior roles in a range of community based children's services.

EXAMPLE 11.1
Reflections on the early childhood profession

Tonia Godhard

What have been the most significant high-level policy changes during your career?

When I graduated I didn't know anything about broader policy issues. I was busy focusing on learning and teaching. I found myself suddenly responsible for working with children and families five days a week. The 'suitcase of tricks', as it was called for short practicums, is quite different to what is required when you start teaching full-time.

I don't remember hearing about any regulations when I graduated but was lucky enough to represent New South Wales overseas at a conference in London where I was introduced to international policy issues. On my return I attended the Australian Preschool Association meetings; too frightened to open my mouth, I listened and learned.

Australian early childhood settings were purely regulations-based until the introduction of the National Childcare Accreditation Council's National Quality Improvement System (QIAS), informed by the United States of America's National Association for the Education of Young Children (NAEYC) voluntary accreditation system. Until then there was a compliance approach to early childhood settings and early childhood professionals had considerable autonomy around curriculum decisions.

Although the profession has always recognised the importance of education in the early years, it is only now with the brain research and a new national curriculum that early childhood programs are finally being recognised by governments as educational. There is still not the recognition for the early childhood professional. For example, poor remuneration and conditions remain. However, this professional recognition cannot be achieved by the early childhood profession acting alone. There must be some alignment of government policy, as well as union involvement and working together with others to achieve change for the better.

Having curricula and nationally consistent standards and regulations including the *Early Years Learning Framework* (EYLF) and *My Time Our Place* is a beginning. The Council of Australian

Governments (COAG) tried for many years to implement consistency in staffing standards without success. There still remain some services that are out of scope.

A lack of professional development to accompany the launch of the *Early Years Learning Framework* has made this significant change more challenging for the profession. This has improved in the last year or so and, of course, requires a significant amount of government resources.

What impact have these changes had upon the early childhood profession?

The introduction of such significant and rapid change has had an impact upon advocacy in the profession. Early childhood professionals are working harder to manage the changes at a service level and simply do not have the *time* for a commitment to advocacy outside their service.

There are always unintentional consequences that require advocacy for the profession. For example, with the introduction of new legislation requiring a Certified Supervisor at all times in each service resulted in the jurisdictions drowning in applications as everyone applied to be a Certified Supervisor. Another distraction was the requirement for all services to advise the regulators of all critical incidents when the definition of such incidents lacked clarity. The change to the *National Quality Standard*, with its required changes to staffing standards, including a changed or new rating system, were, of course, huge.

The early childhood sector has been working *very* hard to implement not only the new *National Quality Standard* but also other changes such as those required for Fair Work Australia and child protection.

The professional commitment and passion for early childhood is remarkable and professionals have risen to the occasion and have not left the profession in huge numbers as some predicted.

It is important that advocacy around the early childhood political agenda is not lost in the implementation phase of the *National Quality Standard*.

What do you believe are the greatest challenges facing experienced early childhood educators in prior-to-school settings?

Tonia identified several challenges:

- Quality Area 1 of the *National Quality Standard* is the area where the Australian Children's Education and Care Quality Authority (ACECQA) Snapshot Reports are currently showing improvement is required. It is important to acknowledge that there is no one right way to implement the national curriculum and *National Quality Standards*. The documents provide a context to work within but having outcomes and pedagogical principles and practices set down in the *Early Years Learning Framework* such as intentional teaching, assessment, reflective practice – to name just a few – are important in giving a focus to teaching and learning in addition to care. However, to enable quality improvement people need professional development.

- Learning to implement the *National Quality Standard* as a reflective practitioner is presenting a challenge for many educators. Many practitioners are expressing anxiety about the expectations of what is required in a Quality Improvement Plan and documentation of children's development and learning.

- Professionals recognising their own expertise and being able to articulate what they have done with confidence in their own knowledge and understanding is also a challenge.

- Strategic review of the *National Quality Standard* is also important. Voices from the sector need to be heard in order to articulate some of the implementation challenges and to ensure the focus in any change gives priority to the impacts on children and the provision of high quality services for them and their families.

- Recruitment and having a choice of staff. This challenge is a direct result of low remuneration and poor working conditions that need to change.
- There is also a need for early childhood educational leaders in all services.
- The final challenge is the acknowledgement of the professional standing of early childhood educators through teacher registration and professional standards.

What advice would you offer to new graduates entering the early childhood profession today?

- Enjoy working with children and families!
- Feel good about working in a team with other reflective practitioners.
- Maintain your professional development and take up all the opportunities you can.
- Advocate in your service first and later in the wider profession.
- Network with others through professional development or informal meetings – this is especially important when you are working in a small or isolated service.
- Seek out a mentor.
- Maintain balance in your life. You can't be a great practitioner without balance.

Source: Tonia Godhard AM, early childhood educator and advocate, 2013

Tonia's journey of change spans the many significant changes in the early childhood profession. Tonia remains a strong advocate for young children and works to raise the quality of services for children and their families.

Example 11.2 from MacDonnell Shire Council Children's Services (the Shire) provides an example of change within a remote Aboriginal context.

The MacDonnell Shire manages 10 centres in Aboriginal communities (including both Budget Based Children's Services and Outside School Hours Care services) across the bottom third of the Northern Territory – an area which is roughly the size of Victoria. The Shire is taking a strategic, proactive approach to the implementation of the *National Quality Framework* as they recognise the importance of qualified early childhood educators who can mentor and support training for local Aboriginal educators to work towards 'closing the gap'.

Belonging, Being and Becoming: The Early Years Learning Framework for Australia and *My Time, Our Place* have a natural synergy with the Central Australian environment. Here, everything important to community members relates to belonging, being and becoming.

The following interview with Margaret Harrison, the Manager of Children's Services, MacDonnell Shire Council, provides insight into a proactive approach to the continuum of change in early childhood education and care from a remote Central Australian perspective.

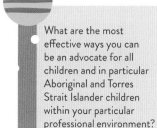

What are the most effective ways you can be an advocate for all children and in particular Aboriginal and Torres Strait Islander children within your particular professional environment?

EXAMPLE 11.2
A Central Australian reflection on the early childhood profession

How has the national early childhood agenda and implementation of the *National Quality Standard* **and curriculum frameworks (***Early Years Learning Framework* **and** *My Time, Our Place***) impacted service delivery in remote Aboriginal communities in Central Australia?**

We have needed to look at the frameworks in a very different light to other services. Positively, we have found that a lot of what we already do relates well to the *Early Years Learning Framework.* The curriculum frameworks are flexible and open-ended enough to relate to all environments and can be adapted for many different contexts. For example, children and families going on cultural bush trips or engaging with elders in art programs strongly supports the *Early Years Learning Framework* Learning Outcome 1: Children have a strong sense of identity.

Central Australian early childhood settings will always be very different to other places. In particular, Indigenous Central Australian services will never look the same as east coast services due to their completely different cultural setting and different environments such as 'not so glossy buildings' (*see* Chapter 10).

How are you preparing for Budget Based Funded Services inclusion in the *National Quality Standard***?**

Firstly we explored the context specific question 'What do we want to do in Early Childhood in MacDonnell Shire?'

To help us on our journey we employed an early childhood consultant to work initially with the head office early childhood coordinators and secondly with the early childhood team leaders based on community. Even though these sessions were independent of each other, the responses were very similar in lots of ways.

We determined that our objective is: 'Creating meaningful and engaging learning for all children, families and educators that reflects local context and community strengths.'

We explored many questions relevant to the context we work within such as:

- Who should be involved? Children, families, community and elders.

- What is important to the community? Family, language, bush tucker, stories, music and art.

- How do we engage? Yarning, sharing information, community involvement, connecting with government and other agencies at all levels.

- What do we bring as early childhood professionals to the team? Our own individual strengths such as creativity, loyalty, energy. We also explored how we could use these strengths.

- Which other professional organisations do we engage with and how? Resource units who are able to work with MacDonnell Shire Council to deliver a program in keeping with our philosophy.

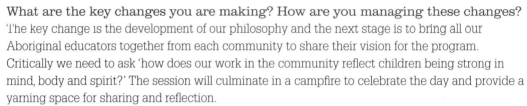

What are the key changes you are making? How are you managing these changes?

The key change is the development of our philosophy and the next stage is to bring all our Aboriginal educators together from each community to share their vision for the program. Critically we need to ask 'how does our work in the community reflect children being strong in mind, body and spirit?' The session will culminate in a campfire to celebrate the day and provide a yarning space for sharing and reflection.

To manage these processes and inevitable changes, we needed to reflect on our management approach. We targeted relationships and support and as a result we:

- decided to utilise specialist skills of head office team across all communities rather than working only with a particular cluster of services. This approach has enabled local Indigenous educators to build stronger relationships with all head office staff resulting in a broader range of expertise available for each educator to tap into.

- decided to step back at strategic points to provide space for local Aboriginal staff to own the program delivery for part of the week, while still offering intermittent and timely support.

- provided training on *My Time, Our Place* for Vacation Care staff and consulted local Aboriginal educators about the most appropriate programs to engage children, families, community and elders. The result was different in every community with some services changing hours of delivery to suit family and community demands, others working closely with the Sport and Recreation team in the community to deliver the program cooperatively.

- employed qualified early childhood educators where possible. We have observed a clear improvement in the quality of programs where a qualified staff member has been successfully recruited and retained.

What are the key challenges to delivery of services in remote locations?

- Recruitment of qualified staff. There is a great need for stronger early childhood programs and more well qualified early childhood teachers in remote communities.

- Staff retention. Time is needed for staff to build relationships with children, families, community and elders. Only then will the program provided reflect the desires and needs of remote Indigenous communities.

- Training local Aboriginal staff. Bringing staff out of their community is not always the answer. Family commitments and lack of transport can often result in non-attendance at centralised training. Clustering communities from similar language groups is one successful strategy. To bring staff together there is a need to have well planned transport solutions that enable remote services to attend.

- Distance. There are challenges of high freight charges for delivery of goods such as food, educational resources, furniture etc. Incidental teaching moments are by necessity more innovative when resources are not at your fingertips, for example where there are no other early childhood educators in the community, no library, no Internet or phone.

- Communication. Frequent telephone failure, exceedingly slow Internet connection, no mobile phone coverage and lengthy travel time (with no phone coverage) can create increased frustration.

What would be your advice to new graduates considering working with Aboriginal communities in Central Australia?

- *Listen* and take time to talk with families.

- Leave east coast ideas behind; don't come with preconceived ideas of what you will do.

- Complete relevant cultural competence training courses.

- Look for the positives. Be generous with your attitudes. Avoid judging from your own values. Ask questions to avoid making assumptions. Ask: What should this service look like for your children and community? One community stated that the program should take the children to the river with the elders.

- What resources are appropriate? In one community I asked if we should buy coolamons. The response was – we don't want that old stuff! A common request from all the communities is – keep our culture and language strong and sing our songs.
- Find a cultural mentor – someone you can ask for cultural advice.

Source: Margaret Harrison, Manager Children's Services MacDonnell Shire Council, 2013

As evidenced in the two examples above, the changes demanded by the implementation of the *National Quality Framework* will continue to have a significant impact upon early childhood service delivery across Australia.

Reflecting on and debating our practices in this time of change is one of our roles as advocates for children.

Organisational culture and change

The changes described above have both challenged and reaffirmed the practices and adaptability of the early childhood profession. They have also prompted organisations to reflect upon and define what makes their organisation unique. When leaders and teams understand their organisation's culture, they are starting from a solid base for successful change management.

Organisational culture refers to the basic assumptions, shared beliefs and orientations that emerge to unite members of a group (Schein, 2004, cited in Jorde Bloom, 2005, p. 6) and which influence how educators, families and children respond to changes.

In Example 11.3, Jenny Green, an early childhood educator and manager, reflects upon her understanding of organisational culture in early childhood settings.

Organisational culture

The basic assumptions, shared beliefs and orientations that emerge to unite members of a group.

CourseMateExpress

Online Example 11.1 'Transitions and changes within an early childhood setting in response to community needs' is available on CourseMate.

► ## EXAMPLE 11.3
Reflection on organisational culture in early childhood settings

I began working with the concept, or idea, of a centre culture, many years ago, as a means of maintaining the practice, feel and 'uniqueness' of a child care centre where I was working, in a time when we were experiencing change. To support this idea of a 'centre culture' I wrote a statement, or a description, of what were the elements or areas that I thought defined the culture of the centre. Many years later, as part of my post-graduate course, I studied the subject Educational Institutions as Organisations. In this subject, I was formally introduced to the concept and theoretical information of an organisational culture. Here was the theory to support my notion of a centre culture. A number of the definitions of organisational culture were perfect for what I had been trying to do in practice. For example, Deal and Kennedy (1982) define culture as 'the way we do things around here' (cited in Bolman & Deal, 2008, p. 269). Denison (1990) states that 'Culture refers to the underlying values, beliefs and principles that serve as a foundation for an organisation's management system as well as the set of management practices and behaviours that both exemplify and reinforce those basic principles' (cited Clayton, Fisher, Harris and Brown, 2008, p. 29).

Although we talk about the 'context' of our centre, a 'culture', in my thinking, is more inclusive, as it underpins the why and where for of what influences the practices, procedures and provision of learning environments in our service.

Just as centre policies are intended to guide and support decision making, so too can a centre culture. The process of developing and documenting the centre's culture affords the team: opportunity for discussion; learning about colleagues; and all voices to be heard, included and valued. Deal and Kennedy described the culture as the way we do things round here, a fantastic starting point for any team in deciding what the important things are at this centre. In terms of growing a team and their professional skills, small groups or individuals can then be responsible for documenting specific areas of the centre's culture. Because the culture is unique to the centre, the staff own and subsequently have a commitment to maintaining and following its principles.

We have a 'culture' that defines how we work and what we do at our centre, but the documenting of these ideas seems to give the centre credibility and importance and a sense of place in the broader organisation. I enjoy referring to the centre culture when showing families, visitors and students through the service because it is unique to us and has been developed by everyone. The culture defines who we are.

Source: Jenny Green, 2013

Developing a shared vision is an important starting point in defining an organisation's culture and reconceptualising our practice.

Shared vision

The EYLF encourages educators to examine what happens in their settings, why they work the way they do, reflect on current views and theoretical perspectives and decide whether there is some aspect of practice that they might change.

H Barnes, *Critical Reflection as a Tool for Change: Stories About Quality Improvement*, p. 1, © 2013 Early Childhood Australia.

When an early childhood education setting, school or outside school hours care setting develops and clearly articulates their shared values and beliefs, there is often a much stronger incidence of shared behaviours. At times of rapid change, shared understandings and behaviours take on even greater importance for the delivery of consistent programs for children, families and community.

While key individuals may play leading parts, effective change means change in the collective attitudes, behaviours and skills of the many (Turner & Crawford, 1998, p. 69). There is no quick fix – leading change and achieving a **shared vision** involves an investment of careful planning, time and energy (*see* Chapter 5).

There are many and varied pathways to developing a shared vision. Deering (2006, p. 41) suggests four key factors that may assist in the development of a shared vision within the staff team: different thinking, challenging current practices, building teams and creating a safe environment.

1. *Different thinking* – Early childhood educators are often so busy managing the day-to-day issues that little time and resources are focused on the long term. A transition to different ways of thinking requires an investment of time and understanding. Potential strategies to inspire educators may include attendance at external professional development sessions (*see* Example 11.4), engaging consultants (*see* Example 11.2) or other service specific strategies (*see* Examples 11.7 and 11.8).

Shared vision

A shared understanding of *what* we do, *why* we do it, *how* we do it and *where* we want to be in the future.

2. *Challenging current practices* – Early childhood educators are often well practised in reflecting on their day-to-day routines. Clearly articulating 'why we do what we do' provides a pathway to enable us to challenge our practice and develop a shared vision for both short and long-term practice. Doing things because 'we've always done it that way' or 'it works' is not a solid rationale. If, however, they have solid theoretical rationale behind their short and long-term practices and these can be articulated within an early childhood framework, these practices will be worth maintaining. Constant reflection on 'why' educators do things and taking care not to 'throw the baby out with the bathwater' will support an informed approach to practice and change (*see* Example 11.4).

3. *Building teams* – Early childhood education and care services often have a continuous turnover of educators as well as families and children. Successful settings manage this turnover skilfully and establish cohesive, but not necessarily homogenous, teams. Leaders should always be mindful of the understandable, but avoidable, tendency to employ people who think, behave and have similar life experience to themselves. Active selection of team members with a diversity of opinions and experience can positively challenge current team practice and build a richer shared vision for the long term.

   Sharing the setting/school philosophy and vision for the future with prospective employees provides the opportunity to reflect on the skills and experience of prospective educators and ask whether they will complement and positively challenge the mindset and cohesion of the team.

4. *Creating a safe environment* – Setting the scene for individuals to express their ideas without fear of judgement is also critical to the process of visioning. When educators are encouraged to offer any idea, including hopes and concerns, without fear of someone invalidating their contribution, they will contribute meaningfully to the setting. Skilful leaders will facilitate free expression of thoughts, fears and vision, listening to and acknowledging each individual within the team (*see* Example 11.5 and Example 11.7).

> Who are the key stakeholders to be engaged in the development of a shared vision for your setting?

In Example 11.4 staff at Ballina Early Intervention describe how they achieved a shared vision and planned for change by undertaking a strategic planning exercise.

EXAMPLE 11.4
Strategic planning in action: an experience in an Early Intervention service

How has the National Early Childhood agenda impacted service delivery in Early Intervention?

Early Childhood Intervention is one of the early childhood services currently not covered by the *Early Years Learning Framework* and *National Quality Standard*. However, as Early Intervention services are part of the early childhood education field and often work with inclusive children's services, Ballina Early Intervention has worked to incorporate the *Early Years Learning Framework* into its practices.

So, in 2011 staff decided it was time to review the services offered to children and families in line with changes in early childhood services and education. In addition to the changes occurring in mainstream settings, there has been a move towards inclusion and inclusive practice both as a reflection of policy and funding changes, as well as research in the early intervention field.

How are you preparing for inclusion and managing change?

Inspired by attending Tim Moore's keynote *Rethinking Early Childhood Intervention Services: Implications for policy and practice* at the Early Childhood Intervention Australia conference in

October 2012 (Moore, 2012), staff returned to our service and started to explore how we could change our current practices to reflect these changes in early childhood intervention and the broader field.

As part of an organisation which develops a strategic plan and reviews this annually, this was our first step in making changes. The organisation has a philosophy, so Ballina Early Intervention undertook a situational analysis, along with other sections of the organisation. This process was a worthwhile experience as it provided a broader picture of our service as part of the larger organisation and also encouraged us to explore how we might reflect inclusive practices and change in early intervention. Our situational analysis showed us that while we had much potential within the service, we were not developing this effectively. This was due to constraints of funding and strategies that had not been evaluated in light of changes in research but had become embedded in our practice. As a result of our situational analysis we developed goals for change for the following year.

What are the key changes that have resulted from this process?

Our first goal focused on developing a mission statement that was reflective of the overall organisation's philosophy. Staff worked together to explore what our purpose as an early intervention service was as we felt that this was the first step before we could make any changes to our practice. After much reflection, we developed the following Mission statement:

It is the mission of Ballina Early Intervention to:

- Provide an educational service to maximise the development and learning of each child
- Support families in accessing appropriate support and specialist services
- Provide family friendly experiences and opportunities to support the child's everyday learning environments
- Strengthen the capacity of other early childhood services in Ballina Shire to meet the needs of children through inclusive programs.

Having a clear purpose supported the team, including families, to move towards more effective practice. Further goals were established which focused on re-evaluating Ballina Early Intervention service direction; reviewing our resource profile, including human resources; providing a clearer focus with our transition to school programs; considering how our documentation requirements could reflect inclusion, family and other stakeholder participation, and elements of the *Early Years Learning Framework*; monitoring new funding policy, including self managed funding; and, reviewing the physical environment to better meet the needs of staff, families and children.

As a result of this process, Ballina Early Intervention has made many changes to practice. These include having fewer centre-based groups at Ballina Early Intervention, instead working with children and supporting early childhood educators in inclusive mainstream settings; providing more family support and discussions while children attend centre-based groups; working more closely with Aboriginal and Torres Strait Islander families by going into the community rather than the focus being on families coming to us; drawing on the strengths of staff within our service, as well as consultant specialists such as therapists and community agencies; working more closely with the school community and families to support the transition to school process; providing professional development for early childhood educators in our region; redeveloping all our documentation to reflect our current approaches; and reorganising our environment, in negotiation with other services within the organisation, to improve the staff work environment and reflect the role of families and children within our service.

What are the key challenges to the delivery of services?

Funding, funding and less funding! There have been challenges to change, particularly in relation to government funding and lack of time. Funding is always limited in early intervention, which leads us to try and balance financial constraints with providing a high quality service to families and the community. All Ballina Early Intervention staff are part time and we have to be constantly monitoring costs within the service. Currently, a very small fee is charged to families, and as there is no subsidy for fees for this type of service, many families have difficulty paying this small fee. Many families have other issues to work through including dealing with emotions after gaining a diagnosis for their child, sitting on long waiting lists for services, and working through the maze of services and agencies accessible in the community. Being situated in a rural area often means limited or no services are available and families have to travel to cities. Another challenge is the growing trend for self managed funding, which in principle is positive, but without further support for families this becomes another part of the maze, creates more administration and increases the need to charge more for services.

What have been the benefits for your service from working towards change through a strategic planning process?

Those participating in working through the strategic planning process and implementing change found the process invaluable in identifying challenges and constraints as well as potential. The process involved stakeholders and encouraged participation in decision making throughout the changes, which has meant that the service is now more dynamic and can make changes to reflect community and policy change. It has made evaluation of the service much more manageable and regular now that a process is in place that stakeholders feel a part of each year.

There are always challenges but using a proactive approach to planning continues to support our service through changes.

Source: Ballina Early Intervention (a service of Rainbow Children's Centre Inc.), a community managed service in North Coast NSW, 2013

Adaptive culture

The ability of the organisation to implement change while maintaining shared values and beliefs will be dependent upon the organisation's adaptability.

> **Adaptive cultures** are those which help an organisation to anticipate and respond to environmental change. They encourage leadership, risk-taking, initiative, innovation, problem identification and problem solving. This adaptive perspective does not emphasise change in any particular direction.

Managing People and Organisations, p.12, Australian Graduate School of Management, © 2010 Australian School of Business.

Adaptive cultures

Help an organisation to anticipate and respond to environmental change. They encourage leadership, risk-taking, initiative, innovation, problem identification and problem solving.

It is therefore important that shared behaviours and outcomes are challenged to reflect current pedagogies and avoid perpetuating inappropriate organisational culture. Active and adaptive leadership (Sachs, 2003) enables educators to take the forms of critical action necessary to lead teams of professionals in a range of service types and to deliver culturally responsive, high quality programs to children and families (Skatebol & Arthur, 2014).

In Example 11.5, Lindy Farrant, an early childhood educator and the Director of Parkes Early Childhood Centre (PECC), reflects upon change and the adaptive organisational culture of a regional community-based service providing long day care, preschool and occasional care.

> **EXAMPLE 11.5**
> Adaptive organisational culture

Lindy Farrant

The approach that our service adopts to change is a reflection of a rich interplay of many factors including:

- our centre philosophy
- the long history of our service as a not-for-profit, community based centre (Parkes Early Childhood Centre opened in 1954)
- our location in Central Western NSW
- the size of our centre – 86 place multipurpose centre with NSW State Government funded preschool and occasional care places and Commonwealth funded Long Day Care places
- inclusion programs within all funded program areas
- collaborative relationships between community, families, management committee, teachers, educators and children
- a rich diversity of experiences, skills, knowledge and expectations that each individual brings to our setting.

We employ a collaborative 'ground up' approach to change, with our centre philosophy providing the framework for all decision making. Our centre culture is one which aims to embrace change, while retaining tried and true best practice. The provision of best practice for each child is our focal point.

PECC Philosophy: 'At all times, our decisions in relation to the entire operation of our centre will be in the best interests of all children'.

A key influence on the culture of our organisation is low staff turn-over. Our staff have a strong sense of belonging and pride in our centre, resulting in our retaining a significant number of very experienced and qualified employees. This allows us to simultaneously focus on the processes that drive and maintain positive change through planning, implementation and evaluation of goals while ensuring that we continue to provide appropriate support and mentoring for our newer, less experienced teachers and educators.

Low staff turn-over has been one of the significant factors contributing to our centre attaining an 'Exceeding' rating for all seven quality areas in the Assessment and Rating process under the *National Quality Framework*. This stability has enabled the consistent implementation of the *PECC Philosophy: 'PECC is committed to promoting a strong sense of physical & psychological well being leading to relationships based on trust, optimism, confidence, respect & engagement'*.

The *National Quality Framework*, Standards, Regulations and the *Early Years Learning Framework* provide us with a clear framework for ongoing, positive change. Our Quality Improvement Plan (QIP) is developed and reviewed in collaboration with families, committee, teachers and educators and is written as a very practical document that allows us to track and record our progress towards planned change. *PECC Philosophy: 'PECC is directed and motivated by the National Quality Framework (NQF) and all other legislation and guidelines supporting best practice in Early Childhood'*.

Leadership is a critical element which supports the management of change at our centre. PECC Philosophy states, 'PECC is committed to the ongoing development of each individual's leadership skills which inspires and empowers others'. The identification of areas of interest and talents of teachers and educators within our team can result in individuals taking on a leadership role for a particular focus area which in turn supports our Quality Improvement Plan (QIP). For example: a teacher has assumed a leadership role to support and in-service our team to meet one of QIP goals – to embed Wiradjuri culture and language into our curriculum. This is being achieved by the leader building community connections between our centre and key members of our local Aboriginal community, collecting teaching resources, accessing journal articles and presenting information at monthly staff meetings etc. The management committee supports this process through the annual budget allocation for in-service. PECC QIP – Quality Area 1, Element 1.1.2 Each child's current knowledge, ideas, culture, abilities and interests are the foundation of the program.

To successfully anticipate and respond to change we embrace an attitude that is open, welcoming and confident about the process of change. As part of this process, we are constantly updating our knowledge and skills. We find that annual appraisals support staff to reflect on their perceived strengths and needs; appraisals are not used as a disciplinary process, but identify areas of interest for professional growth. Professional development helps us to embrace change as a cohesive team through the ongoing growth of our individual skills and knowledge.

Our shared values, beliefs and behaviour continue to strengthen over time. Our centre culture recognises the diversity of individual abilities and their skills to assimilate knowledge. The Director's role is to guide and support the different members of the group with a flexible leadership style that facilitates supports and encourages growth and a willingness to step outside areas of comfort through planned risk taking. Risk taking needs a safe and supportive environment where individuals are confident to try new approaches within trusting and respectful relationships.

Bit by bit, trusting and respectful relationships are built through our everyday interactions, with simple steps such as greeting each other, working towards active listening, sharing personal responses to situations etc. Some individuals embrace change and enthusiastically take hold of new ideas to explore possibilities. Others are keen to observe the processes and outcomes and then contribute to the detail required to further embed the change. As a team managing change we are on the same pathway, just at different points, as we focus on enhancing our strengths to benefit all children.

Source: Lindy Farrant, Director, Parkes Early Childhood Centre, 2013

Within the professional continuum of change, and particularly in the current rapid change climate, every educator within an early childhood setting is a leader. As such, there is a responsibility to engage in reciprocal leadership and two-way learning. This involves both leading and following, learning from and sharing knowledge with, influencing and being influenced by colleagues, children, families and community.

Leadership and change

Leading change is a core role and function for early childhood leaders who are committed to the continuing provision of quality early childhood services.

J Rodd, *Leadership in Early Childhood*, Ch. 10, © 2013 Allen and Unwin.

A leader's attitude has the potential to determine an organisation's appetite for change and risk; that is, how much change and risk the organisation willingly accepts. When there is a mismatch between the leader's appetite for change and that of their team, children or families,

there is increased potential of a stressful change environment. A leader who is overenthusiastic and initiates unilateral change may negatively influence an organisation's change culture. For example, following attendance at a professional development session a leader enthusiastically announces an immediate, innovative change to the delivery of the educational program.

Some of the team may willingly embrace this change while others may react with negativity. A negative response may trigger complaints to coworkers, undermining staff morale and family confidence. They may vent their frustration, anxiety or anger by refusing to participate in the change and performing below their ability. This may result in anxious and stressed educators self-selecting out of the workplace.

Conversely, a leader who is reluctant to initiate change may also negatively influence an organisation's change culture. By actively resisting or deferring decisions for change, the leader may unconsciously develop a change and risk-averse organisational culture where reflection and innovation are discouraged. This may result in proactive and enthusiastic employees becoming frustrated and self-selecting out of the workplace.

In either situation, the resultant disruption to team relationships and the wellbeing, education and care of the children may have been improved by mindful leadership. The astute and mindful leader listens to, acknowledges and accommodates each individual team member's feelings and attitudes to change. The reward will be more focused, reflective and successful change experiences.

Mindfulness

Heightened stress responses at times of change are not uncommon. Any discussion of change can provoke a variety of individual responses from each member of a team.

Leaders are encouraged to reflect upon their own attitudes, be mindful of the impact of their behaviour and be flexible and understanding in their approach to change. This is possible even when leaders have their own automatic, early-learned dysfunctional responses to change. By allowing themselves and their colleagues space to reflect on, and be aware of, their emotional responses to change, a positive and shared journey of change is possible; that is, how they are thinking and physically reacting to stress related to change.

Responses are often automatic and reflective of past experiences – good and bad. Individuals learn how to respond to stressful situations by what worked for them very early in life and these learned responses might become automatic. In many circumstances these behaviours can be effective. However, what the individual learns in a situation that is not positive and functional may result in automatic responses that become problematic in later life. This collection of experiences with learned responses will be influenced by personal circumstances and personal attributes and will determine their desire to support and engage in change.

Mindfulness

The mind is aware *that* it is thinking, *that* it is feeling, *that* it is sensing (Chaskalson, 2011).

Knowledge of our cognitive processes (**mindfulness**) – thinking about how we are thinking – enables us to gain a higher level of awareness of how we personally respond to change and stress. Chaskalson (2011) describes this process as when the mind is 'aware *that* it is thinking, *that* it is feeling, *that* it is sensing'.

Staying in the moment and reflecting upon our own thoughts can help resist the immediate urge to judge other's automatic responses to change. This can enable us to offer productive support to others, including children, families and educators.

In Example 11.6 Bronnie Dean shares her experience of mindful practice as a tool for leadership.

EXAMPLE 11.6
Mindful leadership in an early childhood setting

My career began 11 years ago when as a parent I participated in group times at Parkes Early Childhood Centre. This led to casual work, then work with additional needs children and ultimately, permanent employment as a Child Care Worker. I received my Diploma mostly through Recognition of Prior Learning and completing some modules at TAFE. As part of an Early Workforce Capacity program, I will graduate with my Bachelor of Teaching (Early Childhood) this year. A celebration as I enter my 50th year!

I am currently the leader in the Gumnut Room (birth–2.5-year-olds) having worked with this age group for 7 years. I still love working with the youngest children even though it can be very hectic.

I was lucky enough to attend a workshop about Mindfulness Based Stress Reduction before I commenced studying my Bachelor of Teaching (Early Childhood) (*see* http://www.csu.edu.au/special/teach-ec > Wellness & Wellbeing).

I find that if you allow yourself to remain in a hectic space, the children's anxiety escalates. Exhausting, mind-racing anxiety is something we don't need. At this point I try to be mindful of what is happening, acknowledge and accept my self-talk and remind myself and colleagues that it's not such a bad day. The resultant reduction in my anxiety leads to a reduction in the children's anxiety levels too.

I am lucky to have a supportive workplace where we give each other lots of emotional support as well as a Director who will simply ask me – 'Are you breathing up high or from the bottom of your tummy?' This prompts me when my mind starts to race away to internally say 'stop', draw a big breath and take the time to calmly reflect on my thoughts.

As the room leader, I also feel a responsibility to help my colleagues manage their stress levels. I will often remind them to reflect on 'where are you in this moment'. As part of one of our room meetings, I asked the team if there was anything they were worried about, for example one colleague expressed concern about the possibility of being relocated to work in another room next year. I could sense considerable anxiety and reminded her to be present, that she was here right now, sitting in a chair right next to me and she didn't need to go to that worrying place right now.

Sometimes I find a gentle hand on the shoulder assists them to be mindful, tune into the day and be present in the room and with the children. A colleague who was feeling particularly anxious the other day said 'I might need you to do that a few times today'.

Sometimes my own immediate reaction to change is anxiety. I try to stop and think about how I'm feeling, think about my anxiety as a 'blob' rather than a fixed shape and then allow it to change as needed. I then reflect on where this change might take the playroom and work from there.

I have found the practice of mindfulness very helpful in both my personal and professional life and one of my goals this year is to find out a lot more by reading and attending further training. I really believe it works!

Source: Bronnie Dean, Gumnut Room Leader, Parkes Early Childhood Centre, 2013

CourseMateExpress

Online Example 11.2 'Working with unhelpful thoughts' is available on CourseMate.

Acknowledging and naming unhelpful thoughts that hinder the capacity for change allows educators and families to be more open to change and to consciously guide their reactions for creative results. Chakalson (2011) argues that one of the potential benefits of mindfulness training for change management is increased resilience.

Resilience

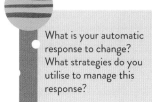

What is your automatic response to change? What strategies do you utilise to manage this response?

Within the current context of change, resilience is a desirable attribute for educators, children, families and communities. Functional organisations demonstrating resilience are in a positive position to predict, embrace and action change.

Resilience is often viewed as our ability to 'bounce back' from a crisis such as excessive and imposed change. Resilience, however, is more than managing crisis or recovering from setbacks; it is also recognising the opportunity or need for change *before* it is imposed or at a crisis point and responding in a timely manner. Trusting others and ourselves to recognise possibilities for change and behaving inclusively will support both individual and team resilience.

Valikangas (2010) challenges educators to think differently about the concept that resilience is purely a 'crisis capability' (Resilience II) and presents an additional definition where resilience is also about 'timely action' (Resilience I).

TABLE 11.1   Conceptions of resilience

RESILIENCE I	RESILIENCE II
The capacity to:	The capacity to:
• Change without first experiencing a crisis • Change without a lot of accompanying trauma • Take action before it is a final necessity	• Recover after experiencing a crisis • Persist in the face of threat; not to yield; tenacity • Survive trauma

Source: L Valikangas, *The Resilient Organization*, Table 2.1, © 2010 McGraw-Hill, USA.

Strategic resilience

The capability to turn threats into opportunities prior to their becoming either (Valikangas, 2010).

Dedicated early childhood educators consistently reflect on pedagogy while looking for opportunities to improve outcomes for children, families and communities. According to the definition provided by Valikangas (2010), this reflects **strategic resilience** as educators demonstrate 'the capability to turn threats into opportunities prior to their becoming either'.

Faces of change

Change has many faces, some slow and gentle, others fast and harsh, some initiated internally, others externally driven. Understanding faces of change raises our awareness and sensitivity to how colleagues, children, families and community can be supported during the change process.

Rodd (2013, Ch. 10) articulates six types of change and potential origins. These are:

1. *Incremental change*, where small changes are introduced slowly and become part of the daily functioning of a setting. This form of change is often carefully planned, introduced and evaluated over time.
2. *Induced change*, which is the result of a conscious decision to implement a change and encompasses changes in people, processes, programs, structures and systems. This type of change can result from new ideas, innovations and research, or as a result of a crisis or change in external influences on the setting.
3. *Routine change*, which is often implemented as part of the daily problem-solving process that occurs in a setting and may mean implementing modifications to daily practice.
4. *Crisis change*, which is often a response to a situation or incident that occurs within a setting. This type of change may result in a quick decision being made by one person due to urgency that does not allow a lengthy process of change to occur.
5. *Innovative change*, which is often the result of creative problem solving that involves many stakeholders within a setting. Ideas and alternatives are explored and a plan of action for changes can be developed. The change is evaluated during the process and modifications may be made to ease the transition of the change.

6. *Transformational change*, which is when an organisation is radically altered at crisis point if it has failed to respond to its demands and often causes stress for those involved. However, if transformational change is viewed as a major shift in philosophy and ideas of children and early childhood practice, which results in a major transformation of the type of setting provided for families and children, then this may be an exciting and positive experience if developed and introduced appropriately.

Frameworks for change

Useful frameworks for managing change involve participants and deepen practice. In this section Prosci ADKAR® Model and action research reflect this focus.

Prosci ADKAR® Model

The **Prosci ADKAR®** (Awareness, Desire, Knowledge, Ability and Reinforcement™) Model was developed by Hiatt (2006). This simple five-element building-block change management framework can be utilised effectively across any organisation. The framework begins with an understanding of change at the individual's level and then extends this understanding to the organisation and community.

Table 11.2 provides an overview of the ADKAR building blocks that constitute a framework

ADKAR

Acronym for 'Awareness, Desire; Knowledge, Ability and Reinforcement'; building blocks for change.

TABLE 11.2   The PROSCI ADKAR Model.

ADKAR® ELEMENTS	FACTORS INFLUENCING SUCCESS
Awareness of the need for change	• A person's view of the current state • How a person perceives problems • Credibility of the sender of awareness messages • Circulation of misinformation or rumors • Contestability of the reasons for change
Desire to support and participate in the change	• The nature of the change (what change is and how it will impact each person) • The organizational or environmental context for the change (his or her perception of the organization or environment that is subject for change) • Each individual person's situation • What motivates a person (those intrinsic motivators that are unique to an individual)
Knowledge of how to change	• The current knowledge base of an individual • The capability of this person to gain additional knowledge • Resources available for education and training • Access to or existence of the required knowledge
Ability to implement required skills and behavior	• Psychological blocks • Physical capabilities • Intellectual capability • The time available to develop the needed skills • The availability to support the development of new abilities
Reinforcement to sustain the change	• The degree to which reinforcement is meaningful and specific to the person impacted by the change • The association of the reinforcement with actual demonstrated progress or accomplishment • The absence of negative consequences • An accountability system that creates an ongoing mechanism to reinforce the change

Source: PROSCI, *A Model for Individual Change*, © 2014 Prosci Inc. http://www.prosci.com/adkar-model/overview-3/

reflections within this chapter and may be adapted to suit different types of change and different environments, including early childhood settings.

The ADKAR elements are discussed below using the example of the implementation of a professional development program at Paddington Children's Centre in Sydney.

EXAMPLE 11.7
Changes to a professional development program using ADKAR

1. *Awareness of the need for change*

Awareness and discussion of change assists early childhood educators, children, families and the community to understand the key reasons and drivers of specific change.

Paddington Children's Centre was engaged in a practitioner research project – Strengths Based Training. As this project progressed, the Director observed an emerging need to make changes to the service's professional development strategy. This approach was proving less and less satisfactory as the motivation of educators to attend workshops diminished and provocative professional sharing with the remaining 28 staff was diminishing. Prompted by the Director, the team discussed and agreed that a change to the professional development program was needed.

Once **A**wareness has been established, the next building block for change is **D**esire.

2. *Desire to support and participate in change*

Each individual will view change through their unique personal lens. Once awareness of the need for change is established the individual's desire to engage will need to be established.

With the introduction of the *Early Years Learning Framework*, there was a lot of language and concept deconstruction and the team (regardless of qualifications and experience) engaged in a shared learning journey. To progress the service's understanding, each room team chose a curriculum area, and researched this over a three-month period culminating in a presentation to the whole team. All team members were consulted and engaged in the process.

At the same time, the Strengths Based Training project created a positive shift in team morale. Each educator became more confident to speak up as the setting had become a 'safe place' to share.

Once **A**wareness and **D**esire are established, the next building block for change is **K**nowledge.

3. *Knowledge of how to change*

Successful training and support to increase knowledge about change should be targeted at where each individual is currently functioning.

The Director was conscious of the varying education levels, learning styles and attitude to change of each team member. The challenge was how to equip staff to feel confident to research and present their learning as well as cover costs and staffing arrangements. The Director commenced resourcing the service with books, articles and information from websites. Much of the time was spent supported each staff member to review their progress, stay on track, sharing and listening to their excitement and fears. There was a shared understanding that some research was completed in their own time as well as some allowance for release from face-to-face responsibilities. Once **A**wareness, **D**esire and **K**nowledge are established, the next building block for change is **A**bility.

4. *Ability to implement required skills and behaviours*

Each individual will require different resources and support.

During the research process the team experienced challenges:
- psychological blocks, such as, fear of looking stupid or fear of presenting
- skill blocks, such as, literacy levels for spelling or written expression

- time, such as, family responsibilities with young children
- resources, such as, money to purchase new texts and additional overtime costs. This was managed by cost saving within the professional development budget.

Each individual required different resources and support, however, commitment was high and staff were buzzing with professional conversation, engaged and involved in their research area both in and out of work.

Once **A**wareness, **D**esire, **K**nowledge and **A**bility are established, the last building block for change is **R**einforcement.

5. *Reinforcement to sustain the change*

Celebrating change in meaningful ways acknowledges actual accomplishments and reinforces positive attitudes to change. The ability to learn from our mistakes and the absence of negative consequences will also reinforce and sustain change.

Constant support and provocation as well as creating time for those who were struggling enabled a positive outcome. Interestingly, when the full day for presentation arrived, *everyone* presented. Those who had previously said they would not present were so engaged and confident in their area of research they couldn't help themselves but be involved. As a result of this process, Paddington Children's Centre now approaches the Quality Improvement Plan review using the methodology above. There is a true culture of learning and trust and professional respect with everyone involved and confident about the process. The team recognizes a constant need for review, improvement, change and celebration.

Source: Natalie Cordukes, Director, Paddington Children's Centre, 2013

CourseMateExpress

A staff reflection as testament to the success of the process, is available on CourseMate in Online Example 11.3.

These five ADKAR building blocks of change provide a positive and shared framework for early childhood educators and organisations as they continue to implement future change within early childhood education.

Canvassing community, family and children's opinions is critical in assisting all aspects of change management. When implementing change, educators, children and families need information about what is happening and why (**A**wareness). Much of the anxiety about change can be dissipated by keeping all participants informed before, during and after any change. Discussing any changes that are going to occur, what has prompted these changes and their possible impact can assist all those affected to adapt to change. When changes are seen to be meeting the goals of the organisation, they are likely to be supported by others (**D**esire, **K**nowledge). Having an awareness of each family, their practices and adaptability is a critical factor when communicating and managing the competing demands of change. Children, too, need to be included in the process in a way that makes sense to them and reassures them of their importance within the program and ability to affect their environment. An educator's image of children influences how they manage change. If they have an image of children as competent and believe they bring understandings and knowledge to any process, the educator will acknowledge children's ability (**A**bility) to respond to change in a positive manner. This is especially true when the changes involve them in an authentic and meaningful experience.

Figure 11.1 shows a visual display of the process that engaged children, families and educators in conversations about changes to their outdoor learning environment at Parkes Early Childhood Centre 2013.

FIGURE 11.1 Playground consultation at Parkes Early Childhood Centre.

How could the ADKAR framework for change support your service to develop a quality improvement plan?

The more people there are strategically involved in the change process, the greater the number of ideas that are generated. Information may be shared with others through meetings, photographs, copies of plans on the noticeboard and in newsletters. A wide-ranging pool of ideas, drawing on a variety of past experiences, can then be called upon to help generate solutions and to foresee possible problems. Such an open process also builds trust between all stakeholders and provides a platform for sustained change (**R**einforcement) (*see* Figure 11.1 and Example 11.7).

Action research for change

Research is a powerful tool that informs, stimulates and enables change within early childhood settings, schools and outside school hours care services. Research is something that all educators engage in on a regular basis, not just something that academics do and educators read about. When educators engage in classroom based, practitioner-led research they are active producers rather than passive consumers of research-based knowledge (Skattebol & Arthur, 2014).

There are many terms that describe this type of research including practitioner inquiry, action research and practitioner research. Skattebol and Arthur (in press) use the term 'collaborative practitioner research' to focus on both the research and the collaborative nature of the activity. Many educators are engaged in practices along a continuum from reflective practice to action research. **Action research** or practitioner research extends on reflective practice by focusing on the action that arises from the reflection. Research differs to reflective inquiry, according to Goodfellow & Hedges (2006) because it involves public sharing of findings. The term 'collaborative practitioner research' identifies the critical role of dialogue within communities of practice as educators work together to support processes of change and transform practices (Skattebol & Arthur, 2014). Educators become more empowered and knowledgeable about their own theory and practice through participation in action research/practitioner research; in other words 'making a difference' (Kemmis & McTaggart, 2003). Skattebol and Arthur (2014) found that collaborative practitioner research, with educators from a range of early childhood settings and schools along with university-based academics as critical friends, supported educators' professional growth and curriculum change. The collaborative nature of the research provided a safe context for educators to share dilemmas and discuss their successes and challenges as they implemented change and developed adaptive and activist leadership skills and dispositions.

Lewin (1946) noted two critical features of action research, namely group decisions and commitment to improvement. Through these features he emphasised that those affected by the planned changes (that is the educators) had the main responsibility for deciding on (and living with) the course of action. More recently, Kemmis and McTaggart (1988) identified two main educational applications of action research: curriculum review and development, and professional growth among educators who seek to improve their theories and practices.

Educators can use action research as evidence of their professional growth and learning in the education community and in the wider community, as evidenced in research published by McNiff (http://www.jean.mcniff.com) and Whitehead (2005). 'Participatory action research is one way to work powerfully, and thoughtfully to bring about changes that improve the rationality and social justice of … [our] own social and educational practices' (Kemmis & McTaggart, 1988, p. 5). As educators do this, they contribute powerfully to their own professional identity and values as well as to collaborative learning among group members (Whitehead, 2005).

The words *action research* imply that what is important is the trying out of ideas in practice (*action*) and learning more about and explaining what is involved (*research*). As educators critically transform their practices they also influence the practices and explanations of other people. The participatory nature of action research focuses on participants' engagement in group processes, taking responsibility for implementing tasks, documenting and analysing, reflecting and reporting back to the group, as well as sharing with wider audiences.

Action research

Extends on reflective practice by focusing on the action that arises from the reflection.

Participatory action research involves:

● *social process*: People (educators, families, managers, children) undertake action research with partners, identifying and responding to their own and other peoples' subjectivities or shared understandings. Researchers therefore are informed 'insiders' of the setting.

● *practical collaboration*: Action research involves people who are affected by the practice, and who maintain collaborative control of the process. Group members establish understandings which other people in the setting take up to improve practices.

● *emancipation*: Action research improves significant social practices; i.e. aspects of early childhood and school curriculum (Kemmis & McTaggart, in Denzin & Lincoln, 2003). People clarify their thinking and practices, taking agency as more empowered educators.

● *critical thinking*: Participants continually consider all perspectives with care since the shared purpose is to improve programs.

● *recursive practices*: The action research process keeps going. Participants refine their focus in the next spiral and investigate emerging issues with modified practice.

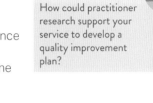

How could practitioner research support your service to develop a quality improvement plan?

(adapted from Kemmis & McTaggart, 2003)

Action research involves continual spirals of self-reflective steps (*see* Kemmis & McTaggart, 2003; Vozzo & Bober, 1997), as shown in Figure 11.2. This is consistent with the *Educators' Guide to the Early Years Learning Framework* (DEEWR, 2010) information about reflective practice, which focuses on continual processes of reflection, action and evaluation.

Reflection and evaluation are integral throughout action research. 'Reflection has an evaluative aspect – to judge whether effects (and issues which arose) were desirable, and suggest ways of proceeding' (Kemmis & McTaggart, 1988, p. 13).

Evaluating and modifying change

Chapter 4 provides a sound coverage of evaluation theory and methodology to enable early childhood educators to gauge the impact of programs and practices on staff, children and families. Educators need to think deeply about their decision making and continue to develop the ability to be reflective (Rand, 2000).

Reflecting on and debating practices is one of the roles of educators as pedagogical leaders and advocates. In Example 11.8, Jo Goodwin challenges our thinking on change for social justice within the broader Australian early childhood context through her reflection on both the incremental and transformational change that is required to achieve cultural competence in an east coast environment.

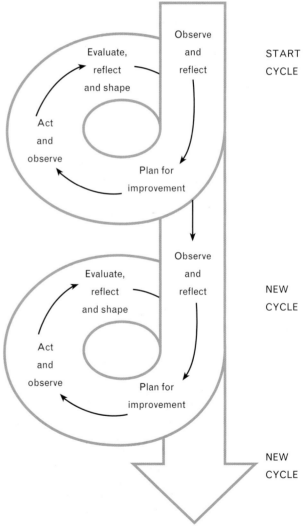

Source: adapted from Kemmis & McTaggart, 2003 in Denzin & Lincoln, 2003, p. 382; Vozzo & Bober, 1997.

FIGURE 11.2 Action research.

EXAMPLE 11.8
Aboriginal and Torres Strait Islander inclusion: when doing
'NAIDOC' is just not enough anymore

An interesting thing happened at the Gold Coast Inclusion Support Agency (ISA) in 2009. Interest, referrals and requests for Aboriginal and Torres Strait Islander inclusion had never been higher, but on examination services that were supported with professional development in the past were still requesting the same support, rather than strengthening inclusion at the centre. How could this be? What was happening? On reflection, it was clear that not a lot was happening in-between support visits and linking services to appropriate resource sites. Change was needed. How to go about this change and ensure that it provided the opportunity for whole team change for all educators at services? How to challenge the thinking that it is a once-a-year consideration at NAIDOC or some stencils of artwork coloured in by children being displayed on the wall? How could these practices allow educators to believe that they are being inclusive of Aboriginal and Torres Strait Islander culture?

One of the most important events occurred on 13 February 2008 when our then Prime Minister, Kevin Rudd, apologised to the Stolen Generations and made a commitment to change:

> A future where we embrace the possibility of new solutions to enduring problems where old approaches have failed. A future based on mutual respect, mutual resolve and mutual responsibility. A future where all Australians, whatever their origins, are truly equal partners, with equal opportunities and with an equal stake in shaping the next chapter in the history of the great country Australia.

Where was our new solution for early childhood services? Such strong words in the apology, spoken with great commitment – how had our practices changed since the apology? What had we committed to? It was with these thoughts that our change began.

We stopped and considered:

- What we had been doing in the past in regards to Aboriginal and Torres Strait islander inclusion?

- Our thoughts about the outcomes and our understanding of the outcomes: was it good enough?

- The applied knowledge, skills, attitudes and different perspectives to our current practices on Aboriginal and Torres Strait Islander inclusion

- Identification of what we might change

- What had we tried to change?

- Our participation in and observed changes we were making, how they affected educators and services and the impact on Aboriginal and Torres Strait Islander inclusion.

We engaged in the cycle of reflective practice to develop new ways of implementing Aboriginal and Torres Strait Islander inclusion.

The process that we now facilitate with services is called, 'Journey of Discovery'.

One of the most important aspects to ensure that real change would happen at services was to consider cultural competence.

The elements which underpin successful cultural competence include:

- Skills:
  - for living and working in the local Aboriginal and Torres Strait Islander contexts (socially)
  - for working in local Aboriginal and Torres Strait Islander contexts (professionally).

- Knowledge:
  - understanding and awareness of Aboriginal and Torres Strait Islander culture, history and contemporary societies
  - understanding that the importance of connectedness to land and spirituality is the core of Aboriginal and Torres Strait Islander cultural identity.
- Attitudes:
  - exploring individual and societal values and attitudes.

DEEWR, 2010, p. 25

The beginning point was a commitment from services to allow an educator to attend a minimum of 5 sessions of 3-hour durations in work hours.

We received an overwhelming response from services to participate in these sessions. We accepted the first 20 services that responded and placed the rest on a wait list.

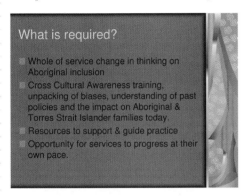

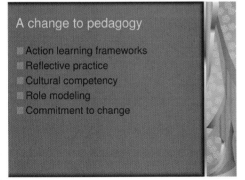

It was decided very early in this process that the Gold Coast ISA team would also participate fully in these sessions, so that we could be involved in and observe the changes within our team.

An action research approach seemed to be the best model to engage with as it involves action with critical reflection: Action > Reflection. The reflection phase includes both review and planning. It is the source of the understanding and learning that allows change to emerge. It allows educators to go back to their services and create a space in which to share their learnings and create their own journeys.

It was with great excitement that we commenced the first session in NAIDOC week 2009.

The first session focused on cross-cultural awareness, identifying our own cultures and identities, timelines of events in world histories, and Aboriginal and Torres Strait Islander histories, past policies and the impact of these policies.

Educators who thought they were coming to get some 'art and craft activities' to ride off into the sunset with were a little shocked. And then, as the sessions progressed, pleasantly surprised that this was not and would never again be the case for Aboriginal and Torres Strait Islander inclusion on the Gold Coast.

It was also at this first session that services were given either an A4 or A3 journal to document their services' journey and a survey for all their team at their service to reflect on all aspects of Aboriginal and Torres Strait Islander inclusion. The commitment was from all educators to ensure that this was completed prior to attendance at the next session. The survey was the tool to bring all team members together and critically reflect on where they were at in regards to Aboriginal and Torres Strait Islander inclusion.

The second session was decided upon by participants in relation to date and frequency of sessions. The action was to share the outcomes of the survey at the next session. This was the defining moment for the group. One of the questions asked was 'Does your service have a specific policy on Aboriginal and Torres Strait islander inclusion?' There were lots of 'No, just a general inclusion policy'. Another question was in relation to the foyer and asked 'Are there any posters, flags, artefacts, paintings, information displays, welcome notices with Aboriginal and Torres Strait Islander perspectives?' One participant stated that they did have, but they were not sure if it was enough. 'How do we know what is enough?' I asked some questions about why they were there, what were the processes, and the feedback was 'I don't know. We don't have any real direction around this at our service'. The journey had officially begun for these participants with lots of 'Ahhs' and 'I get it now'. 'We can't move forward without our whole team knowing where we want to get to with this'; 'It's not a quick fix, we have to develop our own frame of reference for this within our team, it's where we want to go and there is no right or wrong, learning all the way and it will never end'; and a 'Why didn't you tell us we were putting the cart before the horse?'

A reflective cycle of practice had just begun. The journals now made sense. The knowledge that participants had gained from the first session was invaluable information that they wanted to share back at their services; connecting with the local community to include them in their journey had become a huge priority for this group. It was the beginning of cultural competence.

From this point onwards 'Aboriginal and Torres Strait Islander inclusion' had new meaning; the participants went on the Paradise Dreaming Tour and learnt about the rich and diverse histories of the Aboriginal peoples of the Gold Coast.

Based on their experiences, participants advocated for all educators and team members at their services to go on the tour as part of the internal professional development at their individual services. Statements of intent and Aboriginal and Torres Strait Islander inclusion policies have been developed, Traditional Owner acknowledgement is common practice at team meetings, and local Aboriginal services were used – for example, on a health promotions evening one of the services contacted the local Aboriginal Medical Services (AMS) Kalwun, and arranged for the dental nurse to do the display and discussion with the children.

Participating in and supporting all the many and varied community events has become part of these services' everyday plans. Services have developed Reconciliation Action Plans (RAPS), have become members of SNAICC, consult with and use the wealth of knowledge that our local Aboriginal community members can provide for them, but most importantly view Aboriginal and Torres Strait islander inclusion as part of their daily practice.

The Gold Coast Inclusion Support Agency acknowledges the Kombumerri people as the traditional owners and custodians of the Gold Coast region.

We honour and respect their ongoing culture and spiritual connections to this country. We aim to respect cultural heritage, customs, and beliefs of all Aboriginal people.

We currently have two Journey of Discovery sessions running with 56 services actively participating. The support we provide by regular email updates to services with reflective questions are part of this process; for example, coaching and mentoring support, particularly at staff meetings for services if they come to a hump and don't quite know how to get over it. We provide links to the local Aboriginal community through the sessions but how the services use these links is totally up to them.

Some services are in the very beginning stages while other services go ahead at a fast pace. Action learning is totally up to the services – the when, why and how they progress.

The important thing is that we have all progressed and continue to do so.

We don't provide postpacks of resources or culturally appropriate activities. The services now share with us what they are doing and why.

'New solutions to enduring problems where old approaches have failed'

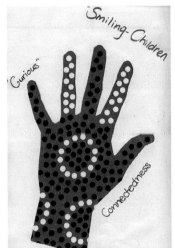

Source: Jo Goodwin, Team Leader, Gold Coast Inclusion Support Agency

Conclusion and reflection

There is no doubt that the early childhood profession will face a challenging and changing landscape in coming years. Our appetite for change and leadership skills will be tested continuously. Successful journeys of change can result when educators appreciate complexities and potentials in change, and manage these new circumstances with useful frameworks that involve participants and strengthen understandings and practice. Early childhood professionals have a responsibility to be open and proactive within their local communities while advocating for high quality early childhood services and schools for *all* children.

Questions for reflection

1. Identify who key stakeholders are for your service or school (for example, children, families, funding bodies, regulators and so on).

2. Within your service or school, reflect on the following with stakeholders:
   - Does your organisation have a shared vision?
   - Do key stakeholders have a voice in planning for change?
   - Is your organisation 'safe' for staff and families, as well as children?
   - Is cultural competence evident in the setting?
   - How do you maintain your awareness of and share current issues and critical changes in the early childhood profession?
   - How can you best develop your abilities to positively influence change?
   - How can you mentor others to share your learning?

3. Reflect on how the ADKAR framework for change will support your service to develop a quality improvement plan to address the seven areas in the *National Quality Standard*.

Key terms

action research, 418

adaptive cultures, 409

ADKAR, 415

mindfulness, 412

organisational culture, 405

shared vision, 406

strategic resilience, 414

Online study resources

Visit http://login.cengagebrain.com and use the access code that comes with this book for 12 months access to the student resources for this text.

CourseMate Express

The CourseMate Express website contains a range of resources and study tools for this chapter, including:

- Online video activities
- Online research activities
- A revision quiz
- Matching pair exercises
- A list of key weblinks
- A chapter glossary, flashcards and crossword to help you revise terminology
- and more!

Search me! education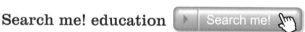

Explore **Search me! education** for articles relevant to this chapter. Fast and convenient, Search me! education is updated daily and provides you with 24-hour access to full text articles from hundreds of scholarly and popular journals, ebooks and newspapers, including *The Australian* and *The New York Times*. Log in to Search me! through http://login.cengage.com and try searching for the following key words:

- change
- organisational culture
- mindfulness
- leadership
- action research
- reflection.

Search tip: **Search me! education** contains information from both local and international sources. To get the greatest number of search results, try using both Australian and American spellings in your searches, e.g. 'globalisation' and 'globalization'; 'organisation' and 'organization'

Recommended resources

Barnes, H 2013, *Critical Reflection as a Tool for Change: Stories About Quality Improvement*, Early Childhood Australia, Canberra.

Bruno, H, Gonzalez-Mena, J, Hernandez, L & Sullivan D 2013, *Learning from the Bumps in the Road*, Redleaf Press, St Paul, Minnesota.

Cartmel, J, Macfarlane, K & Casley, M 2012, *Reflection as a Tool for Quality: Working with the National Quality Standard*, Early Childhood Australia, Canberra

Chaskalson, M 2011, *The Mindful Workplace*, Wiley-Blackwell, UK.

Hiatt, JM 2006, *ADKAR: A Model for Change in Business, Government and Our Community*, Prosci Research, USA.

Johnson, S 2002, *Who Moved My Cheese?*, Vermilion, London.

Jorde Bloom, P 2005, *Blueprint for Action: Achieving Center Based Change Through Staff Development*, 2nd edn., New Horizons, Lake Forest, IL.

Rodd, J 2013, *Leadership in Early Childhood*, 4th edn., Allen & Unwin, Sydney.

Key weblinks

Action research, http://www.jeanmcniff.com/

Action research, http://www.actionresearch.net

Both ways learning, http://www.batchelor.edu.au/about/both-ways-learning/

Budget based funded services, http://education.gov.au/budget-based-funded-programme

Canadian Journal of Action Research, http://cjar.nipissingu.ca/index.php/cjar

Change management, http://www.psctas.org.au/wp-content/uploads/2010/02/Change-Management.pdf

Change management, http://www.change-management.com/Tutorial-ADKAR-series-1.htm

Closing the gap, http://www.dss.gov.au/our-responsibilities/indigenous-australians/programs-services/closing-the-gap

Code of ethics, http://www.earlychildhoodaustralia.org.au/code_of_ethics.html

Council of Australian Governments, http://www.coag.gov.au/early_childhood

Early childhood development strategy, http://education.gov.au/information-national-early-childhood-development-strategy

Mindfulness, http://www.csu.edu.au/special/teach-ec/RESOURCES/html/Wellness.html

Mindfulness, http://www.themindfulworkplace.com

National quality framework for early childhood education and care,
    http://education.gov.au/national-quality-framework-early-childhood-education-and-care

Two-way learning, http://www.csu.edu.au/special/teach-ec/RESOURCES/PDF/Batchelor_presentation.pdf

References

Australian Graduate School of Managment 2010, *Managing People and Organisations*, Australian School of Business, UNSW, Sydney.

Barnes, H 2013, *Critical Reflection as a Tool for Change: Stories About Quality Improvement*, Early Childhood Australia, Canberra.

Bolman, L & Deal, T 2008, *Reframing Organisations: Artistry, Choice and Leadership*, Jossey-Bass, San Francisco, CA.

Chaskalson, M 2011, *The Mindful Workplace*, Wiley-Blackwell, UK.

Clayton, B, Fisher, T, Harris, R, Bateman, A & Brown, M 2008, *Structures and Cultures: A Review of the Literature*, http://eric.ed.gov/?id=ED503353, accessed 30 April 2014.

Council of Australian Governments (COAG) 2009, *The National Early Childhood Development Strategy: Investing in the Early Years*, Commonwealth of Australia, Canberra.

Deering, A 2006, 'Managing organisational change', *Management Today*, Nov/Dec, AIM, Textpacific Publishing, Sydney.

Department of Education, Employment and Workforce Relations (DEEWR) 2010, *Educators Belonging, Being and Becoming: Educators Guide to the Early Years Learning Framework for Australia*, Commonwealth of Australia, Canberra.

Goodfellow, J & Hedges H 2007, 'Practitioner Inquiry', in L Keesing-Styles & H Hedges (Eds.), *Theorising Early Childhood Practice: Emerging Dialogues* (pp. 187–210), Pademelon Press, Castle Hill.

Hiatt, JM 2006, *ADKAR: A Model for Change in Business, Government and our Community*, Prosci Research, USA.

Jorde Bloom, P 2005, *Blueprint for Action: Achieving Center Based Change Through Staff Development*, 2nd edn., Lake Forest Illinois, New Horizons.

Kemmis, S & McTaggart, R (eds.) 1988, *The Action Research Planner*, Deakin University Press, Geelong.

Kemmis, S & McTaggart, R 2003, 'Participatory action research', in N Denzin & V Lincoln, *Strategies of Qualitative Inquiry*, 2nd edn., Sage Publications, Thousand Oaks.

Lewin, K 1946, 'Action research and minority problems', *Journal of Social Issues*, vol. 2, no. 4, pp. 34–46.

Moore, T 2012, *Rethinking Early Childhood Intervention Services: Implications for Policy and Practice*, Pauline McGregor Memorial Address, presented at the 10th Biennial National Conference of Early Childhood Intervention Australia, and the 1st Asia-Pacific Early Childhood Intervention Conference. Perth, Western Australia, 9th August 2012, Murdoch Children's Research Institute and The Royal Children's Hospital Centre for Community Child Health,

Rand, M 2000, *Giving it Some Thought: Cases for Early Childhood Practice*, National Association for the Education of Young Children, Washington, DC.

Rodd, J 2013, *Leadership in Early Childhood*, 4th edn., Allen & Unwin, Sydney.

Turner, D & Crawford, M 1998, *Change Power*, Business and Professional Publishing, Australia.

Sachs, J 2003, *The Activist Teaching Profession*, Open University Press, Buckingham.

Skattebol, J & Arthur, L, 'Collaborative practitioner research: Opening a third space for local knowledge production', *Asia Pacific Journal of Education*, 2014, Vol. 34, No. 3, 341–365.

Valikangas, L 2010, *The Resilient Organization*, McGraw-Hill, USA.

Vozzo, L & Bober, B 1997, 'Improving teacher practice through action research, collaboration and case writing', *Reflect. The Journal of Reflection in Teaching and Learning*, vol. 3, no. 1, pp. 25–33.

Whitehead, J 2005, 'Living inclusional values in educational standards of practice and judgement', *Ontario Action Researcher*, vol. 8, no. 2.1, pp. 1–29, http://www.nipissingu.ca/oar/PDFS/V821E.pdf, accessed 13 January 2014.

Glossary

Ability groups Grouping students according to achievement, skill or ability.

Accommodation Where new schemes, or modified schemes, are constructed to explain the world.

Action plan This plan results from an evaluation. It lists the decision and recommendations/goals, as well as the details of the planned action. This includes the new action, timing, people involved and evaluation criteria.

Action research Extends on reflective practice by focusing on the action that arises from the reflection.

Adaptation The process of adjusting to the environment.

Adaptive cultures Help an organisation to anticipate and respond to environmental change. They encourage leadership, risk-taking, initiative, innovation, problem identification and problem solving.

ADKAR Acronym for 'Awareness, Desire, Knowledge, Ability and Reinforcement'; building blocks for change.

Adult-centred approach This approach occurs when the educator decides what, how and when children will learn in relation to the agenda of the educational setting. There is little consideration for the children's experiences, interests, sociocultural practices or ways of learning.

Agency This refers to a person's ability to act on and shape their own life; when children exercise choice within a given social and cultural context.

Assessment Involves gathering information, reflecting on its meaning and using this analysis to inform future planning. It takes place when educators, families, children, community members and policymakers make sense of all children's learning over time across differing contexts and purposes in order to extend their learning.

Assimilation Where the world is interpreted through current schemes.

Associative play Group play, but without common goals.

Attachment 'The strong, affectionate tie we have with special people in our lives that leads us to experience pleasure when we interact with them and to be comforted by their nearness during times of stress' (Berk, 2009, p. 425).

Bioecological theory A theory of development that emphasises the elements of process, person, context and time.

Buddy programs Programs where older or more experienced members of a community support younger or newer members of that community. Buddy programs often operate in schools where older students are paired with those starting school, providing a friendly face and source of support in the new environment.

Child-centred approach This approach occurs when educators consider each child's strengths, interests and experiences as well as their needs. Children learn through frequently initiating and directing experiences, and educators provide resources and support.

Collaborative partnerships Involves two-way communication and negotiation where educators and family members share information, exchange ideas and work towards shared goals.

Communities of practice Communities of practice are groups of people with shared experiences and interests who interact regularly with each other to engage in collaborative reflection and learning (Wenger, n.d.).

Community of learners approach This approach recognises the significance of the sociocultural contexts of families, peers and communities for children's learning. The emphasis is on children participating as a member of the community of learners, rather than as an individual. Educators organise experiences to extend children's learning.

Conforming approach This approach occurs when the program reinforces the status quo by focusing on the skills needed to achieve national, economic, social and political goals, and the values and practices that enable society to reproduce itself (Mac Naughton, 2003).

Constraints Features that present obstacles to, or negative influences on, practices.

Constructivist approach In this approach educators recognise 'active learning' or 'play-based learning' where children learn across emotional, social, physical and cognitive areas. Children as active learners participate in integrated hands on experiences with open-ended materials as they construct new meanings.

Context In bioecological theory, refers to the immediate contexts in which individuals exist, as well as more general social and cultural contexts.

Cooperative play Group play working towards a shared goal.

Critical reflective practice Reflective practice becomes critically reflective practice when educators continually inspect practice from diverse viewpoints to construct new understandings of, and the connections between, theoretical perspectives, philosophy, ethics and practice.

Critical reflexivity Thinking critically about the impact of our assumptions, values and actions on others in order to develop a more collaborative, responsive and ethical response.

Cultural capital Culture includes ways of being and doing and particular forms of knowledge. Our culture is not always valued in all social fields. What has cultural capital in the playground or at home may not have cultural capital in the early childhood setting.

Cultural competency Includes respect for diversity and a focus on equity and social justice.

Cultural-historical theory Focuses on the role of culture – including values, beliefs and skills – in development. Social interaction with more knowledgeable others is a key driver of development.

Curriculum Constitutes everything that happens across the day in the setting/school.

Curriculum approaches Stances towards curriculum that reflect the stakeholder's beliefs about how children learn and how families, communities and educators support children's learning, as well as what is important for children now and in the future.

Disadvantage Includes people's 'personal capabilities, their family circumstances; the community where they live (and the opportunities it offers); life experiences; and the broader economic and social environment' (McLachlan, Gilfillan & Gordon, 2013, p. 2).

Discourse Socially constructed ways of being, speaking, feeling and acting that represent particular values and world views.

Dispositions These are acquired through experiences within families and communities, including educational settings; habits of mind or tendencies to respond in characteristic ways – for example, with creativity – across different situations.

Educational philosophies A specific vision of education that examines the goals and meaning of education.

Emergent curriculum This approach emphasises and supports children's learning in the potential curriculum by responding to, and extending on, their individual and group interests and questions. Educators document retrospectively what happens, rather than preplanning experiences, as they negotiate the collaboration between children, families and themselves to extend learning.

Evaluation Occurs when educators, families, children, community members and policymakers purposefully collect evidence, analyse and judge the information, and make recommendations that improve the program.

Exclusive approach Educators overlook or ignore diversity and difference among children, families and communities in the curriculum; sometimes diversity and difference is seen as a problem.

Friendship groups Groups formed on the basis of social connections or shared interests.

Functional play Repeated use of objects or actions.

Funds of knowledge The skills, knowledge, networks and everyday practices within families and communities; refers to the understandings, interests and expertise that children acquire as they participate in family and community life.

Gap analysis Identifying the steps that need to be taken in order to move from actual practice to desired practice based on the gap between ideal and reality.

Games with rules Play according to established rules.

Goal A specific statement and measureable accomplishment to be achieved within a specified time and under specified resource constraints.

Guided participation Shared interactions between expert and less expert participants.

Habitus As children engage in the practices of their family, they develop particular ways of thinking, valuing and acting which they use as they move across contexts such as home and school.

Inclusive approach Educators embrace diversity and difference and actively work to reflect the diversity among children, families and communities in the curriculum. Children's learning reflects the importance of understanding and working with diversity and difference in a globalised world.

Individualistic developmental approach Children's learning is emphasised as individuals, with little reference to their family, peers and community contexts. Educators may analyse their learning and link to generalised developmental patterns established from dated research of particular populations, offering little understanding of their learning.

Integrated approach In this approach educators organise learning experiences across combined curriculum learning areas and across various areas in the learning environment. This enables children to learn in ways that are meaningful to themselves as they draw on various curriculum learning areas, knowledge, skills, dispositions, feelings and general capacities.

Intentional teaching Involves deliberate planning of experiences and pedagogies with a clear learning focus.

Internalisation The process by which social activities become mental processes.

Intersubjectivity Shared understandings of a task or situation.

Linguistic capital There are many different languages and different ways of using language. The power and status of Standard English means that diverse languages and ways with language are valued in some social fields but not in others.

Mandates What a service is required to do, or not do, by external authorities.

Metacognition Awareness, understanding and analysis of our own cognitive processes.

Mindfulness The mind is aware that it is thinking, that it is feeling, that it is sensing (Chaskalson, 2011).

Mission A statement about purpose.

Mixed age groups When children of different ages are grouped together.

Monocultural and monolingual approach This occurs when the program is based on a single language and culture. Children and educators may be from one linguistic and cultural group, or the children and families may be from diverse language and cultural groups, but the educators are from a single sociocultural group reflecting the dominant culture and language.

Multicultural and multilingual approach This occurs when the diverse cultures and languages of children and families are integrated into the program. Educators are knowledgeable about children's languages and cultures and the interactions, resources and experiences reflect children's everyday family and community experiences, and children learn to respect and understand their own languages and cultures as well as those of others.

Multiple intelligences approach This approach acknowledges that children learn in different ways, and there are at least seven to nine different ways that intelligence manifests in different individuals and across different cultures. (Gardner, 1983/1993a; 1993b;1998b; 2003).

New basics approach In this approach educators recognise complexity in life and learning as well as change in the world so they support children's participation now and in the future in a flexible knowledge-based society. Children learn how to respond productively, both personally and professionally.

Old basics approach In this approach, commonly interpreted as the traditional 3 Rs, educators may focus on narrow developmental views of children's learning according to fixed patterns at early childhood settings and then focus on the next step. In schools educators may emphasise 'academic' learning areas, or the fragmentation of literacy into phonics, dictation and so on.

Onlooker play Children observe play, but do not seek to enter the play.

Organisation Integration of two or more schemes into a more complex, higher order scheme.

Organisational culture The basic assumptions, shared beliefs and orientations that emerge to unite members of a group.

Parallel play Playing near others, but with no interaction.

Partners The people involved in the setting/school with whom educators work, including children, families, managers, policy makers and community members.

Pedagogical documentation Provides a record of children's experiences and learning that facilitates discussion among children, families and educators and analysis of children's learning from diverse perspectives.

Pedagogies All the actions and processes that educators use to translate philosophy and curriculum approaches into practice.

Person In bioecological theory refers to an individual's physical characteristics include an individual's physical characteristics as well as their resources and individual attributes.

Philosophy Beliefs and values that underpin practice.

Play-based learning A context for learning through which children organise and make sense of their social worlds, as they engage actively with people, objects and representations. (DEEWR, 2009, p. 6)

Play-based pedagogy, Where play is characterised as a planned and purposeful activity, built around a well-resourced environment and rich interactions with adults.

Potentials Features that can facilitate or support the implementation of our philosophy and practices.

Predetermined approaches When educators take a non-responsive approach to curriculum for a particular group of children, they make few connections between the children and the intended learning, concerning children's strengths, interests, capabilities and experiences. Children may complete activities but with little interest and responsibility as they find activities not meaningful.

Private speech Self-directed speech used by children to guide their thinking and behaviour.

Prosocial behaviour Actions to help others, without the expectation of reward.

Proximal processes In bioecological theory, refers to ongoing interactions between the individual and the people, objects and/or symbols in their environment.

Reflection Involves educators, families, children, community members and/or policymakers in thinking about some puzzling aspect of theory and practice that develops new understandings and new ways to strengthen practice.

Reflective practice Occurs when educators and partners regularly examine aspects of practice and theory that puzzle or confound them as they reconsider ideas and construct new understandings of, and the connections between, theoretical perspectives, philosophy, ethics and practice.

Reforming approach This occurs when the individual child moves from a dependant and developing child to a self-realised autonomous adult and free thinker; and a reforming society so that it reflects a greater emphasis on freedom, truth and justice (Mac Naughton, 2003).

Same-sex groups Groups formed on the basis of sex or gender.

Scaffolding A process of providing temporary guidance and support to children moving from one level of competence to another (Mac Naughton & Williams, 2009, p. 370). The level of support provided by a more knowledgeable other as children tackle tasks within the ZPD.

Schemes Strategies for interaction.

Segregated approach If educators understand the curriculum as separate components with clear boundaries, for example separate sets of knowledge and skills, the focus is limited to these aspects, so there may be little flexibility or meaningfulness available for learners. Children may be expected to limit their learning to these boundaries related to curriculum areas, timetable and areas of the setting.

Self-concept The set of attributes, abilities, attitudes and values that individuals use to define themselves.

Self-esteem Evaluative dimension of self-concept.

Self-efficacy Beliefs about the ability to do specific things.

Shared vision A shared understanding of what we do, why we do it, how we do it and where we want to be in the future.

Single or restricted intelligences approach The use of this approach occurs when educators consider only a limited number of intelligences, which reduces children's learning opportunities. Programs and assessment procedures in schools have traditionally reflected linguistic and logico-mathematical intelligences while overlooking the many others.

Situational analysis Collecting and analysing information about an organisation to identify strengths and directions for future planning and implementation.

Social capital Social capital includes relationships, friendships and social networks that provide support to individuals and group solidarity.

Social field Individuals experience different social contexts or social fields depending on where they are, for example, at home, at church, in the classroom, at the park, or out bush and so on. People usually interact and relate in response to functioning of the social field and what is considered important knowledge or capital in that field.

Solitary play Playing alone.

Stakeholders Those involved in the operations of the setting and who should be involved in the decision-making processes.

Strategic planning Describes the goals of the organisation and the strategies that will be used to achieve these goals (Kearns, 2007).

Strategic resilience The capability to turn threats into opportunities prior to their becoming either (Valikangas, 2010).

Sustained shared thinking Educators and children are mutually involved in cognitive constructions.

Symbolic play The use of symbols to represent people and objects.

Time In bioecological theory, refers to the time involved in immediate interactions as well as the impact of historical time on development.

Temperament Characteristic ways of responding to emotional events and novel situations and of regulating their actions.

Thematic approach This approach occurs when the educator decides the topic for children's learning through organising topic-based activities across various curriculum areas of mathematics, language, environmental science or music. Usually these activities do not engage children in deep and meaningful learning as they complete activities about the topic.

Theoretical perspectives A set of principles or propositions drawing on research to explain a particular experience or fact. There may be different perspectives based on different theories.

Transformative relationships Involve educators reflecting on their interactions with families and repositioning families as experts so that there is a two-way exchange of knowledge between the educator and families.

Transforming or transformative approach This occurs when the existing curriculum practices are transformed to achieve greater equity and social justice for all children. Educators engage children in the critique and reconfiguration of dominant discourses so they may learn to operate within the culture of power in mainstream society. This involves explicit teaching of the expected ways of talking and being to gain acceptance (Mac Naughton, 2003).

Transmission approach In this approach children participate in activities involving direct instruction, followed by practice as individuals and in small groups to increase their skills and content knowledge (Schwartz & Copeland, 2010). Educators may also hold behavioural understandings of learning as they use sequenced activities and standardised assessment to provide evidence of how children have learnt the skills taught by educators.

Two-way learning Children and educators learn together through observing, listening to, respecting and incorporating each other's language, culture and ways of learning.

Unoccupied play Children are in the vicinity of play.

Values Beliefs that provide a framework in which decisions are made individually or shared among stakeholders of an organisation.

Vision What things will look like if the mission's purpose is realised.

Zone of proximal development Where tasks are too difficult for a child to perform independently, but are possible with the assistance of more knowledgeable others.

Index

ability 415–18
ability groups 337–8
  advantages and disadvantages 338
  responses to concerns 338
Aboriginal people
  communities 41, 44, 46–7, 403–5
  community Elders 50
  inclusion reflections 420–3
  poverty and 59–60
  spoken languages 89
  Stronger Futures in the Northern Territory program 3
accommodation 84
accountability 11–12, 15, 110–11, 133–4
accreditation 13
achievement 111
acknowledging 322
action research
  critical features 418
  participatory action research 418–19
adaptation 84, 409–11
adaptive organisational cultures 409–11
  reflections 410–11
ADKAR (Awareness, Desire, Knowledge, Ability and Reinforcement) change management model 415–18
adults
  adult relationships in early childhood settings 317–18
  adult–child interactions 334
  relationships 316–17
advocacy 364, 401
age 336–7
age profile (of families) 58
agency 17–19, 76, 148, 264–5
anecdotes 276–80
annual reports 133–5
artefacts 118, 286, 324
assessment 28–9, 107
  authentic assessment 269–70
  collaborative approaches 263–6
  contemporary perspectives 260–7
  formal assessment 11–12
  of learning 236–7, 257–308
  linking assessment and planning 305–6
  methods 275–301
  Program of International Student Assessment 7–8
  purposes 258
  shared understandings about 259–60
  standardised assessment tools 269–70
assimilation 84
associative play 96

assumptions 44, 126–8
attachment 78–9
attitudes 63
Australian Children's Education and Care Quality Authority (ACECQA) 112
Australian Curriculum 112, 114, 131, 208, 266
Australian Curriculum and Assessment Authority (ACARA) 9, 225, 227
Australian Early Development Index (AEDI) 4
  development ratings 6
  developmental domains 4, 6
authentic assessment 269–70
awareness 415–18

babbling 88
behaviour 94, 300
  confidential and ethical behaviour 267–8
  prosocial behaviours 346
behaviourist theory 92–3, 210, 211–12
beliefs 46, 158–9
  of families 57
  philosophy and 151–7
belonging, sense of 37–8, 57, 62
bias 157
bilingualism 89, 270, 288, 340
brain development 2–3, 74–5
brainstorming 158, 203
Bronfenbrenner's theories
  bioecological and ecological theories (child development) 40, 47–8, 71–2
  positive relationships 314
buddy programs 337

capital 17–18
change
  action research for 418–19
  ADKAR model 415–18
  change and experience elements 92–3
  changing worlds 15–16
  designing, implementing and evaluating 121–2
  evaluating and modifying 419–23
  faces of 414–15
  frameworks for 415–19
  journeys of change 200, 400–23
  leadership and 411–14
  managing 407–8
  organisational culture and 405–11
  policy changes 400–1
  professional continuums 400–5
  transition and 40
  see also strategic planning
checklists 260, 300–1
child development theory 23–4

childhood
  changing 15–16
  places and spaces for 169
  reconceptualising early childhood 21–2
  sociology of 20–1
children 156
  adult–child interactions 334
  capable infants 75–6
  children's preparedness for school 4
  with chronic illness 59
  competent/incompetent child binary 28
  curriculum, children's interests at centre of 389–91
  development *see* development (children)
  documentation, contributing to 303–4
  educator-to-child ratios 12–13
  family and community, in context of 37–64
  grouping 244–5
  growth 77
  images of the child 21–2
  information about 183, 188
  interaction with 235–6
  learning 16–22, 91–5, 140–1, 320–6
  play, learning and development 70–102
  prenatal period 74
  relationships 316–17, 318–19
  research *with* and *on* 20–1
  rights of 265
  self-reflections 284–6
  sensorimotor understandings 76
  situational analysis and 192, 196–7
  with special needs 100
  sporting activities for 77–8
  surveillance of 268
  universal child 21
  useful information for collection 181
  views of 26–7
citizenship, democracy and 26–7
classrooms
  situational analysis and 195–6
  supportive classroom environments 250
Closing the Gap strategy 7
co-constructing 260, 264, 323–4, 348, 392
codes of ethics 23, 112, 129, 151
cognition
  cognitive development 84–7
  cognitive skills 4, 6
  learning, cognitive perspectives of 93
  metacognition 99
collaboration 127, 348

Index